Homer from Z to A

Brill's Studies in Indo-European Languages & Linguistics

Series Editors

Craig Melchert (*University of California at Los Angeles*)
Olav Hackstein (*Ludwig-Maximilians-Universität Munich*)

Editorial Board

José-Luis García-Ramón (*University of Cologne*)
Andrew Garrett (*University of California at Berkeley*)
Stephanie Jamison (*University of California at Los Angeles*)
Joshua T. Katz (*Princeton University*)
Alexander Lubotsky (*Leiden University*)
Alan J. Nussbaum (*Cornell University*)
Georges-Jean Pinault (*École Pratique des Hautes Études, Paris*)
Jeremy Rau (*Harvard University*)
Elisabeth Rieken (*Philipps-Universität Marburg*)
Stefan Schumacher (*Vienna University*)

VOLUME 24

The titles published in this series are listed at *brill.com/bsiel*

Homer from Z to A

Metrics, Linguistics, and Zenodotus

By

Claire Le Feuvre

BRILL

LEIDEN | BOSTON

Cover illustration: Venetus A (Marcianus Gr Z 454 (= 822) fol. 12r). Reproduced with permission of the Biblioteca Marciana.

The Library of Congress Cataloging-in-Publication Data is available online at https://catalog.loc.gov
LC record available at https://lccn.loc.gov/2022040004

Typeface for the Latin, Greek, and Cyrillic scripts: "Brill". See and download: brill.com/brill-typeface.

ISSN 1875-6328
ISBN 978-90-04-52233-6 (hardback)
ISBN 978-90-04-52234-3 (e-book)

Copyright 2022 by Claire Le Feuvre. Published by Koninklijke Brill NV, Leiden, The Netherlands.
Koninklijke Brill NV incorporates the imprints Brill, Brill Nijhoff, Brill Hotei, Brill Schöningh, Brill Fink, Brill mentis, Vandenhoeck & Ruprecht, Böhlau, V&R unipress and Wageningen Academic.
Koninklijke Brill NV reserves the right to protect this publication against unauthorized use. Requests for re-use and/or translations must be addressed to Koninklijke Brill NV via brill.com or copyright.com.

This book is printed on acid-free paper and produced in a sustainable manner.

Contents

Acknowledgements IX
Abbreviations X

Introduction 1
1 Homeric Scholarship and Zenodotus' Status 1
  1.1 *Alexandrian Scholarship* 2
  1.2 *Zenodotus* 5
2 Corpus 13

1 Zenodotus' Text: An Overview 19
  1 Types of Variant Readings 19
    1.1 *Unrelated Readings* 19
    1.2 *Related Readings* 20
      1.2.1 Segmentation Divergence 20
      1.2.2 Morphological Divergence 21
      1.2.3 Lexical Divergence 22
      1.2.4 Syntactic Divergence 23
  2 Linguistic Evidence for Zenodotus' Text 27
    2.1 *Psilosis and Accent* 27
    2.2 *Dialect* 31
    2.3 *Recent Forms* 33
  3 Criteria of Discussion of Variant Readings 40
    3.1 *Metrics* 40
    3.2 *Linguistics* 42
      3.2.1 Phonetics 42
      3.2.2 Morphology 44
      3.2.3 Syntax 47
      3.2.4 Mycenaean 49
      3.2.5 Ἀναλογία 50
    3.3 *Semantics* 51
    3.4 *Corpus* 52
    3.5 *Context* 55
    3.6 *Stylistics and Rhetorics* 57
    3.7 *Plausibility of the Emendation* 64
  4 Old Forms in New Clothes 67
    4.1 *ἰογάστριος or ὀγάστριος* 67
    4.2 *φθανέει* 71

	5	Should a Zenodotean Older Reading Be Printed in a Modern Edition? 72
		5.1 *The Problem of the Dual* 73
		5.2 *Heterogeneity of the Corpus* 75
	6	Zenodotus and Historical Linguistics 79

2 **Sitting on an Old Tree** 82
  1 Γ 151–152: The Metrical Problem 82
  2 Zenodotus' Reading 85
  3 Dialectal Trees 87
  4 The Athematic Forms of δένδρεον 89
  5 'Tree' and Its Proto-Indo-European Root 95
  6 Back to Zenodotus 101
  7 Δενδρήεις 102

3 **"Demain, dès l'aube" (Tomorrow at Dawn)** 104
  1 Θ 470: The Metrical Problem 104
  2 Θ 470: The Syntactic Problem 105
  3 Zenodotus' Reading 107
  4 Aeolic αὔα/αὖα 110
  5 Proto-Indo-European Inflection of 'Dawn' 113
  6 Boeotian ἀϝές, Zenodotus' ἄϝας and Sappho's *αὔα 116
  7 Ἄας δή and ἠοῦς δή 119
  8 Θ 525 121
  9 Chronology and Phonetic Evolution 123
  10 Achaean Type τελήεις 128

4 **Stretching Arms** 132
  1 Α 351 132
  2 A Linguistic Fossil 136
  3 Yet Another Fossil 138

5 **Matters of Perception** 142
  1 Ξ 37–38: The Vulgate's Reading 142
  2 Zenodotus' Reading 148
  3 Adverbs and Preverbs 153
  4 μ 438–439 158
  5 Elimination of ὄψ 161
  6 From Zenodotus' Reading to the Vulgate's 162

6   **Cloaks and Coats**   168
    1   Ἔρυμα/ἔλυμα Δ 137   168
    2   Νυκτὶ ἐλυσθείς A 47   176
    3   ϝελυσθείς and ἐλυσθείς   182
    4   ἐλύσθη   186
    5   A New Picture   188
    6   Hesiod's ἔλῠμα   191

7   **Straight Shaft and Straight Flight**   194
    1   The *hapax* ἰθυπτίων   194
    2   Κυλλοποδίων   195
    3   Zenodotus' Reading   198
    4   Reconstruction and Etymology   202
        4.1   *Formal Analysis*   202
        4.2   *Meaning*   206
    5   The Vulgate's Reading   211

8   **Hollow Lacedaemon, Its Reeds, Its Crevices …**   212
    1   Achaean κηώεις?   212
    2   Κοίλην Λακεδαίμονα κητώεσσαν   213
    3   What Was Zenodotus' Spelling?   214
    4   Καιτάεσσαν in Its Context   220
        4.1   *General Pattern of the Catalogue of Ships*   222
        4.2   *B 581*   224
        4.3   *Mycenaean ta-we-si-jo*   226
    5   Reanalysis and Secondary Use   228
    6   Remotivating the New Form   229

9   **Reeds Again**   234
    1   The Vulgate's Reading   234
    2   Zenodotus' Reading   236
    3   The Preposition and the Status of κελάδων   240

10 **Homer the Master of Rhetorics**   243
    1   B 681   243
        1.1   *The Vulgate's Reading*   243
        1.2   *Zenodotus' Reading*   246
    2   A 60   250
        2.1   *The Vulgate's Reading and Conditional Systems in the Iliad*   251
        2.2   *Zenodotus' Reading*   254

3   Ζ 67–71   255
    3.1   *Aristarchus' Reading*   255
    3.2   *Zenodotus' Reading*   260
4   Λ 458   264
5   Γ 210–211   267
6   Ο 190–191   270

Synthesis   275

Conclusion   280

Appendix: The Corpus   293
Bibliography   316
Index Verborum   333
Index Grammaticorum   341
Index Locorum   342
Index Notionum   348

Acknowledgements

This work, which began in the summer of 2016, owes a lot to several people, whom I want to thank here: Ch. de Lamberterie, R. Meyer, D. Petit, G.-J. Pinault and F. Pontani for their remarks and suggestions on the manuscript, from which the text greatly benefited. O. Hackstein, S. Neri and the participants of the Indogermanisches Seminar in Munich, LMU, before whom I presented parts of this work in a series of lectures in June 2019 and whose observations and questions were very helpful. The two reviewers whose thorough work and detailed comments helped me significantly improve the manuscript. The proof-readers who improved my English. And of course the editors of the series Studies in Indo-European Languages and Linguistics, O. Hackstein and C. Melchert, for welcoming the book. Lastly, I owe special thanks to my students at Sorbonne Université, before whom I tested the hypotheses and arguments developed here: their reactions were probably the best touchstone I could get.

Abbreviations

Languages and Dialects

Arc.	Arcadian
Att.	Attic
Av.	Avestan
CSl.	Common Slavic
Dor.	Doric
Got.	Gothic
Hitt.	Hittite
Ion.	Ionic
Lat.	Latin
Lesb.	Lesbian
Latv.	Latvian
Lith.	Lithuanian
Luw.	Luwian
MW	Middle Welsh
Myc.	Mycenaean
OAv.	Old Avestan
OCS	Old Church Slavonic
OIr.	Old Irish
Pal.	Palaic
Pol.	Polish
PIE	Proto-Indo-European
Ru.	Russian
Thess.	Thessalian
Ved.	Vedic

Metrics

H1	first hemistich before the hephthemimeral caesura
H2	second hemistich after the hephthemimeral caesura
P1	first hemistich before the penthemimeral caesura
P2	second hemistich after the penthemimeral caesura
T1	first hemistich before the trochaic caesura
T2	second hemistich after the trochaic caesura
#	line boundary

Translations of Homer, Hesiod and the Homeric Hymns

R.L.   Richmond Lattimore
J.H.   James Huddleston
D.H.   Daryl Hine
Unmarked translations are mine.

References to Homeric lines follow the traditional system in Homeric studies: Α, Β, Γ refer to books 1, 2, 3 of the *Iliad*, α, β, γ to books 1, 2, 3 of the *Odyssey*.

Introduction

1   Homeric Scholarship and Zenodotus' Status

The Homeric text as we know it is the result of a long process which started in Mycenaean times.[1] Professional singers, drawing from a repertoire of stories, of type-scenes, performed before public or private audiences. They used highly formulaic language allowing the singer to improvise within the limits imposed by the metrical constraints. As a consequence, there was no fixed version: oral transmission, in the earliest stage, implied that the singer recreated the epic for each performance, and that variation was important. A progressive crystallisation occurred around a few prominent episodes, and the *Iliad* and *Odyssey* grew out of it. Between the 8th c. and 6th c. BCE, written versions appeared. This changed the status of singers, whose performance progressively became a recitation more than an improvisation. Tradition calls them rhapsodes, once they relied on a written text, and no longer singers.[2] But even after a version was committed to writing, and there was a written authority, so to speak, rhapsodes nevertheless went on orally performing in public recitations, adapting and modifying the text to some extent, and adding new lines.[3] This changing state of the text is witnessed by the preserved papyri. Old papyri, for instance, often bear lines not present in the text as we know it. The percentage of "plus-verses" (extra lines found in Ptolemaic papyri but not in the medieval manuscripts on which our modern editions are based) in the *Iliad* papyri is higher in older papyri and decreases dramatically after the 2nd c. BCE, which is a good testimony of the standardisation of the text.[4] Not only the number of lines, but also the wording was different: textual differences are much more frequent in older

---

1   There is a huge literature on the question of the transmission of the Homeric epics and the edition of the text in Antiquity. It would not be very useful to repeat here what has been written elsewhere. The reader can refer for instance to standard words like Crielaard 1995, Montanari 2002, Fowler 2006, Finkelberg 2011, Morris and Powell 2011.
2   Tradition distinguishes between singers (ἀοιδοί) who composed orally and improvised to a large extent for each performance, drawing from a repertoire of traditional lines, formulae and type scenes, and rhapsodes (ῥαψῳδοί) who took over after the epics had been written down and who were reciting, but not improvising, relying on a written text. On the fact that rhapsodes did not limit themselves to reciting word for word and could modify the text to some extent and create new lines, see Gentili 2011: 22.
3   Gentili 2011: 22.
4   Bird 2010. One version of the *Iliad* was called the πολύστιχος owing to the number of "plus-verses" it had.

papyri.[5] The standardised text that emerged is the one that will be copied in medieval manuscripts. It is known as the vulgate.

1.1 Alexandrian Scholarship

Alexandrian scholarship played an important role in this process. In the Library of Alexandria, founded in 288 BCE, generations of scholars collected different versions of the Homeric epics, studied them and commented on them. The most important name, as far as the Homeric poems are concerned, is Aristarchus of Samothrace, head of the Library from 153 to 145 BCE. He was an influential scholar whose work on Homer was preserved thanks to his successors. But he was by no means the first scholar to work on Homer.

What kind of Homeric text did Aristarchus know? In the Library, he had at his disposal several versions. He had first of all several copies of a mainstream version, probably from Athens. Athens, because of the public recitation of the entire Homeric poems at the Great Panathenaic Games, and because of its cultural importance, was an active diffusion centre. These are probably the ones referred to in the A scholia as αἱ ἀρχαῖαι 'the old copies'. Next to that, Aristarchus had two sets of sources. A first set are local versions, the recensions *kata poleis* 'by city', also called *politikai* 'of the cities', like the Massaliotic one, the Smyrnian one, the Chian one, the Cretan one, so named because a copy of Homer coming from the considered *polis* was kept in the Library in Alexandria. They are Hellenistic versions predating Alexandrian scholarship. Compared to the mainstream version, they displayed differences as far as number of lines, order of lines, wording are concerned. A second set consists of versions known under the name of a grammarian (*kat' andra* 'by man'), produced by Alexandrian scholars, like the recension by Aristophanes of Byzantium, Aristarchus' teacher, or the recension by Zenodotus (3rd c. BCE). They were, rather than an editorial achievement resulting from the comparison of different versions, a particular version, deemed a good one by the considered scholar, on which he wrote comments and corrections and which he used for teaching.[6] The scholar may have written a commentary (*hypomnema*) in which he explained and developed his arguments and interpretations. Aristarchus did write *hypomnemata*, now lost. Zenodotus does not seem to have written any, and his teaching may have been oral (on the basis of the *ekdosis*).[7]

We know very little about those different versions, except through the scholia, thanks to the notes of Aristarchus' successors telling us that "this line is

---

5 Haslam 1997: 64–66.
6 See Montanari 2015.
7 Pfeiffer 1968: 115.

not in Zenodotus," "the Chian recension has a different word." Some of these readings, including Zenodotus', did find their way into the vulgate, against Aristarchus, and are found in modern editions, but most of them did not.

The scholia transmitting those remnants are of several types.

The lexicographical scholia are the oldest type. They go back partly to the classical period and were a classroom tool explaining difficult words for students unfamiliar with the Homeric vocabulary. Those are called D scholia for the *Iliad*.[8] They are often found independently of the text, on papyri or, later on, in manuscripts having only the scholia. They provide semantic explanations but few comments, and variant readings are often not mentioned.

The A scholia, thus named because they are those of a 10th c. manuscript of the *Iliad*, the Venetus A (Marcianus gr. Z 454 (= 822)), are different. The Venetus A contains scholia from several sources, including lexicographical scholia, but its most important source is a compilation of the works of four scholars of the 1st and 2nd c. CE, Aristonicus' treatise on the critical signs in Aristarchus' work,[9] Didymus' treatise on Aristarchus' *ekdoseis* (see below, pp. 5–6), Nicanor's treatise on punctuation, and Herodian's treatise on Homeric accentuation. This compilation, now lost, was probably produced in the 4th c. CE and is known as the VMK, *Viermännerkommentar*. As a consequence, the A scholia transmit Aristarchean scholarship, and the diverging opinions of other scholars are seen through the Aristarchean prism. They consist mainly of scholarly explanations on the Homeric language and text, including questions of what we call textual criticism with the recording of divergent versions: copy X did not bear line *x*, copy Y had a different word in line *y*, scholar Z condemns line *z* as unauthentic (athetesis).[10] They sought to explain the Homeric usage as distinct from the contemporary *koine* and to set rules for it.

The last type of scholia are the so-called exegetical scholia, called for the *Iliad* the bT scholia, because they are found in manuscript T (Townleyanus, 11th c., London, BL Burney 86) and in the manuscripts descending from a lost archetype *b* dated to the 6th c. CE, among which the Venetus B (Marcianus gr. 821,

---

8   Online edition by Van Thiel 2014. They are called D scholia because they were once thought to go back to the work of Didymus Chalcenterus (1st c. BCE–1st c. CE).

9   Aristonicus' comments in the A scholia almost always start with ὅτι "(*diple*), because [...]."

10 The athetesis (ἀθέτησις 'abolition') is the technical term used for condemning a line deemed unauthentic, for a linguistic, metrical, stylistic or any other reason. It was marked with a specific critical sign, the *obelos*, already used by Zenodotus: this allowed the scholar to show he thought the line was unoriginal while not erasing it from the text. The corresponding verb is ἀθετέω 'to reject', 'to athetise'. The question of the consistency of Zenodotus' method as far as condemned lines are concerned is a vexed one and will be dealt with below.

11th c.). They focus on interpretation rather than on textual criticism, whence the name of exegetical scholia. They draw extensively on the works of Porphyry (Ὁμηρικὰ ζητήματα) and Heraclitus (Ὁμηρικὰ προβλήματα).[11] However, the T scholia do preserve indications going back to the VMK and are an important source for textual criticism, albeit less than the A scholia. The Venetus A contains some exegetical scholia.

Another collection, the h scholia, collected in Byzantine times, partly goes back to Hellenistic scholarship.

For the *Odyssey* there are also lexicographical scholia, exegetical scholia and critical scholia, but "because there is no equivalent of Venetus A among the *Odyssey* manuscripts the different types are not so easily separable by manuscript source."[12]

That means that our main source about textual variants are in fact the A scholia deriving from the VMK, and to a lesser extent the T scholia. As a consequence, we know more about the different versions of the *Iliad* than of the *Odyssey* because there is nothing like Venetus A for the *Odyssey*, although there are of course scholia going back to classical and Alexandrian scholarship, but no such collection as the A scholia.[13]

The Homeric scholia are supplemented by other sources. Among the oldest is the *Lexicon homericum* of Apollonius the Sophist (1st c. CE), of which only an Epitome has come down to us: as a lexicographical work, it explains the meaning of words, as the D scholia, but when explaining a word, Apollonius sometimes mentions variant readings. The explanations given in the *Lexicon homericum* often agree with the A scholia, indicating that the *Lexicon* goes back to Aristarchean scholarship. The other two main sources are Byzantine. The *Epimerismi homerici* (9th c.) compile old material, some common with what is found in the Homeric scholia: the *Epimerismi* do not contain much about textual criticism. And above all the two monumental *Commentaries* of Eustathius of Thessalonica (12th c. CE): Eustathius had access to many sources now lost and can occasionally transmit elements not mentioned in the existing corpus of Homeric scholia.

---

11 The A scholia and bT scholia were edited by Erbse 1971–1982 (without the borrowings from Porphyry and Heraclitus).
12 Dickey 2007: 21. For a more detailed picture, see Pontani 2005 and 2016. The old edition of the *Odyssey* scholia by Dindorf is now superseded by the new edition by Pontani (eight books published so far), and the electronic edition of the D scholia by Ernst (2006).
13 The most important manuscripts with ancient scholia are H (Southern Italy, 12th–13th c.) and M (13th c.). See Pontani 2007: xii.

1.2 Zenodotus

Coming back to the different versions known to Aristarchus, Zenodotus' has a special status. Zenodotus, chief librarian in Alexandria, appointed to this position in 284 BCE, produced an *ekdosis* of Homer. This *ekdosis* is the annotated text of a given version taken as a basis; on this text the scholar wrote comments, corrections, maybe variant readings found in other copies,[14] or marked lines considered unauthentic. It is not a composite text created by the scholar out of several copies from which he would pick one line here and another there.[15] The task of correcting Homer (διορθόω) involved sorting out authentic lines from interpolations, and also emending the text—the latter process is already mentioned in Aristotle's *Sophistici Elenchi* 166b3–4. That Zenodotus actually corrected the text by athetising several lines is proved by his use of the *obelos*, an editorial mark signalling a line he deemed unauthentic. That he introduced emendations is possible (and has been assumed by generations of scholars) but this is inferred from the meaning of διορθόω 'to correct'.[16] Now eliminating unauthentic lines is in itself a correction (*diorthôsis*) of Homer: the word *diorthôsis* does not necessarily imply that emendations were suggested and readings changed.

We know Zenodotus produced an *ekdosis* both of the *Iliad* and of the *Odyssey* but, because of the state of the corpus of the Homeric scholia (see above), we have much less information about his readings for the *Odyssey*. Aristarchus, a century later, took as the basis for his own *ekdosis* a different version, probably an Attic one, and constantly compared it to Zenodotus', marking the places of divergence through a specific editorial mark, the *diple periestigmene*.[17] In fact Aristarchus produced two different *ekdoseis* of the *Iliad*, and scholia report several divergences between the two, but they are minor differences, whereas the differences with Zenodotus were sometimes striking. Aristarchus' *diorthôsis*

---

14 There is no agreement on this matter. See a summary of the positions in Rengakos 2012 and Montanari 2015.
15 This still was what Wilamowitz thought (1916: 129): "the Alexandrian scholars took the nice lines from any of their versions."
16 See in particular Pfeiffer 1968: 110: "It is not improbable that Zenodotus, examining manuscripts in the library, selected *one* text of Homer, which seemed to him to be superior to any other one, as his main guide; its deficiencies he may have corrected from better readings in other manuscripts as well as by his own conjectures. Διόρθωσις can be the term for either kind of correction. It is hard to imagine any other way." The word "imagine" is telling.
17 In the A scholia, *diple* alone often stands for *diple periestigmene*. Some scholars think Aristarchus never held in his hands Zenodotus' *ekdosis* and had an indirect knowledge of it, but this is rather unlikely. See Schironi 2018: 549, n. 12.

clearly involved not only athetising unauthentic lines but also changing the reading for a form deemed preferable. But Aristarchus' editorial activity may be different from Zenodotus' a century earlier, and more wide-ranging.

For scholars starting from the standard text, close to Aristarchus' version, which became the vulgate and is the basis of all medieval manuscripts,[18] Zenodotus' variant readings were abnormal, and often attributed to unjustified corrections he made. This conception starts with Greek scholarship: it is already found in Aristonicus' works transmitted by the A scholia, down to Eustathius, who repeatedly states that Zenodotus μεταγράφει 'rewrites' the text of Homer.[19] This can be understood as referring to a change introduced by Zenodotus either as a personal emendation or after another copy of Homer,[20] but it could also refer to a departure from the standard text in Zenodotus' copy kept unchanged. Aristonicus did not have a direct knowledge of Zenodotus' *ekdosis*, and the A scholia do not preserve word for word Aristonicus' text, therefore we do not know exactly what Zenodotus is supposed to have done. We find three different formulations in the scholia going back to Aristonicus:

– γράφει 'he writes', is the most frequent formulation in Aristonicus' comments: *A Schol.* A 8a: ὅτι Ζηνόδοτος 'σφωι' ἔγραφεν "because Zenodotus writes σφῶι." For anonymous copies, Aristonicus uses the same verb: *A Schol.* A 197: ὅτι οὕτως λέγει [...]. ἀγνοήσαντες δέ τινες γράφουσι [...] "because this is what Homer says [...]. But some, unaware of that, write [...]." *A Schol.* I 212: ὅτι ἔν τισι γράφεται 'αὐτὰρ ἐπεὶ πυρὸς ἄνθος ἀπέπτατο, παύσατο δὲ φλόξ' "because it is written in some 'αὐτὰρ ἐπεὶ πυρὸς ἄνθος ἀπέπτατο, παύσατο δὲ φλόξ' ("when the flower of the fire left and the flames died out") (vulgate αὐτὰρ ἐπεὶ κατὰ πῦρ ἐκάη καὶ φλὸξ ἐμαράνθη "but when the fire had burned itself out, and the flames had died out" (R.L.)). A variant of the latter is ἔν τισι γέγραπται.

– μεταγράφει 'he rewrites', which in its technical meaning applies to corrections and emendations, is much less frequent: *A Schol.* A 220: ὅτι Ζηνόδοτος μεταγράφει 'ὣς εἰπὼν πάλιν ὦσε μέγα ξίφος οὐδ' ἀπίθησε' καὶ τοὺς δύο ἕνα ἐποίησεν "because Zenodotus rewrites 'he said, and back he pushed the large

---

18 Although most of the time the vulgate agrees with Aristarchus, in several places it does not and Aristarchus' reading, mentioned by the A scholia, was different. For instance, in I 564 the vulgate has κλαῖ' ὅτε μιν ἑκάεργος ἀνήρπασε Φοῖβος Ἀπόλλων "she cried when Phoebus Apollon abducted her daughter," agreeing with Zenodotus, when Aristarchus had κλαῖεν ὅ μιν "she cried because Phoebus Apollon abducted her daughter."

19 In the scholia, μεταγράφειν is not used for Zenodotus alone, but mainly for him nevertheless.

20 See Montanari 2015: 644–646, for a summary of what we know of pre-Aristarchean scholarship. Some Ptolemaic papyri show several editorial interventions in the text (corrections, insertion of variants), most clearly papyrus 12 (S. West 1967: 136–138).

sword, and did not disobey', and made one line out of two."²¹ Μεταγράφειν is also used for anonymous copies: A Schol. A 211: τινὲς δὲ ἀγνοοῦντες ὅτι [...] μεταγράφουσι [...] "but some, unaware that [...], rewrite [...]."
- no verb: A Schol. H 153a1: θάρσεϊ ᾧ· ὅτι Ζηνόδοτος θάρσει ἐμῷ "because Zenodotus ⟨has⟩ θάρσει ἐμῷ." A Schol. I 3c: βεβολήατο· ὅτι ἔνιοι βεβλήατο, καὶ Ζηνόδοτος οὕτως "because some ⟨have⟩ βεβλήατο, and so Zenodotus."

Two sources can use a divergent formulation, for instance for Γ 206 the A scholion has Ζηνόδοτος γράφει σῆς ἔνεκ'ἀγγελίης, but Apollonius' *Lexicon homericum* (p. 7) has a longer and maybe older formulation Ζηνόδοτος δὲ τοῦτο ἀγνοήσας μεταγράφει ἧς ἔνεκ'ἀγγελίης. This can also occur between two A scholia, for instance A Schol. O 405a ἡ δὲ ἀναφορὰ πρὸς Ζηνόδοτον γράφοντα ῥίμφ' ἐὰ γοῦνα φέρει "this is a reference to Zenodotus who writes ῥίμφ' ἐὰ γοῦνα φέρει (Z 511)," but A Schol. P 700a and A Schol. Σ 148a πρὸς Ζηνόδοτον μεταγράφοντα ῥίμφ' ἐὰ γοῦνα φέρει, alluding to the same line.

Accordingly, when an A scholion going back to Aristonicus has γράφει 'writes' or μεταγράφει 'rewrites, changes', we cannot be certain that the two verbs are properly distinguished. And when there is no verb, we cannot know what the scholar intended. The γράφεται used for anonymous copies refers to the text itself of these copies, not to scholarly emendations. This is also clear from another scholion going back to Aristonicus, A Schol. T 118a: ἐκ δ' ἄγαγε πρὸ φόως δὲ ⟨καὶ ἠλιτόμηνον ἐόντα⟩: ὅτι νῦν ὑγιῶς γράφεται σὺν τῇ προθέσει πρὸ φόως· [...] ὁ δὲ Ζηνόδοτος καὶ ἐπ' ἄλλου (sc. Π 188) οὕτως γράφει "because here we have the correct reading (lit. "it is correctly written"), with the preposition πρὸ φόως; [...] and Zenodotus has this reading in another place, too." This aims at Aristarchus' reading ἐξάγαγεν φόως δέ in Π 188 (see below, pp. 42–43), and γράφεται refers to the text, not to an emendation. Therefore, the active γράφει used for Zenodotus' version, as for all the versions *kat' andra*, can refer to his main text as well as to a marginal comment he wrote or a correction he made.

However, in all three cases the Zenodotean reading can be followed by an explicit indication blaming Zenodotus. As a result, there was a strong tendency to explain any difference between Zenodotus' *ekdosis* and the other versions by a voluntary change introduced by the scholar. This is to a large extent an anachronistic retrospective viewpoint of scholars used to working with a standard version, and forgetting that this version did not become standard until fairly late. Or rather, "forgetting" is not the right word, since they never doubted that there was a poet named Homer who composed the text of the epics, so that

---

21 The vulgate has Ἡ καὶ ἐπ' ἀργυρέῃ κώπῃ σχέθε χεῖρα βαρεῖαν, ‖ ἂψ δ' ἐς κουλεὸν ὦσε μέγα ξίφος, οὐδ' ἀπίθησε "he spoke, and laid his heavy hand on the silver sword hilt and thrust the great blade back into the scabbard nor disobeyed" (R.L.).

any variant was analysed in terms of deviation or alteration or unnecessary addition to the original text. Worse, the A scholia are full of comments like "Zenodotus did not understand" or "Zenodotus ignores that [...]," and picture him not only as an ill-inspired editor, but also as one with a poor knowledge of the epic corpus,[22] and a poor metrician on top of that.[23] As per Schironi: "no doubt, Aristarchus had problems with his predecessor. Yet this impression may also be due to the selection of the material: Aristonicus probably recorded only the instances where Zenodotus was criticized, because Aristarchus himself in all likelihood only reported (and discussed) disagreements in his *hypomnemata*, but not the cases where he shared Zenodotus' choice."[24] This is certainly correct. The same holds true for Didymus: when the two *ekdoseis* of Aristarchus disagree and Zenodotus agrees with one of them, the primary focus of Didymus is on αἱ Ἀριστάρχου, and Zenodotus is sometimes mentioned with a short "the same in Zenodotus."

Notice that, since Zenodotus did not produce a written commentary (*hypomnema*), Aristarchus probably did not have access to the explanations Zenodotus gave. Therefore he tried to understand why Zenodotus had such readings and Aristonicus has formulations like "perhaps because ..." Such comments

---

22 For instance ναῖε δὲ Πήδαιον: ὅτι Ζηνόδοτος γράφει 'ὃς νάε Πήδαιον', ἵνα κατάλληλον τὸν λόγον κατὰ συναφὴν ποιήσῃ. ἀγνοεῖ δὲ ὅτι "Ομηρος διακόπτει τὰς φράσεις, ἵνα μὴ μακροπερίοδος γένηται. ἄλλως τε καὶ κακόμετρον τὸ ἔπος ποιεῖ "because Zenodotus writes 'ὃς νάε Πήδαιον', so that the discourse is syntactically chained. But he ignores that Homer cuts the sentences not to have long sentences. And anyway it makes the line metrically bad" (*A Schol.* N 172a); ἀμέτρως ὁ Ζηνόδοτος ὄπα χαλκέην, οὐ συνεὶς ὅτι παραπλήσιόν ἐστι τὸ σχῆμα τῷ κλυτὸς Ἱπποδάμεια καὶ θερμὸς ἀυτμή "Zenodotus has an unmetrical ὄπα χαλκέην, because he did not understand that the figure is similar to κλυτὸς Ἱπποδάμεια and to θερμὸς ἀυτμή" (*A Schol.* Σ 222b); ὅτι Ζηνόδοτος μὴ νοήσας τὸ σημαινόμενον γράφει ἀδηκότες ἠδέι ὕπνῳ κοιμήσωνται "because Zenodotus, having misunderstood the meaning, writes ἀδηκότες ἠδέι ὕπνῳ κοιμήσωνται" (*A Schol.* K 98b); ὅτι Ζηνόδοτος ὀρῆτο γράφει· ἀγνοεῖ δὲ ὅτι Δωρικὸν γίνεται "because Zenodotus writes ὀρῆτο, but he ignores that this is Doric" (*A Schol.* A 56c). Accordingly, some philologists like Severyns or Van der Valk were very critical towards Zenodotus, thought to have introduced into the text many personal corrections. Suffice it to quote Van der Valk 1964: 20 "so we can see that the alterations of Zenod. in this respect were subjective and were guided by a definite and incorrect principle." Ibid.: 68: "Zenod., as we saw, sometimes offered incorrect emendations, because he had no right idea of Homeric grammar." Such is Van der Valk's bias against Zenodotus that he writes "However, I warn the reader that Wilamowitz has a preference for Zenodotus' text" (1964: 76).

23 For instance ὅτι Ζηνόδοτος γράφει Ἡρακλείη, καὶ ἄμετρον ποιῶν καὶ οὐχ Ὁμηρικὸν τὸ σχῆμα· ἀπὸ γὰρ τοῦ Ἡρακλῆος Ἡρακληείη ἐκπίπτει (*A Schol.* B 658) "because Zenodotus writes Ἡρακλείη, making the form unmetrical and un-Homeric: as a matter of fact, from Ἡρακλῆος, the correct form is Ἡρακληείη."

24 Schironi 2018: 550.

reflect the interpretation of the Aristarchean school, not Zenodotus' own understanding.[25]

In the last decades, however, there has been a trend to rehabilitate Zenodotus' work. Most scholars assume that he did not intervene as much as previously thought and that he did find many of his readings in his working text or in copies he collated. A particular vision is West's, who thinks that Zenodotus did not intervene a lot but relied on an eccentric version of Homer:

> To sum up, we must treat Zenodotus' so-called ἔκδοσις not as the construct of a hare-brained scholar making an unsteady attempt to create order out of a jumble of manuscripts, but as a fourth-century Ephesian rhapsode's text, deformed by many oral variants, arbitrary abridgements, trivializations, modernizations, and so forth, yet drawing on a side-stream of tradition which, having branched off at an early date from the major (Attic) channel, uniquely preserved certain genuine elements of the archaic text.[26]

West may be going too far when he assumes that Zenodotus did not intervene in the text except for atheteses,[27] but he is certainly right on one point, that Zenodotus relied on a text which was different in a number of places from what would become the vulgate, and that the divergences are not all an invention of his, but many are things he did find in his text—which is anyway admitted by most scholars. There is papyrological evidence for readings which scholia say were an abusive correction by Zenodotus, and those papyri are not likely to depend on a scholarly tradition but were "ordinary commercial copies,"[28] confirming that Zenodotus read something different in his sources.

Sometimes Zenodotus' readings are confirmed by literary sources older than the 3rd c. BCE. A well-known example is A 4–5, αὐτοὺς δὲ ἑλώρια τεῦχε κύνεσσιν || οἰωνοῖσί τε δαῖτα "and made them prey to the dogs and banquet for the birds," attributed to Zenodotus by Athenaeus (*Deipn.* 1.21 Kaibel) and by the *Suda* (δ 128), whereas the vulgate has οἰωνοῖσί τε πᾶσι "and for all the birds." In fact, Aristonicus explicitly says that Zenodotus athetised those two lines:

---

25 Schironi 2018: 550: "The scholia do not generally report Zenodotus' arguments, probably because Aristarchus did not know them himself in the first place and thus did not report them in his commentaries."

26 West 2002: 142.

27 For a criticism of West's theory, see the review of West 2001 by Rengakos, BMCR 2002.11.15, and recently Montanari 2015. This study, however, will show that on the points here examined, West was indeed right that Zenodotus did not correct his text.

28 S. West 1967: 27.

A Schol. A 4a: ὅτι Ζηνόδοτος τοὺς δύο ἀθετεῖ. γίνεται δὲ τὸ προοίμιον κόλον.

because Zenodotus athetises both lines; but the introduction becomes truncated thereby.

Zenodotus cannot have introduced the reading δαῖτα into a line which he considered unauthentic anyway.[29] His version already had δαῖτα, and he is not the source of this reading. As pointed out already,[30] and as mentioned in West's apparatus, Aeschylus *Suppl.* 800–801 κυσὶν δ' ἔπειθ' ἕλωρα κἀπιχωρίοις | ὄρνισι δεῖπνον οὐκ ἀναίνομαι πέλειν "thereafter I refuse not to become a booty for dogs and a banquet for the local birds" (transl. H.W. Smyth) are probably modelled after the beginning of the *Iliad*: these lines strongly suggest that the reading δαῖτα was already known in the 5th c. BCE. That does not prove that δαῖτα was the original line and was replaced by πᾶσι, but even if we assume that δαῖτα is an innovation, it remains that this innovation dates back at least to the first half of the 5th c.[31]

Similarly, in Φ 575 Zenodotus read ἐπεὶ κυνυλαγμὸν ἀκούσῃ 'when he hears the dog's barking', vs vulgate ἐπεί κεν ὑλαγμὸν ἀκούσῃ, preferred by Aristarchus. Zenodotus' reading is definitely old, because the word is found in Stesichorus' ἀπειρεσίοιο κυνυλαγμοῖο (*fr.* 255 *PMG*).[32] Aristarchus knew the reading κυνυλαγμός, to which he objected:

bT Schol. Φ 575b: Ἀρίσταρχός τινάς φησι γράφειν "κυνυλαγμόν"· καὶ Στησίχορος δὲ ἔοικεν οὕτως ἀνεγνωκέναι· φησὶ γοῦν "ἀπειρεσίοιο κυνυλαγμοῖο". οὐχ ὁρῶμεν δέ τι πλεῖον ἐκ τῆς συνθέσεως· ὁ γὰρ ὑλαγμὸς καὶ χωρὶς τοῦ προσκεῖσθαι τὸ ὄνομα ἰδίως ἐπὶ κυνῶν ἀκούεται, ὡς ὁ χρεμετισμὸς ἐπὶ τῶν ἵππων.

---

29   This is not the only case in which scholia report Zenodotus had a variant reading in a line he athetised: see also A 47 (chap. 6), B 690 (Zenodotus athetised B 686–694), H 458 (he athetised H 443–464, as did Aristophanes and Aristarchus) among others. This is not specific to Zenodotus: in H 475 the A and T scholia say Aristarchus read ἀνδραπόδοισι vs vulgate ἀνδραπόδεσσι and that he athetised the line, because the word was post-Homeric (νεωτερικός). Most of the time in the passage under consideration only the athetesis is mentioned by the scholion, and the variant reading appears somewhere else as a cross-reference.
30   See a discussion in Bird 1994: 40–42, and in the *BK*, with literature.
31   Pfeiffer 1968: 111–113 considers that Zenodotus' reading is the oldest: "Aristarchus, no doubt, is responsible for οἰωνοῖσί τε πᾶσι having replaced in all our manuscripts the fifth-century and Zenodotean reading δαῖτα" (p. 113).
32   This is acknowledged by most scholars: Nickau 1977: 34–35; Rengakos 2012: 243. Van Thiel 2014a, *sub* Φ 575, assumes κυνυλαγμός is a marginal comment by which Zenodotus compared other poets (Stesichorus among others).

Aristarchus says some write κυνυλαγμόν. And Stesichorus seems to have read it that way, because he says ἀπειρεσίοιο κυνυλαγμοῖο. But we cannot see what is added by the composition: because ὑλαγμός 'barking', even without adding a prefix to the noun, properly refers to dogs, as χρεμετισμός 'whinnying' to horses.

Zenodotus was not alone, and this reading was found in several copies (τινάς). The vulgate's reading is an emendation, which relies on a linguistic reasoning blaming the redundancy of the compound. It is certainly not very old, although it may predate Aristarchus.

In modern scholarship, one radical interpretation must be set aside, that of H. van Thiel (1992 and 2014b). This scholar defended the hypothesis that some "wild" readings attributed to Zenodotus by the A scholia were not variant readings, but comments Zenodotus wrote in the margin of his working text, and which were mistaken by Aristarchus' followers for the reading he advocated. This implies that in fact Zenodotus had the same text as ours, by and large, and no significant variant reading. This also implies that he did not intervene in the text at all—quite the opposite of what the *doxa* says.[33] Van Thiel assumes that Aristonicus was the main person responsible for misinterpreting these marginal comments as genuine variant readings, thus sparing Aristarchus. Nickau (1977) already resorted to explanations of that kind for some Zenodotean readings. But Van Thiel goes a step further and assumes that Zenodotus' marginal comments were metrical and reduced to one word in the margin, with no explanation: "Zenodotus displays a playful approach in so far as he almost always tried to maintain the metrical form, and dressed his comments in a 'Homeric' coat."[34] That supposedly explains why they look like variant readings since they have the same metrical shape as the form on which they comment, and are not accompanied by any comment. They are explained as "experimental modifications" ("experimentelle Wortänderungen") or as implicit references to post-Homeric poets (the νεώτεροι in Aristarchean terminology). For instance, for A 5, Van Thiel assumes that δαῖτα is a marginal comment by Zenodotus meant as a comparison with the tragic poets, Aeschylus (*Suppl.* 800–801) and Euripides (*Hec.* 1077 κυσίν τε φοινίαν δαῖτ'). However, Aeschylus' line does not have the word δαῖτα and it is highly unlikely that Zenodotus made

---

[33] Van Thiel 2014b: 18: "he leaves the text unchanged."
[34] Van Thiel 1992: 5: "einen spielerischen Zug zeigt Zenodotus darin, daß er fast immer die metrische Form zu bewahren suchte, seine Kommentare also in ein 'homerisches' Gewand kleidete."

a comparison without providing the reference, that is, without saying "δαῖτα in Euripides," since in that case the point of the comparison is lost.[35]

Van Thiel's general thesis is highly unlikely and raises many objections.[36] Aristophanes' *ekdosis* had many readings in common with Zenodotus, which Van Thiel can account for either by assuming that Aristophanes himself misunderstood the marginal comments of Zenodotus and integrated them as readings, or found them so interesting that he repeated them himself as marginal comments, which led his followers to misunderstand them for readings. Besides, it is unlikely that Aristarchus invented a specific sign, the *diple periestigmene*, for Zenodotus, whose *ekdosis* he had in his hands,[37] if he did not consider those as variant readings but simply as marginal comments. Van Thiel assumes that many of these marginal comments are in fact references to Hellenistic poets: but what was the source of Hellenistic poets and where do those words come from? The question is not asked. We know that, on the contrary, such forms show up in Hellenistic poetry because poets like Callimachus, Theocritus, Apollonius of Rhodes, and Lycophron were learned poets who were also exegetes of Homer and who integrated into their poetry philological controversies of the time: their sources are the existing variants.[38]

Most scholars nowadays don't subscribe to Van Thiel's hypothesis and assume that what the scholia mention as variant readings by Zenodotus were definitely readings, not marginal comments. The question is: are they old or not, were they in the text or taken from other copies collated by the scholar, are they emendations or not?

The aim of this work is to bring to this discussion new linguistic arguments. As a matter of fact, on linguistic grounds, some of Zenodotus' readings can be shown to be older than the vulgate's readings, and cannot be conjectures. Historical linguistics, not taken into account by Van Thiel, can show that some "experimental modifications" happen to be exactly what Indo-Europeanists can explain as forms no longer analysable in the 3rd c. BCE, but corresponding to a much older state of the language. No scholarly "experimentation" can account for that. Therefore they were not invented. And conversely, I hope this study will bring new philological elements that can improve our knowledge of

---

35 Van Thiel 2014b, *sub* A 5.
36 See a refutation of Van Thiel's thesis in Schmidt 1997. Yet, since Van Thiel persisted on this path and published his monumental commented edition of the *Iliad* scholia (Van Thiel 2014b), his hypothesis will be mentioned in that study.
37 Some scholars assume that Aristarchus did not directly know Zenodotus' *ekdosis* and never had it in his hands, but this is unlikely. He must have had at least a copy of it.
38 See Rengakos 1992, 1993, 1994.

the history of Greek and provide new material for linguists. I will apply here the point of view of the linguist to a material only philologists usually deal with: linguists, most of the time, work on the vulgate's text and neglect this material. In particular, it must be stressed that most of the standard works on Homeric language date back to a time when Zenodotus was seen through the eyes of Aristarchus' followers, so that his readings were most of the time not taken into account. But even in recent studies the tendency remains to stick to the vulgate. This is partly a consequence of the fact that recent studies focus on syntax and make heavy use of electronic corpora such as the *Thesaurus Linguae Graecae* or the "Chicago Homer," which give an even greater weight to the vulgate since only the vulgate's text, on which all modern editions are based with minor variations, is lemmatised and searchable. Those electronic corpora are extraordinary tools, but we should not become prisoners of our tools.

2 Corpus

Zenodotus is mentioned 740 times in Erbse's edition of the *Iliad* scholia—sometimes he is mentioned in two different scholia to the same line, therefore the real number is inferior (see the figures in the Appendix). He is mentioned 88 times in Dindorf's edition of the *Odyssey* scholia.[39] Compared to the 27 802 lines of the Homeric vulgate, the corpus is small, indeed. The difference between the *Iliad* scholia and the *Odyssey* scholia is striking—remember there is no Venetus A for the *Odyssey*.[40]

The variants explicitly attributed to him are only a part of his variant readings. Copyists, in order to spare room on their manuscripts, often did not write down the entire text of their source, and this applies to the A scholia, too. For instance, in B 581, a variant reading is mentioned, without any name, and without the *diple periestigmene*, the critical sign marking divergences from Zenodotus' text in the Aristarchean *ekdosis*, and this same variant reading is found in δ 1, explicitly attributed to Zenodotus by a scholion (see chapter 8). Without the *Odyssey* scholion, we would not know that the reading was Zenodotus', since the A scholia remain silent and the D scholia report the reading without any name. This is obviously not an isolated case, and more than one variant reading left anonymous in our sources can go back to Zenodotus. This

---

39 Not counting the mention in δ 477, eliminated in Pontani's edition as referring to Zenodorus, not Zenodotus.

40 The Geneva scholia were not taken into account here because they repeat the older scholia.

holds true particularly for the *Odyssey*, for which we do not have the equivalent of the Venetus A, our main source on Zenodotus' *ekdosis*. It is also likely that more than one variant reading attributed to one of the *politikai* versions was also found in Zenodotus' text but only the name of the Chian or Massaliotic recension survived.

There also are cases where the Homeric scholia do not give any information whereas a variant reading under the name of Zenodotus is found in another source. Sometimes this coincides with what the scholia say. For instance, in Ξ 40 the vulgate has πτῆξε δὲ θυμὸν ἐνὶ στήθεσσιν Ἀχαιῶν "he abated the heart in the Achaeans' breast" (R.L.). An A scholion mentions a variant reading πῆξε 'he froze', but not under Zenodotus' name, and only Eustathius (*Comm. Il.* 3: 575) says πῆξε was Zenodotus' reading.

Likewise, Eustathius says:

> Eustathius, *Comm. Od.* 2: 90 (*ad* ο 20): τὸ δὲ οἶσθα γὰρ οἷος θυμός, ἐλέγχει Ζηνόδοτον καὶ τοὺς κατ' αὐτόν, κακῶς γράφοντας τὸ οἶσθας παρὰ τῷ ποιητῇ. ἐν τέλει μὲν γὰρ στίχου ἢ καὶ ἐπιφορᾷ φωνήεντος εἴη ἂν γενέσθαι συγχωρηθεῖσαν τοιαύτην γραφήν. ἐνταῦθα δὲ οὐκ ἂν γένοιτο διὰ τὸ κακομέτρητον.

> the οἶσθα γὰρ οἷος θυμός (ο 20), against Zenodotus and his followers who wrongly write οἶσθας in Homer. At the end of the line, or before a vowel, this spelling could be admitted, but here it is impossible because it is unmetrical.

The A scholion to A 85 has ὅτι οἶσθα χωρὶς τοῦ σ· οὕτως γὰρ λέγει διὰ πάντος "οἶσθα without [s], because this is what he uses all along." It confirms the existence of the recent form οἶσθας in some copies but not under Zenodotus' name.[41] In the A scholia, this form οἶσθας is addressed only here and is not repeated for other lines displaying οἶσθα.

Sometimes, the information is not found in the Homeric scholia. For instance, Eustathius (*Comm. Od.* 2: 172, *ad* σ 130 οὐθὲν ἀκιδνότερον) said Zenodotus had οὐθέν instead of οὐδέν. The same indication is found in Herennius Philo (*De diversis verborum significationibus*, omicron 131, quoting the same οὐθὲν ἀκιδνότερον). Οὐθείς is a recent form, like οἶσθας, attested in Attic comedy from the 4th c. on. It is mainly Attic but it soon spread in Ionic and is well attested in 3rd c. inscriptions from Asia Minor. However, the Homeric scholia never mention any variant reading οὐθέν or οὐθείς.

---

41   Van der Valk 1985: 376 thought that Aristonicus' remark for A 85 was aimed at Zenodotus. It was aimed at those who wrote οἶσθας but nothing warrants Zenodotus was one of them.

The loss of written witnesses is of course the main reason for this fragmentary information. For instance, the French humanist Guillaume Budé (1467–1540) annotated his edition of the *Iliad*. The source of the scholia he drew from is unknown. One of his notes reports that two lines were athetised by Zenodotus, which is not reported by any of our sources.[42] This implies that there was a manuscript of the *Iliad* with scholia similar to the Venetus A, but not exactly identical, which preserved different information, including about Zenodotus, and which is now lost.

Moreover, the information we have is not always complete. Not only do the A scholia not mention every single Zenodotean variant reading, but they sometimes mention them in an incomplete way. For example in Σ 198, ἀλλ' αὕτως ἐπὶ τάφρον ἰὼν Τρώεσσι φάνηθι "but go to the ditch, and show yourself as you are to the Trojans" (R.L.). Didymus says that Zenodotus and Aristophanes had not αὕτως but αὐτός:

> A Schol. Σ 198a1: παρὰ Ζηνοδότῳ καὶ Ἀριστοφάνει διὰ τοῦ ο 'αὐτός', ἵν' ᾖ αὐτὸς χωρὶς ὅπλων. καὶ λόγον ἔχει χαρίεντα, καὶ οὐκ ἄλογός ἐστιν ἡ γραφή.
>
> in Zenodotus and Aristophanes αὐτός with omicron, so that it is he alone without his armour. And this reading has an elegant justification, and is not unreasonable.

But with αὐτός the line is unmetrical. That means that Zenodotus and Aristophanes either had a preposition other than ἐπί (ποτί, παρά), or a particle after αὐτός. The scholiast concentrated on what was important to him, the lexical divergence between the adverb and the adjective, and left aside what seemed to him a minor divergence (see below Γ 56, pp. 44–45). Consequently, the exact version of Zenodotus is not given, and we only have a partial recording.[43] A similar case is found in Σ 247. Aristonicus says

> A Schol. Σ 247: πάντας γὰρ ἔχε τρόμος· Ζηνόδοτος φόβος, κακῶς, ἀγνοῶν ὅτι φόβος ἐστὶ καθ' Ὅμηρον ἡ μετὰ δέους φυγή. διὸ ἡ διπλῆ.
>
> πάντας γὰρ ἔχε τρόμος: Zenodotus ⟨has⟩ φόβος, wrongly, because he does not know that φόβος for Homer means the flight caused by fear. Hence the *diple*.

---

42   Pontani 2007: 396; Morantin 2017: 201–202.
43   Van Thiel, who assumes Zenodotus' αὐτός is an "experimental modification," or a "comment," does not comment on the metrical problem.

Zenodotus' reading would require ἔχεν, not ἔχε. There again Aristonicus focuses on the lexical difference, not on the consequence on the preceding word. In this line, we can easily supply the missing information, but such is not always the case. Zenodotus' reading is correctly given in T 14 πάντας δ' ἔλεν φόβος, vs vulgate πάντας ἔλε τρόμος.

Similarly, in E 329 the vulgate has αἶψα δὲ Τυδεΐδην μέθεπε κρατερώνυχας ἵππους "and held the strong-footed team toward the son of Tydeus" (R.L.). Aristonicus says Zenodotus had a dative instead of the accusative: ὅτι Ζηνόδοτος γράφει κρατερωνύχεσι "because Zenodotus writes κρατερωνύχεσι". But of course, Zenodotus had κρατερωνύχεσ' ἵπποις, and his reading is only partially recorded.

On the other hand, Zenodotus was sometimes credited with readings that were not his—only the rich get credit. For instance, in B 111 Ζεύς με μέγα Κρονίδης ἄτῃ ἐνέδησε βαρείῃ "Zeus son of Kronos has caught me fast in bitter futility" (R.L.), with an adverbial μέγα 'greatly', Zenodotus reportedly had μέγας, adjective, epithet of Zeus, instead of μέγα, that is, "great Zeus son of Cronos." But Didymus says: σχολικὸν ἀγνόημα τὸ δοκεῖν Ζηνοδότειον εἶναι τὴν μετὰ τοῦ σ γραφήν "it is an ignorance of the scholiasts to believe that the reading with ⟨s⟩ is Zenodotus'" (A Schol. B 111b), adding that this ignorance is shared by Dionysius Thrax (fr. 14) and that Ptolemy Epithetes did not give μέγας as a Zenodotean reading.[44]

A similar case is found in Δ 3. Didymus says:

> A Schol. Δ 3a1: ἐῳνοχόει· κατ' ἔνια τῶν ὑπομνημάτων "ἐνῳνοχόει" φέρεται. οἱ δέ φασι Ζηνοδότειον εἶναι τὴν γραφήν· ἐν μέντοι ταῖς ἐκδόσεσι χωρὶς τοῦ ν εὕραμεν.

> in some commentaries ἐνῳνοχόει is found; others say it is Zenodotus' spelling. But in the *ekdoseis* we found it without the ⟨n⟩.

Didymus, whose treatise was devoted to the comparison of the two Aristarchean *ekdoseis*, mentions several Zenodotean variant readings: the latter were apparently written down on Aristarchus' *ekdosis*, probably in the margin. Now the form ἐνῳνοχόει is not mentioned in either of Aristarchus' *ekdoseis*. This suggests that it was not Zenodotus' reading, otherwise Aristarchus would have mentioned it. Here, the source saying Zenodotus had ἐνῳνοχόει is not Aristarchus, but an anonymous οἱ δέ. The *diple periestigmene* before the line means

---

44 Ptolemy Epithetes, a near contemporary of Aristarchus whom he frequently criticises, was the author of a treatise on Zenodotus' *ekdosis*.

there was a difference between Aristarchus' and Zenodotus' text, but this difference could bear on another word in the same line.⁴⁵ Centuries later, this reading is presented as Zenodotean by Eustathius, *Comm. Il.* 1: 691 (Ζηνόδοτος δὲ ἐνῳνοχόει γράφει διὰ προθέσεως).

Deviant readings thus tended to be ascribed to the "default culprit," who happened to be Zenodotus. And it is quite possible that the οἶσθας Eustathius attributes to Zenodotus is not a Zenodotean reading but ended up under his name for that reason.

Even atheteses are not always fully reported in the scholia: an A scholion mentions that Zenodotus athetised B 528, but the following line, which cannot be dissociated from B 528, was certainly athetised, too, although the scholion does not mention it.⁴⁶

An illustration of the partial character of the information we have is provided by the front cover of this book. For the first ten lines of the *Iliad*, we know that there were at least three differences between Zenodotus' text and the vulgate's: an athetesis of A 4–5, a variant reading in A 5 (δαῖτα vs πᾶσι, see above, pp. 9–10), and another one in A 8. In the Venetus A, only the athetesis is mentioned in the main scholiastic text of scholia, around the Homeric text (it faces l. 9 in the manuscript), the variant in A 8 was added afterwards in the interval between the Homeric text and the main scholiastic text (it faces l. 8), and the variant in A 5 is not mentioned at all. There is no *diple periestigmene* before A 8, although there is a comment on Zenodotus' reading for this line. On the other hand, there is one before A 5, but it does not match any comment in the scholia: there used to be a comment but it was dropped.

Lastly, our sources sometimes contradict each other. For instance, in Ξ 223 the A scholion says Aristarchus read μέσῳ κόλπῳ and "others" ἑῷ κόλπῳ, but the T scholion says Aristarchus read ἑῷ κόλπῳ and Zenodotus μέσῳ κόλπῳ.

That said, although we know that our Zenodotean corpus is only a fraction of what Zenodotus' Homer text looked like, and that even this fraction contains unauthentic Zenodotean elements, my first criterion will be to examine only variant readings explicitly attributed to Zenodotus by one of our sources. Other variant readings may be old, too, but I will leave them aside in this study.

Within that corpus, mine is a sub-corpus. I will not examine all of Zenodotus' variant readings transmitted under his name, because many of them cannot be judged on linguistic criteria. When a line found in the vulgate is missing in Zenodotus' text, this is most of the time not a linguistic problem.

---

45 Van Thiel 2014b, *sub* Δ 3, assumes Zenodotus really had ἐνῳνοχόει, an artificial poetic word ("ein Kunstwort") and that this is warranted by the *diple periestigmene*.
46 Nünlist 2009: 54, n. 102 (see below, chap. 1, n. 82).

Of course, there are cases when the lines reportedly athetised by Zenodotus display clearly recent features, so that one is tempted to admit that Zenodotus was right in condemning them. However, such a study is more interesting for the vulgate or the Aristarchean recension than for Zenodotus' text. This is also the case when a hemistich or a whole line is different. That may reflect two competing variants, which cannot always be characterised as old or recent.

Among variant readings to which linguistic criteria can apply, I will not study the forms displaying obviously recent features—by "recent" I mean fifth-century or fourth-century Ionic. I will review some of them in chapter 1 but this is not the aim of my work, which is focused on archaic forms. And unfortunately, there are not many. Some of Zenodotus' archaic forms have already been acknowledged as such in the literature. I will survey them in chapter 1, which will seek to provide a general framework on how ancient and modern scholars deal with Zenodotus. The following chapters are devoted each to one specific Zenodotean reading, sometimes to two of them, for which I think previous scholarly discussions missed the point and did not properly evaluate the data.

CHAPTER 1

Zenodotus' text: An Overview

What type of variant readings do we find in Zenodotus? How can we characterise his text through them? How did ancient scholars deal with them and using which criteria? How do modern scholars deal with them? If these readings can be shown to be old, what should editors print? These are the questions I will try to answer in this chapter.

1 Types of Variant Readings

1.1 *Unrelated Readings*

The first type of divergence is found when Zenodotus and the vulgate have altogether different words, as in the following cases. In B 718, Zenodotus has τῶν αὖ ἡγεμόνευε Φιλοκτήτης ἀγὸς ἀνδρῶν "their commander was Philoctetes, leader of men" *vs* vulgate τῶν δὲ Φιλοκτήτης ἦρχεν τόξων ἐῢ εἰδώς "⟨their⟩ leader was Philoctetes skilled in the bow's work" (R.L.). These are two different formulations which can have been created independently out of the familiar stock of formulaic phrases. All one can say is that the latter, making use of the ephelcystic -*n* to make position, cannot be very old,[1] but it does not necessarily depend on the former. Besides, considering that the metrical structure of the noun Φιλοκτήτης assigns as a preferential metrical slot the position after the trochaic caesura, which is the case in Zenodotus' reading (see also vulgate B 725 Ἀργεῖοι παρὰ νηυσὶ Φιλοκτήταο ἄνακτος), but not in the vulgate's reading, this may be another clue hinting at the regularity of Zenodotus' reading, but not at its anteriority, for regular patterns keep being observed even in recent lines. Lastly, one can add that since Philoctetes' bow was famous, it would be conceivable that a singer introduced the formula τόξων ἐῢ εἰδώς as an epithet of the most famous archer in the Achaean army, for there was a mythological motivation for that.[2] Most cases of this type are not relevant for a linguistic study, and they will not be treated here.

---

1 The ephelcystic -*n* was first used before a vowel to prevent an elision and resolve the hiatus, as is the case in Attic prose. It has a linguistic basis. Its use before a consonant to lengthen the syllable is a purely metrical device which has no linguistic basis.
2 The vulgate's reading is attested in a papyrus contemporaneous with Zenodotus. S. West (1967: 47) assumes that Zenodotus' reading is an emendation introduced by him in order to avoid

In the case of Θ 166 the vulgate's πάρος τοι δαίμονα δώσω # "before that comes I will give you your destiny" (R.L.), with its unique and questionable use of δαίμων 'fate' as object of 'to give', can be considered a *lectio difficilior* next to Zenodotus' πάρος τοι πότμον ἐφήσω # "before that I will give you your fate," much better from the semantic point of view, but the relationship between the two readings is too remote to allow us to go very far.

1.2 Related Readings

Related readings are found when the difference between Zenodotus' text and the vulgate lies in a slight change, either in morphology or in syntactic structure or in vocabulary. That means that we are not dealing with two independent wordings, but one is a reformulation, or an emendation, of the other.

1.2.1 Segmentation Divergence

A most conspicuous divergence between Zenodotus and the vulgate can be seen when the identification of word boundaries is not the same in both. There are several instances of that. A scholion to the *Odyssey* tells us that Zenodotus spelled δαμνίον in γ 444 vs vulgate δ' ἀμνίον:

> Schol. γ 444b1 Pontani: ἀμνίον· ἀγγεῖον εἰς ὃ τὸ αἷμα τοῦ ἱερείου ἐδέχοντο. Ζηνόδοτος δὲ ἐν ταῖς ἀπὸ τοῦ Δ γλώσσαις τίθησι τὴν λέξιν. ἅπαξ δὲ ἐνταῦθα παρ' Ὁμήρῳ ἡ λέξις.
>
> ἀμνίον: a vase in which they collected the victim's blood. But Zenodotus lists the word in his *Glossai* under words with initial [d]. This word is found only here in Homer.

The scholiast says the indication Zenodotus had δαμνίον instead of δ' ἀμνίον is drawn from the *Glossai*, a list of rare words which Zenodotus explained, not from his *ekdosis* of the *Odyssey*. This implies that his Homeric text had no word division and that different segmentations were possible. But it also implies that we do not know what Zenodotus' segmentation was unless there is an external indication, in that case the *Glossai*. Any indication given only by the

---

the repetition with τόξων ἐῢ εἰδότες of B 720, reflecting the then dominant conception that most divergences between Zenodotus and the vulgate were innovations introduced by the former. I would suspect that avoiding repetition is a literary concern which was not shared by all epic singers or rhapsodes, and that the emendation may be on the vulgate's side. West 2011: 120 deems Zenodotus' reading "a banal rhapsode's variant" because of which "the point is lost" (that is, the fact that without Philoctetes' bow Troy cannot be taken).

A scholia about a diverging segmentation in Zenodotus' text provides information about how Aristarchus thought the text had to be divided (maybe on the basis of external elements), not about how Zenodotus divided it. This is clear, for instance, from the A scholion to H 127: ὅς ποτέ μ' εἰρόμενος <μέγ' ἐγήθεεν>: ὅτι Ζηνόδοτος γράφει 'μέγα δ' ἔστενεν', ἐξ οὗ φανερός ἐστιν ἀνεγνωκὼς 'μειρόμενος.' "because Zenodotus reads μέγα δ' ἔστενεν, which shows that he read μειρόμενος," with word division inferred from the syntax of the line. Another instance is provided by an A scholion saying that in Π 202 Zenodotus had καὶ μητιάασθε "and you were contriving", vs vulgate καί μ' ἠτιάασθε "and you were blaming me." If the text had no word division, we must understand that Zenodotus' text had ΜΗΤΙΑΑΣΘΕ vs vulgate ΜΗΙΤΙΑΑΣΘΕ, but this need not be a different segmentation: since the iota after a long vowel was no longer pronounced in the 4th c. (this is the iota subscript of modern spelling), the divergence may well be nothing more than a different pronunciation of one and the same word (see below, p. 37). In K 515 the vulgate has οὐδ' ἀλαοσκοπίην εἶχ' ἀργυρότοξος Ἀπόλλων "neither did Apollo of the silver bow keep blind watch" (R.L.), and the A scholion says Zenodotus had ἀλαὸν σκοπιήν in two words, and similarly in Ξ 135. Further examples are given below (p. 27). Of course, a difference in segmentation results in a lexical divergence and sometimes a syntactic divergence.

1.2.2 Morphological Divergence

There are several instances of an aspectual divergence. In O 179–180 most manuscripts have ἠπείλει καὶ κεῖνος ἐναντίβιον πτολεμίξων || ἐνθάδ' ἐλεύσεσθαι "his threat is that he himself will come to fight with you here, strength against strength" (R.L.), with a future participle: Aristarchus had πολεμίξων, but Zenodotus had a present participle πολεμίζων. Similarly in Π 161 where he had an aorist participle λάψαντες 'lapping up' vs vulgate λάψοντες, future participle, and in Φ 335 εἴσομαι ... ὄρσασα θύελλαν "I will go, stirring a storm" vs vulgate ὄρσουσα θύελλαν (Zeodotus' reading with the aorist participle is confirmed by a 3rd c. papyrus for Φ 335). There may be a voice difference: in N 449 and Γ 163 Aristarchus had ὄφρα ἴδη "so that you can see," (middle), whereas Zenodotus had ὄφρα ἴδῃς, (active).[3] Similarly, in A 83 he had the active imperative σὺ δὲ φράσον εἴ με σαώσεις "you, tell me if you will save me" vs vulgate's and Aristarchus' σὺ δὲ φράσαι with the middle. The A scholion μᾶλλον δὲ τὸ φράσαι ἁρμόζει "φράσαι

---

3   For Γ 163 an A scholion reports a variant reading ἴδῃς, not under Zenodotus' name, ὅτι χωρὶς τοῦ σ γράφειν ὁμηρικώτερον "because the reading without the ⟨s⟩ is more Homeric." The comparison with N 449 suggests that the middle aorist ἴδη may have replaced the active ἴδῃς in other places. The middle was felt as characteristic of Homer, because of cases like θαῦμα ἰδέσθαι, and may have been extended for that reason to lines where the older form was the usual active aorist. In particular, it is striking that the Aeolic ἴδωμι is preserved only when metre prohibits its substitution by the middle form ἴδωμαι: the *Iliad* (vulgate) has only two

fits better" suggests Aristonicus rather understood it as "you, decide if you will save me."[4] In Ψ 306–307 ἤτοι μέν σε νέον περ ἐόντ᾽ ἐφίλησαν ‖ Ζεύς τε Ποσειδάων τε, καὶ ἱπποσύνας ἐδίδαξεν "you are young indeed, but Zeus and Poseidon have loved you and taught you horsemanship in all of its aspects" (R.L.), Aristarchus favoured the singular ἐδίδαξεν because the horse is Poseidon's animal, not Zeus', and Zenodotus had the plural ἐδίδαξαν, coordinated with ἐφίλησαν— Zenodotus' reading is syntactically better and Aristarchus' must be a correction prompted by non-linguistic concerns.[5]

As far as nominal inflection is concerned, there may be a divergence between thematic and athematic inflection: Zenodotus had the athematic μάρτυρες Β 302 vs vulgate μάρτυροι, thematic (see pp. 38–39). Zenodotus and the vulgate have the accusative Μίνω (Ξ 322), contraction of the older s-stem Μίνωα, whereas Aristarchus had Μίνων, thematicised and inflected as λεώς. The vocative of the -αντ- stems and of the ā-stems is fluctuating: Zenodotus had a vocative Κάλχα Α 86, as if from an ā-stem, vs vulgate Κάλχαν (stem Κάλχαντ-), but conversely he had Πουλυδάμαν in M 231, where Aristarchus had Πουλυδάμα (stem Πολυδάμαντ-)—the latter form is singled out as irregular in the scholion (αἱ Ἀριστάρχου χωρὶς τοῦ ν, παρὰ τὴν ἀναλογίαν "Aristarchus' ekdoseis spell it without the -n, contrary to ἀναλογία"). This form without -n is kept in the vulgate.

1.2.3 Lexical Divergence

A lexical difference is involved in Α 69 (Zenodotus # μάντις Θεστορίδης "the seer son of Thestor" vs vulgate # Κάλχας Θεστορίδης "Kalchas son of Thestor"): this is typically a case of related readings where linguistics cannot help decide.[6] Another case is Ρ 268, where the vulgate has # φραχθέντες σάκεσιν χαλκήρεσιν

---

cases of ἴδωμι vs six cases of ἴδωμαι, five of which are at the end of the line, and the *Odyssey* has only three cases of ἴδωμαι, all at the end of the line. For the case of ὄφρα ἴδῃ(ς) in Γ 163 and Ν 449, the parallel with ὄφρα ἴδωμαι, attested three times in the *Iliad*, played a role.

4 However, Apollonius' *Lexicon homericum* has (p. 165): φραδέος συνετοῦ, δυναμένου ἐπιφράσασθαι, ὅ ἐστιν ἐπινοῆσαι· "φραδέος νόου ἔργα τέτυκται." ἀπὸ τοῦ αὐτοῦ καὶ τὸ φράσαι, ὅπερ ἀγνοήσας Ζηνόδοτος μεταγράφει "σὺ δὲ φράσαι εἴ με σαώσεις," οὐδέποτε τοῦ ποιητοῦ ἐπὶ τοῦ εἰπεῖν τάσσοντος τὴν λέξιν. διόπερ Ἀρίσταρχος ἐν τῇ Ρ τῆς Ἰλιάδος ἠθέτηκεν "φραδέος 'wise', capable of reflecting, that is, of thinking: 'here is work for a mind that is careful' (R.L.). From the same verb also comes φράσαι; Zenodotus, not aware of that, rewrites 'σὺ δὲ φράσαι εἴ με σαώσεις' whereas Homer never uses this word form with the meaning 'to speak'. And this is why Aristarchus athetised it in book Ρ of the *Iliad*." This seems to refer to the same line Α 83, and to contradict the A scholion which says Zenodotus had φράσον, although Aristonicus and Apollonius agree that φράσαι does not mean 'to say' but 'to think'.

5 Schironi 2018: 331, n. 291, with literature.

6 West 2001: 173.

"fenced beneath their bronze-armoured shields" (R.L.), but Zenodotus # ἀρθέντες σάκεσιν χαλκήρεσιν "with their bronze-armoured shields tightly joined," describing the same military formation. Compare for Zenodotus' reading M 105 οἳ δ ἐπεὶ ἀλλήλους ἄραρον τυκτῇσι βόεσσι "now when these had closed their wrought ox-hide shields together" (R.L.), and for the vulgate's reading N 130 φράξαντες δόρυ δουρί, σάκος σάκεϊ "locking spear by spear, shield against shield" (R.L.). In Λ 86 the vulgate has ἦμος [...] ὁπλίσσατο δεῖπνον "when he prepares dinner," but Zenodotus had δόρπον, and conversely in Λ 730 the vulgate has δόρπον ἔπειθ' ἑλόμεσθα "let us have dinner," but Zenodotus δεῖπνον. In E 898 the vulgate has καί κεν δὴ πάλαι ἦσθα ἐνέρτερος Οὐρανιώνων "long since you would have been dropped beneath the gods of the bright sky" (R.L.), whereas Zenodotus had the superlative ἐνέρτατος. Clearly in all similar cases one reading depends on the other. In some cases linguistic criteria can tell which is older, in other cases non-linguistic criteria may be used, and yet in others there is no cogent argument in favour of one reading rather than the other (see below, pp. 40–67).

1.2.4 Syntactic Divergence

The divergence may also involve a syntactic difference. A typical case is found in E 416, where Dione heals her wounded daughter Aphrodite. The vulgate has ἦ ῥα, καὶ ἀμφοτέρῃσιν ἀπ' ἰχῶ χειρὸς ὀμόργνυ "with both hands she wiped the ichôr out of Aphrodite's hand," whereas Zenodotus had ἦ ῥα, καὶ ἀμφοτέρῃσιν ἀπ' ἰχῶ χερσίν ὀμόργνυ "she said, and with both hands she wiped out the *ichôr*." The only difference is the caseform, hence the function, of the word χείρ.

Similarly, in E 146–147 the vulgate has τὸν δ' ἕτερον ξίφεϊ μεγάλῳ κληῖδα παρ' ὦμον || πλῆξε "and cutting the other beside the shoulder through the collar-bone with the great sword" (R.L.), with a double accusative for the whole (τὸν δ' ἕτερον) and the part (κληῖδα), a frequent construction in Homer. Zenodotus had τοῦ δ' ἑτέρου with a genitive. The same difference is found in E 155–156, vulgate φίλον δ' ἐξαίνυτο θυμὸν || ἀμφοτέρω "he took away the dear life from them both" (R.L.) with a double accusative, but Zenototus ἀμφοτέρων with a genitive. In both cases, the genitive agrees with the usual structure in Attic-Ionic prose where the double accusative of this type has been ousted by the genitive.[7] Accordingly, Zenodotus' readings may be modernisations. The same holds true for Ξ 208 εἰ κείνω γ' ἐπέεσσι παραιπεπιθοῦσα φίλον κῆρ "if I win over with persuasion the dear heart within them" (R.L. modified), for which Zenodotus

---

7 Jacquinod 1989: 222: the double accusative is found in prose with a few verbs only, and ἀφαιρέω τί τινος 'to take something away from someone' is much more frequent in prose than ἀφαιρέω τί τινα.

had not the double accusative, but the genitive κείνων, which was also Aristophanes' reading. Either the genitive is a modernisation or Aristarchus' κείνω is an emendation favouring a 'more Homeric' form (ὁμηρικώτερον).

In A 250–251 τῷ δ' ἤδη δύο μὲν γενεαὶ μερόπων ἀνθρώπων || ἐφθίαθ', οἵ οἱ πρόσθεν ἅμα τράφεν ἠδ' ἐγένοντο "in his time two generations of mortal men had perished, those who had grown up with him and they who had been born to these" (R.L.), Zenodotus had a feminine relative pronoun αἵ οἱ, agreeing with γενεαί, whereas the vulgate has a masculine οἵ οἱ, agreeing with ἀνθρώπων.

Similarly, a minor difference in syntactic structure can be found in Z 53–54 Ἀγαμέμνων || ἀντίον ἦλθε θέων "Agamemnon ran toward him," where the vulgate has ἀντίος: both the adverb (Zenodotus) and the predicative adjective (Aristarchus) are possible in this line. Conversely, in Λ 219 Zenodotus and Aristophanes had ἀντίος and Aristarchus ἀντίον. A similar case is found in Π 155–156, where the vulgate has Μυρμιδόνας δ' ἄρ' ἐποιχόμενος θώρηξεν Ἀχιλλεὺς || πάντας ἀνὰ κλισίας σὺν τεύχεσιν "but Achilleus went meanwhile to the Myrmidons, and arrayed them all in their war gear along the shelters" (R.L.), and Zenodotus has the adverb πάντῃ 'on every side' instead of πάντας agreeing with the object—West prints Zenodotus' πάντῃ, which was already deemed better by Wilamowitz.[8]

A frequent divergence involves number, when the vulgate has a dual and Zenodotus a plural, or conversely. This is a consequence of the early elimination of the dual in Ionic and of the subsequent modernisation replacing duals by plurals. Thus, in Λ 348 the vulgate has a plural ἀλλ' ἄγε δὴ στέωμεν καὶ ἀλεξώμεσθα μένοντες # "let us stand, and hold our ground against him, and beat him off from us" (R.L.), but Zenodotus has a dual participle μένοντε, agreeing with the dual νῶϊν 'the two of us' in Λ 347 but disagreeing with the plural verbs. Similarly in M 127–138, where the vulgate has a string of plurals ἀνέρας ... ἀρίστους / υἷας ὑπερθύμους ... ἔκιον, and Zenodotus and Aristophanes a string of duals (A scholion: Ζηνόδοτος καὶ Ἀριστοφάνης δυϊκῶς ἅπαντα, ἀνέρε, ἀρίστω, υἷε ὑπερθύμω, κιέτην "Zenodotus and Aristophanes have everything in the dual: ἀνέρε, ἀρίστω, υἷε ὑπερθύμω, κιέτην").

In a few cases Zenodotus has a different mode: an instance is Λ 492 where the vulgate has ὡς δ' ὁπότε πλήθων ποταμὸς πεδίον δὲ κάτεισι "as when a swollen river hurls its water" (R.L.) whereas Zenodotus had the subjunctive δίηται instead of the indicative κάτεισι. The variant combines two differences, a syntactic one and a lexical one.

---

8 Wilamowitz 1916: 125, fn 3, who says that "only Aristarcholatry" can discard this reading. See also the comment in West 2001: 236.

The divergence can also be a matter of hierarchisation between two processes. In Θ 526–527 Zenodotus read ἔλπομαι εὐχόμενος Διί τ' ἄλλοισίν τε θεοῖσιν ‖ ἐξελάαν ἐνθένδε κύνας κηρεσσιφορήτους "for in good hope I pray to Zeus and the other immortals that we may drive from our place these dogs swept into destruction" (R.L.), and Aristarchus εὔχομαι ἐλπόμενος, with reversed syntactic hierarchy between the participle and the finite form. The vulgate agrees with Aristarchus.

An instance of such a difference at the interclausal level is B 187–189:

B 187–189
σὺν τῷ ἔβη κατὰ νῆας Ἀχαιῶν χαλκοχιτώνων.
Ὅν τινα μὲν βασιλῆα καὶ ἔξοχον ἄνδρα κιχείη
τὸν δ' ἀγανοῖς ἐπέεσσιν ἐρητύσασκε παραστάς

with this (the sceptre) he went besides the ships of bronze-armoured Achaeans. Whenever he encountered some king, or man of influence, he would stand beside him and with soft words try to restrain him.

R.L.

In the vulgate's reading, σὺν τῷ ἔβη is the beginning of a sentence not syntactically linked with the following one. Zenodotus had σὺν τῷ βάς, with a participle chaining this clause with the following lines.

In Z 34 the vulgate has ναῖε δὲ Σατνιόεντος ἐϋρρείταο παρ' ὄχθας "and his home had been on the shores of Satnioeis' lovely waters" (R.L. modified), with parataxis, and Zenodotus ὃς ναῖε Σατνιόεντος [...] with a relative phrase. Zenodotus' reading requires *correptio epica*,[9] the vulgate's does not. The same difference occurs in N 172, vulgate # ναῖε δὲ Πήδαιον vs Zenodotus # ὃς νάε Πήδαιον, and the scholion going back to Aristonicus explicitly favours parataxis, arguing that Homer "cuts the clauses" (διακόπτει τὰς φράσεις).

Some divergences involve both syntax and morphology, as the well-known case of O 640 where Zenodotus had ἀγγελίην οἴχνεσκε, accusative of the feminine noun ἀγγελίη, syntactically an accusative of aim "he was going for the news," whereas Aristarchus had ἀγγελίης, nominative of the new masculine ἀγγελίης, syntactically an apposition to the subject "he was going as a messenger." The new form ὁ ἀγγελίης arose through a misunderstanding, that is, linguistically speaking, a reanalysis, of a line in which stood the feminine ἀγγελίη, and this is

---

9 *Correptio epica* is the shortening of a long vowel or diphthong if two conditions are met: the vowel must be in hiatus before another vowel and it must not be the first syllable of the foot (it must not be in arsis).

uncontroversial. However, there are two different scenarios accounting for the context of reanalysis and the relative chronology of the considered lines.

For Leumann,[10] the context of reanalysis is Γ 205–206 ἤδη γὰρ καὶ δεῦρό ποτ' ἤλυθε δῖος Ὀδυσσεὺς ǁ σεῦ ἕνεκ' ἀγγελίης σὺν ἀρηϊφίλῳ Μενελάῳ "the divine Ulysses came already here one day, with Menelaus dear to Ares, for an embassy about you." Here ἀγγελίης is a genitive singular regime of ἕνεκα. This led to the erroneous identification of a masculine ἀγγελίης interpreted as an apposition to the subject Ulysses. This masculine was then introduced by the singer who coined Λ 140, where the context is identical. In Γ 206, Zenodotus read σῆς ἕνεκ' ἀγγελίης (erroneously ἧς in Apollonius, *Lexicon homericum*, p. 7), with a possessive and the correct feminine noun: his reading may be an emendation, as the syntax is clearer with a possessive.

For Forssman,[11] on the other hand, the context of reanalysis is Λ 139–141 ὅς ποτ' ἐνὶ Τρώων ἀγορῇ Μενέλαον ἄνωγεν ǁ ἀγγελίην ἐλθόντα σὺν ἀντιθέῳ Ὀδυσῆϊ ǁ αὖθι κατακτεῖναι "who once in the Trojan assembly advised them to kill Menelaus, who had come in embassy with godlike Ulysses, on the spot." Here, according to Forssman, ἀγγελίην is an accusative of direction 'coming for an embassy' (this was already the interpretation of the D scholion: ἀγγελίην: ἀντὶ τοῦ εἰς πρεσβείαν), and it is a feminine noun, but it was reinterpreted as a masculine in apposition to Μενέλαον. In Forssman's view, Γ 206 is not ambiguous, but has a masculine ἀγγελίης, analogical after Λ 140.

The third instance is Ο 640 ὃς Εὐρυσθῆος ἄνακτος ǁ ἀγγελίης οἴχνεσκε βίῃ Ἡρακληείῃ "who went as a messenger of lord Eurystheus to mighty Heracles." It is secondary according to both accounts because it can only be a masculine nominative. However, Zenodotus had for this line ἀγγελίην οἴχνεσκε "who went for an embassy." If Forssman's scenario is correct, Zenodotus' ἀγγελίην, with an accusative of direction as in Λ 140, might be older than Aristarchus' masculine ἀγγελίης. Remember that Zenodotus read σῆς ἕνεκ' ἀγγελίης in Γ 206. That is, he consistently had a feminine ἀγγελίη in the three lines under consideration, without any trace of the masculine ἀγγελίης. Forssman's view that Zenodotus' reading ἀγγελίην in Ο 640 is an abusive emendation introduced by him[12] still relies on the (then widely accepted) conception according to which Zenodotus "rewrites" the text. It may not be justified.

---

10 Leumann 1950: 168–173.
11 Forssman 1974, followed by De Boel 1988: 51–52.
12 Forssman 1974: 59–60.

2 Linguistic Evidence for Zenodotus' Text

On the basis of those divergences, we can have an idea of what Zenodotus' text looked like.[13]

2.1 *Psilosis and Accent*

Zenodotus probably had a psilotic text.[14] This can be deduced from segmentation divergences such as P 368 ἐπὶ τόσσον *vs* vulgate ἐπί θ' ὅσσον, M 75 ἀλλ' ἄγε τὼς ἂν ἐγὼ εἴπω *vs* vulgate ἀλλ' ἄγεθ' ὥς ἂν ἐγὼ εἴπω "do as I say,"[15] Λ 589 Αἴαντος βελέεσσι βιάζεται *vs* vulgate Αἴανθ', ὅς βελέεσσι βιάζεται "Ajax, who is pressed by arrows."[16] Zenodotus' word division in those lines implies a text without initial aspiration and without accentual marks.[17] Or rather, if Zenodotus' text had no explicit word division (see above, pp. 20–21), the segmentation was either known from a distinct source (like the *Glossai*), which did not survive, or deduced by Aristarchus from the fact that Zenodotus had a plain voiceless stop and not an aspirate stop: Zenodotus may have read ἐπί τ' ὅσσον, ἀλλ' ἄγετ' ὥς, Αἴαντ', ὅς with the same segmentation as the vulgate, but the sequences ΕΠΙΤΟΣΣΟΝ, ΑΓΕΤΩΣ, ΑΙΑΝΤΟΣ in *scriptio continua* were identified as ἐπὶ τόσσον, ἄγε τώς, Αἴαντος by a reader who was used to a non-psilotic Homeric text.

Some of Zenodotus' readings are quoted with the effect of aspiration in sandhi, for instance B 160–161 the vulgate has κὰδ δέ κεν εὐχωλὴν Πριάμῳ καὶ Τρωσὶ λίποιεν || Ἀργείην Ἑλένην "and thus they would leave to Priam and to the Trojans Helen of Argos" (R.L.) but Zenodotus had Ἀργείην θ' Ἑλένην "and Helen of Argos." The psilotic form is Ἀργείην τ' Ἐλένην: we may assume that

---

13 This aspect is quickly dealt with in Schironi 2018: 551–556, from a purely Aristarchean point of view. For a summary of Aristarchus' conceptions about Homeric grammar, see Schironi 2018: 601–622.

14 Psilosis is the loss of initial aspiration. Both East Ionic and Lesbian are psilotic dialects.

15 Van Thiel 2014b, *sub* M 75: "here Zenodotus probably wrote ἀλλ' ἄγε and meant that it can also be used before plural verbs, as for instance in N 292 ἀλλ' ἄγε μηκέτι ταῦτα λεγώμεθα. Then τώς or πώς would have been deduced from it because of the supposed hiatus" ("Hier notierte Zenodot vermutlich ἀλλ' ἄγε und meinte, dass es auch vor pluralischem Prädikat stehen könne, wie z.B. N 292 ἀλλ' ἄγε μηκέτι ταῦτα λεγώμεθα. Dann wären τώς oder πώς wegen der vermeintlichen Hiats daraus erschlossen").

16 There was a third reading πώς ἂν ἐγὼ εἴπω. Van Thiel 2014b, *sub* Λ 589, assumes Zenodotus wrote Αἴαντος, meaning Αἴαντος, ὅς βελέεσσι βιάζεται as a marginal comment indicating that Αἴανθ' (elision of Αἴαντι) was the equivalent of a genitive. However, one wonders why here Zenodotus did not try to respect the metrical structure in his comment, whereas he allegedly indulged in that learned play elsewhere (see above, p. 11).

17 West 2001: 259 "Zenodotus' text was unaccented."

Aristarchus restored the θ' because he had no problem with the identification of the form, whereas in the preceding cases he misunderstood Zenodotus' reading, and did not restore the aspiration. The same restoration occurred in P 149 (Zenodotus μεθ' ὁμίλου vs vulgate μεθ' ὅμιλον) and in γ 368 (Zenodotus ἐπεὶ τὰ σὰ γούναθ' ἱκάνει vs vulgate ἐπεὶ τεὸν ἵκετο δῶμα).[18] In other words, the transmitted readings reflect Aristarchus' understanding of Zenodotus' text, rather than the text itself. Aristarchus used the normalised spelling for Zenodotus' readings except when he misinterpreted them.

It is at any rate clear that there was no graphic sign for the initial aspiration, as can be seen from the following lines:

M 294–296
αὐτίκα δ' ἀσπίδα μὲν πρόσθ' ἔσχετο πάντοσ' ἐίσην
καλὴν χαλκείην ἐξήλατον, ἣν ἄρα χαλκεὺς
ἤλασεν

presently he held before him the perfect circle of his shield, a lovely thing of beaten bronze, which the bronze-smith hammered out for him.

R.L.

Aristonicus says

A Schol. M 296: ὅτι Ζηνόδοτος γράφει ἐξέλασ' [...]· ἐξ οὗ φανερός ἐστι τὸ προκείμενον ψιλῶς ἀνεγνωκὼς ἐξήλατον· δεῖ δὲ δασέως, ἵνα ἀριθμὸς δηλωθῇ.

because Zenodotus writes ἐξέλασ' [...]; from where it is clear that he read in the preceding line ἐξήλατον, with smooth breathing; but it must be ⟨ἑξήλατον⟩ with a rough breathing, to express number (Aristarchus' reading was ἑξήλατον "with six layers").

This remark implies that there was no distinctive mark on ΕΞΗΛΑΤΟΝ: the rough or smooth breathing is inferred from the form of the verb at the beginning of l. 296, Zenodotus' ἐξέλασ' instead of vulgate ἤλασεν being taken as proof

---

18   In δ 70 Zenodotus' reading ἵνα μὴ πευθοίαθ' οἱ ἄλλοι # also shows the effect of initial aspiration, but since this is the reading of the vulgate and was the reading of most versions, this is not significant. Similarly, in Σ 154–156 Zenodotus' ll. 156–156a were identical with Σ 176–177: as a result, the reported ταμόνθ' ἁπαλῆς ἀπὸ δειρῆς, reading of the vulgate in Σ 177 and in Zenodotus' reading in Σ 156a, is not significant either, since the copyist probably wrote the line as it appears in Σ 177.

that he also read ἐξήλατον in l. 295, with a *figura etymologica*. This is explicit in another A scholion, probably going back to Herodian:

> *A Schol.* M 295a: Ἀρίσταρχός φησιν ὡς δεῖ δασύνοντας προφέρεσθαι· σημαίνει γὰρ κατὰ ἀριθμὸν ἐκ τοσούτων ἐλασμάτων συγκειμένην αὐτήν. ὁ δὲ Ζηνόδοτος, φησίν, ἔοικε ψιλῶς προφέρεσθαι, ἐκδεχόμενος τὴν ἐξηλασμένην, οὐκ εὖ.
>
> Aristarchus says it must have a rough breathing, because it refers to number and means the shield is made of so many layers; but Zenodotus, he says, seems to have it with a smooth breathing, understanding it as 'spread', erroneously.[19]

However, this is Aristarchus' interpretation: *per se*, the reading ἐξέλασε in M 296 does not imply anything about ἐξήλατον in M 295 and Zenodotus may also have understood 'six-fold'. The T scholion to M 296 assumes ἐξήλατον means ἐξελασθεῖσαν and not 'six-fold' (οὐ γὰρ ἓξ ἔχει) and adds that Nicanor chose the smooth breathing, therefore the meaning 'spread'.

Zenodotus gave indications about initial aspiration in his *Glossai*: an A scholion to A 569 says that χεῖρας ἀάπτους has a smooth breathing (οὕτως ψιλῶς προενεκτέον), and that "Zenodotus too had the same breathing" (ὁ δὲ Ζηνόδοτος ὁμοίως τῷ πνεύματι). The *Glossai* are the only possible source, since Zenodotus' *ekdosis* had no graphic sign for the aspiration.

Psilosis can be deduced from sandhi, but Zenodotus did not have forms like ἀπίκετο for ἀφίκετο found in Herodotus, with the loss of aspiration at the morphological boundary between the preverb and the verb. Preverbs undergo aspiration: for instance Zenodotus had ἐκαθέζετο in A 68 (see below, p. 35), ἀφελέσθαι in A 299. Whether this situation is faithful to Zenodotus' text or results from a normalisation remains open.

In the absence of indication in the *Glossai*, the transmitted breathing and accent are not Zenodotus' but were assigned by Aristarchus. An example is Υ 114 ἣ δ' ἄμυδις καλέσασα θεοὺς μετὰ μῦθον ἔειπεν "and drew the other immortals about her and spoke to them, saying" (R.L). Zenodotus had ἦ δ' ἄμυδις καλέσασα θεοὺς ῥεῖα ζώοντας. Aristonicus comments ἐξ οὗ φανερός ἐστι κατὰ τὸ περισπώμενον ἀνεγνωκὼς ἦ δ' ἄμυδις, ἵν' ἦ ἔφη "from where it is clear that he read ἦ δ' ἄμυδις,

---

19 The *A Schol.* A 567b saying that ἀάπτους has a smooth breathing and means 'which cannot be touched', interpretation of Aristarchus, adds ὁ δὲ Ζηνόδοτος καὶ αὐτὸς ὁμοίως τῷ πνεύματι, εἰς τὰς ἰσχυρὰς δὲ μετελάμβανεν "Zenodotus himself also has the same breathing but he understood it 'strong'." The mention of the breathing does not refer to the *ekdosis* of Zenodotus, but apparently to his *Glossai*, where he may have used the aspiration sign. On the *Glossai*, see Pusch 1890: 188–216.

perispomenon, where ἦ means 'she said'" (*A Schol.* Υ 114a). Didymus adds Ζηνόδοτος δὲ περιέσπασε καὶ ἐψίλωσεν, ῥῆμα ἐκδεξάμενος "Zenodotus reads with a perispomenon and a smooth breathing, taking it as a verb" (*A Schol.* Υ 114b). The indications about the smooth breathing and the accent come from Aristarchus, who deduced them from the syntax of the line. As a matter of fact, Zenodotus' line had no finite verb form, therefore Aristarchus concluded that the verb had to be ἦ. This led him to condemn the reading because "Zenodotus ignores that ἦ is used in Homer after a speech, not at the beginning" (Aristonicus: ἠγνόηκε δὲ ὅτι ἐπί τισι προειρημένοις τίθεται παρ' Ὁμήρῳ τὸ ἦ, οὐκ ἐν ἀρχῇ λόγου).

However, Aristarchus' interpretation of Zenodotus' line might be wrong and Zenodotus may have had here the same ἣ δέ "and she" as the vulgate. As a matter of fact, Greek can introduce a direct speech with a sentence which has no finite verb, then inserting ἔφη into the speech as a parenthetic clause. For instance Plato, *Phaedo* 117d7 Ἐκεῖνος δέ, Οἷα, ἔφη, ποιεῖτε, ὦ θαυμάσιοι "and he: 'what conduct is this, said he, you strange men!'" (transl. Fowler modified); Plato, *Euthyd.* 286b7-8 ἐγὼ δὲ θαυμάσας τὸν λόγον, Πῶς, ἔφην, ὦ Διονυσόδωρε, λέγεις; "and I, wondering at his words: 'what do you mean, said I, Dionysiodorus?'." We could well have the same pattern in Zenodotus' line for Υ 114: the subject (ἣ δ'), an adjunct participle (καλέσασα), and the direct speech in the following line. It would mean "and she, calling together the gods who live an easy life: 'decide, both of you, Poseidon and Athena [...]'." The difference with Plato is that no ἔφη is inserted, but since there is no instance of parenthetic ἔφη in Homer, the singer who coined the line could not use it. Thus, we would have here a hybrid structure, with the introductory line displaying the pattern of the usual type with parenthetic ἔφη while the following line has no ἔφη at all. This must be a recent remodelling, by which a rhapsode introduced the formulaic hemistich θεοὶ ῥεῖα ζώοντες # (Ζ 138, δ 805, ε 122), assuming ἣ δ' ἄμυδις καλέσασα θεούς was a suitable introductory line for a direct speech. This structure is abnormal in Homer—so abnormal that it was not identified by Aristarchus—, but it was familiar to both the rhapsode and the audience. If this hypothesis is correct, there is no ἦ "she said" at all, and Zenodotus did not use ἦ to introduce a speech. Aristarchus was right to condemn the reading, but did so for the wrong reason.

Consequently, if Zenodotus' text had no accentual mark, it is very unlikely that he had any other diacritic. Therefore, when the A scholion to A 129 blames him for writing πόλιν Τροίην ἐϋτείχεον "the well-walled city of Troy" instead of πόλιν Τροΐην ἐϋτείχεον "a well-walled city of Troad," arguing that this refers not to Troy but to a city of the Troad[20] and that the noun is trisyllabic (διὸ καὶ ἐν

---

20 Aristarchus wanted Τροίη to be used for the Troad, whereas Troy itself was always Ilium (Schironi 2018: 302). However, in Homer Τροίη is sometimes used also for the city of Troy.

τρισὶ συλλαβαῖς ἀναγινώσκεται "this is why it must be read in three syllables"), it is an anachronistic remark. Zenodotus had ΤΡΟΙΗΝ, which could be read as dissyllabic or as trisyllabic, and he certainly did not have a diacritic indicating the diaeresis. And we have no means to know whether he understood it as Troy or as a city near Troy.

2.2 Dialect

The classical phase model for the development of the epics holds that the kernel is Mycenaean, which in that case is called Achaean. After the collapse of the Mycenaean world around 1200 BCE, the epic tradition developed in Aeolic, first on the continent (Thessalian) and then in Asia Minor (Lesbian), from where it was passed on to Ionians. In this model, there was no direct contact between Achaean and Ionic, which are two different layers, chronologically distinct. Ionic is therefore the most recent linguistic stratum (except for sporadic Atticisms which are more recent). This view has been increasingly challenged in the last decades, at the benefit of the so-called diffusionist model, which still assumes that the kernel is Achaean, but assumes that there was a contact between the Mycenaean epic tradition and a Proto-Ionic epic tradition and that the diffusion of the epics was a continuous process in all Greek regions, so that no tradition was cut off from the others.[21]

Zenodotus' text displays Ionic forms, not just recent Ionic, when the vulgate has Aeolic ones, as in Π 10 when he read προσδέρκεται vs vulgate ποτιδέρκεται (# δακρυόεσσα δέ μιν ποτιδέρκεται "she looks at him, shedding tears"). His text has the Ionic regular form of the optative aorist where the vulgate has the so-called Aeolic optative (Α 42 τίσ⟨α⟩ιεν Δαναοί vs vulgate τίσειαν Δαναοί "may the Danaeans pay").[22] He has the Ionic infinitive οὐτάσαι (Ε 132) vs vulgate οὐτάμεν with the Aeolic infinitive.[23] Eustathius says that he had a 3sg. ending -έαται for vocalic stems instead of -ηται: καὶ ὅ γε Ζηνόδοτος πολλάκις, φησί, παρὰ τῷ ποιητῇ οὕτω γράφει καὶ τὰ ἑνικά [...], τὸ πεποίηται καὶ νενόηται πεποιέαται γράφων καὶ νενοέαται "and he [*Heracleides, CLF*] says Zenodotus often has this reading in

---

21 Jones 2012.
22 Τίσαιεν is a correction: the text of the scholion reads τίσειεν, which cannot be Zenodotus' reading. Since the form is pinpointed as different from the vulgate's τίσειαν, it follows that it must have been τίσαιεν. Only one other 3rd plural in -σαιεν is mentioned in the A scholia, in Ω 38 (κτερίσαιεν), not under Zenodotus' name. If Zenodotus read τίσαιεν, he probably also had other such forms, but in the scholia only the first occurrence of the feature may have been mentioned once and for all (see below, p. 78).
23 Didymus says he had οὖτασαι, an imperative (*A Schol.* Ε 132), but since Zenodotus' text did not have accentual marks, the accent is either Didymus' or Aristarchus', and Zenodotus probably had an aorist infinitive οὐτάσαι.

Homer also for the singular [...], writing πεποιέαται and νενοέαται for πεποίηται and νενόηται" (*Comm. Od.* 2: 229). This is an Ionic feature: the old 3pl. ending -αται, regular for consonant stems, was extended to vocalic stems after forms like the Homeric κέαται, and such forms are frequent in Herodotus. Zenodotus is said to have used it for the 3sg., not the 3pl. In fact, the scholia report only one such form under Zenodotus' name, ἐπιστέαται in Π 243 (*vs* vulgate ἐπίστηται), and it is not a perfect, contrary to the forms mentioned by Heracleides, but a present subjunctive. If reliable, the form is certainly recent. Zenodotus also had the Ionic κρητός 'of the head' instead of Aeolic/Achaean κρᾶτός (A 530), Ἀμφιάρηος (ο 244) instead of the Atticim Ἀμφιάραος. Psilosis (see above, pp. 27–28) is an Ionic feature, too.

However, he also sometimes has Aeolic forms where the vulgate has the Ionic form, as in A 56 and A 198 ὀρῆτο (Zen., for *ὄρητο, cf. Lesb. ὄρημμι, Sappho, *fr.* 31 LP)[24] *vs* vulgate ὁρᾶτο.[25] In some cases it is more difficult to tell: for instance he had in γ 50 a τοι 'to you', clitic, which might be Aeolic or Achaean, where the vulgate has the Ionic σοί (vulgate τοὔνεκα σοὶ ... δώσω "for that I will give you", *vs* Zenodotus τοὔνεκά τοι ... δώσω). Alexandrian scholars taught that the distribution was between clitic τοι and accented σοί,[26] and for that reason they may have substituted σοί for a number of accented τοί. Zenodotus may well be preserving here a non Ionic form τοί. Aristonicus blames him for using the clitic form, but, if Zenodotus' text did not have accentual marks (see above, pp. 27–28), this reproach is only a consequence of the fact that Zenodotus had the non assibilated form, which for Alexandrian scholars could only be the clitic form, as in Attic-Ionic prose.

This is confirmed by a later source. As a matter of fact, the *Epimerismi homerici* report that Zenodotus taught that τοί had to be accented in E 428 οὐ τοί, τέκνον ἐμόν, δέδοται πολεμήϊα ἔργα "not to you, my child, are assigned the works of warfare." The vulgate has # οὔ τοι with the clitic form.[27] Zenodotus justified

---

24 Since Zenodotus' text did not have accentual marks, ὀρῆτο is the accentuation provided by the scholiast, and analogical after the Attic form ὁρᾶτο. The rough breathing is also secondary, introduced by the scholiast for the same reason since the Aeolic form was marked by both psilosis and barytonesis (all words receive a recessive accent, whatever their morphological category: the systematic recessive accent in Attic-Ionic is limited to finite verbal forms, but in Lesbian it was generalised across the board).

25 The A scholion condemns this form as "Doric": ὁρᾶτο: ὅτι Ζηνόδοτος ὁρῆτο γράφει· ἀγνοεῖ δὲ ὅτι Δωρικὸν γίνεται "because Zenodotus writes ὁρῆτο: but he does not know that this is Doric" (*A Schol.* A 56c).

26 Chantraine, *Gr. hom.* I: 265, mentions only one form of clitic σοι, in the *Odyssey*, in a recent line. West 2001: 173 relies on this distribution to condemn A 170 οὐδέ σ' ὀΐω, preferring οὐδέ τ' ὀΐω but nevertheless leaving οὐδέ σ' ὀΐω in his edition.

27 There is no A scholion for this line, and the surviving T scholion is an exegetical scholion which focuses on the meaning of the line.

his point: ἔστι γάρ, φησί, διαστολή· εἰ δὲ διαστολή, ὀρθοτονητέον "because, he says, there is an opposition, and if there is an opposition, it must be orthotonic" (*Epimerismi homerici*, τ 66). The source of the *Epimerismi* is Herodian (*De enclisi*, Lentz III/1: 556). The opposition here is between Athena and Aphrodite: the πολεμήϊα ἔργα are the former's lot. Thus, Zenodotus explicitly admitted an accented τοί next to the clitic τοι. He probably did not invent it, but he found in his Homeric text several instances where the old Aeolic and Achaean τοί could not be clitic. Aristarchus probably considered the possibility that Zenodotus had an accented τοί but he deemed this use incorrect. Aristonicus, on the other hand, did not know Zenodotus' teaching, and he may not even have considered this possibility.

On the whole, Zenodotus' text is as mixed as the vulgate as far as dialects are concerned, which is not surprising. Van der Valk is right in saying that Zenodotus did not contain more old Ionic forms than the vulgate, neither does the Chian version for instance.[28]

2.3 Recent Forms

It is generally agreed that Zenodotus' text included many recent Ionic forms.
- Pronominal morphology: in A 271 Zenodotus had κατ' ἐμωυτόν with the recent Ionic form of the reflexive pronoun, whereas Aristarchus had κατ' ἔμ' αὐτόν and the vulgate κατ' ἐμαυτόν—similarly in Ξ 162 and P 551 Zenodotus ἑωυτήν vs Aristarchus ἓ αὐτήν. He apparently always had the possessive ἑοῖο where the vulgate has the unmotivated ἑῆος, which Greek scholars analysed either as a possessive or as an adjective meaning 'good' (A 393, O 138, T 342, Ω 528 and 550). Zenodotus had ἑοῖο even in a case like T 342 (Zeus to Athena) τέκνον ἐμόν, δὴ πάμπαν ἀποίχεαι ἀνδρὸς ἑῆος/ἑοῖο "my child, do you completely abandon a brave warrior?", where the interpretation by a possessive is hardly possible, although retained by Lattimore, who translates "have you utterly abandoned the man of your choice?" Chantraine assumes that Zenodotus' ἑοῖο is old and continues the inherited use of the reflexive pronoun for all persons, not only the third person. This use was eliminated by Aristarchus but could still survive in variant readings, not all by Zenodotus (see below, pp. 47–48).[29]
- Nominal morphology: Zenodotus had regularised forms in cases where Homer has a different inflectional type, as in ξ 394 μάρτυρες ἀμφοτέροισι θεοί with the regular athematic nom.pl., where the vulgate has μάρτυροι

---

28   Van der Valk 1964: 54. Petit 1999: 163–174 and 358–359.
29   Chantraine, *Gr. hom.* I: 273–274.

ἀμφοτέροισι θεοί with the rare thematic form—Zenodotus had the same reading in Γ 280 and Ξ 274 (but see below, pp. 38–39).[30] In Θ 349, he had Γοργόνος ὄμματ' ἔχων "having the eyes of the Gorgon," with the recent *n*-inflection Γοργών, vs vulgate Γοργοῦς ὄμματ' ἔχων (for Γοργόος with the older *i*-inflection),[31] and Aristarchus' Γοργοῦς οἴματ' ἔχων. He has several instances of a secondary *n*-less nominative for the comparative: κρείσσω A 80 and Γ 71, γλυκίω A 249, ἀμείνω H 114.[32]

He also has some feminised compounds instead of the epicene old form, as in ἀγχιάλην Ἀντρῶνα B 697 vs vulgate ἀγχίαλον τ' Ἀντρῶνα "and Antron on the shore," or in χερσὶ δ' ἀνίπτῃσιν Z 266 vs vulgate ἀνίπτοισιν 'unwashed hands'—West prints Zenodotus' feminine form, buth this is not justified.[33] Aristarchus condemned ἀγχιάλην because the word is epicene (κοινόν ἐστι τὸ ὄνομα, ὁ ἀγχίαλος καὶ ἡ ἀγχίαλος, A Schol. B 697) and ἀνίπτῃσιν because "the nominative is not ἀνίπτῃ" (A Schol. Z 266).[34] But in E 466 ἀμφὶ πύλῃς εὖ ποιητῇσι, reading of both the vulgate and Zenodotus, is not a compound, whereas Aristarchus corrected it into εὐποιήτοισι, compound and therefore epicene: the A scholion has ποιητοῖσι, because Aristonicus did not understand Aristarchus' point about the link between compound and gender, and West is probably wrong in printing εὐποιήτῃισι.

- Verbal morphology: Zenodotus often has augmented forms where the vulgate has augmentless ones. With elision of the preceding word, he has in P 595 γῆν δ' ἐτίναξε "and he shook the earth" vs vulgate τὴν δὲ τίναξε (with also a lexical divergence), in A 611 ἔνθ' ἐκάθευδ' ἀναβάς "going up to the bed he slept"

---

30 The regular μάρτυρες is also found in papyri, notably the eccentric P.Hibeh 19 (first half of the 3rd c. BCE) for Γ 280. S. West 1967: 51 considers that the papyrus reading and Zenodotus' are independent, which is certainly correct.

31 The replacement of Γοργόος by Γοργόνος is similar to the remodelling of old forms of the comparative, inflected originally as an *s*-stem, and systematically replaced by the younger *n*-form, like μείζονος, μείζονες, μείζονα for *μέζοος, *μέζοες, *μέζοα: the Homeric text as we have it has only scanty traces of the original *s*-inflection, when the long vowel resulting from contraction could not be resolved (ἀρείω # K 237).

32 For an attempt at explaining κρείσσω in A 80 as an accusative agreeing with κότον A 82, which requires the athetesis of A 81, see Nickau 1977: 241–242 (who himself does not subscribe to the hypothesis). However, this is not possible for the other cases.

33 In both cases Van Thiel assumes this is not a variant reading but a marginal comment meaning "the adjective is epicene." Were epicene compound adjectives so rare that Zenodotus felt an explanation was needed?

34 Matthaios 1999 gives the comment on ἀγχιάλην in the sub-section "Genus" (1999: 85), and the comment on ἀνίπτῃσι in the sub-section "Deklination" (1999: 93). But Aristarchus' remark "the nominative is not ἀνίπτῃ" is a different way of saying "the word has no specific feminine and is epicene" (see his comment on ἀγχίαλος, in which he starts from the nominative).

(vulgate ἔνθα καθεῦδ' ἀναβάς).³⁵ The form ἐκάθευδε with augment before the preverb is a younger one, also attested in Attic, as is ἐκαθέζετο (Zen.) in A 68 vs vulgate κατ' ἄρ' ἕζετο "he sat down," clearly older.³⁶ Similarly in O 716 οὐκ' ἐμεθίει "he did not let it go" vs vulgate οὐχὶ μεθίει:³⁷ the original form was οὐκὶ μεθίει, which underwent Atticisation in the vulgate (οὐχί is Attic, vs Ionic οὐκί). In O 716 the position of the augment before the preverb betrays a secondary remodelling.³⁸ Zenodotus' augmented μέγα δ' ἤλπετο νίκην # in N 609 is recent: the older form is ἐϝέλπετο, and ἤλπετο is an augmented form which would fit for a verb with initial /e/, not for a verb with initial /w/, it implies neglect of the digamma and is therefore recent; some papyri preserve the old form καὶ ἐέλπετο νίκην, and most manuscripts have the augmentless καὶ ἔλπετο νίκην. He had the recent form ἤμελλον (M 34) with a long augment: the form, also attested in Hesiod (*Th.* 478 and 898), is found once in the Hippocratic corpus and is usual in Attic—although Aristonicus calls it a barbarism (*A Schol.* M 34 ἔστι δὲ βάρβαρον). It is clearly recent in epic diction.³⁹ However, Zenodotus sometimes has no augment when the vulgate has one, as in ὄτρυνεν P 215 vs vulgate ὤτρυνεν.

He also has recent forms for individual verbs, like the recent aorist ἐσύθη of σεύω, also attested in Hippocrates and in Attic tragedy (E 293 αἰχμὴ δ' ἐξεσύθη παρὰ νείατον ἀνθερεῶνα "so that the spearhead sprang out underneath the jawbone," vs vulgate ἐξελύθη "so that the spearhead came out underneath the jawbone" (R.L.)), next to the old root aorist ἔσσυτο. For ἄγνυμι "to break", he has an aorist ἔηξα for ἔαξα (ξυνέηξε N 166, κατεήξαμεν N 257): Ionic prose has the perfect κατέηγα, with -η-.⁴⁰

---

35 Van Leeuwen's correction καθηῦδ', printed by West, is not necessary, as the augment is not marked for initial εὐ- because of Osthoff's law.

36 Aristonicus condemns the form: ὅτι Ζηνόδοτος γράφει ἐκαθέζετο. οὐκ ἐᾷ δὲ ἑλληνίζειν τὸν Ὅμηρον· ὥσπερ γὰρ οὐδὲ λέγει ἐκατέβαινεν, οὕτως οὐδὲ ἐκαθέζετο "because Zenodotus writes ἐκαθέζετο. But he does not make Homer speak correct Greek: and as ⟨Homer⟩ does not say ἐκατέβαινεν, neither does he say ἐκαθέζετο" (*A Schol.* A 68). The fact that Attic has ἐκαθέζετο (Thuc., Xen., And.) was not an objection, this form is nevertheless deemed "not Greek"—it is definitely not Homeric.

37 There were other comparable instances in Zenodotus, see Schironi 2004: 242, n. 11.

38 In both cases Van Thiel assumes that these forms are comments. Van Thiel 2014b, *sub* O 716: "Here Zenodotus commented by means of an unhomeric, therefore experimental alternative, the Attic οὐχί, which is attested in Homer only in the phrase οὐχὶ μεθίει".

39 The form is reused by Apollonius of Rhodes and Callimachus, cf. Rengakos 1993: 82.

40 The line is quoted by Lucian, *Pseudologista* 27, and Eustathius, *Comm. Il.* 2: 73 with the Zenodotean variant. This reading was found in other versions and was not specific to Zenodotus: the A scholion has ἄλλοι ἐξεσύθη, the indication that it was Zenodotus' reading is found in a bT scholion. Aristarchus' ἐξελύθη 'was broken as it went through', according to the bT scholion 'stopped its rush' (τῆς ὁρμῆς ἐπαύσατο) is hardly plausible. A D scholion

- Article: Zenodotus occasionally has an article where the vulgate has none, when metre allows for a crasis, as in B 1 ὧλλοι μέν ῥα θεοί τε καὶ ἀνέρες ἱπποκορυσταὶ || εὗδον παννύχιοι "now the rest of the gods, and men who were lords of chariots, slept night long" (R.L.) (vulgate ἄλλοι; similarly in K 1); but in δ 70 Zenodotus' reading with the article ἵνα μὴ πευθοίαθ᾽ οἱ ἄλλοι # "so that the others don't learn about it," agreeing with the vulgate, is kept by modern editors against Aristarchus' ἵνα μὴ πευθοίατο ἄλλοι with secondary hiatus, which is a correction aiming at eliminating the article.[41]
- Adverbs: Zenodotus had several cases of κεῖθι 'there' instead of κεῖσε 'thither' (Λ 528, M 368, Ψ 461): the Hippocratic corpus has several cases of (ἐ)κεῖσε in the meaning 'there' (without movement), and the loss of the distinction between the two adverbs may have led to some confusion.
- Syntax: with a neuter plural subject, the verb in Homer displays either singular or plural agreement. The singular tended to be generalised in Attic-Ionic prose, and Zenodotus' τὰ φρονέοντ᾽ ἀνὰ θυμὸν ἅ ῥ᾽ οὐ τελέεσθαι ἔμελλεν "believing things in his heart that were not to be accomplished" (R.L.) in B 36 may be a modernisation of an older ἔμελλον preserved by other versions (bT scholion). The vulgate has ἔμελλεν. However, Aristarchus taught that the plural was regular (A Schol. Π 507: εἴωθε γὰρ τοῖς οὐδετέροις πληθυντικοῖς πληθυντικὰ ῥήματα συντάσσειν, ὡς σπάρτα λέλυνται "because Homer usually uses plural verbs with neuter plural subjects, as σπάρτα λέλυνται"), so that many plurals of the vulgate may be the product of his teaching.
- Phonetically evolved forms: in Δ 478 the vulgate has θρέπτρα 'recompense for rearing due by a child to his parents', but Zenodotus had θρέπτα, a more recent form which arose through dissimilation, as in the case of δρύφακτος

---

understands it as 'it went out': ἐξελύθη· ἐξώρμησεν, διεξῆλθεν (ZYQX), and some modern scholars assumed the form had to be corrected in ἐξέλυθεν (Van der Valk 1964: 139 comments "Aristarchus offers the flat ἐξελύθη" which, however, he understands as 'went out'). The Townleyanus (f. 44ʳ) has ἐξέσυτο in the main text (but the scholion in the margin has ἐξελύθη, a case of discrepancy between the text and the commentary which is not isolated): ἐξέσυτο, unmetrical in the line, is an explanation of ἐξεσύθη integrated into the text instead of the form it was meant to explain.

41 Van Thiel assumes this is a marginal comment by Zenodotus intended to draw the attention to the fact that Homer has no article. Van Thiel 2014b, sub B 1: "Zenodotus' remark ωλλοι (without accent) illustrated the lack of article in Homer" ("Zenodots Notiz ωλλοι (ohne Akzente!) verdeutlichte das Fehlen des Artikels bei Homer"). The same remark can be made as for the epicene compounds: the absence of article in Homer was so familiar to Hellenistic scholars that this is utterly unbelievable. Such marginal comments as imagined by Van Thiel were appropriate in order to explain rare features or difficult forms, certainly not something as trivial as the absence of the article.

from *δρύφρακτος 'wooden barrier' or Arcadian φάτρα from φράτρα 'brotherhood, clan' (Ion. φρήτρη). Aristonicus says:

> *A Schol.* Δ 478: θρέπτρα: ὅτι Ζηνόδοτος γράφει χωρὶς τοῦ ρ. λέγεται δὲ θρεπτά τὰ τεθραμμένα. θρέπτρα δὲ σὺν τῷ ρ τὰ θρεπτήρια, ὥσπερ λύτρα τὰ λυτήρια.
>
> because Zenodotus writes without the [r]. But θρεπτά are the fed ones, whereas θρέπτρα with [r] is the nourishing due by children to their old parents, as in λύτρα for λυτήρια 'ransom'.

If, as is likely, Zenodotus' text did not have accentual marks, he had θρεπτα for θρέπτ(ρ)α, and he certainly correctly understood the meaning of the word— but again the persistent bias against him led younger scholars to think he did not understand properly and mistook the form for a verbal adjective.[42] In that case, the divergence is between an old form and a phonetically evolved one which may be Ionic.

The same cause is likely to explain Ξ 259 Νὺξ δμήτειρα θεῶν ... καὶ ἀνδρῶν "Night, who tames gods and men": Zenodotus and Aristophanes had μήτειρα. This spelling results from a simplification of the initial consonant cluster in a sequence [ksdm], and does not mean that Zenodotus had here a weird variant of μήτηρ, whatever some scholiasts may think (*T Schol.* Ξ 259: ἐπεὶ ἀρχαῖα θεός "because she is an antique goddess").[43] Remember that in Antiquity a text was read aloud, and this certainly also applied to the process of copying a text. Therefore the written form depended not only on what was written in the original text, but also on how it was pronounced.

In O 625–626 ἡ δέ τε πᾶσα || ἄχνῃ ὑπεκρύφθη "and the ship goes utterly hidden under the foam", Zenodotus had ἄχνη without the iota. It is unlikely that he understood the word as a nominative. It must rather witness the loss of the yod in the long diphthong -ηι, which is already achieved in Ionic in the 4th c.[44] This also applies to his μητιάασθε (Π 202, see above, p. 21). A reverse spelling is found in his Ὑρμίνηι in B 616 instead of vulgate # ὅσσον ἐφ' Ὑρμίνη: in the latter case the syntax of the line requires a nominative, but the ἐπί in tmesis may have been interpreted as a preposition governing the dative, no longer phonetically distinct from the nominative.

---

42 Van Thiel 2014a prints θρέπτα after Quintus Smyrnaeus 11.89, who uses the Zenodotean form.
43 Hesychius, μ 1273: μήτειρα· φρονίμη. καὶ ἡ μήτηρ ⟨ὡς παρὰ Καλλιμάχῳ⟩ indicates that Callimachus reused this rare form as a variant of μήτηρ (*fr.* 303 SH). See Rengakos 1993: 82.
44 Lejeune 1972: 227.

In B 532 Zenodotus had Βῆσαν instead of Βῆσσαν: geminate consonants are often written as simple consonants in Greek inscriptions, and this minor divergence results from a spelling convention rather than from a phonetic evolution.

Cases like these, indeed, fuel the conception according to which Zenodotus abusively modernised the received text. However, it is highly unlikely that a scholar familiar with Homer introduced a monster like ὧλλοι 'the other ones' (Β 1) into a text that read ἄλλοι. This can hardly be a spontaneous correction, and this cannot be an emendation introduced after another copy, for the same reason: emendations are supposed to improve the text, and even by 3rd c. standards, this cannot be considered an improvement. Therefore it can only be the reading of his working text, which he left unchanged. The modernisation is real, but it predates Zenodotus.

However, in more than one case the *doxa* may be questioned: for instance, μάρτυρες may be, rather than a regularised form, the older one, since the thematicisation of μάρτυς is a secondary development, metrically motivated in hexametric poetry. As a matter of fact, the only forms attested in the *Iliad* are the nom.pl. μάρτυροι, always before a vowel, in particular in the formula "be witness(es):" in line final position μάρτυροι ἔστων #, or before the trochaic caesura μάρτυροι ἔστε, with the metrical structure [– ⏑ ⏑ – x] of the adonic colon, and the nom.sg. ἐπιμάρτυρος ἔστω # (Η 76). The latter is probably an artificially thematicised form designed to fill the metrical structure, since the athematic μάρτυς would be unmetrical in that phrase, and a singer needs to be able to inflect a given formula without breaking the metrical structure. It can be described as a case of artificial thematicisation *metri causa*, of only one case form, the nom.sg., which was too short by one syllable in the athematic type. This yields a mixed paradigm with both thematic and athematic forms, singular μάρτυρος ἔστω # *vs* plural μάρτυρες ἔστων #, as in ἐρίηρος ἑταῖρος # (Δ 266) *vs* ἐρίηρες ἑταῖροι # (Γ 378), ἐρίηρας ἑταίρους # (Π 363). Then the paradigm was regularised after the singular, see the comment by Aristonicus:

A *Schol.* B 302a: ὅτι Ζηνόδοτος γράφει 'μάρτυρες'. ὁ δ' Ὅμηρος οὕτως ἐσχημάτικεν· 'Ζεὺς δ' ἄμμ' ἐπιμάρτυρος ἔστω' (Η 76), οὗ τὸ πληθυντικὸν μάρτυροί ἐστε.

because Zenodotus writes μάρτυρες. But Homer inflects it thus, 'Ζεὺς δ' ἄμμ' ἐπιμάρτυρος ἔστω', the plural of which is μάρτυροί ἐστε.

The athematic μάρτυρες and the thematic μάρτυροι are metrically equivalent before a vowel (that is, everywhere in the *Iliad*), whereas in Η 76 only the thematic form was possible: therefore morphological regularity and the need to have a consistent paradigm required the remodelling of μάρτυρες into μάρτυροι.[45] So that in fact, Zenodotus can simply preserve here the older, regular athematic form. The *doxa* assumes that he has a regularised form and eliminated older thematic forms: rather, his μάρτυρες can be analysed as a form that predates the systematic application of ἀναλογία and the generalisation of the younger thematic paradigm.[46] It is regular, not regularised: the regularised form is indeed the thematic plural μάρτυροι. The athematic μάρτυρες is attested in several papyri, including P.Hibeh 19 (first half of the 3rd c. BCE), which agree with Zenodotus.[47] The thematic form is not attested in any of the dialects used in the epic language (Ionic, Aeolic, Arcado-Cyprian group), but is epigraphically well attested in North-West Doric dialects from the 3rd c. BCE on: the fact that the Homeric thematic singular μάρτυρος, metrically warranted, met a form familiar from one living dialect at least could help its generalisation in Homer. And the Homeric instances do not prove that the thematic type is old for this word.[48]

Of course, if μάρτυρες is the older form, and attested in a contemporary papyrus, it is more economical to assume Zenodotus' working text had μάρτυρες, not yet the analogised μάρτυροι, and that μάρτυρες is not a correction he imported from another copy.

Zenodotus' awful reputation notwithstanding, modern philologists acknowledge that in several places he does preserve an older reading, and modern editors more than once print Zenodotus' reading rather than Aristarchus' or the vulgate's. This conclusion relies on the use of various criteria.

---

45   The process of regularisation works either way: it can lead to a secondary thematicisation or athematicisation. I discussed a symmetrical case of athematicisation *metri causa* (ἑλίκωπες Ἀχαιοί) in Le Feuvre 2015: 432–436. In a case like ἐρίηρ-, the mixed paradigm is preserved because some case forms required one type rather than the other: ἐρίηρες ἑταῖροι and *ἐρίηροι ἑταῖροι were equivalent, but athematic ἐρίηρας ἑταίρους was the only possible form in the acc.pl. and so was thematic ἐρίηρος ἑταῖρος in the nom.sg. Therefore a complete regularisation was out of reach, contrary to the case of μάρτυρες/μάρτυρος.

46   On ἀναλογία, see below (pp. 50–51). In that case, Greek scholars can lend to Homer, on the basis of an artificial Homeric form (ἐπιμάρτυρος H 76), a whole series of forms. For ἐπιμάρτυρος, Leumann 1950: 71 showed that it results from an erroneous segmentation of ἐπὶ μάρτυρος but did not question the thematic ending.

47   S. West 1967: 51.

48   On the formation and etymology of μάρτυς, see Le Feuvre 2021e.

3 Criteria of Discussion of Variant Readings

3.1 *Metrics*

A widely used criterion to determine which of two variants is older is the metrical effect of an initial digamma. It can lead modern editors to favour Zenodotus' reading.[49] For instance, in N 107 Zenodotus' (and Aristophanes') # νῦν δὲ ἑκὰς πόλιος is rightly preferred by Allen, Leaf, Mazon, West, to Aristarchus' # νῦν δ' ἔκαθεν πόλιος κοίλῃς ἐπὶ νηυσὶ μάχονται "but now far from their city they fight by the hollow vessels" (R.L.) with neglected digamma (ϝεκάς, ϝέκαθεν), although the latter is found in all our manuscripts.

In Θ 526–527 Zenodotus read ἔλπομαι εὐχόμενος Διί τ' ἄλλοισίν τε θεοῖσιν || ἐξελάαν ἐνθένδε κύνας κηρεσσιφορήτους "for in good hope I pray to Zeus and the other immortals that we may drive from our place these dogs swept into destruction" (R.L.), whereas Aristarchus had εὔχομαι ἐλπόμενος, with reversed syntactic hierarchy between the participle and the finite form. Zenodotus' reading, retained by most modern editors (Leaf, Mazon, West among others), is certainly the older one, and not an "experimental word permutation" ("experimentelle Wortumstellung") as per Van Thiel.[50] Aristarchus's reading εὔχομαι ἐλπόμενος implies neglect of the digamma in ἐλπόμενος, whereas Zenodotus' is compatible with the older linguistic form ϝέλπομαι. Besides, εὔχομαι + infinitive normally means 'to boast' or 'to promit', not 'to pray', and here Hector hopes, he does not boast, which is another argument against Aristarchus' reading.[51]

In Λ 437 Zenodotus' reading # πάντα δ' ἀπὸ πλευρῶν χρόα ἔργαθεν "and tore all the skin away from his ribs" (R.L. modified), with an accusative, is better than Aristarchus' χροός "tore everything away from the skin of his limbs," which implies neglect of the digamma in ἔργαθεν and leaves πάντα alone. Aristarchus' genitive may have been introduced to fill the hiatus left by the loss of the digamma.

On the other hand, in A 24, Zenodotus' reading ἀλλ' οὐκ Ἀτρεΐδεω Ἀγαμέμνονος ἥνδανε θυμῷ "but it did not please the Atrid Agamemnon's heart" vs vulgate ἀλλ' οὐκ Ἀτρεΐδῃ Ἀγαμέμνονι ἥνδανε θυμῷ cannot be old: only the vulgate's reading is compatible with the initial digamma of ϝανδάνω—provided we restore

---

49   This is one of the rare cases where Van der Valk accepts a Zenodotean reading "which takes account of the digamma" (Van der Valk 1964: 42) against Aristarchus.
50   Van Thiel 2014b, *sub* Θ 526. Accordingly, in his edition Van Thiel prints εὔχομαι ἐλπόμενος.
51   See also the long discussion in Muellner 1976: 57–62. Even Van der Valk 1964: 76 accepts Zenodotus' reading as better and older than the vulgate's. However, he assumes Aristarchus' εὔχομαι ἐλπόμενος is a conjecture: this is far from certain, and it is more likely that Aristarchus simply found this order in his working text, and did not change it.

the older augmentless ϝάνδανε. Zenodotus' reading in A 24 is posterior to the loss of ϝ, and the vulgate's reading is rightly preferred by modern editors. Similarly for Zenodotus' μέγα δ' ἤλπετο νίκην # in N 609 (see above, p. 35).

In I 537 the vulgate has ἢ λάθετ' ἢ οὐκ ἐνόησεν "either he forgot or he did not think." It requires a synizesis of ἢ οὐκ, for which there is no parallel: this betrays a recent line.[52] Zenodotus had ἐκλάθετ' οὐδ' ἐνόησεν "he forgot and did not think" (which may stand for οὐδὲ νόησεν), which is metrically correct. His reading is condemned by Aristonicus for semantic reasons:

A Schol. I 537a: ἡ διπλῆ ὅτι Ζηνόδοτος γράφει ἐκλάθετ' οὐδ' ἐνόησεν, ὥστε τὸ αὐτὸ διλογεῖσθαι. οὐκ ἐνόησε δὲ ὅτι διαφέρει· τὸ μὲν γὰρ ἐλάθετο, ἑκὼν παρέπεμψεν, τὸ δὲ οὐκ ἐνόησεν, οὐδὲ τὴν ἀρχὴν κατὰ νοῦν ἔσχεν.

diple, because Zenodotus writes ἐκλάθετ' οὐδ' ἐνόησεν, so that the same thing is expressed twice. But he did not see that there is a difference, the ἐλάθετο means 'he voluntarily omitted' and the οὐκ ἐνόησεν means that he did not think of it at all.

---

52   Synizesis, the possibility of scanning as one single syllable a succession of two vowels, arose as a consequence of the quantitative metathesis in Ionic. In A 1, the older *Μῆνιν ἄειδε θεὰ Πηληϊάδᾱ' Ἀχιλῆος (elision of Πηληϊάδᾱο, regular gen.sg. like Ἀτρεΐδᾱο) was modernised with the Ionic ending -εω < *-ηο < -ᾱο, resulting in the transmitted line Μῆνιν ἄειδε θεὰ Πηληϊάδεω Ἀχιλῆος. In order to preserve the metrical structure of the line, this -εω had to scan as one syllable, taking over the metrical value of the ending it replaced, -ᾱ(ο), monosyllabic because of the elision. On that model, the possibility of scanning as one syllable sequences -εω-, -εη- and -εα- was generalised, resulting in new lines like the line final formula Κρόνου πάϊς ἀγκυλομήτεω # (Δ 75) where the ending never was monosyllabic, or Γ 273 # ἀρνῶν ἐκ κεφαλέων τάμνε τρίχας, with the ending -έων of κεφαλέων scanning as a long syllable although there never was a quantitative metathesis in the gen.pl. of ᾱ-stems. The quantitative metathesis itself is posterior to the loss of intervocalic /w/, which dates back to the 9th c. in Ionic (Ion. λεώς 'people' < *ληός < *ληϝός < λᾱϝός). The possibility of synizesis sometimes led to hyperarchaising forms: in Γ 273 ἀρνῶν ἐκ κεφαλέων τάμνε τρίχας, an A scholion tells us that Zenodotus had ἀρνέων ἐκ κεφαλέων, which Aristonicus condemns because ἀρήν is a consonant stem and the latter never have a dissyllabic ending (*A Schol.* Γ 273: ἀπὸ δὲ τῶν κατὰ τὴν ὀρθὴν ληγόντων εἰς ες οὐ γίνονται τοιαῦται διαιρέσεις, ἀλλ' ἀπὸ τῶν εἰς αι· εἰ δὲ ἄρνες, ἀρνῶν. ἀπὸ δὲ τοῦ κεφαλαί κατὰ λόγον κεφαλέων "from nouns ending in -ες in the nominative, such diaereses do not occur, but only for nouns ending in -αι: if ⟨we have⟩ ἄρνες, ⟨then we have⟩ ἀρνῶν, whereas κεφαλέων from κεφαλαί is regular"). This reflects the point of view of a speaker of *koine*: the gen.pl. of κεφαλή is κεφαλῶν, and starting from this contracted form, the spelling κεφαλέων can only be described as a diaeresis, that is, the opposite of the synizesis. The *Epimerismi homerici* (x 56) understand that Zenodotus' spelling was for ἀρνείων, the adjective meaning 'of lambs' (ὡς κτητικὸν αὐτὸ λαβών "taking it as the possessive adjective"), rather than the noun ἀρήν, and in that case, indeed, ἀρνέων should scan with a synizesis.

Zenodotus' reading is better and probably older: this is warranted not only by metrics, but also by the fact that such tautological phrases where a same notion is expressed twice (*hendiadys*) are a common device of formulaic diction: ἐπιτέλλομαι ἠδὲ κελεύω "I order and command" (T 192), κατὰ φρένα καὶ κατὰ θυμόν "in his mind and heart" (*passim*). Such "double" formulations are mostly used in order to obtain a full hemistich. In a variant of this pattern, described by Humbach,[53] the second element is the negated antonym of the first one: A and not non-A. For instance, with two adverbs κρύβδην, μηδ' ἀναφανδά "secretly and not openly" (λ 455), with two verbs, ἤμβροτες οὐδ' ἔτυχες "you missed me and did not reach me" (E 287). Zenodotus' ἐκλάθετ' οὐδ' ἐνόησεν, forming a T1 hemistich, belongs to this type and is a neglected instance of the Humbach pattern. The vulgate's emendation ἢ λάθετ' ἢ οὐκ ἐνόησεν is metrically costly (synizesis) and ruins the old pattern.

The metrical criterion was used by ancient scholars, but not as we use it. They condemned some Zenodotean readings because they were unmetrical, but, having no idea of any chronological heterogeneity of the Homeric corpus, they could not use digamma, metathesis, synizesis or contractions for sorting out older lines from newer ones.

3.2 *Linguistics*

Historical linguistics is a reliable tool when it comes to old and recent forms, and provides arguments favouring one reading over another, or explaining seemingly incorrect forms. I will review here a few cases in which Zenodotus' reading is clearly older than the vulgate's.

3.2.1 Phonetics

In Π 188, modern editors rightly prefer Zenodotus' ἐξάγαγε πρὸ φόως δε "she brought him to the light," modernisation of the original uncontracted φάος δε, to Aristophanes' and Aristarchus' ἐξάγαγεν φώως δέ without πρό (see above, p. 7). As a matter of fact, the long vowel in the first syllable of φώως cannot be old and the use of an ephelcystic -*n* before a consonant to lengthen the syllable in ἐξάγαγεν is recent. Zenodotus' reading, agreeing with the vulgate, does not have the awkward long syllable in φώως but only the regular form with *diectasis*,[54] it does not need the ephelcystic -*n* and probably read

---

53 Humbach 1959.
54 *Diectasis* is the spelling -οω- instead of -αο-, resulting in an artificial compromise between the uncontracted form, metrically necessary, and the contracted one: the long vowel resulting from the contraction is "extended" over two syllables. The device is frequent in participles (ὁρόωντες, scanning as the older uncontracted ὁράοντες, but pronounced as the

ἐξάγαγε, not ἐξάγαγεν, contrary to what modern editors print.⁵⁵ The πρό in Zenodotus' version can be the adverb or the preverb of προεξάγω (Attic) with tmesis:⁵⁶ but Aristarchus seems to have understood it as the preposition, which was incompatible with the lative -δε, hence the suppression and the *ad hoc* lengthening of the first syllable of φώως. There is no reason to believe this is a correction introduced by Zenodotus after another copy, for in this line the modification is on Aristarchus' side. Zenodotus' reading is the older and correct one and it must have been the one of most copies, including his working text.

In B 658 Zenodotus was blamed for producing an unmetrical reading: the vulgate has βίη Ἡρακληείη #, whereas Zenodotus had Ἡρακλείη, lacking a syllable. But the adjective derived from Ἡρακλέης is not Ἡρακλήειος, but *Ἡρακλεέϊος (< *-κλεϝεhιο-). Zenodotus probably had a text where an older Ἡρακλεείη (with -εε- in thesis), with metrically lengthened ῑ,⁵⁷ was spelled with /e/ written only once, yielding the unmetrical Ἡρακλείη. This is the graphic transcription of the phonetic process of hyphaeresis, the loss of a vowel in a sequence of three vowels: hyphaeresis is frequent in the stem of κλέος and its derivatives (ἐϋκλείης Θ 285 from ἐϋκλεείης, nom.pl. ἐϋκλεές P 415 from ἐϋκλεέες M 318).⁵⁸

---

newer contracted ὁρῶντες). Here φόως scans as the older uncontracted φάος and is pronounced as the newer contracted φῶς.

55 Nickau does not comment on this line.
56 As per Petit (2007: 195), no monosyllabic preverb can be found with tmesis and anastrophe, that is, after the verb: this is probably overstated, as there are a few cases—which, granted, have not always been correctly identified.
57 For the metrical lengthening of the suffix -ίη, see Chantraine, *Gr. hom.* I: 101. This mostly happens when the presuffixal syllable is long, in order to avoid a cretic [– ◡ –], for instance Ι 73 # πᾶσα τοί ἐσθ' ὑποδεξίη, χ 374 κακοεργίη, but also when it is short, for instance K 151 κονίη #.
58 The difficult ἐϋκλεῖας in K 281 δὸς δὲ πάλιν ἐπὶ νῆας ἐϋκλεῖας ἀφικέσθαι, scans with a long -ᾱς, irregular for a third declension adjective. The form was interpreted by the Greeks as "grant us to go back to the ships full of glory", that is, a variant for the acc.pl. ἐϋκλεέας, but it is probably the reshaping of an older *δὸς δὲ πάλιν ἐπὶ νῆας ἐϋκλήϝῑς ἀφικέσθαι "grant us to go back to the ship with good benches", old accusative plural of ἐϋκλήϝις, vocalic variant of πολυκλήϝις found in several lines as a traditional epithet of 'ship' (B 74 καὶ φεύγειν σὺν νηυσὶ πολυκλήϊσι κελεύσω, B 175 φεύξεσθ' ἐν νήεσσι πολυκλήϊσι πεσόντες, υ 382 τοὺς ξείνους ἐν νηΐ | πολυκλήϊδι βαλόντες). In K 281, it is the epithet of νῆας, not related syntactically to the subject "us" of ἀφικέσθαι. This form ἐϋκλήϝῑς < ἐϋκλήϝινς is metrically regular in the line, whereas the transmitted ἐϋκλεῖας is awkward, and its restitution fills the empty slot in the formulaic system πολύζυγος (B 293 ἀσχαλάᾳ σὺν νηῒ πολυζύγῳ) / εὔζυγος (ρ 288 τῆς ἕνεκεν καὶ νῆες εὔζυγοι ὁπλίζονται), πολυκλήϊς / ἐϋκλήϊς. But the form was misunderstood for the much more frequent adjective εὐκλεής, probably after the analogy of P 415–416 ὦ φίλοι οὐ μὰν ἥμιν ἐϋκλεὲς ἀπονέεσθαι || νῆας ἔπι γλαφυράς, which has a similar structure "we go back to the ships" and where ἐϋκλεές is 'glorious'. See the details in Le Feuvre 2015: 403–415 (Nussbaum 2017: 284–285 provides an explanation which is not convincing because he keeps the analysis as an accusative of εὐκλεϝής).

The vulgate's Ἡρακληείη goes back to the same form and displays the same hyphaeresis, but underwent a metrical lengthening of the remaining vowel, analogical after Ἡρακλῆος, -κλῆα,[59] and absent in Zenodotus. Since Ἡρακλείη is unmetrical, as underlined in the scholion, it can hardly be an emendation introduced from an other copy, because Zenodotus, too, could see it was unmetrical. Therefore this must be the reading of his working text, which he did not correct and left unchanged.

3.2.2 Morphology

An instance involving derivational morphology is Γ 56, where all modern editors follow the vulgate and print # ἀλλὰ μάλα Τρῶες δειδήμονες "but the Trojans are cowards, indeed." The line is found in a speech of Hector blaming Paris: "And now you would not stand up against warlike Menelaos? Thus you would learn of the man whose blossoming wife you have taken. The lyre would not help you then, nor the favours of Aphrodite, nor your locks, when you rolled in the dust, nor all your beauty. No, but the Trojans are cowards in truth, else long before this you had worn a mantle of flying stones for the wrong you did us" (R.L.). Instead, Zenodotus had Τρῶες ἐλεήμονες "the Trojans are merciful." His reading was condemned by Aristonicus: *A Schol.* Γ 56a: οὐκ ἐλεοῦσι δὲ αὐτόν, ἀλλὰ μισοῦσιν· οὐ μὲν γὰρ φιλότητί γ' ἐκεύθανον· ἶσον γάρ σφιν πᾶσιν ἀπήχθετο ⟨κηρὶ μελαίνῃ⟩ (Γ 453–454) "they don't pity him, but they hate him: 'These would not have hidden him for love, if any had seen him, since he was hated among them all as dark death is hated'" (R.L.).

However, δειδήμων, a *hapax* only known from grammarians and late poets (Nonnos), is morphologically abnormal, for there is no verb *δειδέω, whereas ἐλεήμων form ἐλεέω is regular and usual in Attic-Ionic. The form δειδήμων is derived from δείδω, which is not attested as a present stem in Homer except in the first person at the beginning of the line # δείδω μή, but the form is always resolvable into the older # δέδϝοα μή (perfect *de-du̯oi̯-a).[60] The other persons, as expected, inflect as perfect forms: imperative δείδιθι (E 827, Ξ 342), δείδιτε (Υ 366), indicative 1pl. δείδιμεν (Η 196, Ι 230), recent 1sg. δείδοικα (Α 555, Ι 244, Σ 261), 3sg. δείδοικε (Φ 198), 1sg. δείδια (Ν 49, Ν 481, Φ 536), 3sg. δείδιε (Σ 34, Ω 358), the latter two replacing *dedu̯oi̯a, *dedu̯oi̯e. Now the perfect stem is not a suitable derivation base. Therefore δειδήμων, derived from the modernised form δείδω after the latter was reinterpreted as a present, cannot be old: we have reasons to suspect that Zenodotus' reading is older, and that δειδήμων results from

---

59 Schwyzer, *Gr. Gr.* I: 143. See below, p. 129.
60 Chantraine, *Gr. hom.* I: 55.

an emendation.[61] The new δειδήμων keeps the suffix of the original ἐλεήμων, resulting in a neologism: the morphological irregularity is the consequence of the partial replacement—partial because only the root is changed. As a matter of fact, in Hector's speech, ἐλεήμων makes sense: "the Trojans are merciful, indeed, for you should have been stoned to death and you were not." The merciful behaviour of the Trojans underlines Paris' own cowardice, because he is not on the frontline, although he is the cause of the war. But since in Γ 453–454 the Trojans are said to hate Paris (σφιν πᾶσιν ἀπήχθετο), the apparent contradiction between 'merciful' in Γ 56 and 'he was hated' in Γ 454 was removed: achieving the goal of textual consistency led to the replacement. Modern editors print the vulgate's δειδήμονες, but Zenodotus' ἐλεήμονες must be older.[62]

Besides, Zenodotus' reading as reported by the scholion would yield an unmetrical line with a tribrach in Τρῶες ἐλεήμονες. We can suspect Aristonicus would gladly pinpoint a metrical flaw if there was one, but he does not mention any. This probably means that Zenodotus' text was metrically correct, with an elided particle, for instance ἀλλὰ μάλα Τρῶές γ' ἐλεήμονες "but the Trojans at any rate are merciful, indeed," but the scholion only mentions the lexical divergence, the more significant, and leaves the minor divergence in the dark (see above Σ 198, p. 15).

Linguistics is decisive when it comes to choosing between two competing forms of a same word: in Λ 831 Zenodotus has an archaic δεδάασθαι 'to be taught' where the vulgate has δεδιδάχθαι.[63] The perfect δεδίδαχα, passive δεδιδάχθαι, was secondarily built from the present stem διδασκ- and is clearly recent. The transmitted δεδάασθαι would stand for δεδαέσθαι, found as a *varia lectio*. The indicative δέδαε (ζ 233) is analysed in most grammars as a reduplicated thematic aorist

---

61 This was already seen by Tichy, *Ilias diachronica* Γ 56. However, Tichy in her tentative reconstruction does not consider Zenodotus' reading and she suggests that the older form was μεθήμονες (after μεθήμων Β 241)—which is gratuitous. Bolelli 1953: 9, notices there is no matching verbal form but does not go further: "the frequency of words in -ήμων makes it possible to speak of a suffix -ήμων already in Homer; and as a matter of fact, δειδήμων is formed without any relationship with any attested verbal form in *ē*" ("la frequenza di voci con -ήμων ha fatto sì che già in Omero si possa forse parlare di un suffisso -ήμων; ed infatti, δειδήμων si forma senza che nessuna forma verbale, almeno attestata, in *ē* abbia con essa relazione"). Risch 1974: 52 lists δειδήμων among deverbal adjectives: most display the suffix -μων, hence -ήμων when the basis is a verb in -έω (including μαχήμων 'fighter' derived from μαχέομαι) or -άω. The only other form in -ήμων derived from a thematic verbal stem is ἀλιτήμων 'sinful' (aorist ἤλιτον). The latter may have provided a model for δειδήμων, together with μαχήμων since the form could be related to μάχομαι as well as μαχέομαι.
62 Nickau does not comment on the form.
63 Risch 1974: 243, *LIV*²: 119. Here again Van der Valk 1964: 49 labels δεδάασθαι "a subjective alteration." Wilamowitz 1916: 205, on the other hand, accepted it.

*de-dn̥s-e/o-, with causative meaning 'to make know, to teach'. Zenodotus' form is therefore an aorist, not a perfect, and indeed the aorist is better in the context: (φάρμακα) τά σε προτί φασιν Ἀχιλλῆος δεδιδάχθαι "(medicines) which they say you have been told of by Achilleus" (R.L.) refers to a process, not to a state. The form was replaced by δεδιδάχθαι, which has the same metrical structure, maybe after the new aorist ἐδίδαξε in the following line.

Another instance is I 3 where the passive pluperfect πένθεϊ βεβλήατο 'they had been afflicted by grief' (also found in Ξ 28) is indeed, if not very old, at least older than the vulgate's remodelled βεβολήατο with an abnormal o grade of the root in the passive. Βεβλήατο was found in other versions, not only in Zenodotus (*A Schol.* I 3c: ὅτι ἔνιοι βεβλήατο, καὶ Ζηνόδοτος οὕτως "because some have βεβλήατο, including Zenodotus"). Aristonicus condemns Zenodotus' reading because βεβλήμαι is only used for a physical wound, which is not the case in I 3 because they suffer from grief, πένθεϊ:

> *A Schol.* I 3c: ἐπὶ δὲ τῆς κατὰ ψυχὴν τρώσεως καὶ ἀλγηδόνος ἀεὶ τοῦτο τάττει, ἐπὶ δὲ τῆς κατὰ σῶμα πληγῆς οὐκέτι οὕτως.
>
> for a moral pain and suffering he always uses this form (βεβολήατο), but for a physical wound he no longer does.
>
> *b Schol.* I 3c: τὸ μὲν οὖν βεβολήατο ἐπὶ ψυχῆς, τὸ δὲ "βεβλήατο" ἐπὶ σώματος.
>
> βεβολήατο is used for the soul, and βεβλήατο for the body.

The desire to differentiate between physical wound and moral pain is likely to be fairly recent. The same form is found in the participle in I 9 Ἀτρεΐδης δ' ἄχεϊ μεγάλῳ βεβολημένος ἦτορ "and the son of Atreus, stricken at heart with the great sorrow" (R.L.). No variant reading is reported, but Aristarchus did mark the line with the *diple* and Aristonicus explains the cross-reference: *A Schol.* I 9b (Aim) ὅτι πάλιν τὸ βεβολημένος τὸ διὰ τοῦ ο ἐπὶ ψυχῆς λέγει "because he again uses βεβολημένος with /o/ for the soul." No doubt the copies having βεβλήατο in I 3 also had βεβλημένος in I 9, although the scholion does not mention it— but the scholion is not in the main scholiastic text, it was added in the margin, and is an abridged version of the original comment. The participle is reused in κ 247 κῆρ ἄχεϊ μεγάλῳ βεβολημένος "stricken at heart with great sorrow" (J.H.), and then in Hellenistic poetry (Aratus,[64] Apollonius Rhodius).

---

64 Aratus uses the form only once (*Phaen.* 1.609), and it does not refer to moral pain. There are eight instances in Apollonius, all of them referring to a moral pain.

Some scholars suggested that βεβολήατο, βεβολημένος could be based on a perfect *βέβολε (< *g^we-g^wolh_1-e),[65] of which there is no trace. It is much more likely that this alternative perfect stem was coined through a modification of the regular βεβλήατο after the many compounds in -βόλος and their denominatives in -βολέω (which provide the stem -βολη-), as already seen by Frisk:[66] Herodian derives it from βολέω, and this synchronic explanation may reflect the process that led to the creation of the word.[67] This modification agrees with the theory of accidents (*pathos*): one form is derived from another by several means, insertion of a phoneme, deletion, inversion, or the like. This is typical of the etymological method of the Stoic school. Both the cause (make a distinction between physical wound and moral pain) and the *modus operandi* point to a recent form. Zenodotus' reading preserves the older state of affairs, before the invention of this factitious distinction between two different forms.

3.2.3 Syntax

An example involving syntax is that of the reflexive pronoun. In two cases Aristarchus blamed Zenodotus for using the reflexive possessive ὅς (*suo-) with a dual or plural possessor: the rule in Homer is that ὅς is singular and the plural is σφός or σφέτερος. The first line is Γ 243–244 "Ὣς φάτο, τοὺς δ' ἤδη κάτεχεν φυσίζοος αἶα || ἐν Λακεδαίμονι αὖθι φίλῃ ἐν πατρίδι γαίῃ "So she spoke, but the teeming earth lay already upon them away in Lakedaimon, the beloved land of their fathers" (R.L.), whereas Zenodotus had ἑῇ ἐν πατρίδι γαίῃ. Aristonicus says that the singular does not fit if it refers to Castor and Pollux (*A Schol.* Γ 244 ἑνικὸν οὐχ ἁρμόσει). The second line is Λ 142 νῦν μὲν δὴ τοῦ πατρὸς ἀεικέα τίσετε λώβην "so now your mutilation shall punish the shame of your father" (R.L.), whereas Zenodotus had οὗ πατρός. Aristonicus raises the same objection, that οὗ is a singular and cannot refer to two people. But this objection is only valid in the synchrony of Greek. As a matter of fact, in most Indo-European languages the reflexive pronoun is number insensitive, and so is the reflexive possessive: *suo- is used both with a singular possessor and with a plural or dual possessor. Such was the case in Proto-Greek, too, and the development of a plural reflexive

---

65 Chantraine, *Gr. hom.* I: 435, reported with a question mark in Beekes, *EDG*, s.v. βάλλω.
66 *GEW*, s.v. βάλλω.
67 *Schematismi homerici* 29: Βεβολήατο, παθητικὸς ὑπερσυντέλικος· βολῶ βολήσω βεβόληκα βεβόλημαι ἐβεβολήμην ἐβεβόλητο καὶ Ἰωνικῶς ἐβεβολέατο, εἶτα ἐκβολὴ τῆς ἀρχούσης καὶ τροπῇ τοῦ ε εἰς ⟨η⟩ "Βεβολήατο: passive pluperfect: βολῶ, βολήσω, βεβόληκα, βεβόλημαι, ἐβεβολήμην, ἐβεβόλητο and in Ionic ἐβεβολέατο, and then by deletion of the initial vowel and change of the /e/ into ⟨ē⟩."

pronoun is a Greek innovation.[68] Therefore Zenodotus may be preserving here a syntactic archaism, the number insensitive status of the reflexive, inherited from PIE. It is unlikely that he introduced a singular against the plural or dual agreement in these lines if his text had something different, as already seen by Chantraine.[69] Therefore ἑῇ and οὗ must be the readings of his working text. The vulgate's readings must be corrections: correcting the disyllabic ἑῇ into φίλῃ was easy, and in Λ 142 the vulgate has an article τοῦ πατρός that cannot be old, and τοῦ could have replaced an older οὗ πατρός (with οὗ or *ὅο since the contraction is resolvable in the thesis).[70] Another similar case is found in Λ 76 # σφοῖσι ἐνὶ μεγάροισι (vulg.), where an A scholion simply says γράφεται οἷσι: this may have been Zenodotus' reading, because the pattern—"singular" reflexive possessive for a plural referent—is the same as in Λ 142 and Γ 244.

In P 173 the vulgate has # νῦν δέ σευ ὠνοσάμην "but I blamed you", with *correptio epica*. Zenodotus had νῦν δέ σε ὠνοσάμην with apparently an accusative instead of the regular genitive. However, his reading is old, as σε results from the elision of the uncontracted genitive σεο: West correctly prints σε' ὠνοσάμην. The correct case, the genitive, was restored in the vulgate, with the recent Ionic form σευ instead of σου, but Zenodotus' text is likely to preserve the older state. However, it may have been interpreted as an accusative in the 3rd c.: that is, a purely phonetic phenomenon (elision) could be reinterpreted in terms of a syntactic difference. The same discrepancy between synchronic interpretation and diachronic explanation can be seen in P 368: Zenodotus' ἐπὶ τόσσον vs vulgate ἐπί θ' ὅσσον is caused by a phonetic difference (psilosis, see above, pp. 27–29), and was reinterpreted as a syntactic difference.

---

68   Schwyzer, *Gr. Gr.* I : 601. Petit 1999: 298, draws a distinction, in Homer, between the pronoun ἕ, always singular, and the possessive ὅς which may have preserved the number insensitive status.

69   Chantraine, *Gr. hom.* I: 274: "the vulgate, strongly influenced by Aristarchus, had a tendency to eliminate the instances of a «free» use of ἑός and ὅς. But this use seems to be old. Zenodotus can hardly have arbitrarily introduced it into his text" ("la vulgate homérique fortement marquée de l'influence d'Aristarque a tendu à éliminer les exemples d'un emploi «libre» de ἑός et ὅς. Mais il semble que cet usage soit ancien. Zénodote ne peut guère l'avoir introduit arbitrairement dans son texte"). For Γ 244 the case is not certain because ἑῇ ἐν πατρίδι γαίῃ # is a frequent formula, which might have been introduced mechanically in a context where the possessor was not a singular, but Λ 142 cannot be explained away by means of formulaic diction.

70   A T scholion to Λ 142 mentions another reading σφοῦ πατρός. Tichy in her *Ilias diachronica*, Λ 142, reconstructs *νῦν δὴ τοῖο πατρός and does not consider Zenodotus' reading.

3.2.4   Mycenaean
The decipherment of Mycenaean brought very important linguistic information, leading scholars to revise analyses that were unanimously accepted before that. Mycenaean led to a better understanding of many Homeric forms. But as often, Zenodotus' readings were not examined by linguists. Yet Mycenaean facts can shed a new light on them, too.

A clear case is Σ 222 οἳ δ' ὡς οὖν ἄϊον ὄπα χάλκεον Αἰακίδαο "but the Trojans, when they heard the brazen voice of Aiakides" (R.L.), where Aristonicus tells us that Zenodotus read χαλκέην:

Schol. A Σ 222: ὄπα χάλκεον· ⟨ὅτι⟩ ἀμέτρως ὁ Ζηνόδοτος ὄπα χαλκέην, οὐ συνεὶς ὅτι παραπλήσιόν ἐστι τὸ σχῆμα τῷ κλυτὸς Ἱπποδάμεια καὶ θερμὸς ἀυτμή.

⟨because⟩ Zenodotus has an unmetrical ὄπα χαλκέην, for he did not understand that the figure is similar to κλυτὸς Ἱπποδάμεια and θερμὸς ἀυτμή.

Van Thiel assumes that Zenodotus' χαλκέην was in fact a marginal comment of Zenodotus meaning "χάλκεον is feminine and stands for χαλκέην."[71] Of course, Zenodotus' reading is not metrically correct in the synchrony of Ionic, but neither is the well-known χρυσέη kept in the vulgate (Γ 64 χρυσέης Ἀφροδίτης #, Τ 282 χρυσέη Ἀφροδίτῃ #), and scanned with synizesis, as though it were a contracted form (printed in Χ 470 χρυσῆ Ἀφροδίτῃ #, Υ 272 # τὴν δὲ μίαν χρυσῆν). We now know that χαλκέην, χρυσέη did scan in some dialects as a disyllabic χάλκι̯ᾱν, χρύσι̯ᾱ with the so-called "secondary yod," attested in Aeolic and particularly in Thessalian, but already attested in Mycenaean (ku-ru-sa-pi . o-pi-ke-re-mi-ni-ja-pi PY Ta 707 = /kʰrūssāpʰi/ from *kʰrūsi̯āpʰi 'golden'; ka-za KN Sp 4452 = /kʰaltsa/ < *kʰalki̯a 'made of bronze').[72] Homer has other instances of

---

71 Van Thiel 2014b, sub Σ 222: "Zenodotus did not assume there was a synizesis, but commented the masculine χάλκεον" ("Zenodot las nicht mit Synizese, sondern kommentierte das Maskulinum χάλκεον").

72 In Mycenaean the palatalisation of the velar in that case is visible from the spelling ka-za, in the Homeric form there may be a palatalised but not assibilated [kʲ], or a dispalatalised [k] restored after the substantive χάλκος. Mycenaean has both -i-jo (-ιος) and -e-jo (-ειος) for adjectives of material (ka-ki-jo /χάλκιος/, ka-ke-ja-pi /χαλκει̯ᾱφι/ 'made of bronze', wi-ri-ne-jo /ϝρίνιος/, wi-ri-ni-jo /ϝρίνειος/ 'made of leather'), and also -i̯a, mostly attested in the the feminine (ka-za /χάλκι̯α/). Heubeck 1985, followed by Hajnal 1994, assumed that only the feminine had *-i̯a (from the feminine suffix *-ih₂). This implies that the feminine ka-ke-ja-pi /χαλκει̯ᾱφι/ is remodelled after the masculine. Ruijgh 2011: 286–287 assumes that

disyllabic scansion for χάλκεος for masculine or neuter forms: E 387 χαλκέῳ δ' ἐν κεράμῳ δέδετο τρισκαίδεκα μῆνας "and three months and ten he lay chained in the brazen cauldron" (R.L.), B 490 χάλκεον δέ μοι ἦτορ ἐνείη # "if I had a heart of bronze within me" (R.L.); η 86 χάλκεοι μὲν γὰρ τοῖχοι ἐληλέδατ᾽ ἔνθα καὶ ἔνθα "for walls of bronze had been driven here and there" (J.H.). Zenodotus is therefore likely to preserve here an old form, unknown to Ionic but known in dialects that form the older strata of the epic language, and preserved in some formulas because of the metrical structure. In order to scan properly, the Ionic variant χαλκέην had either to be treated with synizesis or to be turned into a dactyl, hence the replacement of the feminine ending by an epicene form χάλκεον. The metrical problem was solved by a morphological alteration.

Aristarchus and his followers had of course no idea of any such thing as a secondary yod and could not know that centuries ago those forms were pronounced as disyllables. Although the corpus-based argument could have led them to accept Zenodotus' reading, since after all there were parallels in Homer, they interpreted the word along synchronic rules, hence the other instances of epicene adjective adduced by Aristonicus as another corpus-based argument to justify the Ionic form χάλκεον, which is defined as a σχῆμα. This is a recurrent explicative device: a σχῆμα, a "figure" is often the transposition into stylistic terms of the reshaping of an older structure which was no longer clear, that is, the synchronic translation of a diachronic process. Chantraine, writing before the decipherment of Linear B, is still reasoning only in terms of contracted forms or of synizesis, considering that forms like disyllabic χρυσέη are metrically conditioned.[73] It is true in the synchrony of Ionic epic poetry, but it is now clear that the kernel of this type was inherited from Achaean epic poetry as disyllabic and that the device of synizesis is a consequence of the writing down of the lines, which implied the forcing of a spelling χρυσέη, χαλκέη into a disyllabic metrical slot.[74]

3.2.5 Ἀναλογία

The linguistic criterion was used by ancient scholars. But of course their linguistic knowledge was a purely synchronic one and this has little to do with the arguments modern linguists can use. For morphology, they took ἀναλογία as their guideline. Ἀναλογία is the principle of regularity.[75] It is quite different from

---

the adjective ku-ru-so 'golden' is not from *χρύσιος, since this suffix was limited to the feminine, but is built with the stressed thematic vowel ("the Mycenaean adjective for 'golden' is χρῡσός, with the old suffix -ό- instead of -έγο-").

73 Chantraine, *Gr. hom.* I: 65–66.
74 Rutherford 2019: 141 sticks to the traditional view, repeating that Zenodotus' reading is unmetrical.
75 Lallot 1995; Sluiter 2011: 296–298.

what we call analogy in modern linguistics. In the Greek grammatical terminology, it refers to the regularity of linguistic structures. Ἀναλογία can apply to any pattern, either inflectional, derivational, accentual, or syntactic. It can lead Greek grammarians to favour non-existing forms over familiar ones because the former are morphologically more regular according to them. As we have seen above with the case of μάρτυρος, the strict application of this principle can lead to unjustified corrections. In derivational morphology, the fact that Homer had several derivatives in -ήμων was enough to justify the δειδήμονες of Γ 56: the form was regular because it belonged to a well-identified pattern. Similarly, the elimination of the "singular" reflexive possessive in Γ 244 and Λ 142, irregular according to the synchronic rules applied to the Homeric corpus, is caused by ἀναλογία.

3.3 Semantics

The semantic criterion is the easiest to use even for people not trained in linguistics, this is why it can be set apart from the other linguistic criteria. It was widely used by ancient scholars and by modern editors. The reading providing the best meaning is favoured, although of course, "best" is sometimes subjective.

In A 434 Zenodotus' reading ἱστὸν δ' ἱστοδόκῃ πέλασαν προτόνοισιν ὑφέντες "(they) let down mast by the forestays, and settled it into the mast crutch" (R.L.) is retained by all modern editors rather than Aristarchus' ἀφέντες, semantically awkward—and other versions had ἐφέντες (*bT Schol.* A 434d). The two readings, with different preverbs, form a minimal pair, and one is obviously derived from the other. Here again Van Thiel assumes that this is not a matter of variant readings, but of marginal comments: in his view, Aristarchus' ἀφέντες must be "an explanation, not a variant or a conjecture"[76]—that is, Aristarchus too used marginal comments, which were also mistaken by his followers as variant readings of his text.

In Δ 277, Zenodotus has ἰόντι 'going', also found in a few manuscripts, vs Aristarchus ἐόντι 'being' (Δ 277–278 τῷ δέ τ' ἄνευθεν ἐόντι μελάντερον ἠΰτε πίσσα || φαίνετ' ἰὸν κατὰ πόντον "far away though he be he watches it, blacker than pitch is, moving across the sea," R.L.). From a semantic point of view Aristarchus' reading is better and printed in most modern editions. Zenodotus' ἰόντι may have been influenced by the participle ἰόν in the next line. More examples will be provided below (pp. 57–64).

---

76 Van Thiel 2014b, *sub* A 434: (ἀφέντες) "ist vermutlich Deutung, nicht Variante oder Konjektur".

3.4 Corpus

Corpus is used to favour one reading over another according to whether the considered reading has a parallel in the corpus. N 71 is a good example of the use of corpus by Greek scholars:

N 71–72
ἴχνια γὰρ μετόπισθε ποδῶν ἠδὲ κνημάων
ῥεῖ᾽ ἔγνων ἀπιόντος· ἀρίγνωτοι δὲ θεοί περ·

for I knew easily as he went away the form of his feet, the legs' form from behind him.
R.L.

Zenodotus and Aristophanes had a *hapax* ἴχματα 'gait?', which was listed by Diogenianus and ended up in Hesychius (ι 1151: ἴχματα· ἴχνια 'footsteps', which is not an independent witness). Didymus had ἴθματα, probably an emendation of ἴχματα with which it forms a minimal pair, attested in E 778 Αἲ δὲ βάτην τρήρωσι πελειάσιν ἴθμαθ᾽ ὁμοῖαι "these two walked forward, similar in their gait to shivering doves"—unless it is an emendation there, too. Aristarchus had the familiar ἴχνια, which also looks like an emendation of ἴχματα relying on the identical initial sequence ἰχN- (with N a nasal consonant), and also attested in Homer. The word was discussed by West, who concludes it must be an archaism.[77] This is certainly correct. The etymology of the word is unknown: it could belong with οἴχομαι 'to leave' (*$h_3 ig^h$-mn̥*, Watkins' suggestion, reported by West), or with ἱκόμην 'to reach' (*$s(e)ik$-smn̥*), or go back to *$Heig$- 'to move' of Ved. *éjati* (*Hig-smn̥*, the root is *$h_2 eig$- if the connection with αἰγανέη is correct). The meaning itself is not very clear: West is right that 'footsteps' (the vulgate's reading) does not fit in the context, and that 'gait' (Didymus' ἴθματα, and maybe Zenodotus' ἴχματα if it belongs with οἴχομαι) is better. The condemnation of Zenodotus' reading is based on the Homeric corpus: this word is not attested in Homer, neither is it in any Greek dialect—needless to say virtually every *hapax* could be condemned if we followed this line. Therefore, the un-Homeric form was transformed into something which is Homeric, in that case, a word displaying a vague phonetic similarity with the source word (the older ἴχματα), having the same metrical shape, and semantically compatible with the context. There were at least two words meeting those requirements. As a consequence, this results in two competing emendations.

---

[77] West 2001a: 123–124.

A different case is found in α 3, where Zenodotus had πολλῶν δ' ἀνθρώπων ἴδεν ἄστεα καὶ νόμον ἔγνω "he saw many cities of men and he knew their customs" vs vulgate καὶ νόον ἔγνω "and he knew their mind." Now νόμος is not used in Homer: the compound εὐνομίη is found in ρ 487, probably a recent line. The absence of νόμος in the corpus leads all modern editors to retain the vulgate's reading νόον. One may suspect that the coordination with ἄστεα led to a modification of νόον 'mind' into νόμον 'custom', since cities have laws and customs, and both words belong to the same lexical field, whereas the alternative possibility, an emendation of νόμον into νόον 'mind' is not very likely in that context. Therefore, Zenodotus' reading is probably secondary. We cannot know whether it was in his text or imported from another copy.

In B 741 the vulgate has υἱὸς Πειριθόοιο τὸν ἀθάνατος τέκετο Ζεύς "son of Peirithoüs whose father was Zeus immortal" (R.L.), and in Φ 2 Ξάνθου δινήεντος, ὃν ἀθάνατος τέκετο Ζεύς "of whirling Xanthos, a stream whose father was Zeus the immortal" (R.L.). In both lines Zenodotus had ὅν ἀθάνατον τέκετο Ζεύς "whom Zeus begot immortal." Aristarchus condemned Zenodotus' reading because Peirithoüs was not immortal (A Schol. B 741: ὅπερ ψεῦδος "which is a lie"). But Zeus is never called ἀθάνατος in the Homeric corpus, except in this formula. In fact, no individual god or goddess is called ἀθάνατος, there is no "immortal Apollo," "immortal Poseidon" or the like. The phrase θεοὶ ἀθάνατοι is usual, and in the singular θεὸς ἄμβροτος is found, but only the generic noun θεός can be used with an epithet meaning 'immortal', whereas individual theonyms cannot. On the other hand, the Scamander (Xanthus by his divine name) is immortal. Therefore Zenodotus' reading is probably older, at least for the Scamander (Ξ 434, Φ 2, Ω 693): the formula must have been used for semi-gods or lesser gods sons of Zeus. Its use for Peirithoüs may be secondary, due to a mechanical use of the traditional formula, or may refer to a version of the myth according to which Peirithoüs was indeed immortal. The emendation relies on the obvious fact that Zeus is immortal, but the singer, rhapsode or scholar who introduced it did not pay attention to the fact that the Homeric corpus has no instance of ἀθάνατος used as an epithet modifying a theonym (neither does Hesiod). Aristonicus quotes the "immortal gods" (A Schol. Φ 2c: καὶ καθόλου ἀθανάτοισι θεοῖσι "and in general ἀθανάτοισι θεοῖσι"), assuming that this is the same pattern, but the generic θεός and the individual theonyms do not have the same semantic properties and do not combine with the same adjectives.

Corpus-based arguments were used by ancient scholars within certain limits. They often condemn a variant reading because it displays a word which "is not Homeric" (for instance ἴχματα). However, they only do so for unusual words: the idea that a trivial word, like νόμος, could be "un-Homeric" never occurred to them (α 3). In such a case the criterion does not apply, because Homer was supposed to be a speaker of Greek and νόμος is a usual word in Greek. Moreover, they do not use very fine-grain criteria: since ἀθάνατος can be found as an epithet of θεός 'god' in the corpus, they assumed it could be used as an epithet of any god without noticing that in the same corpus, the individual theonyms and the generic word behave differently (B 741, Φ 2).

Corpus is important in so far at it is the domain to which ἀναλογία applies. To stick to the same example, no Greek grammarian would have said that μάρτυρες is irregular in Greek, but they were led to consider it irregular in the Homeric corpus because Homer has the thematic form ἐπιμάρτυρος. There is thus a tension between the rules applied to the specific corpus of epic Greek and the rules of ordinary *koine*. Modern linguists also acknowledge the specificity of the Homeric corpus, and to that extent the approach of Greek grammarians was justified, but the latter did not always draw the correct conclusions because their conception of the Homeric language was exclusively synchronic.

Corpus-based arguments were of course widely used for non-linguistic problems, and this was the basis of Aristarchus' method of "explaining Homer from Homer." I will give only two famous examples. In B 484 the vulgate has ἔσπετε νῦν μοι μοῦσαι Ὀλύμπια δώματ' ἔχουσαι "tell me now, you Muses who have your homes on Olympos" (R.L.). Zenodotus had μοῦσαι Ὀλυμπιάδες βαθύκολποι "deep-girdled Olympian Muses." Aristonicus condemns that with the following corpus-based argument: οὐδέποτε δὲ τὰς Ἑλληνίδας γυναῖκας βαθυκόλπους εἴρηκεν, ὥστε οὐδὲ τὰς Μούσας "Homer never used βαθύκολπος for Greek women, so that he cannot use it either for the Muses" (*A Schol.* B 484). The adjective is allegedly used only for Trojan women (Σ 339 ἀμφὶ δὲ σὲ Τρωαὶ καὶ Δαρδανίδες βαθύκολποι "and beside you women of Troy and deep-girdled Dardanian women" (R.L.), Τρωϊάδων καὶ Δαρδανίδων βαθυκόλπων # Σ 122 and Ω 215). The Muses are definitely Greek deities, therefore are included in the larger group of female Greek characters.

In Θ 562, where Zenodotus has μύρι' ἄρ' ἐν πεδίῳ πυρὰ καίετο "thousands of fires were burning in the plain."[78] Aristarchus observed that in other places the Trojans are said to be fewer than the Achaeans, so that they cannot light as many fires, taking μύρια in its numeral meaning of 'ten thousand' instead of the non-specific meaning 'countless'. This anachronistic reasoning led him to replace μύρια by χίλια, which arguably makes a lesser number—but Homer's line is not about counting. Zenodotus' reading is older.

---

78 Schironi 2018: 455, n. 50. On Aristarchus' insistence on the consistency of the corpus, see Schironi 2018: 225.

3.5 Context

Sometimes context strongly favours one reading above the other. In B 11–12 Zeus is dictating his speech to the Evil Dream:

B 11–12
θωρῆξαί ἑ κέλευε κάρη κομόωντας Ἀχαιοὺς
πανσυδίῃ· νῦν γάρ κεν ἕλοι πόλιν εὐρυάγυιαν

Bid him arm the flowing-haired Achaians for battle in all haste; since now he might take the wide-wayed city.

R.L.

Zenodotus had the third person ἕλοι, so does the vulgate, whereas Aristarchus had the second person ἕλοις: the latter is correct in B 28–29, where the dream speaks to Agamemnon and addresses him in the second person (θωρῆξαί σε κέλευε κάρη κομόωντας Ἀχαιοὺς || πανσυδίῃ· νῦν γάρ κεν ἕλοις πόλιν εὐρυάγυιαν), but in B 12 Zenodotus' reading, agreeing with ἑ in the preceding line, is better because it is an indirect speech.[79]

In O 207 the vulgate has ἐσθλὸν καὶ τὸ τέτυκται ὅτ' ἄγγελος αἴσιμα εἰδῇ "it is a fine thing when a messenger is conscious of justice" (R.L.). Zenodotus had αἴσιμα εἴπῃ "when he speaks just words" (A Schol. O 207b, Didymus). Both αἴσιμα εἰπεῖν and αἴσιμα εἰδέναι are attested in Homer, but in the context what matters is the messenger's speech, not his thoughts, and Zenodotus' reading is better: the vulgate's εἰδῇ must be an emendation prompted by the desire to avoid the repetition of εἰπεῖν found in the preceding line.[80] This case illustrates the conflict between different criteria: Zenodotus' reading is better in this context but stylistically heavier because of the repetition it implies. The stylistic criterion was preferred here.

Context was an important criterion for ancient scholars. An instance of the use of context is the condemnation of Zenodotus' reading in B 196 θυμὸς δὲ μέγας ἐστὶ διοτρεφέων βασιλήων "the wrath of kings born from Zeus is terrible," with a plural that does not agree with the singular in the following line φιλεῖ

---

[79] The two lines are identical: in the first occurrence, Zeus dictates to the evil Dream the words he should speak to Agamemnon—and Agamemnon is referred to in the third person. In the second occurrence, Dream repeats Zeus' words to Agamemnon, who is the addressee, therefore referred to in the second person.

[80] O 206–207: Ἶρι θεὰ μάλα τοῦτο ἔπος κατὰ μοῖραν ἔειπες· || ἐσθλὸν καὶ τὸ τέτυκται ὅτ' ἄγγελος αἴσιμα εἰπῇ/εἰδῇ "Now this, divine Iris, was a word quite properly spoken. It is a fine thing when a messenger speaks just words" (R.L. modified).

δέ ἑ μητίετα Ζεύς "and wise Zeus loves him." The singular διοτρεφέος βασιλῆος, found in other versions, which Didymus calls αἱ χαριέστεραι "the nicest ones" (*A Schol.* B 196c) was therefore favoured by Aristarchus, with the argument that only Agamemnon is intended here (*A Schol.* B 196b, Aristonicus).

Context was widely used as a criterion for non-linguistic matters. For instance, in Δ 139 ἀκρότατον δ' ἄρ' ὀϊστὸς ἐπέγραψε χρόα φωτός "and with the very tip of its point it grazed the man's skin" (R.L.), Zenodotus had χαλκός instead of ὀϊστός (that is, he had δ' ἄρα χαλκός). Aristonicus condemns this because a few lines earlier (Δ 123) Homer uses σίδηρον 'iron'. Zenodotus' reading is likely to be older because heroic weapons were made of bronze and his text agrees with the Homeric use generally speaking. The replacement by ὀϊστός in the vulgate was prompted by a particular attention to internal consistency, context being a decisive criterion.

Sometimes the context does not give an immediate clue. For instance, in A 158–160, the vulgate has

> ἀλλὰ σοὶ ὦ μέγ' ἀναιδὲς ἅμ' ἑσπόμεθ' ὄφρα σὺ χαίρῃς,
> τιμὴν ἀρνύμενοι Μενελάῳ σοί τε κυνῶπα
> πρὸς Τρώων· τῶν οὔ τι μετατρέπῃ οὔτ' ἀλεγίζεις
>
> o great shamelessness, we followed, to do you favour, you with the dog's eyes, to win your honour and Menelaos' from the Trojans. You forget all this or else you care nothing.
> R.L.

Aristonicus says that Zenodotus had the singular ἀρνύμενος in l. 159 and condemned l. 160:

> *A Schol.* A 159: ὅτι Ζηνόδοτος γράφει τιμὴν ἀρνύμενος καὶ τὸν ἑξῆς ἠθέτηκεν. ἠγνόηκε δὲ ὅτι ἡ τιμὴ νῦν ἀντὶ τῆς τιμωρίας κεῖται· καὶ τὸ ἀρνύμενος οὐκ ἔστι λαμβάνων, ἀλλ' ἀντὶ τοῦ εἰσπραττόμενος παρὰ Τρώων.
>
> because Zenodotus writes τιμὴν ἀρνύμενος and athetises the next line. But he ignores that τιμή here is an equivalent for τιμωρία 'punishment', and that ἀρνύμενος does not mean 'to receive', but stands for εἰσπραττόμενος 'making' the Trojans 'pay'.

Zenodotus' reading implies that the subject of ἀρνύμενος is Agamemnon. And in fact it is likely that Zenodotus' version is better. The problem here lies in the meaning of τιμή, as underlined by the scholiast. However, the meaning is different from what the scholion says: here, τιμή means neither 'honour', as usually thought, nor 'punishment', as Aristonicus says, but 'material presents' which were expected as a compensation for the abduction of Helen. Compare Γ 285–286 Τρῶας ἔπειθ' Ἑλένην καὶ κτήματα πάντ' ἀποδοῦναι || τιμὴν δ' Ἀργείοις ἀποτινέμεν ἥν τιν' ἔοικεν "then let the Trojans give back Helen and all her possessions, and pay also a price to the Argives which will be fitting" (R.L.). The correct interpretation of τιμή in this context is a consequence of a revised interpretation of ἄποινα, which did not originally mean 'ransom' but 'Wergeld'. Ἄποινα, applied to abductions, in this case the abduction of Helen, refers to the price the offender (the abductor, here the Trojans) must pay to the offended (Menelaus). As I argued elsewhere, the ἄποινα consisted of two parts, the compensation properly said and an extra payment, the τιμή.[81] Consequently, the meaning is "gaining for Menelaus and yourself the financial reparation."[82]

This makes Zenodotus' reading with the singular ἀρνύμενος more appropriate in the context of the verbal duel. Achilles is not saying that the Achaeans are winning honour and glory for the Atreides, he is simply accusing and insulting Agamemnon alone for his greed, and this echoes Achilles' φιλοκτεανώτατε 'the most cupid of men' (Α 122), hurled at the same Agamemnon. In that case, the clue does not come from the immediate context, but from an element usually considered unrelated to τιμή. The reexamination of the meaning and evolution of a word that is not even in the lines under consideration (ἄποινα) leads to a better understanding of the relationship it has with τιμή and this has a consequence on the evaluation of Zenodotus' reading.

As far as athetesis is concerned here, we don't know whether Zenodotus decided Α 160 had to be deleted for internal reasons or simply marked the line with the *obelos* because it was missing in another copy he had but which he did not use as the main text of his *ekdosis*. In the latter case, we could consider that his version with ἀρνύμενος in l. 159 and no l. 160 is older, and that l. 160 is a secondary addition. The only other instance in Homer of τιμὴν ἄρνυμαι πρός + genitive (Ο 84–85) has a different meaning "to win glory before someone."

3.6 *Stylistics and Rhetorics*

Often Zenodotus' readings were condemned because they were deemed contrary to civilised language or behaviour. This is probably the most commented aspect in ancient and modern scholarship alike. Linguistics can sometimes

---

[81] I discussed the meaning of τιμή as a part of the ἄποινα in Le Feuvre 2021b; however, in this paper I did not mention Α 158–160, but I discussed it in Le Feuvre 2021c: 260.

[82] The reflexive pronoun for the first and second person is rarely used in Homer and the simple pronoun is used instead. See Chantraine, *Gr. hom.* II: 154.

bring new arguments in favour of one reading rather than the other, but not always. The clearest example is A 260–261 ἤδη γάρ ποτ' ἐγὼ καὶ ἀρείοσιν ἠέ περ ὑμῖν ‖ ἀνδράσιν ὡμίλησα "yes, and in my time I have dealt with better men than you are" (R.L.), where ὑμῖν 'you' is Zenodotus' reading, as opposed to Aristarchus' ἡμῖν 'us': the latter is clearly an edulcoration of the direct "better than you are," deemed too brutal. Aristonicus is explicit on that point:

> A Schol. A 260: ἠέπερ ἡμῖν: ὅτι Ζηνόδοτος γράφει 'ἠέπερ ὑμῖν'. ἐφύβριστος δὲ ὁ λόγος. διὰ δὲ τοῦ ἡμῖν καὶ ἑαυτὸν συγκαταριθμεῖ καὶ πάντας τοὺς καθ' αὐτόν.
>
> because Zenodotus writes 'ἠέπερ ὑμῖν' 'than you'. But the discourse is excessive, whereas with ἡμῖν he includes himself and all those around him.

That kind of rewriting on grounds of "decency" is recent, and well described by Leaf in a footnote: "Ar⟨istarchus⟩ read ἡμῖν, thus saving Nestor's politeness at the cost of his point. Ar.'s objection to Zenod. reading is ἐφύβριστος ὁ λόγος; in other words, he wished to import into heroic language the conventional mock-modesty of the Alexandrian court." The reading ἡμῖν may be older than Aristarchus, but it is basically a correction prompted by rhetorical conventions, which most Alexandrian scholars followed because they were trained and educated in a system giving a key role to rhetorics.[83] But we may be almost certain that ὑμῖν was not introduced by Zenodotus, precisely because he, too, was an Alexandrian scholar working in the intellectual framework of third-century Hellenistic culture and was as trained in rhetorics as Aristarchus was a century later. What seemed rude or clumsy to second-century Hellenistic scholars was also rude or clumsy for Zenodotus, and he would certainly not invent such things. Neither would he import it from another copy as an emendation. This implies that when he has such a reading, he found it in his working text. Most of the manuscripts have ὑμῖν with Zenodotus, also found in papyri. Among modern editors, Mazon prints ἡμῖν, Leaf, Allen, Van Thiel and West ὑμῖν. Obviously, if the goal of an edition is to print the original text, an edition of Homer should print, not the original text, which is a mere ghost, but at least the older of the two attested readings, in that case ὑμῖν.[84] Similar cases have been extensively

---

83 See a discussion in Schenkeveld 1970: 170, who has a milder formulation than Leaf but seeks to explain why Aristarchus' opinion about how Homer portrays the heroes (here Nestor) led him to select ἡμῖν.

84 A *b* scholion to A 262 indirectly points to ὑμῖν: οὐ γάρ πω τοίους ⟨ἴδον ἀνέρας οὐδὲ ἴδωμαι⟩: ἀπολογούμενος ὑπὲρ ὧν ἠλάττωσεν αὐτούς, οὐδὲ ἔσεσθαι τοιούτους λέγει "apologising for

discussed in the literature, but not from a linguistic point of view.[85] As a matter of fact, most of the time there is no decisive linguistic argument.

The same applies to P 153 where the Lycian prince Glaucus addresses Hector about the death of Sarpedon: vulgate νῦν δ' οὔ οἱ ἀλαλκέμεναι κύνας ἔτλης "but you did not dare defend him from the dogs." Zenodotus had νῦν δ' οὔ οἱ ἀλαλκέμεναι, κύον, ἔτλης "but you did not dare defend him, you dog," which changes the construction and is above all extremely rude. The insult "dog" can only be hurled at a foe (X 345, Λ 362, Υ 449, and the recent Φ 481). It is unthinkable between allies. The A scholion has only one word: ἄλογον "insane." However, the abnormal character of that insult which is contrary to the πρέπον as defined by rhetorics makes it very unlikely that κύον was introduced by a Hellenistic scholar (that includes Zenodotus). If one reading is a correction, it is almost certainly the vulgate's reading κύνας, not the "ἄλογον" reading κύον, which cannot be Zenodotus' invention and must have been in his working text. Line 153 in the vulgate is modelled after X 348 ὡς οὐκ ἔσθ' ὅς σῆς γε κύνας κεφαλῆς ἀπαλάλκοι "so there is no one who can hold the dogs off from your head" (R.L.).[86]

A similar case is found in O 355–356 προπάροιθε δὲ Φοῖβος Ἀπόλλων ‖ ῥεῖ' ὄχθας καπέτοιο βαθείης ποσσὶν ἐρείπων "and in front of them Phoibos Apollo easily, kicking with his feet the banked edges of the deep ditch" (R.L. modified), for which Zenodotus had χερσὶν ἐρείπων. As Aristonicus says,

> *A Schol.* O 356b: εὐλογώτερον δὲ μὴ κατακύπτειν τὸν θεόν, ἀλλὰ τοῖς ποσὶ συγχεῖν.
>
> it is more appropriate that the god should not bend down, but destroy it with his feet.

The position required to destroy with the hands seemed "less consistent with the dignity of a god," in Leaf's words, and there again it is likely that the vulgate's reading, printed by all modern editors, is an emendation. In that case as in the preceding ones, there is no linguistic criterion allowing us to tell which reading is older, but a simple reasoning: since either reading A is corrected from reading

---

belittling them, he says such men will not exist in the future either." The ἠλάττωσεν αὐτούς probably refers to a second person in Nestor's speech, who has to "apologise," because this second person was too rude.

85   See on individual lines Van der Valk 1964, who summarises the views of his predecessors. More modern discussions can be found in Kirk's *Commentary* and the BK.

86   There again Van Thiel 2014b, *sub* P 153 assumes that κύον is not a variant reading, but a marginal comment by which Zenodotus was alluding to other lines, namely Λ 362 and Υ 449.

B or reading B from reading A, the correction of A into B would make sense in a Hellenistic context, whereas the correction of B into A would be incomprehensible. Therefore A must be older since it is abnormal. Precisely the reason that led Greek scholars to reject a Zenodotean reading as abnormal or contrary to decency is the reason why this reading cannot have been invented by Zenodotus, because Zenodotus was working in the same intellectual framework.

In other cases, the condemnation of Zenodotus' reading relies on the criterion of εἰκός 'likely', which is a sub-criterion of the πρεπόν. Zenodotus had in A 100 αἴ κέν μιν ἰλασσάμενοι πεπίθοιμεν "if we can propitiate and persuade him," also transmitted by the *Epimerismi homerici* (μ 85), vs vulgate τότε κέν μιν "then we might." The "if" was thought unfit in Calchas' mouth (*A Schol.* A 100a: (Aristonicus) γελοῖον δὲ διστακτικῶς λέγειν τὸν μάντιν "it is ridiculous that the seer should speak as voicing a doubt"—γελοῖον means that it goes against the πρέπον). Another reading condemned as γελοῖον is found in Γ 73–74 οἳ δ' ἄλλοι φιλότητα καὶ ὅρκια πιστὰ ταμόντες ‖ ναίοιτε Τροίην ἐριβώλακα, τοὶ δὲ νεέσθων "but the rest of you, having cut your oaths of faith and friendship, dwell, you in Troy where the soil is rich, while those others return home" (R.L.). This is Paris speaking to Hector, and as Aristonicus says, Zenodotus' reading ναίοιμεν instead of ναίοιτε must be condemned because Paris seems to predict that he will win his duel with Menelas, including himself in the ναίοιμεν. But Zenodotus' reading simply means that Paris talks about the two camps, Trojans and Achaeans, and of course he includes himself in the former. The γελοῖον here is not justified.

Another instance is A 204 ἀλλ᾽ ἔκ τοι ἐρέω, τὸ δὲ καὶ τετελεσμένον ἔσται "but I will tell you, and this will be accomplished" vs vulgate ἀλλ᾽ ἔκ τοι ἐρέω, τὸ δὲ καὶ τελέεσθαι ὀΐω, because these are Achilles' words to Athena and this seemed too affirmative in the mouth of a hero speaking to a goddess (*A Schol.* A 204b: (Aristonicus) τοῦτο δὲ τῇ Ἀθηνᾷ ἁρμόζει μᾶλλον διαβεβαιοῦν "it is more appropriate for Athena to be strongly affirmative about that;" *bT Schol.* A 212c: ὁ μὲν ὡς ἄνθρωπος 'ὀΐω' φησίν, ἡ δὲ ὡς θεὸς διαβεβαιοῦται "as a man, Achilles says 'I think', whereas as a goddess, Athena affirms strongly").[87] For Athena's speech in A 212, the vulgate has τὸ δὲ καὶ τετελεσμένον ἔσται, but Zenodotus had τὸ δὲ καὶ τελέεσθαι ὀΐω. That is, the distribution between A 204 and A 212 is reversed. The line may originally have been identical in Achilles' speech and in Athena's, and one of the lines was rearranged in order to mark a difference between the goddess and the hero. In those cases there is no linguistic criterion to say that one

---

87   This is a case where Van Thiel's hypothesis would be plausible: that Zenodotus pointed in a marginal comment to the parallelism between the two lines by giving each time the other formula.

reading is older, but there is a rhetorical criterion to say that one reading, the vulgate's, is probably younger—this is likely in A 100, but less clear for A 204.

In other cases we have a linguistic argument for saying that Zenodotus' reading is older than the vulgate's. An example is Γ 99–100:

[...] ἐπεὶ κακὰ πολλὰ πέπασθε
εἵνεκ' ἐμῆς ἔριδος καὶ Ἀλεξάνδρου ἕνεκ' ἀρχῆς

you have suffered much evil for the sake of my quarrel since Alexandros began it.

R.L.

Zenodotus had Ἀλεξάνδρου ἕνεκ' ἄτης (also found in Z 356 and Ω 28, but in Ω 28 it is probably interpolated). Granted, it was easy to import into Γ 100 the T2 hemistich of the parallel line Z 356 εἵνεκ' ἐμεῖο κυνὸς καὶ Ἀλεξάνδρου ἕνεκ' ἄτης (Helen is speaking), whereas the vulgate's reading has no parallel. Most editors (Leaf, Allen, Mazon, West) stick to the vulgate's version, and invoke a metrical argument: most instances of ἄτη in the *Iliad* can be scanned with the uncontracted form *ἀϝάτη, which is not the case here. There are three exceptions, T 88, Z 356, and Ω 28. However, the vulgate's reading, although metrically correct, poses another problem: in both the *Iliad* and the *Odyssey* ἀρχή is always used with a genitive modifier, 'the beginning of something', except in the prepositional phrase ἐξ ἀρχῆς 'from the beginning', attested only in the *Odyssey*. The construction Ἀλεξάνδρου ἕνεκ' ἀρχῆς "because of the beginning by Alexander" is abnormal—this is why this use is singled out in all Homeric lexica, as meaning 'the initial offense', but this has no parallel and is entirely *ad hoc*. There is no doubt Zenodotus' version is not very old, because of the unresolvable contraction in ἄτη in this metrical position, but there is little doubt the vulgate's version is not old either since the absolute use of ἀρχή, without a genitive, is not attested in Homer (corpus-based argument) and can hardly be considered an old reading.

Aristonicus' comment is illuminating:

A Schol. Γ 100b: ἡ διπλῆ περιεστιγμένη, ὅτι Ζηνόδοτος γράφει ἕνεκ' ἄτης. ἔσται δὲ ἀπολογούμενος Μενέλαος, ὅτι ἄτῃ περιέπεσεν ὁ Ἀλέξανδρος. διὰ μέντοι τοῦ ἕνεκ' ἀρχῆς ἐνδείκνυται ὅτι προκατῆρξεν.

diple periestigmene because Zenodotus writes ἕνεκ' ἄτης. So Menelaus will be excusing Alexander because he fell into ἄτη. With the reading ἕνεκ' ἀρχῆς, clearly, what is made clear is that he started.

This comment "with ἄτη, Menelaus would seem to excuse his rival" is typical of Alexandrian psychological comments, and could be labelled a case of over-interpretation. It is based on the fact that the other instance of the phrase is put in the mouth of Helen in Z 356 εἵνεκ' ἐμεῖο κυνὸς καὶ Ἀλεξάνδρου ἕνεκ' ἄτης. Now Helen could have some reasons to try to excuse Paris (and herself), although in fact she does not in the *Iliad*. For Alexandrian scholars, Helen and Menelaus cannot have the same vision of Paris' crime, as the former shares the guilt whereas the latter is the victim. As a logical consequence, they cannot use the same word, and if Helen uses ἄτη, Menelaus must use another word. The parallelism between both lines is clear, including in the first hemistich (Z 356 # εἵνεκ' ἐμεῖο κυνός / Γ 100 # εἵνεκ' ἐμῆς ἔριδος), but in the vulgate Menelaus' sentence is designed in opposition with Helen's—this can only come from a scholar with a complete written text, not from a singer in the present of performance. In fact, ἄτη could be used in this context, even in Menelaus' words: when Achilles uses ἄτη for Agamemnon who took Briseis away from him and did not honour him (A 412),[88] he is not trying to excuse him at all, and Alexandrian scholars apparently had no problem with this instance of ἄτη. Similarly, that Menelaus uses ἄτη for Paris does not mean that he is excusing him. As Achilles for Agamemnon, he may acknowledge that Paris was not fully responsible, but remains nevertheless accountable. To sum up, there are good reasons to assume that the vulgate's reading, with its abnormal use of ἀρχή, was introduced to replace an older ἄτη (although not very old in this metrical position, see above), in opposition to Helen's speech in Z 356, by *koine* Greek speakers for whom the absolute use of ἀρχή was not a problem.[89] This alleged special meaning of ἀρχή in Homeric lexicons should be at least followed by a question mark in a serious lexicographic presentation which does not limit itself to the transmitted text, but includes different states of the Homeric text.

---

[88] A 411–412 (ἵνα) γνῷ δὲ καὶ Ἀτρεΐδης εὐρὺ κρείων Ἀγαμέμνων ‖ ἣν ἄτην ὅ τ' ἄριστον Ἀχαιῶν οὐδὲν ἔτισεν "(so that) that Atreus' son wide-ruling Agamemnon may recognize his madness, that he did no honour to the best of the Achaians" (R.L.).

[89] Kirk 1985: 277 concedes that ἄτη may be older: he does not object to the unusual use of ἀρχή, which he does not discuss, but he gives only a "psychological" argument, considering it plausible that Menelaus may show some kind of empathy for Paris, thus continuing the tradition of Hellenistic scholarship and assuming that Menelaus "excuses" Paris. But since ἄτη does not imply that the speaker feels empathy (see the preceding footnote), this is not relevant. Similarly, Bowie 2019: 113 writes that "why the less obvious ἀρχῆς should have replaced that is not clear." But he adds "the tone is also wrong with ἄτης," invoking the "shared responsibility," which is a direct continuation of Aristarchus' view.

The syntactic divergence in Ξ 169–171 is a matter of rhetorics, too:

ἔνθ' ἥ γ' εἰσελθοῦσα θύρας ἐπέθηκε φαεινάς.
ἀμβροσίῃ μὲν πρῶτον ἀπὸ χροὸς ἱμερόεντος
λύματα πάντα κάθηρεν, ἀλείψατο δὲ λίπ' ἐλαίῳ

there entering she drew shut the leaves of the shining door, then first from her adorable body washed away all stains with ambrosia, and next anointed herself with [...] olive oil.
R.L.

Zenodotus' reading θύρας ἐπιθεῖσα φαεινάς has two non coordinated participles and the line is part of the sentence developing over the next two lines. The vulgate θύρας ἐπέθηκε φαεινάς has only one participle and a finite verb, and line 169 is a full sentence, syntactically not linked with the following line, which is a different sentence. Aristonicus has the following comment:

A Schol. Ξ 169a: ὅτι Ζηνόδοτος γράφει 'θύρας ἐπιθεῖσα φαεινάς', ἵνα συναφὴς ὁ λόγος γένηται. ὁ δὲ Ὅμηρος ἄλλας ἀρχὰς λαμβάνει, ἵνα μὴ ἀσαφὴς ἡ περίοδος γένηται ἤτοι ὑστεροπερίοδος.

because Zenodotus writes θύρας ἐπιθεῖσα φαεινάς, making the sentence continuous; but Homer takes a new beginning, clearly marking the period, that is, the added period.

That is, Aristonicus uses rhetorical categories, maybe anachronistically, to state that Hera's toilet must be a coherent scene and, as a new scene, must have a new beginning. Therefore the closing of the doors belongs to the preceding scene and the ἀμβροσίῃ μὲν πρῶτον marks the beginning of the new scene, and of the new sentence. Zenodotus' syntax does not mark this "new beginning," therefore it is faulty from the rhetorical point of view. But Zenodotus was probably as familiar with rhetorics as Aristarchus was a century later. Therefore it is not very likely, if his working text had the same reading as the vulgate, that he changed it after another copy. As an emendation is not plausible, the reading must be that of his working text.

In Δ 281–282 the vulgate has πυκιναὶ κίνυντο φάλαγγες || κυάνεαι, σάκεσίν τε καὶ ἔγχεσι πεφρικυῖαι "the compact battalions were going, black, and jagged with spear and shield" (R.L. modified). Zenodotus had for Δ 282 # ἡρώων σάκεσιν with a genitive instead of an adjective in enjambment. Aristonicus explains that γέγονε δὲ ἀντιπαράθεσις τοῦ μέλανος νέφους πρὸς τὸ κυάνεαι "there is a contrast between the black cloud (μελάντερον ἠΰτε πίσσα "(cloud) blacker than pitch is" Δ

277) and the κυάνεαι" (*A Schol.* Δ 282a). In the frame of the comparison, the echo between the *comparandum* and the *comparatum* with two colour adjectives seemed stylistically better. Zenodotus had nothing of the kind: consequently, his reading was condemned. However, the κυάνεαι may well have been introduced into the text for the sake of the parallelism.

Those few cases are interesting because the scholia transmit not only Zenodotus' reading, but also the reason why the latter was condemned. However, it is crystal clear that the reason why it was condemned may also be the reason why it was corrected, and may explain the vulgate's reading. Therefore, the testimony of the scholia, especially the A scholia which epitomise Aristarchus' conceptions, is crucial not only for our knowledge of Zenodotus' text, but also for our understanding of the editing process leading to our transmitted text of Homer. Unfortunately, the latter point is not always taken into account by linguists.

3.7 *Plausibility of the Emendation*

When two readings are obviously related and no clear linguistic or metrical argument can be used, we can try to evaluate the relationship between the two competing variants: is it likely that A was changed into B, or rather B into A? Modern philologists often use this criterion of the *lectio difficilior*: the reading most susceptible of resulting from a correction (*lectio facilior*) is deemed secondary and the reading not susceptible of resulting from a correction (*lectio difficilior*) is deemed older and printed by the editor. The argument is fairly reliable when scholars consider two different manuscripts of one and the same written text, less so when the text is an orally transmitted poem which for centuries was not written down. The philological criteria applying to the process of copying a text cannot be mechanically transposed to the process of orally reciting a poem, let alone orally composing a poem. And Homeric philology has to deal with the text both as a written one and as an oral one. Nevertheless, it can give a clue to help determine which variant can be older.

In Ω 486 Zenodotus had μνῆσαι πατρὸς σεῖο (vulgate σοῖο) "remember your father,"[90] in Ξ 118 πατρὸς ἐμεῖο πατήρ (vulgate ἐμοῖο) "father of my father" vs vulgate σοῖο, ἐμοῖο (see also *Schol. Od.* α 413d Pontani where the erroneous form is blamed on τινές, not on Zenodotus by name, and *Schol. Od.* ζ 256a Pontani, blaming Zenodotus for using the personal pronoun ἐμεῦ instead of the possessive adjective ἐμοῦ in different places). The scholia say Zenodotus is wrong

---

90   The line is quoted by Dionysius of Halicarnassus with σεῖο (*De compositione verborum* 5.21), which means that this version was not only Zenodotus'. And Apollonius of Rhodes uses πατρὸς ἐμεῖο (*Arg.* 1.829, 1.891, 2.776, *fr.* 8.1): "the model is the pre-Aristarchean vulgate" (Rengakos 1993: 111).

(οὐκ ὀρθῶς A Schol. Ξ 118, κακῶς T Schol. Ω 486) because scholars compared his reading to the vulgate's. However, Homer has several instances of the genitive of the accented pronoun instead of the possessive adjective: δᾶερ ἐμεῖο "my brother by marriage" Z 344, σέο δ᾽ ὀστέα "your bones" Δ 174.[91] In Vedic, the accented genitive of the pronoun is the regular means of expressing possession, the possessive being very rare. The use of the genitive is preserved in classical Attic-Ionic, but it is restricted to the unaccented form (ὁ πατήρ μου). This restriction is absent from the Homeric corpus.[92] Therefore Homeric lines with the genitive of an accented pronoun were irregular for speakers of classical Attic-Ionic and *koine*. And obviously, when the head noun was a genitive, the substitution of ἐμεῖο, σεῖο by the metrically equivalent ἐμοῖο, σοῖο, or of ἐμεῦ by ἐμοῦ, was natural. Zenodotus' readings in Ω 486 and Ξ 118 belong with these well-known cases displaying the genitive of the accented pronoun and are probably the older ones, because it was natural to correct πατρὸς σεῖο into πατρὸς σοῖο, whereas the reverse is hardly plausible.[93]

In E 416, Dione heals her wounded daughter Aphrodite. The vulgate has ἦ ῥα, καὶ ἀμφοτέρῃσιν ἀπ᾽ ἰχῶ χειρὸς ὀμόργνυ "with both hands she wiped the ichôr out of Aphrodite's hand," whereas Zenodotus had ἦ ῥα, καὶ ἀμφοτέρῃσιν ἀπ᾽ ἰχῶ χερσίν ὀμόργνυ "she said, and with both hands she wiped out the *ichôr*." In the context, Aristarchus' reading χειρός may be better because Aphrodite is wounded at the hand, and Zenodotus' χερσίν can be influenced by ἀμφοτέρῃσιν, which triggered the agreement of the substantive 'hand' since ἀμφοτέρῃσιν indeed refers to the hands. However, Zenodotus' line is in itself suitable, although less precise than Aristarchus'. The only element leading to the suspicion that Zenodotus' formulation is secondary is that the reorganisation of the line yielding an agreeing syntagm, from χειρός to χερσίν, is more plausible than the reverse process. But on the other hand, ἀμφοτέρῃσι meaning 'with both hands', with implicit χερσίν, is only found in the *Odyssey* (κ 264, λ 594, ρ 356, σ 28) and this would be the only instance in the *Iliad*, where 'hands' is always explicit. However, this passage with Dione is probably not old,[94] and would be consistent with the use of the *Odyssey*.

---

91   See other instances in Chantraine, *Gr. hom.* II: 155.

92   The neutralisation of the opposition between accented and unaccented forms in this function must be an archaism rather than a metrical device.

93   This is explicit in Apollonius Dyscolus' *De pronominibus* (Schneider II/1.1: 108): προκριτέαι μέντοι αἱ κτητικαὶ γραφαί, καθότι αἱ γενικαὶ κτῆσιν δηλοῦσαι ἐγκεκλιμέναι θέλουσιν εἶναι, "the readings with the possessive must be preferred, because the personal pronouns having a possessive meaning are enclitic."

94   Clearly recent forms are Ἀμφιτρύωνος # with *correptio attica* (E 392); παῖδες with [αι] scanning as a long syllable (E 386), which implies that the line was created after the

In Ξ 35–36 the vulgate has καὶ πλῆσαν ἁπάσης ‖ ἠϊόνος στόμα μακρόν, ὅσον συνεέργαθον ἄκραι "and filled up the long edge of the whole sea-coast, all that the two capes compassed between them" (R.L.). Didymus says that Zenodotus and Aristophanes had, not μακρόν, but πολλόν, which was also the reading in one of Aristarchus' *ekdoseis*, while his other *ekdosis* had μακρόν as the vulgate: διχῶς αἱ Ἀριστάρχου, μακρόν καὶ πολλόν. Ζηνόδοτος ⟨καὶ⟩ Ἀριστοφάνης 'πολλόν' "Aristarchus' *ekdoseis* have two different readings, μακρόν and πολλόν. Zenodotus and Aristophanes have πολλόν" (*A Schol*. Ξ 36b). Van Thiel comments "Zenodotus' στόμα πολλόν would not be good as a text," and assumes the πολλόν is a marginal comment, which Aristophanes found interesting, and which was therefore quoted by Aristarchus—that is, it was not Aristarchus' reading.[95] However, Van Thiel did not see that with πολλόν, the syntax of the line can be different: πολλόν can be, rather than an epithet of στόμα, an adverbial neuter meaning 'much' and antecedent of ὅσον. And this may be the reason for the correction: if πολλόν was no longer understood as an adverbial neuter, but as an epithet of the preceding neuter noun στόμα, it was clumsy, to say the least, and even odd, and this could explain why it was replaced by an adjective referring to the physical aspect of the shore, μακρόν 'long'. On the other hand, if μακρόν is older, it is hard to understand how it could have been replaced by πολλόν as an epithet, or, in Van Thiel's framework, how it could have needed such a marginal comment. Zenodotus' reading, shared with Aristophanes and Aristarchus, is likely to be older, although not very old because the thematic type πολλός is recent in Ionic. Which implies that it was in his working text and is not an emendation imported from another copy.

In Β 56–57, the vulgate has θεῖός μοι ἐνύπνιον ἦλθεν ὄνειρος ‖ ἀμβροσίην διὰ νύκτα "a divine dream came to me in my sleep, through the immortal night." Aristonicus understood ἐνύπνιον as adverbial (*A Schol*. Β 56b: ἀντὶ τοῦ κατὰ τοὺς ὕπνους, ἐνυπνίως),[96] but Zenodotus had θεῖόν μοι ἐνύπνιον "a divine vision came to me, a dream through the immortal night," with ἐνύπνιον subject and ὄνειρος in apposition. However, the interpretation as an adverbial neuter for ἐνύπνιον is hardly convincing, among other reasons because one would rather expect a predicative adjective ἐνύπνιος in that case, and Zenodotus' reading may be

---

diphthongisation of πᾶϊς < πάϝις; ἀνήκεστον 'incurable' (Ε 394) with ἀ-νη-, vs older νήκεστος in Hesiod; ωὑτὸς ἀνὴρ Διὸς υἱός (Ε 396) about Heracles (the crasis with the article is secondary, but even assuming the line was created with αὐτός without article, Heracles is never qualified as ἀνήρ in Homer).

95 Van Thiel 2014b, *sub* Ξ 36: "Zenodots στόμα πολλόν wäre als Text nicht gut."
96 Β 56 is repeated in ξ 495.

better than the vulgate's.⁹⁷ If Zenodotus' version is older, the agreement may have been changed by a singer who felt that θεῖος 'divine' was more appropriate for the masculine ὄνειρος than for the neuter ἐνύπνιον, as the former ranks higher on the animacy scale. But one could also assume that an older θεῖος was changed into θεῖον by agreement with the closest form, ὄνειρον. In that case the test of the plausibility of the emendation is not conclusive.

In O 587–588 the vulgate has (θηρί) ὅς τε κύνα κτείνας ἢ βούκολον ἀμφὶ βόεσσιν || φεύγει, πρίν περ ὅμιλον ἀολλισθήμεναι ἀνδρῶν "who has killed a hound or an oxherd tending his cattle and escapes, before a gang of men has assembled against him" (R.L.). Zenodotus had ἀμφί οἱ αὐτῷ instead of ἀμφὶ βόεσσιν. His reading was condemned by Aristonicus because it would create an "un-Homeric" hyperbaton, as he understood ἀμφί as complement of ἀολλισθήμεναι (A Schol. O 587). But Zenodotus' reading probably means "he runs for his life:" ἀμφί οἱ αὐτῷ goes with φεύγει, so there is no hyperbaton. The comment makes it likely that Aristarchus' version is an emendation, drawing βόεσσιν from βούκολον. At any rate, Zenodotus' reading can hardly be an emendation.

This criterion was not used by Greek scholars. Although they themselves suggested emendations, they did not infer from their practice a potential tool for discriminating variant readings.

4 Old Forms in New Clothes

Particularly interesting are cases of related readings when Zenodotus preserves traces of an archaic form, but under an altered appearance.

4.1 ἰογάστριος or ὀγάστριος

West discussed a case of that type in Φ 95, where the vulgate has μή με κτεῖν', ἐπεὶ οὐχ ὁμογάστριος Ἕκτορός εἰμι "do not kill me, since I am not from the same womb as Hector" (R.L. modified), and Aristonicus says Zenodotus read ἰογάστριος:

> A Schol. Φ 95a1: ὅτι Ζηνόδοτος γράφει ἐπεὶ οὐκ ἰογάστριος, παρόσον ἐν ἄλλοις ἔφη ἰῆς ἐκ νηδύος. ἴα δέ ἐστιν ἡ μία, καὶ οὐ τίθησιν Ὅμηρος τὸ μία ἐπὶ τοῦ ὁμοῦ οὐδὲ κατὰ σύνθετον ἐκφέρει.

---

97 Van Thiel 2014b, sub B 56, assumes that there is no variant reading: "θεῖον in the margin in Zenodotus was a comment, concretely formulated 'Homer could have referred the attribute to ἐνύπνιον'" ("θεῖον bei Zenodot am Rande war konkret formulierter Kommentar 'Homer hätte das Attribut zu ἐνύπνιον ziehen können'").

because Zenodotus writes ἐπεὶ οὐκ ἰογάστριος, according to what Homer says elsewhere ἰῆς ἐκ νηδύος "from one and the same womb". But ἴα means μία 'one', and Homer never uses μία in the meaning 'together' nor does he use it in compounds.

A Schol. Ω 47a: πάλιν δὲ ὁμογάστριος λέγει, καὶ οὐχ ὡς Ζηνόδοτος ἔγραφεν ἐκεῖ (Φ 95) μή με κτεῖν' ἐπεὶ οὐκ ἰογάστριος Ἕκτορος.

here again Homer says ὁμογάστριος, not, as Zenodotus writes there, μή με κτεῖν' ἐπεὶ οὐκ ἰογάστριος Ἕκτορος.[98]

Here again one reading is certainly derived from the other and is an emendation. The vulgate's reading ὁμογάστριος is the only one known to the D scholia (ὁμογάστριος: ὁ ἐκ τῆς αὐτῆς γαστρὸς ἀδελφός, ZYQX).

It is not very likely, as West argues, that ἰογάστριος is the original form, for the copulative particle is ἁ- or the Achaean variant ὁ- (ὅπατρος 'having the same father', ὄπατρος λ 257, μ 371), and ἰός 'only one' is never used in composition with the meaning 'same', as Aristonicus correctly writes against Zenodotus' reading. Therefore Zenodotus' reading can hardly be the original form. But on the other hand, it is highly unlikely that an original ὁμογάστριος was modified into the bizarre ἰογάστριος. Accordingly, Zenodotus' working text could not read ὁμογάστριος and his ἰογάστριος must preserve something older than ὁμογάστριος.[99] West's hypothesis is that the older reading was ὀγάστριος, parallel to ὅπατρος: Hesychius has a similar compound ὀγάστωρ· ὁμογάστωρ (ο 31), and Lycophron indeed has ὀγάστριος (*Alex.* 452, given by scholia, and corrected by Tzetzes into ὁπάτριος, found in most editions). According to West, this form is preserved as ἰογάστριος in Zenodotus' recension, with an additional initial /i/, which must result from a resegmentation in the oral chain.

This would be readily understandable if the original was *ἐπεὶ οὐκὶ ὀγάστριος Ἕκτορός εἰμι (cf. Ο 716 οὐκ' ἐμεθίει *vs* vulgate οὐχὶ μεθίει), or *ἐπεὶ οὔ τι ὀγάστριος Ἕκτορός εἰμι "I am to no extent from the same mother as Hector" → *ἐπεὶ οὔτ' ἰογάστριος Ἕκτορός εἰμι—in fact West reconstructs *οὔ τοι, but the resegmentation in the oral chain is unlikely with τοι whereas it is easy with

---

[98] West 2001a: 130–132. But West in his Teubner edition prints ὁμογάστριος. The reading is not discussed by Nickau.

[99] Van Thiel 2014b, *sub* Φ 95: "ἰογάστριος is an experimental neologism, by comparison with Ω 496 ἰῆς ἐκ νηδύος. Zenodotus seems to have formulated himself the comparison" ("ἰογάστριος ist experimentelle Wortbildung, im Vergleich mit Ω 496 ἰῆς ἐκ νηδύος. Zenodot scheint selbst den Vergleich formuliert zu haben").

τι.¹⁰⁰ The resegmentation was possible in a psilotic dialect like Ionic, since the initial aspiration of ὁ-, once lost, could no longer function as a word boundary marker. Thus, Zenodotus' reading is not the original one, but is closer to the original one than the vulgate's, precisely because of the mistake it makes on the old form. The oddity of ἰογάστριος is a clue indicating what the original form was, whereas the vulgate's modernised reading does not give any clue.

However, we cannot not even be certain Zenodotus' form was ἰογάστριος: if his text had no word division and no accentual marks (see above, pp. 20–21, 27–29), it read ΟΥΚΙΟΓΑΣΤΡΙΟΣ, which could be read either οὐκὶ ὀγάστριος, with the old form, or οὐκ ἰογάστριος. And unless there was an external source saying where the word boundary was (the *Glossai* or a commentary), it is quite possible that οὐκ ἰογάστριος is not the way Zenodotus understood it, but the way Aristarchus understood Zenodotus' text, because he thought of ἰῆς ἐκ νηδύος (Ω 496) as the A scholion explicitly says. Zenodotus himself can have understood οὐκὶ ὀγάστριος. In the latter case, the Zenodotean reading not only represents the unaltered old form, but also has an exact match in Lycophron's ὀγάστριος (*Alex.* 452). Lycophron and Zenodotus both lived in Alexandria in the reign of Ptolemy Philadelphus and Lycophron must have known the work of Zenodotus.¹⁰¹ This is a case where Lycophron incorporates into his own poetry a contemporary philological discussion about the Homeric text, and Tzetzes' correction, unjustified on linguistic criteria,¹⁰² should not be printed in modern editions of Lycophron. Therefore, a reading οὐκὶ ὀγάστριος is attested at the beginning of the 3rd c. and it may have been Zenodotus'. The question is whether the competing reading was οὐκ ἰογάστριος or the οὐχ ὁμογάστριος of the vulgate, or both.

Zenodotus' reading, whatever the exact form, is precious also from another point of view, which is the form of the negation. West rejects the hypothesis of an original οὐκὶ ὀγάστριος because οὐκί normally occurs at the end of the sentence in Homer and not in preverbal position.¹⁰³ But O 716, where Zenodotus

---

100 West assumes a wrong segmentation in the written text. But the wrong segmentation can have been produced by a singer in the oral chain, and was then written down in a version that became the working text of Zenodotus. In the oral hypothesis, τοι is impossible, for a diphthong could not be misidentified as a plain vowel, only a syllabic [i] can be reconstructed.
101 Rengakos 1994: 124.
102 Tzetzes justifies the correction by the fact that Ajax and Teucer were not uterine brothers but had the same father.
103 B 238, B 300, K 445 ἠὲ καὶ οὐκί· #; B 349 εἴ τε καὶ οὐκί. #; O 137 ὅς τ' αἴτιος ὅς τε καὶ οὐκί. #; Y 255 # πόλλ' ἐτεά τε καὶ οὐκί· (before the caesura). In all those cases it is found in a binary structure, "X or not," and corresponds to Att. ἢ οὔ.

had Ἕκτωρ δὲ πρύμνηθεν ἐπεὶ λάβεν οὐκ' ἐμεθίει "Hektor would not let go of the stern of a ship where he had caught hold of it" (R.L.) vs vulgate οὐχὶ μεθίει, shows that it may have been preverbal,[104] and was eliminated from that position in the course of time: the misplaced augment in οὐκ' ἐμεθίει is probably an attempt at eliminating this abnormal instance of preverbal οὐχί—whether this is an attempt by Zenodotus himself or by a singer centuries earlier remains open. Significantly, West prints for O 716 οὔ τι μεθίει, with a variant reading τι found in one witness, against the vulgate's οὐχί, because he starts from the principle that there is no preverbal οὐκί. The resegmentation of οὐκὶ ὀγάστριος into οὐκ ἰογάστριος is also an attempt at getting rid of the abnormal non final οὐκί, whether it be Zenodotus' or Aristarchus' (or Aristophanes' in between).

Οὐκί in Herodotus is found in non-final position (ταῦτα λέγων οὐκὶ ἔπειθε ἄλλα οἱ χρᾶν "with those words he did not persuade at all ⟨the god⟩ to deliver him different oracles" Hdt 4.155, καίτοι οὐκὶ ἕνα αὐτὸν δεῖ εἶναι "and ⟨the harbour⟩ must be not at all a single one" Hdt 7.49), as its Attic equivalent οὐχί (πῶς οὐχὶ τἀνάλωμα γίγνεται πικρόν "how can the loss be not painful at all" A., *Suppl.* 476; τὸ πρόσωπον οὐχὶ δεικνύς "not showing his face at all" Ar., *Ran.* 912; καὶ οὐχὶ ἐς ναυμαχίαν μᾶλλον ἢ ἐπὶ στρατείαν ἐπλέομεν "and we did not sail at all for a naval battle rather than for a campaign" Thuc. 2.87.2). The emphatic negation does not undergo elision before a vowel in prose (see Herodotus, Thucydides above): the hiatus was resolved with a glide.[105] In both O 716 and Φ 95 in Zenodotus' reading, the negation is emphatic, for O 716 means "once he had seized it, he would not let it go at all" and Φ 95 "I am not at all the uterine brother of Hector." One could object that non-final instances of οὐκί are post-Homeric and cannot be transposed to Homer. But indeed, the generally accepted explanation of the prevocalic form οὐκ as an elision of οὐκ(ι) < *o̯i̯u-kʷid 'not at all' implies that it could be used in non-final position from old.[106] The negation has a proclitic

---

104 The line is found with a slight change in Π 762 Ἕκτωρ μὲν κεφαλῆφιν ἐπεὶ λάβεν οὐχὶ μεθίει "since Hektor had caught him by the head, and would not let go of him" (R.L.): the vulgate has οὐχί, West prints οὔ τι.

105 In Attic tragedy and comedy, οὐχί is never found before a vowel. For lyric poetry, see Simonides, *fr.* 103.23 Page ὅτι οὐχὶ ἀναιρε[. Attic οὐχί is not a form containing a particle *ĝʰi (Ved. hí), but the result of a simple analogical proportion: οὐκ : οὐκί :: οὐχ : x = οὐχί. That is, its base is the elided variant οὐχ, from οὐκί before initial aspiration. Οὐχί was then generalised at the expense of οὐκί, and then transferred to the assertive particle ναί-χι after the proportion οὐ : οὐχί :: ναί : x = ναίχι (the accentual difference between οὐχί and ναίχι is because ναί is orthotonic). Frisk and Beekes, s.v., assume ναίχι has the emphatic particle and still consider the hypothesis that οὐχί go back to this particle, although they favour the analysis *ou-kʷid.

106 Frisk, *GEW*, Schwyzer, *Gr.Gr.* I: 404, Beekes, *EDG*. Mycenaean has to-pe-za . o-u-ki-te-mi KN V(2) 280.5 "a table, and there is no rim at all," next to a-pe-ti-ra₂ . o-u-te-mi KN V(2)

preverbal variant οὐ and a stressed variant οὔ found only in final position: similarly, the emphatic negation οὐκί normally occurs at the end of the sentence in Homer, as an orthotonic word, especially in binary structures (Att. ἢ οὔ, Hom. ἦε καὶ οὐκί), but could have a preverbal use in which it was presumably proclitic οὐκί (with a graphic accent as in all disyllabic clitics), yet not affected by elision because it had to remain distinct from the regular non emphatic negation οὐκ/οὐχ. The Zenodotean version of Φ 95 backs O 716: both preserve a precious trace of preverbal οὐκί in Homer. And these traces should be recorded in Homeric lexicons, none of which mentions O 716 or Φ 95 under the lemma οὐκί.

Since Zenodotus' reading can be explained as preserving a genuine archaism, which agrees with known facts of linguistic evolution, Van Thiel's "experimental neologism" ("experimentelle Wortbildung") for ἰογάστριος cannot be taken seriously—all the less so if Zenodotus' reading was the regular ὀγάστριος.

4.2 φθανέει

Another case of remodelled old form may be provided by the verb φθάνω. In two lines, the vulgate has a P2 hemistich φθάνει δέ τε πᾶσαν ἐπ αἶαν # "she precedes them everywhere on earth" (Ι 506), φθάνει δέ τε καὶ τὸν ἄγοντα # "(the water) runs faster than the man who guides it" (Φ 262). Aristarchus and the vulgate have the regular Ionic form φθάνει < φθάνϝει with compensatory lengthening. Herodian, taking as its starting point the Attic form φθάνει, without compensatory lengthening, labels it a metrical lengthening (*A Schol.* Φ 262a1: τοῦ δὲ φθάνει ἐκτατέον τὸ α διὰ τὸ μέτρον "the /a/ of φθάνει must be lengthened for metrical reasons")—this must reflect Aristarchus' view. But scholiasts say that Zenodotus had φθάνέει in the two lines under consideration, with a short ᾰ and inflected as φιλέω. This form can hardly be explained as a secondary Atticism in Zenodotus, and in the context it cannot be analysed as a future—the future of verbal stems ending in sonorant is regularly of the φιλέω type—but only as a present.[107] It might be an Aeolicism, because Lesbian does not have the third compensatory lengthening in sequences sonorant + /w/, contrary to Ionic. But that would not explain the φιλέω type. The traditional explanation assumes

---

280.11 "and there is no rim." A reading οὐκί already showing the strong form of the negation may be better than a reading οὔκις 'no one' determiner of te-mi, implying the same reflex as in Thessalian κίς.

[107] Van Thiel 2014a, s.v.: "maybe a reference to the fact that ΦΘΑΝΕΙ (written without accent) can also be a future" ("vielleicht Hinweis darauf, das ΦΘΑΝΕΙ (ohne Akzent geschrieben) auch Futur sein könnte"). Why would Zenodotus have felt the need to write that the form was ambiguous, when the context does not leave room for ambiguity, and spelled this future with uncontracted -εει?

a hyperionicism introduced by Zenodotus, since Ionic has some -έω presents next to -ω presents in Attic.[108] But this is probably not the case.

We know that φθάνϝω results from the thematicisation of an older athematic *φθάνυμι.[109] And this thematicisation can yield either φθάνϝω or *φθανύω, as shown by the pair ἄνϝω vs ἀνύω 'to achieve' in Homer (Ved. *sanóti*), or by τάνυμαι 'to stretch' vs τανύω (imperfect τανύοντο, Ved. *tanóti*), but τίνυμαι 'to make someone pay' vs τίνϝω.[110] Therefore Zenodotus' φθάνέει may simply be the modernisation of an older *φθἄνύει, remodelled because the stem *φθανυ- was not preserved in Ionic. The form would result from a compromise between an older *φθἄνύει and the familiar φθάνει. This is by and large similar to the phenomenon of *diectasis* in forms like ὁρόωντες, a compromise between the uncontracted ὁράοντες and the familiar ὁρῶντες, displaying the metrical structure of the older form with the vocalism of the usual one, extended over two syllables. An alternative hypothesis would be that thematicisation applied to the strong stem *φθανέϝ-ω, which would imply that the form was created when nasal presents still had the *e* grade in the singular, *-neu-/-nu-*. This seems less likely. In either case, Zenodotus cannot have invented such a form, and can hardly have imported it from another copy because it is certainly not better than the vulgate's φθάνει, which displays the regular Ionic form. Therefore he must have found it in his working text.[111]

5 Should a Zenodotean Older Reading Be Printed in a Modern Edition?

The above overview shows that in several cases Zenodotus preserved an older reading, which was sometimes retained by modern editors, but most of the time was not. West did integrate into his Teubner edition of the *Iliad* some of Zenodotus' readings which are clearly older than the vulgate's, as δεδάασθαι 'to be taught' in Λ 831 vs vulgate δεδιδάχθαι, or ἴχματα 'gait?' N 71, vs vulgate ἴχνια 'footsteps', but not all. As a matter of fact, the problem is that, whereas for a case like δειδήμονες in Γ 56 it would be easy to print the Zenodotean reading, because

---

108 Dettori 2019: 136, with literature.
109 Beekes, *EDG*, s.v.; *LIV*²: 135.
110 Originally, the distribution between -νϝω and -νύω was determined by the quantity of the preceding syllable according to Sievers' law (-u̯- after light syllable vs -uu̯- after heavy syllable). Thus, -νυμι (-νυμαι) presents could have a thematic counterpart either in -νϝω or -νύω, and the singers exploited the double outcome to create metrical variants.
111 West 2001: 40 explains φθανέει as a rhapsodic variant.

it is an isolated form and that would not have any consequence on the rest of the line, in other cases this would have far-ranging consequences on the rest of the text.

5.1 The Problem of the Dual

An interesting case is M 342–343 where Zenodotus had the dual Αἴαντε vs vulgate singular Αἴαντα. We know that Αἴαντε is an old elliptic dual compound meaning 'Ajax and Teucros', and indeed Teucros is mentioned in M 350. This type is inherited, compare Ved. *Mitrā́* 'Mitra and Varuna', *dyā́vā* 'Heaven and Earth', and Lat. *Castores* 'Castor and Pollux', borrowed from Greek. But in Greek it was no longer understood, and the "two Ajax" were transformed into two different heroes, with the invention of the "lesser Ajax."[112]

M 342–350
αἶψα δ' ἐπ' Αἴαντα προΐει κήρυκα Θοώτην·
ἔρχεο δῖε Θοῶτα, θέων Αἴαντα κάλεσσον,
ἀμφοτέρω μὲν μᾶλλον· ὃ γάρ κ' ὄχ' ἄριστον ἁπάντων
εἴη, ἐπεὶ τάχα τῇδε τετεύξεται αἰπὺς ὄλεθρος.
[...],
ἀλλά περ οἶος ἴτω Τελαμώνιος ἄλκιμος Αἴας,
καί οἱ Τεῦκρος ἅμα σπέσθω τόξων ἐῢ εἰδώς.

At once he sent Thoötes off as a runner to Aias: "Go on the run, brilliant Thoötes, and call Aias here, or better, both Aiantes, since that would be far the best thing that could happen, since here headlong destruction is building against us [...] But if in their place also hard work and fury have arisen, at least let powerful Telamonian Aias come by himself, and let Teukros follow with him, with his craft in the bow's use."
R.L.

Zenodotus' is clearly the original version[113] but, the elliptic dual being no longer understood, it was replaced by a singular Αἴαντα, with the addition of two lines,

---

112 Β 527–529 Λοκρῶν δ' ἡγεμόνευεν Ὀϊλῆος ταχὺς Αἴας ‖ μείων, οὔ τι τόσος γε ὅσος Τελαμώνιος Αἴας ‖ ἀλλὰ πολὺ μείων "Swift Aïas son of Oïleus led the men of Lokris, the lesser Aias, not great in size like the son of Telamon, but far slighter" (R.L.): Zenodotus athetised l. 528, according to the A scholion (Ζηνόδοτος ἠθέτηκεν αὐτόν), and with it l. 529 although the scholion does not mention it—it cannot stand without the preceding line—and probably l. 530 (Nünlist 2009: 54, n. 102).

113 West 2001: 219 justifies the dual, but seems to assume it refers to the two Ajax, not to Ajax and Teucros. This passage mixes the older state of affairs and the newer one: Teukros is

M 344 starting with # ἀμφοτέρω μὲν μᾶλλον "or rather the two of them," which takes over the old dual and accounts for the presence of Teucros in the following lines. In order to restore as ancient a state of affairs as possible, we should print Αἴαντε in M 342–343 and cancel M 344–345. West prints Αἴαντε but keeps the following line, although ἀμφοτέρω μὲν μᾶλλον after the dual is no longer justified and makes the text unclear. The situation is probably the same in O 301, where Zenodotus' reading Αἴαντε, also found in Aristophanes, is older than the vulgate's Αἴαντα:

O 301–303
οἳ μὲν ἄρ᾽ ἀμφ᾽ Αἴαντα καὶ Ἰδομενῆα ἄνακτα
Τεῦκρον Μηριόνην τε Μέγην τ᾽ ἀτάλαντον Ἄρηϊ
ὑσμίνην ἤρτυνον ἀριστῆας καλέσαντες

They who rallied about Aias, the lord Idomeneus, Teukros, Meriones, and Meges, a man like the war god, closed their order for hard impact, calling on the bravest.
    R.L.

Turning the dual into a singular led to the insertion of O 302 in order to introduce Teucros (who is mentioned next to Ajax in O 446–447). It is hard to escape the conclusion that Zenodotus' reading here is older. West, here, prints the singular Αἴαντα. But since the replacement of the dual by a singular in both cases led to a deeper remodelling and the addition of one or several lines, modern editors cannot print Zenodotus' dual without deleting the added lines, which would be in contradiction with philological principles since those lines are found in all our sources.

On the other hand, in M 127–128 the vulgate has a plural where Zenodotus and Aristophanes had duals δύ᾽ ἀνέρας (ἀνέρε) ηὗρον ἀρίστους (ἀρίστω) ‖ υἷας ὑπερθύμους (υἷε ὑπερθύμω) Λαπιθάων αἰχμητάων "they found two men of the bravest, high-hearted sons of the spear-fighting Lapithai" (R.L.). The dual must be older, although all modern editions have the plural. The dual is also better from the metrical point of view because the dual ἄνερε (with metrically lengthened initial ᾱ) is compatible with the initial Ϝ of εὗρον (*$ue\text{-}ur(h_1)\text{-}e/o\text{-}$

---

mentioned as the companion of his brother Ajax "the greater" in M 363 and 371, but in M 365–369 was inserted a speech of the same Ajax to Ajax "the lesser," so that there are both the original pair Ajax and Teukros, who has an active role in the battle, and the invented pair Ajax the greater and Ajax the lesser, who does not play any role in the episode. Nickau does not discuss those lines.

LIV²), whereas the vulgate's ἄνερας is not. Here the philological rule (all our manuscripts have a plural, therefore editors print a plural) prevailed over the linguistic coherence.

5.2 Heterogeneity of the Corpus

A different kind of problem is posed by very frequent forms belonging to more or less recent lines. A good example is the accusative plural of πολύς. B 3–4 is transmitted in the vulgate as follows: ὡς Ἀχιλῆα ǁ τιμήσῃ, ὀλέσῃ δὲ πολέας ἐπὶ νηυσὶν Ἀχαιῶν "how he might bring honour to Achilleus, and destroy many beside the ships of the Achaians" (R.L.). As in other occurrences in the *Iliad*, the acc.pl. πολέας scans with synizesis, otherwise it would be unmetrical before a vowel, consisting of three short syllables. We know synizesis is recent. For this line, Aristonicus tells us that Zenodotus read πολύς:

> A Schol. B 4b1: πολέας· ὅτι Ζηνόδοτος γράφει πολύς. μόνα δὲ τὰ εἰς υς μονογενῆ δύναται παρὰ τὴν ἔκτασιν ἢ συστολὴν ἑνικὰ καὶ πληθυντικὰ γίνεσθαι, οἷον βότρῠς καὶ βότρῡς.
>
> Zenodotus writes πολύς. But only substantives[114] in υς can, through lengthening or shortening, be both singular and plural, as βότρῠς (nom.sg.) and βότρῡς (acc.pl.).

This comment is of course fully justified in the synchrony of classical Ionic, Attic and for *koine*. But Zenodotus knew as well as Aristarchus that in Homer *u*-stem adjectives had in the acc.pl. -έας, and he would not have invented an acc.pl. πολῠ́ς on the model of βότρῡς. We have to apply here the only valid rule in historical linguistics: what is synchronically regular is not necessarily old, but what is synchronically irregular often, though not always, reflects an older state of the language.[115]

---

114 The Greek word for "substantive" is μονογενής, meaning 'having only one gender': the substantive is here defined through its opposition with the adjective, which has three genders since gender is only an agreement marker in the adjective and not a lexical property.
115 Van Thiel 2014b, *sub* B 4, assumes that πολύς is a marginal note by Zenodotus, and not Zenodotus' reading, and that it is simply the nominative singular, which Zenodotus wrote in the margin in order to indicate that πολέας was a form of πολύς, because that was not the usual form in his time. "Zenodotus can hardly have had the idea of an 'original' acc.pl. πολύς or witness it" ("Zenodot hat kaum ein 'ursprünglich' πολύς acc.pl. gedacht oder es bezeugt"). Can anyone seriously believe that Zenodotus was so unfamiliar with Homer that he had to write in the margin a comment indicating that πολέας was a form of πολύς? And precisely in a line where πολέας poses a metrical problem and must scan

The inflection of ablauting animate substantive and adjective *u*-stems in Greek merged already in Proto-Greek, if not earlier. In the plural, the starting point was the identity of the nominative in *-eu̯-es (Ved. *-avas*, OCS *-ove*) in both types (adj. ἡδέϝες, subst. πήχεϝες). The old acc.pl. *-u-ns > -ῦς, the regular form in nouns, is preserved in Cretan υἱύνς 'sons' (Gortyn, *IC* IV 72, col. 4, l. 40; *IC* IV 51, l. 6).[116] It is also attested in non ablauting *ū*-stems (ὀφρῦς next to ὀφρύας, βότρῦς), where it was borrowed from *u*-stems (the older ending in *ū*-stems was -ῡας < *-uH-n̥s). However, it was soon replaced in *u*-stems by -εϝ-ας, in analogy with the nom.pl. -εϝ-ες < *-eu̯-es. Homer has υἱέας, after υἱέες, and also a more recent υἷας after υἷες < υἱέες with hyphaeresis. Before a consonant (E 159, X 62) or at the end of the line (E 614, Ω 479), υἷας can be a modernisation of the old acc.pl. υἱύς, which before a vowel was modernised as υἱέας and scans as a dactyl.[117] Before a vowel, especially in the many occurrences of the formula υἷας Ἀχαιῶν #, it scans [– ⏑] and can only be analogical after υἷες Ἀχαιῶν #. The inflection of adjectives followed that of the animate nouns, and generalised -εϝ-ες, -εϝ-ας. Now if the old ending -υνς is well attested for animate nouns (υἱύνς, ὀφρύς), it is not for adjectives. Or rather, there is a trace of it in Zenodotus' reading.

Zenodotus' reading πολῦς, mentioned in the apparatus of most editions (although Leaf does not mention it), preserves here the archaic form, as acknowledged by Chantraine and Schwyzer.[118] This form does not pose any metrical problem since it scans [⏑ –], and avoids synizesis. The metrical problem arises from the modernisation of the old πολῦς into the remodelled πολέας. The modernised form could fit into the inherited metrical structure only at the cost of a metrical license, synizesis. And synizesis is systematic whenever πολέας stands before a vowel.

The same applies to cases like acc.pl. πελέκεας Ψ 114, always scanned as a trisyllabic form with synizesis—the form would be otherwise unmetrical, since the stem forms a tribrach. The replacement of the older πελέκῦς by the modernised πελέκεας was possible only at the cost of synizesis.[119] In most instances

---

with synizesis? When there were so many instances of πολέας or πολέες for which he did not provide any marginal comment?
116 See for instance Beekes 2011: 203.
117 The acc.pl. υἷας is certainly not the reflex of an etymological *suHiu̯-n̥s, as argued by Sihler (1995: 326), it is secondary in Homer.
118 Chantraine, *Gr. Hom.* I: 221; same remark in Schwyzer, *Gr. Gr.* I: 572. Curiously, Risch 1974 does not mention the form. Neither does Sihler 1995.
119 Schwyzer, *Gr. Gr.* I: 463. *Pace* Kuiper 1942: 206, who writes "there is no reason for supposing this (= πελέκῦς) to be the earlier form." West does not mention these variants in his apparatus.

there are variants, either the Atticised form πελέκεις Ψ 851, or πελέκυας Ψ 856, which does not solve the metrical problem.

That does not mean that a disyllabic πολύς should be restored under every single πολέας, of course, or πελέκῡς under every πελέκεας. Once synizesis was established as a normal device, new lines with disyllabic πολέας could be created. As a matter of fact, before a consonant πολέας always scans [⌣ ⌣ –], and can never be substituted by πολύς: in that position, only the new form is found, and warranted by metre. There is no reason to suppose that lines with preconsonantal πολέας are all younger than lines with prevocalic πολέας. There was a synchronic complementary distribution, πολέας having two metrical values according to its position.

However, in the case of B 4, there is an agreement between three elements: a philological fact (πολύς is attested in Zenodotus), a metrical fact (this reading does not imply a metrical license) and a linguistic fact (the acc.pl. *-uns > *-ūs is the older form). Therefore, we can be certain that Zenodotus' was the older form and that it was the reading he found in his text, *pace* Van Thiel. If his text had the regular (for Homer) πολέας, he would probably not have corrected the form into an irregular πολύς after another copy (provided another copy had this reading), because he had no means to guess this was an older form and no reason to deem it better. We cannot, however, be certain that Zenodotus had the same reading πολύς in other similar lines. For instance in A 559 he had, according to a T scholion, πολεῖς (*sic*) ἐπὶ νηυσὶν Ἀχαιῶν # (vulgate πολέας), in the same context as in B 4: we can either assume that this πολεῖς is an abusive correction by the scholiast of Zenodotus' form πολύς (which is restored by Erbse), if we take it for granted that Zenodotus' text must have been homogenous, or make the sad constatation that Zenodotus' text was full of inconsistencies and incoherent.[120] Here, however, it is unlikely that Zenodotus ever had an accusative πολεῖς, which is not attested in Ionic, and the intervention of a scholiast is a more plausible explanation. That would make at least two instances of πολύς before a vowel, next to the remodelled πολέας before a consonant, metrically warranted, and for which no divergent form is attested for Zenodotus.

We thus face a well-known problem: the vulgate's reading πολέας was the one known to the Greeks,[121] therefore we should keep it if the aim is to print a text which the Greeks read. But if the aim is to print a text which is as close

---

[120] That, of course, was the conclusion of scholiasts. They give an example of such an inconsistency between Θ 128 Ἐρασιπτόλεμος and Θ 312 Ἀρχεπτόλεμος, two different names for the same warrior.

[121] Known to the Greeks after Aristarchus, known to most Greeks before the *ekdosis* of the latter.

as possible, not to the "original" state of affairs, but at least to the oldest we can reach, that is, which retains the reading transmitting the older form rather than the newer one, we should print B 4 with πολύς. Should we do that for every single occurrence of prevocalic πολέας with West,[122] or only when the older form is in fact attested either in a papyrus or in a scholion? That is, in the latter case, only once, or twice if the T scholion to A 559 is corrupt. It is likely that Zenodotus had πολῦς also in other places, condemned by Aristarchus, but not mentioned in the A scholia because once was enough, so that the problem was mentioned once and for all in B 4.[123] However, we cannot prove that he always had πολύς before a vowel, and this is even unlikely, for it is certain that more than one line with πολέας was coined fairly recently and displayed the synizesis from the start. Printing πολῦς in B 4 and πολέας in other places would introduce a discrepancy between one isolated instance of πολῦς and many more of πολέας. That is, combining the linguistic criterion (the older form) and the philological one (the reading must be attested) results in a fundamental heterogeneity of the Homeric text. This is something linguists are used to, and this heterogeneity is inherent to the Homeric corpus which was elaborated over centuries—but it is something Alexandrian scholars tried to eliminate, and as a rule modern philologists too. Choosing with West to print πολῦς wherever the context is similar to B 4, that is, where there is a synizesis, is probably not faithful to the reality of epic diction, which is dynamic and evolves over time, and to the distance between old lines and new ones. The generalisation of πολέας in all positions in the vulgate can be ascribed either to a spontaneous development in singers' practice, or to the conscious action of ἀναλογία by later scholars working on Homer, after the principle "the Homeric language is consistent, therefore the acc.pl. has one form and not two different forms, and the correct form is πολέας, which is metrically warranted (before a consonant) and regular next to πολέες, πολέων." At any rate, what is clear is that this analogical levelling eliminating one allomorph for the benefit of the other in the Homeric corpus had not occurred yet in the version used by Zenodotus as his working text since he had both πολέας (before a consonant, and probably also before a vowel in recent lines) and πολῦς (before a vowel in old lines).

---

122 West in his edition prints πολύς not only in B 4 and A 559, but in all the lines where πολέας scans with synizesis, see his Introduction, p. XXXIV.

123 Similarly, Zenodotus' reading ἐκαθέζετο vs vulgate κατ' ἄρ' ἔζετο is mentioned by scholia in A 68 but for A 101, B 76, H 354, H 365, Y 149, the vulgate has κατ' ἄρ' ἔζετο and there is no mention of a different reading in Zenodotus. This is not the only case. As it is unlikely that Zenodotus had a different reading only for the first occurrence of a phrase and not for the following ones, it means that scholiasts can mention his readings only under their first occurrence, once and for all. See also the case of τίσαιεν (p. 31).

Similarly, for χάλκεος, χρύσεος, which scan now as trisyllabic, now as disyllabic, the text is fundamentally heterogenous. Here the written form does not change, only the metrical value does, which makes the editors' task easier. For Zenodotus' ὄπα χαλκέην in Σ 222 (pp. 49–50), the same three criteria are met: philological (the form is attested in at least one copy of Homer and has parallels), linguistic (the disyllabic form is inherited from Achaean) and metrical (the line is correct). Therefore, although no modern editor prints Zenodotus' reading, it would be justified to do so.

These readings should be printed in an edition if we were to undertake an edition aiming at reaching as old a state of the Homeric text as we can. This is not the aim of standard critical editions, but it would certainly be worthwhile.[124]

6   Zenodotus and Historical Linguistics

The preceding cases clearly show that historical linguistics can account for some "wild" readings. But conversely, some neglected "wild" readings can also bring new elements for historical linguistics. The following chapters will seek to reevaluate a few Zenodotean readings that have been dismissed by Aristarchus, are either ignored or rejected by modern editors and by linguists, and yet can, with a reasonable degree of certainty, be considered older than those of the vulgate's and bring new elements for Greek historical linguistics and Indo-European studies. At least this is the conclusion to which one is bound to come, provided one examines the facts, without any bias, on the basis of linguistic criteria. Their common point is that the vulgate's reading for most of the

---

[124] This is the aim of E. Tichy in her *Ilias diachronica*, but she is guided by a different principle, which is to bring forth a text conform to the metrical structure she advocates, not to the dactylic hexameter as we know it. The principles are exposed in her 2010 book *Älter as Hexameter?* The framework of my study is instead the dactylic hexameter and I will not try to go into the question of a pre-hexametric versification. In my view Tichy's endeavour is fundamentally flawed by the simple fact that it implies that more or less every single line transmitted in the vulgate existed under a different form in a time prior to the invention of the hexameter. This amounts to a negation of the chronological heterogeneity of the Homeric poems. There is no point in trying to force into a supposedly older metrical structure lines that are clearly recent: this only flattens everything by projecting a developed state of the corpus in a period when the corpus was different. Basically, it is the same problem as that posed by a *Transponat* in Indo-European reconstruction: it counts for nothing the linguistic evolution within the considered language. It can be interesting and stimulating as an exercise, but no more. On the metrical arguments against Tichy's thesis, see the recension of her book by West 2011.

considered lines is metrically, morphologically or syntactically problematic. On those grounds, Zenodotus' readings are generally considered either gratuitous conjectures or emendations introduced by the scholar in order to get rid of the problem.[125] That implies that those readings that would become the vulgate's were already known to Zenodotus. I will try to show that, on the contrary, Zenodotus' readings cannot be an invention of his, but must be something he did find in his text or in copies he collated, and that the vulgate's readings are modernisations or regularisations introduced at the cost either of a metrical license or of a syntactic or morphological oddity. Of course these modernisations need not be attributed to Aristarchus himself, they may be older, and they may have been introduced into a version of the poems by singers at some time well before Zenodotus, but not in the version that eventually became the basis of Zenodotus' *ekdosis*. I do not claim this is the case for all Zenodotean readings, of course: Zenodotus also has a number of modernised forms where the vulgate keeps an older one, but in the considered cases, the archaism is on his side.

At any rate, these readings should be integrated in Homeric lexicography, which deserves some kind of upgrade, and should no longer be ignored by linguists, for they do bring important information about Greek historical morphology and Proto-Indo-European reconstruction. The other point that should not be forgotten is that philology and linguistics are mutually dependent: as linguistics can help establish the correctness of the transmitted form, a careful philological study can also unearth facts that will lead to a renewed picture of linguistic evolution. Zenodotus' readings are never examined by linguists, who rely on the work of philologists of the 19th and first half of the 20th c. But philological facts must also be examined with a linguist's eye, because linguistics is an indispensable tool when it comes to Homeric language. Relying on the work of philologists who established the text and produced the standard modern editions with the general idea that Aristarchus was a wonderful scholar ("the best of the grammarians," as per Schironi 2018) and Zenodotus a fool and an eccentric scholar is no longer permissible. Granted, Aristarchus was a rigorous and systematic scholar, but this systematic approach of his conveys in itself the defects of its qualities, as it leads to a regularisation and systematisation of the text in the name of internal coherence. For Aristarchus, and for all Antiquity, including Zenodotus, there was one poet, Homer, and his use was consistent. But as we now know, this view is not appropriate for a corpus which

---

125 This goes along with the conception inherited from the Greek scholarly tradition that Zenodotus μεταγράφει 'rewrites' the text of Homer.

developed over centuries and has old and obsolete forms next to more recent ones: that consistency which was the aim of Aristarchus leads to the condemnation, or emendation, of many seemingly abnormal forms running counter to ἀναλογία. And in particular of Zenodotus' abnormal forms, which in the eyes of Aristarchus could only be explained as deviations from the consistent text of Homer, introduced by Zenodotus himself. Modern linguists know that archaisms lie in synchronically abnormal forms, not in regular ones. I will therefore apply this principle to Zenodotus' "wild" readings and examine them without any bias to see whether a modern linguistic analysis can do justice to them or not.

The inquiry will lead to a perhaps disturbing conclusion: reading Homer from Z(enotodus) to A(ristarchus), not the other way round, is the only way to understand the making of the *Iliad* and the *Odyssey*.[126]

---

[126] I borrow this from West's titles *The making of the Iliad* (2011) and *The making of the Odyssey* (2015). West did, to some extent, read Homer from Z to A, as the above examples show. However, as a philologist, he did not apply the methods of linguistics, although in several cases he actually saw that Zenodotus' text was older.

CHAPTER 2

Sitting on an Old Tree

1   Γ 151–152: The Metrical Problem

In Γ 151–152 the vulgate reads:

> [...] τεττίγεσσιν ἐοικότες οἵ τε καθ' ὕλην
> δενδρέῳ ἐφεζόμενοι ὄπα λειριόεσσαν ἱεῖσι
>
> as cicadas who through the forest settle on trees, to issue their delicate voice of singing.
> R.L.

As noted from long, line 152 is metrically difficult because the first hemistich scans δενδρέῳ ἐφεζόμενοι [– ⏑ ⏑ – ⏑ ⏑ –] with synizesis of -έῳ which is then shortened in hiatus through *correptio epica*. The fact that the same syllable shows both synizesis and *correptio* indicates that it cannot be very old, and raises suspicion.[1] The problem was already identified in Antiquity, and the two *variae lectiones* transmitted are assumed to be corrections meant to get rid of the metrical problem: the first one, δένδρῳ, found in several manuscripts, implies only *correptio* and avoids the problem of synizesis, but it is clearly a secondary Atticism. The second one, δένδρει, was Zenodotus' reading.

> A Schol. Γ 152a1: ὅτι Ζηνόδοτος γράφει 'δένδρει'. ὁ μὲν οὖν λέγων δένδρος ὡς κάλλος ἐρεῖ δένδρει ὡς κάλλει, ὁ δὲ δένδρον ὡς βάθρον ἐρεῖ δένδρῳ ὡς βάθρῳ. Ὅμηρος δὲ λέγων 'δένδρεον ὑψιπέτηλον' (N 437) ὡς χάλκεον ἐρεῖ καὶ δενδρέῳ ὡς χαλκέῳ.
>
> because Zenodotus has δένδρει. Those who say δένδρος, as κάλλος, will have δένδρει, as κάλλει, those who have δένδρον, as βάθρον, will have δένδρῳ, as βάθρῳ. And Homer, who has 'δένδρεον ὑψιπέτηλον' (N 437), as χάλκεον, will have δενδρέῳ as χαλκέῳ.

---

1   It is impossible to solve the problem thanks to the so-called "Aeolic base" of the glyconic (first two syllables indifferently long or short), in the framework of Tichy 2010. I will not depart here from the framework of the dactylic hexametre, and will try to show that a neat solution is ready at hand within this structure.

Zenodotus' reading is here mentioned by Aristonicus only to be rejected, not as a non-existing word form, but as a non-Homeric one: the reasoning relies on the implication that there are several inflectional types for 'tree' according to dialects, a thematic neuter type in -ον (Attic), a thematic neuter type in -εον (Ionic), and an athematic neuter type in -ος (s-stem) δένδρος, and that within each dialect the inflection is consistent—this is a clear application of the principle of ἀναλογία, because there is a regular pattern in each. That is, the dative δένδρῳ is regular in Attic but cannot match a nominative δένδρεον; neither can a dative δένδρει, although it is regular in at least one dialect. As was the case for μάρτυρες vs μάρτυροι (see above, pp. 38–39), the possibility of a mixed paradigm with both thematic and athematic forms is ruled out from the start. And the second implication is that the base form of the paradigm is the nominative singular, which determines the pattern—this is regular in Greek grammatical analysis, and this is also the reason why the thematic inflection of ἐπιμάρτυρος was applied to the plural forms. Therefore, since Homer has a nominative δένδρεον in N 437, he must have a dative δενδρέῳ, be it at the cost of a synizesis undergoing *correptio*.

A third emendation, suggested by Wackernagel,[2] would be to read # δενδρέῳ ἑζόμενοι without the preverb ἐπι-. Thus we would have only *correptio* and no synizesis. But nowhere in the epic corpus is ἕζομαι used immediately with a dative, it is always used with a preposition (ἐν, ἐπί).[3]

The reading of the vulgate is confirmed by Hesiod, *Op*. 582–583 ἠχέτα τέττιξ || δενδρέῳ ἐφεζόμενος λιγυρὴν καταχεύετ' ἀοιδήν "the noisy cicada, sitting on a tree, pours its melodious song" (there is no *varia lectio*). But of course, since the Homeric reference is crystal-clear, the Homeric reading may have been introduced into Hesiod's text, replacing a different form. West in his commentary[4] tries to justify the awkward combination of synizesis and *correptio* by referring to other instances of the same situation in Homer and the Homeric Hymns, which I shall examine briefly.

A 15 (= A 374) # χρυσέῳ ἀνὰ σκήπτρῳ scans [– ⏑ ⏑ – – –], with synizesis of -έῳ, then shortened through *correptio*, in the same metrical position as

---

2 Wackernagel 1916: 109.
3 Z 354 καὶ ἕζεο τῷδ' ἐπὶ δίφρῳ "and sit down on this chair;" Θ 73–74 ἐπὶ χθονὶ πουλυβοτείρῃ || ἑζέσθην "they seated themselves on the nourishing earth;" O 150 ἕζετο δ' εἰνὶ θρόνῳ "she sat on the throne;" Ω 597 ἕζετο δ' ἐν κλισμῷ πολυδαιδάλῳ ἔνθεν ἀνέστη "and sat down on the elaborate couch from which he had risen" (R.L.); α 437 ἕζετο δ' ἐν λέκτρῳ "she sat on the bed;" μ 425 ἑζόμενος δ' ἐπὶ τοῖς φερόμην ὀλοοῖσ' ἀνέμοισιν "and, sitting on them, I was borne by baneful winds" (J.H.).
4 West 1978: 187, followed by Krieter-Spiro, BK III: 66.

δενδρέῳ ἐφεζόμενοι. The adjective χρύσεος 'golden' is regularly disyllabic in Homer when the ending is long. Some see that as a recent form exhibiting contraction, others argue that this could be a relic of an older *$k^h rus̨ios$, attested in Myc. ku-ru-so, which is clearly an adjective meaning 'golden', coexisting with the noun ku-ru-so 'gold'[5] (see above, pp. 49–50). This "secondary yod" (that is, [i] becoming [y] in hiatus) is well attested in Mycenaean and in Aeolic (Thessalo-Lesbian). Adjectives of material in Mycenaean display either suffix -i-jo or suffix -e-jo. Thessalo-Lesbian generalised -ιος > -ι̯ος.[6] In that case, the spelling χρυσέῳ would be a modernisation of an older disyllabic *χρυσ(σ)ῷ, which can be ascribed either to Achaean or to Aeolic, and there would be no synizesis, but only *correptio*. Another possibility would be to assume that the attested A 15 # χρυσέῳ ἀνὰ σκήπτρῳ results from the Ionicisation of an Aeolic formula # χρυσέῳ ὸν σκάπτρῳ, with the monosyllabic preposition ὸν = ἀνά, and with a trisyllabic χρυσέῳ, in which case only *correptio* would be involved, too, or, with Ruijgh, *χρῡσοῖ ἀνὸ σκάπτροι,[7] but we cannot account for χάλκεον in the above mentioned lines with such a device. Whichever explanation we assume, this syntagm is certainly the modernisation of an older one in which there was no metrical peculiarity: metrical irregularity was created by modernisation (as was the case for the acc.pl. πολέας), and solved by means of a metrical license.

This # χρυσέῳ ἀνὰ σκήπτρῳ is in turn the model of *H.Ap.* 185 # χρυσέου ὑπὸ πλήκτρου, which cannot be used as an old instance of synizesis undergoing *correptio*.[8] The occurrence in Hesiod, *Op.* 144 οὐκ ἀργυρέῳ οὐδὲν ὁμοῖον # quoted by West also involves an adjective of material ἀργύρεος 'silver', that is, an adjective that can behave like χρύσεος and χάλκεος—and the parallelism is clear if one compares *Op.* 129 χρυσέῳ οὔτε φυὴν ἐναλίγκιον οὔτε νόημα, which has the same semantic and syntactic structure "similar to the golden race neither by stature nor by mind" (*Op.* 129) / "similar in nothing to the silver race" (*Op.* 144): *Op.* 144 was built on the pattern of *Op.* 129, where χρυσέῳ can scan as a disyllable, that is, as a contracted form χρυσῷ spelled χρυσέῳ because of the Homeric model, and we should consider ἀργυρῷ also as a contracted form

---

5 PY Ta 714: ta-ra-nu . a-ja-me-no . ku-wa-no . pa-ra-ku-we-qe . ku-ru-so-qe . ku-ru-sa-pi-qe . ko-no-ni-pi 1 "a footstep inlaid with *kyanos* and with turquoise and with gold and with golden X" (the first ku-ru-so-qe = /χρυσōι kʷe/ is the noun 'gold', the second ku-ru-sa-pi-qe = /χρυσιᾱ̓φι kʷe/ is the adjective 'golden', in the feminine).

6 See Alcaeus, *fr.* 357.4–5 LP χ]ά[λκ]ι[αι [...] κνάμιδ[ες.

7 Ruijgh 2011: 287.

8 In fact, # χρυσέου ὑπὸ πλήκτρου is a modification of B 268 # σκήπτρου ὕπο χρυσέου (where χρυσέου is disyllabic but σέου, in arsis, does not undergo *correptio*), aligned on # χρυσέῳ ἀνὰ σκήπτρῳ. This pattern was reused in *H.Lun.* 6 # χρυσέου ἀπὸ στεφάνου.

spelled ἀργυρέῳ because of the Homeric model.[9] All instances of the combination synizesis and *correptio* involving an adjective of material clearly depend on one and the same model, which may have been A 15 or a similar phrase. And in A 15 the metrical difficulty is probably not original, but due to the remodelling in Ionic of an older Aeolic or Achaean phrase.

Γ 152 on the other hand does not involve an adjective of material, therefore it is not directly dependent on A 15, and we must look for another explanation. Contrary to adjectives of material, δένδρεον never had a "secondary yod" since the lost intervocalic consonant was a [w] (δένδρεϝον), and the hiatus is recent. The form does not belong to the same chronological layer as χρύσεος/χρύσιος, and we are not dealing here with an archaism. Either this line is recent, created on the model of cases involving adjectives of material (although 'tree' is not 'wooden' and it is hard to see why adjectives of material should influence a noun), or it is, as A 15, the result of the remodelling of an older phrase which was metrically regular, remodelling made possible by the analogy of the type χρύσεος, χάλκεος disyllabic. Tichy, *Ilias diachronica* Γ 152, gives δενδρέοι ἐφεζόμενοι, reconstructing an original locative. However, as I said, I will be working here within the hexametric metrical structure, and not assume a different structure, and in the framework of the hexameter an old locative δενδρέοι does not change anything to the problem. I think the solution must and can be found within the structure of hexameter.

2   Zenodotus' Reading

Zenodotus' reading # δένδρει ἐφεζόμενοι, on the other hand, is metrically regular, involving only *correptio* if we read δένδρει, and straightforward if we read δένδρε', elision of δένδρεϊ with hiatus preserved.[10] This reading is confirmed by

---

9   Thessalian has ἄργυρρος < *ἄργυριος (*SEG* 36: 548, ll. 9–10), but a form *ἀργύρρῳ would be unmetrical in the attested line.

10 Although elision of the dative singular ending -ι is not frequent, it is attested (see Bowie 2019: 153): Γ 349 # ἀσπίδ' ἐνὶ κρατερῇ; ε 62 χρυσείῃ κερκίδ' ὕφαινεν #; Π 385 # ἤματ' ὀπωρινῷ; Ν 289 οὐκ ἂν ἐν αὐχέν' ὄπισθε πέσοι βέλος οὐδ' ἐνὶ νώτῳ; see other examples in Chantraine, *Gr. hom.* I: 86. Generally speaking, Ionic avoids this elision, and it is possible that some instances are due to the declension of similar syntagms with elided acc.sg. or dat.pl. ending, or nom.acc.pl. for neuters, the metrical structure of which imposed elision in the dative singular. Sometimes two readings coexist: in Γ 349, next to # ἀσπίδ' ἐνὶ κρατερῇ, a papyrus has # ἀσπίδι ἐν κρατερῇ with hiatus filled by a glide. Of course there is no instance of elision for *s*-stems because an elided -ε(ϊ) could always be replaced by a modernised -ει with *correptio epica*, just as in Λ 385 τοξότα λωβητὴρ κέρᾳ ἀγλαὲ παρθενοπῖπα # must be the modernisation of an older κέρα(ϊ) ἀγλαέ. I will come back to this problem below.

Timon of Phlius, who reuses the Homeric line in his poem *Silloi*, thought to have been composed around 260 BCE:[11]

Timon, *fr.* 804.1–3 (*ap.* Diog. L., *Vitae Phil.* 3.7.11)
[...] ἀλλ' ἀγορητὴς
ἡδυεπής, τέττιξιν ἰσογράφος, οἵ θ' Ἑκαδήμου
δένδρει ἐφεζόμενοι ὄπα λειριόεσσαν ἱεῖσιν.

but a sweet-worded speaker, a writer equal to the cicadas who, sitting on the tree of Academos, let flow a delicate voice.

The mocking *simile* aims at Plato. Timon, who died around 230 BCE, is contemporaneous with Zenodotus, and he knew the work of the latter. Indeed, he goes so far as to deter his friend Aratus from using contemporary editions of Homer, which is clearly aimed at Zenodotus' *ekdosis*.[12] Therefore, one cannot expect to find a reading bearing the stamp of Zenodotus in Timon's poem,[13] and the fact that he too has δένδρει means that he had in his possession a version of Homer where Γ 152 read δένδρει. His testimony does not depend on Zenodotus', but is an independent confirmation that this reading was found in a version of the first half of the third century, at least. Therefore it would not be economical to assume δένδρει is a correction Zenodotus took from another copy: as Timon, he probably read it in his text, as already assumed by Wilamowitz.[14]

---

11 Clayman 2009: 20–21: the poem was composed at the earliest in 262/1 because it alludes to Cleanthes as the stoicist scholarch, which he became in 262/1.
12 Clayman 2009: 11: "Aratus asked him how he could obtain a trustworthy text of Homer, and Timon replied that he should be engaged with the ancient copies and not the modern editions (Diog. L. 9.113)."
13 Clayman 2009: 108, n. 97: "Timon's preference for Zenodotus' reading is surprising since he is said to have recommended to Aratus the older, unedited manuscripts of Homer, but it also aligns Timon with the earliest Alexandrian scholars rather than the later ones and so may have some bearing on his date." The problem is not properly formulated: Timon does not show any preference for Zenodotus' reading, but he worked on a version that had δένδρει as Zenodotus' own. The manuscript tradition of Diogenes, who transmits these lines, diverges: manuscripts F and P have δένδρει, and manuscript B has the atticised δένδρῳ (B also has the atticised ἱᾶσιν instead of ἱεῖσι of P and F), see SH p. 379.
14 Wilamowitz 1916: 507. Van Thiel assumes that Timon's δένδρει is original and that Zenodotus quoted him in his marginal notes, which Aristonicus then misunderstood for Zenodotus' own reading. Van Thiel 2014b, *sub* Γ 152: "Zenodotus compared contemporary authors. It must be the case here, too" ("Zenodot verglich zeitgenössische Autoren. Das wird auch hier der Fall sein").

There is a distant echo of this line in Theocritus' *Idyll* 5.47–48:

[...] ταὶ δ' ἐπὶ δένδρει || ὄρνιχες λαλαγεῦντι

on the tree birds are twittering.[15]

The form is usually considered Doric, but it can be a Homeric form identical with Zenodotus' reading: that would be one of the many cases where Theocritus integrates into his own poetry his opinion on a disputed point in Homeric philology. Finally, one finds a nominative πᾶν δένδρος χαρίεν in an elegiac epitaph from Rome (*IGUR* III, 1303f = *Anth. Appendix, Epigr. sepulcr.* 234, end of the first c. CE):[16] the tree full of birds' and cicadas' songs mentioned in the poem is strongly reminiscent of the Homeric and Theocritean contexts, and could ultimately go back to Zenodotus' reading for Γ 152.

3 Dialectal Trees

The dative δένδρει does not agree with the inflectional type attested for δένδρεον in Homer. Scholiasts, followed by modern authors, invoke the existence of an *s*-stem of the γένος type, attested in Herodotus (nom.acc. δένδρος Hdt 6.79) and usual in the dative plural δένδρεσι, regular in Ionic and also known to Attic prose (Thucydides, Xenophon, Plato, Aristotle). The dative singular δένδρει is also found in a fragment by Megasthenes, a historian of the end of the 4th c. BCE, writing in Ionic, quoted by Arrian (ὑπὸ ἑνὶ δένδρεϊ *fr.* 8).[17] In the

---

15 Gow 1952 does not comment on the form.
16 *Epigram. sepulcralia* 234.3–8:
    ἀλλά με πᾶν δένδρος χαρίεν περὶ ῥίσκον ἀνέρπει
    κυκλόθεν εὐκάρποις κλωσὶν ἀγαλλόμενον.
    Ποτᾶται δὲ πέριξ λιγυρὴ μινυρίστρι' ἀηδών
    καὶ τέττιξ γλυκεροῖς χείλεσι λιρὰ χέων,
    καὶ σοφὰ τραυλίζουσα χελιδονίς, ἥ τε λιγύπνους
    ἀκρὶς ἀπὸ στήθο[υς ἡδὺ χέουσα μέλος].
    But the whole gracious tree rises around me, the casket, all around proud of branches heavy with fruit. Around it the melodiously twittering nightingale and the cicada pouring lilies from its sweet lips, and the artfully murmuring swallow, and the clear-voiced cricket, pouring a nice song from its chest.
17 Οὗτοι γυμνοὶ διαιτῶνται οἱ σοφισταί, τοῦ μὲν χειμῶνος ὑπαίθριοι ἐν τῷ ἡλίῳ, τοῦ δὲ θέρεος ἐπὴν ὁ ἥλιος κατέχῃ, ἐν τοῖσι λειμῶσι καὶ τοῖσιν ἕλεσιν ὑπὸ δένδρεσι μεγάλοισιν· ὧν τὴν σκιὴν Νέαρχος λέγει ἐς πέντε πλέθρα ἐν κύκλῳ ἐξικνέεσθαι, καὶ ἂν καὶ μυρίους ἀνθρώπους ὑπὸ ἑνὶ

Hippocratic corpus it appears three times in the *De natura pueri* (chap. 26,[18] no *varia lectio* in the manuscripts), and in the medical literature three times in the *Anonymous Londiniensis*, the longest extant medical papyrus, dating back to the 1st c. CE (*P. Lit. Lond.* 165, Brit. Libr. inv. 137, chap. 33, lines 4, 9, 10).[19] These Ionic forms found among *koine* forms probably betray a hidden quotation: the author compiles a number of textbooks of medicine, most of them written in Ionic, and these forms are certainly not his. The dative appears once in the *Septuagint* (*Deuteronomy* 22.6).[20] The physician Aretaeus of Cappadocia (end of 1st–beg. of 2nd c. CE) has four instances of the genitive δένδρεος:[21] this is clearly an imitation of the language of the Hippocratic corpus, if not an indirect quotation as in the *Anonymous Londiniensis*, and does not mean that the athematic inflection survived in Roman *koine*. But Megasthenes and Hippocrates, together with the imitations of the latter in later medical texts, show that the athematic dat.sg. δένδρει is genuine in several Ionic dialects, as is the dat.pl. δένδρεσι.

From those attestations, the *s*-inflection δένδρος, δένδρεος is usually considered an Ionic feature. But this raises a problem: the *s*-inflection is no more productive in Ionic than it is in Attic, neither dialect can coin neuter nouns of

---

δένδρεϊ σκιάζεσθαι· τηλικαῦτα εἶναι ταῦτα τὰ δένδρεα "these sophists spend their life naked, in the winter they are standing out in the sun, in the summer, when the sun makes it impossible, in the marshes and pastures in the shade of tall trees; Nearchus says their shade reaches up to five plethra around, and that the shade of a single tree could cover ten thousand men, such is the size of those trees" (Megasthenes, *fr.* 8, *ap.* Arrian, *Historia indica* 11.7).

18 The text is given below.
19 Col. 32, l. 53 ἀπὸ τοῦ δένδρους ἀπουσία γί(νεται) "and cut from the tree, the loss occurs;" col. 33, ll. 3–4: καὶ ἐπὶ μ(ὲν) ⟦τ[(ων)] ἐπὶ⟧ τῶι δένδρει "and for those on the tree;" ibid. 33, ll. 8–11: τὰ μ(ὲν) ἀποτμηθέντα ξηραίνεται, τὰ δὲ ἐπὶ τῶι δένδρει οὐ ξηραίνεται· σαφὴς δὲ αὕτη καὶ φαινομένη· τὰ μ(ὲν) γ(ὰρ) ἐπὶ [τῶι] δένδρει οὐ ξηραίνεται [...] "those which have been cut dry out, whereas those which are on the tree do not; and this is obvious and patent, as those on the tree do not dry out [...]."
20 Ἐὰν δὲ συναντήσῃς νοσσιᾷ ὀρνέων πρὸ προσώπου σου ἐν τῇ ὁδῷ ἢ ἐπὶ παντὶ δένδρει ἢ ἐπὶ τῆς γῆς, νεοσσοῖς ἢ ᾠοῖς, καὶ ἡ μήτηρ θάλπῃ ἐπὶ τῶν νεοσσῶν ἢ ἐπὶ τῶν ᾠῶν, οὐ λήμψῃ τὴν μητέρα μετὰ τῶν τέκνων "if you come across a bird's nest beside the road, either in a tree or on the ground, and the mother is sitting on the young or on the eggs, do not take the mother with the young" (*Deuteronomy* 22.6).
21 Aretaeus, *De curatione acutorum morborum* 2.10.4: διὰ τῶν φύλλων τοῦ μαλαβάθρου, τοῦ δένδρεος τοῦ Ἰνδικοῦ "thanks to the leaves of the malabathron, the Indian tree;" ibid. 1.4.5 τερμίνθου τοῦ δένδρεος τῆς ῥητίνης; ibid. 1.4.9 ῥητίνη τερμίνθου τοῦ δένδρεος; ibid. 1.2.8 ῥητίνης τῆς ἀπὸ τῆς τερμίνθου τοῦ δένδρεος "resin coming from the wound of the tree." Three of the four instances are in fact in the same sentence.

the γένος type,[22] only the adjectival type εὐγενής is productive in compounds having a verbal second element—and there is of course no trace of any compound in *-δενδρής with a nominal second element.

Since the s-inflection is considered Ionic, most scholars admit that δένδρει is a recent Ionic form introduced as a correction by Zenodotus into his edition, in order to solve the metrical problem. Thus Chantraine, after Wackernagel: "Zenodotus' reading δένδρει is probably a conjecture. If the text is authentic, it appears to be linguistically recent."[23] Schwyzer mentions δένδρει as a recent Ionic and Doric form but does not mention this variant in Homer: Homer, he says, has only δένδρεον.[24]

Now this explanation is rooted in a general conception according to which Zenodotus introduced emendations wherever he thought it justified and intervened frequently in the text. This now outdated conception of Zenodotus' work is one of the reasons why his readings are not taken into account by linguists, who work primarily with the vulgate. As a matter of fact, Risch does not mention the reading δένδρει,[25] and neither do other scholars, Janda or Forssman, for instance.[26] Still, the facts should be reconsidered, and the question of the inflectional type of δένδρεον examined anew.

4 The Athematic Forms of δένδρεον

The first thing we must underline is that most inflectional forms of δένδρεον attested in Ionic are ambiguous and can be ascribed to several types, as is clear from the table below.

---

[22] The neuter type γένος did have some productivity in Proto-Greek, see forms like τέμενος, πλῆθος or μέγαθος/μέγεθος (Meissner 2006: 51–52). It is noteworthy that all three are built on roots with a final laryngeal, and that an s-stem on *$pleh_1$- for instance would have been *$pleh_1$-os, gen. *$pleh_1$-es-os > **pleos, gen. **plēhos, clearly abnormal. Therefore, rather than assuming that there once was a complex suffix *-$d^h o/es$-, we should rather consider that an original s-stem was remodelled after the *-$d^h e/o$- present πλήθω, which had the advantage of having a consonant preventing hiatus: the same remodelling accounts for the u-stem πληθύς. Μέγαθος/μέγεθος 'large size' could be analogical after πλῆθος 'large quantity'.

[23] Chantraine, Gr. hom. I: 37 ("la leçon de Zénodote δένδρει risque d'être une conjecture. Si le texte est authentique, il apparaît comme linguistiquement récent"), after Wackernagel 1916: 109.

[24] Schwyzer, Gr. Gr. I: 583.

[25] Risch 1974.

[26] Janda 1997; Forssman 2020.

	Singular	Athematic		Thematic	Plural	Athematic		Thematic
		-s-	-u-	-o-		-s-	-u-	-o-
nom.-acc.	δένδρος	+ (γένος)			δένδρεα	+ (γένεα)	+ (ἡδέα, ἄστεα)	+ (ὀστέα)
	δένδρεον			+ (ὀστέον)				
gen.	δένδρεος	+ (γένεος)	+ (ἡδέος, ἄστεος)		δενδρέων	+ (γενέων)	+ (ἡδέων, ἀστέων)	+ (ὀστέων)
	δενδρέου			+ (ὀστέου)				
dat.	δένδρεϊ	+ (γένεϊ)	+ (ἡδέϊ, ἄστεϊ)		δένδρεσι	+ (γένεσι)	+ (ἡδέσι, πώεσι)	
	δενδρέῳ			+ (ὀστέῳ)				(ὀστέοις)

It is generally assumed that in the plural δένδρεα, δενδρέων are thematic forms (because of the thematic singular δένδρεον), but they could just as well be athematic, and could be ascribed to *s*-stems or to *u*-stems. And the dative δένδρεσι is also ambiguous and could be ascribed to *s*-stems (γένεσι) or to *u*-stems (ἡδέσι, πώεσι, remodelling of original *ἡδύσι, *πώϋσι):[27] the only certain thing about the dative plural is that it is athematic in Ionic (*δενδρέοις is not attested in Ionic, but it is true that the material is scarce)[28] and that this is an old feature. Thus, nothing stands against the analysis of the plural forms as being consistently athematic. Nothing, except that the singular is thematic and that in the standard view the inflectional type of the singular determines

---

27   The diminutive δενδρύφιον (first attested in Theophrastus, *Hist. Plant.* 4.7.2 and 3; maybe in Ctesias, *fr.* 63.6 Jacoby) should probably be analysed δενδρ-ύφιον, as ζω-ύφιον 'small animal', with a diminutive suffix analogical after κορύφ-ιον 'summit' (Oribasius, *Coll. med.* 2.58.79) *vel sim.*, rather than δενδρύ-φιον (for an opposite view, see Pinault 2020). It might be traced back to the zero grade of the old *u*-stem if we assume it was created on *δένδρυσι before the latter was remodelled into δένδρεσι, but there is no argument to establish a special relationship between that type of diminutive and the loc.pl.

28   The thematic δενδρέοις is attested in Doric, in the Heraclean Tables, but not in Ionic.

that of the plural. Similarly, in the singular the athematic genitive δένδρεος and the dative δένδρει are ambiguous and could be ascribed to *s*-stems or to *u*-stems. The only unambiguous form is the nom.acc.sg. δένδρος (*s*-stem) or δένδρεον (*o*-stem). Whereas δένδρεον is well attested in Ionic, δένδρος is not: there is only one instance in Herodotus (6.79),[29] and there may be another one in Dioscorides (*Mat. med.* 4.46) where ἰτέα δένδρος 'willow' is a correction accepted by Wellmann for a corrupt form appearing in the lists of synonyms that follow each notice: needless to say the latter must be considered with caution, and, if the correction is reliable, it could be, as the genitive δένδρεος in Aretaeus (see above), a mere imitation of the language of the Hippocratic corpus. Be that as it may, Ionic clearly had a suppletive paradigm for 'tree', mixing athematic forms (δένδρεσι) and thematic forms (δένδρεον), with several ambiguous forms (nom.acc.gen.pl.). The transmitted accent in δένδρεος, δένδρει is that of the thematic type, assigned by Greek grammarians to the athematic variant, and we cannot know whether the athematic forms had a different accent.

In Ionic inscriptions, there is no trace of the athematic inflection in the singular.[30] Such forms, on the other hand, are found in Doric.

In the Epidaurian *iamata*, n°11 (*IG* IV² 1, 121, ca. 350–300 BCE, ll. 90–94)[31] reads as follows (red: athematic inflection; blue: thematic inflection):

> Αἰσχίνας ἐγκεκοιμισμένων ἤδη τῶν ἱκετᾶν ἐπὶ δένδρεόν τι ἀμ-
> βὰς ὑπερέκυπτε εἰς τὸ ἄβατον. καταπετὼν οὖν ἀπὸ τοῦ δένδρεος
> περὶ σκόλοπάς τινας τοὺς ὀπτίλλους ἀμφέπαισε· κακῶς δὲ δια-
> κείμενος καὶ τυφλὸς γεγενημένος καθικετεύσας τὸν θεὸν ἐνε-
> κάθευδε καὶ ὑγιὴς ἐγένετο.

Aeschinas, when the priests had already gone to bed, climbed on a tree and fell into the sanctuary. And when he fell from the tree his eyes hit upon rocks. In a terrible condition and having become blind, he went as a supplicant to the god, he slept in the temple and he was healed.

---

29   Hdt 6.79: ἄτε γὰρ πυκνοῦ ἐόντος τοῦ ἄλσεος οὐκ ὥρων οἱ ἐντὸς τοὺς ἐκτὸς ὅ τι ἔπρησσον, πρίν γε δὴ αὐτῶν τις ἀναβὰς ἐπὶ δένδρος κατεῖδε τὸ ποιεύμενον. Δένδρος is the reading of the majority of manuscripts. There is a *varia lectio* δένδρου in mss S and V, which belong to the same family, but it must be rejected for syntactic reasons.

30   In *TAM* V, 1, 590 (Lydia), δένδρει stands for acc.pl. δένδρη with iotacism. This is not the only case of iotacism in the inscription which also has a future ἕξι for ἕξει.

31   The *iamata* (from ἰάομαι 'to cure') are a series of inscriptions narrating the miraculous healings that occurred in the temple of Asclepius in Epidaurus.

The text is written in a variety of mild Doric and has characteristic Doric forms (ὀπτίλλους l. 92 vs Attic-Ionic ὀφθαλμούς, monosyllabic preverb ἀμ-βάς ll. 90–91, καταπετών l. 91 vs Attic-Ionic καταπεσών, gen.pl. ἱκετᾶν l. 90, the latter three also found in Aeolic).[32] The name of the healed man, Αἰσχίνας, is frequent all over the Greek world, and we do not know where the man came from. What is interesting is that the same text has both an athematic genitive δένδρεος (l. 91) and a thematic nominative δένδρεον (l. 90). One and the same account of a miraculous healing is due to one and the same scribe (before it was entrusted to the lapicide), and probably one and the same redactor: thus, this short text shows a state of language where the word for 'tree' had a suppletive paradigm mixing thematic and athematic forms.[33] A thematic genitive ἀπὸ τοῦ δενδρέου is also found in the *iamata* (*IG* IV² 1, 123, n° 44, l. 2), showing that there was a hesitation between two types.

---

32   For the dialectal study of the language of the *iamata*, which can be considered a form of Doric *koina*, see Méndez Dosuna 2001: 331–332. The few Attic-Ionic features found in those texts must be ascribed to the influence of neighbouring Attic, which can be observed very early in Epidaurus (see Nieto Izquierdo 2014: 82 and Minon 2014 on the evolution of the alphabet), or of early Attic-Ionic *koine* (the so-called "great Attic," see Minon 2014: 53, n. 58), rather than to Ionic. In particular, there is no feature specific to Ionic and alien to Attic, but only common Attic-Ionic ones (ἱερός vs ἱαρός, εἰ vs αἰ, ὀφθαλμοί vs ὄπτιλλοι), or specifically Attic features retained in *koine* but unknown in Ionic. These are: acc.pl. of the ὑγιεῖς type, identical with the nom.pl., whereas Ionic dialects always have a distinct form for nom.pl. and acc.pl. in *s*-stems; five occurrences of the pronoun οὐθείς, not attested in Ionic inscriptions before the 3rd c. BCE, whereas it is attested in Attic inscriptions already in the first half of the 4th c. (*IG* II² 6873; *SEG* 28, 265) and in Attic literature as soon as the 5th c. (Eur., *fr*. 151b.16; Plato); among other instances of reduction of [i] diphthongs in hiatus, we have in the *iamata* ὑός "son," attested in Attic inscriptions from the beginning of the 5th c. (*IG* I³ 730) but not in Ionic; occasional ἐνεγκεῖν instead of ἐνεῖκαι; Attic παρουσία "presence." In Epidauros only the type γίνεται is attested from the 4th c. on (this is not specific to the *iamata*), and not the Attic form γίγνεται: this is probably an early *koineism*, and this development is found in many dialects (Buck 1955: 69). The language is sometimes mixed: τὸν ἄτερον ὀφθα[λμόν (*IG* IV² 1, 124, l. 10) has Doric ἄτερον and Attic-Ionic ὀφθα[λμόν next to each other. This fact casts a doubt on Méndez Dosuna's assumption that the model of the written language of the *iamata* was the Ionic prose of Herodotus, to which he traces back the use of the oblique optative as well as the use of pronouns: the oblique optative is usual in Attic prose and there is no need to seek the model in Herodotus. That we are dealing with a normalised written language is clear, that archaisms are to some extent a stylistic feature of this prose (particularly in the use of pronouns) also seems clear, but clear evidence in favour of a specifically Ionic influence is lacking. Del Barrio 1992: 546, focusing on the lexicon, invokes another Ionic influence, that of the Hippocratic Corpus, next to the influence of *koine*: that would make more sense since it is medical literature, but again the non Doric words found in the *iamata* are common Attic-Ionic.

33   Nieto Izquierdo 2009: 451.

We have a similar situation in some Ionic dialects: in the Hippocratic corpus, chapter 26 of the treatise *De natura pueri* also shows a suppletive paradigm with clearly athematic forms (dat.sg. δένδρει, dat.pl. δένδρεσι), clearly thematic ones (nom.acc.sg. δένδρεον, gen.sg. δενδρέου) and ambiguous ones (plural δένδρεα, δενδρέων). In the text given below, athematic forms (ath.) are in red, thematic ones (th.) in blue, and ambiguous ones in green. There are occasionally secondary Atticisms (δένδρον).

Hippocrates, *De natura pueri* 26 (ed. Littré, vol. 7):

	Ἀναλήψομαι δὲ αὖθις ὅτι τοῦ θέρεος τὸ κάτω τῆς γῆς ψυ-
	χρόν ἐστι, τοῦ δὲ χειμῶνος θερμόν, τὸ δὲ ἄνω τῆς γῆς τοὐναντίον
dat. ath.	τούτου, καὶ δεῖ τῷ δένδρεϊ μὴ δύο θερμὰ ὁμοῦ προσγίνεσθαι, μηδὲ
	δύο ψυχρὰ ὁμοῦ, ἢν μέλλῃ ὑγιαίνειν· ἀλλ᾽ ἢν μὲν ἐκ τοῦ ἄνωθεν
	προσγίνηται θερμόν, ἐκ τοῦ κάτωθεν δεῖ ψυχρὸν αὐτῷ προσγίνεσθαι, 5
	καὶ πάλιν ἢν ἐκ τοῦ ἄνωθεν προσγίνηται ψυχρόν, ἐκ τοῦ κάτωθεν
	δεῖ θερμὸν αὐτῷ προσγίνεσθαι. Αἵ τε ῥίζαι ὅ τι ἂν ἑλκύσωσι, τῷ
dat. ath.–nom. th.	δένδρεϊ προσδιδόασι, καὶ τὸ δένδρεον τῇσι ῥίζῃσι. Καὶ γίνεται οὕτω
	ταμιείη καὶ ψυχροῦ καὶ θερμοῦ· ὥσπερ καὶ τῷ ἀνθρώπῳ ἐσιόντων
	ἐς τὴν κοιλίην σιτίων, ὅσα πεσσόμενα θερμαίνει, δεῖ ψύξιν ἀποδί- 10
dat. ath.	δοσθαι ἀπὸ τοῦ πότου, οὕτω καὶ τῷ δένδρεϊ δεῖ ἀνταποδίδοσθαι ἐκ
nom. th. [Atticism]	τοῦ κάτω πρὸς τὸ ἄνω, καὶ ἀνάπαλιν. Καὶ αὔξεται τὸ δένδρον καὶ
	ἐς τὸ ἄνω καὶ ἐς τὸ κάτω διὰ τόδε, ὅτι οἱ τροφή ἐστι καὶ ἐκ τοῦ
	κάτωθεν καὶ ἐκ τοῦ ἄνωθεν. Καὶ ἕως μὲν ἂν ἁπαλὸν ἔῃ σφόδρα, οὐ
	καρποφορέει· οὐ γάρ ἐστιν αὐτῷ πίειρα δύναμις οὐδὲ παχείη, ἥτις 15
	ἐς καρπὸν ξυμβάλλεσθαι οἵη τέ ἐστιν· ὁκόταν δὲ χρόνος ἐγγένηται,
	τότε ἤδη ἐν αὐτῷ αἱ φλέβες εὐρεῖαι γινόμεναι ποιεῦνται ἐν αὐτῷ ἐκ
	τῆς γῆς πίειραν καὶ παχείην τὴν ῥύσιν· ὁ δὲ ἥλιος διαχέων αὐτὴν
	ποιέει ἐκζεῖν ἅτε κούφην ἐοῦσαν ἐς τὰ ἄκρα καὶ καρποῦσθαι· καὶ
	τὴν μὲν λεπτὴν ἰκμάδα ἀπὸ τοῦ καρποῦ ἀποφέρει, τὴν δὲ παχείην 20
	πέσσων ὁ ἥλιος καὶ θερμαίνων γλυκαίνει· τὰ δὲ οὐ καρποφορέοντα
pl. ambiguous nom. th.	τῶν δενδρέων οὐκ ἔχει πῖαρ ἐν αὐτοῖσιν, ὅσον ἐς τὸν καρπὸν ἐκδώ-
	σεται. Τὸ δὲ πᾶν δένδρεον ὁκόταν ὑπὸ χρόνου στερεωθῇ καὶ λάβηται
	ἐκ τοῦ κάτω τῇσι ῥίζῃσιν ἤδη βεβαίως, πέπαυται αὐξόμενον πάντῃ.
pl. ambiguous dat.pl. ath.	Ὁκόσοισι δὲ ἐς δένδρεα ἀφ᾽ ἑτέρων δενδρέων ὀφθαλμοὶ ἐνετέθησαν 25
	καὶ δένδρεα γενόμενα ἐν τοῖσι δένδρεσι ζῇ καὶ καρποφορέει καρπὸν
	οὐχ ὅμοιον οἷσιν ἐγκείμενά ἐστιν, τρόπῳ τοιῷδε τοῦτο γίνεται. Ξυμ-
	βαίνει τῷ ὀφθαλμῷ πρῶτον μὲν βλαστάνειν, τροφὴν γὰρ εἶχε πρῶτον
gen. th.	μὲν ἀπὸ τοῦ δενδρέου, ἀφ᾽ οὗ ἀπηνέχθη, ἔπειτα ἐν ᾧ ἐνετέθη·
acc. th.	ὁκόταν δὲ βλαστήσῃ οὕτω, μεθίησιν ἐς τὸ δένδρεον ῥίζας ἀπ᾽ αὐτοῦ 30
	λεπτάς· καὶ πρῶτον ἀπαυρίσκεται ἀπὸ τῆς ἰκμάδος τῆς ἐν τῷ δεν-

dat. th.	δρέῳ ἐνεούσης, ἐν ᾧ ἔγκειται· ἔπειτα χρόνου ἐγγενομένου ἀφίησι
	ῥίζας ἐς τὴν γῆν διὰ τοῦ ἐν ᾧ ἐνετέθη, καὶ ἐπαυρίσκεται ἀπὸ τῆς
	γῆς ἕλκον τὴν ἰκμάδα, καὶ τροφὴ αὐτῷ ἐκεῖθέν ἐστιν· ὥστε μὴ θαυ-
pl. ambiguous	μάζειν ἑτερόκαρπα εἶναι τὰ ἔνθετα τῶν δενδρέων, ζῇ γὰρ ἀπὸ τῆς 35
pl. ambiguous	γῆς. Ταῦτά μοι εἴρηται περὶ τῶν δενδρέων καὶ τῶν καρπῶν διὰ
	τόδε, ὅτι οὐχ οἷόν τε ἦν μοι τὸν λόγον ἡμιτελέα καταλιπεῖν.

The dative singular is consistently athematic, except for one δενδρέῳ (ll. 31–32) for which ms V has the Attic form δένδρῳ, which is secondary. The page is missing in the other good manuscript, M, but the reading δενδρέῳ is found in the younger manuscripts derived from M, which means that M must have had δενδρέῳ. Since at the beginning of the chapter we have the athematic dative δένδρει three times, the intrusion of δενδρέῳ can only be a regularisation in favour of the regular thematic Ionic form … which probably means that the process of copying was interrupted for some reason (for lunch or for the mass for instance) and that when the scribe resumed, he did not remember the previous instances of δένδρει and replaced this odd form by the regular one.[34] The text confirms that one and the same writer had in his dialect a suppletive paradigm for 'tree'.

The athematic dative δένδρει is the same form found in Megasthenes, in the *Septuagint* and in the *Anonymous Londiniensis* (see above). Its not so infrequent use in Ionic is probably due to the fact that it was backed by the regular athematic dative plural δένδρεσι.

Now, as we have seen above, neither δένδρει nor δένδρεος inflect unambiguously according to the γένος type, for they could be ascribed to the ἄστυ type. The only unambiguous s-stem form of the paradigm is the nom.acc.sg. δένδρος. This δένδρος is attested once in Greek epigraphy, in a Doric inscription from Cos (*Iscr. di Cos* ED 181, ll. 6–7, 4th c. BCE): κα-]τὰ δένδρος. The inscription is mutilated and its syntax is difficult to restore, but it appears that we have here a distributive κατά + acc. The language is mostly Doric (ᾱ, infinitive ἀνακαθαίρεν), however the editors write an Ionic ἱε[ρός instead of ἱαρός—but this restitution is no more than a restitution and cannot be considered fully reliable. This nom.acc. δένδρος is also found once in Herodotus (6.79), born in Halicarnassus. This city, on the coast of Asia Minor, right in front of Cos, used to be Doric, and was a member of the Doric Hexapolis, like Cos.[35] The agreement

---

34 The *Index hippocraticus* does not mention this δενδρέῳ but only the athematic δένδρει, which should be corrected. I am grateful to C. Magdelaine to whom I owe those indications on the manuscript tradition.

35 The cultural community between Halicarnassus and the Dodecanese goes back to Mycenaean times: Zurbach writes about late Bronze Age Ionia "la péninsule d'Halicarnasse appartient en fait plus au Dodécanèse qu'au continent" (Zurbach 2014: 286).

between the Coan inscription and Herodotus could betray a Doric feature surviving in the Ionic dialect of Halicarnassus. Therefore the presence of δένδρος in Herodotus should not be taken as a proof that the s-inflection is Ionic. Neither should the athematic δένδρει in the Hippocratic corpus for two reasons: this form is not unambiguously an s-stem, and the Hippocratic school is the Coan school. It may not be a coincidence if ancient occurrences of the athematic type in Ionic literature come from the Cos area. At any rate, be it a Doricism in Herodotus' Ionic or an Ionicism in the Cos inscription, it could be ascribed to an areal feature.

To sum up: 'tree' had a suppletive paradigm mixing thematic and athematic forms in several Ionic and Doric dialects at least, and probably also in Attic where the old δένδρεσι is preserved in the otherwise thematic inflection of δένδρον (secondary, from δένδρεον). The unambiguously athematic forms can be assigned either to u-stems or to s-stems. As neither is a productive inflectional type in any Greek dialect, there are two possible conclusions: either the athematic forms are old, and we are not dealing, as usually assumed, with a secondary innovation, or they are analogical after δόρϝος, δόρϝι at a stage when the latter still had the meaning 'tree'. Since analogical reshaping of a thematic form into an athematic one is not frequent, to say the least, and since δόρυ lost the meaning 'tree' very early, the odds are that the first conclusion is correct. That is, we must start from an athematic paradigm in Greek, not from a thematic one. This is the opposite of what handbooks and grammars teach, but this is what an unbiased analysis of the Greek facts shows. The problem is that handbooks and grammars take it for granted that, since Homer only has δένδρεον, thematic, the oldest paradigm is wholly thematic, because Homer is the most archaic form of Greek we have (that was before the decipherment of Linear B).

5   'Tree' and Its Proto-Indo-European Root

In order to solve the morphological problem, we must go back to the PIE paradigm of 'tree', keeping in mind the data from Greek dialects.

The root, or rather, the stem (root + suffix) is *dr-eu̯- 'wood'. The oldest attested type is proterodynamic, and found in Indo-Iranian: nom.acc. *dór-u-Ø, gen. *dr-éu̯-s [Ved. drós, Av. draoš], loc.sg. *dr-éu̯-i (like mádhavi, renewal of an older *dr-éu̯-Ø).[36] As for *ĝón-u 'knee', the old genitive of which was *ĝén-u-s, following the acrostatic inflection, while *ĝn-éu̯-s is a remodelling after the

---

36   Ringe 2006: 48, reconstructs *dréw(i). Neri 2003: 25, reconstructs, after Schindler, a loc.sg. *ĝn-éu̯-Ø for the parallel neuter noun 'knee', and a loc.sg. *dr-éu̯-Ø p. 88. Another neuter

mobile dominant type,³⁷ and the original (unattested) type was probably an acrostatic *dór-u-Ø / **dér-u-s, although there is no trace of **dér-u-s, except maybe in Slavic *dér-u̯-os-Ø (OCS drěvo, drěvese, Ru. dérevo), an s-stem which might go back to an old gen.sg. *dér-u̯-es (see Hitt. genuas), where the ending would have been recategorised as a suffix. The collective was *dr-éu̯-h₂. The loc.pl. was *dr-u-su, with zero grade. We can assume that Greek inherited a paradigm similar to that of Indo-Iranian. In Greek, the zero grade of the gen.sg. ending *-s was replaced by the full grade *-os in all inflectional types. Therefore the old gen.sg. *dr-éu̯-s underwent remodelling into *dr-éu̯-os, of the ἠδέϝος type. In Vedic, through a different remodelling, arose a new gen.sg. *dr-u-n-os (drúṇas) built on the zero grade.

This ablauting paradigm was split into three different ones in Greek, undergoing at the same time a semantic differentiation.³⁸ The generalisation of the strong stem of the nom.acc. *dór-u-Ø yielded δόρυ, δορϝ-ός, which meant originally 'tree' but was restricted to the meaning 'fallen tree, trunk', hence the derived meanings 'beam', 'spear'. The zero grade stem of the loc.pl. is still found in the Homeric loc.pl. δρυσί (Ξ 398), reflex of the inherited *dru-su,³⁹ and from it evolved δρῦς 'oak'. The collective *dréu̯-h₂⁴⁰ is reflected with a modification

noun inflecting according to this pattern in Indo-Iranian is *h₂ói̯-u-, gen. *h₂i-éu̯-s (Ved. áyu-, OAv. āiiu-, gen. yaoš, loc.sg. unattested), see Gotō 2013: 30.

37   On the basis of Hitt. gen.sg. genuas one should reconstruct an original acrostatic *ĝón-u-Ø, gen. *ĝén-u-s (Schindler 1975: 7), but Kloekhorst, EDHIL, s.v., concludes that "the Hittite forms seem to point to a paradigm *ĝén-u-, *ĝnéu̯-s." However, that is a problem of doctrine, the Leiden school being rather skeptical about acrostatic paradigmes. Nevertheless, the existence of an old acrostatic paradigm is certain, as the coexistence of γόνυ, Ved. jánu next to Lat. genu cannot be accounted for otherwise, and since the Hittite form matches the acrostatic type, it is simpler to assume that it is what it looks like, the reflex of the e grade of the root in the weak stem.

38   This is a rather common phenomenon in historical linguistics, going together with the loss of the apophonic alternations inherited from PIE. Compare for instance the case of *deiḱ- in Greek, where the full grade forms specialised in the meaning 'to show' (δείκνυμι) whereas the zero grade forms specialised in the juridical meaning 'justice' (δίκη). Or the case of *di̯eu̯- in Latin, which was split into two different words, diēs 'day', out of the acc.sg. *diēm (Ved. dyám, Gr. Ζήν), and Jūpiter, Jovis 'Jupiter', out of the voc. *di̯éu̯ (Gr. Ζεῦ) and the loc. *di̯éu̯i (Ved. dyávi), the old nom.sg. *di̯éu̯s (Ved. dyáus, Gr. Ζεύς) surviving in nudiūs tertius 'two days ago' (lit. 'today is the third day'), from which was derived the adverb diū 'for a long time'.

39   The zero grade is found in compounds like δρυτόμος 'wood-cutter', δρύφακτος 'wooden barrier', Ved. dru-ṣád- 'sitting on a tree' (which is the compound corresponding to our syntagm δένδρει ἐφεζόμενος).

40   Janda 1997, among others, assumes that the collective was *druh₂ > δρῦς 'oak', but this is less likely, as δρῦς may have been back-formed from other inflectional forms with generalised zero grade after δρυσί and have taken its ū from the type ἰχθύς, ἰχθύος.

in the Greek plural *δένδρεϝα 'trees'. Chantraine, after others, admitted an "expressive" reduplication, but one is at pain to justify an "expressive" derivative for 'tree' unless it was originally a diminutive 'little tree', which is not very convincing. As an alternative, Strunk made the hypothesis of a compound *dem-dreu̯-o- 'tree of the house',[41] referring to the familiar tree in the courtyard, as opposed to those in the forest: this is semantically awkward and neglects the fact that the thematic form originated in the plural (see below). Pinault recently explained the form as an older *dréndru-, abstract derived from a thematic *dr̥ndró- attested in Ved. daṇḍá- 'stick', hence the adjective *dréndreu̯o-, and with dissimilation *déndreu̯o-.[42]

All the previous attempts started from the problem of the reduplication: it is indeed a major one but I suggest we should try from the other end, and focus on the inflectional type, which is the historical problem we face in our study of Zenodotus' Homer. As shown above (pp. 91–95), a characteristic of the paradigm is that it mixes athematic forms (δένδρεσι, and in various dialects athematic forms in the singular) with thematic ones (δένδρεον and all the singular in most dialects), and ambiguous ones (nom.acc.pl., gen.pl.). Among those, only the nom.acc.sg. is unambiguously thematic. This is characteristic of a well-known category, namely, singulatives derived from collectives. As from ἀστήρ 'star' was built a collective ἄστρα, next to the count plural ἀστέρες, and from that collective was derived the singulative ἄστρον, thematic,[43] hence

---

41   Strunk 1976; Janda 1997: 149.
42   Pinault 2020, with a full survey of previous literature. I cannot agree with Pinault's explanation for the reason given above: the athematic inflection being unproductive in Greek dialects, the athematic forms δένδρεσι, δένδρει, found in prose, are necessarily older than the thematic type, whereas Pinault assumes that the starting point in Greek is a thematic derivative *dréndreu̯o—which cannot account for the athematic forms. Athematic forms could be explained if we stop at the stage *dréndru- in Pinault's derivation, but if this is an abstract, as Pinault thinks, it has little chance of providing the neuter plural which is clearly the base of the thematic type in Greek, as the only form in which the reanalysis was possible because the inflectional type is ambiguous.
43   That ἄστρα must be an old collective was contested by Matasović 2006: 113–115, who argues that *h₂ was not used to derive collectives from athematic nouns. There are indeed many collectives built on athematic nouns. The problem is that many of those collectives then generated singulatives, which are always thematic, so that in synchrony one has the impression that only the thematic type is old, since there is most of the time a pair collective vs thematic singular. But the singular is a secondary singulative, and the synchronic pairs do not reflect the diachronic evolution. The collective played a significant role in the thematicisation of old athematic stems. A similar pair in Greek is ἰός, ἰά (Y 68): as shown by Meier-Brügger 1988, the collective is older, derived from the athematic stem íṣu- 'arrow' (fem.) attested in Vedic, and ἰός is a singulative, not the other way round as Matasović argues. Another case of collective built from an athematic animate stem is ἄρρην/ἄρσην

two different paradigms, thematic and athematic, it is likely that the mixing of thematic and athematic forms in 'tree' is due to the same phenomenon. This process also exists for neuter nouns: thus, δάκρυον and ἄλφιτον are the singulatives of δάκρυα, ἄλφιτα, collectives of δάκρυ 'tear', ἄλφι 'wheat flour'. In the latter case both singular and plural are athematic in the original type (δάκρυ/δάκρυα, ἄλφι/ἄλφιτα), and the singulative accounts, not for the shift in gender, as for ἀστήρ/ἄστρον, but only for the coexistence of a thematic type and an athematic one.[44] Now a pattern δόρυ/-δρεϝα/-δρεϝον is exactly parallel to δάκρυ/δάκρυα/δάκρυον.

Therefore, considering that the plural δένδρεϝα matches the old collective *dr-éu̯-h₂ except for the reduplication, and must be an avatar of the collective, it is likely that the starting point of the Greek paradigm is the collective, an athematic δένδρεϝα, which gave rise to an entire athematic declension on the one hand, and to a singulative δένδρεϝον on the other. As a hypothesis, the reduplication could be a secondary feature of the collective. The collective refers to a set or group, for instance a set of wheels (κύκλα, Ved. cakrá̄), a group of stars composing a constellation (ἄστρα).[45] The trees of a forest are a group but cannot be defined as a set. A collective formation, marked by the suffix *-h₂, referring to a large number of items belonging to count nouns, such as the trees of a forest, may conceivably have been secondarily provided with an iconic reduplication indicating a large number. This is a shaky hypothesis because there is no parallel in nominal formations in ancient IE languages. Reduplication was used in verbs to express iteration, probably with an iconic value: the reduplicated present stems derived from telic roots forming a root aorist (Greek type τίθημι, δίδωμι, thematic πίπτω) probably were iterative. But there is no such thing in nouns.[46] In that case, reduplication would be an iconic

---

'male', for which Homer has a collective ἄρσενα next to the count plural ἄρσενες—the word is originally a substantive, not an adjective, contrary to what is found in the literature (Le Feuvre 2021d).

44 Homer has only δάκρυ, δάκρυα, δάκρυσι, athematic, the singulative δάκρυον only in the formula δάκρυον εἴβων # (variant of δάκρυα λείβων), and only once a thematic dative plural δακρύοισι, in a recent line, σ 173 μηδ᾽ οὕτω δακρύοισι πεφυρμένη ἀμφὶ πρόσωπα, with *correptio attica*. The singulative is metrically motivated. Similarly for ἀλφίτου, only form of the singular in Homer (athematic ἄλφι is not found in the Homeric corpus as we have it but only in the Hymns: *H.Cer.* 208).

45 Melchert 2014: 258. In Le Feuvre 2015: 504–514 I suggested that Myc. o-ka is a collective of ὄρχος 'rank' (in the military sense, rank of ten soldiers). Its use in the "o-ka tablets" is consistent with that: a troop is a set of ranks.

46 Reduplication as an iconic means of deriving collectives is known from other languages (Lakoff–Johnson 1980: 128). For instance it is attested in Columbian Salish (Dale Kinkade 1975: 424).

secondary feature subordinate to the collective formation: a "pluralisation" of a collective cannot be achieved through inflectional means, but only through derivational means.[47]

Assuming the reduplication is a secondary feature of the collective, designed to convey the notion of a whole (collective) made up of a large number (reduplication) of items, we can come up with a plausible scenario. For a noun meaning 'tree', the frequency of the collective could give it a particular prominence in the paradigm, and that could account for the generalisation of the reduplicated stem δενδρεϝ-. As a result, the plural forms (gen. *$dréu̯-ōm$), then the old singular forms *$dréu̯-os$, *$dréu̯-i$ built on the same weak stem *$dréu̯-$ acquired the same reduplication through analogy with δενδρεϝα. Δενδρεϝος, δενδρεϝι belong to unproductive inflectional types in Greek (u-stems or s-stems), and they match the PIE forms, except for reduplication. Accordingly, the most economic hypothesis is to assume that they continue the older form with a reduplication borrowed from the collective. The original accent of the athematic forms is unknown (see above). The thematic type is secondary and started with the singulative δένδρεϝον, which received a recessive accent as most e grade neuter thematic nouns.

On the other hand, the strong stem *$dór-u-Ø$ did not acquire the reduplication because it was formally too remote from δένδρεϝα. Then the word underwent differentiation: the reduplicated form took over the meaning '(standing) tree' while the old non reduplicated *$dór-u-$ was confined to the meaning 'fallen tree, trunk'. The semantic differentiation goes together with the splitting of the paradigm into two different words. Thus, the original pattern simple singular vs reduplicated collective was eliminated and surfaces as two differentiated words δόρυ vs δένδρεϝα: the former acquired a new plural δόρϝα, while the latter acquired a new singular, which is in fact a singulative.

The older non reduplicated collective *$dr-éu̯-h_2$ presumably also served as a pivot for the creation of the thematic *$dr-éu̯-o-$ > *$trewa-$ in Germanic (Goth. triu). In Greek as in Germanic, thematicisation must be the result of the creation of a singulative from an originally athematic collective, and the process took place independently in both languages.[48] The result is the intrusion of a thematic form, the nom.acc.sg. in Greek, into an otherwise athematic paradigm, which left clear traces in Greek dialects.

---

47 Since no other Indo-European language has a reduplicated form for 'tree', I assume it is a Greek innovation. Pinault 2020 argues for a reduplicated derivative in Sanskrit, in a word meaning 'stick', not 'tree', which would be related to the Greek form.

48 There is a parallel in the other neuter noun inflecting according to the same pattern, *$ĝón-u-Ø$, *$ĝn-éu̯-s$, with strong stem generalised in Greek (γόνυ, γονϝ-ός) and weak stem

Centuries later, after the loss of intervocalic /w/ in some Greek dialects, the plural δένδρεϝα became δένδρεα, which was even more ambiguous from the morphological point of view and could be analysed as an o-stem, a u-stem or an s-stem. Similarly, gen. *δένδρεϝος and dat. *δένδρεϝι (u-stem) became δένδρεος and δένδρεϊ, which could also serve as a pivot and help reinterpretation of the ambiguous forms as belonging to s-stems. The final step of this reinterpretation is the creation of a new nom.acc. δένδρος. It is not surprising that this process, which implies the loss of intervocalic /w/ and cannot be old, is attested in the Doric dialect of Cos. As a matter of fact, in Rhodes and the Dodecanese, as in East Ionic, the loss of /w/ was very early and predates the first inscriptions. This would not have been possible in the Doric dialects of Peloponnese or Crete, where /w/ was retained until fairly late, which prevented the interpretation of δένδρεϝα as an s-stem.

Once this nom. δένδρος is created and attested, one is tempted to analyse δένδρεος and δένδρεϊ as reflecting the s-inflection, but one should not forget that this synchronic analysis does not necessarily match the diachronic process. Δένδρεος and δένδρεϊ, which originally belong to u-stems, are older than δένδρος. It was easy to create a nom. δένδρος, although the γένος type is not productive in Ionic or in Doric, if the singular already had athematic forms δένδρεος and δένδρεϊ. In that case we are dealing with a straightforward regularisation of a suppletive paradigm, which was done in two different directions: either the thematic inflection was extended to the whole paradigm, starting from the nom.sg., hence δενδρέου and δενδρέῳ—solution of the majority of dialects—, or the athematic inflection was generalised from gen. δένδρεος and dat. δένδρεϊ which continue the original u-stem inflection—solution limited to a few dialects or sub-dialects, notably in the Cos area. Regularisation need not imply that an inflectional type is productive: the creation of a nom.acc. δένδρος was impossible if there were only thematic forms of the δένδρεον type, or ambiguous forms like the plural δένδρεα, δενδρέων, but was very easy if there were unambiguous athematic forms in the paradigm, on the model γένεϊ, γένεος : γένος :: δένδρεϊ, δένδρεος : x = δένδρος.

However paradoxical it may seem, modern linguists never formulate the hypothesis of a u-stem for the athematic forms, although we all know that 'tree' (*dór-u-, *dr-éu̯-) is etymologically a u-stem. They all operate only with an s-stem, which cannot be old, because they hold as a principle that the

---

generalised in Germanic (Goth. *kniu* < **knewa-*, thematicisation of **ĝn-éu̯-*, probably starting in the athematic plural **ĝn-éu̯-a* which took over the value of the lost dual). See already Kuiper 1942: 191.

nominative singular is the basis of the inflection. Therefore, ambiguous forms like δένδρεος, δένδρεϊ are assigned to s-stems because of δένδρος, and for the same reason the ambiguous plural δένδρεα, δενδρέων is assigned to the thematic type because of the nominative singular δένδρεον. Now the diachronic evolution is the opposite one: the nominative δένδρος is secondary after δένδρεος, δένδρεϊ, and δένδρεον is secondary after δένδρεα. The same holds true for the relationship between thematic and athematic forms: athematic forms are assumed to be the result of the reanalysis of an old thematic plural δένδρεα (corresponding to the singular δένδρεον, which is supposedly thematic from the start, because of the Germanic thematic equivalent), whereas historically it must be the opposite, δένδρεα is an athematic collective which was reanalysed as thematic, allowing for the creation of the singulative δένδρεον, and so is probably *trewa- in Germanic. Now if Greek did not inherit a thematic form, but did create it, it follows that the many attempts at reconstructing the preform of this thematic *den/r-dreu̯o- or the like rely on an incorrect basis.

6   Back to Zenodotus

Therefore Zenodotus' reading δένδρει is probably, rather than a recent Ionic form of the γένος type, an old form of the ἄστυ type preserving the original u-stem. We should read δένδρεϝι, parallel to ἄστεϝι (θ 525), with elision δένδρεϝ' ἐφεζόμενοι,[49] of which δένδρει is a modernisation. The coexistence of that athematic form with the thematic nom.acc. δένδρεον simply shows that archaic Ionic had a suppletive paradigm mixing thematic and athematic forms, as do most Ionic dialects (dat.pl. δένδρεσι in all, + dat.sg. δένδρει in some, but nom.sg. δένδρεον everywhere).[50]

In that particular case, three criteria ensuring the correctness of Zenodotus' reading are met: the philological one (Zenodotus' reading is confirmed by an independent source, Timon), the metrical one (this reading yields a correct metrical structure for the beginning of the line), and the linguistic one (the

---

49 See above, p. 85n10. I noted there that the elision was not attested for s-stems: but now that it is clear that 'tree' is not a s-stem but a u-stem, the problem is slightly different, because the intervocalic /w/ was preserved until the beginning of the first millenium, which implies that until then the dative of u-stems could behave in the same way as that of consonant stems.

50 It must be stressed that we only have a partial knowledge of Ionic dialects, so that by "all," I mean all dialects in the actual state of our knowledge. There may have been Ionic dialects where even the dat.pl. was thematic, but we have no such form.

word for 'tree' is etymologically a *u*-stem, therefore one can expect to find traces of the old *u*-stem inflection, and there are other traces of a suppletive paradigm mixing thematic and athematic forms in Ionic and in Doric). Therefore δένδρει, standing for an original elided δένδρεϝ(ι), is almost certainly the older reading. The *u*-inflection being the inherited one, one cannot ascribe the athematic form δένδρεϊ to one dialectal component of the epic diction rather than to another, since it appears that several dialects (Ionic, Doric) in the first millenium still preserve athematic forms in a suppletive paradigm. The vulgate's δενδρέῳ, although it is by far the dominant reading, is a secondary modernisation which relies on the argument that the Homeric language is consistent and that since Homer has a thematic nominative δένδρεον, he cannot have anything but a thematic dative δενδρέῳ (see the A scholion in pp. 82–83)—that is, it rules out the possibility of suppletivism in the name of ἀναλογία. This introduction of the regular (and secondary) Ionic form was made at the expense of metrical regularity, imposing the metrical license that allows for both synizesis and *correptio* on the same syllable, whereas the original form δένδρεϝ(ι) does not show either of those. Thus, this case # δενδρέῳ ἐφεζόμενοι is no more reliable than A 15 # χρυσέῳ ἀνὰ σκήπτρῳ: both result from a secondary modernisation of an older form, and the cost of this modernisation is a metrical license—of course, once this pattern was established, it allowed for other instances of the same license, which back the original instance, but are nevertheless secondary.

The introduction of δενδρέῳ may be old enough to be already the source of Hesiod, *Op.* 583. However, it is more likely that the "new" reading δενδρέῳ ἐφεζόμενοι in Γ 152 was introduced into the Hesiodic text by rhapsodes having both poets in their repertoire, and that Hesiod's original text had δένδρει as Zenodotus'. What is certain is that, as soon as the Hesiodic text also had δενδρέῳ, this backed the reading of the vulgate and the metrical pattern it implies: scholars were all the more inclined to take δενδρέῳ as the genuine form and the abnormal δένδρει as an invention of Zenodotus. But in that case metrics and diachronic linguistics agree with Zenodotus. And together, Zenodotus' δένδρει vs δένδρεον, μάρτυρες vs ἐπιμάρτυρος, πολύς vs πολέας point to an important fact, namely, that his text seems to reflect a state of Homer in which there was no heavy use of ἀναλογία yet.

7   Δενδρήεις

The revisited history of δένδρεον has a consequence on the history of its derivative δενδρήεις, δενδρήεντος 'wooded' (ἄλσεϊ δενδρήεντι ι 200, νῆσος δενδρήεσσα α 51). If we start from a thematic δένδρεϝον, the formation of δενδρήϝεντ- is irregular, "eigenartig" in Risch's words:[51] what would be expected is *δενδρεόεντ-, metrically regular and comparable to λειριόεσσαν Γ 152, δακρυόεσσαν Ζ 455 (for τειχιόεις, see below, p. 130). One could assume that there was a hyphaeresis in *δενδρεόεντ-, yielding *δενδρόεντ-: this altered the metrical structure, which was restored through remodelling after the synonym ὑλήεντ- for instance, hence δενδρήεντ- —since of course it cannot be a regular metrical lengthening.[52]

But the preceding sections imply that we must start, not from an *o*-stem, but from a *u*-stem δένδρεϝ-. Therefore the derivative was *δενδρεϝ-ϝεντ-, with a geminate /ww/. I shall come back below to the phonetic outcome of this sequence. For the time being, let us limit ourselves to the two possibilities put forward by scholars. Either the geminate was simplified with compensatory lengthening, which is the case in most dialects, or a diphthong was formed, which is the case in Thessalo-Lesbian. In hypothesis 1 (compensatory lengthening), Ionic should have *δενδρείεντ- with a spurious diphthong, and the open [ē] of δενδρήεντ- must be explained either as an Achaean form of the τελήεις type, or as a remodelling after ὑλήεντ-. In hypothesis 2 (diphthong), the outcome *δενδρεύεντ-, abnormal, was eliminated and the word remodelled after ὑλήεντ-. I will come back to that point below (pp. 128–130).

51 Risch 1974: 152.
52 "Metrical lengthening" involving a substitution of -η- for -o- is only found in compounds, in the type ἐλαφηβόλος, ἑκατηβόλος. The case of δενδρήεις is different.

CHAPTER 3

"Demain, dès l'aube" (Tomorrow at Dawn)

The title of this chapter is borrowed from a famous poem in Victor Hugo's *Contemplations*. It happens to perfectly summarise the problem posed by an isolated Zenodotean reading.

1 Θ 470: The Metrical Problem

In Θ 470–472 the vulgate reads:

ἠοῦς δὴ καὶ μᾶλλον ὑπερμενέα Κρονίωνα
ὄψεαι, αἴ κ' ἐθέλῃσθα, βοῶπις πότνια Ἥρη,
ὀλλύντ' Ἀργείων πουλὺν στρατὸν αἰχμητάων

> Tomorrow at the dawning, lady Hera of the ox eyes, you will see if you have the heart, a still mightier son of Kronos perishing the ranged numbers of Argive spearmen.
> R.L.

The difficulty lies in the first word of line 470: as Chantraine notices, this is one of the two occurrences where the contraction cannot be resolved in the name of dawn, and where we cannot restore an older ἠόος.[1] The other occurrence is Θ 525:

Θ 523–525
ὧδ' ἔστω Τρῶες μεγαλήτορες ὡς ἀγορεύω·
μῦθος δ' ὃς μὲν νῦν ὑγιὴς εἰρημένος ἔστω,
τὸν δ' ἠοῦς Τρώεσσι μεθ' ἱπποδάμοις ἀγορεύσω

> Let it be thus, high-hearted men of Troy, as I tell you. Let that word that has been spoken now be a strong one, with that which I speak at dawn to the Trojans, breakers of horses.
> R.L.

---

[1] Tichy, *Ilias diachronica* Θ 470, does print ἠϝόος, because she does not work in the framework of Hexameter, but this does not solve the syntactic problem.

Lines 524–525 were condemned by Aristarchus,[2] and are generally thought to be an interpolation by modern scholars. I will come back to these lines below (pp. 121–122), and will not take them into account for the time being.

In all other Homeric occurrences, for the contracted ἠοῦς, ἠῶ, ἠοῖ, non contracted ἠόος, ἠόα, ἠόϊ can be restored. Of course, unresolvable contractions in Homer are not extraordinary: we could admit that this betrays a recent line and move on.

2 Θ 470: The Syntactic Problem

However, besides the minor metrical difficulty, there is another syntactic one: as mentioned in dictionaries, 'at dawn' in Homer is either the adverb ἠῶθεν, always used at the beginning of a line before a consonant, save for two cases in the *Odyssey* which depart from this pattern (γ 366, δ 214), or another adverb ἠῶθι, always found at the end of the line combined with πρό (ἠῶθι πρό # Λ 50, ε 469, ζ 36), in complementary metrical distribution with # ἠῶθεν. Θ 470 and Θ 525 are the only examples of the genitive of the substantive used with the meaning 'tomorrow at dawn'.

Now, the genitive of time is a partitive genitive: it refers to a period of time during which something happens,[3] and never expresses a location in time, which is the function of the dative, older locative. As such, it is frequently used for seasons, for periods of the day, 'by night' or 'by day', 'during the night' or 'during the day'. Compare the following examples:

- ν 278: κεῖθεν δὲ πλαγχθέντες ἱκάνομεν ἐνθάδε νυκτός "but, made to wander from there, we reached here at night" (J.H.).
- Χ 26–27: παμφαίνονθ' ὥς τ' ἀστέρ' ἐπεσσύμενον πεδίοιο, || ὅς ῥά τ' ὀπώρης εἶσιν, "as he swept across the flat land in full shining, like that star which comes on in the autumn" (R.L.).

---

[2] A Schol. Θ 524–525.1: ἀθετοῦνται δύο στίχοι, διότι τῇ ἑξῆς οὐδὲν λέγει καὶ τὸ ὑποτακτικὸν ἄρθρον ἀντὶ προτακτικοῦ παρείληπται, ὃς μέν ἀντὶ τοῦ ὁ μέν "two lines are athetised, because he says nothing the day after, and ⟨the text⟩ has the postpositive article ὅς μέν [*that is, the relative pronoun* ὅς, CLF] instead of the prepositive article ὁ μέν [*that is, the article as we understand it*, CLF]."

[3] Schwyzer–Debrunner, *Gr. Gr.* II: 112–113: "the partitive of time is undetermined for general indications of a period of the day or the year in which something falls, […] and determined (by means of the article etc.) for the indication of a precise time span within which something occurs" ("Der Partitiv der Zeit steht undeterminiert zur allgemeinen Angabe der Tages- oder Jahreszeit, in die etwas fällt, […] determiniert (durch Artikel usw.) zur Angabe eines bestimmten Zeitabschnittes, innerhalb dessen etwas geschieht").

- Ar., *Nubes* 175: ἐχθὲς δέ γ' ἡμῖν δεῖπνον οὐκ ἦν ἑσπέρας "yesterday we had no dinner in the evening."
- Ar., *Eccl*. 796: κἂν ἕνης ἔλθῃς "even if you come the day after tomorrow" (that is, during the day).

Words expressing a period of time cannot be used equally in the genitive of time: for instance the genitive ἑσπέρας 'in the evening' is usual both in prose and in poetry, whereas the genitive ἑσπέρου is found only once with this meaning, in Apollonius of Rhodes' *Argonautica* (*Arg.* 2.1251), and is deliberately unusual. The same distinction exists in French between the feminine *soirée, matinée*, for which *dans la soirée, pendant la soirée* ("during the evening"), *dans la matinée, pendant la matinée* ("during the morning") is usual, and the masculine *soir, matin*, which cannot be found in such a phrase *dans le soir, *pendant le soir, *dans le matin, *pendant le matin, but only in the originally locative *le soir* ('in the evening'), *le matin* ('in the morning'), which express location in time (as shown by the old fashioned *au soir, au matin* with the preposition *à* indicating location in space or time). Greek apparently had the same opposition for 'morning' as for 'evening'. As a matter of fact, ὄρθρον is frequently used in the genitive ὄρθρου, usually translated 'at dawn', as if it were a locative, but ὄρθρου refers to the period during which the sun rises above the horizon (after dawn), and the original meaning must be 'during the first hours of the day', hence 'early in the morning'.[4] On the other hand, Attic ἕως, Ionic ἠώς is never used in the genitive of time, either in prose or in poetry—except in the two abnormal Homeric occurrences here. For 'at dawn', as far as we can tell, Greek only has an adverb (Hom. ἠῶθεν, Attic ἕωθεν).[5] In Homer, ἠῶθεν is normally found at the beginning of the line, before a consonant, whereas the adverb αὔριον 'tomorrow', also used at the beginning of the line (five out of six occurrences in

---

4 For instance in Hesiod, *Op*. 577 # ὄρθρου ἀνιστάμενος "getting up early."

5 The *LfgrE* adduces a unique occurrence of the accusative ἠῶ for 'at dawn': παννυχίη μέν ῥ' ἥ γε καὶ ἠῶ πεῖρε κέλευθον β 434 "she cleaved her way all night and through the dawn" (J.H.). This use is peculiar, and probably results from a clumsy adaptation of an existing model. The model is found in η 288 εὗδον παννύχιος καὶ ἐπ' ἠῶ καὶ μέσον ἦμαρ "I slept all night, even to dawn and midday" (J.H.), and further Θ 508–509 ὥς κεν παννύχιοι μέσφ' ἠοῦς ἠριγενείης || καίωμεν πυρὰ πολλά "so that all night long and until the young dawn appears we may burn many fires" (R.L.). The combination of παννύχιος and ἠώς is characteristic of a pattern "all night long until dawn," and this is also the meaning in β 434: the ἥ γε καὶ ἠῶ must be the remodelling or alteration of an original line where there was a preposition meaning 'until', like the ἐπ' ἠῶ of η 288, and where ἠῶ was a directive accusative. It may be an error for a *κατ' ἠῶ with κατά used as the consonantal variant of ἐπί (see pairs like ἐπὶ νῆας/κατὰ νῆας), misheard or misspelled if this happened on a written text.

the *Iliad*), is used before a vowel: the genitive ἠόος, which has the same metrical value as αὔριον, is never found, which confirms that it could not mean 'tomorrow at dawn'.

Thus, ἠοῦς in Θ 470 and Θ 525 combines a metrical oddity (these are the only examples of unresolvable contraction for 'dawn') and a syntactic irregularity (the genitive of time is incompatible with 'dawn'). This is enough to rouse suspicion.

3   Zenodotus' Reading

For Θ 470 Zenodotus' reading was not ἠοῦς.

> *A Schol.* Θ 470a: ὅτι Ζηνόδοτος γράφει ἄας δή, ἀντὶ τοῦ ἐσαύριον. ἔστι δὲ ἡ λέξις οὐχ ὁμηρική.
>
> because Zenodotus has ἄας δή 'tomorrow'. But this word is not Homeric.

As was the case for δένδρει, Aristonicus does not condemn the reading because the word does not exist, but because it is not found elsewhere in the Homeric corpus. Needless to say one could expell many words according to this principle, since virtually every *hapax* can fall under the accusation of being non-Homeric, having no parallel in the corpus. The reasoning is again that of the homogeneity of the corpus.

Most modern editors mention Zenodotus' reading in their apparatus, with a comment (*"mire"* Mazon) or not (Allen, Van Thiel). A noticeable exception is West, who does not. Leaf has a detailed footnote where he says he hesitated to integrate ἄας δή in the text because "it can hardly have been invented by Zenodotus" and "it has all the appearance of a genuine word of the old Achaian or Proto-Epic dialect, representing ἄϝας."[6] Nickau in his work on Zenodotus also acknowledges that Zenodotus did not invent the form, but he makes a very costly hypothesis about its origin—it would be the deformation of a marginal conjecture erroneously integrated into the text—,[7] which is not justified, as we will see. Van Thiel assumes it is a marginal comment of Zenodotus, "either a dialectal parallel or a quotation of a contemporary poet."[8] Van der Valk sticks to the classical thesis and sees in ἄας an innovation introduced by Zenodotus

---

6   Leaf, *Iliad* 1: 280.
7   Nickau 1977: 43–44.
8   Van Thiel 2014b, *sub* Θ 470: "ἄας ist entweder Dialektparallele oder Zitat eines Zeitgenossen."

"to embellish the Homeric text" through the use of an "uncommon form."[9] Rengakos sees in it a Boeotian form introduced by Zenodotus.[10]

Zenodotus' reading is mentioned by Hesychius (α 23):

ἄας· ἐς αὔριον Βοιωτοί. οἱ δὲ εἰς τρίτην.

ἄας: 'tomorrow'. Boeotian. But for others, 'the day after tomorrow'.

As Latte indicates, this lemma comes from Diogenianus and therefore goes back to the Homeric Alexandrian exegesis. It is not an independent confirmation but has the same source as the A scholion Ζηνόδοτος γράφει ἄας δή, ἀντὶ τοῦ ἐσαύριον "Zenodotus writes ἄας δή for ἐσαύριον" (cf. Θ 538 ἠελίου ἀνιόντος ἐς αὔριον "as the sun goes up into tomorrow" (R.L.)). The wording is the same (ἐς αὔριον), but Hesychius adds a dialectal indication, which is that the word is Boeotian. Moreover, a third element is added, that some understand it as meaning not 'tomorrow' but 'the day after tomorrow' (εἰς τρίτην). Neither Latte nor Hansen comment on this, which is rather strange since it cannot come from the context in Θ 470, where ἄας cannot mean εἰς τρίτην. Thus, the meaning εἰς τρίτην has another source.

Hesychius' *Lexicon* has another interesting gloss (α 1408):

ἀεστητόν· αὔριον. Βοιωτοί (Hansen prints †ἀεστητόν with a *crux*).

ἀεστητόν: tomorrow. Boeotian.

It does not follow the alphabetical order, but is inserted before the series of forms in ἀεσ-, after the series of forms in ἀερ-. That means that it did not belong to Hesychius' *Lexicon* but was added later on. Such out of place additions mostly come from Cyrill, but this one probably does not: at least, it is not in the list of words of Cyrill's *Lexicon* as edited by U. Hagedorn—neither is ἄας.[11] The form is also given as Boeotian, and with the same meaning as ἄας, namely 'tomorrow' (αὔριον). This is why Latte treats this form as a free variant of ἄας. However, it is certainly not a free variant. The lemma is corrupt: the first part ἀεσ- can be identified as corresponding to ἄας, but the end of the word -τητόν is not

---

9   Van der Valk 1964: 49–50.
10 Rengakos 1993: 22. Wilamowitz 1916: 41 assumed Zenodotus had ἄας but not that he introduced it into the text. But he wondered "how a Boeotian provincialism could come into a Homeric text that was the basis of the Ephesian Zenodotus?"
11 Hagedorn 2005.

readily identifiable. Hesychius' *Lexicon* was transmitted through a unique 15th c. manuscript full of material errors and corrupt readings, which does not make the task very easy. But still, it is possible to propose a plausible reading explaining the link between ἄας· ἐς αὔριον Βοιωτοί. οἱ δὲ εἰς τρίτην and ἀεστητόν· αὔριον. Βοιωτοί.

First of all, the fact that ἀεστητόν was inserted between the series in ἀερ- and in ἀεσ- indicates that the ε is authentic, and that a form in /aes/ existed next to Zenodotus' ἄας. It is also likely that this form was Boeotian. The strange mention οἱ δὲ εἰς τρίτην for ἄας echoes the -τητόν of ἀεστητόν. The latter is an adverb, hence the neuter form, whereas the former is a prepositional phrase with understood ἡμέραν, hence the feminine. This means the difference between -ον and -ην can be accounted for and is not an obstacle to the comparison. In fact, the two share a structure [t–to/ān] and only differ by /ē/ vs /ri/. Phonetics cannot account for this difference, but handwriting can. My hypothesis is that -THTON represents a misread -TPITON: in uncials (we know the *Lexicon* was first written in uncials, and the added material not coming from Hesychius was drawn from other lexica also in uncials), if the letters ⟨P⟩ and ⟨I⟩ are written close enough to each other, the sequence ⟨PI⟩ is characterised by a vertical stroke on the left (that of the ⟨P⟩), a vertical stroke on the right (the ⟨I⟩) and at least a horizontal line in the middle (the lower part of the curve of the ⟨P⟩). This sequence has a square shape, and can be confused with a square letter ⟨H⟩, which also has two vertical strokes and a horizontal line in the middle. The confusion would be even easier if the upper part of the ⟨P⟩ was damaged, but even without that, misidentification of ⟨PI⟩ as ⟨H⟩ in a text written in uncials is not unthinkable. This would yield for the Hesychian gloss ἀές τ⟨ρί⟩τον 'the day after tomorrow',[12] which is the source of the strange εἰς τρίτην. The latter can hardly be explained otherwise: 'tomorrow' and 'the day after tomorrow' are quite different and the confusion cannot stem out of a semantic or phonetic confusion, therefore a graphic confusion is the only plausible hypothesis.

If this hypothesis is correct, that means there must have been two different glosses or even three:
- ἄας· ἐς αὔριον (Zenodotus, *via* Diogenianus, who may not have given any dialectal indication because usually there is none in the Hesychian glosses coming from him).
- *ἀές· αὔριον. Βοιωτοί.
- *ἀἐςτ⟨ρί⟩τον· εἰς τρίτην. Βοιωτοί.

---

12 On the accent of ἀές, see below, p. 115. Boeotian has no trace of the ordinal *trit-i̯o-, usually assumed to be the etymon of Thess. τρίττος, τρέττος (but *contra* Nieto Izquierdo 2015, who argues that the Thessalian forms are innovations and not archaisms).

Before we proceed to a tentative reconstruction of the history of these glosses, let us quote Latte's Introduction:

> Lectorem memorem tamen esse decet unumquodque lexicographorum apographon novas glossas inferre, veteres quarum nullus usus videtur omittere, ita ut etiam in Hesychii codice Marciano permulta legantur ab auctore aliena, quorum fontem ignoramus.
>
> The reader should, however, remember that every single copy by lexicographers brings in new glosses, omits old ones which seem useless, so that even in Hesychius' Codex Marcianus much of what we read is alien to the author, and we do not know its source.[13]

Be that as it may, we can nevertheless try to understand what happened.

A first redaction mixed the first two glosses, yielding the attested ἄας· ἐς αὔριον. Βοιωτοί. The result is that ἄας gained a new indication about its dialectal origin, Boeotian, which is not mentioned in the A scholion and was probably not in Diogenianus. The obvious link between *ἀές· αὔριον. Βοιωτοί and *ἀὲς τ⟨ρί⟩τον· εἰς τρίτην. Βοιωτοί led to the erroneous importation onto ἄας of the meaning εἰς τρίτην which is that of ἀὲς τ⟨ρί⟩τον and to the redaction we now have ἄας· ἐς αὔριον Βοιωτοί. οἱ δὲ εἰς τρίτην, which condenses three glosses into a single one. This process of condensation implies deletion of the "useless" lemmata, in that case ἀές and ἀὲς τ⟨ρί⟩τον.

Later on, ἀεστητόν was reintroduced with an altered spelling, probably taken from a compilation of dialectal glosses, with due mention of its dialectal origin (Βοιωτοί). It was given an erroneous meaning, that of ἄας or ἀές alone. Maybe because, as Latte, the scribe identified the obscure ἀεστητόν as a free variant of ἄας.

4   Aeolic αὔα/αὖα

The *LfgrE* does not mention Zenodotus' reading under ἠώς, but under a lemma ἄα (ἡ), which is not attested elsewhere.[14] The *LfgrE* article, by Mette, sees in ἄας the genitive of a feminine ā-stem, comparing Sappho's αὔα (*fr.* 175 LP): both would be the reflex of a contracted *ἀϝοᾱ < *ausos-ā, a resuffixation in *-eh₂ of

---

13   Latte 1953: xv.
14   The form is already mentioned in Bechtel, *GD* I: 52–53.

the name of dawn, which has an exact match in Lat. *aurora*. Voigt (Hamm) has the same analysis and assumes with caution, and with a question mark, that αὔα could be an instance of the contraction οᾱ > ᾱ in Lesbian[15]—there is no other instance of this contraction in Sappho or Alcaeus.

This form αὔα is transmitted by Apollonius Dyscolus, as an example of μεταπλασμός, that is, of a change of morphological paradigm (declension or conjugation):

> Apollonius Dysc., *Adv.* 596
> ὃν τρόπον καὶ ἐπ' ὀνομάτων μεταπλασμοὶ γίνονται καθάπερ τὸ ἐρυσάρματες, τὸ λῖτα, τὸ παρὰ Σαπφοῖ αὖα.

> the way in which changes of inflection also happen for nouns, as for ἐρυσάρματες (Π 370), λῖτα (α 130), in Sappho αὖα.

Αὔα is thus introduced as an abnormal inflectional form of the regular Lesbian αὔως. The form is given without any context, and in the nominative as the other two: that does not mean that Sappho had a nominative αὔα, the word may have been found in a different case, but the rule is to quote nouns under the form of the nominative, this is why Apollonius has ἐρυσάρματες rather than the attested accusative ἐρυσάρματας (Ο 354)—and this is why the *LfgrE* also has a lemma ἄα (ἡ), although no such substantive is known.

The same form is transmitted by the Byzantine *Etymologica*, where it is likely to come from Apollonius or another grammarian.

> *Et. Genuinum*, α 1437: τὴν γὰρ ἠῶ οἱ Αἰολεῖς αὐάν φασι.

> the Aeolians call the dawn αὐαν.

> *Et. Magnum*, Kallierges, p. 174, 40: εἴρηται παρὰ τὴν αὔαν, Αἰολικῶς τὴν ἡμέραν· τὴν γὰρ ἠῶ οἱ Αἰολεῖς αὐάν φασι.

> it gets its name from αὔαν which is the Aeolic for 'day', because the Aeolians call the dawn αὐαν.

There is a hesitation on accentuation, between αὔαν (type ἡμέρᾱ) and αὖαν (type γλῶττᾰ). This probably indicates that the word was never found in a

---

15   Hamm 1957: 33.

context where the quantity of the final vowel could be determined (nom.sg. or acc.sg.), and that the attribution to a given inflectional type is a guess of grammarians, prompted by the rule according to which a substantive must be quoted in the nominative (Apollonius Dyscolus), or in the case implied by its function in the phrase into which it is integrated (*Et. Magnum*, where αὔαν is the regime of παρά in the first occurrence, and the attribute of the direct object ἠῶ in the second one). As a matter of fact, the accentuation αὔα, implying a final short vowel, is incompatible with the hypothesis according to which αὔα results from *αὐόα (*LfgrE*, Voigt).

Unfortunately, the name of dawn is well attested in Sappho's preserved fragments, and it is never αὔα or αὖα, but always the regular form Αὔως (*fr.* 100.13 LP; 104a1 LP; 157 LP). Sappho even has an accusative Αὔων (*fr.* 58.19 LP), instead of the phonetically regular *Αὔοα > Αὔω: this form, remodelled after the nom. Αὔως, confirms that "dawn" was not an *ā*-stem in Lesbian. The regular accusative Αὔω is attested in Orion (*Etymologicum*, alpha, p. 14: Αὔριον, πλεονασμῷ τοῦ ρ· ἐστὶ γὰρ παρὰ τὴν αὔω Αἰολικῶς εἰρημένην φωνήν. οὕτω γὰρ λέγουσι τὴν ἠὼ αὔω· τὴν αὔριον οὖν τὴν ἐπιοῦσαν ἡμέραν, αὔω, αὔϊον, καὶ πλεονασμῷ τοῦ ρ, αὔριον "αὔριον, through addition of [r]; the word comes from the Aeolic form αὔω, because this is how they say 'dawn', αὔω; αὔριον is thus the following day, αὔω, *αὔϊον and through addition of [r], αὔριον").[16] Thus, the hypothesis of a resuffixed *ā*-stem *αὐόᾱ does not rely on anything solid.

Turning back to Zenodotus' ἄας, it obviously has a direct link with the Lesbian form quoted by Apollonius Dyscolus and the *Et. Magnum*, which we have no reason to treat as depending on Zenodotus: the existence of ἄας is thus attested in two different sources, Sappho (on which source depend Apollonius Dyscolus and the Byzantine lexica) and Zenodotus (hence Hesychius' first lemma), and confirmed by Hesychius' ἀεστητόν, however corrupt. Therefore the first criterion is met: Zenodotus' reading is confirmed by other sources independently. But if both ἄας and αὔα come from *αὐόᾱ, which is highly unlikely for Lesbian (see above), we still face the same problem for Θ 470: ἄας from *ἀϝόᾱς would be a contracted form, just as the vulgate's ἠοῦς, and it would be a genitive of time, which is incompatible with 'dawn'. Therefore, the explanation must be different.

---

16   See also *Et. Genuinum*, α 1410: αὔριον παρὰ τὴν αὔω Αἰολικῶς, ὃ σημαίνει τὴν ἡμέραν.

5 Proto-Indo-European Inflection of 'Dawn'

Once again, in order to solve the problem, we must go back to the PIE inflection of the animate s-stem *$h_2(e)us$-os-.

Since Schindler, the paradigm is reconstructed as a holodynamic type nom.sg. *h_2eus-$ós$, acc. *h_2eus-$ós$-$m̥$, gen. *h_2us-s-$és$, loc. *h_2us-$és$.[17] It underwent various remodellings and, in Indo-Iranian, a generalisation of the zero grade allomorph of the root (Ved. nom. uṣā́s, acc. uṣā́sam). The locative *h_2us-$és$-$Ø$ was recharacterised, hence *h_2us-$és$-i (Ved. uṣási). The old genitive *h_2us-s-$é/ós$ is still found in Ved. uṣás (three occurrences in the RV), and the weak stem *h_2us-s- is preserved in the dative and instrumental singular.[18]

This alternating paradigm was regularised in the individual languages. Greek generalised the strong stem of the nom.acc. and has a constant o grade for the suffix: *h_2eus-$ós$ > Dor. ἀϝώς, Ion. ἠώς, Lesb. αὔως, acc. *h_2eus-$ós$-$m̥$ > *ἄϝόα > Ion. ἠῶ, gen. *$h_2(e)us$-$ós$-os > *ἄϝόhος > Ion. ἠοῦς (as *h_2eus- and *h_2us- merge in Greek, the weak stem may have retained the inherited zero grade of the root, or reflect a full grade analogical after the strong stem), loc. *$h_2(e)us$-$ós$-i > *ἄϝόhï > Ion. ἠοῖ; the Attic inflection nom. ἕως, acc. ἕω, gen. ἕω, dat. ἕῳ is the result of quantitative metathesis, except for the gen.sg. which is analogical after the masculine type νεώς. In Italic too the strong stem was the basis of the derivative *h_2eus-$ōs$-eh_2 (Lat. aurōra). In Vedic, on the other hand, the e grade of the locative *h_2us-$és$-i > uṣási was extended to the accusative, hence uṣásam next to the older uṣā́sam (representing the etymological o grade), and to the dative uṣáse, the instrumental uṣásā, as well as to a new genitive uṣásas, replacing the old uṣás with zero grade of the suffix.[19] The acc.sg. uṣā́m (two occurrences in the RV) is no testimony of an old *-eh_2 derivative which could be compared with ἄα, but a secondary form analogical after the nom.sg. uṣā́s—as Sappho's Αὔων is analogical after the nom.sg. Αὔως.[20]

On this stem was built an r-derivative, well attested in most Indo-European languages (Lith. aušrà 'dawn', ONorse austr 'East'), which we find in Greek in the locative *αὖρι (*h_2us-r-i, Ved. usrí 'at dawn'):[21] the old form is preserved in

---

17 Schindler 1967.
18 NIL 357–367. See also on other forms Pinault 2019: 488–491.
19 Stüber 2002: 104–105.
20 Wackernagel, Ai. Gr. 1: 305.
21 Kiparsky 1967. The Baltic and Germanic forms imply a full grade *h_2eus-r-, Vedic a zero grade, and Greek is ambiguous. Most of the time, it shares with Vedic the ablaut variants, therefore I reconstruct here too a zero grade for Greek. But this has no consequence on the analysis of the form. The r-stem may originally be a delocatival form, see Pinault 2017: 646, and a survey of the literature in NIL: 364.

the compound αὐριβάτης 'who walks in the morning' (Aeschylus *fr.* 266)[22] and may be in αὐρίζειν· ῥιγοῦν. καὶ τὸ ἐς αὔριον ὑπερτίθεσθαι "αὐρίζειν: to shiver, and to postpone to the next day" (Hsch., α 8339) (only the second part τὸ ἐς αὔριον ὑπερτίθεσθαι is relevant). In Attic-Ionic it was resuffixed as αὔριον 'tomorrow', neuter because this is the default gender, appropriate for adverbs (see σήμερον 'today', σῆτες 'this year'). The *r*-derivative is found in other words in Greek (ἠήρ < *h_2us-er-*), which are not crucial for the point under examination.

Coming back to the *s*-stem *h_2us-ós-*, Greek generalised the strong stem in the name of 'dawn', as we said, but like Vedic, it preserves a trace of the original paradigm: the adverb ἀϝές of Hesychius' ἀεστητόν, independently of the proposed reading for the second element ?ἀὲς τ⟨ρί⟩τον, is the direct continuation of the endingless locative *h_2us-és-Ø* > *$auh\acute{e}s$* > *$\bar{a}ues$* 'at dawn'. It is one of the many examples of archaic forms driven out of the living paradigm because of an inflectional remodelling and lexicalised as adverbs. From the morphological point of view, we can compare the pair formed by the adverbial loc.sg. ἀϝές and the animate nom.sg. ἀϝώς with other similar ones:

loc. adv. ἀϝές (*h_2us-és-Ø*) nom. ἀϝώς
loc. adv. αἰϝέν (*$h_2(e)i\underset{\cdot}{u}$-én-Ø*) 'always' (Doric) nom. αἰϝών 'lifetime'[23]
†loc. *ἀγκέν (*h_2nk-én-Ø*) (ἐπηγκενίδες, wooden planks fitted on the ribs of the boat, ε 253) nom. ἀγκών 'curve of the arm'

Another pair of this type could be αἰϝές 'always' vs *αἰϝώς found in αἰῶ (Aeschylus, *Ag.* 229, *Ch.* 350) < *αἰϝόα, which lexicographers explain as an apocope of αἰῶνα. This could represent *$h_2ei\underset{\cdot}{u}$-és-Ø* vs *$h_2ei\underset{\cdot}{u}$-ós-m̥*. However, the authenticity of both αἰῶ and αἰϝές as an *s*-stem has been doubted by several scholars.[24]

---

22 Hsch., α 8338: αὐριβάτας· Αἰσχύλος τὸ αὐρὶ ἐπὶ τοῦ ταχέως τίθησι "αὐριβάτας: Aeschylus uses αὐρί in the meaning 'quickly'." The compound is usually translated 'walking quickly', and this is how Hesychius understands it, but the original meaning is 'early' rather than 'quickly'.

23 It has been proposed that αἰϝών is a new formation on the locative αἰϝέν < *$h_2ei\underset{\cdot}{u}$-én*, built with the locatival particle *-en*, so that the *n*-stem would be decasuative. See recently Pinault 2017: 645, with literature. That, however, does not change the picture: the derivation of αἰϝών from αἰϝέν implies that the latter was analysed as an endingless *e* grade locative, even if its origin is different. The radical *e* grade in *$h_2ei\underset{\cdot}{u}$-én* is secondary.

24 Klingenschmitt 1975: 78, followed by Meissner 2006: 150–151. Stüber 2002 does not include αἰές in her study, implying that it is not an old *s*-stem in Greek. On the other hand, Mayrhofer, *EWAia*, and Beekes, *EDG*, assume that αἰῶ is the reflex of *αἰϝόα and is a genuine *s*-stem, corresponding to Ved. *áyu-ṣ-* (neuter).

Greek also has a trace of the recharacterised locative *$h_2(e)us$-es-i in the compound ἠϊκανός· ὁ ἀλεκτρυών (Hsch., η 255), lit. 'singing at dawn', which must be the reflex of an older *ἠϝεϊκανός with contraction (see Hom. ἠριγένεια < ἠϝερι-).[25] It is not very likely that this form relies on a zero grade *$h_2(e)us$-s-i of the Vedic gen. uṣás type,[26] since the old locative had an e-grade suffix and Greek generalised the o-grade suffix, not the zero grade. Accordingly, *h_2us-$és$-i (= Ved. uṣási) or *$h_2(e)us$-os-i can be expected, but not *$h_2(e)us$-s-i. This first element ἠϊ- must rather be the Ionic form matching ἀϝές, and Greek would preserve here both the most archaic form with zero ending and the recharacterised locative. From the semantic point of view, the locative is the expected case for 'singing at dawn'.

The sequences *-u̯s- and *-su̯- are variously reflected in Greek dialects: Thessalian and Lesbian have a diphthong (αὔως < *au̯sōs, ναῦος < *nasu̯os) while other dialects have a compensatory lengthening (Doric, Boeotian and Arcado-Cyprian ἆϝως, Ionic ἠϝώς). The details of the phonetic evolution of *-u̯s- will be examined below. Anyway, ᾱϝές is the expected phonetic outcome in Boeotian.

In that type of endingless locative, the accent was on the suffix, hence ἀϝές—the oxytone type of Hesychius' corrupt ἀεστητόν is not reliable. We have little information on Boeotian accentuation, but non-epigraphic sources (Aristophanes, Acharn. 860 sqq, Corinna) seem to show that Boeotian did not have a systematic barytonesis like Lesbian.[27]

From the semantic point of view, that a word meaning 'at dawn' (locative) should evolve into 'tomorrow' is trivial, and this is precisely the case of *αὖρι/αὔριον—compare also German Morgen 'morning' → morgen 'tomorrow', Pol. jutro 'tomorrow', from CSl. utro 'morning' (Ru. utro 'morning') and many others. This happens when 'at dawn', not necessarily determined, becomes contextually determined, hence 'at this (next) dawn', that is, 'tomorrow'. This old adverb was preserved in Aeolic, at least in Boeotian, whereas it was replaced by αὔριον in Attic-Ionic, except in the compound ἠϊκανός. In Doric it may have been eliminated, maybe because of the homonymy with ἀές (Ar., Lys. 1266, also known from Herodian) < αἰές 'always'—at least we have no trace of it.

Thus, the Hesychian gloss ἀεστητόν, however corrupt the second part may be, preserves a very archaic piece of Indo-European morphology, which should find its due place in handbooks of historical linguistics. If the proposed hypothesis is correct, it should be read ἀὲς τ⟨ρί⟩τον 'the day after tomorrow'. Now as an adverb, ἀές has no gender. Therefore, any modifier will receive the default

---

26 Pace Beekes, EDG, who reconstructs *awhi.
27 Probert 2006: 73.

gender, which is neuter (τ⟨ρί⟩τον), as is the case for αὔριον. The ordinal modifier confirms that the adverb was determined, as it cannot mean 'at a third dawn' but only 'at the third dawn (from now)'.

6 Boeotian ἀϝές, Zenodotus' ἄϝας and Sappho's *αὖα

We now are on firmer ground to examine the various forms mentioned above.

The adverb ἀϝές is reliable, because it has a straightforward etymology and a regular morphology, preserving a very old endingless locative, next to the recharacterised form ἠϊκανός. What about ἄας? It has the same etymology, but cannot go back directly to any old inflectional form of 'dawn'. There is no evidence in Greek for a resuffixation in *-eh_2, as in Italic, and such a resuffixation would imply a contraction. Indeed, there is a rather simple way of accounting for ἄας. As an adverb, ἀϝές 'at dawn' was opposed to ἑσπέρας 'in the evening', a genitive referring to the period of time.[28] There are many examples of influence between members of an antonymic pair, which leads to levelling either in the ending or in the stem, for instance in the adverb ὄπισθεν instead of ὄπιθεν after πρόσθεν. Thus, a remodelling of ἀϝές into ἀϝᾶς after ἑσπέρας would not be extremely surprising: ἀϝές was isolated, whereas ἑσπέρας was morphologically motivated, which may have helped.[29] The result is Zenodotus' ἄϝᾱς.

Now such a form would be in Lesbian αὖας: this is precisely the form attributed to Sappho, which we can now explain. As said above, firstly, the only forms of 'dawn' attested in Sappho's poetry inflect according to the old s-stem, not to an alleged ā-stem, secondly, the nominative αὔα (Apollonius Dyscolus) or αὖα (*Et. Magnum*) is not the form found in Sappho, but the quotation form, and may have been created by grammarians. The solution to this problem is that, next to the substantive αὔως 'dawn', Sappho had an adverb αὖας 'at dawn', remodelling of the old ἀϝές after ἑσπέρας, and showing of course Lesbian barytonesis. Both words were used by Sappho, but they belong to different parts of speech, substantive and adverb. As a matter of fact, Apollonius Dyscolus quotes this αὖα in his treatise *On adverbs*, which probably means that he correctly took αὖας

---

28   'Evening' is masculine in Indo-European languages and in Greek, too. The feminine ἑσπέρᾱ, analogical after ἡμέρᾱ, is attested in various Greek dialects and is not specific to Attic-Ionic. For instance, an inscription from Calydon (Aitolia), from the 6th c. BCE, has πο⟨τ'⟩ ἑσπέρᾱς 'to the west' (*IG* IX, 1² 1:152, c), coupled with ποτ' ἄϝος 'to the east' (*IG* IX, 1² 1:152, a).

29   Kiparsky 1992 assumes the directionality of analogical change reflects a process of optimisation: a motivated form (which is analysable in synchrony) will influence an unmotivated one, not the other way round.

as an adverb, and adduced the fictitious αὔα only as a way of explaining the adverb αὔας, implying that this adverb must be a genitive singular, like ἑσπέρας, hence the idea of a change of inflectional type (μεταπλασμός). But this has been misunderstood by lexicographers, this is why the *Et. Magnum* quotes the form as an existing word. Greek grammarians quoted the form using the quotation form, that is, the nominative which could correspond to this αὔας—and there are two, αὔα (Ap. Dysc.) and αὖα (*Et. Magnum*). Thus, αὔα is a ghost-word, there probably never existed in Lesbian any such substantive meaning 'dawn' next to αὔως: there was in Lesbian poetry an adverb αὔας, matching Boeotian ἀϝές which is more archaic, and from this adverb grammarians wrongly extrapolated a set of inflectional forms, according to their usual practice, which we should not follow. Thus disappears the supposed match with Latin *aurora*, as well as the only hypothetic example of contraction of οᾱ > ᾱ in Lesbian, and so should disappear the lemma ἄα (ἡ) in the *LfgrE*.

Therefore two other criteria are met: the metrical one (ἄας/αὔας is not a case of contraction, therefore Zenodotus' reading is metrically regular) and the linguistic one (ἀϝές is morphologically regular, albeit extremely archaic, and the remodelling into ἄας can be accounted for). There is no doubt Zenodotus' reading is the older one.

The question that arises now is the following. Lesbian poetry (maybe not the Lesbian vernacular) had αὔας, which is indirectly attested through the testimony of Apollonius Dyscolus. Zenodotus' ἄϝᾱς, with compensatory lengthening, is not Lesbian, although the form shows Lesbian barytonesis (but this feature may have been imposed afterwards, since it is unlikely Zenodotus' text had accentual marks). Neither is it Thessalian. This form cannot be Ionic either, because of the preserved ᾱ (the Ionic form is found in ἠϊκανός). It could be Boeotian, as Hesychius' gloss says, but this is unlikely for two reasons. The first one is that there is no characteristic Boeotian form in Homer: the only specific Boeotian forms (that is, Boeotian as opposed to Thessalo-Lesbian) are in fact archaisms preserved only in Boeotian, but which in Homer go back to Proto-Greek and not to Boeotian,[30] and indeed *ἄϝές would belong to this category. The second one is that Hesychius ἀεστητόν shows that Boeotian had *ᾱϝές. Of course, one could object that Boeotian was not homogenous and that some Boeotian dialects may have had the archaic *e* grade *ᾱϝές while others had the remodelled *ᾱϝᾱς. That would explain why Hesychius has the mention Βοιωτοί for both ἄας (ἄας· ἐς αὔριον Βοιωτοί) and ἀεστητόν (ἀεστητόν· αὔριον. Βοιωτοί). However, this indication is not reliable, for the transmitted text of the *Lexicon*

---

30 Wathelet 1970: 371–372.

mixes different glosses, and the mention Βοιωτοί for ἄας most likely comes from either *ἀές or ἀεστητόν/?ἀὲς τ⟨ρί⟩τον, together with the *addendum* οἱ δὲ εἰς τρίτην. Therefore, if we eliminate Boeotian as the source of ἄας, the most likely hypothesis is that Zenodotus' form is an Achaean word.

That would lead to the following scenario. Greek inherited the locative *auhés* 'at dawn', together with the recharacterised *auhés-i*. As the paradigm of 'dawn' was remodelled on the strong stem, this form was expelled from the paradigm and lexicalised as an adverb preserved in Aeolic (Boeotian *ᾱϝές in ἀεστητόν), and in Achaean. In Proto-Attic-Ionic, this adverb was eliminated by αὔριον in the meaning 'tomorrow', and by the derived adverb ἠῶθεν (see below) in the meaning 'at dawn', and survives only as a fossil in the compound ἠϊκανός. However, Achaean *ᾱϝές survived in epic diction in contexts where it could not be replaced by αὔριον. Αὔριον cannot be used before a consonant, and in the *Iliad* it is always used at the beginning of the line except once (Θ 538), as is ἠῶθεν. Therefore we can expect to find the old adverbial locative preserved at the beginning of the line, which is the favourite position for αὔριον, and before a consonant, where αὔριον is impossible: such is the case in Θ 470 (Zenodotus # ἄας δή, vulgate # ἠοῦς δή). There probably was a complementary metrical distribution between prevocalic αὔριον [– ᴗ ᴗ] and preconsonantal *ᾱϝές [– –], of which we can only see a dim trace thanks to Zenodotus.

The adverb was known to Aeolic, and in Lesbian at least it was analogically remodelled after its antonym ἐσπέρᾱς, hence the adverb αὔᾱς which lies under the transmitted αὔα in Sappho, instead of the expected *αὔες 'tomorrow', matching Boeotian ᾱϝές. Zenodotus' ἄας probably results from a contamination of the old Achaean ᾱϝές by the Lesbian adverb αὔᾱς, or from a remodelling of the former after the latter. The initial stress is probably analogical after αὔᾱς, which shows Lesbian barytonesis: if Zenodotus' text was not accented, it is likely the accent was assigned by Aristarchus, who identified the form as Aeolic. In the context of Θ 470 this transformation was not necessary, because the old *ᾱϝές, if it was the original form in # *ᾱϝὲς δή, would yield a metrically correct line, since *ᾱϝές and *ᾱϝᾱς are equivalent before a consonant. However, what makes it unnecessary is precisely what makes it possible, and the older form could be Aeolicised only because that did not alter metre. Whereas *ᾱϝές was completely isolated, at least ἄας was similar to a real form in a living dialect, and thereby no longer isolated.

Now this has an important consequence: if *ᾱϝές, partly Aeolicised into ἄας, is indeed Achaean and was not transmitted through Aeolic (because it does not show the characteristic diphthongisation of *-*uh*- in Thessalo-Lesbian), it follows that we have to admit a direct transmission from the Achaean epic tradition to the Ionic epic tradition (see below, pp. 126–128).

7 Ἄας δή and ἠοῦς δή

This form ἄας, remodelling of *ἀές, is originally a locative, and its function is to express location in time, as in ἠϊκανός: if ἄας, or *ἀές, is the older reading in Θ 470, the syntactic problem caused by the genitive of time disappears. It was from the start dissyllabic: the problem of the abnormal contraction in the name of dawn vanishes. Thus, Zenodotus' reading is on both accounts better than the vulgate's ἠοῦς, which is a secondary Ionicisation, made at the cost of a metrical oddity and a syntactic irregularity. Of course, ἠοῦς was transparent for an Ionian audience, which explains why it was introduced instead of the obscure ἀές/ἄας. However, since the meaning is that of a locative 'at dawn', one would expect rather a replacement by the dative ἠοῖ, and not by the genitive ἠοῦς: compare for instance N 794 # ἠοῖ τῇ προτέρῃ 'the day before, at dawn'.

The problem of the genitive can be solved in the following way. Usually 'at dawn' is expressed by ἠῶθεν, an adverb built with the ablatival morpheme -θεν.[31] Forms in -θεν were used by epic singers as a metrical variant of the genitive: οὐρανόθεν (Α 195 etc.), ἀπ' οὐρανόθεν (Θ 365, Φ 199), ἐξ οὐρανόθεν (Θ 19, Θ 21, P 548), ἐξ οὐρανοῦ (Ζ 108) 'from the sky' are used according to metrical needs. Similarly, the adverb Ἰλιόθεν 'from Ilion' (ἔπλεεν Ἰλιόθεν Ξ 251) commutes with the genitive ἐξ Ἰλίου (Β 230), and Ἰλιόθι πρό # 'in front of Ilion' (Θ 561) with # Ἰλίου προπάροιθε (Χ 6). The parallelism between ἠῶθεν, Ἰλιόθεν, οὐρανόθεν includes the other adverbial form ἠῶθι πρό #, Ἰλιόθι πρό #, with a locative meaning, which was the model of οὐρανόθι πρό # (Γ 3). On that account, ἠῶθεν could be analysed

---

[31] Ἠῶθεν, Att. ἕωθεν is of course not built from the nominative stem (*pace* Chantraine, *Gr. hom.* I: 242–243), but is either built with the allomorph -οθεν abstracted from thematic forms (*ἠϝόh-οθεν > ἑῶθεν > ἕωθεν, with regular reflex of ηοο > ηō > εω as in the thematic genitive λεώ, νεώ < *ληϝόο, *νηϝόο: Stüber 2002: 105), or results from a remodelling of the expected *ἠϝόσθεν, *ἑῶσθεν after the synchronic stem ἕω- (Att. nom. ἕως, acc. ἕω, gen. ἕω, dat. ἕῳ, with secondary integration into the thematic declension for the oblique cases, adjective ἕῳος 'of the dawn', ἕωλος 'of yesterday'). The series of local adverbs ἑτέρωθεν, ἑκατέρωθεν, ἀμφοτέρωθεν, ἄνωθεν, κάτωθεν, ἔξωθεν could provide a model for -ωθεν. Herodotus has the adjective ἑωθινός, which Wackernagel 1916: 104 considers an Atticism, but the Hippocratic corpus has only ἕωθεν, which could plead for a genuine Ionic form. Doric ἀϝθεν (Theocritus, Id. 15.132) is the mere Doricisation of the Homeric adverb and is not significant. Alcman has the theonym Ἀώτῑ (Partheneion, *fr.* 1.87 Page, dat.sg.) which implies a stem ἀϝω-: as it cannot be the outcome of either *ἀϝοh-ο-τι-, which would be morphologically abnormal, or *ἀϝοσ-τι- which would yield *ἄοστις, it means that from the nom.sg. ἀϝώς was abstracted a stem ἀϝω- which became both an inflectional base (acc.sg. Αὔων in Sappho) and a derivational base. This could account for Hom. ἠῶθεν, Ion.Att. ἕωθεν, better than the assumption that the etymon is *ἠϝόh-οθεν, since the allomorph -οθεν is not productive in Attic (adverbs in -οθεν on an athematic base are not attested).

as a variant of the genitive ἠοῦς, and could be substituted by ἠοῦς when metre required it: this proportion οὐρανόθεν : οὐρανοῦ :: Ἰλιόθεν : Ἰλίου :: ἠῶθεν : *x* = ἠοῦς is a purely morphological proportion, it does not take into account semantics and leads to the incongruity that ἠοῦς can be used as an equivalent of ἠῶθεν despite the incompatibility between 'dawn' and the genitive of time. This is what we have in Θ 470, where ἠοῦς used as a variant of ἠῶθεν replaced the older ἀές/ἄας, metrically identical. Thus, it is not surprising that the D scholia have in Θ 470 ἠοῦς· ἔωθεν. ὄρθρου. τῇ ἐπιούσῃ ἡμέρᾳ (ΖΥQΤ). This abnormal use of ἠοῦς with the meaning 'at dawn' is not a spontaneous evolution of the language, it does not belong to the living dialect of Ionian singers, but it was created by the specific conditions of epic diction to provide a metrical variant for ἠῶθεν, and remains artificial. Ὄρθρου may also have provided a model.

The new ἠοῦς early eliminated the old adverb: ἄας is mentioned neither in the D scholia, nor in Apollonius' *Lexicon homericum*, nor in Apion's *Glossai homerikai*, both from the first c. CE—although for the latter one so little survives that this is not very significant. Only Hesychius has not only a trace of it, but also of the Boeotian form in which the solution lies.

As for δένδρει/δενδρέῳ, the problem in ἄας/ἠοῦς is caused by modernisation in the vulgate: this is the opposite of the traditional view which sees in δένδρει and ἄας corrections introduced by Zenodotus to repair a lame line. His readings in both cases are better than the vulgate's not because they are emendations, but simply because they are the older ones. The innovation is on the side of the vulgate, which introduced alterations meant to eliminate forms deemed un-Homeric (δένδρει, ἄας), and creating an irregularity because of that modernisation. And since ἄας ultimately goes back to an Achaean form, it is better to assume that Zenodotus read it in his working text than to hypothesise he imported it from another copy while his own text had ἠοῦς. He would have had no reason to do so since ἠοῦς was clear, unless we follow Van der Valk in assuming that his taste for rare words was the driving force behind his variant readings. He did not have the linguistic tools to evaluate ἄας as an old form better than ἠοῦς. All he could do was a synchronic analysis identifying ἄας as Boeotian, and we can doubt this was enough to justify its introduction into his text at the expense of another reading.

Here again our three criteria are met: the philological one (Zenodotus' form is confirmed by Sappho's αὔας and by Hesychius ἀὲς τ⟨ρί⟩τον), the linguistic one (this old locative is morphologically regular in PIE morphology, its remodelling into *ἀϝᾶς can be accounted for, and an adverbialised locative is syntactically regular in this line), and the metrical one (the only instance of unresolvable contraction in that word is eliminated).

8   Θ 525

Let us now come back to the second occurrence of ἠοῦς 'at dawn' in Θ 523–527.

ὧδ' ἔστω Τρῶες μεγαλήτορες ὡς ἀγορεύω·
μῦθος δ' ὃς μὲν νῦν ὑγιὴς εἰρημένος ἔστω,
τὸν δ' ἠοῦς Τρώεσσι μεθ' ἱπποδάμοις ἀγορεύσω.
ἔλπομαι εὐχόμενος Διί τ' ἄλλοισίν τε θεοῖσιν
ἐξελάαν ἐνθένδε κύνας κηρεσσιφορήτους

> Let it be thus, high-hearted men of Troy, as I tell you. Let that word that has been spoken now be a strong one, with that which I speak at dawn to the Trojans, breakers of horses. For in good hope I pray to Zeus and the other immortals that we may drive from our place these dogs swept into destruction.[32]
> R.L.

Line 523 was not suspected and there is no reason to suspect it. Lines 524–525, on the other hand, were athetised by Aristarchus, as we learn from scholion A:

> (Aristonicus) ἀθετοῦνται δύο στίχοι, διότι τῇ ἑξῆς οὐδὲν λέγει καὶ τὸ ὑποτακτικὸν ἄρθρον ἀντὶ προτακτικοῦ παρείληπται, ὃς μέν (524) ἀντὶ τοῦ ὁ μέν.

> two lines are athetised because he does not say anything the next day and because the postpositive article [*that is, the relative,* CLF] is used instead of the prepositive one [*that is, the plain article,* CLF], ὃς μέν instead of ὁ μέν.

The condemnation relies on two arguments, the logical coherence of the narration, and the use of the article.[33] Both are justified, and one could add with Kirk that these lines display other oddities.[34] This is the only occurrence of ὑγιής in Homer, and it is not applied to an animate with its proper meaning 'in good health', but, in a metaphoric meaning 'sound', to an inanimate (μῦθος), which is not attested before Thucydides—Solon, Simonides, Aesop use ὑγιής only for

---

32   Lines 526–528 are considered interpolated (West 1999: 189).
33   See Schironi 2004: 81.
34   Kirk 1990: 337 "they certainly look like a loose elaboration of 523;" ibid. 337 "ὑγιής of a μῦθος [...] is peculiar;" ibid. 338 "even so the style is clumsy." Kelly 2007: 400 does not comment on the lines.

animates. Another oddity is the perfect passive imperative εἰρημένος ἔστω, also abnormal in the Homeric corpus, clearly induced by ὧδ' ἔστω of line 523, lacking any parallel and semantically awkward (?"let it have been said"). Yet another one is that if the construction is τὸν δ' ἠοῦς 'that of tomorrow', parallel with ὃς μὲν νῦν 'that of today',[35] ἠοῦς is not a genitive of time, but a possessive genitive, and this use of the article to substantivate a possessive genitive has no parallel in Homer and must be considered an Atticism. Modern translators do not agree on the construction of these lines, which pose several problems.

One may hear in these lines a distant echo of δ 214–215:

[…] μῦθοι δὲ καὶ ἠῶθέν περ ἔσονται ǁ Τηλεμάχῳ καὶ ἐμοὶ διαειπέμεν ἀλλήλοισιν.

there'll be stories too, from daybreak on, for Telemachus and me to tell completely to each other.
J.H.

However, although the context is similar (the speaker ceases for the time being and postpones the discussion or the discourse to the following day), and although there are many common elements (μῦθος/μῦθοι, ἠοῦς/ἠῶθεν, future ἀγορεύσω/ἔσονται, dative of the addressee Τρώεσσι/Τηλεμάχῳ), the structure of both is not directly comparable, and that of δ 214–215 is clear.

That lines 524–525 are recent is not a matter of dispute. And the consequence is that ἠοῦς in line 525 is not old either. There is no *varia lectio* transmitted for that line. The use of ἠοῦς with unresolvable contraction in a recent line, if it must be analysed as a genitive of time, which is not certain, implies that ἠοῦς is used as a variant of ἠῶθεν (see above, pp. 119–120). And if it is not a genitive of time but a possessive genitive meaning 'of tomorrow', it is clearly modelled after ἠοῦς 'tomorrow' in Θ 470. That implies that this same ἠοῦς had already replaced ἄας in Θ 470. At any rate, this occurrence is secondary. Of course, the fact that it appears a second time in the Homeric corpus with the same meaning 'tomorrow' backs the occurrence of Θ 470. Likewise, the fact that Hesiod, *Op.* 583 had δενδρέῳ ἐφεζόμενοι as Γ 152 backs the vulgate's reading and marginalises Zenodotus', although it is the older one.

---

35 There is a *varia lectio* μῦθος δ' ὃς μὲν δή, mentioned in the D scholia (ZYQ), which does not make the text much better.

9 Chronology and Phonetic Evolution

The Proto-Greek etymon of 'dawn' is *$au̯sōs$. This yields *$au̯hōs$, reflected in Thessalo-Lesbian as αὔως and in other dialects as ᾱϝώς (> Ionic ἠϝώς). The reflex of intervocalic -$u̯s$- is identical with that of intervocalic -$su̯$- (*$nasu̯os$ > Thess.Lesb. ναῦος, elswhere νᾱϝός), which implies that there was either a metathesis of -$u̯h$- > -$hu̯$- (Kiparsky)[36] or a stage when both merged into an aspirate ϝh. Now the diphthong in the outcome of these sequences is not limited to Thessalo-Lesbian, but is also found once in Arcadian, in the demotic Ἐχευή-θεις < *Ἐχεσϝήθεες (Pausanias 8.45.1), which, as an ethnonym, is probably old since this category is rather conservative. As Arcadian also has sporadic traces of the geminate outcome for sequences -sR-, -Rs- with a sonorant (ἔκριννᾰν IG v, 2. 343, Orchomenos, ca. 360–350 BCE), Ruipérez proposed that the geminate was the first stage of the evolution in all Greek dialects, that this archaic stage was preserved in the peripheral dialects (Thessalo-Lesbian in the North, notoriously archaic Arcadian in the Peloponnesian mountains), whereas the geminate was simplified in central dialects with a compensatory lengthening (Arcadian except for a few remnants with the old geminate,[37] Attic-Ionic, Doric, Boeotian which developed closer to the centre than Thessalo-Lesbian).[38]

For liquids and nasals, the theory that all Greek dialects went through a stage with a geminate is widely accepted now, although not unanimously. Scholars have tried to guess what the situation was in Mycenaean: the Mycenaean syllabary does not have the means to transcribe a geminate consonant. Special syllabograms like ro$_2$ and ra$_2$ may transcribe a geminate /rr/ (ku-pa-ro$_2$ = /kuparr'os/, a-ke-ra$_2$-te = /agerrantes/), but ra$_2$ and ro$_2$ can also transcribe a palatalised /r'/ (kupar'os) not necessarily geminated (me-re-ti-ra$_2$ = /meletr'ai/, alternating with me-re-ti-ri-ja = /meletria/). The fact that ro$_2$ and ra$_2$ reflect both sequences *Rj and *Rs could mean that the pronunciation was identical, which would imply a geminate (and this is what is usually assumed),[39] but it is also possible that Mycenaean scribes, having at their disposal a limited inventory of syllabograms, did with what they had and used the same syllabogram for similar but not identical sounds—the argument is not decisive.[40]

---

36 Kiparsky 1967: 623–624.
37 Of course we have no information for Cyprian since the older inscriptions are written by means of a syllabary which does not transcribe geminates or vowel length.
38 Ruipérez 1972. Accepted for Ἐχευήθεις by Dubois 1986: 58.
39 See for instance Hajnal 2006: 257 *sqq*; García Ramón 2016: 217.
40 Bernabé–Lujan 2020: 178 argue for preserved intervocalic Rh sequences, at least for nasals, yet p. 177 "En micénico es probable—aunque no demostrable—que tengamos la situación

At any rate, the spelling a-ke-ra₂-te implies that the /r/ was not the regular /r/, but probably a geminate /rr/ or aspirate /rh/: this means that the compensatory lengthening (hereafter CL) was not acquired yet, since compensatory lengthening is the result of the elimination of the long consonant /rr/ or /rh/. Ruijgh sought to dismiss a-ke-ra₂-te as displaying a reverse spelling: Mycenaean scribes would have hesitated because in their prononciation /rr/, /rh/ had merged with simple /r/, and would occasionally have used ro₂ and ra₂ where it was not justified. At that cost, he can maintain that CL is an "already accomplished fact[s] in Mycenaean."[41] The objection is that those alleged reverse spellings are found only in words for which we know there was a consonant cluster, and that the few Arcadian cases with a geminate consonant are impossible to explain if CL was already acquired in Mycenaean.[42]

---

de líquida aspirada inicial, y geminada intervocálica." Bartoněk 2003: 147 assumes that the first compensatory lengthening is already acquired. Hajnal 2006 is extremely cautious for liquids and nasals (p. 288 *sqq*), but for /w/, he assumes a geminate /ww/ (p. 237). Rau 2018: 384 leaves the question open.

41   See Ruijgh 2011: 271.

42   Ruijgh's example pi-ra-me-no (KN E 36), a personal name understood /Phīlamenos/, aorist participle of φιλέω representing *b^hil-sa-mh_1no-* is hardly decisive, since the interpretation is far from certain. The sigmatic aorist finds support in the aorist (ἐ)φίλατο (Ε 61, Υ 304). But a personal noun based on a middle aorist participle of an atelic verb meaning 'to love' is unexpected, to say the least: first millenium Greek anthroponymy has only the verbal adjective Φίλητος or the present participles Φιλουμενός (attested first in Athens, 4th c. BCE), Φιλουμένη (several instances in the 4th c. BCE), Φιλήμενος (Magna Graecia, 4th c. BCE), and similarly for the quasi-synonyms Ἀγάπητος, Ἀγαπωμενός, Ἔραστος, Ἐράστη, Ἐρωμένη, Ἐρῶσα, in agreement with the meaning of those verbs. No personal name is formed on the aorist participle. From the semantic point of view, this is easily understandable: one can name a child "Beloved" or "Loving" (Ἐρῶσα), hardly "who has fallen in love", "who has loved." The stative meaning of the verb is the reason why the aorist participle is intrinsically implausible for a proper noun: the only forms that can be used as anthroponyms are either the verbal adjective, which is neutral from the aspectual point of view, or the present participle, which expresses the durative meaning associated to the permanent quality of the person so named. Middle aorist participles are found in anthroponymy, but they are not frequent and they are, as expected, built on telic verbs: Τεισαμενός is the only frequent one in the classical period, Ἐπιλυσαμενός is attested in Athens in the 5th c., Δεξαμενός is attested twice (Chios, 5th c. and Thespies, 3rd c.), and Ἀλεξαμενός (several occurrences in Delphi in the 3rd c.), much less frequent than the older present participle Ἀλεξομενός attested from the 6th c. on, is probably an epicisation of the latter after the infinitive ἀλέξασθαι (N 475)—as Ἀμυναμενός (Hell.) is a modification of the older Ἀμυνομενός. In epic anthroponymy, Ἀκεσσαμενός (Φ 142) is built on a telic verb. And there is no reason to believe that second-millenium anthroponymy followed different principles from first-millenium anthroponymy. So that, if pi-ra-me-no is not /Phīlamenos/ < *b^hil-sa-mh_1no-, Ruijgh's argument can be discarded. As a consequence, we may assume that

As far as the sequence -u̯s- is concerned, it is not clear whether Mycenaean had a geminate /ww/: the famous "tripod tablet" PY Ta 641 spells ti-ri-o-we, qe-to-ro-we, a-no-we for 'with three/four/no handle(s)'. The second element of those compounds is the name of the ear, and can be reconstructed as an s-stem *-ou̯s-es-, an old formation which has an exact match in Slavic. In Greek, as in most languages, geminate consonants are admitted only word-internally, and distributed between two syllables. When the geminate is a semi-vowel, it coalesces into a diphthong with the preceding vowel. Now u-diphthongs /eu/, /au/, /ou/ are consistently written in Mycenaean (a-ro-u-ra = ἄρουρα 'arable land', ke-ka-u-me-no = κεκαυμένος 'burnt', e-re-u-te-ro = ἐλεύθερος 'free'): a geminate *ŏu̯u̯es would result in a diphthong /ou.wes/, and we would expect the spelling *ti-ri-o-u-we, *qe-to-ro-u-we, *a-no-u-we, unless we assume a special rule that u-diphthongs are consistently written except before /w/.[43] A derivative of 'dawn' also illustrates this spelling, the anthroponym a-wo-i-jo (KN Dv 1462.B, PY Cn 599) = /Awhohijos/ or /Ahwohijos/ 'of the dawn', and not *a-u-wo-i-jo. Similarly, pa-ra-wa-jo (PY Sh 737) = /parawhajjo/, name of the piece of the helmet which protects the ears, has no diphthong. The spelling ti-ri-o-we, a-wo-i-jo etc. shows that the /w/ is syllable initial and not in the coda: that implies, if there was a geminate, that the syllabification was tri.o.wwes, a.wwo.hi.jos, which is unlikely since tautosyllabic geminates are unknown. Peters[44] objects that there is no diphthong written in te-o-jo = /tʰehojjo/ (θεοῖο 'of the god'), although we know that there was one, but this objection is not valid since i-diphthongs are not written in Mycenaean except in two cases, through the special syllabograms a₃ for initial /#ai/ and ra₃ for /rai/, none of which is attested before a yod. There was in Knossos an attempt to write i-diphthongs (ko-to-i-na (KN Uf 1031) vs ko-to-na = /ktoinā/ 'land lot', wo-i-ko-de (KN As 1519.11) vs

---

Mycenaean had a long consonant or a palatalised consonant, not yet reduced to a regular simple sonorant, therefore, it had no CL.

43   A case like e-u-wa-ko-ro PY Jn 431, next to e-wa-ko-ro KN V 1005 (Εὔαγρος), quoted by Morpurgo 1972: 94, does not have a true diphthong, but represents [ehu] or [eü] (*h₁su-), followed by a glide; o-u-wo-ze 'does not work' PY Ep 704 has an etymological /u̯/ but may still have a hiatus [o.u], since the negation is from *h₂oi̯u- (cf. a-pe-e-ke = /e-hē-ke/ from *Hi̯eh₁-), although this is not very likely. At any rate, there is a morpheme boundary between /o(h)u/ and /worzei/, so that the case is not strictly speaking comparable with that of stem-internal -su̯- sequences, but it shows that the spelling V-u-wV was not unusual. The spelling e-wa-ko-ro is of the same type as ti-ri-o-we and may transcribe /eh.wagros/ or /e.hwagros/, with the consonantal allophone *h₁su̯-V- across the morpheme boundary.

44   Peters 1986: 306, n. 8.

wo-ko-de (TH Of 36.2) = /woikonde/ 'to the house'), but this is not systematic.[45] Thus, the fact that a geminate /jj/ is not written cannot back the hypothesis that a geminate /ww/ would not be either: the syllabary did not have the means to write a geminate /jj/, but could write a geminate /ww/ since u-diphthongs are consistently written.

Be that as it may, the Arcadian demotic Ἐχευήθεις with gemination and no compensatory lengthening implies that Mycenaean did not have CL for sequences -$u̯h$- and -$hu̯$-. If CL was already effective in the 13th c. BCE, there is no way a form with a geminate could be preserved in the first millenium in a dialect which belongs to the same group as Mycenaean Greek. Therefore, whether Mycenaean had a geminate -$u̯u̯$- or still a sequence -$u̯h$-, simplification of -$u̯u̯$- or -$u̯h$- with CL must be post-Mycenaean.

The consequence for ἆϝές/ἆας/αὖας is clear: since CL is post-Mycenaean and since the form ἆϝές/ἆας with non Ionic CL cannot have been introduced into epic diction from Thessalo-Lesbian because this dialect group does not have CL but gemination, it follows that ἆϝές/ἆας with non Ionic CL is a post-Mycenaean Achaean form. That is to say, it implies that post-Linear B forms of Arcado-Cyprian type could find their way into the epics without going through Aeolic, and that "Achaean" is not a synonym of Linear B Mycenaean, but includes post-Linear B forms of the same dialect. This is impossible within the framework of the phase theory, which assumes there was no contact between Achaean and Ionic, but that all Achaean forms were transmitted through Aeolic. The only way to explain ἆϝές/ἆας in Homer is to assume a direct contact between Achaean and Ionic after the fall of the palatial world: only the diffusionist model can account for this form.[46] It implies that this contact was maintained down to after the first wave of compensatory lengthenings and after the raising of ᾱ > η in Ionic: ἆϝές did not become *ἤϝές because the line-initial adverbial phrase to which it belongs (*ἆϝὲς δή, before the trihemimeral caesura) was borrowed from an Achaean singer after the change took place in Ionic.

Archaeology in the last decades has demonstrated that the collapse of the palatial system was not the end of Mycenaean civilisation, which persisted, reduced to a lesser scale and without the centralised palatial system, in the Peloponnese, Attica, Euboea.[47] During the LH IIIC post-palatial period,[48]

---

45 Hajnal 2006: 45.
46 For a survey of the arguments for and against the diffusionist theory, see Jones 2012.
47 Lemos 2014. Snodgrass 2000: 365–367.
48 Late Helladic IIIC (LH IIIC) is the period that follows the palatial period, from 1200 to

conditions were met for a direct transmission of Achaean epic poems to Proto-Ionic on the Saronic gulf coast, in Attica and Euboea. The likely consequence was the development of a new variant of the epic diction, mixing Proto-Ionic features with Late Achaean ones (that is, post-Linear B Achaean). Besides, the Mycenaean outposts in Asia Minor were not abandoned: on sites like Miletus or Rhodes, where important Mycenaean settlements have been discovered, recent archaeological findings also suggest that there was a continuity, that the sites were not abandoned after 1200—and their population may have increased after the arrival of people from the Peloponnese in the post-palatial period. Rhodes in particular was prosperous during LH IIIC and had clear links with Argolid.[49] Speakers of Proto-Ionic settling in Miletus were thus in contact with Sub-Mycenaean or Post-Mycenaean cultural traditions, including the epic tradition, maybe under a more archaic form in terms of language than in the Peloponnese if we apply here the pattern of a conservative periphery. Of course, Mycenaeans in Asia Minor were in contact with the oriental world and influenced by it, so that their epic tradition could incorporate many motives and even formulae translated from Luwian or Lycian.[50] However, this probably had no real bearing on the language of the epic. Thus, both on the mainland and in Asia Minor, the material conditions made a diffusion of the epic tradition from Achaean to Proto-Ionic possible.

Against this background, it is not surprising to find a form implying a direct contact between the Achaean epic tradition and the Proto-Ionic one.

Let us now test the hypothesis of an Aeolic origin, assuming the Aeolic form was subsequently Ionicised, as the phase model says most Aeolic forms were. Lesbian has an adverb αὔας with the expected geminate. First, Ionicisation is unlikely because Ionic did not have an equivalent, since the Ionic form was αὔριον, and the phase model assumes that Aeolic forms which had no Ionic equivalent were kept unchanged. In that case, we should find αὔας. Secondly, in view of the pairs ἠϝώς/αὔως 'dawn', νηϝός/ναῦος 'shrine, temple', παρειαί, καλλιπάρῃος/παραύαι 'cheek', with a clear correspondence -αυ-/-ηϝ- for usual words, the only possible Ionicisation of the Lesbian form αὔας would yield *ἠϝᾶς, not

---

roughly 1100 BCE. It was followed by the short Sub-Mycenaean period which marks the transition from Late Bronze Age to Early Iron Age. Real changes in the society (new burial practices, destruction of sites or abandon) do not appear before the Sub-Mycenaean period (Lemos 2006: 87). For a recent survey, see Middleton 2020.

49 See Karantzali 2008: 78, with references.
50 See Bachvarova 2016.

*ἆϝᾱς. Those are two reasons to consider that the form cannot have been transmitted through Thessalo-Lesbian.[51]

Therefore the only option is to assume a post-Linear B Achaean CL, and a direct contact between the Late Achaean epic tradition and the Proto-Ionic one since the form was not passed on through Aeolic. Rather than the phase model, we should privilege the diffusionist model, which assumes a continuity in the circulation of the epic poems in second millenium Greece and the possibility of direct borrowings from the Achaean tradition into the Proto-Ionic tradition. If so, this isolated Zenodotean reading, usually ignored by linguists, provides an important argument in favour of the diffusionist model against the phase theory.

10 Achaean Type τελήεις

Ruijgh argued that forms like τελήεις < *teles-ṷent-, found in the formula τεληέσσας ἑκατόμβας #, could not be regular in Ionic, but were Achaean.[52] The fact that possessive derivatives in *-ṷent- are not productive in Aeolic, Ionic, Attic or Doric, whereas they are usual in Linear B, also points to an Achaean form. Ruijgh assumes that Mycenaean already had CL as a result of the elimination of -sṷ-, therefore he admitted that those forms were Mycenaean forms embedded in the epics. But if CL is post-Linear B (see above), that means that the type τελήεις is more recent. This form is always used in the same context, as an epithet of 'hecatomb', and it refers to the fact that the sacrifice is a valid one, with victims that are not damaged by any physical defect.[53] The Ionic corresponding adjective is τέλειος, also found in the same context of a sacrifice consisting of βοῶν αἰγῶν τε τελείων # "of perfect oxen and goats" (Ω 34), ἀρνῶν [...] αἰγῶν τε τελείων # "of perfect goats and sheep" (A 66), also a line final formula, referring either to victims exempt of any defect,[54] or to adult, fully grown animals. Mycenaean also has te-re-ja = /telejjai/ PY Eb 149. For τεληέσσας, Ruijgh is right to stress that this cannot be the Ionic form, which would be *τελειέσσας with a spurious diphthong (phonologically speaking, a

---

51 Thessalo-Lesbian can be understood as the more archaic Aeolic type, whereas Boeotian has developed innovations not shared by Thessalian and Lesbian, mainly through contact with neighbouring dialects.
52 Ruijgh 1985: 176.
53 Probably not with Ruijgh 2011: 278–279 an equivalent of πολυτελής 'very expensive'.
54 It also applies to Zeus' eagle, τελειότατον πετεηνῶν (Θ 247, Ω 315).

long closed /e/).[55] The Homeric language uses both the regular Ionic form and the older Achaean one, the latter in a frozen formula belonging to the religious language.

To Ruijgh's analysis Peters objected, after Brugmann, that -η- instead of -ει- is a conditioned reflex of /ē/ < *-ehe- or *-ehu̯- before /e/ or /i/, where dissimilation applied.[56] He invokes forms like # ἐν σπῆϊ γλαφυρῷ 'in the hollow cave' (Σ 402), # ᾤκεον ἐν σπήεσσι 'they lived in caves' (ι 400), vs # ἷξον δὲ σπεῖος γλαφυρόν 'they came to the hollow cave' (ε 195), περὶ σπείους γλαφυροῖο # 'around the hollow cave' (ε 68), which indicate that ⟨η⟩ is found before /i/ or /e/ or /ei/, and ⟨ει⟩ before other vowels. As a counter-example, the subjunctive δαμείετε (H 72, for older *δαμήετε) does not show the slightest trace of dissimilation before /e/: it is an old /ē/, shortened and then metrically lengthened, but this new /ē/, although identical with the reflex of *-ehe-, is not dissimilated, as it should have been if the rule is that new long /ē/ before /e/ becomes long open /ē/ (⟨η⟩). Now Peters' objection was already answered by Schwyzer.[57] Such forms are artificial spellings under which lie older sequences of non-contracted vowels (σπῆϊ for *σπέεϊ, σπήεσσι for *σπεέεσσι, σπείους for *σπέεος before a consonant) and show no phonetic dissimilation. This spelling device must date back to a time when the Ionic alphabet had acquired the distinction between open /ę̄/ (⟨H⟩) and closed /e/ (⟨E⟩), but not yet the distinction between short closed /e/ (⟨E⟩) and long closed /ẹ/ (⟨EI⟩). Only before /i/ is there a graphic device that writes ⟨ηι⟩ instead of *⟨ειι⟩: dat.sg. χέρηι 'weaker', hence by analogy nom.pl. χέρηες, dat.sg. σπῆϊ 'cave', hence by analogy dat.pl. σπήεσσι. The existence of spellings like Διοκλῆος (E 542), Διοκλῆα (E 547) for -κλέος, -κλέα, shows most clearly that we are dealing with a paradigmatic analogy after the dative -κλῆϊ for -κλέεϊ since before /o/ or /a/ no such dissimilation has ever been claimed. But this explanation cannot apply to τελήεις, since the -η- of the latter is never before /i/: the vowel comes before the suffix, not the ending, and there is no source for a paradigmatic analogy as in σπήεσσι, χέρηες after σπῆϊ, χέρηι. Therefore Ruijgh's explanation must be correct: τελήεις is an Achaean form. Ruijgh considers it a Mycenaean form: we should rather analyse it as a post-Linear B Achaean form since CL is post-Mycenaean.

The situation is the same as for ἆϝές/ἄας, but for the latter, of course, the dissimilation hypothesis between two /ē/ assumed by Peters for τελήεις cannot be invoked. The only possible explanation is a non-Ionic CL since the

---

55   Ruijgh 1970: 320.
56   Peters 1986: 305. Dissimilation is also admitted by Lejeune 1972: 137.
57   Schwyzer, *Gr. Gr.* I: 243.

form cannot have been transmitted through Thessalo-Lesbian. Therefore, ἄας strengthens the analysis of τελήεις and similar forms as post-Linear B Achaean forms, which passed on to the Proto-Ionic epic tradition directly from post-Linear B Achaean.

The same, of course, is true for the parallel adjectives αἰπήεις 'steep', from *αἰπεσ-ϝεντ-, derived from the s-stem αἶπος (Aeschylus, Hippocrates), basis of the derivative αἰπεινός < *αἰπεσ-νός (Hom.), which together with the u-stem αἰπύς belongs to an old Caland system; θυήεις 'fragrant' (Ψ 148), from*θυεσ-ϝεντ-.[58] And for τειχήεις 'fortified' < *τειχεσ-ϝεντ-, preserved by Strabo (*Geogr.* 10.4.11) for B 646 (Γόρτυνά τε τειχήεσσαν) and by a T scholion to Ψ 741a, which has Τίρυνθά τε τειχήεσσαν (B 559), instead of the remodelled τειχιόεσσαν of the vulgate.[59]

That brings us back to the tree from which we started. We have seen above that the etymon of δενδρήεις 'wooded' is not *δενδρεϝο-ϝεντ-, built on the thematic δένδρεϝον, but *δενδρεϝ-ϝεντ- with a geminate /ww/, built on the old athematic u-stem (see above pp. 102–103). Now δενδρήϝεις with etymological *-u̯u̯- is exactly parallel to τελήϝεις and to ἄϝᾱς with etymological *-su̯- or *-u̯s-, which agrees with the idea that those went through a geminate stage *-u̯u̯- before the geminate was simplified. Accordingly, δενδρήεις, too, can be a post-Linear B Achaean form, here again passed on to the Proto-Ionic epic tradition without going through Aeolic, since Thessalo-Lesbian would have maintained *δενδρεύεντ-.

And of course, once we acknowledge that post-linear B Achaean forms could be transmitted directly to the Proto-Ionic epic diction, the same applies for other sequences. Thus, δήνεα 'counsels', the regular reflex of *dens-es-h₂ (Ved. *dáṁsas-* 'skill, magical art') in Achaean, was passed on directly from the Achaean epic tradition to the Proto-Ionic tradition, as argued by Ruijgh[60]—the difference is that Ruijgh saw in it a Mycenaean form (with CL already acquired in Linear B), whereas it should rather be considered a post-linear B Achaean form. There is no need to assume a remodelled *dans-es- with the vocalism of the zero grade and the syllabic structure of the e grade, but the old and

---

59 The same form is given in an erroneous quotation in the *Suda* (Πανὸς τειχήεσσα πιτυστέπτοιο καλιή "the walled hut of Pan crowned with pine," under πίτυς, π 1671): this is *Anth. Gr.* 6.253, l. 3, attributed to Crinagoras, and the line must be read Πανὸς τ' ἠχήεσσα πιτυστέπτοιο καλιή "the resounding hut." Τειχιόεσσα was remodelled after τειχίον (π 165, π 343).

60 Ruijgh 1970: 319. *Contra* Peters 1981, who assumes the form comes from an older *δᾶνος.

morphologically regular *dens-es- can account for the attested form: Hesychius' ἀδανές· ἀπρονόητον 'without premeditation' (α 1004) must be a hyperdoricism coming from an unknown poet.[61]

---

[61] For those who assume that the older form was *δᾶνος, the etymon cannot be equated with the Vedic form and a zero grade root is required. But we know that *s-stems consistently have a radical e grade in Greek as in Vedic. The few cases of zero grade are the result of late analogical remodellings (βένθος → βάθος after βαθύς, κρέτος → κράτος after κρατύς, κρατερός, πένθος → πάθος after ἔπαθον), and if we assume *déns-es- was remodelled into *dn̥s-es- after *dn̥s-i- (δαΐφρων), *dn̥s-eh₁- (ἐδάην), that implies that the nasal was analogically restored in a second step, *das-es- → *dans-es- (Hackstein 2002: 185): not only would that imply two successive analogical remodellings, but there is no source from which a consonantal [n] could be restored in a stem *dn̥s- > *das- since all the verbal forms have a consistent zero grade and the nasal is lost. The hypothesis of a *dn̥s-nes- (Manessy-Guitton 1970), accepted by García Ramón (2021: 21), can be rejected because there is no suffix *-nes-: there was a reshaping of *n-stems after s-stems in several languages independently (on the coexistence with -na-, thematic version of n-stems, in Vedic, see Pinault 2000: 86, after Meillet 1908, and García Ramón 2021), but no *-nes- noun has a direct cognate in other languages. Moreover, the nouns for which this suffix has been assumed display an e-grade stem (Lat. fēnus 'interest' (on capital), pignus 'pledge', vulnus 'wound' (< *u̯elH-), Ved. ápnas- 'belonging, possession', énas- 'sin', réknas- 'material good', Gr. κτήνεα 'goods'), the few Latin forms with apparent o grade are secondary (Vine 1999): this makes a *dn̥s-nes- rather unlikely. On δήνεα, see the different hypotheses in Blanc 2018: 192. After Euler 1979: 220, I argued in Le Feuvre 2007b that the equation between πολυδήνης (Hsch., π 2844: πολυδήνεα· πολύβουλον, and restored in Hesiod, fr. 343.6 MW, Μῆτιν καίπερ πολὺ δινεύουσαν, corr. Bergk πολυδήνε' ἐοῦσαν which is probably correct) and Ved. purudáṃsas- 'of the many arts' is an argument in favour of Ruijgh's explanation: if not only the simple δήνεα but also the compound is inherited, the hypothesis of a double remodelling implying a modification of the metrical structure (*déns-es- → *dn̥s-es- → *dans-es-) is very difficult to defend.

CHAPTER 4

Stretching Arms

One of the criticisms Aristarchus formulated against Zenodotus' readings is that he used "un-Homeric" forms. This is why ἄας was condemned. Aristarchus' argument in that case is based on the known corpus: the form is not attested elsewhere in Homer. But this is the definition of a *hapax*, and of course, every Homeric *hapax* should not be condemned: the condemnation must rely on a linguistic reasoning. Which type of reasoning will be made clear in this chapter.

1   A 351

In A 351 the vulgate has

>   πολλὰ δὲ μητρὶ φίλῃ ἠρήσατο χεῖρας ὀρεγνύς
>
>   many times stretching forth his hands he called on his mother.
>   R.L.

The end of the line is also found in X 37:

>   τὸν δ' ὃ γέρων ἐλεεινὰ προσηύδα χεῖρας ὀρεγνύς
>
>   the old man stretching his hands out called pitifully to him.
>   R.L.

Aristonicus says that Zenodotus read in A 351 χεῖρας ἀναπτάς (*A Schol.* A 351a). We have no mention of a variant reading for X 37.[1] A third variant reading for this line is χεῖρας ἀνασχών, mentioned in a T scholion (*T Schol.* A 351b Erbse: τινὲς 'ἀνασχών' γράφουσιν).

Ἀνασχών and ἀναπτάς are clearly related, and the one is a modification of the other. As Kirk mentions in his *Commentary*, "this form (ἀναπτάς) would be

---

[1] Zenodotus' reading is not discussed in Nickau and not mentioned by Risch 1974, Schwyzer, *Gr. Gr.*, Chantraine, *Gr. Hom.*, or Forssman 2019. Van Thiel 2014b, *sub* A 351, prints †ἀναπτάς with a *crux*.

unique in Homer," which leads him to conclude that ἀνασχών "is a more serious contender against the vulgate's ὀρεγνύς."[2] However, precisely the fact that ἀναπτάς is "unique" makes it important, and an emendation of the "unique" ἀναπτάς into the well-known ἀνασχών is obviously not a problem, whereas the reverse is highly unlikely. Ἀνασχών is trivial, therefore uninteresting, and certainly not a "serious contender" to the vulgate's reading. Ἀναπτάς, unmotivated in Greek, is necessarily older than ἀνασχών, which is transparent, and what must be examined is the relationship between ἀναπτάς and ὀρεγνύς, not between ἀνασχών and ὀρεγνύς. Although ἀναπτάς and ὀρεγνύς do not have anything in common, except for the fact that they are participles and have the same metrical structure, the line is identical, and we can consider that we have here two related readings, an older one and an emendation meant to replace the other form and fitted into a preexisting metrical structure.

The phrase χεῖρας ὀρέγω/ὀρέγομαι is old,[3] but that does not mean that all its formal expressions are old, too. Ὀρέγνυμι is usually considered as the remodelling of an old nasal present found in the Vedic 3pl. r̥ñjate, as ζεύγνυμι matches Ved. yuñjánti, Lat. jungō, and πήγνυμι Lat. pangō, but it could also have been created within Greek, as acknowledged in LIV^2.[4] As a matter of fact, whereas ζεύγνυμι and πήγνυμι are usual, ὀρέγνυμι is only attested in the phrase χεῖρας ὀρεγνύς # in two lines of the *Iliad*. The derived *nu*-present is meant to provide a present participle with the same metrical value as the aorist ὀρέξας (ὀρέξῃ # X 130, E 33), at the end of the line where the inherited thematic present ὀρέγων, the only usual form in Greek, did not fit. This neologism, if it is one, follows a regular pattern in Greek verbal morphology, found in δείξας/δεικνύς, ζεύξας/ζευγνύς, πήξας/πηγνύς: δείκνυμι itself was derived within Greek from the aorist ἔδειξα and does not reflect an old nasal present.[5] And the τὼ καὶ δεικνύμενος

---

2 Kirk 1985: 89.
3 See Covini 2016, who also discusses the phrases with *$peth_2$-.
4 An argument in favour of an inherited *$h_3r̥ĝ$-nu- is Hitt. *harganāu* 'palm of the hand', assuming the latter is a back-formation from this nasal present (Oettinger 2014: 311). However, the Hittite form displays the zero grade expected in a nasal present, whereas Greek has an *e* grade which cannot be old. If the Greek form is secondary, the comparison with Hittite is fragilised. The suffix *-*nu*- in the Hittite noun can be independent from a present formation on the antiquity of which doubt is permitted. The parallel invoked by Oettinger, Ved. *dhr̥ṣṇú-* 'bold', from *dhr̥ṣṇóti* 'to be bold', is not fully convincing because the Vedic form is not a creation *ex nihilo* from the present, but the result of a secondary reshaping of the existing *u*-adjective *$*d^hr̥s$-ú*- (Gr. θρασύς 'bold'), after the *nu*-present (*EWAia*, s.v. DHARṢ-). No *u*-stem is known for *$*h_3reĝ$-.
5 LIV^2: 109. The form is mentioned but not discussed in Forssman 2019: 64.

'welcoming them' (I 196), with a secondary spelling for *δεκνύμενος 'receiving', next to the aorist ἐδέξατο, shows the same productivity of the model.[6]

On the other hand, Zenodotus' ἀναπτάς can hardly be a creation because in Greek the stem πτᾱ-/πτᾰ- is the aorist of πέταμαι/πέτομαι 'to fly', not of πετάννυμι/πίτνημι 'to stretch'. In Homer the stem πτα- is always found as the aorist of πέταμαι/πέτομαι 'to fly', always middle: πταμένη Ε 282, Π 876, Χ 362, ἀποπτάμενος Β 71, πτάτο Ψ 880, ὑπέρπτατο Ν 408, ἔπτατο Ε 99, Ν 587, διέπτατο Ο 83, ἀπέπτατο (I 213, v.l.); after Homer, ἀναπτάμενος 'having flown off' Hdt 2.55, Parm. 2.41, Ar., Av. 1206 (next to ἀναπτόμενος which is retained by most modern editors); active ἀνέπταν in Sophocles (Ant. 1308), participle ἀναπτάς in Aristotle, Hist. An. 613b2. And of course Zenodotus' ἀναπτάς has nothing to do with flying, which is why it was rejected by all ancient scholars.

However, the stem -πτα- also belongs to another verb, πετάννυμι/πίτνημι, of which it provides the perfect, always passive in Homer:

- ἀμφὶ δὲ πέπλοι ‖ πέπτανται Ε 194–195 "and over them blankets lie spread" (R.L.)
- πέπτατο δ' αὐγὴ ‖ ἠελίου ὀξεῖα Ρ 371–372 "and the sharp sunlight had spread"
- πεπταμένας ἐν χερσὶ πύλας ἔχετ(ε) Φ 531 "hold the gates wide open in your hands" (R.L.)

Clearly Zenodotus' ἀναπτάς is a form of 'to stretch', which can only be a root aorist participle. But for πετάννυμι/πίτνημι, the Homeric text only has the s-aorist ἀνὰ ... πέτασσαν Α 480, κατὰ ... πετάσσας Θ 441, and in the same phrase as Zenodotus', χεῖρε πετάσσας # Ξ 495 and Φ 115, and an expanded variant ἄμφω χεῖρε φίλοις ἑτάροισι πετάσσας # Δ 523 and Ν 549. This is another reason why Zenodotus' reading was condemned, because it was irregular for people thinking in terms of synchrony, as did Greek scholars: the aorist in Homer is always πετάσσας, therefore it cannot be ἀνα-πτάς since the poet is consistent in his use. Ἀναλογία, that is, the assumed regularity of the language of Homer in the mind of Greek grammarians, opposed the form ἀνα-πτάς. The linguistic reasoning leading to the condemnation of Zenodotus' form is the application of ἀναλογία.[7]

---

6 *LIV*[2]: 110 assumes the nasal present is old because of Ved. *dāśnóti* 'wartet auf', but this is unlikely: the lengthened grade in the Vedic form is secondary, therefore a secondary form in both Vedic and Greek cannot warrant the reconstruction of a present $*d_e\hat{k}$-nu- (*LIV*[2]). For this root the only old present seems to have been the acrostatic $*d\bar{e}\hat{k}$-ti attested in Ved. *dā́ṣṭi* (after which *dāśnóti*) and Gr. δέγμενος (I 191), δέχαται (M 147).

7 The modern formulation is found in Van der Valk 1964: 46: "Zenod. wished to make use of the verb ἀναπετάννυμι. However, he was not aware of the fact that ἀναπτάς cannot be derived from that verb. Accordingly, the subjective conjecture of Zenod. is unmasked. He coined a new and incorrect form."

However, the phrase is not isolated from the phraseological point of view: in χείρας ἀναπτάς, the participle is the vocalic variant of πετάσσας in χεῖρε πετάσσας.[8] The phrase is found in the present in λ 392 πιτνὰς εἰς ἐμὲ χεῖρας ὀρέξασθαι μενεαίνων "and he spread out his hands toward me, eager to reach me." And the combination with ἀνα- is not found only here, but it is attested in Homer in the passive perfect (πύλας) ἀναπεπταμένας ἔχον "they held the doors wide open" M 122, and after Homer we have τὰν ἐπ' ὄσσοισ' ὀμπέτασον χάριν "spread grace onto her eyes" (Sappho, fr. 138 LP): ἀνα- does not refer to an upward move in either example. In A 480 οἳ δ' ἱστὸν στήσαντ' ἀνά θ' ἱστία λευκὰ πέτασσαν "they set up the mast again and spread on it the white sail" (R.L.), ἀνά does not mean 'up' either, as the sail is deployed downwards from the yard at the top of the mast. A 480 ἀνά ... πέτασσαν and Sappho's ὀμπέτασον are two instances of the active aorist ἀν(α)πέτασα. From this verb was derived an adjective ἀναπετής 'spread out', which is mostly used in the medical lexicon with the meaning 'dilated'.[9]

---

8   That is, ἀναπτάς and πετάσσας have the same meaning and the same metrical structure, they only differ by the fact that the latter has an initial consonant, making it suitable for use after a vowel, whereas the former has an initial vowel, making it suitable for use after a consonant. Epic diction had for most formulae and words two variants, a consonantal one and a vocalic one, allowing to express the same notion in different contexts and to ease versification. For instance, ἔντεα 'armour' is the vocalic variant of τεύχεα 'idem', both scanning as a dactyl, as αἶα 'earth' is the vocalic variant of γαῖα. Such pairs are used to keep the declension of a noun phrase within a given metrical shape: for instance, ἐΰζυγος 'with good benches' is the vocalic variant of πολύζυγος 'with many benches', the former is used when the noun has a consonantal ending as in νῆες ἐΰζυγοι, the latter when the noun has a vocalic ending, as in νηΐ πολυζύγῳ. The metrical shape of the formula does not change and ἐΰζυγος and πολύζυγος, although their meanings are not strictly identical, are used as equivalents to ensure that the noun phrase 'good-benched ship' can be used in different case forms. For nouns, πατρίδα γαῖαν 'fatherland' and πατρίδος αἴης 'idem' provide an example of the use of two different nouns (γαῖα/αἶα) according to the phonetic structure of the ending of the adjective. As is well known, the formula in the nominative takes a different noun, πατρὶς ἄρουρα, because πατρίς is shorter by one syllable, which is compensated by the use of a trisyllabic noun: the semantic difference between ἄρουρα and γαῖα is neutralised in this formula. See a convenient summary in Hainsworth 1968: 123–125.

9   Hippocrates, De glandulis 9.4 συχναὶ γάρ τοι ἀδένες καὶ ἀναπετέες "the glands are dense and dilated;" Aretaeus, De causis et signis acutorum morborum 1.7.4 ὀφθαλμοὶ ἐξίσχοντες, ἀναπετέες, ἐξέρυθροι "the eyes are protruding, dilated, red;" Rufus, De partibus corporis humani 25 Καὶ ὁ μὲν φάρυγξ χονδρώδης τυγχάνει, καὶ ἀναπετής κατὰ τὴν περιφέρειαν, ἐκ μὲν τῶν ἄνω πλατύτερος ὑπάρχων, ἐκ δὲ τῶν κάτω στενότερος "the pharynx is hard and dilated at its periphery, being wider on the upper part and narrower on the lower one." The adjective means 'wide open' in Heliodorus Trag., fr. 472. 14–15 SH ὄμμα διῆναι || ἀμπετὲς ἀκλῄστον "bathe the eye wide open and not shut."

Therefore, since χεῖρας ἀναπτάς is obviously linked with χεῖρε πετάσσας, and since the active aorist with ἀνα- is attested in Homer, we must think in terms of diachrony: one of the two forms is old, the other is not. Active root aorists are not productive in Greek. Therefore ἀναπτάς is not likely to be an inner-Greek creation, even as an archaising form. And the passive perfect, the only form of πετάννυμι/πίτνημι displaying the stem -πτα-, is too narrow a basis for the creation of an active root aorist. Zenodotus cannot have invented the form ἀναπτάς as the aorist of 'to stretch' for there was no model for that, but he found it in his working text or in an old copy which he collated. On the other hand, the s-aorist is the productive formation in all the Greek dialects. Accordingly, if one of the two forms is secondary, it must be the regular ἐπέτασα.

2 A Linguistic Fossil

This is not a new idea. As a matter of fact, Harðarson in his study on the root aorist proposed that the s-aorist ἐπέτασα reflects the remodelling of an older athematic root aorist $*peth_2$-/$*pth_2$- ($*πετᾰ$-/$*πτᾰ$-),[10] as Hesychius' τελάσσαι (τ 395) next to Homeric ταλάσσαι reflects the remodelling of an older athematic root aorist $*telh_2$-/$*tl̥h_2$-, whence, with strong stem analogised after the weak stem, the attested root aorist ἔτλην.[11] His conclusion is accepted in LIV^2.[12] But as usual, Harðarson worked on the vulgate's text and did not take into account variant readings. Had he done so, he would have found in Zenodotus' reading the confirmation that this root aorist did exist: the participle ἀναπτάς is the reflex of a regular $*pth_2$-ént-, of the same type as $*sth_2$-ént- (στάς, στάντος), $*g^wh_2$-ént- (βάς, βάντος), $*d^hh_1$-ént- (θείς, θέντος),[13] and $*tl̥h_2$-ént- (lexicalised neuter plural τάλαντα 'scales', next to the participle τλάς corresponding to the new aorist ἔτλην). Together with $*tl̥h_2$-ént-, it confirms that the participle had the zero grade of the root and that στάντ-, βάντ-, θέντ- are not the reflex of $*steh_2$-nt-, $*g^weh_2$-nt-, $*d^heh_1$-nt- by Osthoff's law, because in that case we would expect $**peth_2$-nt-. With ἀναπτάς, Zenodotus preserves a fossil, which was eliminated later on—and is not mentioned either in LIV^2. This, once more, shows the damage caused by the old idea that Zenodotus' readings were inventions of his which need not be taken seriously: Chantraine, Risch, Schwyzer do not

---

10   Harðarson 1993: 185.
11   Harðarson 1993: 183–184. The original full grade $*telh_2$- is warranted by τελαμών 'baldrick', lit. 'supporter'.
12   LIV^2: 478.
13   Rix 1976: 72.

mention ἀναπτάς, and those reference works are where linguists take their material from—including recent books like Forssman 2019. Worse, Zenodotus' reading is not even mentioned either by Ebeling or in the *LfgrE*, whereas ἄας is.

Yet ἀναπτάς is a linguistic fossil of great interest, which confirms Harðarson's explanation of the *s*-aorist. The suggested correction χεῖρ᾽ ἀναπίτνας (Cobet, accepted by West and Van Thiel) amounts to a desperate attempt to get back to a form which would be synchronically regular (ἀναπίτνημι), but it is useless. The form as it is transmitted is synchronically irregular but quite regular from a diachronic point of view. The old and archaic ἀναπτάς underwent two corrections: the replacement by ἀνασχών was easy and represents a minimal change, as the preverb is kept unchanged and another monosyllabic root aorist with two initial consonants was chosen. The formula χεῖρας ἀνασχών # is found in A 450, Γ 275, E 174, Σ 75, T 254, and in χεῖρας ἀνασχεῖν # Z 257, without any variant—it may be in some of those cases too the replacement of an older ἀναπτάς. The replacement by ὀρεγνύς relies on the formulaic use of ὀρέγω with χείρ as an object and yields a form which has nothing in common with the form it replaces. It is, to my mind, an argument in favour of the explanation of ὀρεγνύς as a Greek innovation: analysing ὀρεγνύς as an old form, remodelling of an inherited nasal present, would imply that the phrase χεῖρας ὀρεγνύς in the present is old, but if ὀρεγνύς there replaced an older ἀναπτάς, which is definitely old, it is not very likely that singers exhumed a *nu*-present which was apparently not very much alive since it is attested only there, and much more likely that they created it after ὀρέξας on the model δείκνυμι/ἔδειξα, because the pre-existing metrical structure did not allow the use of the regular present form ὀρέγων. Metrically conditioned innovations are certainly not unusual in Homer, and this is probably one of them. Next to ὀρέγω, the present stem ὀρεγνυ- may have had an archaic flavour, like δαίνυμι next to δαίω 'to divide' or ἄχνυμαι next to ἄχομαι 'to be distressed', ἐέργνυ (κ 238) next to ἐέργω, and may be an archaising neologism.

That does not mean that Zenodotus' reading is archaic in all respects. As a matter of fact, it has the plural χεῖρας, as the vulgate, not the dual χεῖρε expected in this context and found in χεῖρε πετάσσας Ξ 495. The dual would not be possible before the vowel-initial ἀναπτάς. The attested formula may result from the modification of a formula which originally included a particle, for instance *χεῖρε τ᾽ ἀναπτάς in a coordinative structure (with a complementary distribution between a coordinating formula *χεῖρε τ᾽ ἀναπτάς and a non coordinating one χεῖρας ἀναπτάς), or the result of the declension of a plural formula χεῖρας ἀναπτάντες (impossible at the end of the line, but which may have been found in other metrical positions). If it was a formula with a particle, the suppression of the particle in this context led to the replacement of the dual by the plural to avoid hiatus, which was possible only after the process of loss of the dual had begun, and the introduction of the vulgate's form χεῖρας ὀρεγνύς and of the emendation χεῖρας ἀνασχών took place in a phrase which already had the plural χεῖρας. This may be why the simplest solution by far, the replacement of χεῖρας ἀναπτάς by the well attested χεῖρε πετάσσας #, was not used, because the plural χεῖρας implied that the participle have an initial vowel.

If Zenodotus' working text had ἀναπτάς, he simply left it unchanged. On the other hand, if his working text had ὀρεγνύς or ἀνασχών, it is hardly plausible that he introduced ἀναπτάς as an emendation imported from a copy he collated, because the form was irregular in the synchrony of the Homeric system and could not be deemed better.

The first two cases we studied, δένδρει and ἄας, were a matter of morphological divergence with the vulgate. Yet, ἄας shows that Zenodotus' version preserved lexical archaisms of the highest interest. So does ἀναπτάς: the lexical divergence with the vulgate results from the archaic morphology of the participle, which led to its replacement. For δένδρει and ἄας, the form was attested in Greek independently of Zenodotus: this is not the case for ἀναπτάς, but we have here an interesting case where a theoretical reasoning leads to the assumption that such a form existed at some time in the prehistory of Greek, and the form itself is identified afterwards. Therefore, even though in that case the philological criterion is not met, since the word form is not transmitted by any other source, the linguistic and metrical criteria warrant its authenticity. The linguistic criterion because this is exactly the expected form for the root aorist from which the s-aorist developed, and the metrical criterion because the regular metrical structure of ἀναπτάς is the cause of the morphological singularity of the vulgate's reading ὀρεγνύς, which replaced it.

3 Yet Another Fossil

It is clear, by now, that linguists should not blindly follow Aristarchus and his followers. And that Zenodotus' readings can provide the confirmation that forms that were heretofore only reconstructed did in fact exist in Greek. Another striking example, in the same field of verbal morphology, is provided by Σ 160.

Σ 158–160
[...] ὃ δ' ἔμπεδον ἀλκὶ πεποιθὼς
ἄλλοτ' ἐπαΐξασκε κατὰ μόθον, ἄλλοτε δ' αὖτε
στάσκε μέγα ἰάχων· ὀπίσω δ' οὐ χάζετο πάμπαν

but he, steady in the confidence of his great strength, kept making, now
a rush into the crowd, or again at another time stood fast, with his great
cry, but gave not a bit of ground backward.

R.L.

Zenodotus read # στάσκε μέγα ἀχέων instead of μέγα ἰάχων. Aristonicus condemns this reading as a nonsense:

A Schol. Σ 160a: πρὸς τί δὲ λυπούμενος ἑστήκει, ἀλλ' οὐκ ἰάχων καὶ ἐπεγκελευόμενος τοῖς Τρωσὶν ἀφαιρεῖσθαι τὸν νεκρόν;

why would he stand afflicted, and not shouting and ordering the Trojans to take the corpse out of the fighting?

Zenodotus' reading ἀχέων "afflicted" not only does not make sense, but is also metrically irregular, because before ἀχέω the vowel of μέγα should undergo elision. Instead, far from being elided, the final /a/ scans long. Aristarchus probably pointed to the metrical problem, but the scholion dropped this element because it was secondary: the most important point was that the reading was meaningless. It was, in the eyes of Aristarchus, who knew only one verb ἀχέω and readily identified the form as the participle of the latter.

However, we may legitimately doubt Zenodotus committed so gross a mistake. And we must have a closer look at the form. The vulgate has ἰάχων: we know that ἰάχω behaves like an aorist, not like a present, and linguists agree that it was derived from a thematic aorist *ϝϝαχεῖν, which it replaced in several lines. The irregular behaviour of the form, with ϝϝ now before the reduplication vowel, now between the reduplication and the stem, led Chantraine to the following suggestion: in Σ 219 ὅτε τ' ἴαχε σάλπιγξ # "when the trumpet screamed," an older ὅτε τε (ϝϝ)άχε should be restored and in Σ 228 τρὶς μὲν ὑπὲρ τάφρου μεγάλ' ἴαχε δῖος Ἀχιλλεύς "three times across the ditch brilliant Achilleus gave his great cry" (R.L.), an older μέγα (ϝϝ)άχε.[14] This is certainly correct, and accepted by most linguists.[15] Clearly, Zenodotus' μέγα ἀχέων for *μέγα ϝϝαχέων belongs here.

---

14   Chantraine, Gr. hom. I: 393. Risch 1974: 270. A different genesis for the present stem has been proposed by Schulze, who assumed a metanalysis in sequences *ἐπι-ϝάχω, *περι-ϝάχω reanalysed as ἐπ-ιάχω, περ-ιάχω after the loss of /w/ (Schulze 1888: 247–248).

15   LIV² assumes that ἰάχω was originally a present stem because of the reduplication, and that the aoristic value in Homer is secondary. But Zenodotus' reading ϝϝαχέων confirms that Chantraine was right: the base is a root aorist and the reduplicated present is secondary.

Zenodotus' reading preserves a direct trace of this lost aorist. The participle *ϝϝαχών was unmetrical because the preceding syllable is always long (so in Zenodotus' reading). The participle, therefore, had to be adapted either through the addition of a syllable or through a metrical lengthening. Adding a syllable resulted in the reduplicated form ϝιϝάχω, which is the only one of the vulgate, scanning now ϝϝίϝαχε (Δ 506), now ϝίϝϝαχε (Α 482). But there was another possibility, to transform it into *ϝϝαχέων: as Chantraine says, "from thematic aorists were created -έω presents, with generally a future in -ήσω: from ἔστυγον, στυγέω, from κτυπεῖν, κτυπέει, from ἤκαχον, ἀκαχήσε [...]. It has been suggested that the infinitive aorist in -εῖν provided the input for those forms."[16] To Chantraine's statement we can add that this occurs in particular for verbs sharing a same structure CCV̆C (στυγε/ο-, κτυπε/ο-): for such verbs, the aorist infinitive στυγεῖν, κτυπεῖν and the aorist participle στυγών, κτυπών are unmetrical because they form a cretic. Therefore, they had to be converted into στυγέειν, στυγέων, κτυπέειν, κτυπέων.[17] Then, as Chantraine says, they could be reanalysed as present infinitives, and provide the input for a new present stem inflecting like φιλέω. This CCV̆C structure is also shared by *ϝϝαχε/ο-: as a consequence, the creation of an infinitive *ϝϝαχέειν and a participle *ϝϝαχέων is expected.[18] The latter is Zenodotus' reading in Σ 160.

Zenodotus' reading is therefore metrically regular, semantically fine since it has in fact the same verb as the vulgate, and linguistically very interesting because it confirms the existence of the thematic aorist hypothesised by linguists as the basis of ἰάχω, and it confirms that the latter replaced an older

---

The root is *(s)u̯eh₂ĝʰ-, found in Lat. vagīre 'to cry, to shout', Lith. svagiù 'to resound'. The full grade is found in (ϝ)ἠχή 'noise'. The zero grade of the thematic root aorist *ϝhᾰχ- in Greek was analogised after the full grade *ϝhᾱχ-, with the usual alternation between /ā/ and /ă/. The phonetically regular form would be **hūχ-.

16   Chantraine, Gr. hom. I: 347.
17   The Iliad has seven instances of the verb κτυπέω: four of the root aorist ἔκτυπε (Θ 75, Θ 170, Ο 377, Ρ 595), two of the participle (κτυπέων Η 479, κτυπέουσα Ψ 119, both with the value of an aorist participle), and only one present κτυπέει (Ν 140). The Odyssey has only one, the aorist ἔκτυπε (Φ 413). For στυγέω the present stem is better attested in the Iliad (seven instances), and the root aorist is only found in the Odyssey (ἔστυγον κ 113).
18   Another difficult form of this verb is the feminine participle ἀμφιαχυῖαν Β 316. This perfect participle is clearly "artificial and recent" (Risch 1974: 341). The oldest parchment text with fragments of the Iliad, Ambros. Gr. F 205 inf. (v–vi[th] c.) has ἀμφιάχουσαν: this could be the regular expected feminine aorist participle ἀμφι-ϝαχοῦσαν, rather than the present participle ἀμφ-ιάχουσαν. The accent is not significant: "many accents were added in the early Middle Ages" (West 2001: 88). It would be extraordinary if another direct trace of the radical aorist had survived there, alone against the remodelled and "artificial" perfect ἀμφιαχυῖαν otherwise unanimously transmitted but, although it is more likely that the form has been remodelled into a regular present participle, the possibility cannot be ruled out.

aorist in several ancient lines—after which new lines could be created on this model. And in fact the form is also attested in younger epic poetry: *H.Cer.* 478–479 σεμνά, τά τ' οὔ πως ἔστι παρεξ[ίμ]εν [οὔτε πυθέσθαι,] || οὔτ' ἀχέειν "Mysteries, which are unthinkable either to question or utter or to transgress" (D.H.).[19] But in *H.Cer.* 479 the initial digamma is lost and the verb has an initial vowel, triggering elision. Zenodotus has the older form, with the double ϝϝ preserved.[20] Schulze had already related this ἀχέω to the old aorist ϝϝαχεῖν,[21] and Van Thiel mentions it in his apparatus. Schulze's suggestion is rejected by the *LfgrE* because "the aorist was no longer identifiable under ἴαχε," with the idea that the aorist was deduced from the present stem ἰάχω, and because of the absence of ϝ. Now Zenodotus does provide the form with ϝϝ, which is older than ϝιϝάχω and was not deduced from it, and Schulze's hypothesis proves to be correct. It is all the more regrettable that no one paid attention to Zenodotus' reading: the explanation was found a long time ago, but the central piece remained missing for years.

Aristarchus, knowing no other verb ἀχέω in Homer than 'to grieve', mistook this form for a participle meaning 'suffering, grieving', which of course is meaningless in the context. The morphological difference between Zenodotus' reading and the vulgate's was reinterpreted as a lexical difference. How Zenodotus understood it remains an open question. He probably still understood that it was a form of ἰάχω 'to scream'. If he understood 'grieving' like Aristarchus, thankfully he did not correct the text. At any rate, he cannot have invented this form. Neither could he import it from another copy if his own text had the same ἰάχων as the vulgate, because it would not make any sense to import a reading creating a metrical problem.

---

19   The same form has been assumed for *H.Pan* 18 θρῆνον ἐπιπροχέουσ' ἀχέει μελίγηρυν ἀοιδήν "pouring a melody, she utters a sweet song." However, this reading is an emendation, the manuscripts have ἐπιπροχέουσα χέει, so that this is not a reliable instance.
20   Van Thiel 2014a, *sub* Σ 160, assumes that Zenodotus compared ἰάχων to this ἀχέω in a marginal note. Nickau does not discuss the form.
21   Schulze 1888: 247–248.

CHAPTER 5

Matters of Perception

The application of corpus-based judgements of what is "Homeric" and what is not, together with the constant use of context-based interpretations, can lead to remarkable distortions. Here a striking example will be examined.

1 Ξ 37–38: The Vulgate's Reading

Ξ 37–38
τώ ῥ' οἵ γ' ὀψείοντες ἀϋτῆς καὶ πολέμοιο
ἔγχει ἐρειδόμενοι κίον ἀθρόοι·

These lords walked in a group, each leaning on his spear, to look at the clamorous battle.
R.L.

Οἵ γε are the Achaean kings, Agamemnon, Ulysses and Diomedes. They are coming from their quarters, which are far away from the place where the Achaean wall has been overrun by the Trojans, and therefore from the place where fighting is taking place, inside the Achaean camp. They do not know yet that the Trojans are inside the camp.

Those lines have been commented at length and in fact ὀψείοντες is one of the most disputed problems in Greek verbal morphology. In order to understand them properly we have to take into account ll. 27–31.

Ξ 27–31
Νέστορι δὲ ξύμβληντο διοτρεφέες βασιλῆες
πὰρ νηῶν ἀνιόντες ὅσοι βεβλήατο χαλκῷ
Τυδεΐδης Ὀδυσεύς τε καὶ Ἀτρεΐδης Ἀγαμέμνων
πολλὸν γάρ ῥ' ἀπάνευθε μάχης εἰρύατο νῆες
θῖν' ἔφ' ἁλὸς πολιῆς·

Now there came toward Nestor the kings under God's hand, they who had been wounded by the bronze and came back along the ships, Tydeus' son, and Odysseus, and Atreus' son Agamemnon. For there were ships that had been hauled up far away from the fighting along the beach of the grey sea.
R.L.

There were two competing interpretations for those lines, as we can see from the scholia. The first problem was the understanding of ἀθρόοι in l. 38:

> A Schol. Ξ 38a: (Aristonicus) ἔγχει ἐρειδόμενοι ⟨κίον ἀθρόοι⟩: ὅτι οὐχ ἑνὶ πάντες ἐρειδόμενοι. καὶ ὅτι ἀθρόοι ἐπὶ τῶν τριῶν· ἀρχὴ γάρ ἐστι πληθυντικοῦ ἀριθμοῦ τὰ τρία.
>
> because they are not all leaning on one spear, and because ἀθρόοι applies to the three of them, since 'three' is the beginning of the plural number.

However, a T scholion explains that ἀθρόοι refers to the troops:

> T Schol. Ξ 38d: ἀθρόοι: πλήθους γὰρ ἀρχὴ ἡ τριάς, ἢ ὡς καὶ ἄλλων ἀσημοτέρων αὐτοῖς ἑπομένων.
>
> ἀθρόοι: because the number three is the beginning of the plural, or because there are others, not mentioned, who follow them.

Obviously the second interpretation is correct: despite Aristarchus, who argued for ἀθρόοι applying only to the three kings, ἀθρόοι always refers to large groups. This word implies that the kings are coming with their troops, who are not mentioned because it is customary not to mention the troops but only the heroes, as an epic convention. Notice in particular that ἀθρόοι in military context means not only 'gathered', but 'in military formation', and this is probably the case here.[1]

The second controversial point was the ὅσοι βεβλήατο χαλκῷ. It seems to imply that all three are wounded, and this is why they are leaning on their spears. But as scholia underline it, only Diomedes is wounded.[2] Therefore,

---

[1] This is regularly the case in the *Iliad* when ἀθρόοι applies to troops: T 236–237 ἀλλ' ἀθρόοι ὁρμηθέντες || Τρωσὶν ἐφ' ἱπποδάμοισιν ἐγείρομεν ὀξὺν Ἄρηα "therefore let us drive on, in orderly ranks, and wake the bitter war god on the Trojans, breakers of horses" (R.L. modified); B 439–440 ἡμεῖς δ' ἀθρόοι ὧδε κατὰ στρατὸν εὐρὺν Ἀχαιῶν || ἴομεν ὄφρα κε θᾶσσον ἐγείρομεν ὀξὺν Ἄρηα "and let us, in orderly ranks, as we are, go down the wide host of the Achaians, to stir more quickly the fierce war god" (R.L. modified)—in B 437 the matter is about assembling the army in the camp, and the army is assembled by contingents; O 656–657 (Ἀργεῖοι) αὐτοῦ δὲ παρὰ κλισίῃσιν ἔμειναν || ἀθρόοι, οὐδὲ κέδασθεν ἀνὰ στρατόν "they remained there by the tents, in orderly ranks, and did not scatter along the camp." In those three cases, the army is not simply gathered together, but organised in στίχες. In non-military contexts the word means 'gathered' generally speaking.

[2] A Schol. Ξ 28b: ὅτι συλληπτικῶς εἴρηκεν βεβλήατο ἐπὶ τῶν οὐτασμένων "because he says by syllepsis βεβλήατο for the wounded ones." bT Schol. Ξ 28c: βεβλήατο: καὶ μὴν μόνος ἐν αὐτοῖς

assuming Diomedes is wounded and unable to fight, Ulysses and Agamemnon are not, can fight, and of course so can the warriors who follow them, who are certainly not all wounded.

With this background in mind, we can come to the main problem, the meaning of ὀψείοντες, usually understood 'wishing to see'. Now this interpretation may be endorsed if there are only the three kings, but not if they are coming with their troops. That a whole battalion, and here even three battalions, should come "to see the battle" does not make much sense. The battalion is coming to fight, and this is why they are ἔγχει ἐρειδόμενοι, because they are ready for battle. Since ἔγχος refers to the long spear,[3] not to the light javelin, which is more recent and was borne on the shoulder, the soldiers presumably walked with the spear in vertical position in their hand, which implies that the spear touches the ground when the bearer makes a step forward, much like a walking stick: the bearer leans on it while he walks, and this is what ἐρειδόμενοι refers to—it does not refer to the fact they are wounded.

The form ὀψείοντες, supposedly a desiderative of the root $*h_3ek^w$- 'to see', is a unique formation which has no exact parallel in other Indo-European languages, and which scholars have tried to explain in different ways (see below, pp. 145–146). Thus, for both semantic and morphological reasons, the form is unique. Since such a form can hardly have been created in Greek, because it is completely isolated, Indo-Europeanists would like to see there a very archaic form, but that leaves unsolved the semantic problem.

An A scholion explains the formation as follows:

A Schol. Ξ 37d1: τὸ ὀψείοντες ὁμοίως τῷ 'οἱ μὲν κακκείοντες' (Α 606). ἡ δὲ παραγωγὴ αὕτη ἡ διὰ τοῦ ειω γίνεται ἀπὸ ἐνεστώτων καὶ μελλόντων, ὀκνῶ 'ὀκνείω' (Ε 255), ῥιγείω, θαλπείω, πολεμησείω, βρωσείω.

the ὀψείοντες is similar to οἱ μὲν κακκείοντες: this derivation by means of -ειω is found from presents and from futures, as ὀκνῶ/ὀκνείω (Ε 255), ῥιγείω, θαλπείω, πολεμησείω (Thucydides), βρωσείω (Callimachus).

Διομήδης ἐβέβλητο. οὐκ ἔστιν οὖν σύλληψις "βεβλῆατο: yet only Diomedes among them is wounded, therefore it is not a syllepsis." A T scholion refers to a limping Ulysses: T Schol. Ξ 38b: ⟨ἔγχει ἐρειδόμενοι:⟩ καὶ Ὀδυσσεὺς γὰρ σκάζει, {καὶ} 'τὼ δὲ δύω σκάζοντε βάτην παρὰ νῆας' (Τ 47), obviously trying to save the βεβλῆατο, but Ulysses is not wounded in Ξ.

3 On the difference between older and newer weapons and fighting techniques, see below, p. 209. That ἔγχος originally referred to the long spear is shown in particular by the formulaic phrase δολιχόσκιον ἔγχος 'long-shadowed spear', and the compound δολιχεγχής (Φ 155). Δολιχός is never used as an epithet of the light javelin, αἰγανέη or ἀκών, but only of ἔγχος and δόρυ.

Among the parallels adduced by the scholion, the only ones derived from a future stem, as the scholiast puts it, are post-Homeric (πολεμησείω, βρωσείω). Providing parallels drawn from later authors was not uncommon in Antiquity (and still is nowadays ...), but that goes against Aristarchus' teaching according to which one must explain Homer from Homer. And that goes against what historical linguistics is about, understanding the history of the language and its evolution, and not putting on the same level forms of different ages.

A bT scholion notices that the order in the episode is not the expected one:

bT Schol. Ξ 30–38: πολλὸν γάρ ⟨ῥ᾽⟩ ἀπάνευθε μάχης ⟨—κίον ἀθρόοι⟩· ἐπεξηγεῖται τὸ 'ἀνιόντες' (Ξ 28). ἔστι δὲ περιπαθές, ὅτι καὶ μακρὰν ὄντες ὅμως ᾔεισαν ἐπὶ τὴν μάχην. b(BCE 3)T ἀλλὰ προληπτικῶς τὴν αἰτίαν εἶπεν· ἔδει γὰρ 'ὀψείοντες κίον' (cf. 37–38)· καὶ γὰρ πολλὸν ἀπάνευθε μάχης εἰρύατο νῆες' (cf. 30). T

far away from battle [...] they went together: it explains the ἀνιόντες (l. 28). It is full of passion, the fact that even though they were far away they nevertheless went to battle. But he gave the cause in a proleptic way, and what would have been expected is 'they went in order to see (ll. 37–38), because their ships were drawn far away from the battlefield (l. 30)'.

The D scholia have ὀψείοντες· ὀπτικῶς ἔχοντες (ZYQT, also found in Apollonius' *Lexicon homericum*), ἰδεῖν θέλοντες (ZQE), 'wishing to see'.

Several explanations have been proposed for ὀψείοντες. A convenient review and summary of the previous hypotheses is given in Kölligan (2018a).[4] An old attempt by Wackernagel assumes a periphrasis *ὄψει ἰόντες 'going to see' with a dative of aim,[5] explaining the genitive ἀϋτῆς καὶ πολέμοιο as the complement of ὄψει: this is unconvincing from the semantic point of view (see above) and does not have any parallel. Schwyzer assumed that it is a synthetic form, going back to an old desiderative formation, the suffix being *-seie̯/o-.[6] Lindeman, that *-seie̯/o- is a variant of the regular future suffix *-Hsi̯e/o- yielding Ved. -(i)sya- and the Greek future in -έω.[7] A variant of Lindeman's theory reconstructs the suffix as *-sesi̯e/o-, resulting from a contamination between two allomorphs of the future suffix. Willi starts from *-si̯e/o- and assumes *-sei̯e/o- is a remodelling triggered by the fact that in consonant stems *-si̯e/o- merged with the future

---

4 On the various hypotheses about the sigmatic future and the desiderative, see an overview in McCone 1991: 137–168.
5 Wackernagel, *Kl. Schr.* 1: 626.
6 Schwyzer, *Gr. Gr.* 1: 789.
7 Lindeman 1965: 46 *sqq.*

(*$dei\hat{k}$-$s\underset{.}{i}e$/o- > δείξε/ο-).⁸ Kölligan assumes an etymon *-s-eu-$\underset{.}{i}e$/o-, derived from u-stem adjectives themselves derived from an s-desiderative: this is phonetically unproblematic, but there are no such adjectives in Greek matching a verbal stem with a -σείω desiderative, which undermines the theory, and the only secure -s-u- form of Vedic, d(h)akṣú- 'eager to burn' does not form a denominative verb. Garnier assumes a contamination between two formations, an *ὀψᾶϝων (parallel to ὀπᾶϝων) and the future *$\hat{k}e\underset{.}{i}$-h_1s-e/o-,⁹ which is entirely *ad hoc*.

Other forms in -σείω with a clear desiderative meaning are attested in post-Homeric Greek. It is striking that the great majority of attestations in classical Attic are participle forms, like the Homeric ὀψείοντες. And, like the Homeric form, they are active participles matching a middle future. This has been noted for long, and suggests that either this desiderative formation was somehow restricted to the participle, for which there is no reason, or the post-Homeric forms are modelled after the unique Homeric case, an active participle matching a middle future, and in that case their testimony is not significant for the reconstruction of a PIE formation. That was already stated by Wackernagel, and is for instance assumed by Garnier, and rightly so.

Such forms are mainly found in tragedy: Sophocles has ἀκουσείων 'wishing to hear', *fr.* 991 (next to ἀκούσομαι), symmetrical with ὀψείοντες, δρασείων 'wishing to do', *Aj.* 326 (next to δράσομαι), ἐργασείων 'wishing to act' *Trach.* 1232 (next to ἐργάσομαι). An indicative φευξείω 'I want to flee' in Euripides, *H.F.* 628 (next to φεύξομαι), is a correction for the manuscript φευξίω. Notice that in all those cases, when there is an object, the latter is an accusative, not a genitive as in Ξ 37. Aristophanes' χεσείω 'I want to shit' (next to χέσομαι) (*Nub.* 295 κεἰ θέμις ἐστίν, νυνί γ᾽ ἤδη, κεἰ μὴ θέμις ἐστί, χεσείω "and whether it be lawful, right now, or not lawful, I want to shit"), is not a genuine desiderative: in prominent position at the end of the line, after a typically tragic κεἰ θέμις ἐστίν … κεἰ μὴ θέμις ἐστί, it must be understood as a parody of this tragic use, with a vulgar verb which, of course, no tragic poet would use, and must certainly not be taken as a proof that this kind of formation belonged to real spoken Greek.¹⁰ The comic effect stemming from the contrast between a high style tragic desiderative and the lexical content of the word is maximal. The same holds true for Aristophanes' δρασείει (*Vesp.* 168), δρασείεις (*Pax* 62), both in parodies of tragic speech,¹¹ and Cratinus' χειρονομησείοντας 'wishing to gesticulate' (*fr.*

---

8   Willi 2017: 458, n. 106.
9   Garnier 2020.
10 Similarly for *Eq.* 888 and 998.
11 *Pax* 62: ῏Ω Ζεῦ, τί δρασείεις ποθ᾽ ἡμῶν τὸν λεών; "O Zeus, what are you willing to do to our people?"

453), transmitted by Pollux, without any context. These attestations in comedy must be taken as a witness of the fashionable use of those forms in tragedy, pinpointed by comic poets. In Attic prose, Thucydides uses such forms not only according to the older model, next to a future middle form (ἀπαλλαξείοντες 1.95.7 next to ἀπαλλάξομαι, ξυμβησείοντα 8.56.3 next to συμβήσομαι), but also for active verbs (πολεμησείοντας 1.33.3, παραδωσείοντα 4.28.2, ναυμαχησείοντας 8.79.3). But he uses only participle forms, in agreement with the Homeric form. Plato has once a γελασείοντα 'wishing to laugh' (*Phaedo* 64b), next to the future middle γελάσομαι. It is noteworthy that no such form is used before Attic tragedy: Hesiod, the Homeric Hymns, Ionic poetry, Herodotus, Doric poetry have no trace of this type.

Therefore, since the first attestations are found in tragedy and exactly follow the Homeric model, it is likely that they must be analysed as a conscious Homerism on the part of tragic poets, which later on found its way into prose, rather than as a verbal category in its own right. And when the type became used in prose, it lost its old pairing with a future middle form (Thucydides).

I will not discuss here the various explanations suggested by linguists. All are complicated, all involve either a contamination or a two-storey derivation that has no parallel. The reason why no fully satisfactory solution has been offered is, I think, a consequence of a fact never taken into account. All the previous attemps, whether they assume that the Attic instances are analogical after ὀψείοντες or think they are genuine witnesses of an old inherited formation, have a common point: none of them questioned the reading transmitted by the vulgate, and all took it at face value. But the vulgate's reading is not the only one. Yet this fundamental fact is either not even mentioned in the above studies or

---

Vesp. 165–170: Philocleon—[...] οἴμοι δείλαιος.
πῶς ἄν σ᾽ ἀποκτείναιμι; πῶς; δότε μοι ξίφος
ὅπως τάχιστ᾽, ἢ πινάκιον τιμητικόν.
Bdelycleon—ἅνθρωπος οὗτος μέγα τι δρασείει κακόν.
Philocleon—μὰ τὸν Δί᾽ οὐ δῆτ᾽, ἀλλ᾽ ἀποδόσθαι βούλομαι
τὸν ὄνον ἄγων αὐτοῖσι τοῖς κανθηλίοις.
Philocleon—"Oh! you rascal, how can I kill you? How? Give me a sword, quick, or a conviction tablet.
Bdelycleon—Our friend is planning some great crime.
Philocleon—No, by Zeus! but I want to go and sell my ass and its panniers" (transl. O'Neill). The difference between high-style μέγα τι δρασείει κακόν (mocking Sophocles, *Aj.* 326 καὶ δῆλός ἐστιν ὥς τι δρασείων κακόν "and it is clear that he wants to do a terrible deed") and the very down-to-earth reply ἀποδόσθαι βούλομαι | τὸν ὄνον, with no desiderative at all, underlines the status of the form.

mentioned in a footnote but not taken into account. Nevertheless, it is a fact that the form itself is not philologically secure. And if the form was not ὀψείοντες, all the above hypotheses fall apart.

2   Zenodotus' Reading

As we learn from Aristonicus, Zenodotus had a different reading there.

> *A Schol.* Ξ 37a1: ὅτι Ζηνόδοτος γράφει 'ὀψαῖοντες'. εἴτε δὲ μετὰ πολὺν χρόνον πορευόμενοι ἤθελεν ἀκούειν εἴτε μετὰ πολὺν χρόνον ἀκούοντες, ψεῦδος· εὐθέως γὰρ ἀκούσαντες ὥρμησαν. καὶ τὸ ὀψά ἀνελλήνιστον· οὕτω γὰρ εἴωθε λέγειν 'ὀψὲ δὲ δὴ μετέειπεν' (H 399). ἔστι δὲ τὸ ὀψείοντες ὀπτικῶς ἔχοντες.

> because Zenodotus writes ὀψαῖοντες. Whether he intended that they heard when they were walking after a long time [*reading ὀψα ἰόντες, CLF*], or that they heard after a long time [*reading ὀψ' ἀΐοντες, CLF*], this is false: as a matter of fact, they ran as soon as they heard. And the word ὀψά is not Greek. Here is how Homer usually says, ὀψὲ δὲ δὴ μετέειπεν (with ὀψέ). But the ὀψείοντες means 'disposed to watch'.

The A scholion confirms that Zenodotus' text did not have word division: the scholiast points to two possible interpretations relying on two different segmentations, a consequence of the fact that the Zenodotean *ekdosis* was in *scriptio continua*.[12] A T scholion has a corrupt text with the same argument:

> *T Schol.* Ξ 37a2: τί 'ὄψ' ἀΐοντες'; οὐ γὰρ παρὰ τὸ †ὄψαπος† γὰρ βάρβαρον.

> what is this ὄψ' ἀΐοντες? It cannot come from †ὄψαπος†, for this is a barbaric word (presumably what is "barbaric" is ὀψά, as in the A scholion, and what follows is corrupt).

There was yet another variant, οὐ ψαύοντες, recorded by Didymus:

> *A Schol.* Ξ 37b1: Ἀρίσταρχός φησι Ζηνόδοτον γράφειν 'ὀψαῖοντες', ὁ δὲ Ἐπιθέτης Πτολεμαῖος '{τῷ ῥ' οἵγ'} οὐ ψαύοντες'· καὶ λόγον φησὶν ἔχειν τὴν γραφήν.

---

12   See above, pp. 20–21.

Aristarchus says Zenodotus wrote ὀψαῖοντες, but Ptolemy Epithetes ⟨says Zenodotus wrote⟩ οὐ ψαύοντες. And he says that this reading makes sense.

The latter variant is attributed to Zenodotus by Ptolemy Epithetes, author of a treatise on Zenodotus' *ekdosis*. It is certainly a correction meant to eliminate an abnormal form, but it implies that the starting point is ὀψαῖοντες, that is, Zenodotus' reading, and not the vulgate's ὀψείοντες: from ὀψαῖοντες to οὐ ψαύοντες only one letter is changed in the verb (αι/αυ),[13] whereas from ὀψείοντες one cannot obtain οὐ ψαύοντες (ει/αυ). As a matter of fact, Greek scholars were operating with letters rather than with sounds, and although it is clear that αι and αυ could not be confused phonetically, they were close enough in spelling to make the modification possible.[14] Either Ptolemy Epithetes found this form in a copy of a Zenodotean version (it is likely that there were several copies, which may have had variants)[15] or, in an effort to vindicate Zenodotus, he himself corrected Zenodotus' reading and attributed to him the corrected version.

We are thus left with two abnormal forms: the vulgate's ὀψείοντες, a *hapax* which scholiasts seek to justify, precisely because it is abnormal, and Zenodotus' ὀψαῖοντες, another *hapax* which all scholiasts and modern scholars alike dismiss because it is Zenodotus'.[16] One could not more clearly underline the bias that leads philologists and linguists astray: two *hapax legomena*, two abnormal forms, two different statuses.

---

13 The modification of ὀ- into οὐ may be related to the well-known fact, known to all Alexandrian scholars, that the archaic Ionic alphabet used ⟨ο⟩ both for /ŏ/ and for a closed /ō/, as did the Attic alphabet until the end of the 5th c. BCE. So that it was not a big step to assume that what was written ⟨ο⟩ in ὀψαῖοντες was standing for οὐ, although the latter has an etymological diphthong and is never spelled ⟨ο⟩—but that was unknown to Alexandrian scholars.

14 See already Plato, *Crat.* 434b, on the fact that the primary elements of which words are composed are the letters (στοιχεῖα). The distinction between the graphic level and the phonological level is absent from ancient etymological explanations and from Alexandrian grammatical and editorial practice.

15 Nickau 1977: 6.

16 Van Thiel 1992: 11 assumes it is a (metrical) comment by Zenodotus, integrated into the text: "Zenodotus' remark was on the margin and cannot have been meant to be a textual reading, but it is a comment. Which Zenodotus formulated in his own way, metrical" ("Zenodots Bemerkung stand am Rand und kann nicht als Textvorschlag gemeint gewesen sein, sondern ist ein Kommentar, den Zenodot auf seine Art formuliert, ἐμμέτρως"). This is entirely *ad hoc*. This is repeated in Van Thiel 2014b, *sub* Ξ 37: "Zenodotus gave a wordplay instead of a comment, with an experimental modification of the word and of the segmentation" ("Zenodot bot ein Wortspiel statt eines Kommentars, experimentelle Wortänderung und Worttrennung").

A noticeable exception is West, who assumes Zenodotus' reading is better, but does not analyse the form and does not really answers the objections. However, his remark is worth quoting: "Ancient grammarians seized on ὀψείοντες as the paradigm of a Homeric example of a desiderative form in -σείω. It is the only one in Homer, and it is suspect because there is an older attested variant which makes better sense: the ὄψ' ἀΐοντες reported from Zenodotus. [...] Leaf says hesitantly, 'it is a question if the reading of Zen. should not be preferred to that of Ar.' But most editors are so stepped in the conviction that Zenodotus' variants are never anything but irresponsible errors and conjectures, and cannot be superior to those of Aristarchus and the vulgate, that they reject this one with contumely."[17]

By now we have gone far enough in our Zenodotean journey to be allowed to state the following: Zenodotus' readings deserve an unbiased examination, even when Aristarchus condemned them. And the more bizarre a Zenodotean reading is, the more it deserves examination, because it can mean it has not been corrected into something else. As a matter of fact, Zenodotus' reading in this line, as understood and criticised by Aristonicus, is weird, because ὀψέ 'late', under any form (including the alleged "unhomeric" ὀψά) does not fit in the context. According to the A scholion, in Zenodotus' reading we have two words, ὄψ' ἀΐοντες (verb ἀΐω 'to hear', regular present participle) or ὀψὰ ἰόντες (verb εἶμι, also regular present participle), in Aristarchus' we have one word ὀψείοντες (verb ὄψομαι 'to see', morphologically irregular future, which scholiasts tried to justify as regular after all). The basic difference is thus one of word division. And the correction οὐ ψαύοντες implies yet a third possibility of word division.

The reading 'going late' (ὀψὰ ἰόντες) is condemned by Aristarchus' followers because *ὀψά is unknown. However, a compound ὀψαγόνων 'of the future generations' is attested in a metrical inscription from Crete (*IC* I viii 33, Cnossos, 2nd c. BCE).[18] An anthroponym Ὀψαγένεις is also known in Aspendos, Pamphylia, 2nd c. BCE (Brixhe 49): it is a variation on ὀψάγονος with the frequent replacement of -γονος by -γενής. Both are remodellings of the older ὀψίγονος (Homeric, attested as an anthroponym in Athens in the 4th c. BCE). That may result from

---

17   West 2001: 226.
18   Οὐδὲ θανὼν ἀρετᾶς ὄνυμ' ὤλεσας, ἀλλά σε φάμα
       κυδαίνουσ' ἀνάγει δώματος ἐξ Ἀΐδα,
       Θαρσύμαχε· τρανὲς δὲ καὶ ὀψαγόνων τις ἀείσει
       μνωόμενος κείνας θού[ριδ]ος ἱπποσύνας.
     Even dead you did not lose your renown of excellence, but fame, honouring you, leads you out of the mansion of Hades, Tharsymakhos. With a clear voice one in the future generations, too, will sing you, recalling this impetuous mastery of horses.

a wrong segmentation in compounds like ὀψ-αρότης 'late-ploughman' (Hesiod, *Op.* 490), ὀψ-αμάτης 'late-reaper' (Theocritus, Id. 10.7) modelled after ὀψαρότης. A first member ὀψα- might have been abstracted from such compounds. Or that may be analogical after antonymic adverbs in -α like τάχα 'quickly', αὐτίκα 'right now' and the Homeric αἶψα 'immediately'—but none of these is found in compounds. Zenodotus, of course, knew ὀψαρότης. Did he know forms like ὀψάγονος? That remains unclear. Anyway, even assuming he did, a compound with ὀψα- may not be enough to back an adverb ὀψά in ὀψά ἰόντες. Another objection is that with the reading ὀψά ἰόντες one cannot make anything out of the genitive ἀϋτῆς καὶ πολέμοιο which cannot be the object of ἰόντες or governed by the adverb: Zenodotus was probably aware of that.

The reading 'hearing late' (ὀψ᾽ ἀΐοντες) is also criticised for good reasons by Aristonicus: it is syntactically correct, as ἀΐω regularly takes a genitive object, but semantically not satisfying.[19] But this is precisely where we must follow the same principle: since neither reading is satisfying, neither can be an invention of Zenodotus who was as aware as Aristarchus that there is no word *ὀψά in Homer and in Ionic and who understood as well as Aristarchus that the Achaeans were not coming late but as soon as they could. Here again, it must be a reading he found in his working text and did not correct. There would be no reason for him to introduce into his text something which does not make much sense, unless we are ready to believe with Aristarchus' followers that Zenodotus as a principle "rewrites" Homer according to his fantasy. How he himself understood this reading remains unknown: the interpretation 'late' is that of Aristonicus (and probably already Aristarchus), but it is not necessarily that of Zenodotus himself. As we cannot know how Zenodotus understood it, we have to start from the reading as it is transmitted, and to submit it to modern linguistic analysis.

Zenodotus' reading is straightforward on one point: getting rid of the unnecessary constituents and keeping only the core ones, it means "hearing the clamour and the battle, they set to motion." This is logical and this is what is expected from warriors in that situation. Their ships are far away from the place where fighting is taking place, so that they cannot see the battle, but they can hear it, and consequently they prepare to join it. The verb ἀΐω (ἀϝίω) regularly takes an object in the genitive, therefore ἀϋτῆς καὶ πολέμοιο are regular in that

---

19   Some scholars maintained that Zenodotus changed the ὀψείοντες because one cannot *see* a clamour, therefore he replaced 'to see' by 'to hear'. See Van der Valk 1964: 42, and n. 181. West 2001: 225, on the other hand, is satisfied with 'late': "With Zenodotus' reading we get what the logic requires: 'So they were late in hearing the shouting and the fighting'." The logic requires 'to hear' but certainly not 'late'.

construction. And ἀϋτῆς 'clamor' as the object of a verb meaning 'to hear' is certainly not unexpected. The problem lies in the ὀψ-.

In fact, the problem of Zenodotus' reading can find a surprisingly simple solution. It is clear that he had ἀΐοντες 'hearing', the problem is the preceding two letters, which Aristarchus understood to be an adverb. This is certainly correct, it is an adverb, but not the one Aristarchus thought. The form may stand for an elided ὀψέ, or *ὀψί, although the latter is found only in compounds (ὀψίγονος, ὀψιτέλεστος), as assumed by Aristonicus, but it could also be a non-elided form ὄψ. What would such a form be? Very simply, the adverbial form matching the preposition ἐπί/ὀπί, as ἄψ is the adverb matching the preposition ἀπό. This form with an -s is found in Latin as the preverb obs- next to ob- (cognate with ἐπί/ὀπί), parallel to abs- next to ab- (cognate with ἀπό, and still found as a preposition in Plautus, abs te 'from you'), or subs- next to sub- (cognate with ὑπό, with the s-form also found in the adverb ὕψι 'up, high'). Older forms in Latin show a simplification of the consonant cluster: ostendo < *obstendo 'to put forward, to show', oscen < *obscen 'bird delivering an omen through its song' (cano 'to sing'), but P. Festus has, without simplification, opstrudant: avide trudant (209.9). The same simplificatën is found for subs- > sus- (subscūs 'spit', but sustineo, sustento, suscipio, suspendo) and abs- > as- (abstraho, but asporto). Greek etymological dictionaries (Frisk, GEW, Chantraine, DELG, Beekes, EDG, s.v. ὀψέ) correctly assume that *ὄψ is the adverbial form underlying ὀψέ.[20] Taillardat (DELG[2] p. 1423) suggested that Greek has a thematic derivative of this adverb in ὄψον 'side-dish', lit. 'that which is on the bread': whether this explanation, accepted by Beekes (EDG), is correct or not is not the point here.[21] The point is that linguists agree that there existed in Proto-Greek an adverb *ὄψ, lost in first millenium Greek.[22] Lost, except in Zenodotus' version of the *Iliad*.

This hypothesis implies that ἀΐω may be combined with ἐπί/ὀπί. In Ionic (Herodotus) and in Attic, ἐπαΐω 'to hear of, to know' is usual. The combination is already Homeric, see K 189 [...] ὁππότ' ἐπὶ Τρώων ἀΐοιεν ἰόντων "when they heard the Trojans going," with tmesis and the regular genitive for the object of

---

20 Similarly Schwyzer, *Gr. Gr.* I: 631: "s-derivative with -ε enlargement in Hom. and later ὀψέ" ("Eine Bildung auf -s mit -ε erweitert in hom. usw. ὀψέ").

21 Alternatively, the word has been linked to ὀπτός 'cooked', τὰ ὀπτά. The basic form is the plural ὄψα, a collective, of which ὄψον is a singulative.

22 Dunkel 2014: II. 248 reconstructs an adverb *óp(s) for Italic, but adds in a footnote that "Eine Verbindung mit ὀψέ, ὀψι- 'spät, zu spät' scheidet wegen der Semantik aus," and links these forms with ἀπό (ibid. p. 68), together with ὀπίσσω, ὄπισθεν (p. 70). The identification of ὄψ in ὄψ ἀΐοντες proves that, *pace* Dunkel, these forms are indeed related to Lat. obs- and to ὀπί.

ἐπ-αΐω.²³ Granted, K is a recent book, but as all recent books, it is built from older material. The verb is found in Alcaeus, *fr.* 367.1 LP ἦρος ἀνθεμόεντος ἐπάιον ἐρχομένοιο, "I heard the flowery spring coming" (transl. Campbell): the style of this dactylic line is clearly epic (-ϝεντ- adjective, genitive ending -οιο), and it is a witty reference, with a pun, to P 740–741 ὡς μὲν τοῖς ἵππων τε καὶ ἀνδρῶν αἰχμητάων ‖ ἀζηχὴς ὀρυμαγδὸς ἐπήϊεν ἐρχομένοισιν "so, as the Danaans made their way back, the wearyless roaring of horses, chariots, and spearmen was ever upon them" (R.L.), where ἐπήϊεν is the imperfect of ἔπειμι 'to come to, to assault'. The verb ἐπαΐω cannot be found without tmesis in Homer because of its metrical structure: the first two syllables of the verbal stem are short, so that a preverb like ἐπ- with another short syllable is unmetrical, unless there is an augment. Unmetrical, unless the singer can use a variant of the preverb with a long syllable, yielding a metrically viable combination.

No allomorph of ἐπί/ὀπί is known in Greek, and the *ὄψ we can reconstruct is not attested—except maybe here. But since this *ὄψ is to ἐπί/ὀπί what ἄψ is to ἀπό, a closer look at the behaviour of ἄψ may be illuminating.

3   Adverbs and Preverbs

Ἄψ is an adverb, ἀπό is either preposition or preverb. However, ἄπο can also be used as an adverb and as is known, preverbs and prepositions result from the grammaticalisation and cliticisation of older autonomous particles, which are still found in Homer as autonomous forms, and in that case labelled "adverbial." Similarly, καταί or παραί are adverbs next to κατά, κατα-, παρά, παρα-, preposition and preverb. But epic versification allows the use of the adverb instead of the preverb when metrically necessary. See for instance Ω 771 ἀλλὰ σὺ τὸν ἐπέεσσι παραιφάμενος κατέρυκες "then you would speak and put them off and restrain them" (R.L.), where παραι-, the adverb, is used as a metrical variant of the preverb because *παραφάμενος would be unmetrical. The regular form is found in A 577–578 μητρὶ δ' ἐγὼ παράφημι καὶ αὐτῇ περ νοεούσῃ ‖ πατρὶ φίλῳ ἐπίηρα φέρειν Διί "and I entreat my mother, though she herself understands it, to be ingratiating toward our father Zeus" (R.L.). Another way out was the use of the monosyllabic variant, as in M 248–249 ἠέ τιν' ἄλλον ‖ παρφάμενος ἐπέεσσιν ἀποτρέψεις πολέμοιο "or turn back some other man from the fighting, beguiling him with your arguments" (R.L.), with the same syntagm παρφάμενος (ϝ)ἐπέεσσιν as

---

23   Sophocles uses the verb with an accusative object: τὴν βάρβαρον γὰρ γλῶσσαν οὐκ ἐπαΐω "I can't understand the language of the Barbarians," *Aj.* 1263.

in Ω 771 ἐπέεσσι παραιφάμενος. The same metrical constraints account for παραιβάτης (Ψ 132) instead of παραβάτης with a tribrach. Similarly, Λ 233 has Ἀτρεΐδης μὲν ἅμαρτε, παραὶ δέ οἱ ἐτράπετ' ἔγχος "but the son of Atreus missed him, and his spear was turned aside:"[24] this is a tmesis of παρατρέπω (Ψ 398, Hes., *Th.* 103) with the allomorph παραί, that of the adverb, for metrical reasons. The structure is repeated in α 366 πάντες δ' ἠρήσαντο παραὶ λεχέεσσι κλιθῆναι with a tmesis of παρακλίνομαι 'to lie next to' (cf. Theocr., *Id.* 2.44 εἴτε γυνὰ τήνῳ παρακέκλιται εἴτε καὶ ἀνήρ)—otherwise in Homer παρακλίνω is only attested in the active, 'to incline'.

The same analysis can be made for ὑπαί next to ὑπό. Λ 416–418 (Μ 149–150 repeats Λ 417–418) has θήγων λευκὸν ὀδόντα μετὰ γναμπτῇσι γένυσσιν, ‖ ἀμφὶ δέ τ' ἀΐσσονται, ὑπαὶ δέ τε κόμπος ὀδόντων ‖ γίγνεται "(boar) grinding to an edge the white fangs in the crook of the jawbones, and these sweep in all about him, and the vaunt of his teeth uprises" (R.L.), with a tmesis of ὑπογίγνομαι 'to rise', not attested in Homer as such but known to classical Ionic (Hippocrates, Herodotus). As a matter of fact, ὑπαί here cannot mean 'below', which would not make any sense in the context, but is desemanticised as the preverb in ὑπογίγνομαι. Therefore it is most likely that we have here the adverb used as a metrical variant of the preverb, in tmesis, and that ὑπογίγνομαι is in fact already Homeric.[25] The monosyllabic variant of the preverb is found in Τ 79–80 ἑσταότος μὲν καλὸν ἀκούειν, οὐδὲ ἔοικεν ‖ ὑββάλλειν "it is well to listen to the speaker, it is not becoming to break it on him" (R.L.).

The same pattern applies to ἀμφίς, adverbial form, next to the preverb ἀμφι-. Ἀμφίς can also be used as a preverb, in tmesis or not, for metrical reasons. A clear instance is η 3–4 κασίγνητοι δέ μιν ἀμφὶς ἵσταντ' "his brothers were standing around him," where the accusative μιν is the regular object of ἀμφίσταμαι, next to θ 262–263 ἀμφὶ δὲ κοῦροι ‖ πρωθῆβαι ἵσταντο "young men in their first youth were standing around," with tmesis and the regular form of the preverb, and Ω 712 κλαίων δ' ἀμφίσταθ' ὅμιλος # "the crowd was standing around, weeping" with the preverbed verb. In that case, desemanticisation cannot be used as a criterion, because the preverb is not desemanticised. However, it is in one case: in Σ 254–256 ἀμφὶ μάλα φράζεσθε φίλοι· κέλομαι γὰρ ἔγωγε ‖ ἄστυδε νῦν ἰέναι, μὴ μίμνειν ἠῶ δῖαν ‖ ἐν πεδίῳ παρὰ νηυσίν· "Now take careful thought, dear friends; for I myself urge you to go back into the city and not wait for the divine dawn in the plain besides the ships" (R.L.), we are clearly not dealing with an

---

24   Not "the spear was turned past him" with Lattimore, as οἱ refers to Ἀτρεΐδης, and is not the regime of παραί.

25   I refer to a PhD on tmesis by J. Del Treppo, defended in Paris in December 2018, in which the author correctly analyses this line as a case of tmesis (pp. 657–658).

adverb meaning "on both sides" or "around," but with a tmesis of ἀμφιφράζομαι "to think carefully."²⁶ The same *junctura* recurs in B 13–14 οὐ γὰρ ἔτ' ἀμφὶς Ὀλύμπια δώματ' ἔχοντες ‖ ἀθάνατοι φράζονται· "for no longer are the gods who live on Olympus arguing the matter" (R.L.), with the same tmesis of ἀμφιφράζομαι, and with the adverb ἀμφίς used as a metrical variant of the preverb, exactly as παραι- is used *metri causa* for παρα-.

Let us now turn to ἄψ, which is an adverb, but happens to be also the monosyllabic form of ἀπό. The following lines show that the adverb ἄψ can be used as a metrical variant of the preverb ἀπο-.

- Ο 416–418 οὐδὲ δύναντο ‖ οὔθ' ὃ τὸν ἐξελάσαι καὶ ἐνιπρῆσαι πυρὶ νῆα ‖ οὔθ' ὃ τὸν ἄψ ὤσασθαι, ἐπεί ῥ' ἐπέλασσέ γε δαίμων "and neither was able, Hektor to drive Aias off the ship, and set fire to it, nor Aias to beat Hektor back, since the divinity drove him" (R.L.), and M 419–420 οὔτέ ποτ' αἰχμηταὶ Δαναοὶ Λυκίους ἐδύναντο ‖ τείχεος ἄψ ὤσασθαι, ἐπεὶ τὰ πρῶτα πέλασθεν "nor had the Danaan spearmen strength to push back the Lykians from the rampart, once they had won to a place close under it" (R.L.). The combination ἄψ ὤσασθαι matches the preverbed verb in Π 301 ὡς Δαναοὶ νηῶν μὲν ἀπωσάμενοι δήϊον πῦρ "so when the Danans had beaten from their ship the ravening fire" (R.L.), or in N 367 ἐκ Τροίης ἀέκοντας ἀπωσέμεν υἷας Ἀχαιῶν "to drive back the unwilling sons of the Achaeans from Troy land" (R.L.). The construction is identical, first object in the accusative and second object in the genitive (M 420, Π 301). The verb is found with tmesis in E 308 # ὦσε δ' ἀπό. Α 220 # ἄψ δ' ἐς κουλεὸν ὦσε μέγα ξίφος "and thrust the great blade back into the scabbard" (R.L.), which is usually analysed as displaying the adverb ἄψ and can be analysed as a further example of the same verb ἀπωθέω, with tmesis and use of the variant ἄψ.²⁷

- Π 58 (= Σ 445) τὴν ἄψ ἐκ χειρῶν ἕλετο "whom he took back from his hands" is a variant of A 299 ἐπεί μ' ἀφέλεσθέ γε δόντες "since you took her back from me after giving her" (with the same object, Chryseis),²⁸ and the verb with tmesis is found in I 335–336 ἐμεῦ δ' ἀπὸ μούνου Ἀχαιῶν ‖ εἵλετ' "and I am the only one among Achaeans from whom he took it back" (the γέρας).

- X 276–277 ἀνὰ δ' ἥρπασε Παλλὰς Ἀθήνη, ‖ ἄψ δ' Ἀχιλῆϊ δίδου, λάθε δ' Ἕκτορα ποιμένα λαῶν "but Pallas Athene snatched it, and gave it back to Achilleus,

---

26 This was already seen by Del Treppo, *op. cit.* (p. 387).
27 This is the vulgate's reading: Zenodotus had # ὣς εἰπὼν πάλιν ὦσε μέγα ξίφος with the simple verb.
28 The verb is not ἐξέλετο, but ἀφέλετο: Agamemnon took Chryseis away, out of Achilles' hands (ἐκ χειρῶν). Zenodotus had for this line a different reading, ἐπεί ῥ' ἐθέλεις ἀφελέσθαι, with the same verb.

unseen by Hektor shepherd of the people" (R.L.), tmesis of ἀποδίδωμι with the adverb used as a metrical variant.
- Ν 395–396 οὐδ' ὅ γ' ἐτόλμησεν [...] || ἂψ ἵππους στρέψαι "and he did not dare turn his horses back," and Υ 488–489 ἂψ ἵππους στρέψαντα μετάφρενον ὀξέϊ δουρὶ || νύξ' "as he was turning his horses back, Achilleus stabbed him with the sharp spear in the back" (R.L. modified), tmesis of ἀποστρέφω, next to the preverbed form Ο 61–62 αὐτὰρ Ἀχαιοὺς || αὖτις ἀποστρέψῃσιν ἀνάλκιδα φύζαν ἐνόρσας "let him drive strengthless panic into the Achaians, and turn them back once more" (R.L.).
- Π 394–395 Πάτροκλος δ' ἐπεὶ οὖν πρώτας ἐπέκερσε φάλαγγας, || ἂψ ἐπὶ νῆας ἔεργε παλιμπετές "but Patroklos, once he had cut away their first battalions, was pushing them away, back towards the ships" (R.L. modified), with the adverb, matches Φ 599 αὐτὰρ ὁ Πηλεΐωνα δόλῳ ἀποέργαθε λαοῦ "then by deception he kept Peleion away from the people" (R.L.) with preverb, or Ω 237–238 ὁ δὲ Τρῶας μὲν ἅπαντας || αἰθούσης ἀπέεργεν ἔπεσσ' αἰσχροῖσιν ἐνίσσων "but he drove all the Trojans off from his cloister walks, scolding them with words of revilement" (R.L.). In Π 394–395 the spatial meaning 'back' is clear, but is expressed primarily by the adverb παλιμπετές rather than by ἂψ, and the meaning is that of ἀποέργω 'to separate', lit. 'to enclose sth./so. away from'.
- Γ 324–325 Ὣς ἄρ' ἔφαν, πάλλεν δὲ μέγας κορυθαίολος Ἕκτωρ || ἂψ ὁρόων· "so they spoke, and tall Hektor of the shining helm shook the lots, looking backward" (R.L.), which can be analysed as a tmesis of ἀφοράω 'to look away' (Xen., *Cyr.* 7.1.36, about an army attacked on its back, καὶ εἰσπεσόντες παίουσιν ἀφορῶντας καὶ πολλοὺς κατακαίνουσιν "and falling on them, they beat them who were looking in another direction and killed many;" Theophrastus, *HP* 4.16.6 πάλιν ἀναστρέφειν καὶ ἀφορᾶν ὡς πολεμίας οὔσης τῆς ὀσμῆς "they turn away and look away, as they hate the smell").
- Ι 120 ἂψ ἐθέλω ἀρέσαι δόμεναί τ' ἀπερείσι' ἄποινα "I am willing to placate him and to give an immense compensation," where ἂψ, in tmesis, functions as a preverb for both ἀπαρέσκω (cf. Τ 183 ἄνδρ' ἀπαρέσσασθαι "to placate the man") and ἀποδίδωμι.[29]

Notice that for most of those verbs, the preverbed form is metrically viable. This shows that ἂψ, in tmesis or not, could be used as a metrical variant for verbs of different structures, even when other combinations were possible. The lines quoted above are traditionally analysed not as cases of tmesis, but as displaying the adverb. And they do, but we must add that they display the adverb used as a

---

29   On this line, the meaning of ἄποινα and ἀποδίδωμι, see Le Feuvre 2021b.

metrical variant of the preverb. This is the same case as for παραιφάμενος, which no one hesitates to print as one word, assuming παραι- is a metrical variant for the preverb παρα-. But whereas the use of the adverb instead of the preverb is well identified for παραι-, it is not in the case of ἄψ, which is never considered a possible substitute for the preverb. In fact, ἄψ is mostly found in tmesis, but it can also appear right before the verb, as a preverb would (O 418 and M 420 ἄψ ὤσασθαι, Γ 325 ἄψ ὁρόων).

If *ὄψ next to ἐπί/ὀπί behaved in the same way as ἄψ next to ἀπό, the preceding cases imply that *ὄψ, monosyllabic adverb, could be used as a preverb instead of ἐπί for metrical reasons, in tmesis or not. Now ἀΐω has two initial short syllables, whatever the inflected form, unless there is an augment, as is the case in Alcaeus' *fr.* 367 LP (Aeolic hexameter, see above, p. 153). As a consequence, the combination with ἐπι- is impossible for augmentless forms unless the singer uses either the tmesis or the adverb. Tmesis is found in K 189 [...] ὁππότ' ἐπὶ Τρώων ἀΐοιεν ἰόντων "when they heard the Trojans going." And a unique instance of the use of the adverb is found in Zenodotus' ὄψ ἀΐοντες, metrical variant of ἐπαΐοντες which was unmetrical. The form which puzzled Greek scholars, and led them to condemn it, is not an elided form of ὀψέ 'late', it is the old adverbial ὄψ, symmetrical with ἄψ, meaning 'on, above, after', and having in that line the same meaning as the preverb for which it stands.

That there once was an adverb *ὄψ, matching Lat. *obs-*, has long been acknowledged (see above). If the preceding analysis of Zenodotus' reading is correct, the asterisk should be removed, as ὄψ is indeed attested in Greek, and is no longer a reconstructed form. Zenodotus did not invent his ὄψ ἀΐοντες since this combination, which was abnormal for a Greek scholar like Aristarchus, is indeed consistent with what we modern Indo-Europeanists can expect. It is synchronically weird, but diachronically regular. Zenodotus cannot have been aware of that regularity, because in his time ὄψ as an adverb was certainly extinct. This constitutes the strongest argument that the form ὄψ ἀΐοντες is not an invention of his, but an archaic form preserving a linguistic fossil. The elimination of ὄψ probably goes together with the elimination of ὀπί: as long as the language had a pair ὀπί/ὄψ, it was analysable on the model of ἀπό/ἄψ. But once ὀπί was replaced by ἐπί, as a preverb and a preposition, ἐπί/ὄψ ceased to function as a pair and ὄψ lost its motivation. That this ὄψ was synchronically reinterpreted as an elided form of ὀψέ, as we find in the A scholia for ὄψ ἀΐοντες, was more or less inevitable since only ὀψέ and ὀψι- survive in classical Greek.

The case is similar to ἀναπτάς: a form reconstructed through a theoretical reasoning is afterwards confirmed by the facts. But ἀναπτάς and ὄψ are by no means new findings: these forms are written black on white in texts which have been known to philologists and linguists for a long time, the scholia to the most studied text of Greek literature. Only a persistent bias against the source, Zenodotus, prevented linguists from spotting them.

4 μ 438–439

There may be another trace of the preverb ὄψ in the *Odyssey*:

μ 437–441
νωλεμέως δ' ἐχόμην, ὄφρ' ἐξεμέσειεν ὀπίσσω
ἱστὸν καὶ τρόπιν αὖτις· ἐελδομένῳ δέ μοι ἦλθον,
ὄψ'· ἦμος δ' ἐπὶ δόρπον ἀνὴρ ἀγορῆθεν ἀνέστη
κρίνων νείκεα πολλὰ δικαζομένων αἰζηῶν,
τῆμος δὴ τά γε δοῦρα Χαρύβδιος ἐξεφαάνθη.

> I held on continuously, until she'd vomit back up my mast and keel again, and they came late to me wishing for them, at the time when a man gets up from the assembly for supper, after judging many litigants' disputes.
> J.H.

The unanimous interpretation assumes ὄψ' is the elided form of ὀψέ, which agrees with what follows, at supper time (ἐπὶ δόρπον). This is the only case of elided ὄψ' in Homer, otherwise the form ὀψέ is always used before a consonant. But 'late' in the clause is not necessary, as Ulysses knows that Charybdis is a regular phenomenon and that the remnants of his ship will surface up in due time. Granted, the line "at the time when a man leaves the assembly for supper" obviously goes with ὀψέ, but this may be an addition expanding on the ὀψέ 'late' and justifying it.[30] Syntactically, a reading ὄψ as the preverb of ἐπῆλθον in tmesis, under the form of the adverb, would be better. The verb ἔπειμι/ἐπέρχομαι regularly takes the dative (N 482 ὅς μοι ἔπεισιν # "who comes to me," I 474 ἀλλ' ὅτε δὴ δεκάτη μοι ἐπήλυθε νὺξ ἐρεβεννή "but when came for me the tenth black night," M 200 # ὄρνις γάρ σφιν ἐπῆλθε "a bird came to them," ε 472 γλυκερὸς δέ μοι ὕπνος ἐπέλθοι # "and the sweet sleep may come to me"). And ἐπῆλθον is often found with tmesis (Ψ 65 ἦλθε δ' ἐπὶ ψυχὴ Πατροκλῆος δειλοῖο "the soul of

---

30 Eustathius, *Comm. Od.* 2: 34 (*ad* μ 439): ἐν τούτοις δὲ ἑρμηνεύων καὶ τὸ ὀψέ, περὶ ὃ ἐξεβράσθη ὁ ἱστὸς καὶ ἡ τρόπις, φησίν· 'ἦμος ἐπὶ δόρπον [...]' "in that line, also explaining the ὀψέ 'late', the hour around which the mast and keel were rejected by the sea, he says 'at the time when, at supper time [...]'."

wretched Patroclus came"). For the position of the preverb, if ὄψ is indeed used as a variant of the preverb, compare the structure in Ω 287–288 τῇ σπεῖσον Διὶ πατρί, καὶ εὔχεο οἴκαδ' ἱκέσθαι ‖ ἄψ ἐκ δυσμενέων ἀνδρῶν "here, pour a libation to Zeus father, and pray you may come back home again from those who hate you" (R.L.): this is a tmesis of ἀφικέσθαι, with the adverb used as a metrical variant and placed in enjambment. Also similar is Γ 305–306 ἤτοι ἐγὼν εἶμι προτὶ Ἴλιον ἠνεμόεσσαν ‖ ἄψ "I for one am going back to windy Ilion," with again a tmesis of ἄπειμι and the preverb in the same metrical position.

An argument in favour of ἐπῆλθον is that ἔρχομαι is never used with an inanimate subject unless it has a preverb.[31] The simple verb, used primarily with animate subjects (human or animal), is found with inanimate subjects only when those are abstract entities which can be personified and endowed with motion, like winds (ἄνεμος, θύελλα, Ζέφυρος, νότος), meteorological elements (νύξ, φάος, νέφος, to which we can add ἔτος 'year'), dream (ὕπνος, ὄνειρος), pain

---

31   A search in the TLG for the simple ἔρχομαι in Homer yields the following results: all cases where the subject is an inanimate are in fact cases of tmesis (which the TLG search engine does not integrate). Διῆλθε in Γ 357, Η 251, Λ 435 διὰ μὲν ἀσπίδος ἦλθε φαεινῆς ὄβριμον ἔγχος "all the way through the glittering shield went the heavy spear" (R.L.); Δ 481–482 ἀντικρὺ δὲ δι' ὤμου χάλκεον ἔγχος ‖ ἦλθεν "and the bronze spearhead drove clean through the shoulder" (R.L.); Η 247 ἓξ δὲ διὰ πτύχας ἦλθε δαΐζων χαλκὸς ἀτειρής "and the unwearying bronze spearhead shore its way through six folds" (R.L.); and in Λ 97, Λ 398, Ξ 495, Ρ 49, Υ 473, Χ 327, φ 422, χ 16–17. Ὑπερῆλθε in Ε 16, Π 478 ὑπὲρ ὤμον ἀριστερὸν ἤλυθ' ἀκωκή "the spearhead flew over his left shoulder." Ὑπῆλθε in Ε 67 ἀντικρὺ κατὰ κύστιν ὑπ' ὀστέον ἤλυθ' ἀκωκή "the spearhead passing under the bone went straight into the bladder" (R.L. modified). Διαπροῆλθε in Η 260–261, Μ 404–405 ἣ δὲ διὰ πρὸ ‖ ἤλυθεν ἐγχείη "and the spear went through." Περιῆλθε in Κ 139 τὸν δ' αἶψα περὶ φρένας ἦλυθ' ἰωή "and the clamour immediately rose around his mind;" ρ 261 περὶ δέ σφεας ἦλυθ' ἰωή "the clamour rose around them;" ι 362 ἐπεὶ Κύκλωπα περὶ φρένας ἤλυθ' οἶνος "after the wine had gone around the Cyclops' mind" (J.H.); π 6, τ 444 περί τε κτύπος ἦλθε ποδοῖιν "the sound of feet came around him." Ἐπῆλθε in Ψ 251 ὅσσον ἐπὶ φλὸξ ἦλθε "as much as the flame touched." Κατέρχεται in Ω 82 ἥ τε κατ' ἀγραύλοιο βοὸς κέρας ἐμβεβαυῖα ‖ ἔρχεται "which, along the horn of an ox who ranges the field, goes downward" (R.L.). Ἀνῆλθεν in σ 97 αὐτίκα δ' ἦλθεν ἀνὰ στόμα φοίνιον αἷμα "at once red blood came down into his mouth" (J.H.); χ 18 αὐτίκα δ' αὐλὸς ἀνὰ ῥῖνας παχὺς ἦλθεν ‖ αἵματος "then at once up through his nostrils came a thick jet of blood" (J.H.). In some places the standard editions must be corrected: Ε 658 αἰχμὴ δὲ δι' ἀμπερὲς ἦλθ' ἀλεγεινή "and the agonizing spear drove clean through" (R.L.) (διῆλθε, not διαμπερές with most modern editors); Λ 439 γνῶ δ' Ὀδυσεὺς ὅ οἱ οὔ τι τέλος κατὰ καίριον ἦλθεν "Odysseus saw that the fatal end had not yet come to him" (R.L.) (κατῆλθε, not κατακαίριον with most modern editors; correctly κατὰ καίριον West). The case of ξ 374 ὅτ' ἀγγελίη ποθὲν ἔλθοι "when news comes from anywhere" (J.H.) can hardly be considered a counter-example since the subject ἀγγελίη is an abstract. The only counter-example is Α 120 λεύσσετε γὰρ τό γε πάντες ὅ μοι γέρας ἔρχεται ἄλλῃ "you are all witnesses to this thing, that my prize goes elsewhere" (R.L.): if γέρας is considered an abstract noun, this is no longer a counter-example, and in that case the γέρας is a woman, hence animate.

(ἄχος, ὀδύνη), evil (κακόν, γῆρας, θάνατος, μάχη). The only exception is ναῦς 'ship', but the personification of ships is commonplace (see Engl. "she" for a ship), and a ship is, indeed, 'going'. Nouns referring to an inanimate concrete object like a weapon, a tool, are never found with the simple verb, but always and only with a preverbed form, which is to be expected since they cannot move by themselves. Here the subject are the pieces of the ship (mast and keel), they are not abstract nouns and although they are parts of the ship, they cannot be considered an equivalent for 'ship', therefore we can expect a preverbed form, that is, ἐπῆλθον/ἦλθον ὄψ.

This reading, incidentally, would eliminate the alleged "dative absolute" ἐελδομένῳ δέ μοι, as ἐπέρχομαι regularly takes the dative. The dative here is governed by the preverb or the adverb used as a metrical variant of the preverb, it is neither a dative of interest nor a dative absolute.

If so, that would be another archaic line. The difference with Ξ 37 is that in the context of μ 438–439 a synchronic reinterpretation of ὄψ as ὀψέ was possible and did not seem too far-fetched: Ulysses, suspended to the tree like a bat (ὡς νυκτερίς μ 433) felt that it took an awfully long time before he could at last take hold of what was left of his ship, and indeed this reinterpretation adds to the pathos of the episode, with the ὀψέ (synchronic analysis) in prominent line-initial position and sentence-final position. The addition of "at the time when a man leaves the assembly for supper," posterior to the reinterpretation, explains the ὀψέ and thereby integrates it into a broader context. In the context of Ξ 37, on the other hand, the reinterpretation as ὀψέ was ill fitted, as rightly noticed by Aristonicus, and this is why a singer got rid of that oddity and remodelled the form.

This reading of μ 438–439, if correct, would provide another attestation of the adverb ὄψ: in that case the philological criterion would be met, as Zenodotus' reading would be confirmed by another source, namely another Homeric line displaying the same structure. This kind of confirmation a posteriori does not have the same weight, of course, as for instance the coexistence of ἄας, αὔας, ἀεστητόν, where the same form is explicitly found in another source, but it is interesting because it cannot depend on the Zenodotean reading. The linguistic criterion is met (ὄψ ἀΐοντες and ἦλθον ὄψ are linguistically regular for an archaic state of the language), and the metrical criterion is met, too, because metrical constraints are the only reason why this archaic type was preserved, although no longer understood by singers, and the preexisting metrical structure of ὄψ ἀΐοντες accounts for the morphological singularity of the vulgate's reading ὀψείοντες which replaced it.

5 Elimination of ὄψ

The question that logically arises, then, is: are there other cases where an old ὄψ can be suspected? Under the form ὄψ, probably not. But under another form, maybe: some of the attested ἄψ could be modernisations of an older ὄψ.[32] It only took a change of /o/ into /a/ to get rid of an obsolete form and to turn it into a familiar one, and this certainly was an easy modification. A plausible candidate is E 502–505:

> [...] ὣς τότ' Ἀχαιοὶ
> λευκοὶ ὕπερθε γένοντο κονισάλῳ, ὅν ῥα δι' αὐτῶν
> οὐρανὸν ἐς πολύχαλκον ἐπέπληγον πόδες ἵππων
> ἂψ ἐπιμισγομένων· ὑπὸ δ' ἔστρεφον ἡνιοχῆες.

> So now the Achaians turned white underneath the dust the feet of the horses drove far into the brazen sky across their faces as they rapidly closed and the charioteers wheeled back again.
>
> R.L.

The ἄψ in l. 505 can only be understood as temporal 'again', but an adverbial *ὄψ ἐπιμισγομένων 'mixing together one against the other' might be better. In particular, if we consider the frequent combination of ἄψ with the preverb ἀπο- (ἄψ ἀπονοστήσειν A 60, Θ 499, M 115, P 406, ἄψ ἀπιών K 289, ἄψ ἀφελέσθαι Π 58, ἄψ ἀπονάσσωσιν Π 86, ἄψ ... ἀπέλυσε Z 427, ἄψ ... ἀποίσειν K 337, ἄψ δ' ἀπὸ τείχεος ἆλτο M 390—where ἀπό can also be interpreted as a preposition), restoring ὄψ here would yield a similar pattern combining ὄψ with the preverb ἐπι-. The same combination could also occur in P 543:

> P 540–544
> Ὣς εἰπὼν ἐς δίφρον ἑλὼν ἔναρα βροτόεντα
> θῆκ', ἂν δ' αὐτὸς ἔβαινε πόδας καὶ χεῖρας ὕπερθεν
> αἱματόεις ὥς τίς τε λέων κατὰ ταῦρον ἐδηδώς.
> Ἂψ δ' ἐπὶ Πατρόκλῳ τέτατο κρατερὴ ὑσμίνη
> ἀργαλέη πολύδακρυς

> So he spoke, and took up the bloody war spoils and laid them inside the chariot, and himself mounted it, the blood running from hands and feet,

---

32   This was suggested to me by R. Meyer, whom I thank here for his insight.

as on some lion who has eaten a bullock. Once again over Patroklos was close drawn a strong battle weary and sorrowful.

R.L.

Ἄψ here cannot have its local meaning 'back', since Hector is driving away and not returning to battle. Therefore it is understood with the temporal meaning 'again', but this would imply a new event and is hardly compatible with the perfect stem of τέτατο 'was extended'. On the other hand, ἐπιτείνω is a usual verb in Attic-Ionic, although unattested in Homer, meaning 'to stretch over' (Hdt.) and also 'to prolong, to extend', or 'to intensify' (Hippocrates). And the perfect stem τέταμαι starting with two short syllables cannot be used with the preverb except if there is a tmesis. Here also an older *ὄψ δ' ἐπὶ Πατρόκλῳ τέτατο κρατέρη ὑσμίνη "and over Patroclus the strong battle was intensifying/extending" may be preferable.

Perhaps other lines, too, could be read with ὄψ, like Θ 335: Ἄψ δ' αὖτις Τρώεσσιν Ὀλύμπιος ἐν μένος ὦρσεν "Now once again the Olympian filled the Trojans with fury" (R.L.). The line with ὄψ would read: "thereupon once again ..."[33]

On the whole, the presence of an older ὄψ in those cases remains hypothetical: there is no variant reading and ἄψ is more or less fitting. We can suspect that in some lines ὄψ was, indeed, replaced by ἄψ, especially when ἄψ in the transmitted text displays a purely temporal meaning. The preposition ἐπί, adverb ἔπι, can have a temporal meaning 'after', whereas this is not the case of ἀπό in Homer. The temporal meaning of ἄψ 'again' might be imported from an older ὄψ 'after that'. On the other hand, the frequent combination ἄψ δ' αὖτις 'back again', in which the originally local αὖτις assumed a temporal meaning, could also account for the temporal meaning of ἄψ. This remains speculative, however plausible it may be.

6 From Zenodotus' Reading to the Vulgate's

The older form, preserved in Zenodotus' text, was abnormal and semantically not logical if it contained ὀψ(έ) 'late', which was the only possible analysis in the synchrony of Ionic. If one rules out the reading ὀψ(έ) 'late', only one possibility

---

33 This could not be a tmesis ὄψ ... ὦρσεν matching the verb ἐπόρνυμι, also found with μένος in the phrase ὅς μοι ἐπῶρσε μένος "who stirred up my spirit" (Υ 93), ὅς οἱ ἐπῶρσε μένος (Χ 204), because the verb is ἐνῶρσεν. Should we assume that the line once had ὄψ, it would have to be an adverb.

was left: since it was no longer possible to analyse ὄψ as an adverb, let alone a preverb, ὀψ- had to be the root. This implied a morphological reanalysis of the sequence, the adverb/preverb being reanalysed as the root, and the root as a suffixal element.[34] This was possible because ὀψ- 'to see' is frequently used in Homeric Greek[35] and is also usual in Attic-Ionic. The frequency of a morpheme is of course a major factor in reinterpretations and reanalyses because the frequent morpheme is much more present in the mind of speakers than the rare one, therefore spontaneously the speakers' first interpretation will be that it is the frequent morpheme. The second factor is, as usual, context.

In the context, identifying ὀψ- as the root of 'to see' was rather natural. At the beginning of Ξ, Nestor is in his tent and hears the fighting (Ξ 1 Νέστορα δ' οὐκ ἔλαθεν ἰαχὴ πίνοντά περ ἔμπης), which is now taking place inside the Achaean camp, after the Trojans managed to overrun the wall. He then goes out to see what is happening (Ξ 8 αὐτὰρ ἐγὼν ἐλθὼν τάχα εἴσομαι ἐς περιωπήν).[36] The parallelism is obvious: the Achaean kings whose ships are far away from the place where the wall has been overrun "come to see" (ὀψείοντες ... κίον) as Nestor "goes to look around" (εἴσομαι ἐς περιωπήν). Notice there is also a parallelism with Zenodotus' reading: as Nestor hears the fighting first (Ξ 1 Νέστορα δ' οὐκ ἔλαθεν ἰαχή) and goes out (Ξ 8 εἴσομαι), the Achaean kings hear the fighting (Ξ 37 ὄψ

---

34 An instance of the opposite reanalysis is found for instance in καμμονίην, understood by scholiasts and modern linguists alike as a variant of κατ(α)-μονή (Preverb-Root), whereas it is an old derivative of a *ḱn̥s-mon-, animate noun matching the inanimate *ḱn̥s-mn̥ (Ved. śásman- 'praise'), where *ḱn̥s- is the root and -mon- the suffix (Le Feuvre 2008). Καμμονίη means 'praise' and belongs to the formulaic system of κλέος/εὖχος/κῦδος. It has nothing to do with μένω 'to stay'.
35 The *Iliad* has 14 instances of the future ὄψομαι.
36 Ξ 1–8: Νέστορα δ' οὐκ ἔλαθεν ἰαχὴ πίνοντά περ ἔμπης,
    ἀλλ' Ἀσκληπιάδην ἔπεα πτερόεντα προσηύδα·
    φράζεο δῖε Μαχᾶον ὅπως ἔσται τάδε ἔργα·
    μείζων δὴ παρὰ νηυσὶ βοὴ θαλερῶν αἰζηῶν.
    ἀλλὰ σὺ μὲν νῦν πῖνε καθήμενος αἴθοπα οἶνον
    εἰς ὅ κε θερμὰ λοετρὰ ἐϋπλόκαμος Ἑκαμήδη
    θερμήνῃ καὶ λούσῃ ἄπο βρότον αἱματόεντα·
    αὐτὰρ ἐγὼν ἐλθὼν τάχα εἴσομαι ἐς περιωπήν.
    Now Nestor failed not to hear their outcry, though he was drinking his wine, but spoke in winged words to the son of Asklepios: 'Take thought how these things shall be done, brilliant Machaon. Beside the ships the cry of the strong young men grows greater. Now, do you sit here and go on drinking the bright wine, until Hekamede the lovely-haired makes ready a hot bath for you, warming it, and washes away the filth of the bloodstains, while I go out and make my way till I find some watchpoint'.
        R.L.

ἄϊοντες ἀϋτῆς καὶ πολέμοιο) and come (Ξ 38 κίον). The parallelism is displaced in the remodelling of the line: in Zenodotus' version, it implies the cause, hearing, whereas in the vulgate, it implies the consequence, going to see.

Therefore the context oriented the interpretation towards a form of the verb 'to see', and backed the spontaneous interpretation that ὀψ- belonged with ὄψομαι. As the form was clearly a participle, the only problem was to provide a likely explanation for the second syllable. And as the A scholion makes clear, a parallel was drawn with κακκείοντες. Of course, the scholion uses κακκείοντες as a parallel to justify ὀψείοντες, but this parallel works both ways: we know that the Alexandrian school was working with analogy, that is, tried to find parallel formations or syntactic constructions, but we also know that singers work with analogy, and that very often a line is modelled after another one, and a word after another one. Here κακκείοντες, also a participle, may have provided a model for remodelling the form. And we modern scholars must be aware of that possibility, and not follow blindly what Aristarchus said.

Κακκείοντες is a participle of κεῖμαι, which has an etymological diphthong. It is found twice in the *Iliad*, in Α 606 = Ψ 58 οἳ μὲν κακκείοντες ἔβαν κλισίην δὲ ἕκαστος "they went away each to sleep in his home" (R.L.). It is used as an apposition to the subject of a motion verb, which is the same syntactic configuration as Ξ 37–38, it is used in the same metrical position as ὀψαίοντες/ὀψείοντες, with the same pronominal subject οἳ μὲν/οἵ γε, and it expresses goal. It must go back to a future *k̂ei-s-e/o- (*LIV*^{2}) but in synchrony the future is the remodelled κείσομαι (Σ 121 etc.), therefore κακκείοντες was understood as meaning 'desiring to go to bed' with a desiderative value distinct from the future. Now the weird ὀψαίοντες could only be interpreted as a participle of ὄψομαι, but the /a/ was abnormal. The model of κακκείοντες next to κεῖμαι, κείσομαι could back the analysis as an active participle next to the middle ὄψομαι, and account for the transfer of the /e/ of κακκείοντες to the problematic form. Since the future is thematic, the stem ὀψε- of ὄψεαι, ὄψεται, ὄψεσθαι was the closest candidate.

This prompted a remodelling, which was a minimal one: replacement of /opsaïontes/ by /opseiontes/ implied only changing one vowel and making use of isochrony (one long syllable equals two short syllables). This replacement was certainly easier in a written text, as there was no diacritic sign to indicate that /aï/ were two vowels in hiatus and not a diphthong. In a written text, there is only one step from ΟΨΑΙΟΝΤΕΣ to ΟΨΕΙΟΝΤΕΣ. Such modifications of demotivated forms are known: compare the case of χθονὸς εὐρυοδείης "earth of the broad roads," remodelling of an older χθονὸς *εὐρυεδείης "earth of the broad basis," derivative of a regular εὐρυεδής compound of ἕδος 'seat' and preserved in Simonides (*fr.* 37.24–25 εὐρυεδέος ὅσοι | καρπὸν αἰνύμεθα χθονός) after εὐρυάγυια "of the broad streets," epithet of Troy and other cities.[37] The remodelled form was afterwards introduced into the Hesiodic text. In both cases a demotivated form was remodelled because of a synchronic etymology, by changing one phoneme. In both cases the remodelled form is morphologically irregular (ὀψείοντες as εὐρυοδείης) whereas the older one is regular (ὄψ ἀΐοντες as *εὐρυεδείης). In both cases the antiquity of the older form is warranted by other languages (*urú sádas* "wide foundation" RV 1.85.6, said of earth and sky, and *obs-* in Latin). Granted, the remodelling of *εὐρυεδείης into εὐρυοδείης has no incidence on the morphological boundaries and the morphological analysis of the form, whereas the remodelling of ὄψ ἀΐοντες into ὀψείοντες does, because in the latter case we have two successive steps, first reanalysis, which yields a new morphological segmentation, and subsequently remodelling, within the limits of the new morphological segmentation.

Once the form was remodelled after κακκείοντες, it could have acquired a future meaning, as future participles expressing goal are regular. It did not, because the future was ὄψομαι, not **ὀψείω. The new form ὀψείοντες took from its model κακκείοντες the desiderative value 'desiring to see'. In addition, another factor may have played a role. The desiderative value may be a consequence of the syntax of the line, namely, the presence of the genitive ὀψείοντες ἀϋτῆς καὶ πολέμοιο. The genitive is regular with Zenodotus' reading, as the object of ἐπαΐω. This genitive is not regular as the object of ὄψομαι, but verbs meaning 'to desire' do govern a genitive object (ἐπιθυμέω, ἱμείρω, ἔραμαι, ἐρατίζω, ἔλδομαι, λιλαίομαι). Therefore, assuming ὀψείοντες meant 'desiring to see' and not 'going to see' was a simple way of accounting for the genitive object, provided the feature [+ GENITIVE] was transferred from the lexical level (verbs meaning 'to desire') to the morphological one (desiderative morpheme added to any verb). Scholars usually justify the genitive object by the desiderative value of ὀψείοντες, but in fact things developed the other way round. The preexisting genitive (required by the verb of perception) imposed the desiderative value on a verbal form which was not desiderative. Once this was done, of course the only possible analysis is that the genitive is required by the desiderative morpheme: the synchronic analysis reverses the diachronic process.

But ὀψείοντες is not alone, and several similar forms are found in Attic tragedy and even in prose (see above, pp. 146–147). They are modelled after ὀψείοντες, which gives a *terminus ante quem* for the creation of this form: since

---

37 Schmitt 1967: 246, after Schulze 1892 and Bechtel 1914. Poltera 2008: 464 considers Simonides' εὐρυεδής is secondary and modelled after εὐρυοδείης, which is incorrect. Another case of such incorrect analysis and remodelling of an old form is the plural accusative ἐϋκλεῖας in K 281 (see above, p. 43, n. 58).

the desiderative participle in -σείων is already well attested in Sophocles, it means that the remodelling of ὄψ ἀΐοντες into ὀψείοντες occurred at the latest in the first half of the 5th c. Notice Aeschylus has no such form, at least in what survives of his works. The argument *e silentio* is not a valid one, but the fact remains, nevertheless. Although those forms seem to strengthen the case of ὀψείοντες, which is not isolated since there are other forms of that type in post-Homeric Greek, they are worthless if they are analogical after ὀψείοντες. They merely show the internal logic of verbal creation in epic poetry and Greek poetry in general, on the model of Homer, but they cannot prove the authenticity of the Homeric form. Homer must not be explained in the light of post-Homeric facts: Aristarchus' principle that one must explain Homer from Homer is sound and must be observed. The problem here is to know what "Homer" was—and in that case the vulgate is only one of the possible Homers.

The modification of ὄψ ἀΐοντες into ὀψείοντες is probably linked to the Athenian version of the poems—whether or not one believes in the "Pisistratid recension" reported by tradition. The offshoots of ὀψείοντες are only found in Attic literature, first of all in tragedy (and in a parody of tragic use, in comedy). The only prose writer who uses them is Thucydides, and that may be a feature of his mannerism, at any rate a conscious use of a marked poetic form allowing a maximal condensation of the expression (πολεμησείοντες instead of πολεμεῖν βουλόμενοι), which is typical of Thucydides. The limitation to Attic tragedy is likely to indicate that the modification was introduced by an Athenian rhapsode. As a matter of fact, this looks like a correction by a rhapsode working with a written text (see above) rather than by a singer in an entirely oral framework. First of all because correcting ΟΨΑΙΟΝΤΕΣ into ΟΨΕΙΟΝΤΕΣ in a text with no word division and no diacritic sign was very easy, and secondly because the parallelism with κακκείοντες in the same structure whereas the two lines do not have any phonetic similarity but only a structural one probably implies the existence of a written text allowing comparisons within a corpus. That scenario would agree with West's thesis according to which Zenodotus' copy of Homer was a text which was distinct from the Athenian tradition at an early date. If the modification is specific to the Athenian version, Zenodotus' text can be expected not to have any trace of it.

To sum up, there is no point in trying to explain the vulgate's ὀψείοντες if this form results from the remodelling within Greek of an utterly different form. All the attempts at solving the problem of ὀψείοντες are bound to fail if this form is not authentic. Zenodotus' form is old and is almost certainly the older one. It is neither an invention of his nor an emendation he introduced, but it is an archaism, regular on all accounts (morphology, syntax, metrics, semantics), which agrees with what we modern Indo-Europeanists know. This form, as in the preceding case, vindicates a reconstruction which had been so far only proposed as such, that of the adverb ὄψ, in both adverbial and preverbal use. This form, hereto known from Latin only, is indeed also attested in Greek—which implies that it is not a "relatively recent" creation in Latin (*pace* de Vaan 2008). It was preserved in epic diction for metrical reasons, as a variant of ὀπί/ἐπί when the verbal stem could not combine with the regular preverb. The form was no longer synchronically understandable, therefore it was reinterpreted, either without any formal change (μ 438–439) when the reinterpretation was compatible with the context, or with a remodelling when the reinterpretation was ill-fitted for the context (Ξ 37–38). But once again, the archaism is on Zenodotus' side, and it is useless to try to integrate the vulgate's ὀψείοντες into the rules of PIE morphology, although that is what linguists have sought to do until now, since this is a remodelling prompted by an erroneous synchronic analysis. Granted, ὀψείοντες cannot have been created within Greek, but we have to beware of the argument "the form X cannot have been created within Greek, therefore it must be inherited." In that case, as in many others, the form results from the alteration of an older inherited form, alteration that has nothing to do with a regular linguistic evolution. It is all the more so remarkable that this artificial form, imitated by the tragic poets, found its way into Attic prose and became part of the (learned) Greek language. Another proof of the ubiquitous influence of Homer.

CHAPTER 6

Cloaks and Coats

1   Ἔρυμα/ἔλυμα

Another case where Zenodotus' reading and the vulgate's form a minimal pair is found in Δ 137:

Δ 136–138
καὶ διὰ θώρηκος πολυδαιδάλου ἠρήρειστο
μίτρης θ', ἣν ἐφόρει ἔρυμα χροὸς ἕρκος ἀκόντων,
ἥ οἱ πλεῖστον ἔρυτο· διὰ πρὸ δὲ εἴσατο καὶ τῆς.

> into the elaborately wrought corselet the shaft was driven and the guard which he wore to protect his skin and keep the spears off, which guarded him best; yet the arrow plunged even through this also.
>   R.L.

In that case, the vulgate's reading seems unproblematic: there is no metrical or morphological problem with ἔρυμα. But there is a slight semantic oddity: in Attic-Ionic prose and poetry, ἔρυμα is never used for a piece of clothing, but only as 'fence, defence', including metaphorically for a person defending a land or a box protecting a music instrument (Eur., *fr.* 12.47 Page). The use for a piece of clothing has no parallel. In this line, both Zenodotus and Aristophanes of Byzantium had ἔλυμα instead of ἔρυμα. The minimal pair is a true one, as there is no difference in segmentation between Zenodotus' reading and the vulgate, as was the case for ὀψ ἀΐοντες/ὀψείοντες.

A *Schol.* Δ 137a1: ἡ Ζηνοδότου καὶ Ἀριστοφάνους 'ἔλυμα' εἶχον, οἱονεὶ εἴλημα.

> the recension of Zenodotus and Aristophanes had ἔλυμα, as though it were εἴλημα 'wrapping'.

Van Thiel assumes that ἔλυμα is an "experimental modification by Zenodotus, who probably started from the comparison of ἔρυμα—ἕρκος—ἔρυτο."[1] Then

---

[1] Van Thiel 2014b, *sub* Δ 137: "experimentelle Wortänderung Zenodots, der wohl aus dem Vergleich von ἔρυμα—ἕρκος—ἔρυτο hervorgegangen ist."

Aristophanes wrongly took ἔλυμα for the correct reading and integrated it into his text. But assuming that there was in the text a *figura etymologica* between ἔρυμα (Δ 137) and ἔρυτο (Δ 138), it is hard to understand what could have suggested ἔλυμα, which ruins the etymological relationship. On the contrary, it is much more likely that an older ἔλυμα was replaced by ἔρυμα for the sake of the *figura etymologica*.

Ἔλυμα is not attested elsewhere in the Homeric corpus. A homonym ἔλυμα is found in Hesiod (*Op.* 430, 436) with the meaning 'stock of the plough', that is, a wooden piece into which the ploughshare is fitted.[2] This meaning is also given by lexicographers (Pollux, *Onomasticon* 1.252), but obviously cannot be the meaning in Δ 137. Besides, ἔλυμα 'stock of the plough' has a long ῡ in *Op.* 430 (ἐν ἐλύματι πήξας # "having fitted it in the stock"), whereas in Δ 137 the ῠ must scan short. This could be a simple case of metrical lengthening in Hesiod, since the rule is that in a sequence of four short syllables the second one is lengthened to allow its use in hexametric poetry, which would be the case for ἐλύματος and ἐλύματι in the singular, ἐλύματα and ἐλύμασι in the plural. But this lengthening is mostly used in the metrical position before the bucolic, which is not the case in *Op.* 430. *Op.* 436 has # δρυὸς ἔλυμα, πρίνου δὲ γύην "so is a plough-share of oak as well as a plough-tree of holm-oak" (D.H.) which is both metrically awkward and probably corrupt, for the absence of any coordination with the preceding sentence poses a significant syntactic problem, hence West's proposal # δρυὸς ⟨δ'⟩ ἔλυμα. West's choice (1978) to scan δρυός with synizesis counting for a long syllable and followed by two short syllables ἔλῠ (the μα, long through position, is the first syllable of the second foot), for which West acknowledges that there is no parallel, is an attempt at solving something which is probably more a textual problem than a metrical one, or rather, a metrical problem resulting from a corrupt text. The correction proposed by Schäfer and accepted by Mazon (CUF) # δρυὸς ἔλυμα, γύης πρίνου [⌣ ⌣ ⌣ – ⌣ ⌣ – – –] yields a better text: it is an acephalous line, of which there are other instances, without any coordination because we are dealing with a list, and with the same long ῡ as in ἐλῡματι of l. 430. Besides, the line may not be acephalous: the forms δρῦς and δρῦν have a long ῡ. It is conceivable that the poet extended this ῡ to the genitive, in order to provide the required long first syllable—the ῡ is shortened before a vowel, but the epic language has so many cases of long

---

2 *Schol. vetera in Hesiodi* Opera 430: ἔλυμα δὲ παρὰ τὸ ἐλύειν ὅ ἐστι καλύπτειν, ἐξ οὗ καὶ ἔλυτρον τὸ περικάλυμμα "Ἔλυμα is derived from ἐλύειν which means 'to cover', from which is also derived ἔλυτρον, the wrapping."

vowel in hiatus that the model was easily found. Therefore we should not rely on this instance, and at any rate not take it as contradicting l. 430. The word in Hesiod has no initial digamma.

A noun ἔλῠμα 'wrapping' is regularly formed from the root *$u̯el$-u-, 'to cover, to wrap', found in Arm. *gelum* 'to turn', Lat. *volvō* 'to turn', Ved. *vr̥ṇóti* 'to cover, to envelop', Goth. causative *walwjan* 'to revolve'. Armenian, Latin and Germanic imply a present stem *$u̯el$-u- (causative *$u̯ol$-u-$ei̯e/o$-). The -u- may be an enlargement. Whatever the exact origin, synchronically *$u̯el$-u- behaves as a root forming a present stem and nominal derivatives. In Greek, the -u- is found in all the aspectual stems, and the perfect is εἴλυμαι. Vedic has a nasal present with which εἰλύω has been compared, although the structure of the Greek form does not match the Vedic one because Greek has an *e* grade which cannot be old.[3] A possibly inherited derivative of this root is ϝέλῠτρον 'wrapping, scabbard', matching Sanskrit *varutra*- 'cloak' mentioned by lexicographers (*EWAia*, s.v. VAR-). However, since *-tro- is productive in both languages, this can also be an independent formation. Orion has ἔλυτρον. τὸ ἔλυμα τοῦ τόξου (*Etymologicum*, epsilon, p. 63), in which ἔλυμα is used to explain ἔλυτρον, further implying that it was not a particularly difficult word. Primary *-$mn̥$ neuters inflected according to the proterodynamic type. In Greek the strong stem is generalised and *-$mn̥$ neuters mostly display the *e* grade of the root, which is the case of ϝέλυμα.

In Δ 137 ἔλυμα applies to a μίτρη, a belt, which is, indeed, wrapped around the waist. The word is found in Hesychius, ε 2225: ἔλυμα· τὸ τοῦ ἀρότρου †πέριον. νύσσα. καὶ τὸ ἱμάτιον. καὶ ἡ ἀϊών "the ? of the plough [reference to Hesiod, *Op.* 430], the turning-post [in a chariot race], and also the cloak, and also the sea shore." The meaning 'turning-post' does not come from Homer, at least in the preserved state of the corpus. The gloss ἱμάτιον 'cloak', that is, a garment wrapping the body, is not very likely to be an explanation of Zenodotus' ἔλυμα in Δ 137. Even if we take ἱμάτιον as meaning 'piece of cloth' and not specifically 'cloak', this does not fit very well for the Homeric μίτρη. The gloss must rather be drawn from a lost poem in which ἔλυμα meant 'cloak'. The meaning 'sea shore' must likewise be a reference to an unknown piece, wherein the word seems to have been used with the meaning 'rolling of the waves', but since the source is lost, we cannot make more than a hypothesis. At any rate, in the gloss of Hesychius, two meanings at least, νύσσα and ἀϊών, apply to neither Δ 137 nor

---

3 LIV[2] separates two roots, 'verhüllen' (*vr̥ṇóti*) and 'drehen, rollen' (*volvo, gelum*, ἐλυσθείς 'curled up'), adding that the two may ultimately be one and the same root, and that the Greek forms can be assigned to either one. Lubotsky 2000 argues for an initial laryngeal in *$Hu̯el$- 'verhüllen'.

Hesiod, *Op.* 430, nor does the third meaning, ἱμάτιον. This may be taken as a philological confirmation of the Zenodotean reading, if ἔλυμα 'coat' does not depend on Zenodotus but comes from an unknown poet or is a dialectal word.

The semantic and formal differences between Hesiod's ἔλῦμα and Zenodotus' ἔλῠμα which must go back to ϝέλυμα suggest that ἔλῦμα 'stock of the plough' is a different word.

The vulgate's reading ἔρυμα is not better attested in the Homeric corpus, where it is a *hapax*. It is also found in Hesiod (*Op.* 536), in the same syntagm ἔρυμα χροός (see pp. 175–176), and in Attic-Ionic with the meaning 'defense' (Aeschylus, *Eum.* 701; Eur., *Med.* 1322; Hdt 7.223 etc.; Thuc. 1.11.1 etc.). It is regularly derived from ἐρύω, and is synchronically motivated.

Now, while ἔρυμα from ἐρύω is synchronically regular, ἔλυμα from εἰλύω is not. As Alexandrian scholars observed, 'to wrap' in Homer is always εἰλυ-, not ἐλυ-. The verb 'to wrap' is attested almost always in the passive perfect εἴλῦμαι < *ϝε-ϝλῦ-.[4] The present εἰλύω is not attested in Homer but first in the fifth century. Only found in poetry, it was remodelled after the perfect, or it represents the thematicisation of the perfect reanalysed as an athematic present (εἴλυμαι as γάνυμαι). The *Iliad* has the future εἰλύσω (Φ 319), which implies a present stem εἰλυ-.[5] The present is attested in a variant reading only: in Ψ 135 an A scholion says there was a reading θριξὶ δὲ πάντα νέκυν καταείλυον "they covered all the corpse under the locks of their hair" (R.L.) instead of the vulgate's καταείνυον (καταέννυμι) and Aristarchus' καταείνυσαν (καταέννυμι).[6] The only form in

---

4   The long [ū] remains unclear. Some admitted a *seṭ* variant *ṷeluH- (Peters 1980: 45–46, with the laryngeal between brackets; laryngeal with a question mark in *LIV*²). The long [ū] is also found in Vedic *varūtár-* 'protector', but the Indian grammarians quote a *varutra-* 'cloak', exact match of ϝέλυτρον, with a short [ŭ] (see Mayrhofer, *EWAia*). Tichy 1995: 41, assumes that *varūtár-* does not belong with *vṛṇóti*. In Greek the long [ū] is probably a metrical lengthening: εἴλυμαι, εἴλυσαι, εἴλυται (Μ 286), εἴλυσθε, εἰλύσθαι could be used only if the vowel was metrically lengthened, and εἰλυμένος (five occurrences in Homer) was also aligned on the dominant pattern of -μενος participles with a dactylic ending. This dominant pattern in the perfect was extended to the pluperfect although it was not necessary (εἴλῡτο Π 640, ε 403).

5   This is the vulgate's reading. There was a reading ἰλύσω ψαμάθοισιν: A Schol. Φ 319a: εἰλύσω· ἐὰν μὲν διὰ τοῦ ει, εἰλύσω, δηλοῖ τὸ εἰλήσω· ἐὰν δὲ διὰ τοῦ ι, τὸ σκεπάσω, ἀφανίσω, παρὰ τὴν ἰλύν, ὡσεὶ ἔλεγε 'τῇ ἰλύϊ καλύψω'. διχῶς οὖν ἡ γραφή "if it is spelled with ει, εἰλύσω, it means 'I will wrap it'; if it is spelled with ι, it means 'I will cover, I will make disappear', from ἰλύς, as if he were saying 'I will cover with mud'; thus, there are two spellings." This reading is also mentioned by Apollonius Soph., *Lexicon homericum*, p. 91 ἰλύσω· ἰλύϊ περικαλύψω (in the alphabetical order with ι), and also appears in Hesychius (ι 597), Orion (*Etymologicum*, iota, p. 76), *Et. Magnum* (Kallierges, p. 470), Eustathius (*Comm. Il.* 4: 507). It is not associated with Zenodotus' name. No denominative ἰλύω is known otherwise.

6   Homer also has two derived present stems εἰλῠφάω (Λ 156 # πάντῃ τ' εἰλυφόων ἄνεμος φέρει "and the roll of the wind carries it everywhere," R.L.) and εἰλῠφάζω with ῡ *metri causa* (Υ

ἑλυ- is a passive aorist ἐλύσθη, which is used in Homer with the meaning 'to curl up', not 'to wrap'. Thus, it was clearly separated from the group of εἰλύω by Greek scholars (see below, pp. 176–177).

The stem εἰλῡ- is also found in the neuter derivative εἴλῡμα in ζ 178–179 δὸς δὲ ῥάκος ἀμφιβαλέσθαι, ‖ εἴ τί που εἴλυμα σπείρων ἔχες ἐνθάδ' ἰοῦσα "and give me a rag to throw about me, if by chance you had a wrapper for cloths when you came here" (J.H.). The line as it is transmitted is recent, for it shows neglect of the digamma of ϝεῖλυμα. The word is only known from Homer, Anacreon, Apollonius Soph. and lexicographers,[7] with the exception of one instance in the Pseudo-Galen.[8] In itself, εἴλῡμα can be either a recent derivative of the new present stem εἰλυ-, or a remodelling after εἴλῡμαι, εἰλύω of an older -μα derivative which was directly built from the root, since *-mn̥ neuters are primary derivatives, as ϝέλυτρον. A primary *-mn̥ neuter would have the form *u̯el-u-mn̥ 'wrapping': this form is the etymon of Lat. volūmen (the long vowel of volūmen is secondary, see de Vaan 2008, s.v. volvo).[9] Its reflex in Greek would be ϝέλῠμα, the form Zenodotus had in his text.

In fact, Mycenaean provides a clear confirmation of the antiquity of Zenodotus' form. PY Ub(1) 1318, a list of leather pieces, has:

(l. 4): wi-ri-no . we-ru-ma-ta . ti-ri-si . ze-u-ke-si 1.

Scholars agree that the meaning is "one ox-hide (ϝρῑνός) ⟨for⟩ we-ru-ma-ta." The latter word is a *hapax*, the interpretation of which is difficult. The first

---

492 πάντῃ τε κλονέων ἄνεμος φλόγα εἰλυφάζει "and the blustering wind lashes the flame along" (R.L.), which seem to imply a nominal stem *εἰλυφή (Schwyzer's suggestion (*Gr. Gr.* I: 645) of a verbal compound εἰλύω + ὑφάω, must be rejected). But the meaning here is clearly 'to roll, to wind', not 'to wrap, to cover'. The verb εἰλυσπάομαι 'to roll in a spasm' (Hippocrates, Galen), ἰλυσπάομαι 'to crawl like a worm' (Plato, with the derivatives ἰλύσπασις, ἰλυσπαστικός Aristotle) is a recent creation.

7 Hsch., ε 917: εἴλυμα· ἐνείλυμα. περίβλημα. σκέπασμα "εἴλυμα: garment, coat, blanket."
8 Ps.-Galen, *Definitiones medicae* 19.367: Περιόστεοι ὑμένες εἰσὶν εἰλύματα λεπτά, ἰνώδη ὥσπερ ἐνδύματα τῶν ὀστῶν "the periosteal membranes are thin wrappings, tendinous, like the bones' garments."
9 Although de Vaan maintains the comparison with ἔλυμα 'stock of the plough', the connection must be rejected (*pace* Beekes, *EDG*, s.v. εἰλύω): ἔλυμα, which has no ϝ, does not belong to this root (see below, pp. 192–193). But of course de Vaan does not take into account Zenodotus' ϝέλυμα. Euler 1979: 113–114 compares εἴλυμα with *volūmen* to conclude that they are independent analogical creations in each language, but maintains that εἴλυμα and Ved. *várman*- 'defence' could go back to a same PIE etymon, reconstructing a *u̯el(ū)mn̥. This is clearly impossible.

interpretation understands ϝέρυμα 'bridles', from ϝερύω.[10] This is correctly rejected by Bernabé–Luján for several reasons. They themselves suggest that the phrase refers to three pairs of sandals, because in l. 3 the list mentions pe-di-ra /πέδιλα/ 'sandals'.[11] However, in that case the use of the dative 'by three pairs' (ti-ri-si . ze-u-ke-si /τρισὶ ζεύγεσι/) would be strange. Another interpretation, followed by most scholars, understands it as εἴλυμα 'wrapping' and compares it with ζ 179.[12] The word would refer to a leather bag, or to wrappers—but why "in three pairs?"[13] However, since εἴλυμα is a recent form derived from what is ultimately the perfect stem *ϝεϝλυ- (see above), it is clear that the Mycenaean word we-ru-ma-ta cannot have anything to do with the perfect stem (we would expect *we-wu-ru-), but must be read /ϝελύματα/. That is, Mycenaean agrees with Zenodotus. And introducing Zenodotus' reading into the discussion sheds a new light on the meaning of the Mycenaean form. In Δ 137, the μίτρη is a leather belt with a kind of leather apron covered with metal pieces, that is, the waist-piece protecting the belly and the genitals. The line says the μίτρη is worn as ϝέλυμα. In Greek *-m̥ neuters have a concrete meaning, and, indeed, the Mycenaean we-ru-ma-ta are very concrete.

Accordingly, I suggest that the we-ru-ma-ta of PY Ub(1) 1318 are that kind of protecting belts, and match the use of the word in Δ 137 in Zenodotus' reading. One ox-hide (wi-ri-no 1) is definitely enough to cut several of these protecting belts (we-ru-ma-ta, plural). Moreover, this has a consequence on the interpretation of the whole phrase and the meaning of ti-ri-si . ze-u-ke-si 'ϝελύματα for/in three ζεύγεσι'. If ϝέλυμα is a belt, ζεῦγος 'pair' has nothing to do with horses, but can simply refer to the fasteners of the belt (buckles or hooks) made of two matching pieces, one at each end of the belt. The we-ru-ma-ta . ti-ri-si . ze-u-ke-si would be 'leather belts for three pairs of fasteners'. This must be an indication of the width of the belt because the fasteners are one above the other, and a belt with one pair of fasteners is narrower than one with three.[14] Such a belt would be strong enough to bear the metal pieces added to it, and fit for a warrior. Therefore Zenodotus' text in Δ 137 is a perfect match for the Pylos tablet.

---

10 Ruijgh 1966: 133, 145 we-ru-ma-ta . ti-ri-si . ze-u-ke-si "bridles for three yokes" ("brides pour trois attelages"). Alternatively, Ruijgh suggests ϝελύματα 'envelopes', but rejects it because a single hide cannot provide an envelope for three yokes.
11 Bernabé–Luján 2016: 575, with literature.
12 Bartoněk 2003: 389 (εἴλυμα), 615 (wĕl(l)ūmata?). Panagl 1992: 509 (εἴλυμα). Piquero Rodríguez 2019: 198 (ἔλῡμα 'a part of the sandal').
13 Olsen 2014: 151 translates 'ox-hide wrappers'.
14 It is less likely to refer to three different positions of the buckle, allowing to tighten the belt more or less, because in that case ze-u-ke-si, which implies there are three pairs, would be difficult to understand.

Not only is his ϝέλυμα confirmed by we-ru-ma-ta, but it also provides a better meaning for the Mycenaean word. Piecing the two together provides a new picture.

In first millenium epic Greek, the old Achaean word ϝέλυμα was replaced by μίτρη, which is the usual word in Homer for that kind of belt. Zenodotus' line has both, and the older word is used to explain the function of the μίτρη. But once μίτρη was generalised, ϝέλυμα became obsolete and was eliminated. Its preservation in Zenodotus' line is exceptional. The replacement by ἔρυμα in the vulgate loses the concrete meaning: ἔρυμα is an abstract noun meaning 'protection', instead of the name of a concrete piece of military equipment, warranted by Mycenaean.

Both phonetically and morphologically regular, attested in Mycenaean, and warranted by an exact counterpart in Latin, ϝέλυμα is clearly old. Εἴλυμα 'wrapper' (ζ 179) can be either the modernisation of the older ϝέλῠμα, or rather, a new word derived from the new present stem εἰλυ- abstracted from the perfect εἴλῡμαι. On the other hand, a εἴλῡμα could not have been remodelled into ϝέλῠμα after a present *ϝελύω because the latter is not attested in Greek. The presence of a remodelled form in the *Odyssey* contra the old form in the *Iliad* (in Zenodotus' version) is not surprising. And the fact that the creation of the new form led to the elimination of the old form for the sake of consistency is even less surprising. The *ἔλῡμα given as a lemma by Piquero Rodríguez (ῡ after εἴλῡμα and Hesiod) does not exist.

So far, we have on the one hand a noun (ἔρυμα) that is usual in Attic-Ionic and synchronically regular, while on the other hand a noun (ἔλυμα) that is not usual at all, does not correspond to the verbal stem bearing the same meaning, but is diachronically regular and attested in Mycenaean. Under these conditions, it is much more likely that an older ἔλυμα was modified into ἔρυμα, than that an older ἔρυμα was modified into ἔλυμα. The new form ἔρυμα forms a *figura etymologica* with ἐρύω in the next line, a stylistic feature appreciated by poets and valued by rhetorics. Moreover, it is also synonymous with the following ἕρκος ἀκόντων. This is an effect of what I called the principle of reduplication.[15] That is, the unusual word is replaced by a word which has more or less the same meaning as an adjacent one. Both words then form a redundant formulation, in that case "defense and fence." Therefore, replacing the old and obscure ἔλυμα by the regular and usual ἔρυμα was not only linguistically justified, but also stylistically more interesting. On the contrary, the modification of an old ἔρυμα into ἔλυμα, which is not attested elsewhere with this meaning and no

---

15   Le Feuvre 2015: 45–46.

longer connected to the verbal base, is highly unlikely.[16] This word ἔλυμα 'wrapping' cannot have been invented by Zenodotus or any Alexandrian scholar, or by any rhapsode, because it could not be created within the state of language of fourth or third century Greek. And since Mycenaean confirms that it is an archaic form, the only possible conclusion is that Zenodotus and Aristophanes preserve here an older reading, as already seen by Rengakos. The older reconstructible state of the line is μίτρης θ', ἥν ἐφόρει ἔλυμα χροὸς ἕρκος ἀκόντων "and the belt he was wearing, wrapping around his skin, fence against spears." There is no reason to think Zenodotus took it, as an emendation, from a copy he collated, since ἔλυμα does not represent an obvious improvement over ἔρυμα if such was the reading of his working text. Therefore ἔλυμα must be the reading of his text, which he left unchanged.

How old is the "new" form ἔρυμα? It depends on the relationship between Δ 137 and Hesiod, *Op.* 536, which both have ἔρυμα χροός.

Hesiod, *Op.* 536–537
Καὶ τότε ἕσσασθαι ἔρυμα χροός, ὥς σε κελεύω,
χλαῖνάν τε μαλακὴν καὶ τερμιόεντα χιτῶνα·

Furthermore, take my advice, put on for your body's protection a soft cloak and a tunic that comes all the way to your ankles.
D.H.

There is no variant reading. If ἔρυμα is original in Hesiod's line, it may be the source for the correction in Homer. But ἔρυμα could also be borrowed from Homer. This does not mean that the correction ἔρυμα dates back to the eighth century, but that the new reading from Homer could have been introduced into Hesiod's text by later editors. In Hesiod, ἔρυμα χροός is the object of the verb ἕσσασθαι 'to dress', and in this context ἔλυμα would probably be better understood as referring to a piece of clothing. Hine's translation takes it not as the object, but as the attribute of the object, which he assumes is the cloak and the tunic. But the three nouns are coordinated, so that ἔρυμα/ἔλυμα may be understood as the name of a third piece of clothing. Since we-ru-ma-ta in Mycenaean and ϝέλυμα in the *Iliad* refer to a piece of clothing, the protecting belt, it is likely

---

16 This has already been seen by Rengakos 1993: 59–60, against Düntzer and Van der Valk. Rengakos' formulation "it is therefore not very likely that ἔλυμα is a conjecture by Zenodotus" ("nicht sehr wahrscheinlich ist demnach, daß ἔλυμα eine Konjektur Zenodots darstellt") can be more firmly reformulated as "it is impossible." Nickau does not discuss the form.

that this is the case in Hesiod, too. If so, since in Hesiod the context has nothing to do with war, this 'belt' can only refer to the underwear, which was a piece of cloth wrapped around the waist and covering the belly and the genitals, and ἔλυμα is appropriate for that. The line should rather be translated "put on a waist-piece, following my advice, and a soft cloak and a tunic." Accordingly, it is plausible that Hesiod originally had ἔλυμα χροός, which was replaced by ἔρυμα χροός after the Homeric phrase when the latter was remodelled. Additionally, we may have a clue about the date of this remodelling: Herodotus' περιβαλέσθαι ἕρκος ἔρυμα τῶν νεῶν "to build around a wall, protection for the ships" (Hdt 9.96) is strongly reminiscent of the structure of ἔρυμα χροός ἕρκος ἀκόντων, and may find its source in the Homeric line. If so, it implies that Herodotus, the Ὁμήρου ζηλωτής (Dion. Hal., *Epistula ad Pompeium Geminum* 3.11), the Ὁμηρικώτατος (Ps.-Longinus, *Subl.* 13.3), knew the line with ἔρυμα. The lexical replacement would then date back to the mid-5th c. BCE at the latest.

2   Νυκτὶ ἐλυσθείς A 47

Now this has a consequence that has not been noticed, as far as I know. The authenticity of ἔλυμα 'wrapping, piece of clothing' means that Zenodotus had a text in which the stem ἐλυ- was used with the etymological meaning 'to wrap'. And this brings us to another of his readings, the well-known ὃ δ' ἤϊε νυκτὶ ἐλυσθείς # "he went, wrapped in night" *vs* vulgate ὃ δ' ἤϊε νυκτὶ ἐοικώς # "he went, similar to night" in A 47. Zenodotus athetised l. 46 and 47, as we learn from Aristonicus, but he had a different reading for l. 47, which is not transmitted under A 47, but under M 363, also going back to Aristonicus.

> *A Schol.* A 46–47: ὅτι Ζηνόδοτος ἀμφοτέρους ἠθέτηκεν, οὐ καλῶς (Aim).

because Zenodotus athetises both lines, wrongly.

> *A Schol.* M 463a: νυκτὶ θοῇ ἀτάλαντος: ὅτι τὰ φοβερὰ νυκτὶ ὁμοιοῖ. πρὸς τὸ 'ὁ δ' ἤϊε νυκτὶ ἐοικώς' (A 47), ὅτι Ζηνόδοτος γράφει 'νυκτὶ ἐλυσθείς'.

'similar to the swift night': because he assimilates frightful things to night: this aims at the 'ὁ δ' ἤϊε νυκτὶ ἐοικώς', because Zenodotus writes 'νυκτὶ ἐλυσθείς'.

Nickau rejects Zenodotus' reading with the following argument: "but ἐλυσθείς is not original because in Homer the meaning 'to wrap', which we would have to favour here, is always expressed by means of the form of the verb εἰλύω beginning with εἰλ-."[17] Although Nickau is followed by Rengakos,[18] this argument has no weight from the linguistic point of view for two reasons. The first is that the aorist stem is of course not identical with the present stem, and Chantraine for instance clearly and rightly states that the (unaugmented) passive aorist of εἰλύω is ἐλύσθη, since the root is *ṷel-u-, not *εἰλύσθη, unless there is an augment. The second is that this reasoning is based on the assumption that Homer is a homogenous text, which it is not. We know that our text has old forms as well as recent ones (for instance, for the considered root, ϝέλῠμα vs εἴλῡμα), and that old forms, when they were too odd, were modernised when metre allowed it or simply replaced by a different word. The very principle of making Homer as homogenous as possible was that of Greek scholars, notably Aristarchus', because for them there was a poet named Homer and this poet had one consistent use. As a logical consequence, this principle leads to a homogenisation of the text, through the elimination of deviant uses, even though the latter can be older uses, which Aristarchus was not always able to recognise as such. Here too, we must apply the basic principle of historical linguistics, that synchronically irregular forms may preserve the older state of things, whereas regular forms are not significant because they may have been regularised. And, to be sure, in the realm of ἀναλογία, Aristarchus did regularise a lot.

17 Nickau 1977: 45: "unoriginal ist ἐλυσθείς aber deshalb, weil bei Homer die Bedeutung 'verhüllen', die hier zu fördern wäre, durchgehend durch die mit εἰλ- anlautenden Formen des Verbums εἰλύω ausgedrückt wird." Kirk 1985: 58 does not mention Zenodotus' variant, although he comments "like night" as "effective."
18 Rengakos 1994: 77: "a further parallel for the improper use of ἐλυσθείς ('curled up') [...] is the Zenodotean reading in A 47" ("Eine weitere Parallele zu uneigentliche Verwendung von ἐλυσθείς ("verhüllt") [...] ist die zenodoteischen Lesart zu A 47"). Apollonius in *Arg.* 1.254 ἐνὶ κτερέεσσιν ἐλυσθείς "wrapped in the funerary gifts" is probably taking up Zenodotus' use of ἐλυσθείς in the considered line, but this is not an "improper use" (except in the eyes of some modern scholars), this is a deliberate means of taking sides with Zenodotus' reading against others. When Rengakos says that Hellenistic Homeric scholarship distinguished properly between the two stems εἰλυ- and ἐλυ-, he adopts a synchronic principle, that of Hellenistic Homeric scholarship seeking to rationalise and to homogenise the Homeric use, which is appropriate in order to analyse the Hellenistic poets' relationship with Homer and contemporary scholarship, but not to analyse the relationship between Zenodotus, for instance, and the Homeric text(s) he could read. See Apollonius, *Arg.* 1.1034–1035 ὁ δ' ἐνὶ ψαμάθοισιν ἐλυσθείς || μοῖραν ἀνέπλησεν "and he, wrapped down under sand, met his fate," which echoes Φ 318–319 κὰδ δέ μιν αὐτὸν || εἰλύσω ψαμάθοισιν "and himself I will wrap down under sand." Apollonius thereby shows that for him ἐλυσθείς is the aorist participle of εἰλύω 'to wrap, to cover'—which can be contrasted with Oppian, *Hal.* 2.124 ἐν ψαμάθοισιν ὑπ' ὀστράκῳ εἰλυθεῖσα "curled up beneath a shell in the sand."

To that may be added a philological argument: we know that Zenodotus athetised A 46–47 (*A Schol.* A 46 ὅτι Ζηνόδοτος ἀμφοτέρους ἠθέτηκεν, οὐ καλῶς). That implies that ἐλυσθείς is not an emendation of his since he considered the line unauthentic, but rather something he found in his working text.[19] Van Thiel suggests that, since the reading is not mentioned under A 47, it may be that it was, not Zenodotus' reading in that line, but a comparison he suggested in the margin, maybe with E 186.[20] However, it is very unlikely that ἐλυσθείς is a suggestion by a third-century scholar since, as Nickau notices, the passive aorist participle ἐλυσθείς does not mean 'wrapped' in its Homeric attestations, so that the alleged comparison would be lame. The reason why Zenodotus' reading is not mentioned under A 47 must rather be that this was a secondary indication, compared to the athetesis. Aristonicus may have mentioned the reading νυκτὶ ἐλυσθείς, but the copyist who integrated the VMK into the Venetus A probably found that this was at best a secondary element which could be dropped for lack of space: what was the point in mentioning Zenodotus had a different reading since Zenodotus himself condemned the lines where this reading appeared? This is parallel to A 4–5, where the A scholion does not mention the Zenodotean reading οἰωνοῖσί τε δαῖτα instead of the vulgate's οἰωνοῖσί τε πᾶσι because the scholiast's main concern is that Zenodotus athetised the two lines, wrongly: ὅτι Ζηνόδοτος τοὺς δύο ἀθετεῖ. γίνεται δὲ τὸ προοίμιον κόλον "because Zenodotus athetises both, but the prologue becomes lame" (*A Schol.* A 4a).[21]

From the etymological point of view, the passive aorist of *$\mathit{\mu el\text{-}u}$- is regularly ϝελύ(σ)θη, always attested with inorganic -s- ἐλύσθη, and found in Homer twice in the participle ἐλυσθείς, meaning 'curled up, bent down', and once in the indicative: Ψ 393 ῥυμὸς δ' ἐπὶ γαῖαν ἐλύσθη #, Ω 510 κλαῖ' ἀδινὰ προπάροιθε ποδῶν Ἀχιλῆος ἐλυσθείς (Priam before Achilles; a D scholion has ἐλυσθείς. εἰλυθείς), ι 433 λασίην ὑπὸ γαστέρ' ἐλυσθείς # (Ulysses hidden under the ram). In none of those three instances does ἐλύσθη mean 'wrap(ped)'. Moreover, the meaning is not identical in all three: the meaning 'curled up' can fit in Ω 510 and ι 433,[22] but it cannot be correct for Ψ 393, as noticed in the *LfgrE* which translates 'it swung'. I will come back to those later (see below, pp. 182–187).

---

19 This argument, while accepted by most modern scholars, is rejected by Van der Valk 1964: 16: "we must bear in mind that the Alexandrian critics, even if they athetised lines, nevertheless sometimes made alterations in these lines."
20 Van Thiel 2014b, *sub* M 463.
21 See above, pp. 9–10.
22 The Homeric line was the model of Archilochus' *fr.* 191.1 ἔρως ὑπὸ καρδίην ἐλυσθείς # "love, curled up in his heart."

Thus, those three instances are not even a homogenous group. To that must be added that Zenodotus' ἐλυσθείς in A 47 can be read with the etymological digamma, whereas in all three other instances the digamma is neglected, which implies that the lines are recent. It is not methodologically sound to condemn a synchronically abnormal use (Zenodotus') after a clearly recent use (the other three). This, of course, was normal for Greek scholars, but modern scholarship should not follow them on that point but rather always try to distinguish between ancient lines and recent ones.

Once again, we are faced with a case in which Zenodotus' reading is synchronically abnormal, but diachronically regular. It is the expected form with the expected meaning, and it is consistent with the fact that the same Zenodotus read (ϝ)ἔλυμα 'wrapping, piece of clothing' in Δ 137, with the same stem ϝελυ- 'to wrap, to cover'. Thus, there is no reason to see in νυκτὶ (ϝ)ἐλυσθείς "wrapped in night" a conjecture stemming from a confusion between 'curled up' (ἐλυσθείς) and 'wrapped' (ϝειλυμένος). As Zenodotus' text preserved in (ϝ)ἔλυμα an old form, synchronically irregular, it also preserved the old etymological meaning of (ϝ)ἐλυσθείς. His νυκτὶ ἐλυσθείς 'wrapped in night' is precisely one of those old forms which could not be modernised for metrical reasons, because it was impossible to replace ἐλυσθείς by *εἰλυσθείς, which would conform to the synchronic pattern alluded to by Nickau and Rengakos.[23] Therefore it was eliminated and replaced by a different reading, the vulgate's νυκτὶ ἐοικώς.[24] The obvious motivation for replacing νυκτὶ ἐλυσθείς by νυκτὶ ἐοικώς was the specialisation of the stem εἰλυ- for 'to wrap' that had occurred at some point in the history of Greek, whereas there was no motivation for replacing νυκτὶ ἐοικώς by a synchronically irregular νυκτὶ ἐλυσθείς.

There are indeed parallel formulations in the *Iliad*, where a god is 'wrapped' or 'cloaked' in a cloud (Ε 186 νεφέλῃ εἰλυμένος ὤμους # "mantling in mist his

---

23 Nickau 1977: 46, acknowledges that the "confusion" may be anterior to Zenodotus and that the conjecture need not be his : "one can assume that a semantic change could have occurred long before Zenodotus" ("Man wird also zugeben, daß ein Bedeutungswandel lange vor Zenodot möglich war").

24 There are so many occurrences of a structure [– ◡] ἐοικώς # in Homer that νυκτὶ ἐοικώς could have been created at any time. Aristarchus justified the reading νυκτὶ ἐοικώς by comparing it to similar formulae, as νυκτὶ θοῇ ἀτάλαντος # "similar to the quick night." See *A Schol.* M 63: νυκτὶ θοῇ ἀτάλαντος: ὅτι τὰ φοβερὰ νυκτὶ ὁμοιοῖ. πρὸς τὸ 'ὁ δ᾽ ἤϊε νυκτὶ ἐοικώς', ὅτι Ζηνόδοτος γράφει 'νυκτὶ ἐλυσθείς' "because Homer compares frightening things to the night; it aims at the 'ὁ δ᾽ ἤϊε νυκτὶ ἐοικώς', because Zenodotus writes 'νυκτὶ ἐλυσθείς'." In a different metrical position, lines like Κ 547 αἰνῶς ἀκτίνεσσιν ἐοικότες ἠελίοιο "strikingly similar to the rays of the sun," Λ 27 ἴρισσιν ἐοικότες "similar to the rainbows" may also have provided a model for ἐοικώς + abstract noun referring to a natural element.

shoulders," Ο 308 # εἱμένος ὤμοιιν νεφέλην "wearing a mist about his shoulders," Υ 150 ἀμφὶ δ ἄρ' ἄρρηκτον νεφέλην ὤμοισιν ἕσαντο "and gathered a breakless wall of cloud to darken their shoulders," Ξ 350 ἐπὶ δὲ νεφέλην ἔσσαντο # "and they drew about them a cloud" [all translations by Lattimore]) or in mist (Ξ 282 # ἠέρα ἐσσαμένῳ).[25] This is an inherited mythological element, also found in Vedic (RV 5.57.4a *marúto varṣánirṇijas* "the Maruts whose dress is rain"; RV 5.63.6c *abhrā́ vasata marútaḥ* "the Maruts dressed in clouds"). Further, the inherited motive of the veil of Night could be mentioned although it is different from what is meant here.[26] Verbs meaning 'to dress with' a meteorological noun as their complement are used for gods only, and νυκτὶ ἐλυσθείς fits into this pattern.

The symmetrical formula, which is used when humans are dissimulated by a god, has the verb καλύπτω 'to cover'. We find in the second hemistich either the formula νυκτὶ καλύψας # (Ε 23), νυκτὶ καλύψαι # (Ν 425),[27] or κάλυψε δ' ἄρ' ἠέρι πολλῇ # (Γ 381, Υ 444, Φ 597), καλύψας ἠέρι πολλῇ # (Λ 752), and in the first hemistich the passive formula # ἠέρι καὶ νεφέλῃ κεκαλυμμένοι/-αι (θ 562, λ 15), which is also used for a god (# ἠέρι γὰρ πολλῇ κεκαλυμμένος Π 790). That is, with καλύπτω we can see a metrical complementary distribution between a short formula with 'night' used in the adonic colon (νυκτὶ καλύψας #), a longer T2 formula with 'mist' (κάλυψε δ' ἄρ' ἠέρι πολλῇ #, καλύψας ἠέρι πολλῇ #), and a long formula where the verb stands in the same metrical position as in the T2 formula—however, the reduplication of the perfect stem moves the caesura, which becomes penthemimeral, and as a consequence the first hemistich is filled by a P1 phrase # ἠέρι καὶ νεφέλῃ. The reason for the distribution in the second hemistich is that the trisyllabic dative ἠέρι in the adonic colon could only be used with a disyllabic word form. As few verbal forms meaning 'dress', 'wrap', 'cover' *vel sim.*, are disyllabic, the metrical slot is invariably filled by the adjective πολλῇ, whereas the dative νυκτί leaves room for a trisyllabic word form, which makes it easier to use a verb.

---

25 See also Aeschylus, *fr.* 216 *TrGF* εἴ μοι γένοιτο φᾶρος ἶσον οὐρανῷ "if I had a coat similar to the sky."

26 See Dardano 2010, with references to previous literature.

27 In this line the formula is used not for a god hiding a man, but for a warrior eager to kill an enemy. A regular metaphoric expression of death is "night covered his eyes" (ὄσσε ... νὺξ ἐκάλυψε #). Ν 425 νυκτὶ καλύψαι # arose from the conjugation of νὺξ ἐκάλυψε # aligned on the model of the "rescue formula:" this is the only case where the "death formula" is used with a causative meaning, and the line is clearly secondary, as well as the use of δουπῆσαι in the meaning 'to fall' in the following line. The rescue formula is disjoined in Ε 506–507 ἀμφὶ δὲ νύκτα || θοῦρος Ἄρης ἐκάλυψε μάχῃ Τρώεσσιν ἀρήγων "as violent Ares defending the Trojans mantled in dark night the battle" (R.L.).

On this model, we can expect that next to the P2 formula 'wrapped in mist/cloud' (νεφέλῃ εἰλυμένος ὤμους # E 186) a shorter formula 'wrapped in night' will exist, with the structure νυκτί [⏑ – x] fitted for the adonic colon. Νυκτὶ ἐλυσθείς # is that formula, working as the passive of νυκτὶ καλύψας # (E 23). A variant is found in the *Odyssey*, where we read (υ 351–352) νυκτὶ μὲν ὑμέων ‖ εἰλύαται κεφαλαί τε πρόσωπά τε νέρθε τε γοῦνα "your heads, your faces and the knees beneath you are wrapped in night" (J.H.). Here we are dealing with the metaphorical night of death, but we nevertheless have a syntagm "wrapped in night" (νυκτί ... εἰλύαται), with νυκτί in the expected metrical position at the beginning of the adonic colon, and the verb displaced to the beginning of the next line because of the different metrical structure of the perfect tense verb εἰλύαται. Zenodotus' reading νυκτὶ ἐλυσθείς # and νυκτί [⏑ – x] ‖ εἰλύαται are two realisations of one and the same formula, the difference being a consequence of the conjugation of this formula. Zenodotus' reading appears to be consistent with the economy of the formulaic system in the Parryan sense,[28] whereas the vulgate's reading takes A 47 out of the system here described.

In E 186 we have a perfect participle, while in A 47 we find an aorist participle. The difference is partly due to the metrical position, but the aorist is not isolated, as we also have one in Ξ 282, and can be justified by the context. E 186 is a description, the finite verb is perfect and has a stative meaning (ἔστηκε) and the participle too is stative.[29] Whereas A 47 and Ξ 282 are dynamic, the finite verb is a verb of motion in a past tense (βήτην, ἤϊε)[30] and part of a sequential process: the god puts on his magical meteorological garment and sets off.

The perfect εἴλυμαι can also be used with the meaning 'covered by' something which is not a garment and may be rigid, as in Σ 522 εἰλυμένοι αἴθοπι χαλκῷ "shrouding themselves in the bright bronze" (R.L.), ξ 479 σάκεσιν εἰλυμένοι ὤμους "wrapping their shoulders in their shields" (J.H.), ε 403 εἴλυτο δὲ πάνθ' ἁλὸς ἄχνῃ "all was wrapped in sea's spray" (J.H.), and even Π 639–640 ἐπεὶ βελέεσσι καὶ αἵματι καὶ κονίῃσιν ‖ ἐκ κεφαλῆς εἴλυτο διαμπερὲς ἐς πόδας ἄκρους "since he was covered by arrows and blood and dust, from head to toe, all around."

---

28 In Parry's conception, *economy* refers to the fact that one formula may appear under different forms, but there is only one form for one metrical structure (Parry 1928, *passim*). In other words, there are no doublets within a system, each formulation filling one specific metrical position.

29 E 185–186 ἀλλά τις ἄγχι ‖ ἔστηκ' ἀθανάτων νεφέλῃ εἰλυμένος ὤμους "but some one of the immortals, mantling in mist his shoulders, stands close beside him" (R.L.).

30 Ξ 281–282 τὼ βήτην Λήμνου τε καὶ Ἴμβρου ἄστυ λιπόντε ‖ ἠέρα ἑσσαμένω ῥίμφα πρήσσοντε κέλευθον "the two went away from Lemnos, and the city of Imbros, and mantled themselves in mist, and made their way very lightly" (R.L.).

3 ϝελυσθείς and ἐλυσθείς

Now the recognition that νυκτὶ ἐλυσθείς preserves the old participle of the verb 'to wrap, to cover' must lead to a reexamination of the other two occurrences of ἐλυσθείς 'curled up'. Clearly those forms cannot be separated, and the reintegration of ϝελυσθείς 'wrapped' into this set means that the picture may be different from what was previously thought.

As was stressed above, the two cases of ἐλυσθείς 'curled up' have no initial /w/, implying that they are recent. Now how can we account for the meaning 'curled up'? This is compatible with a general meaning 'to roll', but not with a specific meaning 'to envelop, to wrap' which is that of ϝελυσθείς in A 47, and of ϝέλυμα.

> Ω 509–510
> τὼ δὲ μνησαμένω ὃ μὲν Ἕκτορος ἀνδροφόνοιο
> κλαῖ᾽ ἀδινὰ προπάροιθε ποδῶν Ἀχιλῆος ἐλυσθείς,
>
> and the two remembered, as Priam sat huddled at the feet of Achilleus and wept close for manslaughtering Hektor.
>
> R.L.

> ι 432–435
> ἀρνειὸς γὰρ ἔην μήλων ὄχ᾽ ἄριστος ἁπάντων,
> τοῦ κατὰ νῶτα λαβών, λασίην ὑπὸ γαστέρ᾽ ἐλυσθεὶς
> κείμην· αὐτὰρ χερσὶν ἀώτου θεσπεσίοιο
> νωλεμέως στρεφθεὶς ἐχόμην τετληότι θυμῷ
>
> there was a ram, the best by far of all the sheep, that I grabbed by the back and lay curled beneath his shaggy belly. Then, turned around, I held onto his abundant fleece with my hands continuously with a steadfast heart.
>
> J.H.

The participle is in the same position at the end of the line in both (as in νυκτὶ ἐλυσθείς), and in both there is a prepositional phrase referring to a place (προπάροιθε ποδῶν Ἀχιλῆος ἐλυσθείς, ὑπὸ γαστέρ᾽ ἐλυσθείς). The one may be modelled after the other.

The dominant interpretation by Greek scholars was that the participle means 'curled up': Ἐλυσθείς. Εἰλυθείς (*D Schol.* Ω 510), ἐλύσθη: συνερρύη, κατειλήθη, ὡς "λασίην ὑπὸ γαστέρ᾽ ἐλυσθείς" (*bT Schol.* Ψ 393b), ἐλυσθείς: παρεθεὶς ἢ συνειληθεὶς ἢ κυλισθείς (*bT Schol.* Ω 510), ἐλυσθείς· ἑλίξας ἑαυτόν (Hsch., ε 2109), "προπάροιθε ποδῶν Ἀχιλῆος ἐλυσθείς", ὅ ἐστι συστραφείς (Eustathius, *Comm. Il.* 4: 942), ὑπὸ γαστέρα ἐλυσθεὶς ὅ ἐστι κρυβείς, εἰληθείς (Eustathius, *Comm. Od.* 1: 354). But there were others, for instance 'light': ἐλυσθείς· κουφισθείς. ἐλισθείς (Hsch., ε 2232); 'pulled down': ἐλυσθεὶς δὲ κατενεχθείς, ἀπὸ τοῦ ἔλω ἐλύω ὡς ἕλκω ἑλκύω (*Et. Genuinum*, λ 152); 'stretched out': ἐλυσθείς: ἐκταθείς (*Scholia vetera in Ap. Rh. Arg.*, p. 256, *ad Arg.* 3.1313). The word is never explained as meaning 'wrapped'. And as often, the interpretation of ancient scholars prevented modern scholars from understanding the original meaning of the verb. From the morphological point of view, it is clear that ἐλυσθείς is the participle of *ἐλύω 'to wrap', and Zenodotus' reading νυκτὶ ϝελυσθείς, morphologically regular, preserves the original meaning. The other two instances must therefore result from a semantic shift.

I suggest the key is in the *Odyssey*'s line. Here, as a matter of fact, the older meaning of ἐλυσθείς would fit, since Ulysses is literally 'covered, wrapped' in the fleece of the ram. Thus, this instance is not at odds with Zenodotus' reading νυκτὶ ἐλυσθείς "wrapped in night" as applied to Apollo. The night is no more a garment than the fleece, yet the use of the verb meaning 'to wrap' with a magical thing normally not used as a garment to convey the notion of invisibility is traditional. The fleece also wraps or covers Ulysses with the same result, it makes him invisible to the Cyclops. Besides, εἴλυμαι is regularly used with nouns which do not refer to clothes (shield, armour, see above) and have no magical power, but have the same function of covering the body. Therefore, this line is fully consistent with the formulaic instances studied above (pp. 179–181). It is a terrestrial transposition of a formula otherwise used for the gods, in which the magical cloud is replaced by the material and down-to-earth fleece of the ram. However, the fleece keeps a flavour of supernatural magic because of its thickness (ἀώτου θεσπεσίοιο 'prodigious fleece'). This line hints at the traditional formula on which it is a playful variation.

On the topic of variation, an interesting one is found in Euphorion (3rd c. BCE) in a description of Cerberus: Οἱ δ' ὄπιθεν λασίῃ ὑπὸ γαστέρι πεπ[τηῶτες] || οὐραῖοι λιχμῶντο περὶ πλευρῇσι δρά[κοντες] "and lurking under his shaggy belly behind him the snakes of his tail licked round his ribs [...]" (*fr.* 51 Powell, ll. 5–6; transl. Lightfoot). The quotation and the distorsion are obvious, so is the modernisation replacing ἐλυσθείς 'curled up' by πεπτηώς 'idem'. The interesting point is that the "shaggy belly" is in the dative. Either it is a modification made by Euphorion as a consequence of the introduction of πεπτηώς, or it means that he had a Homeric text where ι 433 had a dative prepositional phrase instead of an accusative one.[31] Archilochus' *fr.* 191.1 ἔρως ὑπὸ καρδίην ἐλυσθείς #

---

31 The problem of the relationship with ι 433 is not discussed by Powell 1925, Clúa 2005 (*fr.* 84), Lightfoot 2009 (*fr.* 71), Acosta-Hughes–Cusset 2012 (*fr.* 87), White 1993: 193.

"love, curled up in his heart", which also depends on the Homeric model, apparently implies that he knew the line with the accusative, provided Stobaeus (*Anth.* 4.20b.43) quotes faithfully—the dative would be metrically equivalent. From the Homeric line, Euphorion reuses the prepositional phrase but changes the participle, Archilochus reuses the participle but changes the prepositional phrase. Of course Archilochus is much older and his testimony is of greater weight, but the fact he knew the line with the accusative does not mean there was no variant. The construction with ὑπό + dative is also found in Apollonius Rhodius, *Arg.* 3.281–282: αὐτῷ δ' ὑπὸ βαιὸς ἐλυσθείς || Αἰσονίδῃ 'crouching low beneath Jason himself'. The same Apollonius, alluding to Archilochus' line, has a dative: τοῖος ὑπὸ κραδίῃ εἰλυμένος αἴθετο λάθρῃ || οὖλος ἔρως "such, curled up under her heart, was burning secretly a funest love" (*Arg.* 3.296–297). The dative is expected with the perfect εἰλυμένος, which expresses a state, not a motion, but this does not apply to *Arg.* 3.281 with the aorist ἐλυσθείς. This means that Apollonius considers the dative as the regular case, and this may point to a Homeric reading with the dative, of which Euphorion would preserve a record.[32]

Nevertheless, let us test the dative hypothesis. The dative in Homer is either γαστρί (E 539, E 616, P 519, Ionic inflection) or γαστέρι (Z 58, N 372, N 398, T 225, Aeolic inflection). A formula with the dative would be parallel to νυκτὶ ἐλυσθείς, the dative-instrumental of the magical garment being turned into a dative-locative. Better: the dative would be compatible with the older form ϝελυσθείς with preserved ϝ, under the form *γαστρὶ ϝελυσθείς #, modification of the formula νυκτὶ ϝελυσθείς # and filling the same adonic colon. This formula was then expanded to form a P2 hemistich *λασίῃ ὑπὸ γαστρὶ ϝελυσθείς || κείμην "beneath his shaggy belly I lay covered," where the prepositional phrase can modify κείμην as well as ἐλυσθείς.[33] Euphorion's version with the dative is not reported as a variant reading for ι 433 in the scholia, therefore caution is required: that the Homeric line originally had a dative remains a hypothesis, but it would fit well in the pattern studied here.[34]

Coming back to ἐλυσθείς, in ι 433 the participle could also be understood in a different way, namely that Ulysses is crouching to creep under the animal in

---

32   Incidentally, the use of the perfect here is for Apollonius a means of saying "ἐλυσθείς and εἰλυμένος are one and the same verb" (see n. 18 above).

33   In that case Euphorion's γαστέρι instead of γαστρί would be a consequence of the replacement of ἐλυσθείς by πεπτηώς, since *γαστρὶ πεπτηώς would be unmetrical. In the three instances of γαστρί in Homer, the word is placed right before the trochaic caesura and never in the adonic colon, but that cannot be considered an objection.

34   The Sorbonne papyrus of the *Odyssey* (P.Sorb. Inv. 2245A), from the second half of the 3rd c. BCE, has ἐρεισθείς corrected in ἐλυσθείς but no variant for the accusative λασίην ὑπὸ γαστέρα (S. West 1967: 228).

CLOAKS AND COATS 185

order to remain undetected. That is, the invisibility ensured by the prodigious fleece in the older version becomes the result of the man's action in the newer interpretation. If the original case form was the dative *λασίῃ ὑπὸ γαστρί, it was then modified into an accusative expressing motion: Ulysses slips under the ram, and the prepositional phrase modifies only ἐλυσθείς. It is hard to visualise, though, how a man could be 'curled up' below the ram while the text itself says that he is in supine position under the belly of the animal while his hands are holding the back of the ram above (τοῦ κατὰ νῶτα λαβών). This is clearly not a position that could be described as 'curled up'.[35] If one really thinks about the material situation, which has to be plausible even in a mythological context, the translation 'curled up' is suspect. Nevertheless, this is how it was interpreted. The presence of στρεφθείς in ι 435 may have played a role in the reinterpretation (αὐτὰρ χερσὶν ἀώτου θεσπεσίοιο || νωλεμέως στρεφθεὶς ἐχόμην) because it refers to the position of Ulysses.[36] With that new meaning it was used by the singer who created Ω 510: in this line ἐλυσθείς refers to the bodily position of the character, not to the fact that he may be wrapped in a cloak. The evolution is as follows:

	ϝ	Wrapped	Invisible	Bodily position
νυκτὶ ϝελυσθείς #	+	+	+	
?*λασίῃ ὑπὸ γαστρὶ ϝελυσθείς #	+			
		+	+	+
λασίην ὑπὸ γαστέρ' ἐλυσθείς #	−			
προπάροιθε ποδῶν Ἀχιλῆος ἐλυσθείς #	−			+

We see thereby how the participle acquired in ι 433 a new feature [+BODILY POSITION]. This new feature, which was peripheral in ι 433, and contextually induced, was reinterpreted as central and displaced the older central feature

---

35 Notice that all the archaic representations of the scene show Ulysses not 'curled up', as in later iconography, but lying in horizontal position with straight legs (bronze of the museum of Delphes, Inv. 2560, ca. 540–530; Proto-Attic jug of Aegina, Inv. 1754, ca. 675–650; crater of the Cahn collection, Basel, Inv. HC 1418, ca. 570; cup of Munich's Antikensammlung, Inv. J26, ca. 550; jug, Stockholm, Medelhavsmuseum, Inv. 303287, ca. 550–500; Attic cup, Toledo Museum, Inv. 1927.97, ca. 530–520). This shows that in the 7th and 6th centuries the iconographic type disagrees with the interpretation 'curled up'.

36 However, a scholion understands it differently, and gives as an equivalent συστρέψας τὰς χεῖρας "having intertwined my hands ⟨and the wool⟩" (Schol. vet. B.Q.).

[+WRAPPED]. Then the participle was applied to a new context where only the feature [+BODILY POSITION] is relevant and the older feature [+WRAPPED] is not (Ω 510).[37]

This is a classical case of reinterpretation: ι 433 is the context of reinterpretation, while Ω 510 is the context where the reinterpretation becomes visible as it is actualised.[38] As a consequence, since Λ 47 νυκτὶ ἐλυσθείς is not compatible with the feature [+BODILY POSITION], relevant in Ω 510 and ι 433, this phrase becomes synchronically irregular. As always in the case of a reinterpretation, the new meaning (result of the reinterpretation) supersedes the older one and eventually eliminates it. Logically, νυκτὶ ἐλυσθείς had to be eliminated—and it was. But there again it proves more archaic than the two lines displaying the recent reinterpreted meaning. If Zenodotus' reading had not be preserved by chance, in a scholion which is not even about the line where this reading was found, how could we understand what happened? In this case, we are lucky that the textual tradition provides a clue, but there are, for sure, many similar cases in which the vulgate keeps only the reinterpreted line(s), but not the oldest line(s), and for which the textual tradition is mute.

4 ἐλύσθη

The last form belonging to this group is the aorist ἐλύσθη in Ψ 393:

Ψ 392–394
ἵππειον δέ οἱ ἦξε θεὰ ζυγόν· αἳ δέ οἱ ἵπποι
ἀμφὶς ὁδοῦ δραμέτην, ῥυμὸς δ' ἐπὶ γαῖαν ἐλύσθη.
αὐτὸς δ' ἐκ δίφροιο παρὰ τροχὸν ἐξεκυλίσθη,

and she, a goddess, smashed his chariot yoke, and his horses ran on either side of the way, the pole dragged, and Eumelos himself was sent spinning out beside the wheel of the chariot.
R.L.

It is certainly not old: the word must scan without ϝ. Ancient lexicographers did not know how to understand the word. Apollonius' *Lexicon homericum* has ἐλύσθη παρεχύθη καὶ ἔπεσεν (p. 67). Some understand that the pole got tangled in

---

37 Macleod 1982: 130: "ἐλυσθείς 'curled up' or perhaps 'crouching'."
38 On the notion of actualisation of the reinterpretation or reanalysis, see Timberlake 1977.

the reins, for instance Eustathius, *Comm. Il.* 4: 753 (*ad* Ψ 393) Τὸ δὲ ἐλύσθη ἀντὶ τοῦ συνεστράφη τοῖς ἡνίοις, ἀπὸ τοῦ εἰλῶ εἰλύω ἀπελεύσει τοῦ ι "ἐλύσθη for συνεστράφη 'got tangled' in the reins, from εἰλῶ εἰλύω, by dropping of the [ι]"—the same explanation is found in *Et. Magnum*, and in the *Lexicon* of the Pseudo-Zonaras.[39] This must probably be ascribed to a comparison with Π 470, where the death of the third horse (the παρήορος, 'one-horn') makes it impossible to drive the chariot and the reins get tangled (κρίκε δὲ ζυγόν, ἡνία δέ σφι || σύγχυτ(ο)). Yet the reins are not mentioned at all in Ψ 393 or in the following line, and ἐλύσθη alone can hardly mean 'got tangled' with no overt complement. Therefore the semantic problem remains.

The evolution outlined above can provide a solution. In Ω 510, Priam is 'curled up' at Achilles' feet (προπάροιθε ποδῶν Ἀχιλῆος). From this context a new feature can be drawn, the local indication [DOWN]: that is, the line can be interpreted as 'fallen on the ground at Achilles' feet'. And this is the meaning in Ψ 393: the pole falls on the ground. Therefore the line is probably derived from Ω 510: ἐλύσθη occupies the same metrical position as ἐλυσθείς, it has no ϝ either and it refers to someone or something that fell on the ground (Priam at the feet of Achilles, the pole). This is a further step in the evolution: in Ψ 393, the feature [+BODILY POSITION] of Ω 510 is lost since the verb has an inanimate subject. What remains is the idea of a downward move.

That is, we would have here two successive cases of hyperanalysis—the incorporation of a contextual feature into the meaning of the word itself.[40] A first one integrates the contextual feature [+BODILY POSITION] (ι 433), and a second one integrates the contextual feature [DOWN] (Ω 510). Accordingly, one cannot rely on ἐλύσθη in Ψ 393 to reconstruct the original meaning of the verb since this line is the product of several successive reinterpretations. What we have here is a chain where each link depends on the previous one:

Α 47 → ι 433 → Ω 510 → Ψ 393.

We must first reconstruct the chain and the relative ordering of the lines, so that we can rely on the older uses to understand the proper meaning of the verb, without allowing recent connotations to disturb the picture.

Furthermore, this process can shed light on the only occurrence of ἐλυσθείς in prose:

---

39   *Et. Magnum*, Kallierges, p. 333; Ps.-Zonaras, *Lexicon*, epsilon, p. 696.
40   Croft 2000: 121.

Hippocrates, *De mulierum affectibus ii*, 15 (Littré 124)
"Ἢν δὲ πρὸς τὴν καρδίην προσιστάμεναι πνίγωσιν αἱ ὑστέραι, καὶ ἀνάσσυτος ἴῃ ὁ ἠὴρ βιώμενος, ἀλησθύει καὶ εἰλέει, καὶ ἔστιν ᾗσιν αὐτίκα ἐλυσθεῖσα κάτω χωρέει καὶ φῦσα ἔξεισιν, ἢ καὶ ἐμέει ἀφρώδεα, ἡ δὲ παῦλα ἥδε γίνεται.

if the uterus moves close to woman's heart and provokes suffocation, and her breath rushes upward under force, she will be restless and convulsed. In some cases the coiled up uterus immediately moves downward, and wind is expelled, or the patient vomits frothy material and the disease ends.

transl. POTTER, LCL

Bourbon's text (forthcoming edition of *De mulierum affectibus ii*, CUF) is

[...] καὶ ἀνάσσυτος ἴῃ ὁ ἠὴρ βιώμενος, ἀλὴς θύει καὶ εἰλέει, καὶ ἔστιν ᾗσιν αὐτίκα ἐλυσθεὶς κάτω χωρέει καὶ φῦσα ἔξεισιν [...]

the air, pressed, gathered, rushes and winds up, and for some, immediately falling, it moves downwards and wind is expelled.

Bourbon's text is better. Ἐλυσθείς here applies to the air and not to the womb (Potter ἐλυσθεῖσα). This text of the Hippocratic corpus displays several Homerisms, and it is noteworthy that they all come from Ψ (F. Bourbon, personal communication). The participle, preceding κάτω χωρέει, refers to a downward move, and the meaning 'falling' is consistent with the meaning of ἐλύσθη in Ψ 393. Alternatively, ἐλυσθείς could work as the passive of εἰλέω 'to roll' of the preceding clause (εἰλέει 'is convulsed').[41] In that case the meaning would be 'and for some, right after winding up, it goes down', closer to the meaning of Ω 510. However, the first translation 'falling' is preferable. At any rate, in this text the original meaning is of course lost and the meaning is the one matching the last stage of the reinterpretation chain.

5   A New Picture

Unless we study together ἔλυμα in Δ 137 and ἐλυσθείς in Α 47, we miss the important point, namely, the consistency of Zenodotus' text, which must be

---

41   Neither *ἐλύω nor εἰλύω/εἴλυμαι is attested in the Hippocratic corpus.

underlined. The two readings of Zenodotus are not two independent conjectures, but they back each other. Together they point to a state of language anterior to the generalisation of the stem εἰλυ- for 'to wrap', in the verb (ἐλυσθείς) as well as in the nominal derivatives (ἔλυμα). Granted, Zenodotus seems to have had the future εἰλύσω as the vulgate: at least the A scholia do not mention any different reading under his name for Φ 319. That means his text was not fully consistent, but the coexistence between forms of differing age is expected anyway, and the examples above (δένδρει vs δένδρεον, μάρτυρες vs μάρτυρος, ἀναπτάς vs πετάσσας) prove that he tolerated such inconsistencies as εἰλύσω vs ἐλυσθείς without a problem. However, the consistency between the verb (ϝ)ἐλυσθείς and the noun (ϝ)ἔλυμα can certainly not be ascribed to "experimental" forms coined by Zenodotus, whose version proves more archaic than the vulgate. Here again a lexical divergence between Zenodotus' ἐλυσθείς and vulgate ἐοικώς results from a lexical replacement in the vulgate due to the seemingly archaic morphology of the participle ἐλυσθείς—although it is certainly not as archaic a form as ἀναπτάς or ὄψ—, and to the semantic difference with the other two instances of ἐλυσθείς 'curled up'. But precisely, taking into account Zenodotus' reading in A 47 provides the starting point which allows us to understand the semantic evolution of the participle ἐλυσθείς and how it took on the meaning 'curled up'. This contextual meaning arose in one specific line, ι 433 (the context of reinterpretation), and afterwards the new meaning was transferred to Ω 510. As mentioned above, this is a recent development because of the absence of initial /w/ in Ω 510 and already in ι 433 as we read it now (but maybe not in an earlier state of the line). It is one of the rare cases where the context of reinterpretation is a line of the *Odyssey* while the context of actualisation is a line of the *Iliad* (but Ω is not an old book).[42]

The elimination of ἐλυσθείς is similar to the elimination of ἀναπτάς in A 351, replaced by ὀρεγνύς (pp. 136–137). Ἀναπτάς dates back to a time when the root aorist of πίτνημι was still alive in Greek. When this root aorist was restricted to the verb 'to fly', while the stem -πτα- survived for 'to spread' only in the perfect πέπταμαι, the form ἀναπτάς had to be either modernised or replaced by a different word. It could not be replaced by the newer form ἀναπετάσσας for metrical reasons, hence the replacement by ὀρεγνύς, which has the same meaning. Similarly, ϝελυσθείς could not be kept because in the meantime ἐλυσθείς had taken over a different meaning in another context, neither could it be replaced by the new εἰλυσθείς because the modernisation was metrically impossible, hence the replacement by ϝεϝοικώς. But whereas in the case of ἀναπτάς/ὀρεγνύς the

---

42   I studied a similar case in Le Feuvre 2015: 283–303.

meaning of the inserted form is more or less the same as that of the replaced form, in the case of ἐλυσθείς/ἐοικώς the meaning is very different.

It may be noteworthy that Aristophanes of Byzantium, who had ἔλυμα as did Zenototus in Δ 137, apparently did not have νυκτὶ ἐλυσθείς in A 47, according to the testimony of the scholia. His name is not associated with this reading— granted, many things have been lost, so that this is not decisive. This suggests that ἐλυσθείς was eliminated early on because of the semantic evolution described above, and that the elimination of ἐλυσθείς was the factor leading to the replacement of ἔλυμα, once the latter was isolated. Aristophanes' version would reflect this intermediate stage.

From the etymological point of view, new conclusions can be drawn once the picture has been completed and reorganised. LIV^2 has under $*u̯el$- a note "Eine detaillierte Untersuchung aller $*u̯el$-Wurzeln wäre hilfreich." My point here is certainly not to undertake an exhaustive study. But the findings of our Zenodotean inquiry already bring new elements. Zenodotus' ϝέλυμα 'wrapping' and ϝελυσθείς 'wrapped' are old forms and clearly belong with vṛṇóti 'to cover, to envelop'. The avatar of ϝελυσθείς, ἐλυσθείς 'curled up', is not reliable in order to establish the original meaning of the verb because its meaning is secondary, and ἐλύσθη is even less reliable because it is even more remote from the original meaning. As a consequence, ἐλύσθη 'rollte, krümmte sich' and εἰλύομαι 'krümme mich' should be withdrawn from the list of forms in LIV^2. The Zenodotean forms, which were not taken into account by linguists, unfortunately, confirm that in Greek the root was $*u̯el$-u-, that there is no trace of any initial laryngeal in Greek, and they provide a new argument against the distinction made by LIV^2 between two roots. If ϝελυσθείς belongs with vṛṇóti (LIV^2 1. $*u̯el$- 'einschließen, verhüllen') and ϝέλυμα, cognate of *volumen*, with *volvō* (LIV^2 2. $*u̯el$- 'drehen, rollen'), that implies that vṛṇóti and *volvō* belong to one and the same root meaning 'to roll, to wrap', and that vṛṇóti also is derived from the enlarged root $*u̯el$-u-. Whether the -u- must be considered an enlargement of the root or an old present morpheme no longer analysable as such in synchrony is not fundamental: in Greek, $*ϝελυ$- behaves as a root.[43] Together, ϝέλυμα and ϝελυσθείς confirm that εἰλύω is the remodelling of an older $*ϝελύω$,[44] matching Arm. *gelum*, Lat. *volvō* and implied by the Gothic causative *walwjan*. In the course of time, the stem εἰλῡ- was generalised from the perfect, not only to the verbal paradigm but also to nominal derivatives (*Od.* εἴλῡμα). The relative

---

43 See on this problem of the *u*-present formations and the enlargements García Ramón 2018.
44 The expected syllabification would be $*u̯elu̯e/o$-: a vocalic /u/ can have been restored after other forms of the paradigm.

prominence of the perfect stem in a verb meaning 'to wrap', and particularly frequent in the passive perfect 'wrapped' (nine occurrences in Homer, vs only one for the future εἰλύσω and none for the present and aorist), is semantically plausible. If a nasal present was inherited in Greek, it may be εἰλέω (*LIV*² **u̯el-neu-*, accepted by Beekes, *EDG*) rather than εἰλύω, provided one assumes that the *e* grade is analogical after the aorist. The reduplicated present ἴλλω was created within Greek. As a consequence, the forms with a long augment or a lengthened preverb (Ved. *ví āvar* 'hat enthüllt') quoted by *LIV*² under either root **u̯el-* must belong to root **Hu̯er-* (*LIV*² 'einschließen, stecken, hineintun'), found in Lat. *aperiō* 'to open', *operiō* 'to close', OCS *ot-voriti* 'to open'.[45]

6   Hesiod's ἔλῡμα

Piecing together ϝέλῠμα and ϝελύσθεις, both built from **u̯el-u-* 'to wrap', means that we must disconnect Hesiod's ἔλῡμα 'stock of the plough', which has no ϝ, probably has a long ῡ and can hardly mean 'wrapping' of the ploughshare, which is not appropriate for a rigid wooden piece. Now in the primitive form of the plough, the ard, the draft-pole into which the share is fitted and from which the stock will evolve through technical progress is the long wooden piece the ploughman drives while the animal drags it. That means that 'stock' cannot be the original meaning since the stock is a relatively late invention. Hesiod still mentions two different types of ard (*Op.* 433), one αὐτόγυος and the other one πηκτός. The αὐτόγυος type, the "one-piece" ard, is the older: it has no stock, technically speaking, as a distinct piece, but only a single long wooden piece which is used to move the ard and into which the share is fitted. Hesiod gives the indication that it must be a bent piece of wood: *Op.* 427–429 πόλλ᾽ ἐπικαμπύλα κᾶλα· φέρειν δὲ γύην, ὅτ᾽ ἂν εὕρῃς, || ἐς οἶκον, [...] || πρίνινον "there is plenty of bent fire wood; bring home, if you find one, [...] a holm-oak" (D.H.). This applies to the αὐτόγυος ard, in which there is only one wooden piece, naturally bent.

Now Hesychius has a word which refers to a long wooden piece in ἐλύμνιαι· δοκοὶ ὀρόφιναι 'roof-beams' (ε 2227), a technical term which is old, and found already in Mycenaean under the form *e-ru-mi-ni-ja* PY Vn 46.3 (nom.pl.), unanimously understood as referring to wooden pieces used in carpentry, more specifically in naval carpentry.[46] For a ship, carpenters need bent pieces of wood. The required curve was obtained by means of a stove, whereas the peasant had

---

45   *LIV*² mentions this as a possibility in a footnote under 2. **u̯el-*.
46   See the literature in *DMic.*, s.v., and Piquero Rodríguez 2019: 199.

to rely on nature to find a suitably bent piece of wood for his ard. Bent wooden pieces can also be used as roof beams, for instance as connecting elements between opposite straight beams, and that would agree with Hesychius' definition δοκοὶ ὀρόφιναι. In a previous study, I argued that these words were derived from a *-men stem, either neuter or animate.[47] I can go a step further now: the *-men stem is attested in Greek, it is Hesiod's ἔλυμα, which I had not included into this set of forms. The word probably referred first to the αὐτόγυος type of ard before it was restricted to the meaning 'stock' when technical progress invented the composite ard. The suffix *-ih₂ is found in many nouns referring to material artifacts (μάχαιρα, σφαῖρα, γέφυρα, τράπεζα): ἐλύμνιαι certainly belongs to this category. The derivative, displaying the same reflex as πότνια after heavy syllable, must be old enough.

I also linked this *-ih₂ derivative with the compound προθέλυμνος of I 541 (πολλὰ δ' ὅ γε προθέλυμνα χαμαὶ βάλε δένδρεα μακρά "and he threw down to the ground high trees προθέλυμνα"), which I think is a neo-compound resulting from a resegmentation of a line in which προθ- is a preverb with tmesis, and *ἔλυμνα the adjective modifier of δένδρεα (or δούρατα in a *varia lectio* which may be older), that is, uncut wood.[48] I understood προθέλυμνα as referring to the trunk of the tree, as a consequence of the etymology I suggested, but προθέλυμνα could as well refer to the branches, and indeed, if ἔλυμα and its derivative ἐλύμνιαι refer to bent pieces of wood, the branches would be a better candidate. What is clear, at any rate, is that *ἔλυμνα refers to long and strong pieces of wood suitable for woodwork.

I will not go into the discussion of προθέλυμνος again. The point I am interested in here is that, once we acknowledge that Hesiod's ἔλυμα has nothing to do with *u̯el-u- and does not mean 'wrapping', because this is the meaning of ϝέλυμα, this form provides a clear derivational base for ἐλύμνιαι, and brings the new information that the latter has a long /ū/, which is of course impossible to see in a closed syllable. Conversely, ἐλύμνιαι confirms that the absence of initial ϝ in ἔλυμα in Hesiod is old since Mycenaean *e-ru-mi-ni-ja* proves that there is no /w/ at the beginning of the word. At any rate, the word is not isolated within Greek, since it has a derivative which goes back to second millenium Greek, and probably another one in the Homeric neo-compound προθ-έλυμνος.[49]

---

47 Le Feuvre 2015: 586–593.
48 Kölligan (2018b) since then has proposed a different interpretation, with a segmentation προ-θέλυμνος, and links the second element with the group of θάλλω.
49 In theory, Sievers' law implies that, if ἔλυμα has a /ū/, ἐλύμνιαι cannot be derived directly from ἔλυμα, but only from a thematicised *ἔλυμνος. However, the application of Siever's law in Greek is not without exceptions.

As a consequence, the etymology I had tentatively proposed at the time for ἐλύμνιαι and προθέλυμνος can no longer be maintained. I had argued for a relationship with root *h_1leud^h- 'to grow'. Now if ἔλυμα is indeed the base of ἐλύμνιαι, that is impossible, because of the /ū/ and because in ἔλυμα the *d^h of *h_1leud^h- would be preserved. It can be lost in a consonant cluster like *-d^h-mn-o-, but it cannot in *-d^h-m̥n. The assumption that it was lost in the derivative ἐλύμνιαι and that the base ἔλυμα was subsequently reshaped after the derivative is very unlikely. I will leave aside here the etymological analysis of ἔλυμα, since that would lead us away from Zenodotus, and will come back to it elsewhere.

CHAPTER 7

Straight Shaft and Straight Flight

Greek grammarians had a synchronic vision of their language as well as of Homeric language. Therefore, faced with unfamiliar forms, they were prone to either replace them (ἄας, ἀναπτάς, νυκτὶ ἐλυσθείς) or correct them (ὄψ ἀΐοντες). Of course, the first source of those corrections was the Homeric corpus itself. This will be particularly clear with the next weird Zenodotean reading.

1   The *hapax* ἰθυπτίων

In Φ 169–170 the vulgate reads:

> δεύτερος αὖτ' Ἀχιλεὺς μελίην ἰθυπτίωνα
> Ἀστεροπαίῳ ἐφῆκε κατακτάμεναι μενεαίνων
>
> throwing second Achilleus let fly at Asteropaios with the straight-flying ash spear in a fury to kill him.
> R.L.

The compound ἰθυπτίων 'straight-flying' is a *hapax*. It is explained by scholiasts as the compound corresponding to the syntagm 'ἰθὺ βέλος πέτεται' "the spear flies straight" (Υ 99), and a bT scholion even says explicitly that the former is derived from the latter: ἰθυπτίωνα· ἀπὸ τοῦ 'ἰθὺ βέλος πέτεται', "it comes from ἰθὺ βέλος πέτεται" (*bT Schol.* Φ 169a). The correspondence between a compound and a syntagm is a well-known principle of epic diction, already identified by Greek scholars.

The same explanation is given by a D scholion: ἰθυπτίωνα· ἐπ' εὐθείας φερομένην, καὶ οἷον ἱπταμένην "straight going, and like flying" (Ζ): ἱπταμένην refers to ἰθὺ βέλος πέτεται.

A spelling ἰθυπτείωνα is attested, probably a mere iotacising spelling itself. Hesychius also has a spelling εἰθυπτίωνα (ε 801), in a series of several glosses with εἰθυ- for ἰθυ-.

The problem with the standard explanation is that, from the root of πέτομαι 'to fly', no derivative in -ίων is known, nor an *i*-derivative. Most forms in -ίων are derived from *-io-* adjectives, but there is no *-πτιος adjective, except ὕπτιος which does not belong with πέτομαι. Schulze admits the word is a neologism: "we must think the poet adapted to the line by an artificial neologism."[1] However, such a neologism requires a model. The only other compound in -ίων in Homer is κυλλοποδίων. Risch says that those two compounds result from an extension of the suffix -ίων, extracted from the οὐρανίων type, which is patronymic in Homer,[2] but the reason for this extension remains to be identified. Moreover, the patronymic suffix yields substantives, not adjectives, and ἰθυπτίων is certainly not a substantive. Lastly, κυλλοποδίων cannot have a patronymic value: Hephaistos is not "son of the lame-footed" as Zeus Κρονίων is the son of Cronos or Achilles Πηληίων the son of Peleus. Hephaistos is lame-footed himself. The question therefore deserves to be reexamined.

2 Κυλλοποδίων

Now the question is *should* the two words be compared? Κυλλοποδίων is Hephaistos' nickname, a substantive, or substantivised adjective, whereas ἰθυπτίων is an adjective, and certainly not a nickname. Κυλλοποδίων has a short-vowel stem κυλλοποδιον-, metrically warranted in Φ 331, while ἰθυπτίων has a generalised long vowel (acc. ἰθυπτίωνα). Κυλλοποδίων is attested only at the end of an hemistich, before the trochaic caesura (Φ 331) or at the end of the line (the other two instances), but ἰθυπτίων is not found in that position. To sum up, morphologically, semantically and metrically, they do not belong together. This is confirmed by a closer examination of κυλλοποδίων.

Κυλλοποδίων is attested three times in the *Iliad*:
- Φ 331 # ὄρσεο κυλλοπόδιον ἐμὸν τέκος "rise up, god of the dragging feet, my child" (R.L.). This is Hera speaking to Hephaistos. The line was athetised on grounds of decency, the form deemed too familiar.[3]
- Σ 371 ὃν ῥ' αὐτὸς ποιήσατο κυλλοποδίων # "built for himself by the god of the dragging footsteps" (R.L.).
- Υ 270 ἐπεὶ πέντε πτύχας ἤλασε κυλλοποδίων # "since the god of the dragging feet had made five folds on it" (R.L.). Υ 269–272, a digression, were

---

[1] Schulze 1892: 309: "ἰθυπτίωνα poeta artificiali productione versui adaptasse putandus est."
[2] Risch 1974: 57. Forssman 2020: 128 and 131 gives the form among derivatives in -ων (not -ίων).
[3] T Schol. Φ 331b: ἄκαιρον καὶ ἀπρεπὲς τὸ ἐπίθετον "the epithet is untimely and not decent." A Schol. Φ 331a: †ἀθετεῖται†, ὅτι [...] ἄκαιρον τὸ ἐπίθετον· ἡ γὰρ φιλανθρωπευομένη καὶ λέγουσα ἐμὸν τέκος οὐκ ὤφειλεν ἀπὸ τοῦ ἐλαττώματος προσφωνεῖν "it is athetised, because [...] the epithet is untimely. Because Hera who is being gentle and saying 'my child' should not call him after his physical defect."

athetised by Aristarchus among others, and were missing in several redactions, according to scholia.[4]

The iota is metrically lengthened in all three instances. The regular κυλλόπους was unmetrical in the nominative, and in the vocative, if κυλλόπους was also the form used in that function (cf. vocative Οἰδίπους Soph., *OR* 646). It could be replaced by the variant *κυλλόπος, as ἀελλόπος (which, however, is not attested as a vocative, but only as a nominative), or by a derivative: the latter solution was preferred and the result is κυλλοποδίων. The word apparently shows the individualising suffix *-on- often used to build nicknames derived from adjectives, as in Γλίσχρων (from γλισχρός 'sticky') or Στράβων (from στραβός 'squinting'). That would imply that the second element is -πόδιος, but no compound in -πόδιος is attested in Homer. This may be for metrical reasons, but in fact, it appears that this is a general fact in Greek, for the compounds in -πόδιος listed in Buck-Petersen are all hypostatic compounds derived from prepositional phrases (παραπόδιος Pind., ἐμπόδιος Hdt, ἐπιπόδιος Soph.). *Κυλλοπόδιος, however, is not of this type.

The only other productive category is that of the neuter substantives in -πόδιον, which are found with a numeral first member (Antiphanes τριπόδιον 'small tripod', Dinarchus ἡμιπόδιον 'measure of a half foot'—well attested in inscriptions—, Xenophon τριημιπόδιον, πενθημιπόδιον 'measure of one/two feet and half'—also attested as adjectives τριημιπόδιος, πενθημιπόδιος 'of one/two feet and half' in inscriptions), or are regular derivatives of compounds with a nominal first element (Hipponax χυτροπόδιον 'small cauldron', Hyperides ἀνδραπόδιον 'small slave', Theophrastus μελαμπόδιον 'black-foot', name of the black hellebore). This category includes substantivised prepositional compounds like ὑποπόδιον 'step' (*IG* II² 1394, beginning of the 4th c. BCE). These compounds in -πόδιον may or may not have a diminutive meaning.

According to the derivational pattern of compounds in -πόδιος and -πόδιον, κυλλοπόδιον, based on κυλλόπους, must belong to the latter type. Schulze proposed that Κυλλοποδίων is the derivative of a neuter noun κυλλοπόδιον,[5] but Greek does not derive nouns in -ων from nouns in -ιον. In Homer, -ιον derivatives from compounds are well attested, without diminutive meaning, and -ιον derivatives with basically the same meaning as their base are attested, too, see θηρίον 'beast' (κ 171) which is metrically but not semantically different from the animate θήρ, or ἰνίον 'tendon' (Ε 73), next to the animate plural ἶνες. But one

---

4 *A Schol.* Υ 269–272a1: ἀθετοῦνται στίχοι τέσσαρες; *T Schol.* Υ 269–272b1: οὗτοι καὶ προηθετοῦντο παρ' ἐνίοις τῶν σοφιστῶν, ἐν ἐνίοις δὲ οὐδὲ ἐφέροντο "those were already athetised by some sophists, and in others they were not even present."

5 Schulze 1892: 307–308, followed by Hackstein 1992: 156.

cannot help but think of the type Φειδιππίδη, Φειδιππίδιον 'Pheidippides, my dear Pheidippidion' (Ar., *Nub.* 80). The use of a -ιον diminutive for the vocative of a name is usual and probably old. In Φ 331 we are in fact dealing with a similar context, that of a father (*Nub.* 80) or a mother (Φ 331 # ὄρσεο κυλλοπόδιον ἐμὸν τέκος) calling his/her son. Moreover, κυλλοπόδιον is a nickname, and a diminutive is expected for this category.[6] Now if κυλλοπόδιον is a neuter noun of the θηρίον type, whether it is a diminutive or not, it has -ιον both in the vocative and in the nominative. It is noteworthy, although it remained unnoticed, that the only line where vocalic quantity is warranted by metre is Φ 331 where the form is in the vocative before the trochaic caesura. In the other two, one of which is probably interpolated, the epithet is at the end of the line: since the last syllable is of indefinite quantity, a form κυλλοπόδιον would fit in this context. As it happens, in the archaic Ionic alphabet, both were spelled -ION. Accordingly, nothing, except the weight of tradition, warrants the nominative κυλλοποδίων, which could be an erroneous reanalysis of the vocative κυλλοπόδιον, or κυλλοποδῖον,[7] as belonging to the εὐδαίμων type instead of the θηρίον type. Next to the graphic identity of both, a stylistic factor may have played a role, namely that diminutives in -ιον were deemed too familiar for high-style epic poetry (there again a typically Hellenistic concern)—see above what the scholiasts say about it.

The parallelism with ἰθυπτίων appears to be not only very fragile, but maybe utterly erroneous if κυλλοπόδιον is in fact a neuter noun. As a consequence, we must study ἰθυπτίων *per se*. Hackstein already saw that the latter cannot be from πέτομαι, and proposed an alternative etymology. He derives it from the root of πταίω 'to strike' (παίω as a doublet), assuming that -πτι- is the reflex of the zero grade $*pih_2$- 'to strike', "with -π- replaced by -πτ- after the full grade $*p{i̯}eh_2$-."[8] The meaning would be 'Gerad-Schläger', 'straight-striking'. But the implied remodelling of the root remains hypothetical, and would be isolated. Nowhere in epic phraseology do we have a combination of 'to strike' and 'straight': ἰθύς combines with verbs of motion, not with verbs meaning 'to strike'. The main objection to this explanation, however, is that it can be questioned for the simple reason that it takes the vulgate's reading at face value.

---

6 Rutherford 2019: 171: "the ending -ίων suggests a diminutive." The diminutive value is correct, but the suffix is not -ίων.

7 There was a discussion on the accentuation of the form, some having, like Aristarchus and Herodian, a proparoxytone κυλλοπόδιον (*A Schol.* Φ 331), while others preferred a properispomenon κυλλοποδῖον. Anyway, not one doubted that the word belonged to the εὐδαίμων type.

8 Hackstein 1992: 156: "-πτι- setzt die schwundstufige Wurzelgestalt $*pih_2$- von uridg $*p{i̯}eh_2$- 'schlagen' fort mit Ersatz des Wurzelanlauts -π- durch -πτ- nach dem nicht-schwundstufigen Wurzelformen mit lautgesetzlichem πτ- aus $*p{i̯}$-."

3   Zenodotus' Reading

Aristonicus says that Zenodotus had a different form, ἰθυκτίωνα. The form is not mentioned by Nickau.

> *A Schol.* Φ 169b1: ὅτι Ζηνόδοτος γράφει 'ἰθυκτίωνα' διὰ τὸ κτηδόνας λέγεσθαι τῶν ξύλων τὰς γραμματοειδεῖς διαφύσεις. παρέλκει δὲ νῦν τὸ περὶ τῆς τοῦ ξύλου φύσεως εἰπεῖν. τὸ μέντοι ἰθυπτίωνα εἰς εὐθὺ φερομένην, ἀναφερομένου τοῦ ἐπαίνου εἰς τὸν ἀκοντίζοντα· 'καὶ δ' ἄλλως τοῦ γ' ἰθὺ βέλος πέτεται' (Υ 99).

> because Zenodotus writes ἰθυκτίωνα, from the fact that the line-looking divisions in the wood are called κτηδόνες. But it is redundant here to talk about the nature of the wood. In fact ἰθυπτίωνα refers to ⟨the spear⟩ which is thrown straight, the praise being referred to the spear thrower, ⟨compare⟩ 'καὶ δ' ἄλλως τοῦ γ' ἰθὺ βέλος πέτεται' (Υ 99).

This scholion gives three different points of informations. The first is Zenodotus' reading. The second is the semantic and etymological explanation of this word. The third is about the context of use, a consequence of the semantic interpretation of the word—ἰθυκτίωνα applies to the material of the weapon, ἰθυπτίωνα to the throw.

The word is also found in an A scholion by Aristonicus:

> *A Schol.* Υ 273–274a1: ὅτι Ζηνόδοτος μετεποίησεν οὕτως 'μελίην ἰθυπτίωνα ἀσπίδα νύξ' εὔχαλκον ἀμύμονος Αἰνείαο'. οὐκ ἐκ χειρὸς δὲ ἐπέτυχεν ὁ Ἀχιλλεύς, ὅπερ διὰ τοῦ νύξε σημαίνεται, ἀλλὰ βέβληκε τὸ δόρυ· διὸ καὶ ἑξῆς (sc. Υ 283) 'βέλος' αὐτὸ εἴρηκε.

> because Zenodotus changed it as follows, 'with his spear ἰθυπτίωνα he hit the bronze shield of noble Aeneas'. But Achilles did not hit him by thrusting from his arm, which is what νύξε means, but he threw the weapon, and this is why he says afterwards βέλος.[9]

This variant is also given by a T scholion:

---

[9] The vulgate reads (Υ 273–274) Δεύτερος αὖτ' Ἀχιλεὺς προΐει δολιχόσκιον ἔγχος, || καὶ βάλεν Αἰνείαο κατ' ἀσπίδα πάντοσ' ἐΐσην "after him Achilleus let go his spear far shadowing and struck the shield of Aineias along its perfect circle" (R.L.).

T Schol. Υ 273–274a2: Ζηνόδοτος 'δεύτερον αὖτ' Ἀχιλεὺς μελίην ἰθυπτίωνα ἀσπίδα νύξ' εὔχαλκον ἀμύμονος Αἰνείαο' ὥστε ἐκ χειρὸς τετρῶσθαι, ἀλλὰ μὴ βεβλῆσθαι.

Zenodotus has δεύτερον αὖτ' Ἀχιλεὺς μελίην ἰθυπτίωνα ἀσπίδα νύξ' εὔχαλκον ἀμύμονος Αἰνείαο, so that he is hit by a thrust, but the spear is not thrown.

In the latter scholion the word is quoted under the form of the vulgate ἰθυπτίωνα. This is most probably not the exact line of Zenodotus, who is not likely to have used twice the same syntagm with two different spellings. However, the copyist may have corrected the condemned form in his commentary since what was at stake there was not the spelling of the compound but the fact that Zenodotus had a different line. Therefore this testimony is not reliable, except for the fact that it tells us that in Zenodotus' *ekdosis* the compound was not a *hapax* but a formular epithet of μελίη. Van Thiel assumes that since it is a mere "experimental modification of the word" in Φ 169, "even Zenodotus ignored his own conjecture" in Υ 273,[10] but this is unlikely.

The spelling ἰθυκτίωνα is confirmed by other scholia:

bT Schol. Φ 169b2: ἄλλως· ἰθυπτίωνα· †ἀρίσταρχος† 'ἰθυκτίωνα', ὅ ἐστιν ἐπ' εὐθείας ἔχουσαν τὰς κτηδόνας καὶ τὰς ἐν τοῖς ξύλοις διαφύσεις.

other: ἰθυπτίωνα. †Aristarchus writes ἰθυκτίωνα, that is, which has straight fibres and wood veins.

Geneva Schol. Φ 169c: ἰθυπτίωνα: ἐπ' εὐθείας φερομένην ὑπὸ τῆς εὐστοχίας τοῦ Ἀχιλλέως. | οἱ δὲ γράφοντες 'ἰθυκτίωνα' φασὶ κτηδόνας καλεῖσθαι τὰς κατ' εὐθεῖαν διαφύσεις τῶν ξύλων οἷον ἶνας. ἰθυπτίωνα δὲ λέγει τὴν ἐπ' εὐθείας πετομένην καὶ πορευομένην. | ὅτι Ζηνόδοτος γράφει 'ἰθυκτίωνα' καὶ Καλλίστρατος. | Ἑρμαπίας περισπᾷ τὴν παρεσχάτην, 'ἰθυπτιῶνα' ὡς 'Ἑλικῶνα.[11]

ἰθυπτίωνα: the straight-flying one because Achilles aimed straight. And those who write ἰθυκτίωνα say the veins of the wood are called κτηδόνας, as blood veins. But Homer says ἰθυπτίωνα, the straight-flying one and

---

10   Van Thiel 2014b, *sub* Φ 169: "übrigens ignorierte auch Zenodot seine vermeintliche Konjektur an anderer Stelle." On the other hand, Renehan 1975: 110 correctly states that in Υ 273, too, Zenodotus probably had ἰθυκτίωνα.
11   The scholion is a patchwork of different sources, separated by |.

straight-going. | Because Zenodotus writes ἰθυκτίωνα, and so does Callistratus. | Hermasias has a properispomene ἰθυπτιῶνα as Ἑλικῶνα.

We see here that Callistratus, a student of Aristophanes of Byzantium and rival of Aristarchus, had the same reading as Zenodotus, or retained Zenodotus' reading. Accordingly, we cannot be sure that his testimony is independent. In that case the philological criterion is not met, as there is no independent attestation. Likewise, the metrical criterion is ineffective, since neither reading is metrically better. Only the linguistic criterion remains for our consideration.

The two readings only differ by one phoneme, which raises the suspicion that the one is a modification of the other—either a correction or an alteration. Each camp justified their reading with a semantico-etymological explanation, which may be correct or not. Therefore, we must not rely on these explanations, but we must try to see which of the two spellings is morphologically sound.

We have seen above that ἰθυπτίωνα was morphologically abnormal if derived from πέτομαι, and that there was no directly comparable formation. But similarly, ἰθυκτίωνα cannot be related to the group of κτηδών, whatever scholiasts may say. The only common point is the initial sequence /kt/. This was enough for Greek etymologists, but we cannot be satisfied with that.

Wackernagel, in trying to find a solution for Zenodotus' reading, proposed to correct ἰθυκτίωνα into *ἰθυκτείωνα or ἰθυκτήωνα,[12] and to link it with glosses found in Hesychius:

> Hsch., ι 405: ἰθυκτέανον· τὸ ἰθὺ πεφυκὸς καὶ ὀρθὸν δένδρον "the tree which has grown straight and upright."
> Hsch., ε 6881: εὐθυκτέανον· εὖ πεφυκυῖαν, εἰς ὀρθόν "well grown, upright."

The compound εὐθυκτέανον may be compared with εὐκτέανον, which is attested twice in Plutarch as an epithet of "tree" (δρυὸς γὰρ εὐκτεάνου πρέμνον ὄρθιον καὶ μέγα τεμών "cutting a straight and large stump of a tall oak," *Marcel.* 8.2; ἐκ τῶν περὶ Τίρυνθα δένδρων ὄγχνην τεμὼν εὐκτέανον, "Ἥρας ἄγαλμα μορφῶσαι "he cut a tall pear-tree from the trees around Tirynth, to carve a statue of Hera," *fr.* 158.13–15 Sandbach). However, in Plutarch it is unlikely that the meaning is 'with good fibres', for it is not a technical term, but a general one meaning rather something like 'well-grown, tall'.

In Wackernagel's analysis, the -d- in κτηδών 'fibre' is an enlargement, and the non-enlarged root is preserved in εὐθυκτέανος, εὐκτέανος and *ἰθυκτείωνα.

---

12   Wackernagel 1916: 242.

However, the latter is a correction of Zenodotus' reading. This explanation, which is now outdated, clearly has its roots in the semantic explanation found in the scholia. Scholiasts explain ἰθυκτίωνα as a compound of a word meaning 'fibre' (κτηδών), therefore Wackernagel tried to justify this and sought for other words that had the same meaning, or at least supposedly so, all the while taking for granted that scholiasts actually knew the meaning of the word. But what if the scholiasts' explanation is fanciful, and if ἰθυκτίωνα does not mean 'with straight fibres'? We know that scholiasts often invent a meaning and an explanation for words which were not clear to them. If ἰθυκτίωνα is one of those words, we cannot rely on the explanation found in the scholia. That does not mean that the form itself is fanciful and unreliable: the etymological explanation must be rejected because obviously it is not correct,[13] but the form should not be rejected together with it. The preceding cases show that more than once Zenodotus' forms considered fanciful by most scholars are in fact archaic words that were no longer understandable. The general practice of the scholia shows through a host of examples that scholiasts readily provide a fanciful etymology—and a fanciful interpretation—for an existing word.

Rather, it seems that, faced with an obscure word ἰθυκτίωνα, scholiasts did indeed try to explain and etymologise the word by means of a word semantically compatible with the context and the first element ἰθυ- as well as phonetically close—by their criteria—, whence κτηδών, possibly because, just as Wackernagel, they had in mind the compounds εὐκτέανον and εὐθυκτέανον—although they do not mention them. Therefore, we should proceed the other way round and start from the transmitted form, without any attempt at guessing its meaning, then see if we can propose a convincing morphological analysis, which may then lead to a semantic interpretation.

At any rate, if one of the readings is an emendation, it must be the vulgate's. Obviously one could easily correct ἰθυκτίωνα into ἰθυπτίωνα after ἰθὺ βέλος πέτεται (and ἰθὺς πέτετο X 143), as a remotivation, but not the other way round since ἰθυκτίωνα cannot be related to anything in Greek and is completely isolated. Accordingly, the older form is almost certainly ἰθυκτίωνα. It is pointless to seek an alternative etymology for ἰθυπτίωνα if the latter results from an old emendation. The form we must seek to analyse is ἰθυκτίωνα.

---

13 For instance Leaf "Zenodotus ἰθυκτίωνα, said to mean *straight-grained* and derived from κτηδών or κτιδών, the fibre of wood, which is impossible."

4 Reconstruction and Etymology

4.1 Formal Analysis

There is no reason to doubt that the first element of the compound is ἰθυ-, the Ionic variant of εὐθυ-. The second element can be the reflex of *kti-$ōn$ or *tki-$ōn$, which by metathesis yields /kt/ (*ti-tk-e/o- > τίκτω). The former analysis was the only possible one for Greek scholars, hence the link with κτηδών. We could also think of root *$tk̂ei$-, that of κτίζω 'to found', but this does not lead to a viable semantic combination with ἰθύς 'straight'. However, modern linguistics tells us that the second element can in principle be reconstructed either as *kti-$ōn$ or as *$Hkti$-$ōn$ (or *$Htki$-$ōn$). Of course, the possibility that there was a phoneme before the sequence -κτ- was out of reach for Greek scholars, but it must be considered in a modern reconstruction. As a matter of fact, a structure *$īd^hu$-$Hkti$-$ōn$[14] would yield *ἰθῡκτίων with regular lengthening of the final vowel of the first element of the compound. This lengthening is not perceptible since the syllable is long, anyway, and there is no graphic difference between ῡ and ῠ in the Greek alphabet. Since the word was obscure and unknown to Greek speakers, they had no means to determine the quantity of the vowel. But if this does not make a phonetic difference, it does make a morphological one, on the grounds that if the etymon is *$īd^hu$-$Hkti$-$ōn$, then the morphological boundary does not lie before /kt/ but in the middle of the /ū/.

Does such a structure lead to a different etymology? Indeed, it does. I would suggest the second element of ἰθυκτίωνα is linked with another word of difficult etymology, ἀκτίς, ἀκτῖνος 'ray of light'. The word has been compared previously with Vedic aktú- 'twilight', but this is now almost unanimously abandoned.[15] J. Jouanna proposed to see in ἀκτίς a derivative from root ἀκ- 'pointed, sharp', reconstructed as *$h_2ek̂$-.[16] He relied on the phraseology involving ἀκτίς in scientific Greek terminology, and optical theory in particular, wherein the ray of light is described as ὀξύς, as well as relying on the many instances in poetry where the sun "hits" the earth with its rays (ἀκτῖσιν ἐβάλλεν # E 479, τ 441, ἀκτίς ... ἔβαλλε γαῖαν Eur., Suppl. 641) assimilated to arrows (ἀκτῖν᾽ ἐφῆκας Eur., Phoen.

---

[14] The Ionic form ἰθύς is certainly secondary, the older form is Attic εὐθύς. I do not intend to go into the question of the etymology of this adjective here (see the literature in Beekes, *EDG*, s.vv.), and my "etymon" *$īd^hu$- is a mere Transponat, for the sake of convenience.

[15] Beekes, *EDG*. On the etymology of aktú-, see Mayrhofer, *EWAia*. The etymology linking aktú- and ἀκτίς is still found, however, in Mallory–Adams 2006: 302. The word is almost certainly a derivative with zero-grade stem of the name of 'night' (*$n̥k^w$-t-$ú$-), the older meaning of which is 'darkness'. The association of the morning twilight with dawn led to a secondary drift toward the notion of shining.

[16] Jouanna 2002.

5). The word is also used for the thunderbolt, Zeus' weapon: ὦ Διὸς ἀκτίς, παῖσον Soph., *Trach*. 1086. This phrase belongs here too:"Ἥλιος ὀξυβελής in Empedocles (*fr*. 40, transmitted by Plutarch, *Mor*. 920c10), where βέλος 'arrow' stands for the ray of light. More remote, Euripides' τόξα θ' ἡλίου τάδε "and (I see) the sun's arrows here" (Eur., *HF* 1090), is another formulation of the same idea.

To that we may add the occurrence in Mimnermus, *fr*. 11. 5–6 D (11a. 1–2 West) Αἰήταο πόλιν, τόθι τ' ὠκέος Ἠελίοιο || ἀκτῖνες χρυσέωι κείαται ἐν θαλάμωι "city of Aietes, where the rays of swift Helios are lying in a golden room." The formulation is strikingly reminiscent of the description of the θάλαμος in which Ulysses' weapons are stored: χ 109 βῆ δ' ἴμεναι θαλαμόνδ', ὅθι οἱ κλυτὰ τεύχεα κεῖτο "and made his way to the chamber where the splendid armor lay" (J.H.); φ 11–12, (θάλαμος) ἔνθα δὲ τόξον κεῖτο παλίντονον ἠδὲ φαρέτρη || ἰοδόκος, πολλοὶ δ' ἔνεσαν στονόεντες ὀϊστοί "and there lay a back-bent bow, and a quiver holding arrows, and in it were many arrows that cause groans" (J.H.). That is, Mimnermus describes the rays of Helios as arrows or javelins stored in a devoted room, as there was one in every palace.[17] Be it a direct influence of the *Odyssey* or not, this is another element in the assimilation of rays to arrows.

Of course a phraseological collocation does not imply an etymological relationship. However, since many words applying to various sharp things were derived from the root *$*h_2ek$-, it is possible that ἀκτίς, which is sharp, indeed, is another one. As I will try to show, Jouanna's suggestion can be backed by the Zenodotean form ἰθυκτίωνα.

Ἀκτίς is first attested in the plural, which is not surprising for a word referring to the rays of the sun. In Homer, Hesiod and the Homeric Hymns it is only used in the dative plural ἀκτῖσι, or with the Aeolic ending ἀκτίνεσσι. The singular is first attested in Pindar. The word belongs to an old layer of epic poetry and apparently comes from a non-assibilating dialect. It is also possible that the process of assibilation was blocked to prevent a potential homonymy with ἀξίνη 'axe', a probable loanword, as is usual in Attic-Ionic. Ἀκτίς is not used in prose before fourth century scientific literature, especially Aristotle.[18] It seems to be

---

17 In the narrative of the *Odyssey*, the weapons are stored there because Telemachus removed them from the megaron under a pretext. There were armour-rooms in Mycenaean palaces, and the device of having Telemachus removing shields and spears from the megaron to lock them up in a special room is a means of reconciling the traditional element of weapons in the armour-room and the reality of the archaic period where there was no such room. In the *Iliad* the storage room is the κλισίη (N 260–265), as expected for a campaigning army.

18 The word is found once in Plato, *Tim*. 78d6 τὰς ἐντὸς τοῦ πυρὸς ἀκτῖνας: the 'rays of fire' is an adaptation of the 'rays of the sun' and this can be considered one of the many poeticisms of Plato.

a poetic word, which was borrowed by philosophers in this period of building up of a new scientific language.

The suffix *-īn- is rare. It can characterise loanwords (so Beekes, *EDG*), but can also be analysed as *-i-Hn-, with the zero grade of *-$h_3on(H)$-, the Hoffmann suffix. The Hoffmann suffix is a suffixalised second element of a compound, which acquired the status of a suffix early enough in Indo-European languages. The ablaut opposed a strong stem *-$h_3on(H)$- and a weak stem *-$h_3n(H)$-, as shown by Ved. *yúvan-*, gen. *yūnás* 'young man' (strong *$h_2i̯u$-h_3on- / weak *$h_2i̯u$-$h_3n(H)$-*ós*), lit. 'provided with vital strength', and also by the old Umbrian ablative *natīne* 'patrician family', built on the weak stem *$ǵn̥h_1$-ti-h_3n-, lit. 'provided with a (common) birth', corresponding to Latin acc. *nātiōnem* 'people', built on the strong stem *$ǵn̥h_1$-ti-h_3on-. In most languages the ablaut was eliminated, and Latin for instance has a non-alternating paradigm for nouns in *-tiō, *-tiōnis, with the strong stem generalised. The combination of the Hoffmann suffix with the abstract suffix *-ti- attested in Italic languages is also found in Greek in a few forms, like δωτίνη 'liberality' (*deh_3-ti-$h_3n(H)$-eh_2), προμνηστῖνος 'thoughtful, cautious', lit. 'provided with thought (μνῆστις)' (*$mn̥h_2$-sti-$h_3n(H)$-o-).[19]

The comparison of ἀκτῖν- with ἰθυκτίων would point to a paradigm nom. *$h_2ḱti$-h_3on-, gen. *$h_2ḱti$-h_3n-os, with the weak stem generalised in ἀκτῖνες, ἀκτίς, and the strong stem preserved as a fossil in the compound ἰθυκτίων, maybe because the *o* grade in compounds is frequent (see φρήν/ἄφρων, ἀνήρ/ἀγήνωρ, πῆμα/ἀπήμων). The generalisation of the weak stem in the substantive is not surprising. As a matter of fact, Greek, like most languages, has a strong tendency to eliminate apophonic alternations. The word is above all attested in the plural and appears first in the dative plural. The weak stem is predominant in the plural—the only case built on the strong stem was the nominative, nor is an inanimate noun frequently used in the nominative, so that the latter was analogised after the other cases. Therefore the nom. singular ἀκτίς probably does not continue the old form but was also remodelled after the plural. For the opposition between a compound built on the strong stem and a simple form with generalised zero grade, compare πολύρρην, -ενος 'rich in lambs' next to ἀρήν, ἀρνός 'lamb' (and, remodelled after the simple, πολύαρνι B 106). The same tendency to eliminate apophonic alternations led to the inflection nom.sg. ἰθυκτίων, acc. ἰθυκτίωνα, as in χειμών, -ῶνος 'winter', ἄκμων, -ωνος 'anvil', ἀγκών, -ῶνος 'curve of the arm'. Moreover, for a poetic compound, the need to have a stable metrical

---

19   On those forms, see Le Feuvre 2015: 194–195. On the identification of the root that gave rise to the Hoffmann suffix, see Pinault 2000.

structure in the inflectional paradigm probably played a role in that generalisation of -ων-.[20] The divergent evolution of ἀκτῖνες and ἰθυκτίων led to a complete demotivation of the compound.

Can this etymon reconstructed on the basis of Greek alone be backed by other forms outside Greek? A perfect match is found in Celtic languages: Middle Welsh has a phytonym *eithinn* 'broom (plant), furze', matching OIr. *aittenn* 'id.', for which two reconstructions have been proposed, either *$h_2ek̂$-ti-h_3n-o-* (McCone, NIL)[21] or *$h_2ek̂$-sti-Hn-o-* (Matasović).[22] The latter reconstruction relies on Lith. *akštìs/akstìs* 'spit, thorn', but this form is secondary. The sequence *$k̂s$ yields /š/ in Lithuanian, and not /kš/ (*ašìs* 'axle' < *$h_2ek̂s$-i-*), therefore the expected Lithuanian form would be *aštìs*, either from *$h_2ek̂$-sti-* or from *$h_2ek̂$-ti-*, and the /k/ is a later addition.[23] The Slavic counterpart *ostь* 'sharp point, awn' can be the reflex either of *$h_2ek̂$-sti-* or of *$h_2ek̂$-ti-*: in Slavic *$k̂s$ yields /s/ (*osь* 'axle' < *$h_2ek̂s$-i-*), as *$k̂$. Since none of these forms is a proof of a *-sti- suffix (or of an underlying s-stem), and since Greek has a form without /s/, it is safer to reconstruct *$h_2ek̂$-ti- and *$h_2ek̂$-ti-h_3n-o- for *aittenn*, *eithinn*. The difference lies in the apophonic grade of the root: Celtic implies an *e* grade, Greek ἀκ- can go back to both an *e* grade as well as to a zero grade, for both *#h_2C- and *#h_2eC- yield #aC-, and ἰθυκτίων implies a zero grade.

The pattern in which a Hoffmann form has a zero grade for the first element is found in Vedic, Italic and maybe Anatolian: see Ved. *yúvan-* < *h_2iu-$h_3$on- next to *ā́yu-* (*$h_2ói$-u-*), Ved. *dámūnas-* 'master of the house', remodelling of an older *damūna-* 'provided with a household' < *$dm̥$-u-h_3n-o-, next to *dom-u-*,[24] Ved. *kanyā̀* 'young woman', older *kan(i)yān-*, weak stem *kanīn-*, < *$kn̥i$-$h_3$on-, next to *kon-* in OCS *iskoni* 'from the beginning' (zero grade also in Gr. καινός),[25] Lat. *nātiōn-* < *$ĝn̥h_1$-ti-$h_3$on- next to *gens*, *gentis* (*$ĝenh_1$-ti-*), Pal. *malitanna-*

---

20   The long ī cannot be phonetic, and can be either a simple metrical lengthening or a real /ī/ analogical after the weak stem ἀκτῖν- < *$h_2ek̂$-ti-h_3n- and preserved by the metrical structure.
21   McCone 2005: 409.
22   Matasović, EDPC, s.v.
23   Derksen, EDBIL, s.v. *akstis*. In Le Feuvre 2015: 264, I accepted the reconstruction *$h_2ek̂$-s-ti- for Baltic and Slavic, and assumed that the form was derived from an s-stem: the existence of the s-stem is undisputable, but it is not certain that it lies at the basis of the Baltic and Slavic derivatives.
24   On *dámūnas-* and the *u*-derivative of *dom-* 'house', see Pinault 2000.
25   Pinault 2000 reconstructs *kon-Hi-$h_3$on-, but now accepts a zero grade *$kn̥$-i-$h_3$on- (*per litteras*, August 2018). The question whether *$dm̥$-u-, *$kn̥$-i- reflect a Lindeman variant or a resyllabification of the zero grade after the full grade remains open.

'provided with honey' < *mlit-h₃on-, next to Hitt. militt- (*meli-t-).²⁶ Of course, if the first element is thematic, the Hoffmann form will show the same apophonic grade as the base and not the zero grade, as in Av. *mąθrān-* 'he who knows formulas' from *mąθra-* (Ved. *mántra-*), and from there the older pattern was lost. There are indeed a few cases with a full grade athematic first element, for instance OCS *junъ* 'young', Lith. *jáunas* (*h₃ieu-h₃n(H)-o-*)—itself a probable secondary *e* grade derived from the weak stem *h₃iu-h₃n(H)-os, next to Lat. *juvenis*, Ved. *yúvan-*; Gr. δωτίνη 'liberality' (*deh₃-ti-h₃n(H)-eh₂), unless the latter is a Greek creation on the old stem δωτ- (δώς Hesiod, *Op.* 354) with what was already a complex suffix -ῑνος, -ῑνᾱ. Therefore we may reconstruct *h₂eḱ-ti-, *h₂ḱ-tei-* for the derivational base and *h₂ḱ-ti-h₃on-* for the Hoffmann form. If so, it would not be surprising were Greek only to preserve the older form, as it was phonetically unproblematic in this language, whereas Celtic generalised the strong stem *h₂eḱ-ti-*, or remodelled the word after the other words belonging to the same root and displaying the *e* grade, in order to preserve the phonetic shape and the motivation of the word when the initial laryngeal was lost.

4.2 Meaning

Now how about meaning? From root *h₂eḱ-*, the derivative *h₂eḱ-ti-* must mean 'point' or the like (Slavic 'sharp point, awn', Baltic 'spit, thorn'). This could be an abstract, originally meaning 'pointedness', derived through the suffix *-i-* from a thematic *h₂eḱ-to-* 'pointed, sharp' attested through the substantivised ἀκτή 'promontory'.²⁷ The Hoffmann suffix has a possessive meaning, accounting for the Celtic word, 'thorny', substantivised 'broom, furze'. The initial meaning of *h₂ḱ-ti-h₃(e)n-* must therefore be 'provided with a point, sharp', *vel sim.* It was subsequently substantivised as 'point'. This agrees with the use of the epithet ὀξύς for ἀκτίς, as noticed by Jouanna. It is a substantivised adjective applying to something 'sharp', 'point-like', and the rays of the sun are metaphorically described as points. Compare the use of Latin *radius* 'ray of light', the first meaning of which is 'pointed stick', but which also designates various pointed objects like the weaver's shuttle, the rooster's spur, the spine of certain species of fish. In Homer ἀκτῖνες is never used alone, but always in syntagmatic association with ἠέλιος 'sun' and possibly yet to be specialised into the meaning

---

[26] Eichner 1980: 147, accepted by Pinault 2000. For *malit-* representing the old zero grade, see Kloekhorst 2008, s.v. *militt-*.

[27] On this type of derivative, see Vine 2006. On the oxytone type, see Dieu 2016: 230–231. The name Ἄκτιον, better known under its Latin form *Actium*, is a diminutive of ἀκτή and must be analysed Ἄκτ-ιον, not Ἄκτι-ον.

'ray of light'. The word also has a technical meaning: it designates the teeth of a toothed gear (*Anth. Gr.* 9.418, l. 5, attributed to Antipater of Thessalonica),[28] which radiate outside the circle of the wheel like the rays of the sun. The derived adjective ἀκτινωτός means 'toothed' (gear),[29] 'radiated' (ornament),[30] 'decorated with rays' (vase).[31] The technical meaning 'tooth' is metaphoric after the rays of the sun, but it strikingly preserves the proper meaning 'pointed', for a toothed wheel is indeed provided with points, whereas the meaning 'sunray' is more remote from the etymological one.

Another *t*-derivative from the same root is ἀκτηρίς, -ίδος 'stick, staff', attested in the 5th century poet Achaeus (*apud* Pollux, *Onomasticon* 10.157). According to the same Pollux, it also means 'wooden pole': ἀκτηρίδα δὲ τὴν βακτηρίαν Ἀχαιὸς ἐν "Ἴριδι ὠνόμασεν· καλεῖται δὲ οὕτως καὶ τὸ τὸν ῥυμὸν τοῦ ἅρματος ἢ τῆς ἁμάξης ἀνέχον ξύλον, ὅταν ἄζευκτος ᾖ, ὃ στήριγγα καλεῖ Λυσίας "Achaeus called the staff ἀκτηρίδα in *Iris*; this is also the name of the piece of wood supporting the shaft of a chariot or of a waggon, when it is unyoked, which Lysias calls στήριγγα." Chantraine, after Frisk, explains the word as a compound, the second element of which would belong with ἐρείδω 'to support', but that is impossible and correctly rejected by Beekes, who does not offer any alternative proposal.

---

28   It does not apply to the spokes of an ordinary wheel, *pace* LSJ, DGE, Frisk, Chantraine, and Beekes, but to the teeth of a gear. This poem by Antipater is famous as the first mention in Greek literature of a watermill. The text is the following:

Ἴσχετε χεῖρα μυλαῖον, ἀλετρίδες, εὕδετε μακρά,
    κἢν ὄρθρον προλέγῃ γῆρυς ἀλεκτρυόνων·
Δηὼ γὰρ Νύμφαισι χερῶν ἐπετείλατο μόχθους·
    αἱ δὲ κατ' ἀκροτάτην ἁλλόμεναι τροχιὴν
ἄξονα δινεύουσιν· ὁ δ' ἀκτίνεσσιν ἑλικταῖς
    στρωφᾷ Νισυρίων κοῖλα βάρη μυλάκων.
γευόμεθ' ἀρχαίου βιότου πάλιν, εἰ δίχα μόχθου
    δαίνυσθαι Δηοῦς ἔργα διδασκόμεθα.

Hold back your hand from the mill, you grinding girls; even if the cockcrow heralds the dawn, sleep on. For Demeter has imposed the labours of your hands on the nymphs, who leaping down upon the topmost part of the wheel, rotate its axle; with encircling cogs, it turns the hollow weight of the Nisyrian millstones. If we learn to feast toil-free on the fruits of the earth, we taste again the golden age.
    transl. LEWIS

29   Hero of Alexandria (*Pneum.* 2.32), πρὸς δὲ τῷ T ἀκτινωτὸν τύμπανον ἐμπεπληγμένον τῷ M τυμπάνῳ "against T a toothed drum imbricated into the M drum."

30   Philo of Alexandria (*Legatio ad Gaium* 103), στέφανον ἀκτινωτὸν φορεῖ "he bears a radiated crown."

31   Φιάλαι χρυσαῖ ἀκτινωταί in Delos (*ID* 104, l. 34, 364/3 BCE), φιάλην ἀκτινωτήν (*ID* 1408, D, col. II, l. 17, 162/1 BCE), (ὁλκή) ἄλλη ἀκτινωτή Didyme 19, l. 36, 288/7 BCE.

It is likely that ἀκτηρίς is one of the many derivatives of *$h_2ek̂$-. Deriving the name of the stick from a word meaning 'spit, point' is not particularly difficult, since a stick is a long pointed piece of wood. The suffix is probably analogical after βακτήριον/βακτηρία 'stick, staff', and we can suspect that in Achaeus the word was a mere metrical variant of βακτηρία. However, an analogy of that kind implies a minimal formal and semantic similarity. The basis of ἀκτηρίς must be a lost substantive *ἀκ-τ-V- designating a long and pointed object, either *ἀκτι- from which stem the Balto-Slavic forms meaning 'spit, awn, thorn' (see above) or ἀκτῑν-. Since, when a word specialises into a metaphoric meaning, the older proper meaning is often not lost, but taken over by a new derivative or a new word, we could then hypothesise that when *$h_2k̂ti$-$h_3(o)n$- was specialised to mean 'sun ray', the older meaning 'pointed shaft or stick' was taken over by a new derivative, namely ἀκτηρίς, borrowing its suffix from a synonym.

So, the Zenodotean *hapax* ἰθυκτίωνα can be accounted for in a satisfying way, from the phonetic, morphological, etymological point of view. It is a regular possessive compound with a substantive second element. If we assume the meaning of ἀκτῑ́ν- is similar to that of ἀκτηρίς (in the hypothesis where ἀκτηρίς is a renewal of ἀκτίς), the ἰθυκτίωνα μελίην is the 'spear with a straight point', or 'with a straight shaft'. This meaning combines well with the first element 'straight' and the compound is appropriate as an epithet of 'spear'. In both cases it is the condition for the weapon to be usable—a twisted or bent spearhead makes it useless,[32] a shaft which is not perfectly straight does not allow the warrior to control the direction. If it refers to the spearhead, the second element *$h_2k̂$-ti-$h_3(e)n$- is an equivalent for αἰχμή or ἀκωκή. Ἀκωκή and αἰχμή are used in metrical complementary distribution, so that a potential semantic difference is impossible to grasp in the epic corpus. Αἰχμή is old and attested in linear B (a₃-ka-sa-ma PY Jn 829.3); ἀκωκή cannot be very old because of its morphological structure and may have replaced an older *$h_2k̂$-ti-$h_3(e)n$-.[33]

---

32   See Γ 348 = H 259 = P 44 ἀνεγνάμφθη δέ οἱ αἰχμή # "the spearhead bent back." For the opposition between 'to bend' and 'to straighten', see Aristotle, *Meteor*. 385b26–29 ἔστι δὲ καὶ τὰ μὲν τῶν σωμάτων καμπτὰ καὶ εὐθυντά, οἷον κάλαμος καὶ λύγος, τὰ δ' ἄκαμπτα τῶν σωμάτων, οἷον κέραμος καὶ λίθος "some bodies can be bent and straightened (εὐθυντά), as the reed and the wicker, some cannot be bent, as pottery and stone."

33   From the same root, another name of the point of a weapon is ἀκίς, specialised for 'arrowhead' (Ar., *Pax* 443; Hippocr., *Morb. pop*. 5.1.46), not attested in Homer. The formulaic ἔγχος ἀκαχμένον ὀξέϊ χαλκῷ # "spear with a point of sharp bronze" (O 482) is too remote to be directly compared, except that it implies the existence of a derivative of ἀκ- as a name of the spearhead, which may be ἀκωκή or another word. On the formation of ἀκωκή, see Vine 1998.

It may be of some significance that ἰθυκτίωνα is an epithet of μελίη, the ash spear of Achilles, which is an archaic type of spear, heavier and longer,[34] meant not for throwing but for thrusting (see above the discussion by scholiasts under Υ 273–274, pp. 198–199). If so, it would be expected that the head of that kind of spear be different from that of the lighter spear, meant to be thrown (of which the warrior had two, as for instance Paris in Γ 18, Agamemnon in Λ 43 or Idomeneus in Ν 241), and bear a different name. In particular, the spearhead had to be smaller and lighter for a throwing spear, in order to maintain balance during the flight. As a matter of fact, Mycenaean spearheads vary greatly in size and form, and a burial from the first quarter of the 14th c. BCE contained a spearhead three times as long as the ones which become usual in the 12th c. BCE. But the distinction was lost for singers of the first millenium, who use αἰχμή and ἀκωκή as synonyms for ἔγχος and δόρυ according to metrical needs, without understanding that the two words designated two different weapons, as σάκος and ἀσπίς are two different types of shield but became more or less interchangeable in epic diction for metrical reasons. This would make the interpretation 'with a straight spearhead' preferable to 'with a straight shaft'.

The fact that in Homer ἰθύς, as an adverb, is mostly used with motion verbs and refers to the straight direction of the movement, is not an objection. The phrases ἰθείῃσι δίκῃσι (Hesiod, Th. 86) 'straight sentences', ἰθεῖα (δίκη) 'straight justice' (Ψ 580, Hesiod, Op. 224), do not imply motion.[35] In compounds, ἰθυ- means 'straight' as opposed to 'curly' (ἰθύθριξ Hdt 7.70), or 'flaccid' (ἰθύφαλλος), without motion, and the same holds true for Attic compounds in εὐθυ- like εὐθύγραμμος 'rectilinear' (Aristotle), εὐθύκαυλος 'having a straight shaft', εὐθύρριζος 'having straight roots' (both in Theophrastus). But of course, the frequent use with motion verbs could favour the remodelling into ἰθυπτίωνα, since this compound is modelled on a syntagm with a motion verb.

To sum up, ἰθυκτίωνα is not an invention of Zenodotus, but a very old word which was preserved by epic diction even though it was no longer well

---

34   See Π 141–142 "(spear) huge, heavy, thick, which no one else of all the Achaians could handle, but Achilleus alone knew how to wield it, the Pelian ash spear which Cheiron had brought to his father" (R.L.). Such a spear is also described in Hector's "eleven cubits long spear" (Θ 494), and such is Aias' spear (he has only one spear, not two). The formula δολιχόσκιον ἔγχος "far-shadowing spear" must have initially referred to this kind of spear. On the association of the long spear with the σάκος, most conspicuously for Aias, and the iconographic evidence of Mycenaean time showing that the long spear had to be wielded with both hands, see Greco 2002: 564, 569. The difference between the two types of spear was no longer understood by singers for whom any spear can be thrown and who often use δολιχόσκιον ἔγχος as the object of προΐει 'he threw'.

35   See Lamberterie 1990: 272–281.

understood. This also makes it very unlikely that Zenodotus introduced it as an emendation from another copy if his text had the same reading as the vulgate, because it is hard to see what replacing ἰθυπτίωνα by ἰθυκτίωνα could improve. The proposed etymology by a compound of ἀκτίς implies that the form is old, indeed, since the compound must have been coined before the elimination of laryngeals. It was synchronically unmotivated and, for that reason, it does not conform to the synchronic pattern of Wackernagel's lengthening which applies to the initial vowel of the second member—and here the /a/ of ἀκτίς is lost. Motivated compounds could be remodelled, like *πρόσῑπον (*proti-h₃kʷ-o-, Ved. prátīka-), remodelled into πρόσωπον after the κύκλωψ type, or *εὐρῦπα remodelled into εὐρύοπα after the αἰθίοψ type,[36] but this one could not, since it was cut from its base. I do not mean, however, that it is highly archaic in every respect. As a matter of fact, it underwent a remodelling: the first element of the compound displays the regular Ionic variant ἰθυ- which is probably not the inherited form. As long as a word is motivated, it undergoes the regular evolution. The first element of the compound was unmistakably the adjective meaning 'straight', and accordingly took on the Ionic form ἰθυ-.[37] The second element was no longer analysable as a form of ἀκτῑν-, therefore it was frozen in its archaic form.

Coming back to κυλλοπόδιον, if the above analysis is correct for ἰθυκτίωνα, it confirms that the parallelism between the two compounds is only a superficial similarity. Once we have recognised that ἰθυκτίωνα contains an old form built with the Hoffmann suffix, it becomes impossible to see there, with Risch

---

36   The original compound was *h₁urHu-h₃kʷ-, with zero grade of the second element as in *proti-h₃kʷ-o-, *kʷe-kʷl(h₁)o-h₃kʷ-, but in the phonetically regular outcome *εὐρῦπα the second element was not identifiable, which prompted the remodelling. The form has an exact match in Ved. urūcí 'wide spreading', preserving the regular phonetic outcome of *-u-h₃kʷ- at the compound boundary (EWAia, s.v. urú-, Olsen 2020: 407–410). Another instance, with the same root, is παρθεν-οπῖπα 'spying on girls' (vocative), ὀπῑπεύω 'to spy', from *opi-h₃kʷ-: in the latter case it is likely that the form was indeed motivated in synchrony, with the initial ὀπ- analysed as the root, instead of the preverb, which can explain why it was not remodelled.

37   U-adjectives are not supposed to be found as first members of a compound in PIE, but they were used in that function early enough in Greek, see Hom. ἡδυεπής 'sweet-speaking', ταχύπωλος 'having swift horses', βαθύζωνος 'deep-girded', θρασυκάρδιος 'stout of heart', εὐρύοπα Ζεύς 'far-seeing Zeus', Homeric Hymns. βαρύφθογγος 'having a resounding voice'. Similarly in Vedic urucákṣas- 'far-seeing', svādurāti- 'bestowing sweet presents', dhṛṣṇvòjas- 'having a bold might' (whereas Avestan still has compounds in dərəzi- with the Caland form). Avestan vourucašānē (Y 33, 13) matches Ved. urucákṣas-, which suggests that the innovation dates back to Indo-Iranian times—and is probably even older in view of the phraseological equation with Greek εὐρύοπα Ζεύς (Schmitt 1967: 157–159).

and Chantraine (who consider only the vulgate's reading ἰθυπτίωνα), a secondary extension of the οὐρανίων type suffix. That leaves Hephaistos' nickname alone, and since it is highly unlikely that this nickname received its suffix from ἰθυκτίωνα/ἰθυπτίωνα, the only solution left is the one suggested above, that is, κυλλοπόδιον is a neuter of the θηρίον type, and the only old form is the vocative of Φ 331, which may be used with a diminutive meaning, the nominative -ίων resulting from a morphological reanalysis.

5   The Vulgate's Reading

Now we can come back to the vulgate's reading ἰθυπτίωνα. As acknowledged in the literature, it is semantically clear, but morphologically awkward. Now that we have seen that Zenodotus' reading ἰθυκτίωνα could not be an emendation, it appears that there was indeed an emendation, but it is the vulgate's form, not Zenodotus'. The old and obscure ἰθυκτίωνα was remotivated and remodelled into a clearer ἰθυπτίωνα, after the line 'ἰθὺ βέλος πέτεται' (Υ 99) quoted by scholiasts to justify the form. The remodelling is minimal, it changes ony one phoneme, and preserves the structure of the original form. As a result, the morphological structure of the remodelled form is abnormal because it is that of a preexisting different word.

The explanation 'straight-flying' for ἰθυπτίωνα, and the parallel with the line ἰθὺ βέλος πέτεται are consistent in the synchrony of the Homeric poems, because the compound was designed to match this line and can be considered to have been generated out of Υ 99. Therefore, adducing ἰθὺ βέλος πέτεται as a parallel does not confirm in any way the spelling ἰθυπτίωνα, because this phrase is not an independent parallel, it is the very source of ἰθυπτίωνα. The pair is secondary, but from a synchronic point of view it is a pair, which imposes the meaning of the phrase to the compound. Only the abnormal morphology of ἰθυπτίωνα, which cannot be derived from πέτομαι, betrays the fact that the synchronic interpretation cannot be correct from the diachronic point of view. In that case, again, Zenodotus preserved a linguistic fossil, which was eliminated and transformed into something more understandable.

If Zenodotus' reading had not been preserved, it is likely that we would not even suspect the form ἰθυπτίωνα itself is a remodelling any more than for ὀψείοντες. Unfortunately, this is certainly not an isolated case, and there must be in Homer other words resulting from a remodelling, either old or not, for which we have no element pointing to a different form.

CHAPTER 8

Hollow Lacedaemon, Its Reeds, Its Crevices ...

1   Achaean κηώεις?

Let us begin this chapter with a form for which, as far as we know, Zenodotus had the same reading as the vulgate, κηώεις 'sweet-smelling'. It is a derivative from καίω < *καϝιω 'to burn' and refers to odorous fumigations or incense burning. Next to κηώεις (Γ 382, Ζ 288 = Ω 191 = ο 99) Homer has a synonym κηώδης 'sweet-smelling', which implies a thematic *κᾱϝο-: Ζ 483 [...] ἣ δ᾽ ἄρα μιν κηώδεϊ δέξατο κόλπῳ "who took him back again to her fragrant bosom" (R.L.). A possessive -ϝεντ- adjective derived from *κᾱϝο- would be *κᾱϝόϝεντ-, unmetrical unless it is lengthened—but metrical lengthening in Ionic yields ου, not ω. Thus, κηώεις shows a non-Ionic lengthening. Could it be an Achaean form? The synonym κηώδης, with which κηώεις stands in complementary metrical distribution,[1] has a phonetically regular ω, as do all forms in -ώδης (*-o-h₃d-es-), and provides an obvious source for an analogical extension of ω. Therefore, κηώεις was probably built directly on κηώδης through suffix permutation, as a metrical variant suitable for the end of the line where κηώδης could not fit. See in particular Γ 382 κὰδ δ᾽ εἷσ᾽ ἐν θαλάμῳ εὐώδεϊ κηώεντι "and set him down again in his fragrant perfumed bedchamber" (R.L. modified), where κηώεις is associated with a compound in -ώδης. The presence of two contiguous synonymous adjectives is a frequent device in Homer (A Schol. Ε 194: ἐνίοτε παραλλήλως τάσσει τὰς ἰσοδυναμούσας λέξεις "Homer sometimes uses words having the same meaning next to each other"). In a formula *εὐώδεϊ κηώδεϊ the replacement of κηώδης by κηώεις would be almost mechanical. This line could have provided the model for Ζ 288 = Ω 191 = ο 99 αὐτὴ δ᾽/αὐτὸς δ᾽ ἐς θάλαμον κατεβήσετο κηώεντα "while she/he descended into the fragrant store-chamber" (R.L.), which has the same structure but does not keep the association with εὐώδης, the metrical slot of the latter in Γ 382 being occupied by the verb in Ζ 288. A similar process accounts for θυῶεν· εὐῶδες (Hsch., θ 980), a metrical variant of Homeric θυόεις (θυόεν νέφος Ο 153) borrowing its ω from θυώδης (δ 121, ε 264, φ 52).[2] Therefore,

---

[1] Κηώεις is always the last word of the line (Γ 382, Ζ 288 = Ω 191 = ο 99), a position where κηώδης cannot be used except in the animate nom.sg.

[2] The older form is θυήεις (Ψ 148, see p. 130), found only in Homer, Hesiod and the Homeric Hymns, whereas younger θυόεις is found in Pindar, Euripides, Callimachus and the Hellenistic poets. The poet who created θυώεις clearly had θυόεις as his point of departure, and had forgotten the older θυήεις.

© CLAIRE LE FEUVRE, 2022 | DOI:10.1163/9789004522343_010

κηώεις cannot be considered a reliable instance of Achaean lengthening since its ω is imported from κηώδης, where it is the reflex of a laryngeal, and this creation need not be very old.

2   Κοίλην Λακεδαίμονα κητώεσσαν

The interesting form here is κητώεις, an epithet of Sparta in Homer, found in the final formula κοίλην Λακεδαίμονα κητώεσσαν # (Β 581, δ 1). It is similar to κηώεις, but more difficult to explain. One cannot see here a derivative of κῆτος 'sea monster, seal', however hard scholiasts may try in this direction.[3] Ruijgh acknowledges that it cannot be derived from the attested κῆτος, because it would be morphologically irregular, but his hypothesis of a substantive *κητώς (animate s-stem) does not rely on anything.[4] In her electronic edition of Ilias diachronica, Tichy maintains the vulgate's reading κητώϝεσσαν in Β 581, while suggesting it could stand for an older *κητόϝεσσαν, which would be morphologically correct only if one assumes that it were derived from an unattested thematic *κῆτος—which would nonetheless not solve the semantic problem. Next to the κητώεσσαν of the vulgate, there was a reading κηώεσσαν (Schol. Od. δ1h1 Pontani), which is probably not a misspelling, but an emendation bringing the word back to the similar and more familiar κηώεις discussed above (p. 212).

---

3   This literal interpretation 'full of sea creatures' was advocated by Morris 1984, who understands that κοίλη refers to the curve of the Laconian gulf, so that both epithets refer to the sea. Visser 1997: 96 "Auch die Bezeichnung als κητώεις scheint auf den Raum zwischen Parnon und Taygetos hinzudeuten," with reference to Morris 1984.

4   Ruijgh 1971: 173 "as derivative of the neuter κῆτος, one would expect *κητήεις (cf. τελήεις : τέλος). The ⟨suffix⟩ of κητώεις is found in εὐρώεις (εὐρώς 'mould') and ἰδρώεις (ἰδρώς 'sweat'). Now ἰδρώς originally was an -οσ-stem, so that ἰδρώεντ- can be explained starting from *swidros-went-. The result of the compensatory lengthening is ω, not ου because -(ϝ)εντ- adjectives no longer existed in Ionic but had been inherited as they were from Mycenaean singers [...] On the other hand, one could also legitimately think of an ō-stem borrowed from a Pre-Greek language (like ἥρως, ἄλως). Thus we may assume a noun *κητώς or *κήτως 'abyss', which could be compared with κῆτος 'sea monster'" ("comme dérivé du neutre κῆτος, on attendrait *κητήεις (cf. τελήεις : τέλος). La finale de κητώεις se retrouve dans εὐρώεις (εὐρώς) et ἰδρώεις (ἰδρώς). Or, ἰδρώς était originellement un thème en -οσ-, de sorte qu'on peut expliquer ἰδρώεντ- à partir de *swidros-went-. Le résultat de l'allongement compensatoire est ω, non pas ου parce que les adjectifs en -(ϝ)εντ- n'existaient plus en ionien mais avaient été hérités tels quels des aèdes mycéniens [...] D'autre part, il est aussi légitime de penser à un thème en -ω- emprunté à un parler préhellénique (type ἥρως, ἄλως). On peut donc poser un substantif *κητώς ou *κήτως «gouffre», qui pourrait bien être rapproché de κῆτος «monstre marin»"). I studied εὐρώεις elsewhere (Le Feuvre 2007a), and argued for a metrical lengthening in this form, on the model of ἰδρώεις, which is the only one with a regular -ώεντ- < -os-went- through Achaean compensatory lengthening.

Thus we have "sweet-smelling Lacedaemon," which is not very satisfying from the semantic point of view, but not absolutely impossible.

3 What Was Zenodotus' Spelling?

Zenodotus had not κητώεσσαν, but καιτάεσσαν (*Schol. Od.* δ 1i Pontani) or καιετάεσσαν (Strabo 8.5.7).[5] The philological facts are somewhat messy, and require a detailed exposition.

The variant καιτάεσσαν is found in a D scholion to B 581, attributed, not to Zenodotus, but to "some:"

> *D Schol.* B 581: τινὲς δὲ γράφουσιν και⟨ε⟩τάεσσαν, ἵν᾽ ᾖ τὴν καλαμινθώδη. και⟨έ⟩τα γὰρ παρ᾽ αὐτοῖς ἡ καλαμίνθη ⟨ἥ⟩ ἐστὶ πολλὴ ἐν Σπάρτῃ (ZQR).
>
> some write και⟨ε⟩τάεσσαν, so that it means 'rich in reeds': they explain that και⟨έ⟩τα is the reed, of which there is plenty in Sparta.[6]

The text above is what Van Thiel prints in his edition of the D scholia. However, the reading of all three manuscripts ZQR is καιτάεσσαν, not και⟨ε⟩τάεσσαν, which is a correction after an *Odyssey* scholion to δ 1 in Dindorf's edition. For the form from which καιτάεσσαν is derived, mss Z and R have καίτα, not και⟨έ⟩τα which is a correction after Hesychius, and Q has the faulty κατά, obviously an alteration of καίτα and not of και⟨έ⟩τα. Thus, the material witnesses of the D scholia agree on the spelling καίτα, καιτάεσσαν. In his 1996 edition of the *Iliad*, Van Thiel does not mention the variant καιτάεσσαν in his apparatus.

The same reading is also found in the *Odyssey* scholia, explicitly attributed to Zenodotus:

---

5 Zenodotus' reading is mentioned in the *Odyssey* scholia. There is nothing under B 581 in the *Iliad* A scholia or bT scholia, and the *Iliad* D scholia mention the reading καιτάεσσαν but without mentioning Zenodotus. It makes sense to admit that if Zenodotus read καιτάεσσαν in δ 1, he also read καιτάεσσαν in B 581, but it is not impossible that he found two different readings in the texts he used (see West's apparatus, who leaves the question open). Apollonius' *Lexicon homericum*, of which we have only an abridged version, does not quote the line, which makes it impossible to know whether it refers to δ 1 or to B 581. Strabo does not quote the line *in extenso* either, so that we cannot know which line he is referring to—as for Apollonius, probably both. Nickau 1977 does not discuss the form. Tichy 2010: 45, prints κητώϝεσσαν.

6 Van Thiel 2014a. Van Thiel 2014b, *ad* B 581, maintains the same spelling, even after the publication of the scholia to δ by Pontani 2010.

Schol. Od. δ 1i Pontani: κητώεσσαν· Ζηνόδοτος γράφει 'καιτάεσσαν', ἀντὶ τοῦ καλαμινθώδη. δοκεῖ δὲ καὶ Καλλίμαχος ἐντετυχηκέναι τῇ γραφῇ δι' ὧν φησιν 'ἵππους καιτάεντος ἀπ' Εὐρώταο κομίσσαι'. (HMᵃ).

Zenodotus writes 'καιτάεσσαν', for 'rich in reeds'; it seems Callimachus also knew this reading, this is why he has 'ἵππους καιτάεντος ἀπ' Εὐρώταο κομίσσαι' (*fr.* 639 Pf. = SH 286.6 = Hec. *fr.* 47.6 Hollis).

Dindorf here prints καιετάεσσαν and καιετάεντος, which is not the reading of the manuscripts but a correction after Eustathius. Thus, Dindorf's καιετάεσσαν after which Van Thiel corrected the καιτάεσσαν of the D scholia to και⟨ε⟩τάεσσαν, both in his D scholia online edition and in his *Odyssey* 1991 edition, is itself a correction. In fact, both the D scholia to B 581 and the scholion to δ 1 agree on the form καιτάεσσαν without ε.[7]

Callimachus' line is quoted in Eustathius:

Eustathius, *Comm. Od.* 1: 140 (*ad* δ 1)
τινὲς δὲ ὧν καὶ Ζηνόδοτος, καιετάεσσαν γράφουσιν. ὅθεν παρὰ Καλλιμάχῳ τὸ 'ἵππους καιετάεντας ἀπ' Εὐρώταο'.

but some, including Zenodotus, write καιετάεσσαν, hence by Callimachus 'ἵππους καιετάεντας ἀπ' Εὐρώταο'.

Eustathius makes a misspelling on the ending -ας instead of -ος, maybe because he read ἵππους χαιτάεντας 'with a thick mane', and has the extra ⟨ε⟩ both for the Homeric καιετάεσσαν and Callimachus' occurrence. But the reading καιτάεντος for Callimachus' line has been confirmed by a papyrus,[8] which is why

---

[7] Most scholars ignore the real form. Kirk 1985: 213 writes "the scholiast states (for δ 1, *CLF*) that Zenodotus read καιετάεσσαν." Bechtel 1914: 195 also gives καιετάεσσαν and not the form of the manuscripts, without mentioning that this is a correction. So do Leaf and Mazon. And so does Van Thiel 2014b. S. West in Heubeck's *Commentary to the Odyssey* (vol. 1, p. 193) gives both spellings.

[8] Lloyd-Jones–Parsons 1983: 125 admit this καιτάεντος belongs to the line quoted by Eustathius and *Schol. Od.* δ 1i Pontani and accordingly print ἵππους₁ καιτάεντος ₁ἀπ' Εὐρώταο κομίσσαι (n° 286, POxy. 2377, 3rd–4th c. CE, in fact καιταεντος). See also Rengakos 1992: 27 and footnote 21, who quotes this form as an illustration of the fact that Callimachus agrees more than once with Zenodotus' *ekdosis* and correctly gives the two different spellings, although in Rengakos 1993: 29 he only quotes καιετάεσσαν.

Pontani prints καιτάεσσαν, καιτάεντος for *Schol. Od.* δ1i. It is not very likely that Callimachus' reading is independent from Zenodotus. As Callimachus is used to integrating into his own poetic composition a point of philological scholarship,[9] we may assume he is thereby taking sides with Zenodotus against a different reading.

Eustathius also mentions the reading for B 581:

> Eustathius, *Comm. Il.* 1: 454 (*ad* B 581): γράφεται δὲ καὶ ἄλλως παρὰ τοῖς παλαιοῖς 'καιετάεσσα', ἤγουν καλαμινθώδης, φασί· πολὺ δὲ ἐν Σπάρτῃ τὸ τοιοῦτον φυτόν· οἱ δὲ ὅτι εὔσειστος ἡ Λακωνική· Καιετοὶ γὰρ οἱ ἀπὸ τῶν σεισμῶν ῥωχμοί, ὅθεν Καιέτας δεσμωτήριον παρὰ Λακεδαιμονίοις, σπήλαιόν τι· τινὲς δὲ κώους τὰ τοιαῦτα κοιλώματά φασιν, ἀφ' οὗ 'φηρσὶν ὀρεσκῴοισιν' φησὶν Ὅμηρος.

> it is differently written by the Ancients 'καιετάεσσα', that is, 'rich in reed', as they say; because this plant is abundant in Sparta. But others think it means that Laconia was particularly exposed to earthquakes, because καιετοί are the name of the crevices created by earthquakes, whence the name of the prison Καιέτας in Sparta, which was a cave; yet others call such hollows κῶοι, whence the 'beasts ὀρεσκῴοισιν' (A 268) in Homer.

Eustathius confirms the antiquity of the reading καιτάεσσα or καιετάεσσα for B 581, but he neither quotes Zenodotus (because his source probably did not give that information), nor is his spelling that of the scholia. He gives the same explanation as the D scholion that the word would be derived from a local name of the reed, which Eustathius does not quote. Moreover, he gives an alternative explanation—namely that the word means 'full of crevices', also derived from a local name of the crevice, καιετοί.

The same two explanations are found in Strabo, with the same spelling as in Eustathius, and without any variant:

> Strabo 8.5.7, ll. 1–8
> Γραφόντων δὲ τῶν μὲν 'Λακεδαίμονα κητώεσσαν' τῶν δὲ 'καιετάεσσαν', ζητοῦσι, τὴν κητώεσσαν τίνα δέχεσθαι χρή, εἴτε ἀπὸ τῶν κητῶν, εἴτε μεγάλην, ὅπερ δοκεῖ πιθανώτερον εἶναι· τὴν δὲ καιετάεσσαν οἱ μὲν καλαμινθώδη δέχονται, οἱ δέ, ὅτι οἱ ἀπὸ τῶν σεισμῶν ῥωχμοὶ καιετοὶ λέγονται, καὶ ὁ καιέτας τὸ δεσμωτήριον

---

9 Rengakos 1992.

ἐντεῦθεν τὸ παρὰ Λακεδαιμονίοις, σπήλαιόν τι· ἔνιοι δὲ κώους μᾶλλον τὰ τοιαῦτα κοιλώματα λέγεσθαί φασιν, ἀφ᾽ οὗ καὶ τὸ 'φηρσὶν ὀρεσκῴοισιν'. εὔσειστος δ᾽ ἡ Λακωνική.[10]

since some write 'Λακεδαίμονα κητώεσσαν', and others 'καιετάεσσαν', scholars try to find how to understand κητώεσσαν, either from the name of the seals or as meaning 'large', which is more plausible. As for καιετάεσσαν, some understand it as meaning 'rich in reeds', others say it is because the crevices caused by earthquakes are called καιετοί, and καιέτας, the prison in Sparta, comes from there, it is a cave. Some say that such caves are better called κῶοι, whence the 'beasts ὀρεσκῴοισιν' (A 268). Laconia is particularly exposed to earthquakes.[11]

Eustathius' formulation is almost word for word the same as Strabo's.[12] Whether it is a direct quotation or both authors independently drew from a common source, Strabo and Eustathius are not two independent witnesses, but they represent one and the same testimony. The ultimate source of both had the spelling καιετάεσσαν, not καιτάεσσαν.

The last pieces of evidence come from lexicographers.

---

10 Ed. Baladié 1978 (CUF).
11 The "prison in Sparta" is mentioned by Thucydides (1.134.4, l. 2) under the form Καιάδας, not as a prison, but as a pit where men sentenced to death were thrown; the same pit is named Κεάδας by Pausanias (4.18, sections 4, 5 and 7) and Dion of Prusa (*Or*. 80.9). Strabo quotes the same word καιέτας in 5.3.6, ll. 37–39, about the gulf called Καιάτας: καὶ τὸν μεταξὺ δὲ κόλπον ἐκεῖνοι Καιάταν ὠνόμασαν· τὰ γὰρ κοῖλα πάντα καιέτας οἱ Λάκωνες προσαγορεύουσιν "and they call the guf in between Kaiatas; for Laconians call every hollow thing καιέτας," meaning that the word applies both to a vertical break (the crevice) and to a horizontal hollow (the gulf); Strabo does not comment on the different vocalism, because by Greek etymological standards it was not an objection to the identity of the two forms Καιάτας and καιέτας. The word for 'crevice' appears in Hesychius under a different form (Hsch., κ 208: καίατα· ὀρύγματα. ἢ τὰ ὑπὸ σεισμῶν καταρραγέντα χωρία "holes, or places with crevices caused by earthquakes"). Thus, there are three attested stems, καιετ-, καιατ-, καιαδ-, and we cannot know which is the original one.
12 In bold print the common wording (with slight variations in the relative order):

Strabo: οἱ δὲ ὅτι οἱ ἀπὸ τῶν σεισμῶν ῥωχμοὶ καιετοὶ λέγονται· καὶ ὁ **καιέτας τὸ δεσμωτήριον ἐντεῦθεν τὸ παρὰ Λακεδαιμονίοις, σπήλαιόν τι· ἔνιοι δὲ κώους μᾶλλον τὰ τοιαῦτα κοιλώματα λέγεσθαί φασιν, ἀφ᾽ οὗ καὶ τὸ 'φηρσὶν ὀρεσκῴοισιν'**. εὔσειστος δ᾽ ἡ Λακωνική.

Eustathius: οἱ δὲ ὅτι **εὔσειστος ἡ Λακωνική**· Καιετοὶ γὰρ οἱ ἀπὸ τῶν σεισμῶν ῥωχμοί, ὅθεν **Καιέτας δεσμωτήριον παρὰ Λακεδαιμονίοις, σπήλαιόν τι**· τινὲς δὲ κώους τὰ τοιαῦτα κοιλώματά φασιν, ἀφ᾽ οὗ **'φηρσὶν ὀρεσκῴοισιν'** φησὶν Ὅμηρος.

Apollonius Soph., *Lexicon homericum* p. 99
κητώεσσαν τὴν Λακεδαίμονα. [...] τινὲς δὲ καλαμινθώδη· καιέτας γὰρ φυτὸν ἡ καλάμινθος ὑπ' ἐνίων καλεῖται.

but some understand 'full of reeds', for καιέτας is the name given by some to the καλάμινθος plant.

Apollonius gives here the same explanation as the scholia, Strabo or Eustathius, namely that the word means 'rich in reeds' and is derived from a word καιέτας. This is obviously not a common word but rather apparently a dialectal one (ὑπ' ἐνίων καλεῖται), albeit without further indication. A similar, but not identical form is given by Hesychius καιέτα· καλαμίνθη. Βοιωτοί "καιέτα: reed, Boeotian" (Hsch., κ 219), with a (possibly unreliable) indication about the dialect but no allusion to the Homeric adjective, although the word was obviously included in order to explain καιετάεσσαν and must come from Diogenianus.[13]

On that basis, one could be tempted to imply that, if the derivational base is καιέτα(ς) 'reed', the derivative must have had the form καιετάεσσαν with the extra ⟨ε⟩ attested in the common source of Strabo and Eustathius, which would then gain a new weight. However, the explanations in Apollonius and Hesychius do not necessarily imply a reading καιετάεσσαν: it was not a problem for ancient scholars to derive a Homeric form καιτάεσσαν from a noun καιέτα or καιέτας, through a syncope—this is even a frequent device in ancient etymology. Technical operations like syncope, apocope, prothesis, metathesis or the like, underlying ancient Greek etymologies, often remain implicit in the wording of scholiasts.[14] But we should not project our modern conceptions about derivation onto the conceptions of Greek scholars. To restore και⟨ε⟩τάεσσαν because the base is καιέτα(ς) according to Apollonius and Hesychius is a

---

13   The same phytonym may be attested with a variant καιατας in the plural καιατῶν in the *Anonymous Londiniensis* (36, 57), in Diel's edition καιατῶν ἢ κάπν(ων), but Ricciardetto 2016 has an altogether different wording καὶ αἰονήματα. Therefore this doubtful occurrence should be left out.

14   Le Feuvre 2021a. Compare for instance two redactions of a same bT scholion to E 672: 672a1 Erbse has προτέρω διώκοι· προσωτέρω διώκοι (T), 672a2 Erbse has ἀπὸ τοῦ προσσωτέρω γέγονεν ἐν συγκοπῇ (b(BCE)); the second one states explicitly that there was a syncope, the first one does not. The entry κητώεσσαν in Apollonius' *Lexicon homericum*, known to us only as an epitome and not in its original state, is very elliptic: it does not mention the alternative reading καιτάεσσαν which has to be inferred from the etymological explanation through καιέτας, since the latter cannot explain the vulgate's κητώεσσαν which is Apollonius' lemma, and one should not wonder if it does not say anything about the technical means of derivation.

modern way of reasoning, not the Greek way of etymologising.[15] Besides, the D scholion to B 581 also quotes this name of the reed, and all three manuscripts write καίτα, not καιέτα (on the misspelling κατά, see above). Van Thiel here again introduces a correction and prints και⟨έ⟩τα instead of the καίτα of the manuscript, on the basis of Hesychius' testimony.

Greek scholars obviously hesitated about both spelling and meaning of the Homeric adjective. Strabo (1st c. BCE–1st c. CE) is our first secure source for the spelling καιετάεσσαν. This source is later than the two sources having καιτάεσσαν (Zenodotus, 3rd c. BCE, known of course from late manuscripts but which all agree on the spelling καιτάεσσαν; Callimachus, 3rd c. BCE, confirmed by a papyrus). The spelling καιετάεσσαν is probably a consequence of the various etymologies proposed, καιέτας 'reed' or καιετός 'crevice', and the fact that Strabo mentions this reading not alone, but together with the assumed derivation base καιετός is significant. That is one of the numerous instances of remodelling of an obscure word according to a synchronic etymology. This spelling may have been the form known to Apollonius, but as we have seen, it cannot be automatically deduced from the etymology relating it to καιέτας. Thus, Apollonius' testimony remains ambiguous, probably because it has been abbreviated and important information has been cut out. Moreover, the existence of a word καιέτα(ς) or καίτα 'reed' is not even certain. As a matter of fact, this word is quoted by lexicographers and scholiasts in order to explain the Homeric word, and it may well be a ghost form, invented in order to provide a base to the attested adjective—Hesychius' *Lexicon* has several cases of this type, sometimes even with an indication about dialect which is mere fantasy.[16]

However, the metrical criterion here leaves little doubt as to which form is older. Whatever the meaning of the adjective,[17] καιετάεσσαν, scanned as

---

15 To these can be added a form καλάμινθον [...] καιτήεσσαν in a scholion to Nicander, *Ther.* 60, for καλάμινθον [...] χαιτήεσσαν "reed [...] with beautiful mane:" according to Jacques 2002, it is a conjecture of the scholiast rather than a *varia lectio*. The form should be left out, but we can notice that it has the disyllabic stem καιτή- without the extra ⟨ε⟩.

16 For instance Hsch., κ 4314 κτιδέα· γένος περικεφαλαίας. καὶ κτὶς δέ ἐστι ζῷον ὅμοιον γαλῇ, οὗ τὸ δέρμα εὔθετον εἰς περικεφαλαίας "κτιδέα: a type of helmet. And κτίς is an animal similar to the weasel, whose hide is convenient to make helmets." Κτιδέα (κτιδέη Κ 458) results from an erroneous segmentation of ἰκτιδέα, derivative of ἴκτις 'marten', in the phrase (ἕσσατο) κρατὶ δ' ἐπ' ἰκτιδέην κυνέην "and on his head set a cap of marten's hide" (R.L.) K 335 (Leumann 1950: 53). The name of the animal is ἴκτις, and κτίς is a ghost-form invented for the sake of explaining κτιδέη. Homeric rare words often gave rise to this kind of lexical creativity, in so far as it was legitimate for Greek grammarians to assume a non-existing word as the derivational base of an existing one.

17 In Callimachus, the adjectif qualifies the river Eurotas and can only be understood 'rich in reeds', which is a recurrent epithet of this river: cf. Theognis 1.785 has Σπάρτην δ'

[– ⏑ ⏑–⏑] with a short ᾰ, cannot be the original form in Homer. On an *ā*-stem (if καιέτᾱ(ς)), one can only derive -ᾱϝεντ- (> -ήϝεντ- in Ionic), which never undergoes *correptio epica* in the attested corpus, on a thematic one, -όϝεντ-, on a *-d*-derivative (if καιέτᾰδ-), *-αδϝεντ-. This is acknowledged by Bechtel, who thinks the form must be corrected and restores *καιατόεσσαν.[18] Yet this correction of a correction (καιτάεσσαν → και⟨ε⟩τάεσσαν → *καιατόεσσαν) is not necessary, for the form given by the manuscripts καιτᾰ́εσσαν is metrically correct and morphologically not irregular, although clearly non-Ionic because of its ᾰ. Thus, the spelling of the scholia, also found in Callimachus, was most probably Zenodotus'. Modern editors who correct the scholia after Eustathius (Dindorf, followed by Van Thiel) are wrong, the correction is abusive, and Pontani is right to print καιτάεσσαν. Eustathius and Strabo reflect a source which did not have the original word form, but an altered one, resulting from an early emendation, probably by Alexandrian scholars. Unfortunately, most modern linguists and philologists take it without further examination and write that Zenodotus' reading was καιετάεσσαν, which is thus found in most editions (Allen, Mazon, Leaf, Van Thiel for Homer, Pfeiffer for Callimachus), commentaries (Kirk) and etymological or specialised dictionaries (Bechtel, Chantraine, Buck–Petersen, Beekes, *LfgrE*).

Therefore one cannot say with Beekes, *EDG*, s.v. κητώεσσα, that Zenodotus read καιετάεσσαν and Callimachus καιετάεις. Any attempt to find an etymology on this basis is pointless, since καιετάεσσαν is a correction which is not justified on philological grounds, and which, as I will try to show, is not justified on linguistic grounds either.

4 Καιτάεσσαν in Its Context

Such a form καιτᾰ́εσσαν is abnormal in Homer, where we only find derivatives in -ήϝεντ-. It is generally agreed that derivatives in -ϝεντ- were inherited from the Achaean tradition, since this suffix is no longer productive in Ionic. Thus, the only possible explanation for καιτᾰ́εσσαν is that it is an Achaean word which

---

Εὐρώτα δονακοτρόφου ἀγλαὸν ἄστυ "Sparta, splendid city of reed-growing Eurotas," Euripides has δονακόχλοον ... Εὐρώταν "the reed-green Eurotas" (*I.T.* 399–400), δονακόεντος Εὐρώτα "the reed-rich Eurotas" (*Hel.* 209), τοῦ καλλιδόνακος ... Εὐρώτα "the Eurotas with beautiful reeds" (*Hel.* 493), ἀπ' Εὐρώτα δονακοτρόφου "leaving reed-growing Eurotas" (*I.A.* 178–179). However, that tells us how Callimachus understood the word, not what the original meaning is.

18   Bechtel 1914: 195, after Döderlein.

was not ionicised into *καιτήεσσαν because the word *καιτᾶ was unknown in Ionic. But *καιτᾶ is not better known in other dialects, either from epigraphy or from lexicographers—Hesychius has καιέτα, not *καίτα. Therefore it is highly unlikely that we are dealing with a correction introduced by Zenodotus instead of the vulgate's κητώεσσα,[19] since the word καιτάεσσαν is even more obscure than κητώεσσα and has no identifiable base. Only the non Zenodotean spelling καιετάεσσα can be linked with other forms, but this is a secondary spelling, as we have seen. The conclusion to which we are bound to come is that Zenodotus found this form in his working text.

A recently published Arcadian inscription dating back to the second quarter of the 5th c. BCE has a Καίταο, genitive of a proper name Καίτας, which the editors interpret as a heronym.[20] The latter has no better etymology than Zenodotus' καιτάεσσαν. The striking similarity between both forms raises the question of a possible etymological connection. If καιτάεσσαν is derived from an ᾱ-stem, it cannot be the basis of a masculine Καίτας, for this pattern has no parallel. Καίτας could, on the other hand, be a hypocoristic of a compound of which *καίτα was the first element, but this is unlikely. The segmentation is most probably Καί-τας, that is, the stem may have nothing to do with *καιτά-ϝεσσαν. The name may be an agent noun of the Ἀμύντας type, or a hypocoristic of the Θερσίτης type.[21]

---

19 This traditional conception of Zenodotus introducing corrections into the text is still found in Zucker 1997: 426–427 for κητώεσσα. Similarly in the LfgrE, s.v. κητώεσσα, "reich an Meerungeheuern, was für Lak⟨onien⟩ abwegig erscheinen, daher wohl Zen⟨odot⟩s Les⟨un⟩g" (notice by B. Mader). A more measured view is found in the LfgrE, s.v. καιετάεσσα, "Auch wegen Unklarheit von κητώεσσα kein Kriterium für oder gegen Priorität" (notice by M. Schmidt).

20 Carbon–Clackson 2016. The inscription has ἰν Καίταυ (l. 16) = ἐν Καίταο "in ⟨the sanctuary⟩ of Kaitas."

21 Dubois 2018: xv thinks the stem και- is the present stem of καίνυμαι 'to excel, to be renowned' and translates "Victorieux" (but καίνυμαι does not mean 'to win', see on this root in Greek Le Feuvre 2008). This is unlikely to my mind, as agent nouns imply an active verb, and an agent noun can hardly be derived from a medium tantum, intransitive καίνυμαι. For that reason the parallelism invoked by Dubois with δαίτης vs δαίνυμαι is flawed because the latter is an active, transitive verb, δαίω, δαίνυμι. Besides, in Arcadian non-compound agent nouns have the old suffix -τήρ, not -τᾱς. However, on the same root, one could think of a different formation, namely the hypocoristic of a compound *ḱn̥s-i-X 'of the renowned X', with a Caland form, yielding *Καῖ-X, hence *Καῖ-τᾱς (of the same type as Θερσίτης, hypocoristic of a Θερσί-X). This would allow a comparison with the name Καίβων, only attested in Delos within one and the same family, for which no explanation is convincing: it could be the hypocoristic of a *Καῖ-βιος 'of the renowned strength', (βία) or 'of the renowned bow' (βιός, cf. # ἐγχείῃ δὲ κέκαστο "he was renowned for his spear" B 530). An objection is that no Caland form is known for this root.

4.1 General Pattern of the Catalogue of Ships

I will therefore suggest a new hypothesis, which approaches the problem from an altogether different end. One of the two lines featuring the syntagm κοίλην Λακεδαίμονα κητώεσσαν # is found in the *Catalogue of ships*, a piece which probably originates in Aeolic tradition. As an enumeration of the troops, this famous passage follows a fixed pattern like most enumerations, which is repeated for every new contingent. Namely, "those who inhabit region X, and cities Y and Z, those were lead by hero W," or "those who inhabit cities X and Y, those were lead by hero W." The basic pattern has the verb ἔχω 'to hold' with two coordinated toponyms; depending on the metrical structure of the toponyms, there is or is not an expansion, epithet, apposition or adverbial constituant, or a coordinated third toponym (in what follows, Top stands for Toponym, N for any common noun and V for verb):[22]

- epithet, structure # V + Top₁ + [Top₂–Adj.] #

    B 519: οἳ Κυπάρισσον ἔχον Πυθῶνά τε πετρήεσσαν

    B 559: οἳ δ᾽ Ἄργός τ᾽ εἶχον Τίρυνθά τε τειχιόεσσαν

    B 646: οἳ Κνωσόν τ᾽ εἶχον Γόρτυνά τε τειχιόεσσαν

    B 729: οἳ δ᾽ εἶχον Τρίκκην καὶ Ἰθώμην κλωμακόεσσαν

    B 695: οἳ δ᾽ εἶχον Φυλάκην καὶ Πύρασον ἀνθεμόεντα

    B 632: οἵ ῥ᾽ Ἰθάκην εἶχον καὶ Νήριτον εἰνοσίφυλλον

    B 584: οἵ τ᾽ ἄρ᾽ Ἀμύκλας εἶχον Ἕλος τ᾽ ἔφαλον πτολίεθρον

    B 683: οἵ τ᾽ εἶχον Φθίην ἠδ᾽ Ἑλλάδα καλλιγύναικα

- the second city appears in the genitive and is not the head of the syntagm which constitutes the second element, structure # V + Top₁ + [Top₂gén.–N] #:

    B 735: οἵ τ᾽ ἔχον Ἀστέριον Τιτάνοιό τε λευκὰ κάρηνα

- apposition, structure # V + Top₁ + Top₂ + N_app. #:

    B 562: οἵ τ᾽ ἔχον Αἴγιναν Μάσητά τε κοῦροι Ἀχαιῶν [expansion of the subject]

- prepositional phrase, structure # V + Top₁ + [Prep. Top₂] #:

    B 711–712: οἳ δὲ Φερὰς ἐνέμοντο παραὶ Βοιβηΐδα λίμνην Βοίβην καὶ Γλαφύρας καὶ ἐϋκτιμένην Ἰαωλκόν

- third toponym, structure # V + Top₁ + Top₂ + Top₃ #:

    B 500: οἵ τ᾽ Ἐλεῶν᾽ εἶχον ἠδ᾽ Ὕλην καὶ Πετεῶνα

    B 676: οἳ δ᾽ ἄρα Νίσυρόν τ᾽ εἶχον Κράπαθόν τε Κάσον τε

With a synonymous verb, νέμω or ναίω, we find:

- no expansion, structure # V + Top₁ + Top₂ #:

    B 716: οἳ δ᾽ ἄρα Μηθώνην καὶ Θαυμακίην ἐνέμοντο

---

22 See the different patterns in Kirk 1985: 170, who does not quote all the instances. The examples given here are taken from Allen's edition.

- epithet, structure # V + Top₁ + [Top₂–Adj.] #:
    B 496: οἵ θ᾽ Ὑρίην ἐνέμοντο καὶ Αὐλίδα πετρήεσσαν
    B 591: οἳ δὲ Πύλον τ᾽ ἐνέμοντο καὶ Ἀρήνην ἐρατεινήν
    B 511: οἳ δ᾽ Ἀσπληδόνα ναῖον ἰδ᾽ Ὀρχομενὸν Μινύειον
    B 615: οἳ δ᾽ ἄρα Βουπράσιόν τε καὶ Ἤλιδα δῖαν ἔναιον
- third toponym, structure # V + Top₁ + Top₂ + Top₃ #:
    B 531: οἳ Κῦνόν τ᾽ ἐνέμοντ᾽ Ὀπόεντά τε Καλλίαρόν τε
    B 639: οἳ Πλευρῶν᾽ ἐνέμοντο καὶ Ὤλενον ἠδὲ Πυλήνην
    B 682: οἵ τ᾽ Ἄλον οἵ τ᾽ Ἀλόπην οἵ τε Τρηχῖνα νέμοντο

Of course, this pattern "those who held X and Y" allows for some variation:
- the name of the second town is delayed until the next line by an apposition which occupies the second hemistich of the first line, structure # V + Top₁ + N_app. # + Top₂ + Top₃ + Top₄ #:
    B 536–537 [expansion of the subject]:
    οἳ δ᾽ Εὔβοιαν ἔχον μένεα πνείοντες Ἄβαντες
    Χαλκίδα τ᾽ Εἰρέτριάν τε πολυστάφυλόν θ᾽ Ἱστίαιαν
    B 505–506 [expansion of the object]:
    οἵ θ᾽ Ὑποθήβας εἶχον ἐϋκτίμενον πτολίεθρον
    Ὀγχηστόν θ᾽ ἱερὸν Ποσιδήϊον ἀγλαὸν ἄλσος
- the verb is delayed until the next line, structure # Top₁ + [Top₂–Adj.] # + Top₃ + V #:
    B 573–574: οἵ θ᾽ Ὑπερησίην τε καὶ αἰπεινὴν Γονόεσσαν
    Πελλήνην τ᾽ εἶχον ἠδ᾽ Αἴγιον ἀμφινέμοντο
- the second element is a full clause with a different verb (the first hemistich is metrically irregular when ἔχον stands before a vowel), structure # V₁ + Top₁ + V₂ + Top₂ #:
    B 738: οἳ δ᾽ Ἄργισσαν ἔχον καὶ Γυρτώνην ἐνέμοντο
    B 504: οἵ τε Πλάταιαν ἔχον ἠδ᾽ οἳ Γλισᾶντ᾽ ἐνέμοντο
    B 585: οἵ τε Λάαν εἶχον ἠδ᾽ Οἴτυλον ἀμφενέμοντο
    B 634: οἵ τε Ζάκυνθον ἔχον ἠδ᾽ οἳ Σάμον ἀμφινέμοντο
    B 539: οἵ τε Κάρυστον ἔχον ἠδ᾽ οἳ Στύρα ναιετάασκον
- the second element is an elliptic clause, structure # V₁ + Top₁ + (V₂) + Top₂ #:
    B 734: οἳ δ᾽ ἔχον Ὀρμένιον, οἵ τε κρήνην Ὑπέρειαν
- there is no second element at the end of the enumeration in the sub-sequence, structure # V + Top + N_app. # or # V + Top + [Prep. N] #:
    B 523: οἵ τε Λίλαιαν ἔχον πηγῇς ἔπι Κηφισοῖο
    B 730: οἵ τ᾽ ἔχον Οἰχαλίην πόλιν Εὐρύτου Οἰχαλιῆος

The pattern appears most of the time at the beginning of the sub-sequence, but can also be found within the enumeration of the sub-sequence. For instance, the two following lines are the final two of the enumeration of the Arcadian contingent:

B 607–608: καὶ Τεγέην εἶχον καὶ Μαντινέην ἐρατεινὴν
Στύμφηλόν τ' εἶχον καὶ Παρρασίην ἐνέμοντο

This long list of examples clearly shows the basic pattern "those who held X and Y" and its modifications.[23]

4.2 B 581

Having this background in mind, we can now come back to B 581:

B 581–582
οἳ δ' εἶχον κοίλην Λακεδαίμονα κητώεσσαν (vulgate) / καιτάεσσαν (Zenodotus)
Φᾶρίν τε Σπάρτην τε πολυτρήρωνά τε Μέσσην

Zenodotus' reading can easily be integrated into the general pattern: it belongs to the type # V_1 + Top_1 + Top_2 # "those who held X and Y" which represents the majority of cases, οἳ δ' εἶχον κοίλην Λακεδαίμονα καὶ *Τάϝεσσαν "those who held hollow Lacedaemon and *Tāwesa*." Lacedaemon may be the name of the region rather than the name of the city,[24] and is followed by a list of various towns in Laconia, including Sparta. The pattern displaying first a coordination through καί followed by other elements coordinated through τε is also found in B 496–497: for instance, οἵ θ' Ὑρίην ἐνέμοντο καὶ Αὐλίδα πετρήεσσαν || Σχοῖνόν τε Σκῶλόν τε πολύκνημόν τ' Ἐτεωνόν; see also B 695–696. Καιτάεσσα is not one word, but two words: the first syllable is the coordination, and the last three are an unknown Laconian toponym.[25] We probably have here the result of an erroneous segmentation, which is not unfrequent at all, and was all the

---

23   Interestingly enough, the lines devoted to the Athenians (B 546 *sqq*) do not follow this pattern. This is another fact setting those lines apart from the rest: they were considered a later interpolation already in Antiquity.

24   So Hope Simpson 1970: 74, who argues that "κοίλη and κητώεσσα are hardly appropriate epithets for a town." For the possibility of coordinating the name of the region with that of the cities of that region, see the case of Euboea, B 536–537, which would thus no longer be isolated—for names like Pylos or Argos, it is likely that they refer to the city rather than the region dominated by this city. Visser (1997: 479–492) does not comment on the epithet.

25   This is not an isolated case: in the list of Laconian cities, Augeiai is unknown (Kirk 1985: 213), and its identification with Aigiai, defended by Strabo 8.364, not certain (Hope Simpson 1970: 77) and many other toponyms of the *Catalogue* are unknown. For a recent survey of the confrontation of archaeological facts with the Laconian place names in the *Catalogue*, see Chapin and Hitchcock 2007: 262, who conclude that "the evidence supporting the identification of the sites named in the Catalogue of Ships remains woefully weak."

more expected if the toponym was indeed unknown to singers. The first morpheme involved is the conjunction καί, which is a proclitic and forms a single phonological word with what follows. The incorporation of clitic functional morphemes, prepositions, preverbs or conjunctions, into neo-compounds resulting from a resegmentation in the oral chain, is well attested in epic diction.[26] Here we are not dealing with a neo-compound, since καιτάεσσαν cannot be analysed as a compound and never was, but the process of univerbation of a clitic element with its host is the same. Such a resegmentation implies, of course, that the toponym was preserved as a toponym down to the generalisation of καί as the regular coordinative conjunction.[27]

Since unknown words are often recategorised as epithets, because formulaic diction allows for epithets of obscure meaning in many formulae, as long as the head substantive is clear (which is the case with Λακεδαίμονα here),[28] this new [kaitāwessan] was transformed into an epithet, through a syntactic reanalysis. That aligned B 581 with the variant mentioned above, in which the name of the second city is delayed to the following line and the end of the first line is occupied by an expansion of the toponym, V + [Top.₁–Adj.] # + Top₂ (see B 505–506 οἵ θ᾽ Ὑποθήβας εἶχον ἐϋκτίμενον πτολίεθρον ‖ Ὀγχηστόν θ᾽ ἱερὸν Ποσιδήϊον ἀγλαὸν ἄλσος with V + [Top₁–N_app.] # [Top₂–N_app.]), although this structure is much less frequent than the dominant one # V₁ + Top₁ + Top₂ #. As the most frequent expansion is an epithet, and as, among epithets, adjectives in -ϝεντ- are especially numerous (see the first examples above, and the generally remarkable concentration of city-epithets in -ϝεντ- in the *Catalogue*), the toponym could have been remodelled into a -ϝεντ- adjective, whatever its exact original shape. Thus, the syntactic reanalysis goes along with a morphological reanalysis, isolating a new stem *kaitā- and the familiar feminine suffix -ϝεσσα. It stands isolated in the series because normally -ϝεντ- adjectives derived from ā-stems are in -ήϝεντ-, not in -ᾱϝεντ-, but this one had no ā-stem identifiable as its base, therefore it could preserve the [ā]. It may be an Achaean form which, as ἄας, was integrated in post-Mycenaean times, after Ionic had known the raising of /ā/ > /æ/ > η.

If this hypothesis is correct, καιτάϝεσσαν would be an old form preserved under disguise in Zenodotus' reading, as West thinks is the case for ἰογάστριος (pp. 67–71), a fossil trapped in a new form produced through the resegmentation of the line. Notice that metrically the line could be old, for # οἵ

---

26 Leumann 1950: 71–92. Le Feuvre 2015: 28–32, 663.
27 Mycenaean only has -*qe*.
28 Le Feuvre 2015: 660 *sqq*.

δ' εἶχον κοίλην is compatible with an older scansion *οἳ δ' ἔεχον κοϝίλην, anterior to contraction or diphthongisation.

I do not imply thereby that the toponym was exactly [Tāwes(s)a]. It may have been a [Tāwes(s)os] which, as soon as it was reanalysed as an epithet of the feminine Λακεδαίμονα, received the feminine ending. In other words, the form transmitted by Zenodotus may be the result of a morphological remodelling due to the reanalysis of *καὶ T. as a single word belonging to the category "adjective" (*καὶ Τᾰϝεσσον → *καιτᾰ́ϝεσσον through resegmentation and univerbation → καιτᾰ́ϝεσσαν because it must agree in gender with Λακεδαίμονα). One may in particular think about pre-Hellenic toponyms in -ησσος, mostly found in Asia Minor (Μαρπησσός, Ἁλικαρνασσός, Λυρνησσός) but also in Greece (Μυκαλησσός in Boeotia, the Thessalian river Τιταρησσός mentioned in B 751, Παρνασσός) or elsewhere (Τυλησσός, mountain in Italy). A sequence [kai Tāwēsson] could be feminised into (Λακεδαίμονα) *καιτᾱ(ϝ)ησσαν, which would anyway be spelled ΚΑΙΤΑΕΣΣΑΝ in the archaic Ionic alphabet. This spelling ΚΑΙΤΑΕΣΣΑΝ, being in agreement with the regular feminine of -ϝεντ-adjectives, had no reason to be spelled differently once the Ionic alphabet was improved by the new distinction between ⟨H⟩ for open /ẹ̄/ and ⟨E⟩ for closed /ẹ̄/ (and afterwards ⟨ει⟩), because the original form of the toponym was no longer recoverable.[29]

4.3 Mycenaean ta-we-si-jo

It is always dangerous to explain an obscure word through a proper name, toponym, hydronym or else, for proper names need not be motivated, therefore this can seem an easy solution. However, the objection is not so strong here since the *Catalogue* is a list of toponyms.

Besides, one element could be in favour of an old toponym in -ησσος, -εσσος, or -εσσα. Linear B has an anthroponym ta-we-si-jo, attested in Pylos (PY An 261, PY An 616) and in Cnossos (KN Dv 1332.B, KN Dv 7908).[30] Ruijgh proposed

---

29 In Mycenaean the feminine of *-u̯ent- adjectives, originally *-u̯n̥t-i̯a > *-u̯assa, has been remodelled after the masculine and is attested as -we-sa = -ϝεσσα, as in Ionic: to-qi-de-we-sa, pi-ti-ro₂-we-sa, mi-to-we-sa.

30 In PY An 616 (side 2 of the tablet) the text reads:
    ta-we-si-jo-jo . ke-ro-si-ja VIR 20[
    a-pi-qo-o . ke-ro-si-ja VIR 17 [(correctly written a-pi-qo-ta-o . ke-ro-si-ja VIR 17 in PY An 261)
    a-pi-o-to . ke-ro-si-ja VIR 18
    o-to-wo-o . ke-ro-si-ja VIR 13
    The first word is in all cases a man's name in the genitive. PY An 261 (of which PY An 616 seems to be a draft) has the same structure: the name is mutilated in all three occurrences on side 1, but complete on side 2. The structure of the beginning of PY An 261 is PN in the

to read *Θᾱϝήσιος 'admirable', from θηητός,[31] similar to -γνητός/γνήσιος type. However, this is unlikely: *Θᾱϝήσιος would be derived from θᾱϝητός (cf. Pindar θᾱητός), of the Ionic type θηέομαι, but the θηέομαι type is recent and evolved from the original type in -άομαι. It is found in several dialects, including Cyprian (e-ta-we-sa-to = ἐθᾱϝέσατο *ICS*² 379), but this remodelling occurred in the present stem after the loss of the intervocalic yod, therefore it is a post-Mycenaean development. The base is *$t^hāu̯ā$, the denominative is *$t^hāu̯ā$-i̯e/o-, the verbal adjective is *$t^hāu̯ā$-to-, and that could only be reflected by *ta-wa-to, *ta-wa-si-jo in Mycenaean, not by ta-we-si-jo. Other scholars keep *Ταϝέσιος, without any attempt at an interpretation.[32]

Now this ta-we-si-jo could be an ethnonym 'from *Τᾱϝἔσσός/*Τᾱϝἔσσα'. The city of *Τᾱϝἔσσός/*Τᾱϝἔσσα in B 581 is part of the enumeration of Laconian places, therefore it was located in Laconia, and a man coming from there was a foreigner both in Pylos, Messenia, and in Cnossos, Crete, and would rightly be referred to through the ethnonym. Derivation of ethnics in -ιος from toponyms in -ησσος is old.[33] Moreover, ethnonyms are often used as nicknames, and eventually as names, in second millenium Greek as in first millenium Greek. In Pylos we have for instance a ko-ri-si-ja (= Κορινθία, Corinthian), in Cnossos an a₃-ku-pi-ti-jo (= Αἰγύπτιος, Egyptian), in Thebes a ra-ke-da-mi-ni-jo (= *Λακεδαίμνιος, "Lacedemonian)," in Mycenae a za-ku-si-jo (= Ζακύνθιος, "Zacynthian)."[34]

It is true that analysing ta-we-si-jo as the ethnic from an unknown toponym removes motivation, since we cannot find an equivalent in the lexicon of first millenium Greek. Therefore it can also seem an easy solution. But taken

---

genitive + ke-ro-si-ja + PN in the nominative + VIR 1 (individual names) "from the council of Elders of (that is, headed by) X, one man, Y;" the structure at the end of the text is PN in the genitive + ke-ro-si-ja + VIR plural (total of men for each γερουσία) "from the council of Elders of X, N men."

31 Ruijgh 1967: 153.
32 Bernabé–Luján 2006: 338.
33 Herodian, *De prosodia catholica* (Lentz III/1, 121) has a whole list of ethnics derived from toponyms in -ησσος, all in -ήσσιος, which would be coherent with ta-we-si-jo: Ἁλικαρνάσσιος (attested in several 5th c. Attic inscriptions, next to Ἁλικαρνασσεύς which is the only form found in Ionic inscriptions), Παρνάσσιος, Ἥσσιος, Ἀγήσσιος, Ἀσσήσιος, Καρδήσσιος, Λυρνήσσιος, Μαρπήσσιος, Μερμήσσιος, Μυκαλήσσιος, Σαρδήσσιος, Σαλμυδήσσιος, Ταρτήσσιος, Τελμήσσιος (but Herodotus has Τελμησσεύς), Τεγήσσιος, Τυλήσσιος. The list includes ethnics from toponyms in -ϝεσσα, also in -ιος: Ἐλαιούσσιος, Πιτυούσσιος, Ποιηέσσιος. Several are confirmed by inscriptions: Ἥσσιοι *IG* I³ 100, Ἕσσιοι *IG* I³ 259, Ποιήσσιοι *IG* II² 43, Ποιασσίων *IG* XII, 5, 568, [Τ]ελεμέσσιο[ι] *IG* I³ 71, Μυέσσιοι *IG* I³ 266. See also the name Παρνάσσιος, derived from the ethnic via the epithet of Apollo Parnassios, and the adjective ὑμήττιος 'from Hymettus'.
34 García Ramón 2006:41. See other instances in Bartoněk 2003: 418 and 427–428.

together, those two "easy solutions" draw a coherent picture, because a unique hypothesis provides a plausible explanation for two otherwise isolated forms found in different types of texts. This amounts to a confirmation a posteriori for the philological criterion. That is, the form would indeed be attested in an independent source, but that cannot be recognised until a new analysis has been proposed for the Zenodotean reading.

Thus, the form transmitted by Zenodotus can receive a rather simple explanation, which agrees with the prevailing syntactic pattern found in the *Catalogue*, at a morphological cost which is not very high (feminisation of the ending if the original toponym was masculine, which is not even certain) and this explanation is compatible with Mycenaean facts. It remains a hypothesis, which cannot be proven, but if this hypothesis is correct, it is a further argument against the correction καιετάεσσα found in Strabo and Eustathius and confirms that the form καιτάεσσα transmitted by the Homeric scholia and by Callimachus is the authentic Zenodotean reading. Secondly, it confirms that this reading is not a Zenodotean correction, but the one he found in his text. And thirdly, it implies that this reading is much older than the vulgate's κητώεσσαν, thus answering the question left open in the *LfgrE*.[35] Of course Zenodotus never understood this word as a sequence conjunction + toponym. He may have understood καιτάεσσαν as 'rich in reeds', as did Callimachus, or not. At any rate, the original meaning was certainly lost, even though his reading preserves by and large the original word form.

5   Reanalysis and Secondary Use

Under this altered form, the line was reused in the *Odyssey*, in a different context: δ 1 Οἱ δ' ἷξον κοίλην Λακεδαίμονα καιτάεσσαν/κητώεσσαν, where the end of the line is identical, but the verb was changed, and "those who held Lacedaemon" became "and they reached Lacedaemon." With a verb of motion like ἷξον, Λακεδαίμονα could be either the city or the region, but what is certain is that the travellers reach one city, not two, which means a coordinative structure "Sparta and X" is highly unlikely here. Καιτάεσσαν can only be understood here as an epithet of Λακεδαίμονα. Therefore, this line was created after the reanalysis took place in B 581—and probably, then, after the integration of the *Catalogue* into the *Iliad*. The reanalysis is actualised in δ 1, and the syntax of δ 1 backs the

---

35   *LfgrE*, s.v. καιετάεσσα, "Auch wegen Unklarheit von κητώεσσα kein Kriterium für oder gegen Priorität."

analysis of καιτάεσσαν as an epithet of Λακεδαίμονα also in B 581. As always, when there is a reanalysis or reinterpretation within the Homeric corpus, the younger occurrences, which display the secondary meaning (and, here, the secondary syntax), overcome the older occurrence, which is the context of reanalysis and admits of both interpretations.[36] Thus the only possible analysis for δ 1 was applied to B 581, according to the rule that one and the same syntagm must have one and the same meaning in all its occurrences. This is generally true, but not always, and particularly not when a reanalysis has taken place.

6 Remotivating the New Form

Afterwards, scholars struggled to find a plausible meaning to this καιτάεσσαν. The explanations referring it to a dialectal name of the reed (Apollonius, Hesychius) or to a dialectal name of the crevice (Strabo) are attempts to remotivate an obscure word. They are synchronic etymologies, which should not be taken for more than what they are.[37]

The explanation linking it with a Laconian word for 'crevice' deserves further comment. The interesting fact is the use of the word ῥωχμός (οἱ ἀπὸ τῶν σεισμῶν ῥωχμοὶ καιετοὶ λέγονται, Strabo 8.5.7). Before Strabo, ῥωχμός is not attested in prose, but only in poetry (Homer, Apollonius Rhodius, Bion). In the Roman period, it appears more regularly in medical prose, in a metaphoric use. Thus, the word is clearly marked. The same phrase with the same word is repeated in Eustathius (see above p. 217), which means that it belonged to the common source of Strabo and Eustathius, a commentary on Homer. Now there is only one occurrence of ῥωχμός in Homer, in Ψ 419–420, στεῖνος ὁδοῦ κοίλης ἴδεν Ἀντίλοχος μενεχάρμης. ‖ ῥωχμὸς ἔην γαίης [...] "battle-stubborn Antilochos saw where the hollow way narrowed. There was a break in the ground [...]" (R.L.). In fact, the translation "hollow way" is probably erroneous. The way (the path for the horses' race) is not hollow *per se*, but it becomes narrow (στεῖνος) because it becomes hollow (κοίλης) due to the crevice (ῥωχμός). A better translation would be "A. saw a narrowing of the path, which was hollow, there being a crevice in the ground [...]." In these lines, the syntagmatic association between κοίλη 'hollow' and ῥωχμός is natural, the one being the consequence of the other. In our two lines B 581 and δ 1, the same adjective κοίλην is associated with καιτάεσσαν. We may suggest that the interpretation of the obscure καιτάεσσαν associated

---

36 Le Feuvre 2015, *passim*, and in particular 703–706.
37 And one should definitely not with Beekes, *EDG*, follow Strabo and link the word with καιέτας, καιάδας 'crevice'.

with κοίλην as meaning 'full of crevices' was influenced by the association of the same κοίλη with ῥωχμός 'crevice' in Ψ 419–420, although the syntactic structure is different. If so, this is a typically scholiastic interpretation relying on what I called the "principle of contextual permutation." It operates as follows: if A is associated with B in a given line, in which the meaning of B is unclear, but associated with C in another line, in which the meaning of C is clear, scholiasts often draw the erroneous conclusion that B and C are synonymous and explain the association A–B after the meaning of C.[38] Here A (κοίλη) is associated with unclear B (καιτάεσσαν) in B 581, but with semantically clear C (ῥωχμός) in Ψ 419–420. In that case, even though this explanation is found in Strabo, a serious writer, it is nevertheless a fantastic explanation, as reliable as most scholiasts' elucubrations—because Strabo is quoting here a commentary on Homer.

A more radical option, however, was chosen by the singer or rhapsode who substituted the κητώεσσαν transmitted by the vulgate to this obscure form. He was successful, obviously, although this substitution does not make more sense. The two readings κητώεσσαν and καιτάεσσαν are clearly not independent readings—one is derived from the other. Since the latter is isolated, while the former is irregular but motivated, the derived one must be the motivated one. However, it is difficult to understand how it could arise.

A first hypothesis would be that the modification reflects a phonetic change, namely the monophthongisation of /ay/ into an open mid-vowel /ɛ̄/, attested in Boeotian as early as the 4th c. BCE.[39] But in other dialects there is no trace of monophthongisation before the 2nd c., and this process goes together with the raising of η into closed /ē/ first (in Boeotian ⟨ει⟩) and /i/ next.[40] Therefore, when /ay/ was monophthongised into /ɛ̄/, κῆτος was pronounced [kētos] with closed /ē/, or even [kitos]. The reason for the modification must be sought in the formulaic system rather than in the phonetic evolution.

There is an indication of what happened in Apollonius' *Lexicon*:

> Apollonius Soph., *Lexicon homericum*, p. 99
> κητώεσσαν τὴν Λακεδαίμονα. οὕτως ἐξ ἐπιθέτου λέγεται· 'Λακεδαίμονα κητώ-
> εσσαν'. τὸ μὲν ὑγιὲς μέγα κύτος ἔχουσαν, ὡς καὶ ἐπὶ τῆς νηός· τινὲς δὲ ὅτι εἰς ἣν
> κήτη ἐκβράσσεται. τινὲς δὲ καλαμινθώδη· καιέτας γὰρ φυτὸν ἡ καλάμινθος ὑπ'
> ἐνίων καλεῖται.

---

38   See Le Feuvre 2015: 37 *sqq*.
39   Lejeune 1972: 230–231. However, Teodorsson 1974: 286–299, assumes the changes occurred much earlier, already in the 4th c. BCE. Horrocks 2010: 164–165, sticks to the traditional view that these changes are not anterior to the 3rd or 2nd c.
40   Lejeune 1972: 237.

Thus he says with an epithet 'Λακεδαίμονα κητώεσσαν'. The proper meaning is 'which has a large hollow', as is also said of the ship. Others, because it is where seals (κήτη) come ashore. Others think that it means 'abounding in reeds', because the reed is called by some καιέτας.

The notice gives as first and proper meaning 'hollow', and adds an important element, ὡς καὶ ἐπὶ τῆς νηός "as is also said of the ship." Apollonius' (abridged) formulation can be understood in two ways. First, it may imply that the epithet of Lacedaemon κητώεσσα 'hollow' was also found as an epithet of the ship. Or second, it may mean simply that there was an epithet of the ship built on the same stem and meaning 'with a large hollow'. Other interpretations, given next, are not correct according to Apollonius.

Ships are never qualified with the epithet κητώεσσα in the Homeric corpus as we know it, but in two identical lines a ship is qualified with the epithet μεγακήτης 'with a large hollow'. Θ 222 = Λ 5: στῆ δ᾽ ἐπ᾽ Ὀδυσσῆος μεγακήτεϊ νηΐ μελαίνῃ "and stood beside the black huge-hollowed ship of Odysseus" (R.L.). This corresponds to Apollonius' formulation μέγα κύτος ἔχουσαν, ὡς καὶ ἐπὶ τῆς νηός, the compound μεγακήτης being hinted at by μέγα κύτος ἔχουσαν.[41] Originally, μεγακήτης is an epithet of the sea, 'which has large sea creatures' (μεγακήτεα πόντον γ 158), reinterpreted as meaning 'which has large depths', and transferred abusively to the ship.[42] Besides, it may be more than a coincidence if the ship so qualified is Ulysses', the seafarer. The meaning 'hollow' for μεγακήτης probably comes from the following series:

- Θ 222 = Λ 5: στῆ δ᾽ ἐπ᾽ Ὀδυσσῆος μεγακήτεϊ νηΐ μελαίνῃ
- γ 365: ἔνθα κε λεξαίμην κοίλῃ παρὰ νηΐ μελαίνῃ
- κ 272: ἔσθων καὶ πίνων κοίλῃ παρὰ νηΐ μελαίνῃ
- δ 761: ὁππότε κεῖνος ἔβη κοίλην ἐπὶ νῆα μέλαιναν

The principle of contextual permutation, in this series where the 'black ship' was now 'hollow' (κοίλη), now μεγακήτης, led to the interpretation of the latter as a synonym of the former, hence 'huge-hollowed'.

---

41 See also Eustathius, Comm. Il. 3: 261 (ad Λ 600): "Ὅρα δὲ καὶ ὧδε τὸ 'μεγακήτεϊ νηΐ' συντελοῦν εἰς τὸ Λακεδαίμονα κητώεσσαν, ὡς οἶδεν ὁ νοῶν τεχνικῶς. καὶ ἄλλως δὲ οἰκεῖον μεγακήτεα ὀνομάσαι τὸν θαλάσσιον τοῦτον ἵππον κατὰ τὸ 'αἵ θ᾽ ἁλὸς ἵπποι'." "Notice that thus, the μεγακήτεϊ νηΐ 'huge-hollowed ship' belongs with Λακεδαίμονα κητώεσσαν, as the wise knows, skillfully. And otherwise, it is proper to call μεγακήτεα this 'horse of the sea', according to the 'and the horses of the sea' [the ships, CLF]."

42 DELG, s.v. κῆτος. We do not have the line in which the reinterpretation took place. That the reinterpretation is old is also confirmed by Hesiod who mentions a goddess Κητώ, daugther of Pontos (Th. 238), whose name probably means 'depth' and not 'seal' or the like.

Besides, κητώεις is attested as an epithet of the sea (# βένθεα κητώεντα), in Marcellus' poem *De piscibus* (l. 5). This late attestation (2nd c. CE) shows that in late hexametric poetry, there was a metrical complementary distribution between μεγακήτης and κητώεις as epithets of the sea. Since there is an equivalence between possessive compounds and possessive -ϝεντ- adjectives, seen for instance in the pairs νιφόεις vs ἀγάννιφος, δινήεις vs βαθυδίνης, τειχήεις (τειχιόεις) vs εὐτειχής, δενδρήεις vs πολυδένδρεος, στονόεις vs πολύστονος,[43] the creation of a new pair κητώεις (modelled after κηώεις) vs μεγακήτης was not difficult. We don't know whether this metrical distribution is old or not. The adjective in Marcellus stands before the trochaic caesura (T). One of the reasons for the frequency of the trochaic caesura is that the first hemistich (T1) then ends with the same metrical structure as the end of the line, so that it allows final formulae to be transposed before T, making them more flexible. Thus, the position of κητώεντα before T in Marcellus agrees with the position of κητώεσσα at the end of the line in Homer. The meaning in Marcellus can be either 'deep, hollow', or 'full of sea creatures', 'full of seals'. Be that as it may, if κητώεις was used as a metrical variant of μεγακήτης as an epithet of the sea, so could it be as an epithet of the ship. This implies that a syntagm *νηῦς κητώεσσα was possible, meaning 'hollow ship', next to μεγακήτεϊ νηΐ μελαίνῃ 'black huge-hollowed ship' (Θ 222). This syntagm is not attested in Homer but may have been used by other poets before Marcellus.

Once this was acquired, it was possible to turn the paradigmatic association between κοῖλος and μεγακήτης, understood as near-synonyms 'hollow' and 'huge-hollowed', into a syntagmatic one, in a line displaying the sequence κοίλην Λακεδαίμονα καιτάεσσαν # where the last word was obscure. It was straightforward as soon as there was an adjective κητώεις 'hollow' next to μεγακήτης. In that case the transformation of κοίλην ... καιτάεσσαν into κοίλην ... κητώεσσαν was an easy way out because the first adjective suggested its synonym. This was made plausible by the many instances of hendiadys, where two synonymous adjectives are used together, as in Σ 479–480 περὶ δ' ἄντυγα βάλλε φαεινὴν || τρίπλακα μαρμαρέην "and ⟨he⟩ threw around it a shining triple rim that glittered" (R.L.). It was less straightforward if the only adjective was μεγακήτης, but still, it is conceivable that the association with κοίλην suggested an epithet meaning 'hollow', hence the transformation of μεγα-κήτης into κητώεσσαν with the metrical structure of the preexisting form. In that case, later poets like Marcellus borrowed it from the remodelled Homeric line.

---

43   On the equivalence between -ϝεντ- adjective and possessive compounds in πολυ-, see Risch 1974: 153. But in fact this equivalence extends to other possessive compounds, in εὐ-, μεγα- /ἀγα- for instance.

This was not enough. As a matter of fact, a third interpretation is found in late texts. The Pseudo-Herodian understands 'large' (*Partitiones*, p. 210: πλὴν τοῦ κητώεις, ὁ μέγας "[...] except κητώεις 'large'"). This meaning is also found in Quintus' *Posthomerica* 12.314–315 (Πρῶτος μὲν κατέβαινεν ἐς ἵππον κητώεντα || υἱὸς Ἀχιλλῆος "before others Achilles' son mounted his tall horse"), in an epigram of the Anthology (*Anthologiae graecae Appendix* 264, l. 51) quoted by Eusebius' *Constantini imperatoris oratio ad coetum sanctorum* 20.10, 15 (Κόσμου κητώεντος ὁρῶν εὔπηκτα θέμεθλα "seeing the firm foundations of the large universe," freely translated from Virgil's *Aeneid* 4.50–59), and in Himerius' *Oratio* 41, ll. 66–69 ("Ομηρος μὲν οὖν τὸ τῆς Σπάρτης μέγεθος ὀνόματι καιρίῳ δηλῶσαι θέλων κατὰ τὴν ποίησιν, κητώεσσαν αὐτὴν ὡς εὐμήκη προσείρηκεν "Homer, wishing to show through an appropriate adjective the size of Sparta in his poetry, called it κητώεσσαν, that is, 'large'"). 'Large', 'great' or the like are default meanings for an epic adjective of unknown meaning, which can fit almost any context. This interpretation does not rely on a specific Homeric use, but is a very general one.

To sum up, neither κηώεις nor κητώεις are genuine Achaean forms. Rather, the latter was built on the model of the former, which itself is a metrical variant of κηώδης, from which it borrowed its ω. It was not the original form in B 581. Here again, Zenodotus is likely to preserve with καιτάεσσαν the older reading— a form which has been altered by a resegmentation in the oral chain, but which is closer to the original form than the morphologically irregular κητώεσσαν of the vulgate. And as for other cases, the resegmentation and reanalysis preserves a very old element (if the hypothesis developed here is correct, a toponym *Tāwĕssos or *Tāwĕssa, maybe pre-Hellenic, attested in Linear B through the derived ethnonym ta-we-si-jo), fossilised in a larger chunk.

CHAPTER 9

Reeds Again

In Σ 576, the vulgate has a reading that has for long raised questions. Two lines belonging to the long *ekphrasis* of the Shield of Achilles describe a pastoral scene where cattle are reaching the meadows near a river.

1 The Vulgate's Reading

Σ 575–576
(βόες) ἐπεσσεύοντο νομὸν δὲ
πὰρ ποταμὸν κελάδοντα, παρὰ ῥοδανὸν δονακῆα

(the cattle) thronged in speed to a pasturing place by a sounding river, and beside the moving field of a reed bed.
R.L.

There are two problems. First, δονακεύς 'grove of reeds' is not otherwise known (although it was taken over by later poets) and its formation is not regular, as there is no other noun in -εύς derived from an athematic noun (δόναξ, -ακος) and referring to a place. Perpillou is very cautious about it, writing "if we keep this epic form, which, however, is not absolutely secure."[1] The second problem is that ῥοδανός is not better known. It is also a *hapax* in Homer, and there are several variants for that word. The vulgate's ῥοδανόν looks like a correction after the name of the river Rhodanos (mod. *Rhône*), running into the Mediterranean near Massalia, a Greek colony, and was probably suggested by ποταμόν. The whole sentence is in fact a problem because both words are questionable.

Scholia mention various readings for ῥοδανός, which are all interpreted along the same line. It is an adjective meaning something like 'moving' (because of the wind).

---

[1] Perpillou 1973: 331: "si l'on retient cette forme épique, qui n'est cependant pas pleinement assurée." The problem is not even mentioned in Forssman 2020: 221.

A Schol. Σ 576a1: παρὰ ῥοδανὸν δονακῆα· παρὰ Ζηνοδότῳ 'διὰ ῥαδαλόν'. ὁ δὲ Ἀριστοφάνης 'παρὰ †ῥαδηλόν†'. ῥαδαλὸν δὲ ἀκουστέον τὸν εὐκράδαντον δι' ὕψος. φησὶ δὲ Διονύσιος (*fr.* 47 S.) γράφεσθαι καὶ 'δονακῆεν' κατὰ τὸ οὐδέτερον, ὡς καὶ τὸν πευκῶνα πευκᾶεν.

Zenodotus has διὰ ῥαδαλόν. And Aristophanes παρὰ †ῥαδηλόν†. Ῥαδαλόν must be understood as the one moving easily because of its height. And Dionysius (*fr.* 23) says there is also the spelling δονακῆεν with the neutre, as in πευκῶνα πευκᾶεν.[2]

The reading ῥαδηλόν is unmetrical, and therefore can be eliminated. It is erroneously attributed to Aristarchus in the *Et. Magnum* (Kallierges, p. 701: Ἀρίσταρχος δὲ ῥαδηλόν). It is likely to be a correction for the obscure ῥαδαλόν after δῆλος, διάδηλος, ἔκδηλος, ἔνδηλος, in which the first element was compared with ῥᾴθυμος. That is, it is a remotivation of an obsolete form linking the word with a familiar group. That Aristophanes' reading and Zenodotus' are related is not a surprise since Aristophanes often agrees with Zenodotus. A T scholion erroneously attributes the reading ῥοδανόν to Zenodotus (Σ 576a2 Erbse), while a bT scholion explains the word as follows

bT Schol. Σ 576b: παρὰ ῥοδανόν· τὸν ῥᾳδίως ἀναφύοντα· ἢ τὸν εὐκίνητον διὰ λεπτότητα· καὶ ῥοδανίζειν γὰρ αἱ γυναῖκες τὸ συνεχῶς τινάσσειν τὴν κρόκην. b(BCE3E4)T οἱ δὲ ῥοανόν, ῥευστικόν.

παρὰ ῥοδανόν: the easily growing one, or the easily moving one because of its slenderness. And women call ῥοδανίζειν the action of constantly shaking the weft. Others have ῥοανόν 'flowing'.

The D scholia have only ῥοδανόν· Εὐδιάσειστον, εὐκίνητον. διὰ τοὺς ἐν αὐτῷ πεφυκότας καλάμους "ῥοδανόν: easily waving, easily moving, because of the reeds growing in them." The scholiast does not mention any variant reading.

Eustathius gives the form as ῥοδαλόν:

Eustathius, *Comm. Il.* 3: 500: καθὰ καὶ ῥοδαλὸν ἐρεῖ που ποταμὸν δονακῆα, ἤτοι κραδαλόν, ὅ ἐστιν εὐκράδαντον διὰ τοὺς ἐκεῖ δόνακας.

---

[2] Nickau does not comment on the line.

as he will call ῥοδαλός a river rich in reeds, that is, waving, moving because of the reeds there.

It seems all our sources understand the form, whatever the exact reading, as an adjective. This is also the case for the unmetrical innovation ῥαδηλόν. If it is analogical after δῆλος, it implies that the form was analysed as an adjective. But Eustathius' formulation seems to point to a different syntax, in which δονακῆα is analysed as an adjective meaning 'rich in reeds', epithet of ποταμόν, and ῥοδαλόν would be a noun, attribute of ποταμόν.

The interpretation of δονακῆα, meanwhile, is not controversial, and all our sources understand it as 'provided with reeds'. A D scholion has Δόνακας ἔχοντα, ἤγουν καλάμους, the *Et. Magnum* has Καὶ αὐτὸν τὸν καλάμους ἔχοντα, Ἰλιάδος ς', 'παρὰ ῥοδανὸν δονακῆα'. Τὸν καλαμώδη, ἢ εὐδιάσειστον, εὐκίνητον, διὰ τοὺς ἐν αὐτῷ πεφυκότας καλάμους "(δόνακες) and the same word means the one rich in reeds, *Ilias* Σ, 'παρὰ ῥοδανὸν δονακῆα'. The reed-like, of well-moving, mobile, because of the reeds that grow there" (Kallierges, p. 283). The problem lies therefore in the relationship between δονακῆα and ῥαδαλόν/ῥοδανόν: if δονακῆα is the equivalent of an adjective, as scholiasts understand it, it has to be substantivised in order to function as the head of the noun phrase and accept the modifier ῥοδανόν, therefore it must refer to a reed-bed. The alternative is Eustathius' syntax, where ῥοδαλόν is a noun and δονακῆα an adjective.

2   Zenodotus' Reading

The A scholion is crucial. It tells us that Zenodotus had not only ῥαδαλόν, from which arose the remodelled form ῥαδηλόν, but also a different preposition διά, whereas the vulgate has παρά. And it adds an indication coming from Dionysius Thrax, that there was not δονακῆα but δονακῆεν. Was this Zenodotus' reading? The scholion is not explicit on that point, and can be understood either as "Dionysius says that there is also a variant reading δονακῆεν" or as "Dionysius says it was also (in Zenodotus' *ekdosis*) written δονακῆεν." However, the fact that the scholion is centered on Zenodotus' text, since after mentioning Aristophanes' ῥαδηλόν it discusses the meaning of the Zenodotean ῥαδαλόν, makes it likely that the information given by Dionysius also applied to Zenodotus, in the continuity of the preceding sentence. Otherwise, we might expect something like φησὶ δὲ Διονύσιος γράφεσθαι ἐν ἄλλοις 'δονακῆεν'. Dionysius, a student of Aristarchus, knew Zenodotus' *ekdosis*, and accordingly he could have preserved here a piece of evidence which was also preserved in Aristonicus' work, or which in Aristonicus' work was explicitly said to come from Dionysius. The scholiast chose one version, and it happened to be Dionysius', maybe because it was more complete due to the parallel πευκῶνα πευκᾶεν.[3]

If so, Zenodotus' text was διὰ ῥαδαλὸν δονακῆεν. That makes a big difference to the vulgate—a difference not mentioned by scholars who most of the time concentrate only on διὰ ῥαδαλόν and do not discuss δονακῆα/-εν.[4] First of all, δονακῆεν 'rich in reeds' is a regular derivative of δόναξ in the epic language, which uses the allomorph -όϝεντ- after long syllable and -ήϝεντ- after short syllable, whatever the morphological type of the base, for metrical reasons. Therefore in the epics, δονακήϝεις is the expected form (Euripides has δονακόεις, in a different metrical frame).[5] Granted, as a regular form, it could stem from a regularisation and be a correction introduced by Zenodotus to get rid of the awkward δονακῆα, which should be preferred as *lectio difficilior*. But this is probably not the case, for the good reason that these lines are found in the *ekphrasis* of the Shield of Achilles, of which Zenodotus kept only the beginning (A Schol. Σ 483a: ὅτι Ζηνόδοτος ἠθέτηκεν ἀπὸ τούτου τοῦ στίχου τὰ λοιπά, ἀρκεσθεὶς τῇ κεφαλαιώδει προεκθέσει "because Zenodotus athetised all the rest starting from this line, being satisfied with the initial introduction"). Σ 576 is in the part he athetised. Therefore he is unlikely to have introduced any correction.

The reading δονακῆεν fits with the unanimous interpretation of the word by the Greeks themselves for δονακῆα: it means 'rich in reeds'. There is no need to assume that the adjective was substantivated. An adjective it was, an adjective it remained, and an adjective it is in Zenodotus' text.[6] The corollary is that, since δονακῆεν is an adjective, the substantive must be ῥαδαλόν, which is usually taken as an adjective. This is the syntactic structure assumed by Eustathius (see above). This form is a *hapax* Zenodotus cannot have invented. It is possible that he corrected another earlier form into ῥαδαλόν, but he would need a model for that, for which there is none. Moreover, the fact that he kept unchanged forms like ἄας, ἀναπτάς, ὀψ᾿ἀΐοντες, ἰθυκτίων, καιτάεσσα would rather indicate that he did not correct his text as a rule. Greek has several neuter nouns in

---

[3] West 2001a: 133–134 quotes Dionysius' text but does not make any link between the δονακῆεν and Zenodotus. Rather, he assumes δονακῆεν goes together with the reading 'Ῥόδανον and that it is a gross mistake: "the scholar responsible ignored the fact that the river-name is otherwise a masculine, not a neuter." Therefore he still operates with δονακῆα as the noun and tries to find a suitable meaning for ῥαδαλόν/ῥοδανόν.

[4] See for instance the discussion in Van der Valk 1964: 44–46.

[5] Risch 1974: 158 does not mention the form δονακῆεν. Neither does Forssman 2020.

[6] Substantivization of -ϝεντ- adjectives is common, in particular in toponyms like Οἰνοῦσσα, Ἐλαιοῦς, Πιτυοῦς. However, it is different to substantivate as a toponym and to substantivate as a common name, and there is no example of such a substantivization for a -ϝεντ- adjective in Homer.

-αλον, mostly names of instruments but not exclusively. In that case, the word would fall into a known category. Those nouns are paroxytona, and we would expect rather *ῥάδαλον. If Zenodotus' *ekdosis* did not bear accentual marks,[7] the oxytone ῥαδαλός transmitted by the scholia alone is not reliable: it goes back to Aristophanes or Aristarchus and reflects their own theory about the accentuation of the word, not Zenodotus'.

Now two questions arise: what does *ῥάδαλον, a *hapax*, mean and why was the noun phrase N–Adj. reanalysed as Adj.–N? In fact the two questions are linked. In Zenodotus' version διὰ *ῥάδαλον δονακῆεν, the noun phrase consists of an unclear noun and a well-identified adjective. That is, the head of the noun phrase is unanalysable whereas the modifier is motivated. This is the main problem. As a matter of fact, epic diction preserves many noun phrases with an obscure word, thanks to the inertia of formulaic composition, but the obscure word is never the head, the noun, it is always the modifier, the adjective.[8] As long as the head of the noun phrase is clear, the modifier can be obscure.[9] But when the head becomes obscure, the noun phrase has to be changed. In that case, there was a very simple way of reshaping the noun phrase into something understandable: to turn the adjective 'rich in reeds' into a noun which would become the head. Hence we find the minimal modification of δονακῆεν into δονακῆα, made possible because, at the end of the line, the modification had no metrical consequences. This turned *ipso facto* *ῥάδαλον into an adjective, and as is well-known, adjectives in -αλός are oxytone, hence the ῥαδαλόν transmitted by the A scholion. The oxytone type reflects the morphosyntactic category of the word in Aristarchus' mind, namely, an adjective. At this stage, we have a noun phrase 'a reed-bed ῥαδαλόν'.

The last step of the evolution is that a meaning had to be found for ῥαδαλόν, compatible with 'reed' and accounting for the form of the word. This meaning was drawn from κραδαίνω 'to brandish, to shake', because it shared with ῥαδαλόν

---

7 Tradition attributes to Aristophanes of Byzantium the invention of accentual marks, but it is possible that he only improved a preexisting system.
8 See for instance Λ 754 διὰ σπιδέος πεδίοιο (Zenodotus' reading), δι' ἀσπιδέος πεδίοιο (Ptolemy of Ascalon): Greek scholars all understood (ἀ)σπιδέος as an adjective, all had a different idea about the meaning of this word, but the phrase was nevertheless kept because a plain is a plain, and this is what matters. Another well-known case is the formula ἕλικας βοῦς: although Greek scholars disagreed on the meaning of ἕλικας, it was enough that it was in relation with 'to twist' and that the phrase was unambiguously referring to oxen. See on that phrase Le Feuvre 2015: 445–463.
9 See Le Feuvre 2015: 660–663. This was already stated by Parry 1928b, that ornemental epithets may be of unknown meaning since they have no structural role in the sentence and are used for their metrical and poetic value.

the sequence [rada], and the only formal manipulation needed was to remove the initial [k]. This is something Greek etymologists did without any scruples, since it was in line with their theory of *pathos*, the formal accident that can affect any word, such as addition or loss of a letter/phoneme, inversion of two letters/phonemes, 'change' of a letter/phoneme into another one.[10] Hence the explanations in Eustathius (*Comm. Il.* 3: 500: καθὰ καὶ ῥοδαλὸν ἐρεῖ που ποταμὸν δονακῆα, ἤτοι κραδαλόν, ὅ ἐστιν εὐκράδαντον διὰ τοὺς ἐκεῖ δόνακας), the bT scholia (τὸν εὐκίνητον διὰ λεπτότητα), T scholion (Σ 576a2 Erbse: τὸν εὐκράδαντον διὰ τὸ ὕψος), the *Et. Magnum* (Kallierges, p. 701: 'Ραδαλὸν δὲ ἀκουστέον τὸ εὐκράδαντον καὶ εὐδιάσειστον διὰ τὸ ὕψος). That yielded the meaning 'waving' in the wind. The adjective is reused with this meaning by the epic poet Nicaenetus (3rd c. BCE): γείνατο δὲ ῥαδαλῆς ἐναλίγκιον ἀρκεύθοισι | Βυβλίδα "she gave birth to Byblis, similar to the supple juniper" (*fr.* 1.4 Powell). Van Thiel quotes this line as a proof that Zenodotus has ῥαδαλόν as a marginal comment, a form taken from a contemporary poet,[11] but does not ask the question where Hellenistic poets could have taken this form from … The correct scenario is probably the opposite. Nicaenetus took this adjective ῥαδαλός from Homer, and may echo a controversy between two competing analyses, ῥάδαλον δονακῆεν N–Adj. (Zenodotus) and ῥάδαλὸν δονακῆα Adj.–N. He takes sides with the latter, in which ῥαδαλός is analysed as an adjective, epithet of a plant name.

An alternative solution to the problem was to replace the word with another one, in that case ῥοδανόν, which is not much better but was at least an existing word, and moreover the name of a real river, so that it could be deemed appropriate in that context.

Now if *ῥάδαλον was originally a noun, what does it mean? Can modern linguistics come up with a satisfying explanation for this Zenodotean form which the Greeks did no longer understand? After others, Risch compares the word with the adjective ῥαδινός 'tender, flexible, soft', because it is appropriate as an epithet of 'reed-bed' (Risch does not consider the possibility that the

---

10 On the theory of *pathos*, see Lallot 1995. Greek scholars do not make any distinction between the graphic level (letter) and the phonological leven (phoneme). Deleting the initial consonant, a customary way of dealing with words for Greek scholars, is what Leaf assumes Zenodotus did: "Zen. derived his ῥαδαλόν from κραδαλόν = εὐκράδαντον, εὐκίνητον." Always the same old idea that Zenodotus is wildly imaginative. But Zenodotus did not create this word out of κραδαλόν since the A scholion shows that for him the adjective was δονακῆεν and ῥαδαλόν was a noun, not an adjective, so that he could not understand it as 'moving': this meaning is valid only once the syntax of the noun phase has been reversed and ῥαδαλόν has been reanalysed as an adjective, and Zenodotus' text predates the reanalysis.

11 Van Thiel 2014b, *sub* Σ 576: "wohl auf zeitgenössische Poesie."

syntagm is N–Adj.).¹² From the formal point of view, this is reasonable. Beekes considers the group to be Pre-Greek, while for others it should be compared with Ved. *ávradanta* (RV 2.24.3, *hapax*) 'they became mellow',¹³ implying a root **u̯red-* (also attested in Iranian, cf. *LIV²*). The zero grade of this root regularly yields **u̯r̥d-i-no-* > ῥαδινός, **u̯r̥d-°lo-* > **ῥαδαλο-*. The relationship between ῥαδινός and **ῥαδαλον* is comparable to that between πυκ-ι-νός 'thick, dense' and πευκ-άλ-ιμος 'shrewd' (always used metaphorically), or κύδ-ι-μος 'glorious' and κυδ-άλ-ιμος 'glorious', or **ἀλγ-ι-νός* in ἀλγινόεις 'painful' (Hesiod) and **ἀλγ-αλ-έος* > ἀργαλέος 'painful'. It is an old structure in Caland systems. Reconstructing a Caland system on the basis of the pair ῥάδαλον vs ῥαδινός would be possible. However, the pair may have been built in Greek on the model of old Caland forms. This would confirm that περιρρηδής (χ 84), of unclear meaning, has nothing to do with this root **u̯red-*, **u̯r̥d-*.¹⁴ If this hypothesis is correct, **ῥαδαλος* originally was an adjective, and was later on substantivated, *via* a syntagm **ῥαδαλὸν πέδον* for instance, which would explain the neuter. The root means 'to be weak, soft'. Accordingly, the word could apply to a soft and muddy ground, the kind of soil in which reeds grow.

3   The Preposition and the Status of κελάδων

The last difference lies in the preposition: Zenodotus' reading was διὰ **ῥάδαλον δονακῆεν, vs vulgate παρὰ ῥοδανὸν δονακῆα. The preposition διά is expected if **ῥάδαλον* refers to the soil through which the river flows, so that it is logical in Zenodotus' syntax. However, as soon as the head of the noun phrase was the new noun 'reed-bed', διά was no longer appropriate because the river does not flow through the reeds but along the reeds growing on its banks (παρά). Thus, the change of preposition could be a consequence of the reanalysis of the noun phrase.

In addition, another factor may have played a role, namely, a change in the semantic structure of the line itself. The verb κελάδω is in fact not used in Homer except in the participle κελάδων, for the personal forms Homer has only κελαδέω. Zenodotus' reading διὰ **ῥάδαλον δονακῆεν implies that the prepositional phrase refers to the river, and that κελάδοντα is a verb, 'a river murmuring through a **ῥάδαλον*', the circumstant διὰ **ῥάδαλον δονακῆεν modifying the verbal

---

12   Risch 1974: 108.
13   This is the received meaning, but Gotō 1987: 301 suggests the form may be transitive factitive.
14   See Blanc 2018: 276.

predicate κελάδοντα. However, the participle was soon lexicalised as an adjective. This can be seen from Aristonicus' remark on another line:

A Schol. H 133–135a: ὠκυρόῳ κελάδοντι: ὅτι ἰδίως τὰ ἐπίθετα προτάξας τὸ κύριον ἐπήγαγεν (H 135) Ἰαρδάνου ἀμφὶ ῥέεθρα.

because having unusually put the adjectives first, he then added the proper noun 'along the stream of the Iardanos'.

Here τὰ ἐπίθετα 'the adjectives' includes κελάδοντι.[15] As an adjective, κελάδων lost its ability to govern a circumstant. The river can be 'murmuring in a valley', but not *'sonorous in a valley'.[16] Therefore the prepositional phrase was understood as referring not to the river, but to the subject of the sentence, βόες, and the latter do not graze through the reed-bed but near it. The choice of the preposition παρά may have been influenced by the beginning of the line # πὰρ ποταμὸν κελάδοντα, since apparently the two prepositional phrases were understood as parallel. Aristophanes already had παρά. This would explain the presence of two prepositional phrases in asyndeton. In Zenodotus' reading, the two prepositional phrases are not on the same level, since διά N modifies κελάδοντα, itself belonging to a prepositional phrase παρά N modifying ἐπεσσεύοντο. In the vulgate, both are on the same level, without coordination. The absence of coordination is the consequence of the reanalysis of a structure in which they were on different syntactic levels. The change of the preposition is in fact the most substantial modification from the formal point of view, although it is not commented by scholiasts.

In the case of Σ 576, the morphologically abnormal form of the vulgate δονακῆα is again due to metrical constraints because it replaces a preexisting form.

---

15   See also Eustathius, Comm. Il. 2: 423: Ἐν δέ γε τῷ 'πόντος κελάδων' ἐπιθετόν ἐστιν ἡ τοιαύτη λέξις; ibid., 4, 263 (Τὸ δὲ 'κελάδων' ὥσπερ ἀλλαχοῦ ἀνέμου καὶ πόντου, οὕτω καὶ ποταμοῦ ἐνταῦθά ἐστιν ἐπίθετον). Similarly, for β 420–421 τοῖσιν δ' ἴκμενον οὖρον ἵει γλαυκῶπις Ἀθήνη, ‖ ἀκραῆ ζέφυρον, κελάδοντ' ἐπὶ οἴνοπα πόντον, the participle κελάδοντα is understood as a verbal form of which the prepositional phrase ἐπὶ οἴνοπα πόντον is a complement, but scholia also mention that it can be an adjective epithet of πόντον and not a participle of which ζέφυρον is the subject: κελάδοντ' ἐπὶ οἴνοπα πόντον: ἤτοι ἠχοῦντα κατὰ τὴν θάλασσαν, τὸν ἄνεμον, ἢ κατὰ τὸν κελάδοντα πόντον πνέοντα (Schol. Od. β 421f1 Pontani), δύναται καὶ 'κατὰ τὸν κελάδοντα καὶ οἴνοπα πόντον' (Schol. Od. β 421f2 Pontani).

16   Adjectives can be used with circumstants, for instance "white on the edge," "ugly from head to toe," "clumsy in his moves" and so on; this depends on the meaning of the adjective and of the circumstant. Adjectives referring to a sound do not combine with a spatial circumstant as a rule.

This form is probably recent, and the older δονακήεις should be reintegrated into the series of -ϝεντ- adjectives. The interesting point is the syntactic change, and the reanalysis of a noun phrase N–Adj. as Adj.–N, owing to the ambiguity of ῥαδαλόν/ῥάδαλον, which could be analysed either as a substantive or as an adjective.

CHAPTER 10

Homer the Master of Rhetorics

So far, we have examined Zenodotus' readings that differ from the vulgate's either from the lexical or the morphological point of view. Those are of course the most conspicuous. However, there are also variant readings in which the main problem is syntax. Syntax was involved in several of the previous cases, but as a secondary problem. This chapter will examine some cases where syntax is central.

1   B 681

1.1   *The Vulgate's Reading*

B 681–685
Νῦν αὖ τοὺς ὅσσοι τὸ Πελασγικὸν Ἄργος ἔναιον,
οἵ τ' Ἄλον οἵ τ' Ἀλόπην οἵ τε Τρηχῖνα νέμοντο,
οἵ τ' εἶχον Φθίην ἠδ' Ἑλλάδα καλλιγύναικα,
Μυρμιδόνες δὲ καλεῦντο καὶ Ἕλληνες καὶ Ἀχαιοί,
τῶν αὖ πεντήκοντα νεῶν ἦν ἀρχὸς Ἀχιλλεύς.

Now all those who dwelt about Pelasgian Argos, those who lived by Alos and Alope and at Trachis, those who held Phthia and Hellas the land of fair women, who were called Myrmidons and Hellenes and Achaians, of all these and their fifty ships the lord was Achilleus.
R.L.

This is the beginning of the third part of the *Catalogue of ships*, which lists cities of Northern Greece. The *Catalogue* is usually divided into three sub-tours of Greece: the mainland (from B 490 to B 644: Boeotia and south), the Aegean islands, starting with Crete (from B 645 Κρητῶν δ' Ἰδομενεὺς δουρὶ κλυτὸς ἡγεμόνευεν to B 680), then Thessalia and Northern Greece.

There are several problems with the vulgate's reading. The first one is the use of the article in ὅσσοι τὸ Πελασγικὸν Ἄργος ἔναιον. This is the only use of the article with a toponym in the entire *Catalogue*.[1] The order article + adjective

---

[1] See *BK* II: 221: "the use of the article together with the geographic name is unique. It must be explained because of the exceptional metrical structure of the semantic determiner

+ noun makes it all the more suspect as in cases when a toponym may refer to two different places which have to be distinguished by means of a geographical adjective, the adjective is placed after the noun in spoken Greek as in Homer, e.g. Σάμος Θρηϊκίη (Σάμου ὑληέσσης ‖ Θρηϊκίης N 12–13), Σαμοθράκη in prose, Κύμην Αἰολίδα (Hesiod, *Op*. 636). Ornemental epithets, which can be removed, may be placed before the noun, but distinctive epithets are part of the toponym itself and regularly follow it.[2] Alexandrian scholars knew that Homer as a rule does not use the article. Yet there are cases of a fully developed article in Homer, so that this must not have bothered them too much, and anyway that was not a reason for them to condemn the line. Apparently, they did not pay attention to word order.

The second problem in the vulgate's reading is the general structure of the sentence. In τοὺς ὅσσοι [...] ἔναιον [...], τῶν αὖ πεντήκοντα νεῶν ἦν ἀρχὸς Ἀχιλλεύς, the τούς remains *pendens*, as it has no function in the sentence. The sentence starts as though there were a cataphoric τούς, in correlation with the following series of relative pronouns, but the main clause in line 685 τῶν αὖ πεντήκοντα νεῶν ἦν ἀρχὸς Ἀχιλλεύς has an anaphoric pronoun τῶν, syntactically correct. There cannot be one cataphoric and one anaphoric pronoun in correlation with the same relative pronouns, in two different cases, accusative and genitive. Should we assume an anacolouthon? Did the singer start with one structure and forget within four lines the beginning of his sentence? This is not likely. Let us reiterate that the enumerations of the *Catalogue* always have the same structure (see above, pp. 222–224) and that there is no correlation with a cataphoric pronoun before the relative clause but only correlative systems with the relative clause first and an anaphoric pronoun in the main clause. This is the pattern of l. 685 τῶν αὖ πεντήκοντα νεῶν ἦν ἀρχὸς Ἀχιλλεύς, but l. 681 creates an irregular and incorrect syntax.

Scholiasts tried to explain that structure as best they could. Another A scholion going back to Nicanor for the first part and to Herodian for the second part explains it by the fact that there are two different sentences, not one:

Πελασγικὸν Ἄργος" ("Im Zusammenhang mit geogr. Angaben ist die Verwendung des Artikels singulär; sie dürfte durch die auffällige metr. Struktur der semantischen Determinante Πελασγικὸν Ἄργος zu erklären sein"). The problem is correctly identified but the solution proposed is an easy solution (metrics), relying on a weak argument (the metrical structure of Πελασγικὸν Ἄργος is not exceptional), and Zenodotus' reading is not even mentioned. Tichy, *Ilias diachronica*, rewrites the line in the following fashion: *νῦν αὖθ᾽, οἵ ῥα Πελασγικὸν Ἄργος ναιετάεσκον.

2 The exception of *H.Ap*. 34 # Θρηϊκίη τε Σάμος Ἴδης τ᾽ὄρεα σκιόεντα, in an unmetrical line, is metrically conditioned as Σάμος could not be used at the beginning of a line.

A Schol. B 681–685: (Nicanor) νῦν αὖ τοὺς ὅσσοι τὸ Πελασγικὸν Ἄργος ἔναιον 〈—Ἀχιλλεύς〉: μακρόθεν ὑπακούεται τὸ 'ἔσπετε' (B 484) ἢ τὸ 'ἐρέω' (B 493)· καὶ τὰ τοιαῦτα τοῖς αἰτήμασιν ὑποπίπτει. στικτέον δὲ ἐπὶ τὸ ἔναιον, ἵν' ᾖ τὸ ἐπιφερόμενον 'οἵ τ' Ἄλον †τε καὶ Ἀλόπην† ἐνέμοντο'· τὸ γὰρ οἵ κατ' ἐπανάληψιν περισσεύει. δύναται δὲ καὶ ὑποστίζεσθαι ἕκαστος στίχος ἕως τοῦ Ἀχαιοί κατὰ τέλος. ἡ δὲ συνήθεια συνάπτουσα τὰ τοιαῦτα τοῖς ἐπάνω οὐ κατορθοῖ· οὐ γὰρ μόνοι τὸ Πελασγικὸν Ἄργος κατοικοῦσιν οἱ ὑπ' Ἀχιλλεῖ τεταγμένοι. | (Herodian) τὸ δὲ τούς ἀντωνυμία ἐστί· διὸ περισπαστέον τὸ νῦν καὶ τὸ αὖ.

(Nicanor) from afar is understood the ἔσπετε (B 484) or the ἐρέω (B 493). And such verbs can be deduced from their objects. There must be a dot after ἔναιον, so that what is added is οἵ τ' Ἄλον †τε καὶ Ἀλόπην† ἐνέμοντο' because the οἵ, in epanalepsis, is unnecessary. But each line can also end with a dot up to Ἀχαιοί down to the end. The general use linking those lines to the preceding ones is not correct, because those whose Achilles is the commander are not the only ones living in the Pelasgian Argos. (Herodian) The τούς is a pronoun, and this is why the νῦν and the αὖ must be circumflex.

This way of getting rid of the accusative is entirely *ad hoc* and utterly impossible. Τούς cannot be the object of a verb meaning 'to speak' used two hundred lines earlier in the invocation to the Muses. The point is that, since Achilles is the leader of only a fraction of the people living in Pelasgian Argos, l. 681 must not belong with l. 685, and there must be two different sentences, one consisting of l. 681 alone, with no main verb (hence the idea that there is an implicit verb of speech), and the second one consisting of ll. 682–685. Leaf repeats nevertheless this explanation and comments on τούς: "as though the poet meant to continue ἔσπετε (484) or ἐρέω (498)."

Thirdly, there are two features without any parallel in the *Catalogue* in the vulgate's reading. First, the enumeration is introduced by ὅσσοι. Although the latter point has gone unnoticed, there is no other ὅσ(σ)οι at the beginning of a list in the highly stereotyped structure of the *Catalogue*, which has only simple relative pronouns, and the vulgate departs here from the regular structure. Last, at the beginning of l. 681, νῦν αὖ of the vulgate has no parallel in the *Catalogue*,[3] and the αὖ is redundant with the one in l. 685 τῶν αὖ πεντήκοντα νεῶν ἦν ἀρχὸς Ἀχιλλεύς. The second αὖ alone is regular and has parallels in the *Catalogue* (τῶν

---

3 See BK II: 221: "unique beginning of an entry in the Catalogue" ("singulärer Beginn eines Eintrags im NK"). Then comes the usual justification by the beginning of a new sub-tour of Greece.

αὖ or τῶν αὖθ' B 540, 552, 563, 601, 618, 627, 678, 698, 731, 740). The first one is probably influenced by the line introducing the *Catalogue*, B 493 ἀρχοὺς αὖ νηῶν ἐρέω νῆάς τε προπάσας.

1.2 Zenodotus' Reading

Aristonicus says that Zenodotus had a different version for l. 681:

> *A Schol.* B 681a: ὅτι Ζηνόδοτος μετέγραφεν οὕτως 'οἳ δ' Ἄργος τ' εἶχον τὸ Πελασγικόν, οὖθαρ ἀρούρης', τοῦ Ὁμήρου φιλοτέχνως ὥσπερ προοιμιαζομένου διὰ τὸ μεταβαίνειν ἀπὸ τῶν νήσων καὶ τῆς Πελοποννήσου ἐπὶ τὰ κατὰ Θεσσαλίαν, οὐκ ὄντα συναφῆ τοῖς προειρημένοις.

> because Zenodotus rewrote the line as follows: οἳ δ' Ἄργος τ' εἶχον τὸ Πελασγικόν, οὖθαρ ἀρούρης, whereas Homer, skillfully, is making a prelude, because he is crossing from the islands and the Peloponnese to cities in Thessaly, which are not contiguous with the ones mentioned before.

The Zenodotean version is not commented upon by Nickau or by Leaf, and not mentioned by Kirk in his *Commentary* of the *Catalogue* or by Van der Valk. Yet it is much better than the vulgate's variant. Van Thiel assumes it is not a variant reading but a marginal comment in which Zenodotus compared I 141 (= I 283) εἰ δέ κεν Ἄργος ἱκοίμεθ' Ἀχαιϊκὸν οὖθαρ ἀρούρης and B 559 οἳ δ' Ἄργος τ' εἶχον Τίρυνθά τε τειχιόεσσαν ("Zenodotus drew the reader's attention to the exceptional formulation of the beginning of the second part of the Catalogue, while quoting the formal parallel").[4]

Compared to the line of the vulgate with its article, Zenodotus' line οἳ δ' Ἄργος τ' εἶχον τὸ Πελασγικόν, οὖθαρ ἀρούρης is certainly older, as the τό here is used with its anaphoric value in order to introduce a distinctive epithet modifying a noun already mentioned in the context, "Argos, the Pelasgian one," as opposed to Argos, city of Achaia. It is not the article but the anaphoric pronoun, and this use is old.[5] Compare, with a similar structure Noun–Determiner–Adjective:

– Π 358 Αἴας ὁ μέγας "Ajax, the great one"
– B 595 Θάμυριν τὸν Θρήϊκα "Thamuris, the Thracian one"
– Z 201 πεδίον τὸ Ἀλήϊον "the plain, the Alean one"

---

[4] Van Thiel 2014b, *sub* B 681: "Zenodot machte auf die abweichende Formulierung zu Beginn des zweiten Katalogabschnitts aufmerksam, indem er die formelhafte Parallele zitierte."

[5] Schwyzer–Debrunner, *Gr. Gr.* II: 22, assumes the determiner has a deictic value. At best it is internal deixis, that is, anaphora.

- Κ 11 ἐς πεδίον τὸ Τρωϊκόν "the plain of Troy"
- Ξ 278–279 θεούς [...] τοὺς ὑποταρταρίους "the gods, those under the Tartar."[6]

As far as toponyms are concerned, this structure with only one "article" between the noun and the distinctive epithet is also that of classical prose:
- παρέπλευσαν ἐς Λοκροὺς τοὺς Ἐπιζεφυρίους (Thuc. 7.1)
- ἐν Λοκροῖσι τοῖσι Ἐπιζεφυρίοισι (Hdt. 6.23)
- Λοκροῖς τοῖς Ἐπιζεφυρίοις (Aristotle, *Pol.* 1274a)
- ἀπὸ Κύμης τῆς Αἰολίδος (Hdt 7.194)
- Κύμην τὴν Αἰολίδα (Thuc. 3.31.1)
- ἐν Ἡρακλείᾳ τῇ Ποντικῇ (Dioscorides, *De materia medica* 2.82.4)
- Κέρκυρα ἡ μέλαινα (Scylax, *Periplus* 23).

Similarly, when the information is conveyed by another element than an adjective, a genitive or a prepositional phrase, the latter follows the noun:
- πέμψας ἐς Θήβας τὰς Βοιωτίας (Hdt. 5.67)
- ἐκ Χαλκίδος τῆς Εὐβοίας (Thuc. 7.29.2)
- Μεσσήνην τὴν ἐν Σικελίᾳ (Thuc. 4.1.1)
- Ἡράκλειαν τὴν ἐν τῷ Πόντῳ (Aristotle, *Meteor.* 367a1)
- ἐν Ἡρακλείᾳ τῇ ἐν Τραχῖνι (Thuc. 4.78.1)
- περὶ τὴν Κύμην τὴν ἐν Ἰταλίᾳ (Aristotle, *Mirabilium auscultationes* 839a)
- Σαλαμῖνα τὴν ἐν Κύπρῳ (Strabo 14.6.3)
- Φωκαίη Ἰωνίης (Hdt 1.163)
- ἐς Σαλαμῖνα τῆς Κύπρου (Hdt. 4.162)
- ἐν Θήβαις τῆς Βοιωτίας (Diod. Sic. 1.23.1).[7]

However, it becomes possible in Hellenistic and imperial Greek to use the customary structure for a qualificative adjective, article + adjective + noun:
- περὶ τὴν Ποντικὴν Ἡράκλειαν (Arius Didymus, *fr.* 13)
- εἰς τὴν Ποντικὴν Ἡράκλειαν (Plutarch, *Lucullus* 13.3)
- αἱ Βοιώτιαι Θῆβαι (Ptolemy, *Geogr.* 8.12.15)
- ἐς τὰς Βοιωτίας Θήβας (Pausanias 8.33.2).

Or with a prepositional phrase
- τῆς ἐν Κύπρῳ Σαλαμῖνος (Athenaeus, *Deipn.* 12.41 Kaibel).

One can add νῆσος ἡ μέλαινα Κέρκυρα καλουμένη (Strabo 7.5.5) to this list. Here, the article modifies the participle, not μέλαινα Κέρκυρα, but the order

---

6 See other instances in Chantraine, *Gr. hom.* II: 163.
7 Compare, with a geographical name having a common noun and not a toponym as its head, ἀπίκοντο τῆς Κιλικίης ἐς τὸ Ἀλήιον πεδίον (Hdt 6.95), ἐς τὸ Ξάνθιον πεδίον (Hdt 1.176). In that case the adjective can be placed before the noun, which is not the case in classical texts when the head is a toponym.

in the toponym is adjective + noun, as opposed to noun + adj. in Scylax' Κέρκυρα ἡ μέλαινα. Therefore, a structure τὸ Πελασγικὸν Ἄργος instead of Ἄργος τὸ Πελασγικόν was not a problem for Hellenistic scholars.

The structure of Zenodotus' line is parallel to I 141 (= I 283) εἰ δέ κεν Ἄργος ἱκοίμεθ᾽ Ἀχαιϊκὸν οὖθαρ ἀρούρης, without the anaphoric because Argos of Achaia is the "default" Argos, so to speak, but with the adjective regularly placed after the noun, as in T 115 καρπαλίμως δ᾽ ἵκετ᾽ Ἄργος Ἀχαιϊκόν, γ 251 ἦ οὐκ Ἄργεος ἦεν Ἀχαιϊκοῦ;

Compared to the isolated ὅσσοι of the vulgate, Zenodotus' reading agrees with the expected structure, as it has οἵ τε ... οἵ τε, with the regular simple relative. And compared to the awkward τούς ... τῶν of the vulgate, it is syntactically correct, it has the relative clause in first position and only one anaphoric pronoun in the correlation, in the required case. The formulation with ἔχω 'to hold' a land is the traditional one and the one most frequently found in the *Catalogue* (see above, pp. 222–224), and here the contraction in εἶχον can be resolved in *ἔεχον. Moreover, there is no repetition of αὖ with his reading. To sum up, none of the problems posed by the vulgate's reading may be found in Zenodotus' reading.

Does that mean that Zenodotus' version is an emendation? That is unlikely in view of the first problem, the presence of an article in the vulgate's τὸ Πελασγικὸν Ἄργος, betraying a recent line, as opposed to an older structure in Zenodotus. The innovation probably lies on the side of the vulgate. Now why was such a change introduced? Probably because, as the scholiast of 681a Erbse underlines (followed by Kirk centuries later), there is a geographical discontinuity between Thessaly and what precedes (the Aegean islands). Rhetorics teaches that when there is a new topic (here a different part of Greece, Thessaly), this must be made visible in the wording of the narration or of the discourse, and that there must not be a continuity with the preceding topic (here the islands). That is, the line as it is transmitted in the vulgate obeys rhetorical rules rather than linguistic concerns. A new development implies an introduction. This is explicit in the formulation of several scholia: τοῦ Ὁμήρου φιλοτέχνως ὥσπερ προοιμιαζομένου (*A Schol.* B 681a), ἐπιστρέφει ἠθικῶς τὸν Κατάλογον ἐπὶ Ἀχιλλέα, δευτέραν ἀρχὴν Καταλόγου ποιούμενος "he turns the *Catalogue* toward Achilles, in agreement with rhetoric use, making a second opening for the *Catalogue*" (*b Schol.* B 681b), with the technical word ἠθικῶς, referring to the correct rhetorical use since Aristoteles (*Rhet.* 1418a38–39).[8] Alexandrian

---

8   See above the discussion of Ξ 169–170 (pp. 62–63). See also Schenkeveld 1970: 175–177 (on Homer φιλότεχνος) and 171. Schenkeveld argues that Aristarchus defended this reading

HOMER THE MASTER OF RHETORICS 249

scholars were very sensitive to that, even at the expense of syntactic correctness—and that is why they tried to justify with *ad hoc* arguments a patent syntactic irregularity. Zenodotus' reading, on the other hand, runs counter to the rhetorical rules by having no rhetorical opening for the new development. What was considered a flaw by scholars informed by rhetorical concepts can be considered an old, pre-rhetorical feature.

It is worth noticing that the opening of the second part of the *Catalogue*, moving from mainland Greece to the Aegean islands, has no such introductory line. The second "sub-tour" starts with B 645 Κρητῶν δ᾽ Ἰδομενεὺς δουρὶ κλυτὸς ἡγεμόνευεν. This line has the same structure as B 638 Αἰτωλῶν δ᾽ ἡγεῖτο Θόας Ἀνδραίμονος υἱός, which does not mark the beginning of a block and belongs to the first part. Now if there has to be a prologue at the beginning of each part, part two should be treated as part three, and it is not. Apparently Homer was skillful for part three (φιλοτέχνως) but forgot to be for part two, and that did not bother Alexandrian scholars.[9]

Therefore, it is safe enough to consider that we have here again the older reading preserved in Zenodotus and a modified text in the vulgate. This modification was introduced not for linguistic reasons as was the case in the preceding examples, but for stylistic reasons.[10] The reason why part three was given a special treatment, whereas part two was not, is that it starts with Achilles' troops. Such special status is a consequence of the prominence of the hero, and this, again, agrees with rhetorical principles. The second part of the *Catalogue*

---

because the line under this form had a function in the Catalogue, it was an introductory line, whereas Zenodotus' line was not, and Aristarchus was focused on the function of the lines: "his real concern is whether ⟨the lines⟩ are functional in the context of the story."

9   Neither did it bother West 2011: 113: "The Cat. Begins from Boeotia … From Elis it continues up to the western isles and from there back to Aetolia. Now surely it will come to Thessaly? But no, it leaps down to Crete, passing on from there to Rhodes and the smaller Dorian islands. Only then, with a marked transition at 681, does it take account of Ach.'s kingdom and the other more northerly contingents, which are appended in a less orderly sequence. It may be that this arrangement goes back to an earlier stage of the tradition at which Ach. had not yet been integrated into the story of Troy and the catalogue of those who took part in the war did not extend north of the Malian Gulf." West 2011: 119 comments on B 681 "a conscious transition."

10 Besides, Zenodotus' reading was similar to another line mentioning Argos, I 141 (= I 283) εἰ δέ κεν Ἄργος ἱκοίμεθ᾽ Ἀχαιϊκὸν οὖθαρ ἀρούρης: that probably implies a common formulaic prototype, but it would also be consistent with the practice of Alexandrian scholars to judge that the phrase οὖθαρ ἀρούρης could not be used for two different cities bearing the same name, so that if it was the epithet of Argos in Achaia, it could not be that of Pelasgian Argos, which was a further reason to modify the end of the line. However, this argument is not found in the scholia and it would have been easy to change the adonic colon without changing the rest of the line.

starts with Idomeneus, king of Crete, who is arguably a far lesser hero in the *Iliad* than Achilles. The beginning of part two remained unmarked, that of part three could not. As a consequence, any subtle comment on the skillful construction of the *Catalogue* relying on B 681 is deprived of any basis if the line as we have it in the vulgate's formulation is not earlier than the 4th c.: needless to say it is not "Homer's."[11]

2   A 60

Another interesting case, which is much less conspicuous and therefore most of the time left aside, is found in A 60. The vulgate has

> A 59–61
> Ἀτρεΐδη νῦν ἄμμε παλιμπλαγχθέντας ὀΐω
> ἂψ ἀπονοστήσειν, εἴ κεν θάνατόν γε φύγοιμεν,
> εἰ δὴ ὁμοῦ πόλεμός τε δαμᾷ καὶ λοιμὸς Ἀχαιούς

> Son of Atreus, I believe now that straggling backwards we must make our way home if we can even escape death, if fighting now must crush the Achaians and the plague likewise.
> R.L.

As Aristonicus says,

> *A Schol.* A 60: ὅτι Ζηνόδοτος οἵ κεν γράφει, οὐ καλῶς· καλὴ γὰρ ἡ ἀπόγνωσις τῆς σωτηρίας.

> (*diple periestigmene*) because Zenodotus writes οἵ κεν, wrongly. Because desperation about salvation is beautiful.

This is a stylistic reason, not a linguistic one.[12] Zenodotus' οἵ κεν instead of εἴ κεν (αἴ κεν in one manuscript), meaning "those of us who can escape death," implies that Achilles acknowledges that some will escape death caused by πόλεμος and

---

11   This is one of the reasons why Tichy's principle in her *Ilias diachronica* cannot be followed: she starts from the vulgate and adapts it to her conception of what the original metrical structure was. But if the text of the vulgate is not old, the attempt is meaningless.

12   Van Thiel's hypothesis (2014b, *sub* A 61) that οἵ κεν is an "experimentelle Wortänderung" by Zenodotus is gratuitous (but consistent in Van Thiel's framework).

λοιμός of l. 61 while others will not. It is a restrictive relative clause, isolating a subset within the group ἄμμε. The vulgate's formulation εἴ κεν (αἴ κεν in one manuscript) "if we can escape death" is less brutal, because Achilles puts all the Achaeans on a par, including himself, and may have been preferred for that reason.

2.1 The Vulgate's Reading and Conditional Systems in the Iliad

However, in the vulgate's reading we have a conditional protasis with the optative and the modal particle. There are several instances of such a structure in Homer, but they are found almost only in a regular conditional system displaying the optative with the particle in both the protasis and the apodosis. As Chantraine puts it, "the particle κε underlines the parallelism with the main clause."[13] There are eleven instances in the *Iliad*, all with a clear potential value. Cases of iotacism left aside, there is a variant reading on the particle of the protasis in one case, and on the mode of the protasis in one case. That leaves nine instances without any variant reading.

- Β 123–128: εἴ περ γάρ κ' ἐθέλοιμεν ... πολλαί κεν δεκάδες δευοίατο οἰνοχόοιο "since if both sides were to be willing ... still there would be many tens left without a wine steward" (R.L.). There is no variant reading.
- Ε 273: εἰ τούτω κε λάβοιμεν, ἀροίμεθά κε κλέος ἐσθλόν "if we might only take these we should win ourselves excellent glory" (R.L.). There is no variant reading.
- Η 28: ἀλλ' εἴ μοί τι πίθοιο τό κεν πολὺ κέρδιον εἴη "but if you might only do as I say, it would be far better" (R.L.). There is no variant reading.
- Θ 205–207: εἴ περ γάρ κ' ἐθέλοιμεν ... αὐτοῦ κ' ἔνθ' ἀκάχοιτο "for if all of us were willing ... he would be desperate there" (R.L.). There is no variant reading.
- Ψ 592–594: εἰ καί νύ κεν ... ἐπαιτήσειας ... ἄφαρ κέ τοι αὐτίκα δοῦναι βουλοίμην "and if you asked something ... I should still be willing at once to give it to you" (R.L. modified). The only variant reading is an ἀπαιτήσειας, which is not relevant for the syntactic structure.
- Ν 288–289: εἴ περ γάρ κε βλεῖο ... οὐκ ἂν ἐν αὐχέν' ὄπισθε πέσοι βέλος "even were you to be wounded ... the weapon would not strike behind your neck" (R.L.). There is a reading καὶ βλεῖο in some manuscripts and papyri, which may simply stem from a confusion with monophthongised καί and a variant βλῆο in others, but no source has a subjunctive.
- Θ 196: εἰ τούτω κε λάβοιμεν, ἐελποίμην κεν "could we capture these two things, I might hope [...]" (R.L.). The only variant reading is a γε instead of κε in the

---

13 Chantraine, *Gr. hom.* II: 277: "La particule κε souligne parfois le parallélisme avec la principale." "Sometimes" is in fact weak, as this applies to the great majority of instances.

protasis in one manuscript and one Ptolemaic papyrus (papyrus 7 West, 3rd c. BCE).
- I 141–142 = I 283–284: εἰ δέ κεν Ἄργος ἱκοίμεθα ... γαμβρός κέν μοι ἔοι (οἱ ἔοις I 285) "and if we come back to Achaian Argos, he may be my son-in-law" (R.L.). One commentary on papyrus (h68 West, from the 2nd c. BCE) has the subjunctive ἱκώμεθα in I 141, there is no variant reading for I 283.
- Z 49–50 = K 380–381: τῶν κέν τοι χαρίσαιτο ... εἴ κεν πεπύθοιτο "and he would be grateful to you ... if he learned" (τῶν κ' ὕμμιν χαρίσαιτο K 380). This is the only case where the apodosis comes first, but the two lines could easily be inverted. One manuscript has τῶν καί τοι χαρίσαιτο in Z 49 (probably a iotacising spelling), there is no variant for K 380.

Next to that is found a consistent series of negated conditional clauses, all starting with # οὐδ᾽ εἴ κεν, after which we find now the optative, now the subjunctive, most of the time metrically interchangeable. The apodosis is negative, too, and the particle is not systematic. The negative clause introduced by οὐδ᾽ εἴ κεν always comes after the apodosis. It does not express the condition of realisation of the process of the main clause, but confirms the impossibility of this process under any circumstance. Here are the instances with the optative:

- I 444–445: ὡς ἂν ἔπειτ᾽ ἀπὸ σεῖο φίλον τέκος οὐκ ἐθέλοιμι || λείπεσθ᾽, οὐδ᾽ εἴ κέν μοι ὑποσταίη θεὸς αὐτός [...] "Therefore apart from you, dear child, I would not be willing to be left behind, not were the god in person to promise [...]" (R.L.). The modal particle is found in both clauses. There is no variant reading.
- T 321–322: οὐ μὲν γάρ τι κακώτερον ἄλλο πάθοιμι ... οὐδ᾽ εἴ κεν ... πυθοίμην "for I could not suffer anything worse ... even if I learned." There is no modal particle in the main clause. However, this may be secondary and the line may have replaced an older *οὐ μὲν γάρ κε with a modal particle (as in I 545), although there is no variant reading.
- X 348–352: ὡς οὐκ ἔσθ᾽ ὃς σῆς γε κύνας κεφαλῆς ἀπαλάλκοι, || οὐδ᾽ εἴ κεν δεκάκις τε καὶ εἰκοσινήριτ᾽ ἄποινα || στήσωσ᾽ ἐνθάδ᾽ ἄγοντες, ὑπόσχωνται δὲ καὶ ἄλλα, || οὐδ᾽ εἴ κέν σ᾽ αὐτὸν χρυσῷ ἐρύσασθαι ἀνώγοι || Δαρδανίδης Πρίαμος "so there is no one who can hold the dogs off from your head, not if they bring here and set before me ten times and twenty times the ransom, and promise more in addition, not if Priam son of Dardanos should offer to weigh out your bulk in gold" (R.L.). The two εἰ clauses display two different modes, subjunctive in l. 350, optative in l. 351—the subjunctive would metrically fit.[14] There is no variant reading.

---

14 Chantraine states at the beginning of his chapter on the moods that "many variant readings lead us to wonder whether we are dealing with a subjunctive or an optative, the

- X 219–220: οὔ οἱ νῦν ἔτι γ' ἔστι πεφυγμένον ἄμμε γενέσθαι, || οὐδ' εἴ κεν μάλα πολλὰ πάθοι ἑκάεργος Ἀπόλλων "now there is no way for him to get clear away from us, not though Apollo who strikes from afar should be willing to undergo much" (R.L.). The vulgate has an optative but several manuscripts have a subjunctive πάθῃ.
- Ψ 345–347: οὐκ ἔσθ' ὅς κέ σ' ἕλῃσι μεταλμένος οὐδὲ παρέλθῃ, || οὐδ' εἴ κεν μετόπισθεν Ἀρίονα δῖον ἐλαύνοι || Ἀδρήστου ταχὺν ἵππον "there is none who could sprint to make it up, nor close you, nor pass you, not if the man behind you were driving the great Arion, the swift horse of Adrestos" (R.L.). The vulgate has οὐδὲ παρέλθοι in the main clause.

The *Iliad* has three exceptions not agreeing with either of the described patterns. The first one is A 60, the other two are the following:

- H 386–388: ἠνώγει Πρίαμος [...] || εἰπεῖν, αἴ κέ περ ὔμμι φίλον καὶ ἡδὺ γένοιτο, || μῦθον Ἀλεξάνδροιο "Priam [...] has bidden me give you, if this message be found to your pleasure and liking, the word of Alexandros" (R.L.). The order αἴ κέ περ betrays a recent line: the regular order is εἴ πέρ κε (A 580, B 123, Θ 205, Λ 113, M 140, M 302, N 288), εἴ περ ἄν (B 597, Γ 25–26, E 224–225, E 232). There is no variant reading.
- B 597–598: στεῦτο γὰρ εὐχόμενος νικησέμεν εἴ περ ἂν αὐταί || Μοῦσαι ἀείδοιεν κοῦραι Διὸς αἰγιόχοιο "for he boasted that he would surpass, if the very Muses, daughters of Zeus who holds the aegis, were singing against him" (R.L.). This is the only case of εἴ περ ἄν followed by an optative, against three cases with a subjunctive (Γ 25–26, E 224–225, E 232). The subjunctive would metrically fit. There is no variant reading.

The vulgate's reading in A 60 does not agree with the regular pattern (conditional system with the optative and the particle in both the protasis and the apodosis, and protasis before the apodosis). It does not belong to the sub-series # οὐδ' εἴ κεν with negation. Kirk's comment "εἴ κεν with the optative in 60 is a remoter condition than εἰ with the future indicative in 61" (after Leaf) misses the point because in A 61 εἰ does not express condition but cause.[15] Basset's interpretation "if thus (that is, going back) we could escape death"[16] relies on an *ad hoc* value of κεν. And of course, Zenodotus' reading is never mentioned.

---

endings of the two modes [...] being easily liable to confusion" (*Gr. hom.* II: 205: "de nombreuses variantes nous font souvent nous demander si nous avons affaire à un subjonctif ou à un optatif, les finales de ces deux modes [...] pouvant être aisément confondues").

15 Kirk 1985: 59.
16 Basset 1989: 166–167: "«Je crois que nous ferons demi-tour si *ainsi* nous devions échapper à la mort.» Ici κεν, traduit par «ainsi», pourrait être développé par «si nous faisions demi-tour»" ("Here κεν, translated 'thus', could be developed by «if we did go back»").

2.2 Zenodotus' Reading

On the other hand, in Zenodotus' reading, we have a potential optative with the modal particle in a relative clause. Here are other instances of the same structure in the *Iliad*:[17]

- Α 62–64 ἀλλ' ἄγε δή τινα μάντιν ἐρείομεν [...] ὅς κ' εἴποι "but let us ask a seer who could tell [...]." Porphyry has the subjunctive εἴπῃ.
- Γ 234–235 νῦν δ' ἄλλους μὲν πάντας ὁρῶ [...] οὕς κεν ἐῢ γνοίην καί τ' οὔνομα μυθησαίμην "and now I see all the others, whom I could well recognise and name." There is no variant reading (but l. 235 is missing in several witnesses).
- Ε 456–457 οὐκ ἂν δὴ τόνδ' ἄνδρα μάχης ἐρύσαιο [...] Τυδεΐδην, ὃς νῦν γε καὶ ἂν Διὶ πατρὶ μάχοιτο "you could not hold back this man from the fighting [...] Tydeus' son, who would now fight even against Zeus father" (R.L. modified). There is no variant reading, but l. 457 is missing in one papyrus.
- Ο 39–40 καὶ νωΐτερον λέχος αὐτῶν || κουρίδιον, τὸ μὲν οὐκ ἂν ἐγώ ποτε μὰψ ὀμόσαιμι "and the bed of marriage between us: a thing by which I at least could never swear vainly" (R.L.). There is no variant reading.
- Ξ 90–91 σίγα, μή τίς τ' ἄλλος Ἀχαιῶν τοῦτον ἀκούσῃ || μῦθον, ὃν οὔ κεν ἀνήρ γε διὰ στόμα πάμπαν ἄγοιτο "do not say it: for fear some other Achaian might hear this word, which could never at all get past the lips of any man" (R.L.). There is no variant reading.

In these examples the relative clause follows the main clause. The use of the potential in the relative clause is that found in an independent clause, not in a conditional protasis. The structure of Zenodotus' reading in A 60 is similar. The only difference is that the relative clause expresses a restriction on the subject of the process, "we will go back, those of us who can escape death."[18]

Zenodotus' reading, fully agreeing with a regular pattern, is better from the syntactic point of view, and probably older—but it was not as good from the stylistic point of view, because there is less pathos in "those of us who can escape" than in "if ever we can escape" (see the A scholion καλὴ γὰρ ἡ ἀπόγνωσις τῆς σωτηρίας). This may have led a singer to replace the relative pronoun οἵ by the conditional conjunction εἰ—a minimal change, involving one phoneme. Since, indeed, Homer has other instances of the optative with the particle in a conditional protasis, nothing opposed it. However, Homer has other instances of this, but the only secure ones are in complete potential systems (see above). And the singer or rhapsode who changed the line was not

---

17 Schwyzer–Debrunner, *Gr. Gr.* II: 326, and Chantraine, *Gr. hom.* II: 244.
18 This relative clause is not discussed in Probert 2015 because it is not in the vulgate. However, Probert (personal communication) agrees that Zenodotus' reading is better than the vulgate's.

aware of that. Besides, the following clause (A 61) is introduced by εἰ. This may have provided the input. The result is an isolated syntactic pattern, which scholars try to explain as they can.[19] And regrettably, they forget Zenodotus' reading, which is probably older.

In this case, it is not unthinkable that the reading was introduced by Zenodotus after another copy, but since there is no positive element pointing to that, it is simpler to assume that it was the reading of his working text.

3   Z 67–71

Another nice case of "rewriting" in the vulgate in application of the rhetorical principles puzzled Greek scholars.

3.1   *Aristarchus' Reading*

Z 67–71
ὦ φίλοι ἥρωες Δαναοὶ θεράποντες Ἄρηος
μή τις νῦν ἐνάρων ἐπιβαλλόμενος μετόπισθε
μιμνέτω ὥς κε πλεῖστα φέρων ἐπὶ νῆας ἵκηται,
ἀλλ' ἄνδρας κτείνωμεν· ἔπειτα δὲ καὶ τὰ ἕκηλοι
νεκροὺς ἂμ πεδίον συλήσετε τεθνηῶτας.

O beloved Danaan fighters, henchmen of Ares, let no man any more hang back with his eye on the plunder designing to take all the spoil he can gather back to the vessels. Let us kill the men now, and afterwards at your leisure all along the plain you can plunder the perished corpses.
R.L.

Scholia comment at length on the change of person between this line and the preceding one (κτείνωμεν but συλήσετε). The vulgate's reading was considered problematic because of this inconsistency, which scholiasts tried to justify, quoting other instances.

A Schol. Z 71a1: νεκροὺς ἂμ πεδίον συλήσετε τεθνηῶτας: οὕτως Ἀρίσταρχος. ὁ δὲ Ζηνόδοτος 'Τρώων ἂμ πεδίον συλήσομεν ἔντεα νεκρούς'. Ἀθηνοκλέους δὲ

---

19   Chantraine, *Gr. hom.* II: 277 "the particle seems to insist on a specific case." Willmott 2007: 222 labels the optative "specific", but does not analyse the line.

ἐν τῷ Περὶ Ὁμήρου παρατηρήσαντος ὅτι τῷ μὲν καμάτῳ καὶ ἑαυτὸν ὁ Νέστωρ ὑποβάλλει λέγων 'κτείνωμεν' (Z 70), τὸ δὲ κέρδος ἴδιον ποιεῖται τῶν στρατιωτῶν ἐν τῷ συλήσετε, ὁ Χαῖρις (*fr.* 3 B.) Ὁμηρικὸν εἶναί φησι τὸν τῆς ἑρμηνείας χαρακτῆρα ὡς ἐν τούτοις· 'ἄλλοι μὲν γὰρ πάντες, ὅσοι θεοί εἰσ' ἐν Ὀλύμπῳ, || σοί τ' ἐπιπείθονται καὶ δεδμήμεσθα ἕκαστος' (E 877–878)· ἔδει γὰρ δέδμηνται ὡς πείθονται ἢ ἀνάπαλιν. καὶ πάλιν· 'ἀλλ' ἄγεθ', ὡς ἂν ἐγὼ εἴπω, πειθώμεθα πάντες· || νῦν μὲν δόρπον ἕλεσθε κατὰ στρατόν' (Σ 297–298), καὶ ἀλλαχοῦ· οὐδὲ γὰρ ἄλλως ἀκμάζει ὁ Νέστωρ, ἀλλ' ὑπὸ γήρως ἔοικεν ἀπειρηκέναι. ταῦτα ὁ Δίδυμος.

νεκροὺς ἂμ πεδίον συλήσετε τεθνηῶτας: this is Aristarchus' reading; but Zenodotus has Τρώων ἂμ πεδίον συλήσομεν ἔντεα νεκρούς. As Athenocles observed in his *On Homer* that Nestor includes himself into the labour, saying κτείνωμεν 'let us kill', but makes the booty proper to the soldiers in his συλήσετε 'you will spoil', Chaeris says the character of this interpretation is Homeric, as in the following lines: ἄλλοι μὲν γὰρ πάντες, ὅσοι θεοί εἰσ' ἐν Ὀλύμπῳ, || σοί τ' ἐπιπείθονται καὶ δεδμήμεσθα ἕκαστος (E 877–878) because what would have been requested is ⟨the 3pl.⟩ δέδμηνται as for πείθονται, or conversely [that is, with two 2pl. verbs, *CLF*]; and also ἀλλ' ἄγεθ', ὡς ἂν ἐγὼ εἴπω, πειθώμεθα πάντες· || νῦν μὲν δόρπον ἕλεσθε κατὰ στρατόν (Σ 297–298), and elsewhere. Because Nestor is otherwise not in the full strength of age, but seems to have given up because he is old. This is what Didymus says.

The scholion, going back to Didymus, explicitly opposes Zenodotus' text and Aristarchus', commenting on the inconsistency between the 1st plural κτείνωμεν and the 2nd plural συλήσετε. So do modern scholars,[20] with the exception of Van Thiel who assumes that συλήσομεν in Zenodotus is not a variant reading but a marginal note by which he says "συλήσετε stands for συλήσομεν, notice the change of person."[21]

However, the scholion says that Zenodotus' reading differed not only on the verb, but also on the end of the line, ἔντεα νεκρούς, on which Van Thiel does not comment, although obviously the two facts are linked. The 2nd plural συλήσετε implies that Nestor leaves the spoils to others and is above that, so to speak. It goes with the general portrayal of Nestor as the old and noble king full of wisdom as opposed to the younger Achaean leaders. Zenodotus' text is

---

20 Nickau does not comment on this variant. Kirk 1990: 162, comments only, together with the A scholion, on the change of person between this line and the preceding one (κτείνωμεν—συλήσετε). So does Stoevesandt *in* Latacz, *BK* IV: 33.

21 Van Thiel 2014b, *sub* Z 71.

given in the A scholion because it has a 1st pl. συλήσομεν in l. 71. That implies, although it is not said explicitly, that he also had a 1st pl. κτείνωμεν in l. 70 and that the inconsistency did not exist in Zenodotus' version, which has κτείνωμεν and συλήσομεν.

Modern commentators usually dismiss Zenodotus' reading, because it is Zenodotus' and because of a reason very clearly stated in Graziosi–Haubold: "Nestor switches back from the 1st to the 2nd pers. plur. This is unusual at the end of an exhortation, but effectively makes the point that Nestor does *not* care about the spoils. Zenodotus preferred to read Τρώων ἂμ πεδίον συλήσομεν ἔντεα νεκρούς, apparently because he wanted Nestor to join the others in the taking of the spoils. His text is less convincing rhetorically than that of the vulgate."[22] This is typical of Alexandrian scholarship. Rhetorical effectiveness was a criterion according to which Alexandrian scholars did judge Homeric lines, but was it the case for archaic singers? It is understandable that for a Hellenistic scholar killing the enemies was worthy of Nestor, as a proof of his valiance despite his old age, but that leaving the spoils to others was a proof of magnanimity and of disdain for material goods: that builds an image of Nestor as a Hellenistic philosopher, but that is miles away from archaic conceptions in which the spoils are considered first for their material price, because bronze was expensive, and secondly, and more importantly in the epic context, as the proof of victory, often given as an offering to a god. The disdain for the spoils is anachronistic for archaic times. Killing the enemy and taking the spoils are indissociable.[23] Thus, the formal problem (the inconsistency in the verbal person) is not the only one.

Scholiasts also comment on the redundant νεκρούς ... τεθνηῶτας:

bT Schol. Z 71b: τὸ δὲ νεκρούς τεθνηῶτας ὡς 'τάφρον ὀρυκτήν' (Ι 67).

the νεκρούς τεθνηῶτας is similar to τάφρον ὀρυκτήν 'the dug ditch' (Ι 67).

---

22   Graziosi–Haubold 2010: 94. The formulation "preferred to read [...] because he wanted" illustrates very clearly the *doxa*: Zenodotus arbitrarily changed the text according to his fantasy and his personal taste. Zenodotus did not "prefer to read," he *did* read in his text, which is entirely different.

23   See Λ 755 where Nestor is speaking of his prowesses when he was younger: κτείνοντές τ' αὐτοὺς ἀνά τ' ἔντεα καλὰ λέγοντες "killing the men themselves, and picking up their magnificent armour;" Λ 432 τοιώδ' ἄνδρε κατακτείνας καὶ τεύχε' ἀπούρας "for having killed two such men as we and stripping our armour;" Ε 435 ἵετο δ' αἰεὶ || Αἰνείαν κτεῖναι καὶ ἀπὸ κλυτὰ τεύχεα δῦσαι "but ⟨Diomedes⟩ forever forward drove, to kill Aineias and strip his glorious armour" (R.L. in all three lines). To which one may add, of course, the meaning of ἐναρίζω, ἐξεναρίζω 'to strip of his weapons', which came to mean simply 'to kill in combat'.

As a matter of fact, this same redundancy occurs elsewhere: Π 526, 565 ἀμφὶ νέκυι κατατεθνηῶτι #, Σ 173 νέκυος πέρι τεθνηῶτος #, Κ 343 νεκύων κατατεθνηώτων #, Σ 540 # νεκροὺς ... κατατεθνηῶτας #, the latter with the same position of νεκρούς and τεθνηῶτας at the beginning and end of the line. This can be used to back Aristarchus' reading, but one could also assume that the latter was modelled on those cases, in particular Σ 540. Zenodotus' reading, on the other hand, is free from that redundancy.

Now the inconsistency in verbal person, the anachronistic disdain for the spoils and the redundancy are not the only problems. In Aristarchus' reading, we have a double accusative, τά and νεκρούς; τά is anaphoric, referring to ἔναρα 'spoils' in the preceding sentence (ἐνάρων Ζ 68). However, this is semantically problematic, although no ancient or modern scholar seems to have noticed it.

The construction of συλάω 'to strip' in the *Iliad* is the following: it is used with a double accusative, as its first object τεύχεα 'weapons', and as its second object the body of the dead enemy (N 201–202, Ο 427–428, Π 499–500, Χ 258, Ρ 59–60). Often the dead enemy is implicit because it is already the object of the preceding clause and we have a zero anaphora (Δ 466, Ε 164, Ε 618, Ζ 28, Η 78, Η 82, Ο 524, Ο 544–545, Ο 583, Χ 368, Ν 640–641). Λ 110 has the prepositional construction ἀπὸ τοῖιν ἐσύλα τεύχεα καλά, after the regular ὁ δ' ἀπ' ὤμων τεύχε' ἐσύλα # (Ο 524, Χ 368). The weapons are always mentioned, almost always under the form τεύχεα, once as the vocalic variant ἔντεα (N 640–641 "Ὣς εἰπὼν τὰ μὲν ἔντε' ἀπὸ χροὸς αἱματόεντα || συλήσας ἑτάροισι δίδου Μενέλαος ἀμύμων "so Menelaos the blameless spoke, and stripping the bloody armour away from his body gave it to his companions", R.L.). The verb is found once with the second object (the man) only, in a recent line from the Doloneia (ἤ τινα συλήσων νεκύων κατατεθνηώτων "or to strip some one of the perished corpses" Κ 343 = Κ 387, R.L.).[24]

However, the verb is *never* used with ἔναρα as an object, either in Homer or after Homer. This is not surprising, for ἔναρα refers to the spoils after the enemy has been stripped of his weapons, never to the armour on the body. One can strip an enemy of his τεύχεα or ἔντεα, not of his ἔναρα because there are no ἔναρα before stripping. This is also the reason why the denominative verb ἐναρίζω 'to strip' is used with τεύχεα as an object.

---

24 The doublet συλεύω is used only twice, with an animate object only. In Ε 48 it has the same meaning as συλάω. In Ω 435–436 it means, not 'to strip someone of his arms', but 'to deprive' (here to deprive Achilles of part of the ransom destined to him): this is an extended use.

Clearly, from the semantic point of view, the vulgate's reading is problematic, although this has gone unnoticed, for ἔναρα cannot be the object of συλάω, and consequently τά, object of συλάω, cannot be anaphoric of ἔναρα. It is highly unlikely that the semantic distinction between ἔναρα and τεύχεα was lost, and the only way out would be to assume that from the ἔναρα 'spoils' of line 68 was inferred the hyperonym τεύχεα, also a neuter plural, which is the real referent of the anaphoric pronoun τά.[25] This is probably the analysis underlying Aristarchus' reading, but it must be secondary. The line cannot have been created with a τά object of συλάω and referring to ἔναρα, and Aristarchus' reading must be the rearrangement of an older structure in which τά had a different function, or a different referent.

The semantic evolution of συλάω confirms that the vulgate's reading is not old. As a matter of fact, συλάω came to mean 'to seize' with an object other than the name of a weapon. This is the meaning of the verb in Greek inscriptions of the classical period. A first step of the evolution can be seen in the *Iliad*. The word is supposed to mean 'to denude' an object (*LfgrE*), in Δ 105 # αὐτίκ' ἐσύλα τόξον ἔϋξοον "straightway he unwrapped his polished bow" (R.L. modified). In this line Pandaros takes his bow to shoot at Menelaus, yet the bow was certainly not in a bowcase, but on his shoulder, since he is on the battlefield. Thus, it cannot be 'unwrapped' or 'denuded'. It is likely that this line was taken from a context where the meaning of συλάω was regular, that is, when a warrior strips the killed enemy of his weapons, τόξον occupying the position of τεύχεα as first object. Then the line was secondarily reused in a new context, which implies a semantic distortion of the verb, not fitting well in the new context. Here the most likely meaning is "he took from his shoulder," the distortion being that in the regular use the shoulders are the dead enemy's (see Z 28 = O 524 = X 370: [...] ἀπ' ὤμων τεύχε' ἐσύλα), whereas here they are his own. The *LSJ* rightly translates 'take off'.[26] The other abnormal use, from the same episode, is Δ 116 # αὐτὰρ ὁ σύλα πῶμα φαρέτρης "he stripped away the lid of the quiver" (R.L.), where the meaning is reduced to 'take away from', 'take off', and is derived from the preceding one. Both lines show the same extended meaning of συλάω and could be due to one and the same singer. The compound ἱερόσυλος 'stripping the sacred' (Attic), that is, stealing sacred objects from a sanctuary, shows the

---

25 Jacquinod 1989: 216, does not mention Zenodotus' reading but only the vulgate and assumes explicitly that τά is anaphoric of ἔναρα.
26 A bT scholion has an interesting interpretation: ἐσύλα τόξον: ὅτι ἡσυχῇ μέλλει κλέπτειν τὴν πρᾶξιν ἢ θεῶν πίστιν λύειν ὡς ἱερόσυλος "because silently he is going to steal the deed or to destroy the gods' truce as a sacrilege thief" (*bT Schol.* Δ 105a), where the compound ἱερόσυλος lends to ἐσύλα τόξον the idea of theft.

extension of use to another object than the weapons, outside a military context. In Greek inscriptions συλάω means 'to seize', 'to take hold of' a man and the original meaning is lost.[27]

Now in Z 71 ἔναρα cannot be the object of συλάω if the verb has its proper meaning, but the problem disappears once συλάω has evolved towards the meaning 'to seize', 'to take away from', as it appears in Δ 116 # αὐτὰρ ὁ σύλα πῶμα φαρέτρης. One cannot 'strip the spoils' but one can 'seize the spoils'. This means that ἔναρα could be reanalysed as the object of συλάω only after this semantic evolution of the verb was acquired. This is a confirmation that the line as it appears in the vulgate is not old.

3.2   Zenodotus' Reading

Zenodotus' text was different in several respects, as mentioned above, and in particular for the use of συλάω:

Z 70–71 (Zen.)
ἀλλ' ἄνδρας κτείνωμεν· ἔπειτα δὲ καὶ τὰ ἔκηλοι
Τρώων ἂμ πεδίον συλήσομεν ἔντεα νεκρούς

> Let us kill the men, and afterwards at leisure, in the Trojan plain, those we will plunder, the armours of the dead.

We have no indication of a variant reading for l. 70. Since Zenodotus' text is given as different for l. 71 only, the default assumption is that in his text l. 70 was identical with the vulgate's text. For l. 71, Zenodotus' # Τρώων ἂμ πεδίον is a modification of the usual prepositional phrase ἐν πεδίῳ Τρώων (Λ 836, Ο 739, λ 513) which is never line-initial, whereas Aristarchus has two nouns with no direct syntactic link between them.

With Zenodotus' reading, assuming l. 70 was not different from the vulgate's, there is no problem of reference because the referent of τά is ἔντεα, regular object of συλάω as the vocalic variant of τεύχεα. This reading is compatible with the proper meaning of the verb, and the pronoun is cataphoric. The old cataphoric value of *to- is lost in classical and *koine* Greek, where it was taken over by the recharacterised form ὅδε, τόδε, but can still be seen in several Homeric lines.

The pattern is similar to that of the following lines, which display a right dislocation. The noun, whatever its function, is postponed to the end of the clause,

---

27   On the use of συλάω in classical texts and in epigraphy, see Bravo 1980.

and its logical position within the clause is filled by a cataphoric pronoun in the required case.[28] In the following examples, most of which are already quoted by Chantraine,[29] the cataphoric pronoun is in blue, and the referent is in red.

- N 83–84 τόφρα δὲ τοὺς ὄπιθεν γαιήοχος ὦρσεν Ἀχαιούς, || οἳ παρὰ νηυσὶ θοῇσιν ἀνέψυχον φίλον ἦτορ "meanwhile the earth-encircler stirred them up behind, the Achaians, who were cooling the heat of the inward heart back beside their vessels" (R.L. modified): the preceding lines are a dialogue between the two Ajax, and the rest of the army is not mentioned;
- ο 54–55 τοῦ γάρ τε ξεῖνος μιμνήσκεται ἤματα πάντα || ἀνδρὸς ξεινοδόκου, ὅς κεν φιλότητα παράσχῃ "for a guest remembers all his days that man, the host who furnished him with friendship" (J.H.);
- Φ 89–91 τῆς δὲ δύω γενόμεσθα, σὺ δ' ἄμφω δειροτομήσεις, || ἤτοι τὸν πρώτοισι μετὰ πρυλέεσσι δάμασσας || ἀντίθεον Πολύδωρον "we are two sons who were born to her. You will have cut the throat of both, since that one you beat down in the forefront of the foot-fighters, Polydoros the godlike" (R.L. modified).

This pattern is particularly frequent when there is a particle, as in

- E 321 ἀλλ' ὅ γε τοὺς μὲν ἑοὺς ἠρύκακε μώνυχας ἵππους "but he held them, their own single-foot horses" (R.L. modified): the horses have not been mentioned previously, and τούς is cataphoric;
- Ω 472–475 ἐν δέ μιν αὐτὸν || εὗρ', ἕταροι δ' ἀπάνευθε καθήατο· τὼ δὲ δύ' οἴω || ἥρως Αὐτομέδων τε καὶ Ἄλκιμος ὄζος Ἄρηος || ποίπνυον παρεόντε "he found him inside, and his companions were sitting apart, as those two only, Automedon the hero and Alkimos, scion of Ares, were busy beside him" (R.L. modified): Automedon and Alkimos have not been mentioned before, and this cannot be analysed as a case of an article with the numeral like οἱ τρεῖς 'the three of them';
- A 408–409 αἴ κέν πως ἐθέλῃσιν ἐπὶ Τρώεσσιν ἀρῆξαι || τοὺς δὲ κατὰ πρύμνας τε καὶ ἀμφ' ἅλα ἔλσαι Ἀχαιούς "if perhaps he might be willing to help the Trojans, and pin those back against the ships and the water, the Achaians" (R.L. modified);
- Ω 281–282 Τὼ μὲν ζευγνύσθην ἐν δώμασιν ὑψηλοῖσι || κῆρυξ καὶ Πρίαμος πυκινὰ φρεσὶ μήδε' ἔχοντες "for them in the high house the yoking was done, for the herald and Priam, men both with close counsels in their minds" (R.L. modified): the preceding lines are about Priam's sons, and the pair Priam and the

---

28 See on those problems of right and left dislocation in Homer Bakker 1990 who, however, deals almost exclusively with cases where the dislocated element is the subject.

29 Chantraine, *Gr. hom.* II: 161.

herald has not been mentioned before. Τώ can be understood here as the adverb 'therefore', with most translators (Lattimore translates "now"), but it can as well be understood as the dual pronoun, cataphoric of κῆρυξ καὶ Πρίαμος, and subject of ζευγνύσθην, as in Ω 473–474 above: this dual pronoun could be easily reinterpreted as the adverb, and probably was in more than one case;[30]

- Λ 723–724 ὄθι μείναμεν Ἠῶ δῖαν ‖ ἱππῆες Πυλίων, τὰ δ' ἐπέρρεον ἔθνεα πεζῶν "There we waited for the divine Dawn, we horsemen among the Pylians, and they were streaming, the troops of infantry" (R.L. modified):
- Ε 519–520 Τοὺς δ' Αἴαντε δύω καὶ Ὀδυσσεὺς καὶ Διομήδης ‖ ὄτρυνον Δαναοὺς πολεμιζέμεν "and them the two Aiantes and Odysseus and Diomedes were stirring to fight, the Danaans" (R.L. modified): lines 512–518 are about the Trojans, not the Achaeans;
- Ε 508–509 τοῦ δ' ἐκραίαινεν ἐφετμὰς ‖ Φοίβου Ἀπόλλωνος χρυσαόρου, ὅς μιν ἀνώγει ‖ Τρωσὶν θυμὸν ἐγεῖραι "of him he was carrying out the commandments, of Phoibos Apollo of the golden sword, who had bidden him wake the heart in the Trojans" (R.L. modified): Apollo has not been mentioned since E 460;
- Ι 587–589 ἀλλ' οὐδ' ὣς τοῦ θυμὸν ἐνὶ στήθεσσιν ἔπειθον, ‖ πρίν γ' ὅτε δὴ θάλαμος πύκ' ἐβάλλετο, τοὶ δ' ἐπὶ πύργων ‖ βαῖνον Κουρῆτες καὶ ἐνέπρηθον μέγα ἄστυ "but even so they could not persuade the heart within him until, as the chamber was under close assault, those were mounting along the towers, the Kouretes, and set fire to the great city" (R.L. modified): the τοί cannot be anaphoric because the plural subject of the preceding clause are Meleager's relatives, not the Kouretes.

With a particle, those τοὺς μέν or τοὺς δέ were readily analysed in the synchrony of classical or *koine* Greek as the anaphoric pronoun, followed by an apposition, and not as a cataphoric element. In A 408–409 one can infer from l. 408 ἐπὶ Τρώεσσιν ἀρῆξαι that τοὺς δέ refers to the other side, the Achaeans, so that the cataphoric value may have been lost. In I 588–589 in the context of the war one can infer from ἐβάλλετο that τοὶ δέ refers to the enemy, that is, the Kouretes. Cases where there was no particle, however, which are less frequent, were probably odd for rhapsodes and for scholars alike because they were not matched by a similar structure in classical or *koine* Greek. In N 82–83 the presence of a relative clause may have led to the interpretation of τούς as correlative of οἵ, according to a frequent pattern where the cataphoric pronoun is preserved. In Φ 89–91 the presence of ἄμφω in l. 89 could lead to the interpretation of τόν in

---

30 Probably also in δ 20–21, ο 301–302, π 1–2, π 333, τ 31.

l. 90 as anaphoric rather than cataphoric. Thus, on the whole, cataphoric *to-, except when followed by a relative clause, was not well preserved unless combined with a particle.

Zenodotus' version ἀλλ' ἄνδρας κτείνωμεν· ἔπειτα δὲ καὶ τὰ ἕκηλοι || Τρώων ἂμ πεδίον συλήσομεν ἔντεα νεκρούς is then syntactically and semantically regular, but displays a pattern which is old and not productive. The position of the cataphoric pronoun after an adverb and not in clause-initial position matches that of N 82–83 (τόφρα δὲ τοὺς ὄπιθεν γαιήοχος ὦρσεν Ἀχαιούς), and the position of the noun in the right periphery, after the verb, is that of almost all the instances quoted above. To that can be added that the postponed noun or syntagm is often found in a metrically prominent position, after the bucolic (Z 70–71, E 321, Λ 723–724), at the end of the line (N 82–83, A 408–409, in both cases the adonic colon is V + O) or in line initial position (o 54–55, E 508–509). Therefore it is not likely that Zenodotus used this rare and old pattern in a conjecture of his, on the contrary it must be an old reading he found in his working text. Kirk assumed that Zenodotus' text was "perhaps designed to explain τά in 70, which must otherwise refer to 68 ἐνάρων as a double acc."[31] That is to say that, once more, he assumes that Zenodotus modified (for the worse, of course) the correct text. But in either case there is a double accusative, regular with συλάω, and the problem is precisely that τά cannot be anaphoric of ἐνάρων, which cannot be the object of συλάω in the regular Homeric construction of the verb.

If Zenodotus' version is old, there was already a τά in the line, which did not refer to ἔναρα but to a noun which is the regular object of συλάω, that is, ἔντεα. As anaphoric *to- is much more frequent than cataphoric *to-, this τά, not combined with a particle, may have been reanalysed as anaphoric, and referred to the only compatible element in the preceding context, namely ἔναρα. Although this is semantically abnormal for Homer, it is not unusual for classical Attic-Ionic where the meaning of the verb has evolved. That is, the semantic irregularity would be secondary, being the result of a wrong interpretation of a pre-existing structure, whereas if we take Aristarchus' reading as older, the semantic irregularity would be primary, which is rather unlikely. Then ἔντεα, which felt odd and superfluous since there was already an object, was eliminated. This, however, was done at the cost of a redundancy (νεκρούς ... τεθνηῶτας, on the model of Σ 540, since νεκρούς was already present in the line and τεθνηῶτας could occupy the adonic colon, as a metrical filler) and of a change of the 1pl. in l. 70 into a 2pl. in l. 71 since before τεθνηῶτας a vowel-final word is required. Those are the points scholiasts tried to justify, which shows

---

31 Kirk 1990: 162.

that they were aware of the problem, but they did not see that below this problem was lying a hidden inconsistency which was a bigger one.

I would therefore reverse Kirk's hypothesis: Zenodotus' reading cannot be a creation of his, and Aristarchus' reading is an emendation—maybe older than Aristarchus—prompted by two reasons. The first reason is linguistic: the cataphoric use of *to- was no longer usual except when combined with a particle, or followed by a relative clause; that explains why the pronoun was reanalysed as anaphoric. The second one is stylistic: as Graziosi–Haubold put it, Zenodotus' reading "is less convincing rhetorically than that of the vulgate." We must not forget that the reason why Aristarchus' text was deemed better than Zenodotus' may be that it suited Alexandrian taste better—because it was designed for Alexandrian taste. As we have seen above (pp. 57–60), rhetorical conventions did intervene in Aristarchus' *ekdosis* and in the vulgate, as is the case for A 260 (ὑμῖν/ἡμῖν), O 356 (χερσίν/ποσσίν), B 681 (the new beginning for the list of Thessalian cities, pp. 243–250). Those conventions were responsible for emendations aiming at making the discourse more persuasive or at conforming it to the contemporary rules of rhetorics. Although here the rhetorically correct formulation is obtained at the expense of the syntactically and semantically correct one, as in B 681, it was nevertheless defended by scholiasts who saw everything through the prism of rhetorics. That does not mean that Zenodotus did not care about rhetorics, as he received the same education and training as all Hellenistic scholars, but that could mean that he was more conservative and did not alter his working text so easily—the exact opposite of the reputation he has gained thanks to Aristarchus.

4   Λ 458

In some cases Zenodotus' readings have a consequence for historical syntax, although this is not taken into account by linguists. This is the case in particular for some uses of the absolute participle, as in the following lines:

Λ 456–458
Ὣς εἰπὼν Σώκοιο δαΐφρονος ὄβριμον ἔγχος
ἔξω τε χροὸς ἕλκε καὶ ἀσπίδος ὀμφαλοέσσης·
αἷμα δέ οἱ σπασθέντος ἀνέσσυτο, κῆδε δὲ θυμόν.

So he spoke, and dragged the heavy spear of wise Sokos out of his flesh and out of the shield massive in the middle, and as it was torn out the blood sprang and his heart was sickened.
    R.L.

Line 458 has a striking feature, the use of what looks like a genitive absolute, without any subject, σπασθέντος. This is rare in the Homeric epics. This line, among others, was used by Chantraine, after Meillet, as an argument in favour of the free use of the participle in an older state of the language,[32] before definite case forms were grammaticalised as the regular means of expressing circumstantial relationships.

However, Zenodotus had for this line a different reading.

> *A Schol.* Λ 458a: (Didymus) αἷμα δέ οἱ σπασθέντος: οὕτως Ἀρίσταρχος οἱ, αἷμα δὲ αὐτῷ τῷ Ὀδυσσεῖ. Ζηνόδοτος δὲ γράφει 'αἷμα δὲ οὗ σπασθέντος'· γίνεται δὲ τὸ ἑαυτοῦ, ὃ οὐχ ἁρμόζει.
>
> αἷμα δέ οἱ σπασθέντος: this is Aristarchus' reading, with οἱ, the blood of Odysseus himself. But Zenodotus writes αἷμα δὲ οὗ σπασθέντος: it becomes 'himself', which does not fit.

Here again Zenodotus is credited with an incorrect reading in the context. But once more, assuming that one reading is derived from the other, it is hard to see why οἱ, if it was the original reading, would have been corrected into οὗ, which does not make sense, as the scholiast says, whereas one can easily understand that a bizarre οὗ was corrected into οἱ. Accordingly, it is likely that Zenodotus' reading is older.

Aristarchus here does not take into account the existence of two different forms, the reflexive pronoun οὗ, stressed, and the anaphoric pronoun οὐ, clitic. Aristarchus is right that the form here cannot be the reflexive pronoun. But what if it were the anaphoric pronoun? Zenodotus' text probably did not have accentual marks, and at any rate before accentual marks were written down, the form was simply ⟨ΟΥ⟩. This genitive obviously goes together with the participle σπασθέντος, and refers to the object of the preceding phrase, ἔγχος, subject of σπασθέντος. Although the anaphoric pronoun *s*ᵤ*e-* > ἑ mostly refers to an animate, it can refer to an inanimate: in Α 236 it refers to σκῆπτρον, in Φ 523 to κάπνος, in Λ 29 to ξίφος. As a result, we obtain a regular structure "and the spear having been pulled out, blood gushed out, and wounded his heart." That can be interpreted as a genitive absolute, with the anaphoric subject of the participle, or as a structure with a dominant participle:[33] blood gushed out from the pulling out of the spear. The second hypothesis is much better: the subject of

---

32   Chantraine, *Gr. hom.* II: 322–323.
33   On the dominant participle in Greek, see Denizot 2017. The structure is so named after the fact that the participle is formally the modifier of the head noun but is in fact the

a genitive absolute cannot be a clitic pronoun, whereas a verbal complement can. Compare a similar structure in O 199 οἵ ἕθεν ὀτρύνοντος ἀκούσονται "who obey his orders," with the Aeolic variant of ἑο, a dominant participle functioning as the object of ἀκούσονται. The construction of ἀνασεύομαι with an ablatival genitive is expected, although unattested in Homer (contrary to ἐκσεύομαι + genitive). It is found much later in Nonnos, *Dion.* 42.441 ἀνεσσύμενος δὲ θαλάσσης # "leaping out from the sea." Nonnos may be imitating here another epic poet.

That means that Zenodotus' reading is not a nonsensical one, but is syntactically and semantically correct, save for the fact that the form was transmitted as a stressed οὗ instead of a clitic οὑ—probably not by Zenodotus himself but because of Aristarchus' misinterpretation of Zenodotus' reading. The vulgate has no instance of clitic οὑ, but has anaphoric (clitic) εὑ and ἑο.[34] As it is certain that this form did exist, it means that it was eliminated everywhere by Alexandrian scholars, replaced by εὑ or οἱ. Needless to say, "everywhere" would include this line.

Now the line cannot be very old with οὑ, the contracted form. We know that Zenodotus systematically had ἑοῦ or οὗ for the genitive of the reflexive pronoun and the anaphoric pronoun where the vulgate had the uncontracted form (B 239, T 384, Y 261, η 217). If we restore the uncontracted form ἑο < *ϝεho < *sṷeso, we obtain # *αἷμα δ' ἑο σπασθέντος with neglect of the initial ϝ of ϝεο. That can mean either that the line is fairly recent, created after the loss of ϝ, or that it results from a modification of an older line. In the latter case, I would suggest that the older line was # *αἷμά ϝεο σπασθέντος ἀνέσσυτο, and that the problem arose when the coordinating conjunction δέ was added because the general structure of the sentence required it. That could generate either # αἷμα δ' ἑο σπασθέντος ἀνέσσυτο, with neglect of the ϝ, or *αἷμα δέ οὑ σπασθέντος ἀνέσσυτο with ϝ and a contraction, which could have been remodelled into αἷμα δέ οἱ σπασθέντος ἀνέσσυτο (Aristarchus' reading), with a possessive dative referring to an animate, Ulysses. The interest of the reading οἱ is that it underlines the fact that Ulysses himself spills his own blood, adding to the pathos of the scene, as underlined by the scholiast (αἷμα δὲ αὐτῷ τῷ Ὀδυσσεῖ). This reading may have been considered stylistically more expressive, therefore better.[35]

---

semantically dominant element: Hdt 1.34.1 μετὰ Σόλωνα οἰχόμενον "after the departure of Solon" (lit. "after Solon leaving").

34   See the examples in Petit 1999: 20–22.
35   See comments like the A scholion to Λ 841 ἀλλ' οὐδ' ὥς περ σεῖο μεθήσω τειρομένοιο: Ζηνόδοτος '†δὲ† ἀμελήσω'. ποιητικώτερον δὲ τὸ ἕτερον "Zenodotus ⟨has⟩ †δὲ† ἀμελήσω 'I will neglect', but the other one is more poetic."

To sum up: Zenodotus' reading may well be older than Aristarchus', and it is likely that there was here a structure with a dominant participle. Therefore, if the reading αἷμα δέ οἱ σπασθέντος ἀνέσσυτο is secondary, one should not rely on it as a proof of the syntactic freedom of the participle in early Greek.

5 Γ 210–211

This leads to another remark about the absolute participle. In Γ 211 the vulgate has what seems to be a nominative absolute, taken at face value by all linguists:

Γ 210–211
στάντων μὲν Μενέλαος ὑπείρεχεν εὐρέας ὤμους,
ἄμφω δ' ἑζομένω γεραρώτερος ἦεν Ὀδυσσεύς

of the two standing Menelaus was bigger by his broad shoulders, but Odysseus was the more lordly when both were seated.
    R.L. modified

Aristonicus says:

A Schol. Γ 211a1: ἄμφω δ' ἑζομένω, γεραρώτερος ἦεν Ὀδυσσεύς: ὅτι Ζηνόδοτος σὺν τῷ ν γράφει ἑζομένων. τὸ δὲ ἄμφω δύο πτώσεις ἔχει, ἀμφότεροι ἢ ἀμφοτέρους. καὶ νῦν λέγει ἀμφότεροι δὲ καθήμενοι, κατ' ἐναλλαγὴν πτώσεως, ἀντὶ τοῦ καθημένων δὲ ἀμφοτέρων, καὶ ἔστι σύνηθες, ὡς ἐπ' ἐκείνου 'οἱ δὲ δύο σκόπελοι, ὁ μέν' (μ 73), ἀντὶ ⟨τοῦ⟩ τῶν δύο σκοπέλων.

because Zenodotus writes ἑζομένων with -n. But ἄμφω only has two cases, nominative and accusative. Here Homer says 'both sitting' in the nominative (ἀμφότεροι δὲ καθήμενοι), with a change of case form, instead of καθημένων δὲ ἀμφοτέρων in the genitive. And this is customary, as in the οἱ δὲ δύο σκόπελοι, ὁ μέν (μ 73), instead of τῶν δύο σκοπέλων.

T Schol. Γ 211a2: ὡς τὸ 'σὺν δὲ δύ' ἐρχομένω' (Κ 224) καὶ 'οἱ δὲ δύο σκόπελοι'.

as the 'σὺν δὲ δύ' ἐρχομένω' (Κ 224) καὶ 'οἱ δὲ δύο σκόπελοι' (the σὺν δὲ δύ' ἐρχομένω was dropped in the A scholion, which retains only one of the two examples provided by Aristonicus).

This line has been cited in commentaries as a clear example of a nominative absolute: Holland compares Γ 210 στάντων μὲν Μενέλαος ὑπείρεχεν εὐρέας ὤμους, with the genitive, and states that these lines "demonstrate the equivalence of nominative and genitive absolutes in Greek"[36] (which is not correct because στάντων is not a genitive absolute but is required by ὑπερ-).[37] Holland, as always, does not mention Zenodotus' reading, but Zenodotus does have the expected genitive, consistent with στάντων in the preceding line. In line 211 the genitive is triggered by γεραρώτερος, a comparative instead of a superlative because there are only two elements compared. In fact, it is a partitive genitive, which is the inherited construction of superlatives. With Zenodotus' reading, there is no absolute participle at all, neither nominative absolute nor genitive absolute.

Is Zenodotus' reading an emendation of the vulgate's, replacing the abnormal nominative by a regular genitive? The nominative is clearly the *lectio difficilior*—given the genitive is the expected case, replacement is certainly a possibility. On the other hand, it is not very likely that a consistent syntagm ἄμφω δ' ἑζομένω was replaced by ἄμφω δ' ἑζομένων with internal inconsistency and lack of agreement between the participle and its subject. That means that Zenodotus probably found this reading in his working text and did not invent it. I suspect that the problem is rather with ἄμφω, the old genitive of which, ἀμφοῖν, had been lost (it is unattested in Homer, but attested in *H.Merc.* 50, and well attested in lyric poetry), so that a regular genitive *ἀμφοῖν δ' ἑζομένοιν, with the loss of the dual, had to be remodelled in Ionic. Ionic, as is well known, lost the dual early on, whereas Attic is more conservative and preserves the dual. This was Aristarchus' main argument to assert that Homer was an Athenian, because the dual is typically Attic (*A Schol.* N 197 ὅτι συνεχῶς κέχρηται τοῖς δυϊκοῖς. ἡ δὲ ἀναφορὰ πρὸς τὰ περὶ τῆς πατρίδος. Ἀθηναίων γὰρ ἴδιον "because he consistently uses the dual. This is a reference to his fatherland: because ⟨the dual⟩ is specifically Attic"). There are countless instances of hesitations and inconsistencies between dual and plural in the vulgate, because singers had inherited lines with a dual in their repertoire, which could not always be modernised (from the point of view of Ionic) into a plural because of their metrical structure.[38]

---

36 Holland 1986: 176. Same analysis as a *Nominativus pendens* in Maiocco 2005: 5, without any mention of Zenodotus' variant reading.
37 *Pace* Vasilaros 1993: 88–89 who analyses it as a subjectless genitive absolute.
38 For verbal forms, the A scholia report that Zenodotus had in several lines the secondary dual ending -την where the primary ending -τον is expected (K 545, Λ 782), which points to the loss of functional oppositions for the dual in Ionic.

A first (and trivial) modernisation is the shift to the plural in Zenodotus' version because of the loss of the dual, with the genitive case maintained for the participle (ἑζομένων, metrically equivalent to ἑζομένοιν) and an indeclinable form ἄμφω for the numeral. In Zenodotus' *ekdosis* the confusion between oblique and direct dual case forms is frequent in pronouns (A 336 σφῶϊ (vulgate) *vs* σφῶιν (Zenodotus), Θ 377 and X 216 νῶϊ (vulgate) *vs* νῶιν (Zenodotus)), a consequence of the early loss of the dual in Ionic. Another consequence of the latter is the confusion between second person and third person dual pronouns: Zenodotus had in A 8 σφωι 'the two of you' *vs* vulgate σφωέ 'the two of them'. It is of course pinpointed by Aristonicus as a proof that Zenodotus was not good at Homeric morphology and syntax. In Θ 139, Zenodotus had Τυδείδη, ἄγε νῶι φόβον δ' ἔχε μώνυχας ἵππους "son of Tydeus, see, he threw our horses into panic" *vs* vulgate Τυδείδη, ἄγε δ' αὖτε φόβον δ' ἔχε μώνυχας ἵππους. Aristonicus condemns, saying that νῶι "is nominative or accusative, none of which fits."[39] Zenodotus' reading implies that the direct case νῶι was used for the dative νῶιν. Therefore the use of ἄμφω as an oblique case form would not be very surprising.

Then a second modernisation took place. As the A scholion states, "ἄμφω has only two cases, nominative and accusative" (see above), so that the genitive could not be maintained with ἄμφω and was changed into a secondary nominative ἑζομένω agreeing with ἄμφω, but στάντων in the preceding line remained unchanged. This is the result of a regularising process based on the observation of the occurrences of ἄμφω (61 in the vulgate including this one), which leads to the elimination of this abnormal occurrence where ἄμφω would be neither nominative nor accusative. This reading cannot have directly replaced an original *ἀμφοῖν δ' ἑζομένοιν but implies the intermediate step of Zenodotus' reading ἄμφω δ' ἑζομένων, of which it is a correction. The correction may be by Aristarchus himself, or may be due to a singer who mechanically applied agreement with the subject ἄμφω, with this version ending up as Aristarchus' working text. The use of analogy to back this reading by a similar structure is Aristarchus'. However, μ 73 is a clear case of *nominativus pendens*, but not a case of absolute participle, and K 224, which has a participle, is found in the notoriously recent Doloneia and is a problematic line.[40] Moreover, K 224 has, as Γ 211,

---

39 A *Schol.* Θ 139: ὅ ἐστιν ἡμεῖς ἢ ἡμᾶς, ὧν οὐδέτερον ἁρμόζει.
40 K 224–226 in the vulgate read σύν τε δύ' ἐρχομένω καί τε πρὸ ὃ τοῦ ἐνόησεν ‖ ὅππως κέρδος ἔῃ· μοῦνος δ' εἴ πέρ τε νοήσῃ ‖ ἀλλά τέ οἱ βράσσων τε νόος, λεπτὴ δέ τε μῆτις "when two go together, one of them at least looks forward to see what is best; a man by himself, though he be careful, still has less mind in him than two, and his wits have less weight" (R.L.). There again there was a variant ἐρχομένων. The vulgate's reading is quoted by Plato, *Prot.* 348d, which provides a *terminus ante quem*. The contracted τοῦ in arsis is not old, and there is no instance in all the Homeric corpus of a sequence *πρὸ ὅ/ὅ (here προνοέω in tmesis). Moreover, K 226 cannot be old, which suggests the three lines are a late addition.

a numeral meaning 'two' as the head of the participial clause (δύο/ἄμφω), followed by a main clause where the subject, singular, is one of the 'two' of the participial clause, of which the participle belongs to the same lexical field of verbs expressing a position in space, with the same metrical structure and in the same position before the penthemimeral caesura (σύν τε δύ' ἐρχομένω καί τε πρὸ ὃ τοῦ ἐνόησεν / ἄμφω δ' ἑζομένω γεραρώτερος ἦεν Ὀδυσσεύς). The parallelism is so obvious that we may suspect one line was modelled after the other. The use of analogy is difficult: Greek grammarians used it as a proof that the form was regular, but of course they could not take into account the diachronic factor and have the idea that one line may have been modelled after another line. Moreover, they sometimes use the existence of a similar structure in the corpus to condemn a different reading, wrongly, as for instance in the case of ὄπα χάλκεον (see above, pp. 49–50), which they favoured for the sake of the σχῆμα. This is unavoidable. Modern linguists, myself included, do the same. To sum up, if K 224 was modelled after Γ 211, it cannot prove anything.

There again, if Zenodotus' reading is older than the vulgate's, which is likely, this alleged "nominative absolute" would not be old at all. The only argument in favour of the vulgate's reading is the fact that the nominative is the *lectio difficilior*. That may not be enough. As a matter of fact, Alexandrian scholars, and probably rhapsodes before them, were prone to favour an unusual form, provided it could find a parallel in Homer, as a σχῆμα.

6   O 190–191

I will end this review of problematic participles with an example not linked to Zenodotus, but which I think is linked to the rhetorical lens through which Homer was studied from the sophists onwards.

O 187–193
τρεῖς γάρ τ' ἐκ Κρόνου εἰμὲν ἀδελφεοὶ οὓς τέκετο Ῥέα
Ζεὺς καὶ ἐγώ, τρίτατος δ' Ἀΐδης ἐνέροισιν ἀνάσσων.
τριχθὰ δὲ πάντα δέδασται, ἕκαστος δ' ἔμμορε τιμῆς·
ἤτοι ἐγὼν ἔλαχον πολιὴν ἅλα ναιέμεν αἰεὶ
παλλομένων, Ἀΐδης δ' ἔλαχε ζόφον ἠερόεντα,
Ζεὺς δ' ἔλαχ' οὐρανὸν εὐρὺν ἐν αἰθέρι καὶ νεφέλῃσι·
γαῖα δ' ἔτι ξυνὴ πάντων καὶ μακρὸς Ὄλυμπος.

Since we are three brothers born by Rheia to Kronos, Zeus, and I, and the third is Hades, lord of the dead men. All was divided among us three ways, each given his domain. I when the lots were shaken drew the grey sea to live in forever; Hades drew the lot of the mists and the darkness, and Zeus was allotted the wide sky, in the cloud and the bright air. But earth and high Olympos are common to all three.

R.L.

The text is transmitted without any variant reading. So why include it in this study? The problem here lies in l. 191 with the participle παλλομένων. It is explained by Debrunner as an instance of subjectless genitive absolute (ἡμῶν) παλλομένων, where the subject has to be deduced from the context.[41] Vasilaros on the other hand treats παλλομένων as a partitive genitive modifying ἐγών,[42] which is better, yet not completely satisfying. However, here the transmitted text may not be the original version.

As a matter of fact, the enumeration of the three Olympian brothers follows the relative order of birth in l. 188: Zeus, the last born, is both the youngest of the three and the eldest. Hades was the first born and the first swallowed by his father, then came Poseidon, then Zeus, who escaped the fate of his elder siblings. When Cronus released his children by vomiting them, they were born in reverse order, Hades, the first swallowed, being the last born on this second birth. This is stated explicitly for Hestia, first born and then last born, in *H.Ven.* 22–23: Ἱστίη, ἣν πρώτην τέκετο Κρόνος ἀγκυλομήτης, || αὖτις δ' ὁπλοτάτην, βουλῇ Διὸς αἰγιόχοιο "Hestia, eldest begotten of Cronus whose counsels are crooked, youngest, again, the last born at the instance of shield-bearing Zeus" (D.H.). Coming back to the *Iliad*, the mention of Hades τρίτατος 'the third one' in l. 188 makes it clear that the order of birth is decisive. Therefore, we expect a chiasma disposition between l. 188 (order of the second birth, Zeus first, then Poseidon, then Hades τρίτατος 'the third one') and ll. 189–191 which should display the order of the first birth (Hades, then Poseidon, then Zeus), as in Hesiod, *Th.* 455–458.[43] But only Zeus stands as expected in third position (l. 192), the other two do not. Anyway, the order in which the three brothers drew lots must be in agreement with either order of birth. By all accounts, Poseidon must be second.[44] And this would give a better text, with the order 191–190–192:

---

41   Schwyzer–Debrunner, *Gr. Gr.* II: 400.
42   Vasilaros 1993: 90.
43   Hesiod, *Th.* 455–458: "(Rhea gave birth to) powerful, strong-armed Hades who under the earth makes his dwelling (pitiless his disposition), Poseidon the crashing earth-quaker as well, and Zeus the far-planner, father of gods and of men too, under the force of whose thunder the wide earth shivers in terror" (D.H.).
44   The order was traditional also in prose. Maxime of Tyre has (*Diss.* 40.6) ἐγὼ καὶ τῶν θεῶν τὴν ἰσοτιμίαν ἀφαιρῶ· πείθομαι γὰρ Ὁμήρῳ λέγοντι· 'τριχθὰ δὲ πάντα δέδασται, ἕκαστος

τρεῖς γάρ τ' ἐκ Κρόνου εἰμὲν ἀδελφεοὶ οὓς τέκετο Ῥέα
Ζεὺς καὶ ἐγώ, τρίτατος δ' Ἀΐδης ἐνέροισιν ἀνάσσων.
τριχθὰ δὲ πάντα δέδασται, ἕκαστος δ' ἔμμορε τιμῆς
*παλλομένων· Ἀΐδης (δ'/γ') ἔλαχε ζόφον ἠερόεντα,[45]
*αὐτὰρ ἐγὼν ἔλαχον πολιὴν ἅλα ναιέμεν αἰεί,
Ζεὺς δ' ἔλαχ' οὐρανὸν εὐρὺν ἐν αἰθέρι καὶ νεφέλῃσι·

all was divided in three parts, and each of us who were drawing lots obtained his realm: Hades drew the lot of the mist and the darkness, I obtained for my part to inhabit the grey sea forever, and Zeus obtained the wide heaven, to live in ether and in clouds.

Not only does this different relative order of l. 190 and 191 restore the traditional and expected logical structure (Zeus–Poseidon–Hades / Hades–Poseidon–Zeus), but it also removes the alleged non agreeing adjunct participle or subjectless genitive absolute παλλομένων: if the Hades line was the first one, παλλομένων is simply a partitive genitive modifying ἕκαστος in the preceding line. The head of the partitive genitive is explicit, whereas Vasilaros assumes it is implicit. Moreover, this order accounts better for the ἐν αἰθέρι καὶ νεφέλῃσι which in fact depends on ναιέμεν, whereas in the transmitted text it is not linked to anything. The syntagm αἰθέρι ναίων # is a regular qualification of Zeus (see B 412; Δ 166; O 523; Hes., Op. 18), and ναίειν can be construed with an accusative (πολιὴν ἅλα), with a dative or with ἐν + dative (ἐν αἰθέρι καὶ νεφέλῃσι). Here ναιέμεν is common to the Poseidon line (l. 190 in the transmitted text, but which should be l. 191) and l. 192, but not repeated in l. 192. The fact that the Poseidon line was moved to the first position cuts the verb from the complement.

If this is correct, there must be a reason why two lines underwent inversion in the vulgate,[46] and indeed there is an obvious one. Whenever there are three

---

δ' ἔμμορε τιμῆς· τιμῆς οὐκ ἴσης, οὐδὲ γὰρ ἀρχῆς ἴσης· οὐ γὰρ ἴση ἡ νομὴ οὐρανοῦ πρὸς θάλατταν καὶ θαλάττης πρὸς Ἄιδην· θεὸς δὲ ὁμοίως καὶ Κρόνου παῖς καὶ Ἄιδης καὶ Ποσειδῶν καὶ Ζεύς "I for one would take the equal honour from the gods. Because I trust Homer when he says 'everything was divided in three, and each got his lot'; the honor is not equal, and neither is the power, since the empire of the heavens is not equal to the empire of the sea, and the latter is not equal to Hades; but all are gods and sons of Cronos, Hades, Poseidon and Zeus." The hierarchy in dignity, with the sea in second position, mirrors the canonic succession Zeus–Poseidon–Hades, and so does the list at the end in the reverse order.

45 With this order of lines, the connecting particle may have been different.
46 Scholia as well as Ptolemaic papyri show that the relative order of lines was subject to some hesitation in more than one case—and of course many such variations were not transmitted to us. Aristarchus used a special diacritic sign, the antisigma, for such

items, the second position is the least prominent, and from a rhetorical perspective the marked positions are the first one or the last one. Here, as Poseidon is making his claim to equal rights with his brother, his claim could not be kept in a second position which did not give it full strength. This is a basic requirement of rhetorics. Therefore it was in a way logical to place Poseidon's claim in first position. In classical Greek, the regular order is ἐγὼ καὶ αὐτός, and the first position is the most prominent. The line begins with # ἤτοι ἐγών. Most of the time ἤτοι is in first position in the correlation ἤτοι ... δέ.[47] It is not absolutely ruled out that # ἤτοι ἐγών, as an equivalent for ἐγὼ μέν, impossible at the beginning of the line, might also serve as an equivalent for ἐγὼ δέ, just as impossible in that position, and that ἤτοι was already the particle used when Poseidon's line was in second position. More probably, ἤτοι replaced a different particle like αὐτάρ, metrically equivalent, and normally used in second position (# αὐτὰρ ἐγών Γ 290, Η 237, Η 296, Η 361, Ι 103 = Ι 314 = Ν 735, Λ 747, Μ 368, Ν 752, Ξ 8, Ο 260, Υ 208, Φ 187, Φ 334, Χ 390, Χ 479, Ω 110, Ω 117, Ω 493), when the Poseidon line was moved to the first position. And since ἤτοι has an assertive value which αὐτάρ does not have, the replacement was in keeping with rhetorical requirements. This permutation separated the participle παλλομένων from its head ἕκαστος, but that was not a problem in a state of the language where a subjectless genitive absolute was admitted, which is the case in classical prose.

The relative order of the lines is the same in all our sources. There are no variants in the manuscripts, the papyri, the scholia or in the indirect tradition. That means that this order was fixed early enough, it predates the vulgate and it may predate Zenodotus, too, because no Zenodotean variant is transmitted for these lines. Thus, there are no philological reasons to suspect that this order is not original. However, there are linguistic reasons to do so, and there is a stylistic reason why the order needed to be changed: rhetorical effectiveness. Since Homer was the Poet, his lines had to be perfect also from a rhetorical point of view. This clearly led to changes in the transmitted text, because at this stage we are dealing with a written text. Here the conflict between the mythological logic (the traditional order Zeus–Poseidon–Hades) and the rhetorical logic (Poseidon's claim must appear in a prominent position) was solved at the expense of the former. The important lesson the examples above teach us is that the requirements of rhetorics were strong enough to be placed above syntax, for in more than one case this emendation on rhetorical criteria creates

---

inversions. That there is no antisigma in those lines means that the inversion occurred early enough and that Aristarchus did not have access to a version with a different line order.

47   Ruijgh 1981.

a syntactic problem. That could be due to the fact that for Alexandrian scholars, Homeric syntax was admittedly different from the regular syntax of *koine* Greek, so that divergences could be justified, whereas rhetorical principles are universal and timeless. This was probably also true for rhapsodes who received the same *paideia*.

I will not develop further with similar exemples, for fear of being accused of μεταγράφειν Homer myself as light-heartedly as Zenodotus allegedly did. But when it comes to μεταγράφειν, I hope the cases studied here will convince readers that Zenodotus was certainly not the main culprit for the many alterations the received text underwent.

Synthesis

Before I conclude, I will provide a synthetic summary of the new elements brought by this study. The facts are presented in the order of the Homeric text.
- A 47 (chapter 6, section 2): Zenodotus' reading ὁ δ' ἤϊε νυκτὶ (ϝ)ἐλυσθείς "and he went, wrapped in night" is old, and probably older than the vulgate's ὁ δ' ἤϊε νυκτὶ ἐοικώς "and he went, similar to night." Ἐλυσθείς is the old participle meaning 'wrapped', from PIE *u̯el-u- (Ved. *vr̥ṇóti* 'to cover'), which was eliminated because for this verb the stem εἰλυ- had been generalised and the form could not be modernised. Its condemnation by Alexandrian scholars relies on its synchronically abnormal character, but the form is diachronically regular. It belongs with ἔλυμα Δ 137. 'Curled up' is a secondary meaning of ἐλυσθείς, which arose in ι 433 (Ulysses hiding beneath the ram), and the form was then reused with the secondary meaning in Ω 510 (Priam prostrated at Achilles' feet). Ψ 393, the only occurrence with an indicative ἐλύσθη, was then created after Ω 510, with a further semantic twist, and the meaning seems to be 'fell on the ground'.
- A 60 (chapter 10, section 2): Zenodotus' reading οἵ κεν θάνατόν γε φύγοιμεν "those of us who can escape death" is syntactically better than the vulgate's αἴ κεν "if we can escape death." It agrees with a regular pattern in relative clauses, whereas the vulgate's reading does not agree with the regular pattern in conditional clauses. The remodelling was justified by stylistic concerns and must date back to a time when rhapsodes assumed that a conditional clause can have the modal particle or not independently of the structure of the main clause.
- A 351 (chapter 4): Zenodotus' reading χεῖρας ἀναπτάς "stretching his hands upwards" is old, and probably older than the vulgate's χεῖρας ὀρεγνύς "stretching his hands." The form is the old aorist participle of the archaic root aorist of ἀναπίτνημι/ἀναπετάννυμι, later on eliminated by ἐπέτασα. The root aorist can be reconstructed as *peth₂-/*pth₂-, participle *pth₂-ént-. Ὀρεγνύς is probably an inner-Greek creation *metri causa*, on the model δείξας : δεικνύς :: ὀρέξας : *x* = ὀρεγνύς, rather than a very archaic form.
- B 4 (chapter 1, section 5.2): Zenodotus' πολύς is the old acc.pl. of πολύς, from -υνς (see Cret. υἱύνς), much better than the vulgate's πολέας with synizesis. This has been known for a long time and cannot be doubted. West is right to print πολύς in that line, but probably not to print it in every line where the transmitted text has a πολέας scanned with synizesis before a vowel.
- B 581, δ 1 (chapter 8): Zenodotus' reading Οἳ δ' εἶχον κοίλην Λακεδαίμονα καιτάεσσαν (not καιετάεσσαν although most modern editions print it thus) is

certainly older than the vulgate's κητώεσσαν, which does not make any reasonable sense. The original line in B 581 was probably *Οἳ δ' εἶχον κοίλην Λακεδαίμονα καὶ Τάϝησσαν/Τάϝησσον "those who held hollow Lacedaemon and Tawessa/Tawessos," with a toponym referring to an unknown city in second-millenium Laconia. The line conforms to the dominant pattern in the *Catalogue of ships*, "those who held cities X and Y." The original form of the toponym remains unclear, but it may be a pre-Hellenic toponym in -ησσος. Mycenaean has an anthroponym ta-we-si-jo, which could be an ethnic *Τἄϝησσιος used as anthroponym.

- B 681 (chapter 10, section 1): Zenodotus' reading οἳ δ' Ἄργος τ' εἶχον τὸ Πελασγικόν, οὖθαρ ἀρούρης "those who held Argos, the Pelasgian city, the earth's womb" is older than the vulgate's νῦν αὖ τοὺς ὅσσοι τὸ Πελασγικὸν Ἄργος ἔναιον "now again all those who inhabited Pelasgian Argos," which is abnormal in the *Catalogue* and linguistically recent. The vulgate's reading is a remodelling obeying the laws of rhetorical composition, according to which the beginning of the third part of the *Catalogue*, especially the lines introducing Achilles' troops, had to be marked as a new development and could not have the default formulation found in the rest of the *Catalogue*.

- Γ 56 (chapter 1, section 3.2): Zenodotus' reading ἀλλὰ μάλα Τρῶες ἐλεήμονες "but the Trojans are merciful, indeed" is older than the vulgate's δειδήμονες, which is a recent form, morphologically irregular.

- Γ 100 (chapter 1, section 3.6): Zenodotus' reading εἵνεκ' ἐμῆς ἔριδος καὶ Ἀλεξάνδρου ἕνεκ' ἄτης "because of my quarrel and of Alexander's error," although certainly not very old, is older than the vulgate's εἵνεκ' ἐμῆς ἔριδος καὶ Ἀλεξάνδρου ἕνεκ' ἀρχῆς "because of my quarrel and Alexander's initiative," which seems to be due to a late remodelling contrasting this line with the parallel Z 356. The meaning of ἀρχή in the vulgate's reading cannot be old.

- Γ 152 (chapter 2): Zenodotus' reading δένδρει ἐφεζόμενοι "sitting on a tree" is older than the vulgate's δενδρέῳ ἐφεζόμενοι "idem." It points to the fact that, in Ionic as in several dialects, the name of the tree had a suppletive paradigm mixing thematic and athematic forms (Ionic dat.pl. δένδρεσι). A systematic review of the Greek forms is provided, and the analysis concludes that all the forms in Greek developed from an athematic paradigm, not from a thematic one as is always assumed in reference works. Δένδρεον is the singulative of a collective δένδρεα which is originally athematic and preserves to a large extent the athematic inflection of the old *u*-stem **dóru, *dréu̯-*. Later on, after the loss of intervocalic [w], forms like δένδρεα, δενδρέων, δένδρεος, δένδρει became ambiguous and could be analysed as reflecting an *s*-stem (γένος) as well as a *u*-stem (ἄστυ): one dialect innovated by creating a nom.acc.sg. δένδρος, which seems to be specific to the Cos area (including Halicarnassus).

- Γ 211 (chapter 10, section 5): Zenodotus' reading ἄμφω δ' ἑζομένων "both sitting" could be older than the vulgate's ἄμφω δ ἑζομένω "idem," thus eliminating an alleged case of nominative absolute. The basic problem is the agreement with ἄμφω after the loss of the dual in Ionic. K 424 is probably modelled after Γ 211 and therefore not conclusive.
- Δ 137 (chapter 6): Zenodotus' reading ἔλυμα χροός "wrapping around his skin" is older than the vulgate's ἔρυμα χροός "protection of his skin," as already seen by Rengakos. It is a regular derivative (ϝ)ἔλῦμα, which is a different word from the ἔλῦμα 'stock of the plough' found in Hesiod, although the two are usually considered one and the same word, erroneously. /ϝελῠματα/ is the correct reading for Mycenaean we-ru-ma-ta (PY Ub(1) 1318): we-ru-ma-ta is usually compared with Homeric εἴλῦμα (ζ 179) but in fact it matches Zenodotus' form and probably means 'belts', not 'leather bags' or the like. (ϝ)ἔλῦμα 'wrapping', not ἔλυμα 'stock of the plough', is the cognate of Lat. volūmen, from PIE *u̯el-u- (Ved. vr̥ṇóti 'to cover', Lat. volvō). This reading cannot be dissociated from νυκτὶ (ϝ)ἐλυσθείς in A 47, and shows that Zenodotus' text was consistent in preserving the old stem ϝελυ-, later on eliminated by the new stem εἰλυ- abstracted from the perfect εἴλῦμαι, hence εἴλῦμα in ζ 179. Together, the two provide a new argument against the distinction between two roots *u̯el- and the separation between vr̥ṇóti 'to cover' and the present stem *u̯el-u-e/o- reflected in Lat. volvo, Arm. gelum, etc. Hesiod's ἔρυμα χροός (Op. 536) could well be an older ἔλυμα χροός identical with the old Homeric phrase, and the remodelling of the latter led to the introduction of the new ἔρυμα χροός into the Hesiodic line.
- Ζ 71 (chapter 10, section 3): Zenodotus' reading Τρώων ἂμ πεδίον συλήσομεν ἔντεα νεκρούς "in the plain of Troy we will strip the dead of their armour" is older than the vulgate's νεκροὺς ἂμ πεδίον συλήσετε τεθνηῶτας "you will take the spoils from the dead, in the plain, the fallen warriors," which on linguistic criteria is recent (because of the meaning of συλάω) and results from a rewriting due to rhetorical conventions.
- Θ 470 (chapter 3): Zenodotus' ἄας is an archaic form going back to an endingless locative ἀϝές 'at dawn', hence 'tomorrow', attested under a corrupt form by Hesychius with the label "Boeotian." It is probably not a Boeotian form in Homer, but an Achaean one. Zenodotus' form appears to reflect a contamination of the authentic Achaean form ἀϝές by the Lesbian adverb αὔας (Sappho), remodelled after the antonym ἑσπέρας. The form αὔα/αὖα given by the Byzantine *Etymologica* and by Apollonius Dyscolus is a ghost form coined by Apollonius as an intermediate step in order to explain the adverb αὔας, the only genuine Lesbian form. The form ἄας in Zenodotus cannot have been transmitted via Thessalo-Lesbian, therefore is a strong argument

in favour of the diffusionist model assuming a direct transmission from the Achaean epic tradition to the Proto-Ionic one. The vulgate's ἠοῦς with unresolvable contraction is linguistically recent.

- I 506 and Φ 262 (chapter 1, section 4.2): Zenodotus' reading φθάνέει 'she precedes' vs vulgate φθάνει (< φθάνϝει) probably results from the modernisation of an older *φθάνύει, with a pair similar to ἄνϝω vs ἀνύω 'to achieve', from an older *φθάνυμι.
- Λ 458 (chapter 10, section 4): Zenodotus' reading αἷμα δὲ οὗ σπασθέντος ἀνέσσυτο cannot be very old as transmitted, but could be the remodelling of an older *αἷμά ἑο σπασθέντος ἀνέσσυτο "blood sprang forth from its removal" with a dominant participle, ἑο being the anaphoric pronoun, referring to the spear. The insertion of δέ prompted the contraction οὗ (the accent transmitted by Aristonicus is probably not original), and in the vulgate the remodelling to οἱ, understood as referring to Ulysses. The latter was deemed stylistically better.
- Ξ 37 (chapter 5): Zenodotus' reading ὄψ ἀΐοντες 'hearing' is older than the vulgate's ὀψείοντες 'wishing to see'. Zenodotus' form was not understood by Aristarchus and his followers. It is the verb ἐπαΐω 'to hear', with, instead of ἐπι-, impossible for metrical reasons, the adverbial form ὄψ. This form, matching Lat. *obs-*, is postulated by all etymological dictionaries of Greek as the base of ὀψέ, ὀψι-, but was not attested in any Greek document. It is now. It may also be in μ 438–439 ἦλθον || ὄψ, where it was easily reinterpreted as the adverb ὀψέ 'late' with elision before a vowel. In Ξ 37, however, it could not be understood as meaning 'late'. Consequently, the form was modified and understood as a form of 'to see' with a desiderative meaning. The remodelling is old because forms built on that model are well attested in Attic tragedy of the second half of the 5th c., and the occurrences in comedy or in prose depend on this fashionable use in tragedy.
- Ο 190–192 (chapter 10, section 6): these lines are transmitted without any variant reading and not associated with Zenodotus, but it is likely that the original ordering of the lines was 191–190–192. This order agrees with the expected one when it comes to the three brothers Zeus–Poseidon–Hades, and it would eliminate the abnormal participle παλλομένων, which is with the order 191–190–192 a regular partitive genitive depending on ἕκαστος in l. 189. The interchange of l. 190 and 191 is probably due to rhetorical concerns.
- Σ 160 (chapter 3, section 3): Zenodotus' στάσκε μέγα ἀχέων is the older reading. It does not mean "he stood in grief," but "he stood, screaming," as the vulgate's στάσκε μέγα ἰάχων. Zenodotus preserves here a direct trace of the old root aorist *ϝϝάχον, reconstructed by linguists as the base from which

the present ϝιϝάχω/ἰάχω was derived. Aristonicus, and probably Aristarchus before him, misunderstood the verb.
- Σ 222 (chapter 1, section 3.2): Zenodotus' ὄπα χαλκέην "brazen voice" is the older form which preserves a case of "secondary yod" as χρυσέη Ἀφροδίτη. Aristarchus' ὄπα χάλκεον with a masculine adjective is a more recent form.
- Σ 576 (chapter 9): Zenodotus' reading was *πὰρ ποταμὸν κελάδοντα, διὰ ῥάδαλον δονακῆεν, vs vulgate πὰρ ποταμὸν κελάδοντα, παρὰ ῥοδανὸν δονακῆα. In Zenodotus' version, which is older, ῥάδαλον is a neuter noun, and δονακῆεν is the regular adjective 'rich in reeds', whereas in the vulgate ῥοδανόν is a masculine adjective and the noun is a morphologically irregular *δονακεύς. The change of construction, the head of the noun phrase becoming the modifier and conversely, is probably due to the fact that the meaning of ῥάδαλον was lost and that a noun phrase can be kept only if its head is semantically clear.
- Φ 95 (chapter 1, section 4.1): Zenodotus' reading was ἰογάστριος 'from the same womb' (West 2001) or ὀγάστριος, also found in Lycophron. The latter possibility may be better. At any rate, whatever the reading, it is older than the vulgate's ὁμογάστριος 'idem'. Even assuming that Zenodotus had ἰογάστριος, West's reconstruction is probably not correct and the older phrase was *ἐπεὶ οὐχὶ ὀγάστριος Ἕκτορός εἰμι "since I am not at all from the same womb as Hector," not *ἐπεὶ οὔ τοι ὀγάστριος Ἕκτορός εἰμι. This is a rare but reliable instance of preverbal οὐχί in an older state of the Homeric text.
- Φ 169 (chapter 7): Zenodotus' reading μελίην ἰθυκτίωνα is older than the vulgate's μελίην ἰθυπτίωνα, which is a remodelling of the unclear ἰθυκτίωνα after the phrase ἰθὺς βέλος πέτετο. This is a remotivation of an old obscure word. Zenodotus' ἰθυκτίωνα can be etymologised as 'with a straight spearhead', or, less convincingly, 'with a straight shaft'. The second member of the compound is identified as the word ἀκτίς, ἀκτῖνος, which in Greek was specialised in the meaning 'rays' of the sun, but must have meant originally 'point, spike' and belongs to the root $*h_2ek̑$-. The stem ἀκτῖν- can be analysed as the weak stem with "Hoffmann's suffix" in the zero grade $*h_2k̑$-ti-h_3n-, while the strong stem with full grade $*h_2k̑$-ti-h_3on- is preserved in the compound ἰθυκτίων.
- Φ 331 (chapter 7, section 1): Κυλλοπόδιον 'lame-footed' is a neuter diminutive and the two instances of a nominative Κυλλοποδίων at the end of the line are the result of a remodelling transferring the noun to the δαίμων type.
- δ 1 (chapter 8): see B 581.
- ι 433 (chapter 6, section 3): see A 47.
- μ 438–439 (chapter 5, section 4): see Ξ 37.

Conclusion

Let us go back to West's formulation:

> To sum up, we must treat Zenodotus' so-called ἔκδοσις not as the construct of a hare-brained scholar making an unsteady attempt to create order out of a jumble of manuscripts, but as a fourth-century Ephesian rhapsode's text, deformed by many oral variants, arbitrary abridgements, trivializations, modernizations, and so forth, yet drawing on a side-stream of tradition which, having branched off at an early date from the major (Attic) channel, uniquely preserved certain genuine elements of the archaic text.[1]

How can we evaluate it after this inquiry?

That Zenodotus' *ekdosis* is not "the construct of a hare-brained scholar" is clear. That it "uniquely preserved certain genuine elements of the archaic text" is certain, provided we take "archaic text" as one of the early written versions of the epics, not as *the* text. Those elements were preserved in the version that became Zenodotus' working text, rather than corrected or replaced by something altogether different as they were in the vulgate. The readings examined in this study cannot be emendations introduced by Zenodotus because no Hellenistic scholar had the linguistic knowledge necessary to produce those forms. Therefore, he did not intervene in his text as much as the *doxa* kept repeating for centuries.

Now the forms could have been, rather than the ones he read in his text, variants he found in other copies, which he found interesting and which he wrote down in the margins of his *ekdosis*, not because he deemed them better but for the sake of recording the divergence, in a kind of primitive *apparatus criticus*. This is unlikely because the A scholia report only one reading under Zenodotus' name for each considered line. Therefore his aim was not to record variant readings, otherwise he would probably have recorded more than one for lines for which there were competing readings—unless we assume that he collated a very small number of copies. Was it to provide a better text? If so, we have to assume that the variants he took from other copies seemed preferable to the readings of his working text. But the overview provided in chapter 1 makes it difficult to believe that he preferred such forms as ὧλλοι for οἱ ἄλλοι

---

[1] West 2002: 142.

in B 1 because he knew that a crasis with the article is not found elsewhere in Homer, or οὐκ ἐμεθίει in O 716 because he was a native speaker of Greek who knew that the imperfect of μεθίημι is not ἐμεθίει, or Ἡρακλείη in B 658 because he could see it was unmetrical. This also applies to the many cases where he has a reading contrary to the πρέπον: such readings cannot have been meant to improve the text. The most likely hypothesis is that these readings were in his text and that he did not correct them.

The same holds true for cases where his reading is known from contemporary papyri or other texts: if readings like μάρτυρες or δένδρει were found in 3rd c. copies, they could clearly be found in Zenodotus' working text. Assuming that his text had the same recent forms as the vulgate (μάρτυροι, δενδρέῳ with synizesis and *correptio*, both clear products of ἀναλογία) and that he corrected them after contemporary copies is unnecessary.

Now for the archaic forms studied in this book, we face a similar question: assuming they were not in his text but were introduced by him from other copies implies that he thought they were preferable. But it is impossible that he deemed the isolated ἔλυμα, the irregular ἀναπτάς, the unclear ἰθυκτίωνα, the ambiguous ἀχέων, better than ἔρυμα, ὀρεγνύς, ἰθυπτίωνα or ἰάχων, assuming Zenodotus' working text agreed with the vulgate[2]—except if we follow Van der Valk in assuming that Zenodotus had an immoderate taste for rare words. A Hellenistic scholar, whether in the 3rd c. or in the 2nd c., could not use the linguistic criterion to state that the irregular or isolated form was better. And on the other hand, if he had an immoderate taste for rare words, he would not have chosen a flat ὀψ' ἀΐοντες 'hearing late' (since this was the only possible synchronic meaning) at the expense of the unique ὀψείοντες, or the regular ἐλεήμονες, δονακῆεν at the expense of the *hapaxes* δειδήμονες, δονακῆα. Accordingly, the most economical hypothesis is that those were the readings of his text and do not result from an editorial intervention.

Is it likely that his text could have so many archaisms, next to many recent forms (see above, pp. 33–38)? Such was also the case of Aristarchus' text: every version was bound to be linguistically heterogenous because such is the nature of the epic corpus. Furthermore, it would make sense to believe that, the older the copy, the more heterogenous the text, because it had not yet been homogenised by generations of scholars who had defined what was Homeric and

---

[2] The very slight difference between the vulgate and Zenodotus makes it unlikely that the latter had in his text something altogether different: ἔλυμα/ἔρυμα, ἰθυκτίωνα/ἰθυπτίωνα are minimal pairs, ἀχέων and ἰάχων are two forms of the same verb, so that it would be very costly to assume that there was an unattested third reading when the two attested ones are so obviously related.

what was not. Zenodotus was supposed to correct Homer, that is, first of all, to eliminate unauthentic lines. For that purpose, if he had at his disposal in the Library several copies, he probably chose as his working text one of the oldest, because it was closer to Homer's time in his view, and an Ionian copy because Homer was said to have been an Ionian.[3] And, having this old copy in his hands, he apparently respected the text, even when the latter displayed obviously un-Homeric forms like ὦλλοι or unmetrical ones like Ἡρακλείη. There may have been other old copies in the Library, on which he may have relied for some variant readings, but we have no information about that. As it is not unlikely that the 'wild' readings here studied were found in one and the same copy, the simplest hypothesis may be the best.

Rengakos objects that, since Apollonius of Rhodes and Callimachus clearly knew several readings, therefore several copies, this must have been the case for Zenodotus, too.[4] That he knew several versions is uncontroversial, but that does not imply he used several versions for his *ekdosis*: he may have chosen one in particular for his *ekdosis* and used the other versions only for his oral teaching.

That does not mean he did not intervene at all, but we have no means of knowing what his interventions were. The picture that emerges is rather that he did not behave as a grammarian aiming at a linguistically consistent text: otherwise he would probably not have kept such archaic elements as the acc.pl. πολύς in B 4 while other lines required a trisyllabic πολέας. Such inconsistencies were apparently not a problem for him. Aristarchus, "the best of the grammarians," regularised the text according to principles which he believed were valid, either by correcting the text or by selecting a reading agreeing with those principles. We could say we are lucky that Zenodotus was *not* a grammarian, and in particular that he did not apply the rules of ἀναλογία to his text, preserving synchronic inconsistencies like δένδρει vs δένδρεον, μάρτυρες vs μάρτυρος, πολύς vs πολέας, ἀναπτάς vs πετάσσας, ἐλυσθείς vs εἰλυμένος, the old reflexive pronoun οἱ αὐτῷ (O 587) with the two elements inflected vs the univerbated recent form ἑωυτήν (Ξ 162), or the inherited use of the reflexive possessive as number insensitive (see above, p. 47).

Accordingly, we should definitely read Homer from Z to A: Zenodotus' readings are in many cases older than Aristarchus', and sometimes definitely archaic, as the linguistic study demonstrates.

---

[3] Aristarchus' opinion that Homer was an Athenian because of his use of the dual (see above, p. 268) is late. Zenodotus, himself an Ionian, most probably subscribed to the common view that Homer was an Ionian.

[4] Rengakos 2012: 243.

CONCLUSION

That the version on which Zenodotus' *ekdosis* relies "branched off at an early date from the major (Attic) channel" is supported by the case of ὄψ ἀΐοντες, since the vulgate's form ὀψείοντες, much older than Aristarchus, seems to be specific to the Attic version, in so far as it provided a model for a type of desiderative formations found only in Attic, and clearly dependent on the Homeric model in the earliest attestations. Sophocles' *Ajax*, staged between 450 and 440 BCE, and *Trachinian women*, maybe posterior to *Ajax* but still one of his oldest plays, give a *terminus ante quem* in the middle of the 5th c.[5] The absence of this innovation in Zenodotus' *ekdosis* fits the pattern of two already independent traditions, stemming from the same version, in the second half of the 5th c. BCE.

Also on the lexical level, if Herodotus' περιβαλέσθαι ἕρκος ἔρυμα τῶν νεῶν (Hdt 9.96) has its source in Δ 137 ἔρυμα χροὸς ἕρκος ἀκόντων, as is likely, it means Herodotus knew the line in its secondary shape: this also points to two diverging versions already in the 5th c.

The reading δένδρει is, as argued here, older than the vulgate's δενδρέῳ: its preservation is coherent with an Ionic version since δένδρει was preserved in Ionic prose too, but this feature cannot be used to provide a chronological estimation, except for the fact that the new form δενδρέῳ is posterior to the quantitative metathesis which gave rise to the metrical licence of synizesis. I suspect that it was in fact introduced in the Attic version: the replacement of δένδρει ἐφεζόμενοι by δένδρῳ ἐφεζόμενοι was metrically straightforward, since δένδρει and δένδρῳ have the same metrical value, and since Ionic has δένδρεον, not δένδρον, the form δένδρῳ was ionicised in δενδρέῳ since synizesis for εω was commonplace in dactylic poetry. That yields this awkward combination of synizesis and *correptio epica*, backed by a few other such examples involving the adjectives χρύσεος, χάλκεος, ἀργύρεος, in which the epic diction has many cases of synizesis which in fact go back to an Aeolic or Achaean "secondary yod." The Attic form provides an intermediate step between the older δένδρει and the new δενδρέῳ. If this pattern δένδρει → δένδρῳ → δενδρέῳ is correct, that means that the new form was secondarily introduced also in Hesiod, *Op.* 583. Yet, while the odds are that the vulgate's reading δενδρέῳ ἐφεζόμενοι arose in an Attic version, this could have occurred any time between the 8th and the 5th c. A clue, notwithstanding, could be provided by the fact that the thematic dat.pl. δένδροις is not attested before the 4th c. in Attic, and that 5th c. authors only have δένδρεσι: this points to the fact that the inflection of δένδρον remained suppletive down to the 5th c.[6] A dat.pl. δένδρεσι could back a dat.sg. δένδρει (as it did in Ionic),

---

5 Finglass 2011: 7–11.
6 That, of course, depends on the textual transmission, which may have a modernised δένδροις for an older δένδρεσι. However, there is no trace of that for 5th c. writers.

but as soon as the dat.pl. δένδροις was generalised, the pressure to regularise the odd athematic dat.sg. was strong. Accordingly, this modernisation could also date back to the 5th c.

Other archaic forms like ἀναπτάς, ἄας or οὐκ ἰογάστριος/οὐκὶ ὀγάστριος, vs vulgate οὐχ ὀμογάστριος are not exploitable for chronology: ὀρεγνύς could have replaced ἀναπτάς any time, and ἠοῦς was available to replace ἄας as soon as the contractions were made. The loss of the dual occurred early in Ionic and the version from which both the Attic text and Zenodotus' text derive probably already had ἄμφω in Γ 211 (otherwise ἀμφοῖν would have been kept in the Attic version), and this case cannot be used for dating either.

However, one can argue from the many cases where Zenodotus' readings diverge from the vulgate's by not conforming to rhetorical principles that this version was distinct from the Attic one when sophistics and rhetorics arose in Athens, and that also points to the 5th c., more specifically the second half of the 5th c. Similarly, the fact that Zenodotus' version had for Α 4–5 οἰωνοῖσί τε δαῖτα, a version which Aeschylus probably knew, means that the replacement by οἰωνοῖσί τε πᾶσι in the Attic version occurred after Aeschylus. It can probably also be attributed to the growing influence of sophists, who paid special attention to the question of the propriety of words, and deemed 'banquet' (δαῖτα) inappropriate for animals.[7] The elimination of the redundant compound κυνυλαγμός (Φ 575), preserved in Zenodotus' text, may date back to the first theoretical reflections on language and the appropriateness and correctness of words. The semantic distinction between ἐλάθετο and οὐκ ἐνόησεν in Ι 537 (Zenodotus ἐκλάθετ᾽ οὐδ᾽ ἐνόησεν vs vulgate ἢ λάθετ᾽ ἢ οὐκ ἐνόησεν), and the invention of a formal difference between βεβόλημαι referring to a moral wound and βέβλημαι to a physical wound (Ι 3, Ι 9) are of the same type. In all those lines, Zenodotus' reading is the older one. And from this point of view, too, Homer must be read

---

7   This is explicit in a comment from Athenaeus, *Deipn.* 1.21.24–30 Kaibel: καὶ ἐπὶ μόνων ἀνθρώπων δαῖτα λέγει ὁ ποιητής, ἐπὶ δὲ θηρίων οὐκ ἔτι. ἀγνοῶν δὲ ταύτης τῆς φωνῆς τὴν δύναμιν Ζηνόδοτος ἐν τῇ κατ᾽ αὐτὸν ἐκδόσει γράφει 'αὐτοὺς δὲ ἑλώρια τεῦχε κύνεσσιν ‖ οἰωνοῖσί τε δαῖτα᾽ "Homer uses δαίς only for men, but not yet for animals. And Zenodotus, ignoring the true meaning of this word, writes in his *ekdosis* 'αὐτοὺς δὲ ἑλώρια τεῦχε κύνεσσιν ‖ οἰωνοῖσί τε δαῖτα᾽." This goes back to Aristarchean scholarship, which distinguishes Homer from the post-Homeric poets (οἱ νεώτεροι), referred to by the οὐκ ἔτι: Zenodotus has allegedly here taken this δαῖτα from one of the νεώτεροι, which includes Aeschylus. This is repeated in the *Suda*, delta 128 ὅτι ἐπὶ ἀνθρώπων λέγεται δαίς, ἐπὶ δὲ θηρίων οὔ. ἀγνοῶν δὲ Ζηνόδοτος τῆς φωνῆς ταύτης τὴν δύναμιν ἔφη· ἑλώρια τεῦχε κύνεσσιν οἰωνοῖσί τε δαῖτα) and in Eustathius (*Comm. Od.* 1: 35 ὅτι δὲ ἐπὶ μόνων ἀνθρώπων ἡ δαίς κἂν ὁ Ζηνόδοτος ἄλλο τι βούληται, καὶ ἐν τοῖς εἰς τὴν Ἰλιάδα δεδήλωται "that δαίς is used only for men, even though Zenodotus thinks differently, was shown in the *Commentary* to the *Iliad*"). But the replacement of δαῖτα by πᾶσι is certainly older than Aristarchus.

from Z to A: Zenodotus' text remained exempt from many sophistic emendations, whereas Aristarchus' text displays re-elaborated lines in agreement with sophistic concerns.

So, Zenodotus' text was an Ionic version (this was already known), which was distinct from the Attic one already in the second half of the 5th c. but goes back to the same source. Which one "branched off" from the other remains a point under discussion, however. Was it an "Ephesian rhapsode's text"? To answer this question, one would have to examine the typically recent Ionic features in Zenodotus' text, in order to see whether there are features that can be ascribed to one Ionic sub-dialect rather than another one. This was not the aim of my study, which concentrated on the archaic features, and a study of recent Ionic features would probably not be conclusive, anyway. That it was an Ionic version is clear, that it came from Ephesus relies only on the fact that Zenodotus was born in Ephesus: the argument is weak. That it was a rhapsode's text is simply impossible to prove and only relies on the obvious fact that rhapsodes were more likely to own a complete copy of Homer than a private individual.

The conclusions reached here confirm that Van Thiel's thesis about Zenodotus' forms being comments and not readings cannot be defended. It would indeed be remarkable that so-called "experimental" forms like ἰογάστριος or ἔλυμα, "puns" like ὄψ ἀΐοντες, or "corrupt" forms like ἀναπτάς, printed with a *crux* by Van Thiel, happen to be regular from the linguistic point of view, not for the state of language of the 3rd c. BCE, but for a much older one. Zenodotus was remarkably inspired when he crafted such forms in Van Thiel's theory, so much so that the only plausible explanation is that his working text did preserve here archaic forms that had been eliminated in other versions.

There may be others yet: I studied here Zenodotean readings for which I think there are strong arguments in favour of the priority of Zenodotus compared to the vulgate and which are interesting for historical linguistics. There are other cases for which I do not have decisive arguments. For instance, in E 31 the vulgate reads Ἆρες Ἆρες βροτολοιγὲ μιαιφόνε τειχεσιπλῆτα "Ares, Ares, manslaughtering, blood-stained, stormer of strong walls" (R.L.). Zenodotus had τειχεσιβλῆτα. The A scholion condemns Zenodotus' reading:

> ὅτι Ζηνόδοτος γράφει τειχεσιβλῆτα, ὁ τείχη καταβάλλων. Ποσειδῶνος δὲ ἔργον τὸ ἐκ θεμελίων καταβάλλειν καὶ τὰ ἐπίγεια σείειν, Ἄρεως δὲ τοῖς τείχεσι προσπελάζειν· καὶ ἔστιν ἐπίθετον ἀνάλογον τῷ παρὰ Στησιχόρῳ πυλεμάχῳ.

> because Zenodotus writes τειχεσιβλῆτα, the one who brings down the walls. But it is Poseidon's work to throw down from the foundations and

to shake what is on earth, wherehas it is Ares' to march to the walls. And it is an epithet similar to the πυλεμάχος 'fighting at the doors' in Stesichorus (*fr.* 242 PMG).

The argument is of course weak, and has nothing to do with linguistics. War can bring down city walls, and only the traditional roles and mythology of Ares and Poseidon account for the condemnation of the scholiast. And the meaning of τειχεσιβλῆτα may be different, for instance 'wall-beating' (relying on the construction βάλλειν τινὰ λίθῳ): the scholiast considers it an equivalent of καταβάλλω, but the meaning of βάλλω and καταβάλλω is not the same. However, from a linguistic point of view there is no decisive argument to decide between the two readings. It is likely that the older form was *τειχεσ-π/βλῆτα, and that the remodelling of the compound with an inflected form in the first element is secondary, as in ὀρεσίτροφος next to ὀρεσκῷος. The remodelling implies that the word scan with *correptio attica*, confirming it is rather recent. And as soon as the first element was interpreted as a dative-locative, a verb indicating a position in space or a motion verb could be more appropriate. This could explain why a τειχεσιβλῆτα (see -βλησις, -βλητος and the Homeric βλῆτρον) was modified to τειχεσιπλῆτα (see πλῆτο 'he came near'). If the older form was *τειχεσ-βλῆτα, -βλητης must have been selected as a metrical alternative to the usual agent noun in compounds, -βόλος, impossible at the end of the line. However, it is also possible that a *τειχεσ-πλῆτα with a rare second element was modified under the influence of the more usual stem -βλη-.[8]

Another form for which a convincing solution has yet to be found is the notoriously difficult βουγάϊε (vulgate) in N 824, for which Zenodotus had βουγήϊε. Its meaning was unknown and the various meanings suggested by Greek scholars result from different synchronic etymologies.

The confirmation that Zenodotus did not heavily correct his text and kept archaic forms (ἀναπτάς, ἔλυμα) as well as apparent inconsistencies (δένδρει *vs* δένδρεον, πολὺς *vs* πολέας) as he found them, and that he did not attempt to emend "pre-sophistic" readings, so to speak, running counter to the rules of decency and rhetorics advocated by Alexandrian scholarship, has a consequence on the problem of atheteses. Zenodotus used a specific sign, the *obelos*, to mark a line he condemned, and Aristonicus in that case uses the technical term ἀθετεῖ. Zenodotus also used brackets to mark lines he deemed spurious, but did not athetise: in that case Aristonicus uses the technical term

---

[8] Hesychius has a πλήτης· πλησιαστής (π 2595), probably a form abstracted from τειχεσιπλῆτα and therefore not reliable.

περιγράφει.⁹ However, the same Aristonicus also says in a several places "Zenodotus does not write (οὐ γράφει) this line." He clearly makes a difference between ἀθετεῖ and οὐ γράφει: *A Schol.* A 488 ὅτι Ζηνόδοτος ἠθέτηκεν ἕως τοῦ 'αὖθι μένων' (A 492). Τὸν δὲ 'οὔτε ποτ᾽ ἐς πόλεμον' (A 491) οὐδὲ ἔγραφεν "because Zenodotus athetised until 'αὖθι μένων' and did not even write the line 'οὔτε ποτ᾽ ἐς πόλεμον'." *A Schol.* B 673–675 ὅτι ἐκ τῶν τριῶν τοὺς δύο ἠθέτηκε Ζηνόδοτος, τὸν δὲ μέσον οὐδὲ ἔγραφεν "because Zenodotus athetised two of the three lines (B 673 and 675) and did not even write the second one (B 674)."

The question is: are we also dealing with an athetesis in that case, with Zenodotus purely and simply deleting the line instead of using the *obelos*, or does it mean that Zenodotus' working text did not have the line under consideration? Of course Aristarchean scholarchip favours the former, because it considers every deviation from Aristarchus' text as a proof of Zenodotus' intervention, and this opinion still prevails in modern scholarship.¹⁰ If so, the reason why Zenodotus at times kept the line, marking it with the *obelos*, and at times deleted the line remains unknown: this erratic handling of spurious lines fits the *doxa* according to which Zenodotus did not follow any logic and was inconsistent.

However, this is difficult to understand if the *ekdosis* is not a new copy made by a scholar with his own readings, but a preexisting copy of the text on which the scholar wrote his comments and emendations:¹¹ Zenodotus could not choose not to write a given line if he did not produce a new copy. If he used an existing text, all he could do was to comment on his working text, which had the line under consideration or not. He could add a line in the margin or between the lines, but he could not erase an existing line. Therefore οὐ γράφει probably means that the line was not in his working text, not that he decided not to write it down.

Granted, there are occasional inconsistencies. For instance, in T 388–391 four lines were athetised by some because they are allegedly transferred from Π 141–144. Aristonicus says that Zenodotus leaves the lines under consideration in

---

9   *A Schol.* Θ 493: ὅτι Ζηνόδοτος περιγράφει ἀπὸ τούτου τέσσαρας στίχους κατὰ τὸ ἑξῆς (sc. Θ 493–496) διὰ τὸ καὶ ἐν ἄλλῳ τόπῳ γεγράφθαι (cf. Z 318–320) "because Zenodotus encloses in brackets four lines starting from this one, because they are also found in another place (Z 318–320)."

10 For instance Pontani 2005: 48–49: "Aristophanes limited himself to athetesis and abandoned the method of οὐ γράφειν, that is, of physically not writing the lines, still used by Zenodotus, it seems" ("Aristofane si limitò all'atetesi e abbandonò il metodo dell'οὐ γράφειν, cioè del non scrivere materialmente i versi, di cui Zenodoto, a quanto pare, ancora si serviva"). See a summary in Montanari 2015: 654–655.

11 Montanari 2015.

T but athetises them in Π (*A Schol.* T 388–391: ὅτι ἐνταῦθα μὲν αὐτοὺς Ζηνόδοτος καταλέλοιπεν, ἐπὶ δὲ Πατρόκλου ἠθέτηκεν), whereas he said earlier Ζηνόδοτος τοῦτον ἀθετήσας τοὺς ἑξῆς τέσσαρας οὐκ ἔγραφεν "Zenodotus athetised this line (Π 140) and did not write the following four lines" (*A Schol.* Π 140). The same lines Π 141–144 are said to be missing in one scholion and to be athetised in the other. Perhaps Aristonicus did not check the first passage while dealing with the second one, which would solve the contradiction if we assume that οὐ γράφει means that the lines never were in Zenodotus' working text. Or the copyist retained only the ἀθετήσας applying to the first line and extended it to the whole sequence.

Similarly, when Aristonicus says Zenodotus 'abridges' or 'summarises' (συντέμνω) an episode, it does not necessarily mean that he did it on purpose: it can simply mean that his working text had a shorter version.

On this vexed question of Zenodotus' atheteses, we may add one argument: our inquiry shows that Zenodotus followed the text he had, rather than not, as far as linguistic matters (morphology, syntax, lexicon) are concerned. If he was rather conservative on these issues, he probably was conservative on textual matters (number of lines), too. Accordingly, when a scholion says "Zenodotus does not write this line," it is probably not because Zenodotus chose not to write it down because he condemned it (he used the *obelos* for that purpose) or deemed it spurious (he used the brackets for that purpose), but rather because the line was missing in his working text from the start. That is no longer a linguistic problem, but the linguistic inquiry suggests that Zenodotus's handling of spurious lines must be reexamined. It seems his version of the *Iliad* significantly differed from Aristarchus' in that respect, too, and that the latter included added lines not found in older versions: in other words, the vulgate itself contains plus-verses, like the Ptolemaic papyri, but since it became the vulgate, they are not counted as such. And for that matter, too, it is legitimate to read Homer from Z to A.

At any rate, one point must be stressed. This study confirms to what extent our Homeric text is a construction and underlines that it must not be sacralised as a genuine reflex of a very archaic state of language, which could almost be transposed back into Proto-Indo-European. Reconstructing a nasal present for *$h_3reǵ$- on the basis of ὀρεγνύς compared with Ved. *r̥ñjáte* is already questionable because, as underlined in LIV², both can have been independently created in Greek and Vedic. It becomes even more hazardous when one acknowledges that ὀρεγνύς replaced an older ἀναπτάς preserved in Zenodotus, which cannot have been created in first millenium Greek and which imposed the metrical structure leading to the creation of ὀρεγνύς after ὀρέξας on the model of δεικνύς, δείξας. And trying to figure out what the PIE origin of the desiderative ὀψείοντες could have been is simply vain if this form is a remodelling resulting from the misunderstanding of an older structure preserved in Zenodotus, which cannot have been created in first millenium Greek but reflects an old pattern lost for a long time in the 5th c. BCE.

The Homeric corpus is a repository of archaic forms, but it is also full of innovations, and, more important in the case we are studying, full of remodellings, which convert an old unmotivated form into a newer one through a process of remotivation. This remotivation has nothing to do with correct diachronic linguistic rules, it is only a matter of synchronic relationship between Greek words: as when an unmotivated and obscure ἰθυκτίων, which cannot have been invented by Zenodotus because it was unanalysable in his time, is remodelled into a clearer ἰθυπτίων, after ἰθὺς βέλος πέτετο which is the source of the remotivation.

The vulgate in all those cases keeps the motivated form and rejects the unmotivated one: this is to be expected, as speakers spontaneously choose the meaningful form, and singers and rhapsodes naturally obeyed this law. To that must be added the role of Alexandrian scholars, who of course sought to have the best text from their point of view, that is, the most consistent one, meaning that they got rid of many obscure or irregular forms. Ἰθυπτίων is certainly not immediately understandable and remains a rare word, but it was consistent with ἰθὺς βέλος πέτετο and that was enough. But modern linguists must not be content with that and must not trust the reasonings underlying Aristarchus' and his followers' editorial decisions. We must never forget that our Homer text is a Hellenistic text in so far as the editorial choices are those of Hellenistic scholars, and that Hellenistic scholars simply did not have the tools we now have in historical linguistics.

Every Homeric form must first of all be checked from the philological point of view, and the vulgate must be questioned. The variant readings must be examined, carefully, and without the bias induced by centuries of Aristarchean scholarship. We are lucky that some variant readings clearly preserving a much older state of the lines under consideration were preserved in the Homeric scholia, be it under Zenodotus' name or not, or in other sources. But we also know that this is only a fraction of the variant readings that were in Zenodotus' text, not to mention the other versions, and we know that Zenodotus' text itself had eliminated many old forms, replaced by newer and clearer ones or remodelled through remotivation because this process is inherent to oral tradition. Generations of epic singers constantly modified older lines and created new ones, and generations of rhapsodes introduced into their recitation modernisations and variations. Conversely, they also introduced new "old" forms on the model of existing ones, and we also have to beware of hyperarchaisms, of which ὀρεγνύς may be an instance (a metrically motivated one). This process did not stop when written versions came into being, it was certainly slowed down but not halted. The versions on which Alexandrian scholars worked were the product of this process of permanent recreation. In other words, the archaic state of the epic corpus is out of reach: many archaisms were preserved down to versions circulating in the 4th or 3rd c. BCE, but many others were not.

The lesson we can draw from the cases examined here is that many Homeric forms for which we have no variant reading and which are deemed philologically secure may in fact be, like ὀψείοντες, ἰθυπτίων or δονακεύς, remodellings of older forms that were lost without any trace: they may not constitute a firm basis for reconstruction. Other forms deemed archaic because they are found only in Homer can nevertheless be innovations, like ὀρεγνύς, and do not constitute a firmer basis. Linguists are tempted to analyse such forms as archaisms because of their singularity and because "Homer is the earliest form of Greek we have," after Linear B, of course, but Mycenaean documents display a rather limited lexicon and even more limited grammar, which could not dethrone Homer. Nevertheless, this idea that Homer is necessarily archaic is a bias we must fight. I don't imply thereby that reconstruction is a desperate task, and of course authentic archaic forms were transmitted down to us and are precious for Indo-Europeanists. But we must be aware of the limits: we are dependent not only on the text that was transmitted, but also on how that text was established, and this is something linguists tend to forget.[12] This holds true for everything: lexicon, phonology, morphology, syntax, and even stylistics. If we do not pay attention to the principles underlying this editing process, we cannot properly evaluate the transmitted forms. The transmitted text must be studied as what it is, not an intangible sacred text, but the result of a dynamic process which lasted for centuries and was completed in the second century BCE: in the course of this process Homeric lines underwent countless modifications.

The other lesson is a consequence of the nature of this constantly reinvented corpus. In order to explain many linguistic facts, we must first of all reconstruct the internal chronology of the epic corpus, whenever we can, and distinguish older lines from recent ones, the model from the copy. This is a fundamental principle. Here, Zenodotus' "wild" readings preserving an older state clearly

---

12 This is blatantly the case in Forssman 2019 and 2020: not only are those volumes a series of mere lists of forms without any analysis, but there is not a single word on variant readings and on the textual tradition. As though the text had been given to us engraved in marble and immutable from the start. Considering the forms of the vulgate only, without questioning them, is a pure and simple negation of the specificity of the Homeric corpus.

show how we can tell the old from the new and how important it is. In such cases the starting point of linguists should be Zenodotus and not Aristarchus. But even when no beautifully archaic variant reading is transmitted, only a stratigraphic study of the corpus can bring new solutions to old problems. We must not deal with Homer as a synchronically homogenous corpus: this is the way Greek scholars dealt with it, but this led to a homogenisation of the text of which we must be aware, because this process almost always aligns the text with the more recent state and sometimes wipes out all the traces of the older state—the case of ἐλυσθείς is a telling one. But next to one ἐλυσθείς where fortunately a Zenodotean reading transmitted by scholia preserves the original meaning whereas the vulgate only has the secondary meaning resulting from a reinterpretation, there are many cases for which only the reinterpreted meaning is kept in our text, sometimes because the text was modified according to the reinterpreted meaning (ἦλθον || ὄψ in μ 438–439, with the addition of "at the time when a man …" expanding on the meaning 'late'). This allows us to search for a possible reinterpretation whenever there is a discrepancy between the morphology of a word and the transmitted meaning, and, taking linguistics as our guideline, to restore a meaning sometimes very different from the transmitted one, as is the case for ὀψείοντες, or at least significantly different, as for ἐλυσθείς. In the cases studied here, we have a textual witness, Zenodotus, pointing to the problem, but the same principles and method can also apply when there is no variant reading—in the latter case we must be all the more cautious.[13]

There is no good linguistics without precise philology, in Homeric Greek as in any ancient Indo-European language. And conversely, Homeric philology is half blind without linguistics. The problem is that in the case of Homer the philological questions are a world unto themselves, so that Indo-Europeanists do not venture in it. They definitely should, starting from Z.

---

13   On this problem, see Le Feuvre 2015, *passim*.

APPENDIX

The Corpus

Tables of the Zenodotean Corpus

Below are listed all the lines about which Zenodotus is mentioned. For the *Iliad*, the source is Erbse's edition of the scholia, and the origin of the scholion is mentioned according to his edition: the Geneva scholia are taken into account only when they are listed in Erbse, that is, when they do not merely repeat an A scholion or a T scholion. Within this corpus, I took into account only scholia explicitly mentioning Zenodotus: if an A scholion mentions reading X as Zenodotus', and a T scholion mentions the same reading but not under Zenodotus' name, only the A scholion is in the table. The column "other source" is used when the variant reading is attested under Zenodotus' name in in a source other than the scholia. Among those other sources, Herodian is taken into account only if his text does not come from the Homeric scholia.

For some lines there are two entries because there are two independent differences.

Under Type, the "missing line(s)" refer to the cases for which Aristonicus says that Zenodotus "does not write" and Didymus that "the line is not in Zenodotus". It is therefore distinct from the athetesis. When our sources disagree, it is marked by missing line/athetesis (meaning for instance that the A scholion says οὐ γράφει, whereas the T scholion says ἀθετεῖ).

Under Subtype, the categories refer to the scholiast's analysis, not to the modern one:

a difference in case is labelled "syntax" except after preposition (see below),

a difference in number or in person is labelled "syntax,"

a difference in gender in adjectives (epicene type or overt feminine suffix) is labelled "morphology," in nouns it is labelled "lexicon,"

metrical problems like Ἡρακλείη/ Ἡρακληείη are labelled "morphology,"

the differences involving the pronominal and verbal dual endings are labelled "syntax," because this is how they were understood by scholiasts (either as a different case or as a different person) although they merely show the inconsistency in the use of obsolete form no longer clearly distinguished,

the variation between ἑοῖο and ἑῆος is labelled "morphology" (since ἑοῖο results from the regularisation of ἑῆος understood as an irregular genitive),

a difference in verbal tense or aspect is labelled "morphology," if this is the same verb in both readings,

a difference in voice between active and middle is labelled "morphology,"

a difference in mode is labelled "syntax,"

© CLAIRE LE FEUVRE, 2022 | DOI:10.1163/9789004522343_015

the presence or absence of the modal particle κε/ἄν is labelled "syntax,"

differences in segmentation are labelled "syntax" because this is how they were understood by scholiasts, even though this may be a mere phonetic difference,

differences resulting from elision are labelled "syntax" if they result in a different structure, as in P 173 Zenodotus' σε ὠνοσάμην (from σε(ο)) vs vulgate σευ ὠνοσάμην,

phonetic differences such as μήτειρα/δμήτειρα, θρέπτα/θρέπτρα, κρητός/κρατός are labelled "lexicon," for the same reason,

cases for which Zenodotus had a different form of the same word which was understood as a different word (such as ἀχέων Σ 160) are labelled "lexicon,"

a different preposition is labelled "lexicon," whether it governs the same case or a different one,

two variants of one and the same proper noun are labelled "lexicon,"

"agreement" refers to cases when Zenodotus is said to agree with the vulgate.

Statistics

For the *Iliad*, there are 623 references.

Source: 396 are transmitted by the A scholia alone, 16 by the A and bT scholia, 134 by the A and T scholia, 1 by the A and b scholia, 52 by the T scholia alone, 7 by the b scholia alone, 2 by the bT scholia alone, 2 by the A and Geneva scholia and 1 by the Geneva scholia alone. 12 are transmitted by other sources than the scholia.

Distribution according to the books of the *Iliad*: A: 63 – B: 60 – Γ: 31 – Δ: 11 – E: 23 – Z: 12 – H: 14 – Θ: 32 – I: 28 – K: 19 – Λ: 40 – M: 28 – N: 40 – Ξ: 45 – O: 32 – Π: 33 – P: 25 – Σ: 41 – T: 9 – Υ: 10 – Φ: 10 – X: 2 – Ψ: 6 – Ω: 9.

Type: 435 are variant readings, 40 are cross-references, 47 are atheteses, 39 are missing lines, 7 are spurious lines or passages, 14 are different lines, 5 are cases in which Zenodotus' text was "cut," that is, had one line instead of three or four in the vulgate, 6 mention plus-verses, 5 mention line inversions, 3 mention displaced lines, 1 is about book division. The few remaining ones mention comments or interpretations attributed to Zenodotus.

Sub-type: among variant readings, 5 are different hemistichs, 168 involve lexical divergences, 84 involve morphology, 5 spelling, 134 syntax, 35 syntax and lexicon, 1 syntax, lexicon and morphology, 1 syntax and morphology, 1 morphology and lexicon, 1 syntax or morphology.

TABLE 1   *Iliad*

Line	Scholia	Other source	Type	Sub-type
A 1	bT		comment	
A 4		Epim.	comment	
A 4		Athenaeus, Suda, Eust.	variant	lexicon
A 4–5	A		athetesis	
A 8	A	Ap. Dysc.	variant	morphology
A 24	A		variant	syntax
A 34	A		variant	lexicon
A 42	A		variant	morphology
A 46–47	A		athetesis	
A 56	A		variant	morphology
A 60	A		variant	syntax
A 63	A		athetesis	
A 68	A		variant	morphology
A 69	A		variant	lexicon
A 73	A		different line	
A 80	b		athetesis	
A 80	A, bT		variant	morphology
A 83	A	Ap. Soph.	variant	morphology
A 86	A		variant	morphology
A 91	A, T		agreement	
A 97	A, T		variant	different hemistich
A 100	A, bT		variant	lexicon/syntax
A 117	A		athetesis	
A 129	A		variant	spelling
A 143	A		athetesis	
A 143		Hrd., Et. M.	interpretation	
A 159	A		variant	syntax
A 160	A		athetesis	
A 163	A		variant	syntax
A 169	A		agreement	
A 198	A, bT		variant	morphology
A 203		Epim.	variant	morphology
A 204	A		variant	lexicon
A 208–209	A		athetesis	
A 212	A		variant	lexicon
A 216	A		cross-reference	

TABLE 1 *Iliad (cont.)*

Line	Scholia	Other source	Type	Sub-type
A 219–220	A		2 lines in 1	
A 225–234	A		athetesis	
A 249	A		variant	morphology
A 251	A		variant	syntax
A 260	A		variant	lexicon
A 271	A		variant	morphology
A 294	A		cross-reference	
A 299	A		variant	lexicon/syntax
A 336	A		variant	morphology
A 351	A		variant	lexicon
A 393	A		variant	morphology
A 396–406	A		athetesis	
A 400	A	Eust.	variant	lexicon
A 404	A	Eust.	variant	different hemistich
A 405	A	Eust.	plus-verse	
A 434	bT, Ge		variant	lexicon
A 446–448	A		3 lines in 1	
A 488–492	A		athetesis	
A 491	A		missing line	
A 508		Eust.	variant	different hemistich
A 530	A		variant	lexicon
A 559	T		variant	morphology
A 567	A		variant	syntax
A 567	A		agreement	
A 598	A		agreement	
A 609	A, T	Ap. Dysc.	variant	morphology
A 611	A		variant	morphology
B 1	A, b	Ap. Dysc., Hrd., Et. M.	variant	syntax
B 4	A		variant	morphology
B 12	A		variant	syntax
B 36	bT		variant	syntax
B 53	A, bT		variant	syntax
B 55	A		different line	
B 56	A		variant	syntax
B 60–70	A	Eust.	missing lines	
B 111	A	Dion. Thrax	variant	syntax

TABLE 1   *Iliad (cont.)*

Line	Scholia	Other source	Type	Sub-type
B 144	A		variant	lexicon
B 156–169	A		spurious lines	
B 161	A		variant	syntax
B 187	A		variant	syntax
B 196	A, T		variant	syntax
B 220–223	A		athetesis	
B 225	T		variant	lexicon
B 226	A		variant	lexicon/syntax
B 227–228	A		athetesis	
B 231–234	A		athetesis	
B 239	A		variant	morphology
B 258	b		variant	syntax
B 297	A		variant	lexicon
B 299	A		variant	lexicon
B 302	A, bT		variant	morphology
B 314	A	Eust.	variant	lexicon
B 318	A		variant	lexicon
B 435	A, bT		variant	lexicon
B 448	A		variant	morphology
B 484	A	Eust.	variant	lexicon
B 502	A		variant	lexicon
B 507	A	Strabo, Eust.	variant	lexicon
B 520	A	Eust.	variant	morphology
B 528	A		athetesis	
B 529–530		Eust.	athetesis	
B 532	A		variant	spelling
B 553–555	A		athetesis	
B 571	A		variant	lexicon
B 579	A		agreement	
B 579–580	A		athetesis	
B 612–614	A		athetesis	
B 616	A		variant	syntax
B 626	A		variant	syntax
B 634	A		variant	morphology
B 641–642	A		athetesis	
B 658	A		variant	morphology

TABLE 1   *Iliad (cont.)*

Line	Scholia	Other source	Type	Sub-type
B 667	A		variant	lexicon
B 673–675	A	Eust.	athetesis	
B 674	A		missing line	
B 681	A		different line	
B 686–694	A		athetesis	
B 690	A		variant	syntax
B 694	A		variant	morphology
B 697	A	Hrd.	variant	morphology
B 718	A		different line	
B 724–725	A		athetesis	
B 727	A		variant	syntax
B 741	A		variant	syntax
B 801	A		agreement	
B 851		Eust.	variant	lexicon
B 852	A	Strabo, Eust.	variant	lexicon
Γ 17–18	A		athetesis	
Γ 18	b		variant	syntax
Γ 28	A		variant	syntax
Γ 51	A		variant	syntax
Γ 56	A		variant	lexicon
Γ 57	A		agreement	
Γ 71	A		variant	morphology
Γ 74	A		variant	syntax
Γ 92	A		variant	morphology
Γ 99	A		variant	syntax
Γ 100	A		variant	lexicon
Γ 126	A	Eust.	variant	lexicon
Γ 152	A		variant	morphology
Γ 155	A		variant	lexicon
Γ 163		Epim.	variant	morphology
Γ 206	A	Ap. Soph.	variant	syntax
Γ 211	A		variant	syntax
Γ 236	T		comment	
Γ 244	A		variant	syntax/lexicon
Γ 259	A		agreement	
Γ 273	A	Ap. Dysc., Hrd., Epim.	variant	morphology

TABLE 1   *Iliad (cont.)*

Line	Scholia	Other source	Type	Sub-type
Γ 279	A		comment	
Γ 280	A		variant	morphology
Γ 334–335	A		athetesis	
Γ 334–338	A		line inversion	
Γ 339	A		cross-reference	
Γ 361	A		cross-reference	
Γ 364	A		variant	lexicon
Γ 423–426	A		line inversion	
Γ 453	A		cross-reference	
Γ 459	A		variant	syntax
Δ 3	A	Eust.	variant	lexicon
Δ 87	A		variant	lexicon
Δ 88	A		missing line	
Δ 123–124	A		line inversion	
Δ 137	A, T		variant	lexicon
Δ 139	A		variant	lexicon
Δ 161	A		variant	morphology
Δ 277	A, T		variant	lexicon
Δ 282	A		variant	lexicon
Δ 339	A		variant	lexicon
Δ 478	A		variant	lexicon
E 31	A		variant	lexicon
E 53	A		variant	lexicon
E 128	A		variant	lexicon
E 132	A, T		variant	morphology
E 146	A		variant	syntax
E 156	A		variant	syntax
E 162	A		variant	lexicon
E 187	A		athetesis	
E 194	A		2 lines in 1?	
E 227	A, bT		variant	lexicon
E 249–250	A		athetesis	
E 263	A		variant	morphology
E 293	T		variant	lexicon
E 323	A		variant	morphology
E 329	A		variant	syntax

TABLE 1   *Iliad (cont.)*

Line	Scholia	Other source	Type	Sub-type
E 416	T		variant	syntax
E 466	T		variant	morphology
E 638	A		variant	morphology
E 708	A		variant	lexicon
E 734–736	A		athetesis	
E 807a	A		plus-verse	
E 898	A, T		variant	morphology
E 906	b		athetesis	
Z 34	A		variant	syntax
Z 54	b		variant	syntax
Z 71	A, bT		variant	syntax/lexicon
Z 112	A		different line	
Z 121	A		variant	syntax
Z 135	A		variant	lexicon
Z 155		Eust.	variant	lexicon
Z 226	A, T		variant	syntax
Z 266	A		variant	morphology
Z 285	A, T		variant	lexicon
Z 511	A		variant	syntax
Z 514	A		cross-reference	
H 9	A		cross-reference	
H 32	A, T		variant	morphology
H 114	A		variant	morphology
H 127	A, T		variant	lexicon/syntax
H 153	A		variant	lexicon
H 198–199	A, T		athetesis	
H 256–257	A		missing lines	
H 390	A		cross-reference	
H 428	A, T		variant	syntax
H 443–464	A, T		athetesis	
H 451	T		variant	syntax
H 458	A		variant	syntax
H 475		Eust.	athetesis	
H 482	A		book division	
Θ 1	A	Eust.	displaced line	
Θ 10	A		variant	lexicon

TABLE 1   *Iliad (cont.)*

Line	Scholia	Other source	Type	Sub-type
Θ 25–26	A		athetesis	
Θ 37	T		missing line	
Θ 53	A		cross-reference	
Θ 56	A		cross-reference	
Θ 109	A		variant	syntax
Θ 128	A		variant	lexicon
Θ 139	A		variant	lexicon/syntax
Θ 166	A, T		variant	lexicon
Θ 207	A, T		variant	syntax
Θ 213	A, T		variant	syntax
Θ 284	A, T		missing line	
Θ 290	A		variant	syntax
Θ 291	T		variant	lexicon
Θ 304	A, T		variant	lexicon
Θ 312	A		cross-reference	
Θ 349	A, bT	Eust.	variant	morphology/lexicon
Θ 371–372	A, T		missing lines	
Θ 377	A		variant	morphology
Θ 378	A, T		variant	syntax
Θ 385–387	A, T		missing lines	
Θ 448	A		variant	syntax
Θ 470	A		variant	lexicon
Θ 493–496	A		spurious lines	
Θ 501	A		variant	different hemistich
Θ 503	A		variant	syntax
Θ 526	A		variant	syntax
Θ 528	A, T		missing line	
Θ 535–537	A		missing lines	
Θ 557–558	A, T		missing lines	
Θ 562	A		variant	lexicon
Ι 3	A		variant	morphology
Ι 14	A		different line	
Ι 15–16	A		spurious lines	
Ι 23–25	A, T		missing lines	
Ι 26–31	A		different lines	
Ι 36	A		variant	lexicon

TABLE 1   *Iliad (cont.)*

Line	Scholia	Other source	Type	Sub-type
I 88	A		variant	lexicon
I 128	T		variant	syntax
I 130	T		variant	syntax
I 131	A		cross-reference	
I 158	A		variant	lexicon
I 271	A		cross-reference	
I 404	A		interpretation	
I 405	A		variant	lexicon
I 416	A, T		missing line	
I 447	A		variant	syntax
I 506	A		variant	morphology
I 537	A		variant	syntax/lexicon
I 564	A, T		variant	syntax
I 594	A		variant	lexicon
I 612	A		variant	syntax/lexicon
I 616	A		cross-reference	
I 638	A		cross-reference	
I 641	A		variant	syntax/lexicon
I 660	T		variant	syntax/lexicon
I 664	A		variant	lexicon
I 692	A		athetesis	
I 694	A, T		missing line	
K 1	A	Ap. Dysc.	variant	syntax
K 10	A, T		variant	lexicon
K 25	A		cross-reference	
K 45	A		displaced hemistich	
K 98	A		variant	syntax/lexicon
K 127	A		variant	syntax
K 175	A		cross-reference	
K 240	A, T		missing line	
K 253	A		missing line	
K 291	A, T		variant	morphology
K 291	A		variant	lexicon
K 306	A, T		different line	
K 317	A		variant	morphology
K 497	A		missing line	

TABLE 1   *Iliad (cont.)*

Line	Scholia	Other source	Type	Sub-type
K 515	A		variant	syntax
K 520	A		line inversion	
K 534	T		missing line	
K 545	T		variant	syntax
K 546	A, T		variant	syntax
Λ 13	A, T		missing line	
Λ 27	A		variant	lexicon
Λ 32	A		cross-reference	
Λ 78–83	A, T		missing lines	
Λ 86	A		variant	lexicon
Λ 94	A		variant	syntax
Λ 101	A, T		variant	syntax
Λ 104	A, T		variant	syntax
Λ 106	A		cross-reference	
Λ 111	A		cross-reference	
Λ 123	A		variant	lexicon
Λ 132	A, T		variant	syntax/lexicon
Λ 138	T		variant	lexicon
Λ 142	A		variant	syntax
Λ 179–180	A, T		missing lines	
Λ 219	A		variant	syntax
Λ 222	A, T		variant	lexicon
Λ 348	A, T		variant	syntax
Λ 356	A, T		missing line	
Λ 368	A		variant	morphology
Λ 413	A		variant	syntax/lexicon
Λ 437	A, T		variant	syntax
Λ 439	A, T		variant	lexicon
Λ 451	A		variant	lexicon
Λ 458	A		variant	syntax
Λ 480	A		variant	lexicon
Λ 492	A		variant	syntax/lexicon
Λ 515	A, T		missing line	
Λ 528	A		variant	lexicon
Λ 548–557	A		athetesis	
Λ 589	A		variant	syntax

TABLE 1   *Iliad (cont.)*

Line	Scholia	Other source	Type	Sub-type
Λ 705	A, T		missing line	
Λ 730	A		variant	lexicon
Λ 754	A	Et. M.	variant	lexicon
Λ 782	A, T		variant	syntax
Λ 794–795	A		spurious lines	
Λ 799	T		variant	spelling
Λ 831	A, T		variant	morphology
Λ 838	A, T		variant	syntax
Λ 841	A		variant	lexicon
M 11	T		variant	spelling
M 34	A		variant	morphology
M 59	A, T		variant	lexicon
M 66	A, T		variant	syntax
M 75	A, T		variant	syntax
M 79	A		variant	syntax
M 127–138	A, T		variant	syntax
M 153	A, T		variant	lexicon
M 161	T		variant	syntax
M 175–180	A, T		missing lines	
M 230	A		different line	
M 231	A		variant	morphology
M 246	A, T		variant	lexicon
M 295	A	Hrd.	variant	lexicon
M 296	A		cross-reference	
M 340	A		variant	syntax
M 342	A, T		variant	syntax
M 346	A		cross-reference	
M 348	A		variant	lexicon
M 359	A, T		variant	lexicon
M 365	A		variant	lexicon/syntax
M 366	A	Ap. Dysc.	variant	syntax
M 368	A		variant	lexicon
M 423	A		variant	lexicon
M 428	A, T		variant	morphology
M 444	A		variant	different hemistich
M 450	A		missing line	

TABLE 1   *Iliad (cont.)*

Line	Scholia	Other source	Type	Sub-type
M 463	A		cross-reference	
N 2	A		variant	lexicon
N 2	T	Eust.	variant	lexicon
N 68	A		variant	morphology
N 71	A, T		variant	lexicon
N 107	A, T		variant	lexicon
N 148	A		variant	syntax/lexicon
N 166	A		variant	morphology
N 172	A		variant	syntax
N 191	A, T		variant	morphology/syntax
N 198	T	Eust.	variant	syntax
N 203	A		variant	lexicon/syntax
N 222	A		cross-reference	
N 229	A, T		variant	syntax/lexicon
N 237	A, T		variant	lexicon
N 245	A, T		variant	lexicon
N 246	A, T		variant	lexicon
N 257	A		variant	morphology
N 315	A		variant	syntax
N 351	A		variant	lexicon
N 367	T		variant	lexicon
N 374	A		variant	morphology
N 423	A, bT		variant	syntax
N 446	A		variant	spelling
N 447	A		variant	lexicon
N 449	T		variant	morphology
N 450	A		interpretation	
N 485	A		variant	syntax
N 546	A, T		variant	lexicon
N 551	A, T		variant	lexicon
N 609	A		variant	syntax/lexicon/morphology
N 610	A		variant	syntax/lexicon
N 627	A		variant	syntax
N 643	T		variant	syntax

TABLE 1   *Iliad (cont.)*

Line	Scholia	Other source	Type	Sub-type
N 643		Eust.	variant	lexicon
N 692	A		cross-reference	
N 694	A		cross-reference	
N 702	A, T		variant	lexicon
N 712	A	Eust.	variant	lexicon
N 808a	A, T		plus-verse	
N 824	A, T	Eust.	variant	lexicon
Ξ 16	A, T		variant	syntax
Ξ 36	A		variant	lexicon
Ξ 37	A		variant	lexicon
Ξ 40	A, T		variant	lexicon
Ξ 40		Eust.	variant	lexicon
Ξ 89	A, T	Eust.	variant	lexicon
Ξ 95	A, T		variant	syntax
Ξ 114	A, T		athetesis	
Ξ 118	A, T	Eust.	variant	syntax
Ξ 135	A		variant	syntax
Ξ 136a	A		plus-verse	
Ξ 162	A		variant	morphology
Ξ 169	A		variant	syntax
Ξ 177	A		variant	lexicon
Ξ 208	A, T		variant	syntax
Ξ 223	T		variant	lexicon
Ξ 229	A, T		variant	lexicon
Ξ 236	A, T		variant	lexicon
Ξ 249	A		variant	syntax
Ξ 259	A		variant	lexicon
Ξ 274	A		variant	morphology
Ξ 276	A		variant	syntax
Ξ 285	A		variant	syntax
Ξ 299	A		variant	syntax
Ξ 304–306	A, T		athetesis	
Ξ 310	A, T		variant	lexicon
Ξ 322	A, T		variant	morphology
Ξ 340	A		variant	syntax
Ξ 349	A		variant	syntax/lexicon

TABLE 1   *Iliad (cont.)*

Line	Scholia	Other source	Type	Sub-type
Ξ 351	A, T		variant	lexicon
Ξ 366	A		variant	lexicon
Ξ 376–377	A, T		missing line/athetesis	
Ξ 394–396–398	A		line inversion	
Ξ 398	T		variant	syntax
Ξ 400	A		variant	syntax
Ξ 412	A, T		variant	morphology
Ξ 427	A, T		variant	lexicon
Ξ 437	A		variant	lexicon
Ξ 442	A		cross-reference	
Ξ 445	T		variant	syntax
Ξ 469	A, T		variant	syntax
Ξ 470	T		variant	morphology
Ξ 485	A, bT		variant	lexicon
Ξ 499–500	A, bT	Eust.	variant	lexicon
Ξ 505	A		variant	lexicon
O 18–31	A		missing lines	
O 33	A, T		missing line	
O 64–77	A, T		missing lines	
O 79	T		variant	lexicon
O 86	b		variant	lexicon
O 134	A, T		variant	lexicon
O 138	A, T		variant	morphology
O 139	A		variant	syntax
O 169	A, T		variant	lexicon
O 179	T		variant	morphology
O 192	A		variant	lexicon
O 206	T		critical sign	
O 207	A		variant	lexicon
O 225	A, T		variant	morphology
O 266–268	T		missing lines	
O 277	T		variant	syntax
O 301	A, T		variant	syntax
O 307	A, T		variant	lexicon
O 336	T		variant	lexicon
O 347	A		variant	syntax

TABLE 1   *Iliad (cont.)*

Line	Scholia	Other source	Type	Sub-type
Ο 356	A		variant	lexicon
Ο 377	A, T		variant	lexicon
Ο 405	A, T		cross-reference	
Ο 439	A, T		variant	lexicon
Ο 459	A		variant	syntax
Ο 470	A, bT		variant	lexicon
Ο 480	A		cross-reference	
Ο 587	A		variant	lexicon
Ο 610–614	T		missing lines	
Ο 626	A, T		variant	syntax
Ο 640	A		variant	syntax
Ο 716	T		variant	morphology
Π 10	A		variant	lexicon
Π 89–90	A, T		athetesis	
Π 91	A		variant	lexicon
Π 92	A		variant	lexicon
Π 93–96	A, T		4 lines in 1	
Π 97–100	T		spurious lines	
Π 140	A		athetesis	
Π 141–144	A		missing lines	
Π 141–142	b		interpretation	
Π 150	A		variant	morphology
Π 156	A		variant	syntax
Π 160	A		interpretation	
Π 161	A, bT		variant	morphology
Π 188	A, T		variant	syntax/morphology
Π 202	A		variant	syntax/lexicon
Π 223	A, T		variant	syntax/lexicon
Π 233	A, T	Hrd.	variant	lexicon
Π 234	T		variant	lexicon
Π 237	T	Hrd.	missing line	
Π 243	A		variant	morphology
Π 281	T		variant	syntax
Π 432–458	A, T	Heracleides	spurious lines	
Π 507	A		variant	syntax
Π 515	A, bT		variant	syntax

TABLE 1   *Iliad (cont.)*

Line	Scholia	Other source	Type	Sub-type
Π 666	A, T		different line	
Π 666–683	A		athetesis	
Π 667–668	A, T		athetesis	
Π 677	A		spurious line	
Π 697	A, T		variant	syntax
Π 710	A		variant	lexicon
Π 748	A, T	Eust.	variant	syntax
Π 807	A		variant	lexicon
Π 812	A		cross-reference	
P 7	A		variant	syntax
P 15	A		cross-reference	
P 51	A		variant	lexicon
P 54	A		variant	lexicon
P 103	A		variant	syntax
P 134–136	A, T	Eust.	missing lines	
P 149	A, T		variant	syntax
P 153	A		variant	syntax
P 171	A, T		variant	lexicon
P 173	A		variant	syntax
P 214	T		variant	syntax/lexicon
P 215	A		variant	morphology
P 260–261	A		athetesis	
P 268	A, T		variant	lexicon
P 364–365	A		athetesis	
P 368	A, T		variant	syntax
P 392	T		variant	syntax
P 404–425	T		missing lines	
P 456	T		variant	lexicon
P 456a	T		plus-verse	
P 545–546	T		athetesis	
P 551	A		variant	morphology
P 582	A		different line	
P 595	A		variant	lexicon
P 700	A		cross-reference	
Σ 34	A, T		variant	lexicon
Σ 39–49	A		athetesis	

TABLE 1   *Iliad (cont.)*

Line	Scholia	Other source	Type	Sub-type
Σ 142	A		variant	syntax
Σ 148	A		cross-reference	
Σ 154	A		variant	lexicon
Σ 155	A		variant	syntax/lexicon
Σ 156	A		different line	
Σ 156a	A		plus-verse	
Σ 160	A		variant	lexicon
Σ 174	A		variant	syntax/lexicon
Σ 175–177	A		displaced lines	
Σ 198	A, T		variant	syntax
Σ 210	A, T		variant	lexicon
Σ 222	A		variant	morphology
Σ 230	A		variant	lexicon
Σ 231	A		variant	syntax/lexicon
Σ 247	A		variant	lexicon
Σ 287	A		variant	syntax
Σ 339	T		cross-reference	
Σ 364	A		variant	morphology
Σ 385	A, T		variant	syntax
Σ 400	A		variant	lexicon
Σ 424	A		variant	syntax
Σ 466	A		variant	syntax/lexicon
Σ 477	A, T		variant	morphology
Σ 483–606	A		athetesis	
Σ 485	A		variant	syntax/lexicon
Σ 492	A		variant	lexicon
Σ 499	A		variant	lexicon
Σ 501	A		variant	lexicon
Σ 502	A, T		variant	syntax
Σ 528	A		variant	lexicon/syntax
Σ 563	A		variant	morphology
Σ 564	T		interpretation	
Σ 565	A		variant	lexicon
Σ 570	A		variant	syntax/lexicon
Σ 576	A, bT	Et. M.	variant	syntax/lexicon
Σ 579	A, T		variant	lexicon

THE CORPUS   311

TABLE 1   *Iliad (cont.)*

Line	Scholia	Other source	Type	Sub-type
Σ 581	A		variant	syntax
Σ 584	A		variant	lexicon
Σ 592	A, T		variant	lexicon
T 14	A		variant	lexicon
T 15	A		cross-reference	
T 26	A		variant	lexicon
T 76–77	A		2 lines in 1	
T 118	A		cross-reference	
T 246	T	Eust.	variant	lexicon
T 342	A		variant	morphology
T 384	A		variant	morphology
T 388–391	A		cross-reference	
Υ 11	A		variant	lexicon
Υ 114–115	A, T		variant	syntax/lexicon
Υ 138	A		variant	syntax
Υ 261	A	Ap. Dysc.	variant	morphology
Υ 273–274	A		different lines	
Υ 283	A		cross-reference	
Υ 331	A, T		variant	lexicon
Υ 346	A, T		cross-reference	
Υ 481	T		variant	lexicon
Υ 484	A, T		variant	morphology
Φ 2	A		variant	syntax
Φ 17	A		cross-reference	
Φ 95	A, T		variant	lexicon
Φ 169	A, Ge		variant	lexicon
Φ 195	A, Ge		missing line/athetesis	
Φ 262	T		variant	morphology
Φ 288	Ge		comment	
Φ 335	A		variant	morphology
Φ 538–539	A, T		athetesis	
Φ 575	T	Hrd.	variant	syntax/lexicon
Χ 216	A		variant	syntax
Χ 378	A		different line	
Ψ 307	A		variant	syntax
Ψ 461	A, T		variant	lexicon

TABLE 1   *Iliad (cont.)*

Line	Scholia	Other source	Type	Sub-type
Ψ 527	A		variant	syntax
Ψ 533	A		variant	syntax/lexicon
Ψ 753	A		variant	syntax
Ψ 759	A		variant	lexicon/syntax
Ω 47	A		cross-reference	
Ω 110	A		variant	lexicon
Ω 269	A, T		missing line	
Ω 293	A, T		variant	morphology
Ω 486	T	Ap. Dysc., Polybius	variant	syntax
Ω 512	A		variant	lexicon
Ω 528	A		variant	morphology
Ω 550	A		variant	morphology
Ω 725	A, T		variant	syntax

For the *Odyssey*, there are 91 references.

Sources: 8 are transmitted by other sources than the scholia.

Distribution according to the books of the *Odyssey*: α: 5 – β: 4 – γ: 18 – δ: 11 – ε: 2 – ζ: 4 – η: 6 – θ: 3 – ι: 1 – κ: 6 – λ: 8 – μ: 7 – ν: 1 – ξ: 7 – ο: 1 – π: 2 – ρ: 2 – σ: 2 – τ: ∅ – υ: 1 – φ: ∅ – χ: ∅ – ψ: ∅ – ω: ∅.

Type: 69 are variant readings, 8 are atheteses, 2 are missing lines, 3 are spurious lines, 1 is a different line, 7 are cross-references.

Sub-type: 1 is a different hemistich, 37 involve a lexical divergence (probably 38 since λ 364 with a corrupt text is likely to belong here), 14 involve morphology, 1 morphology and lexicon, 11 syntax, 4 syntax and lexicon.

TABLE 2   *Odyssey*

Line	Other source	Type	Sub-type
α 3		variant	lexicon
α 38		variant	syntax/lexicon
α 93	Eust.	variant	lexicon
α 261		variant	syntax/lexicon
α 337		variant	morphology
β 41		variant	syntax

THE CORPUS 313

TABLE 2   *Odyssey (cont.)*

Line	Other source	Type	Sub-type
β 42		variant	lexicon
β 81		variant	lexicon
β 404		athetesis	
γ 11		variant	lexicon
γ 50		variant	morphology
γ 216–217		variant	syntax
γ 228		variant	syntax
γ 230		different line	
γ 276		variant	lexicon
γ 296		variant	syntax/lexicon
γ 307		variant	lexicon
γ 313		cross-reference	
γ 335		variant	morphology
γ 349		variant	lexicon
γ 362		variant	morphology
γ 368		variant	lexicon
γ 378		variant	lexicon
γ 380		variant	lexicon
γ 400–401		spurious lines	
γ 444		variant	lexicon
γ 489		cross-reference	
δ 1	Eust.	variant	lexicon
δ 62–64		athetesis	
δ 70	Hrd.	variant	syntax
δ 159	Eust.	variant	lexicon
δ 162		variant	lexicon
δ 353		athetesis	
δ 366	Eust.	variant	lexicon
δ 370		variant	lexicon
δ 379		variant	morphology
δ 465	Eust.	cross-reference	
δ 498		spurious line	
ε 132		variant	lexicon
ε 459		variant	morphology
ζ 1		variant	morphology
ζ 137		variant	lexicon

TABLE 2 *Odyssey (cont.)*

Line	Other source	Type	Sub-type
ζ 256		cross-reference	
ζ 290		variant	morphology
η 13		athetesis	
η 15		cross-reference	
η 41		variant	syntax
η 140		cross-reference	
η 217		variant	morphology
η 222		variant	syntax
θ 23		athetesis	
θ 142		missing line	
θ 251		variant	syntax
ι 116		variant	lexicon
κ 41		variant	morphology
κ 70		variant	lexicon
κ 124		variant	lexicon
κ 160		variant	lexicon
κ 239		variant	lexicon
κ 351		variant	syntax
λ 26		variant	morphology
λ 38–43		athetesis	
λ 93		variant	lexicon
λ 193		variant	morphology
λ 245		missing line	
λ 249		variant	morphology
λ 364		variant	? (corrupt text)
λ 498		variant	syntax
μ 15		variant	different hemistich
μ 209		variant	lexicon
μ 284		variant	lexicon
μ 290		variant	lexicon
μ 297		variant	morphology/lexicon
μ 388		variant	lexicon
μ 422		variant	lexicon
ν 213		variant	syntax
ξ 8		variant	syntax/lexicon
ξ 22		spurious line	

TABLE 2   *Odyssey (cont.)*

Line	Other source	Type	Sub-type
ξ 171		variant	lexicon
ξ 231		variant	syntax
ξ 295		variant	lexicon
ξ 318		agreement	
ξ 394		variant	morphology
ο 244		variant	lexicon
π 104		athetesis	
π 281–298		athetesis	
ρ 111		variant	lexicon
ρ 221		variant	lexicon
σ 130	Her. Philo, Eust.	variant	lexicon
σ 197		variant	lexicon
υ 106	Eust.	cross-reference	

Bibliography

Sources

Acosta-Hughes, Benjamin, and Christophe Cusset. 2012. *Euphorion. Œuvre poétique et autres fragments*. Paris: Les Belles Lettres (coll. Fragments).

Allen, Thomas W. 1920. *Homeri opera* I–II; *Iliad* (3rd ed.). Oxford: Clarendon Press.

Allen, Thomas W. 1917–1919. *Homeri opera* III–IV; *Odyssey* (2nd ed.). Oxford: Clarendon Press.

Baladié, Raoul. 1989. *Strabon, Géographie*, tome V (Livre VIII). Paris: Les Belles Lettres (Collection des Universités de France).

Bekker, Immanuel. 1833. *Apollonii sophistæ lexicon homericum*. Berlin: Reimer (repr. Hildesheim: Olms. 1967).

Bethe, Erich. 1900–1931. *Pollucis onomasticon*, 2 vols. Leipzig: Teubner (*Lexicographi Graeci* 9.1 et 9.2).

Bowie, Angus M. 2019. *Homer. Iliad. Book III*. Cambridge: Cambridge University Press.

Brixhe, Claude. 1976. *Le dialecte grec de Pamphylie, documents et grammaires*. Paris: Maisonneuve.

Clúa Serena, Josep Antoni. 2005. *Estudios sobre la poesía de Euforión de Calcis*. Cáceres: Universidad de Extremadura.

Cunningham I.C.: see Latte.

Dettori, Emanuele. 2019. *Antidorus, Dionysius Iambus, Epigenes, Lysanias, Parmenon, Silenus, Simaristus, Simmias*. Leiden: Brill (*Supplementum Grammaticum Graecum* 1).

Dindorf, Wilhelm. 1855. *Scholia græca in Homeri Odysseam, ex codicibus aucta et emendata*. Oxford (repr. Amsterdam: Hakkert. 1962).

Dyck, Andrew. 1983. *Epimerismi homerici, pars prior epimerismos continens qui ad Iliadis librum A pertinent*. Berlin: de Gruyter.

Dyck, Andrew. 1995. *Epimerismi Homerici: Pars altera. Lexicon αἱμωδεῖν*. Berlin–New York: de Gruyter.

Erbse, Hartmut. 1971–1982. *Scholia græca in Homeri Iliadem (scholia vetera)*. Berlin: de Gruyter.

Ernst, Nicola. 2006. Die D-Scholien zur Odyssee. Kritische Ausgabe. Cologne. Online edition, URL: https://kups.ub.uni-koeln.de/1831/1/D-Scholien.pdf

Finglass, Patrick J. 2011. *Sophocles. Ajax*. Cambridge: Cambridge UP.

Gaisford, Thomas. 1848. *Etymologicum magnum*. Oxford.

Gow, Andrew S.F. 1952. *Theocritus, edited with a translation and commentary*. Cambridge: Cambridge UP.

Hagedorn, Ursula. 2005. *Das sogenannte "Kyrill"-Lexikon in der Fassung der Handschrift*

E (*Codex Bremensis* G11), online edition by U. Hagedorn, URL http://kups.ub.uni
-koeln.de/1813/

Hansen P.A.: see Latte K.

IC: Guarducci, Margherita. *Inscriptiones Creticae*, 4 vols. Rome: Libreria dello stato. 1935–1950.

IG I³: *Inscriptiones Graecae I: Inscriptiones Atticae Euclidis anno anteriores*. 3rd ed. Berlin. 1981, 1994. Fasc. 1, ed. David Lewis, *Decreta et tabulae magistratuum* (nos. 1–500); fasc. 2, ed. David Lewis and Lilian Jeffery, *Dedicationes. Catalogi. Termini. Tituli sepulcrales. Varia. Tituli Attici extra Atticam reperti. Addenda* (nos. 501–1517).

IG IV² 1: Hiller von Gaertringen, F., *Inscriptiones Graecae, IV. Inscriptiones Argolidis*. 2nd ed. Fasc. 1, *Inscriptiones Epidauri*. Berlin. 1929.

IG V, 2: Hiller von Gaertringen, F., *Inscriptiones Graecae, V, 2. Inscriptiones Arcadiae*. Berlin. 1913.

Iscr. di Cos: Segre, Mario. *Iscrizioni di Cos*. Rome: L'Erma. 1993.

Jacques, Jean-Marie. 2002. Nicandre, vol. II. *Les Thériaques*. Paris: Les Belles Lettres (Collection des Universités de France).

Lasserre François, and Nikolaos Livadaras. *Etymologicum magnum genuinum. Symeonis etymologicum una cum magna grammatica. Etymologicum magnum auctum*. Vol. 1, Rome. 1976. Vol. 2, Athens. 1992.

Latte, Kurt. 1953–1966. *Hesychii alexandrini lexicon*. Copenhague: Munksgaard (vol. 1 & 2, A–O; vol. 3, Π–Σ by Peter A. Hansen, 2005; vol. 4, T–Ω by Ian C. Cunningham, Peter A. Hansen, 2009; 2nd ed. of vol. 1 by Peter A. Hansen, 2018).

Leaf, Walter. 1900–1902. *The Iliad. Edited with apparatus criticus, prolegomena, notes and appendices* (2nd ed.). London: MacMillan.

Lentz, August. 1867–1870. *Grammatici Graeci*. Vol. III/1 and III/2, *Herodiani technici reliquiae*. Leipzig (repr. Hildesheim. 1965).

Lightfoot, Jane. 2009: *Hellenistic collection: Philitas, Alexander of Aetolia, Hermesianax, Euphorion, Parthenius*. Cambridge, Mass.–London: Harvard UP (Loeb CL).

Linke, Konstanze. 1977. *Die Fragmente des Grammatikers Dionysios Thrax*. Berlin: de Gruyter.

Lloyd-Jones, Hugh, and Peter J. Parsons. 1983. *Supplementum hellenisticum*. Berlin–New York: de Gruyter.

Lobel, Edgar and Denys L. Page. 1955: *Poetarum Lesbiorum Fragmenta*. Oxford: Clarendon Press.

Macleod, Colin W. 1982. *Homer. Iliad. Book XXIV*. Cambridge: Cambridge UP.

Mazon, Paul. *Homère. L'Iliade*. Paris: Les Belles Lettres (Collection des Universités de France).

Nicole, Jules. 1891. *Les scolies genevoises de l'Iliade*. Paris: Hachette.

Page, Denys L. 1962. *Poetae melici Graeci*. Oxford: Clarendon Press.

Poltera, Orlando. 2008. *Simonides Lyricus. Testimonia und Fragmente*. Basel: Schwabe.

Pontani, Filippomaria. 2010. *Scholia Graeca in Odysseam*. Vol. II *Scholia ad libros γ – δ*. Rome: Edizioni di Storia e Letteratura.

Powell, Johannes U. 1925. *Collectanea alexandrina. Reliquiae minores Poetarum Graecorum Aetatis Ptolemaicae, 323–146 A.C.* Chicago: Ares publishers (repr. 1981).

Ricciardetto, Antonio. 2016. *L'Anonyme de Londres. P.Lit.Lond. 165 Brit. Libr. Inv. 137. Un papyrus médical grec du Ier siècle après J.-C.* Paris: Les Belles Lettres (Collection des Universités de France).

Rutherford, Richard B. 2019. *Homer. Iliad. Book XVIII*. Cambridge: Cambridge UP.

SH = *Supplementum hellenisticum*, see Lloyd-Jones and Parsons.

Schneider, Richard. 1878. *Grammatici graeci*. Vol. II/1. *Apollonii Dyscoli quae supersunt*. Leipzig: Teubner (repr. Hildesheim: Olms. 1965).

Stallbaum, Johann. 1825–1826. *Eustathii archiepiscopi thessalonicensis commentarii ad Homeri Odysseam*. Leipzig: Weigel.

Sturz, Friedrich. 1820. *Orionis Thebani etymologicon*. Leipzig: Weigel.

Van der Valk, Marchinus. 1971–1987. *Eustathii, archiepiscopi thessalonicensis, Commentarii ad Homeri Iliadem pertinentes*. Leiden: Brill (4 vol.).

Van Thiel, Helmut. 1991. *Homeri Odyssea*. Hildesheim–Zürich–New York: Olms (Bibliotheca weidmanniana I).

Van Thiel, Helmut. 1996. *Homeri Ilias*. Hildesheim–Zürich–New York: Olms (Bibliotheca weidmanniana II).

Van Thiel, Helmut. 2014a. *Scholia D in Iliadem, proecdosis aucta et correctior 2014, secundum codices manu scriptos*, online edition: http://www.uni-koeln.de/phil-fak/ifa/vanthiel/scholiaD.pdf

Van Thiel, Helmut. 2014b. *Aristarch, Aristophanes Byzantios, Demetrios Ixion, Zenodot. Fragmente zur Ilias gesammelt, neu herausgegeben und kommentiert*. Berlin: de Gruyter.

West, Martin L. 1972. *Iambi et elegi Graeci*. Oxford: Clarendon Press.

West, Martin L. 1978. *Hesiod, Works and Days*, edited with Prolegomena and Commentary by M.L. West. Oxford: Clarendon Press.

West, Martin L. 1998–2000. *Homeri Ilias* (2 vol.). Leipzig–Stuttgart: Teubner.

West, Martin L. 2017. *Homeri Odyssea*. Leipzig–Stuttgart: Teubner.

West, Stephanie. 1967. *The Ptolemaic papyri of Homer* (*Papyrologica coloniensia* vol. 3). Cologne: Westdeutscher Verlag.

Commentaries and Translations

BK: Latacz, Joachim (ed.). *Homers Ilias. Gesamtkommentar*. Münich–Leipzig: Saur (references are given to books of the *Iliad*, not to volumes of the BK).

Graziosi, Barbara and Johannes Haubold (eds.). 2010. *Homer. Iliad. Book VI*. Cambridge: Cambridge UP.

Heubeck, Alfred (ed.), et al. 1988–1992. *A commentary on Homer's Odyssey* (vol. 1, books 1–8, S. West, J.B. Hainsworth, 1988; vol. 2, books 9–16, A. Hoekstra, 1989; vol. 3, books 17–24, M. Fernandez-Galiano, A. Heubeck, J. Russo, 1992). Oxford: Clarendon Press.

Hine, Daryl. 2005. *Works of Hesiod and the Homeric Hymns*. Chicago: University of Chicago Press.

Huddleston, James. *Odyssey*, translation available online on the Chicago Homer. http://homer.library.northwestern.edu

Kirk, Geoffrey S. (ed.), et al. 1985–1993. *The Iliad: a Commentary* (vol. 1, books 1–4, G.S. Kirk, 1985; vol. II, books 5–8, G.S. Kirk, 1990; vol. 3, books 9–12, B. Hainsworth, 1993; vol. 4, books 13–16, R. Janko, 1992; vol. 5, books 17–20, M. Edwards, 1991; vol. 6, books 21–24, N. Richardson, 1993). Cambridge: Cambridge UP.

Lattimore, Richmond. 2001. *The* Iliad *of Homer*, translated by R. L., introduction and notes by R. Martin. Chicago: University of Chicago Press.

Dictionaries and Lexicons

Buck, Carl D. and Walter Petersen. 1970. *A reverse index of Greek nouns and adjectives*. Hildesheim–New York: Olms.

DELG: Pierre Chantraine. 1968–1980. *Dictionnaire étymologique de la langue grecque. Histoire des mots*. Paris: Klincksieck. 2nd ed. 1999.

De Vaan, Michiel. 2008. *Etymological Dictionary of Latin and the other Italic languages*. Leiden: Brill.

Derksen, Rick. 2015. *Etymological dictionary of the Baltic inherited lexicon*. Leiden: Brill.

DMic.: Francisco Aura Jorro (ed.). 1993–1999. *Diccionario Micénico*. Madrid: Consejo Superior de Investigaciones Cientificas. Supplement 2020.

Dunkel, George. 2014. *Lexikon der indogermanischen Partikeln und Pronominalstämme* (2 vols.). Heidelberg: Winter.

Ebeling, Heinrich. 1874–1885. *Lexicon homericum*. Leipzig: Teubner.

EDG: Robert S.P. Beekes. 2010. *Etymological Dictionary of Greek*. Leiden: Brill.

EWAia: Manfred Mayrhofer. 1992–1996. *Etymologisches Wörterbuch des Altindoarischen*. Heidelberg: Winter.

Kloekhorst, Alwin. 2008. *Etymological Dictionary of the Hittite inherited lexicon*. Leiden: Brill.

Kroonen, Guus. 2013. *Etymological Dictionary of Proto-Germanic*. Leiden: Brill.

LfgrE: Bruno Snell and Michael Meier-Brügger (eds.). *Lexikon des frühgriechischen Epos*. Göttingen: Vandenhoeck & Ruprecht, 1955–2010.

LIV²: Helmut Rix (ed.). 2001. *Lexikon der indogermanischen Verben*, 2nd ed. Wiesbaden: Reichert.

Matasović, Ranko. 2009. *Etymological Dictionary of Proto-Celtic*. Leiden: Brill.

NIL: Dagmar Wodtko, Britta Irslinger, and Carolin Schneider (eds.). 2008. *Nomina im Indogermanischen Lexikon*. Heidelberg: Winter.

Piquero Rodríguez, Juan. 2019. *El Léxico del griego micénico. Index Graecitatis. Étude et mise à jour de la bibliographie*. Nancy: ADRA.

Grammars

Bartoněk, Antonin. 2003. *Handbuch des mykenischen Griechisch*. Heidelberg: Winter.

Bernabé, Alberto, and Eugenio Luján. 2020. *Introducción al griego micénico. Gramática, selección de textos y glosario*, 2nd ed. Zaragoza: Zaragoza UP.

Chantraine, Pierre. *Gr. hom.*: *Grammaire homérique. I. Phonétique et morphologie*, 1948. *II. Syntaxe*, 1953. Paris: Klincksieck.

Forssman, Bernhard. 2019. *Die homerische Verbalformen, unter Mitarbeit von M. Brust und J. Habisreitinger*. Munich: Röll (*MSS Beiheft* 28).

Forssman, Bernhard. 2020. *Die homerische Nominalformen, unter Mitarbeit von M. Brust und J. Habisreitinger*. Munich: Röll (*MSS Beiheft* 29).

Hajnal, Ivo. 2006. *Grammatik des mykenischen Griechisch* (online publication). https://web.archive.org/web/20080514121722/http://www.uibk.ac.at/sprachen-literaturen/sprawi/mykgr.html

Hamm, Eva Maria. 1957. *Grammatik zu Sappho und Alkaios*. Berlin: Akademie Verlag.

Schwyzer, Eduard. 1953. *Griechische Grammatik*, Bd I (2nd ed.). Munich: Beck.

Schwyzer, Eduard, and Albert Debrunner. 1971. *Griechische Grammatik*, Bd II (2nd ed.). Munich: Beck.

Sihler, Andrew. 1995. *New comparative grammar of Greek and Latin*. Oxford: Oxford UP.

Wackernagel, Jacob. *Ai. Gr. = Altindische Grammatik*. Göttingen: Vandenhoeck & Ruprecht. 1896–1957.

Weiss, Michael. 2009. *Outline of the historical and comparative grammar of Latin*. Ann Arbor: Beech Stave.

Secondary Literature

Bachvarova, Mary. 2016. *From Hittite to Homer: The Anatolian Background of Ancient Greek Epic*. Cambridge: Cambridge UP.

Bakker, Egbert. 1990. Homeric discourse and enjambement: a cognitive approach. *Transactions of the American Philological Association* 120.1–21.

Basset, Louis. 1989. *La syntaxe de l'imaginaire. Étude des modes et des négations dans l'Iliade et l'Odyssée*. Lyon: Maison de l'Orient.

Bechtel, Friedrich. 1914. *Lexilogus zu Homer. Etymologie und Stammbildung homerischer Wörter.* Halle (repr. Hildesheim: Olms. 1964).

Bechtel, Friedrich. GD: *Die griechischen Dialekte*, 3 vol. Berlin. 1921–1924.

Beekes, Robert S.P. 2011. *Comparative Indo-European linguistics. An introduction* (2nd ed.). Amsterdam–Philadelphia: Benjamins.

Bernabé, Alberto, and Eugenio Luján. 2016. Testi relativi a pelli e manufatti in pelle. In Mario del Freo and Massimo Perna (eds.), *Manuale di epigrafia micenea. Introduzione allo studio dei testi in lineare B*. Padova: libreriauniversitaria.it. 567–588.

Bird, Graeme D. 1994. The textual criticism of an oral Homer. *Prudentia* 26/1.35–52.

Bird, Graeme D. 2010. *Multitextuality in the Homeric Iliad. The witness of the Ptolemaic papyri*. Washington, DC: Center for Hellenic Studies.

Blanc, Alain. 2018. *Les adjectifs sigmatiques en grec ancien : un cas de métamorphisme dérivationnel*. Innsbruck: Institut für Sprachen und Literaturen der Universität Innsbruck (*IBS* 160).

Bolelli, Tristano. 1953. Origine e sviluppo delle formazioni greche in men/mon. *Annali della Scuola Normale Superiore di Pisa* (serie II) 22.5–74.

Bravo, Benedetto. 1980. *Sulân*: représailles et justice privée contre les étrangers dans les cités grecques: étude du vocabulaire et des institutions. Pisa: Scuola Normale Superiore.

Buck, Carl D. 1955. *The Greek dialects*. Chicago: University of Chicago Press.

Carbon Jan-Mathieu, and James P.T. Clackson. 2016. Arms and the boy: on the new festival calendar from Arcadia. *Kernos* 29.119–158.

Clayman, Dee L. 2009. *Timon of Phlius. Pyrrhonism into Poetry.* Berlin–New York: de Gruyter (*Untersuchungen zur antiken Literatur und Geschichte* Bd 98).

Covini, Andrea. 2016. Griechisch ὀριγνάομαι, 'sich ausstrecken'. *Münchener Studien zur Sprachwissenschaft* 70/1.7–32.

Crielaard, Jan Paul (ed.). 1995. *Homeric Questions.* Amsterdam: Gieben.

Croft, William. 2000. *Explaining Language Change. An Evolutionary Approach.* London: Longman.

Dardano, Paola. 2010. La veste della sera: echi di fraseologia indoeuropea in un rituale ittito luvio. *Quaderni di vicino oriente* 5.75–84.

De Boel, Gunnar. 1988. *Goal accusative and object accusative in Homer. A contribution to the theory of transitivity.* Brussels: Koninklijke Academie voor Wetenschappen, Letteren en Schöne Kunsten van Belgie.

Del Barrio Vega, Maria Luisa. 1992. La medicina hipocrática y los iámata de Epidauro. In Juan Antonio López Férez (ed.), *Tratados hipocráticos: Estudios acerca de su contenido, forma e influencia.* Actas del VII Coloquio Internacional Hipocrático (Madrid, 24–29 de septiembre de 1990). Madrid: Universidad nacional de educación a distancia. 541–547.

Del Treppo, Julia. *Syntaxe de la tmèse : étude de l'autonomie des prépositions-préverbes dans la phrase homérique.* PhD defended in Sorbonne Université, Paris (12-08-2018).

Denizot, Camille. 2017. Les constructions dites à participe dominant en grec ancien : motivations sémantiques et pragmatiques. In Claire Le Feuvre, Daniel Petit, Georges-Jean Pinault (eds.), *Verbal Adjectives and Participles in Indo-European Languages*. Bremen: Hempen. 29–49.

Dickey, Eleanor. 2007. *Ancient Greek scholarship*. Oxford: Oxford UP.

Dieu, Eric. 2016. *L'accentuation des noms en -ā (*-eh₂) en grec ancien et dans les langues indo-européennes : étude morphologique et sémantique*. Innsbruck: Institut für Sprachen und Literaturen der Universität Innsbruck (*IBS* 156).

Dubois, Laurent. 1988. *Recherches sur le dialecte arcadien*. Louvain: Peeters.

Dubois, Laurent. 2018. Une nouvelle inscription arcadienne. *Revue des Etudes Grecques* 131.XIII–XVII.

Egetmeyer, Markus. 2010. *Le dialecte grec ancien de Chypre*. Berlin: de Gruyter.

Eichner, Heiner. 1980. Phonetik und Lautgeschichte des Hethitischen—ein Weg zur ihrer Entschlüsselung. In Manfred Mayrhofer et al. (eds.), *Lautgeschichte und Etymologie*, Akten der VI. Fachtagung der Indogermanischen Gesellschaft, Vienna, 24.–29. Sept. 1978. Wiesbaden: Reichert. 120–165.

Eichner, Heiner. 1985. Das Problem des Ansatzes eines urindogermanischen Numerus „Kollektiv" („Komprehensiv"). In Bernfried Schlerath and Veronica Rittner (eds.), *Grammatische Kategorien. Funktion und Geschichte*. Akten der VII. Fachtagung der Indogermanischen Gesellschaft, Berlin, 20.–25. Februar 1983. Wiesbaden: Reichert. 134–169.

Euler, Wolfram. 1979. *Indoiranisch-griechische Gemeinsamkeiten der Nominalbildung und deren indogermanische Grundlagen*. Innsbruck: Institut für Sprachwissenschaft der Universität Innsbruck (*IBS* 30).

Finkelberg, Margalit. 2011. *The Homer encyclopedia*. Malden–Oxford: Wiley–Blackwell.

Forssman, Bernhard. 1974. Zu homerisch ἀγγελίης 'Bote'. *Münchener Studien zur Sprachwissenschaft* 32.41–64.

Fowler, Robert (ed). 2006. *The Cambridge companion to Homer*. Cambridge: Cambridge UP.

García Ramón, José Luis. 2006. Zu den Personennamen der neuen Texte aus Theben. In Sigrid Deger-Jalkotzy and Oswald Panagl (eds.), *Die neuen Linear B-Texte aus Theben*. Vienna: Verlag der Österreichischen Akademie der Wissenschaften. 37–52.

García Ramón, José Luis. 2016. Il greco miceneo. In Mario del Freo and Massimo Perna (eds.), *Manuale di epigrafia micenea. Introduzione allo studio dei testi in lineare B*. Padova: libreriauniversitaria.it.

García Ramón, José Luis. 2018. Root enlargement or stem-forming -u-? *Historische Sprachforschung* 31 (Beiträge des Workshops der 15. Fachtagung der idg. Gesellschaft "Proto-Indo-European Root Extensions"). 145–178.

García Ramón, José Luis. 2021. Formations en *-nes- et en *-no-, formations en *-on/en- : védique °bharṇas- et grec φερνή, mycénien *po-re-na*. In Alain Blanc and Isabelle

Boehm (eds.), *Dérivation nominale et innovations dans les langues indo-européennes anciennes*. Lyon: MOM éditions. 19–44.

Garnier, Romain. 2020. Genèse du type homérique ὀψείοντες «désireux de voir». In Claire Le Feuvre and Daniel Petit (eds.), *Ὀνομάτων ἵστωρ. Mélanges offerts à Charles de Lamberterie*. Louvain: Peeters. 283–289.

Genevrois, Gérard. 2017. *Le vocabulaire institutionnel crétois d'après les inscriptions (VIIe-IIe s. av. J.-C.). Étude philologique et dialectologique*. Geneva: Droz.

Gentili, Bruno. 2011. *Poesia e pubblico nella Grecia antica. Da Omero al V secolo* (2nd ed.). Milan: Feltrinelli.

Gotō, Toshifumi. 1987. *Die I. Präsensklasse im vedischen. Untersuchung der vollstufigen thematischen Wurzelpräsentia*. Vienna: Österreichische Akademie der Wissenschaften (Phil.-Hist. Klasse Sitzungsberichte 489).

Gotō, Toshifumi. 2013. *Old Indo-Aryan morphology and its Indo-Iranian background*. Vienna: Österreichische Akademie der Wissenschaften (Phil.-Hist. Klasse Sitzungsberichte 849).

Greco, Alessandro. 2002. Aiace Telamonio e Teucro. Le tecniche di combattimento nella Grecia micenea dell'età delle tombe a fossa. In Franco Montanari and Paola Ascheri (eds.), *Omero tremilla anni dopo*. Rome: Edizioni di storia e letteratura. 561–578.

Hackstein, Olav. 1992. Eine weitere griechisch-tocharische Gleichung: Griechisch πτῆξαι und tocharisch B *pyāktsi*. *Glotta* 70.136–165.

Hackstein, Olav. 2002. *Die Sprachform der homerischen Epos*. Wiesbaden: Reichert.

Hainsworth, J. Brian. 1968. *The flexibility of the Homeric formula*. Oxford: Clarendon Press.

Hajnal, Ivo. 1994. Die frühgriechische Flexion der Stoffadjektive und deren ererbte Grundlagen. In George Dunkel et al. (eds.), *Früh-, Mittel-, Spätindogermanisch, Akten der IX. Fachtagung der indogermanischen Gesellschaft*. Wiesbaden: Reichert. 77–109.

Harðarson, Jón Axel. 1993. *Studien zum urindogermanischen Wurzelaorist und dessen Vertretung im Indoiranischen und Griechischen*. Innsbruck: Institut für Sprachwissenschaft der Universität Innsbruck (IBS 74).

Haslam, M.W. 1997. Homeric papyri and transmission of the text. In Ian Morris and Barry Powell (eds.), *A new Companion to Homer*. Leiden: Brill. 55–100.

Heubeck, Alfred. 1985. Zu den mykenischen Stoffadjektiven. *Münchener Studien zur Sprachwissenschaft* 46.123–138.

Hope Simpson, John, and John F. Lazenby. 1970. *The Catalogue of ships in Homer's Iliad*. Oxford: Clarendon Press.

Horrocks, Geoffrey. 2010. *Greek. A History of the Language and its Speakers*. Malden–Oxford: Wiley–Blackwell.

Humbach, Helmut. 1959. Aussage plus negierten Gegenaussage. *Münchener Studien zur Sprachwissenschaft* 14.23–33.

Jacquinod, Bernard. 1989. *Le double accusatif en grec d'Homère à la fin du V{e} siècle avant J.-C.* Louvain-la-neuve: Peeters (BCILL 50).

Janda, Michael. 1997. *Über "Stock und Stein." Die indogermanischen Variationen eines universalen Phraseologismus.* Dettelbach: Röll (MSS Beiheft 18).

Jones, Brandtly. 2012. Relative chronology and an 'Aeolic phase' of epic. In Ø. Andersen, D.T. Haug (eds.), *Relative chronology in early Greek epic poetry.* Cambridge: Cambridge UP. 44–64.

Jouanna, Jacques. 2002. «Soleil, toi qui vois tout» : variations tragiques d'une formule homérique et nouvelle étymologie de ἀκτίς. In L. Villard (ed.), *Couleurs et vision dans l'Antiquité classique.* Rouen: Université de Rouen. 39–56.

Karantzali, Efi. 2008. The transition from EB I to EB II in the Cyclades and Crete: Historical and Cultural Repercussions for Aegean Communities. In Neil J. Brodie, Giorgos Gavalas and Colin Renfrew (eds.), *Horizon, A colloquium on the prehistory of the Cyclades.* Cambridge: McDonald Institute for Archaeological Research. 241–260.

Kelly, Adrian. 2007. *A referential commentary and lexicon to Homer,* Iliad VIII. Oxford: Oxford UP.

Kinkade, Marvin Dale. 1975. The lexical domain of anatomy in Columbian Salish. In Marvin Dale Kinkade, Kenneth L. Hale and Oswald Werner (eds), *Linguistics and anthropology, in honor of C.F. Voegelin.* Lisse: de Ridder. 423–444.

Kiparsky, Paul. 1967. Sonorant clusters in Greek. *Language* 43.619–635.

Kiparsky, Paul. 1992. Analogy. *International Encyclopedia of linguistics.* Oxford: Oxford UP.

Klingenschmitt, Gert. 1975. Altindisch śaśvat-. *Münchener Studien zur Sprachwissenschaft* 33.67–78.

Kölligan, Daniel. 2018a. A new look at the Greek desiderative. *Indo-European linguistics* 6.95–116.

Kölligan, Daniel. 2018b. προθέλυμνος, θαλύσια und ein griechisches u-Präsens. In G. Mensching et al. (eds.), *Sprache–Mensch–Maschine. Beiträge zu Sprache und Sprachwissenschaft, Computerlinguistik und Informationstechnologie für J. Rolshoven aus Anlass seines sechsundsechzigsten Geburtstages.* Cologne. 219–230.

Kuiper, Franciscus B.J. 1942. *Notes on Vedic noun-inflexion.* Amsterdam: Mededelingen der Koninklijke Nederlandse Akademie van Wetenschappen.

Kuryłowicz, Jerzy. 1949. La nature des procès dits 'analogiques'. *Acta linguistica* 5.15–37.

Lakoff, George, and Mark L. Johnson. 1980. *Metaphors we live by.* Chicago–London: Univ. of Chicago Press.

Lallot, Jean. 1995. Analogie et pathologie dans la grammaire alexandrine. *Lalies* 15.109–123.

Lamberterie, Charles de. 1990. *Les adjectifs grecs en -υς : sémantique et comparaison.* Louvain: Peeters.

Le Feuvre, Claire. 2007a. Grec γῆ εὐρώεσσα, russe *syra zemlja*, vieil islandais *saurr*, 'la terre humide' : phraséologie indo-européenne et étymologie. *Bulletin de la Société de Linguistique de Paris* 102/1.101–129.

Le Feuvre, Claire. 2007b. La reprise décalée, un procédé de renouvellement formulaire dans la poésie lyrique et épique grecque ; sur les composés grecs πολυδήνης / skr. *púrudaṃsas-* (sic), *μελιϝεπής / skr. *mádhuvacas-*. In Alain Blanc and Emmanuel Dupraz (eds.), *Procédés synchroniques de la langue poétique*. Bruxelles: Safran. 123–137.

Le Feuvre, Claire. 2008. La forme homérique καμμονίη, le parfait κέκασμαι et le groupe de skr. *śáṃsati* 'louer'. *Revue de Philologie, de littérature et d'histoire ancienne* 82.305–320.

Le Feuvre, Claire. 2015. Ὅμηρος δύσγνωστος. *Réinterprétations de termes homériques en grec archaïque et classique*. Geneva: Droz.

Le Feuvre, Claire. 2021a. Implicit elements in scholiasts' etymological reasoning. In Arnaud Zucker and Claire Le Feuvre (eds.), *Ancient and Medieval Greek Etymology: Theory and practice I*. Berlin: de Gruyter (*Trends in Classics Supplementary Volumes* 111). 55–82.

Le Feuvre, Claire. 2021b. Νήποινος, νηποινεί, ἀνάποινος, ἄποινα, and ποινή. *Glotta* 97.107–157.

Le Feuvre, Claire. 2021c. A propos du supposé ποι[ν]ίον «amende» de la loi de Cadys : retour sur le groupe de ποινή, ἄποινα et leurs composés dans le vocabulaire juridique grec. *Ktèma* 46.249–265.

Le Feuvre, Claire. 2021d. Védique *vádhri-*, *vŕ̥ṣan-*, *dhārú-*, grec *ἔθρις, ἄρσην / ἔρσην et θῆλυς. Conversion et dérivation, In Hannes Fellner, Melanie Malzahn and Michael Peyrot (eds.), *Lyuke wmer ra. Indo-European Studies in Honor of Georges-Jean Pinault*, Ann Arbor, Beech Stave. 319–330.

Le Feuvre, Claire. 2021e. Greek μάρτυς 'witness', σειρά 'rope' and PIE *$t\underline{u}er(H)$- 'to bind'. *Historische Sprachforschung* 134.

Lejeune, Michel. 1972. *Phonétique historique du mycénien et du grec ancien*. Paris: Klincksieck.

Lemos, Irene. 2006. The 'Dark Age' of Greece. In E. Bispham, B. Sparkes, T. Harrison (eds.), *The Edinburgh companion to Ancient Greece and Rome*. Edinburgh: Edinburgh UP. 87–91.

Lemos, Irene. 2014. Communities in transformation. An archaeological survey from the 12th to the 9th century BC. *Pharos* 20.161–191.

Leumann, Manu. 1950. *Homerische Wörter*. Basel: Reinhardt.

Lindeman, Fredrik O. 1965. Notes sur quelques formes verbales du grec ancien. *Bulletin de la Société de Linguistique de Paris* 60/1.46–52.

Lubotsky, Alexander. 2000. The Vedic root *vr̥-* 'to cover' and its present. In Bernhard Forssman and Robert Plath (eds.), *Indoarisch, Iranisch und die Indogermanistik*.

Arbeitstagung der Indogermanischen Gesellschaft vom 2. bis 5. Oktober in Erlangen. Wiesbaden: Reichert. 315–325.

McCone, Kim. 1991. *The Indo-European origins of the Old Irish nasal presents, subjunctives and futures*. Innsbruck: Institut für Sprachwissenschaft der Universität Innsbruck (*IBS* 66).

McCone, Kim. 2005. Mögliche nicht-indogermanische Elemente in der keltischen Sprachen. In Gerhard Meiser and Olav Hackstein (eds), *Sprachkontakt und Sprachwandel. Akten der XI. Fachtagung der Indogermanischen Gesellschaft*. Wiesbaden: Reichert. 395–435.

Maiocco, Marco. 2005. *Absolute participial constructions. A contrastive approach to the syntax of Greek and Latin*, Alessandria: Edizioni dell' Orso.

Mallory, James P., and Douglas Adams. 2006. *The Oxford introduction to Proto-Indo-European and the Proto-Indo-European world*. Oxford: Oxford UP.

Manessy-Guitton, Jacqueline. 1970. Grec δῆνος, skr. *dáṃsas*. *Annales de la Faculté des Lettres et Sciences humaines de Nice* 11.3–14.

Matasović, Ranko. 2006. Collective in Proto-Indo-European. In K. Jones-Bley et al. (eds.), *Proceedings of the seventeenth UCLA Indo-European conference*. Washington DC: Institute for the Study of Man. 107–121.

Matthaios, Stephanos. 1999. *Untersuchungen zur Grammatik Aristarchs: Texte und Interpretation zur Wortartenlehre*. Göttingen: Vandenhoeck & Ruprecht (*Hypomnemata* 126).

Mazon, Paul. 1940. Notes sur quelques passages du XXIIIe chant de l'*Iliade*. *Revue des Etudes Anciennes* 42.254–262.

Meier-Brügger, Michael. 1988. Zu griech. ἰός 'Pfeil'. *Münchener Studien zur Sprachwissenschaft* 49.75–77.

Meillet, Antoine. 1908. Sur le suffixe indo-européen *-nes-. *Mémoires de la Société de Linguistique de Paris* 15.254–264.

Meissner, Torsten. 2006. *S-stem nouns and adjectives in Greek and Proto-Indo-European. A diachronic study in word formation*. Oxford: Oxford UP.

Melchert, H. Craig. 2014. PIE *-*eh$_2$ as an "individualizing" suffix and the feminine gender. In Sergio Neri, Roland Schuhmann (eds.), *Studies on the Collective and Feminine in Indo-European from a Diachronic and Typological Perspective*. Leiden: Brill. 257–271.

Méndez Dosuna, Julian. 2001. L'optatif oblique dans les iamata d'Epidaure. In René Hodot (ed.), *Les modes dans les dialectes grecs anciens*. Nancy: Presses universitaires de Nancy.

Middleton, Guy. (ed.), 2020. *Collapse and transformation: the Late Bronze Age to Early Iron Age in the Aegean*. Oxford–Philadelphia: Oxbow.

Minon, Sophie. 2014. Les mutations des alphabets péloponnésiens au contact de l'alphabet attique ionisé (ca. 450–350 av. J.-C.). In Sophie Minon (ed.), *Diffusion de l'attique et expansion des koinai dans le Péloponnèse et en Grèce centrale*. Geneva: Droz. 29–55.

Montanari, Franco, and Paola Ascheri (ed.). 2002. *Omero tremila anni dopo*. Roma: Edizioni di storia e letteratura.

Montanari, Franco. 2015. Ekdosis. A product of the ancient Scholarship. In Franco Montanari, Stephanos Matthaios and Antonios Rengakos (eds.), *Brill's Companion to Ancient Greek Scholarship*. Leiden: Brill. 641–672.

Morantin, Patrick. 2017. *Lire Homère à la Renaissance. Philologie humaniste et tradition grecque*. Geneva: Droz.

Morpurgo, Anna. 1972. Greek and Indo-European Semiconsonants: Mycenaean *u* and *w*. In Martin S. Ruipérez (ed.), *Acta Mycenaea* 2. Salamanca: Universidad de Salamanca. 80–121.

Morris, Ian, and Barry Powell (eds.). 2011. *New companion to Homer*. Leiden: Brill.

Morris, Sarah. 1984. Hollow Lakedaimon. *Harvard studies in classical philology* 88.1–11.

Muellner, Leonard C. 1976. *The meaning of Homeric εὔχομαι through its formulas*. Innsbruck: Institut für Sprachwissenschaft der Universität Innsbruck (*IBS* 13).

Neri, Sergio. 2003. *I sostantivi in -u del gotico: morfologia e preistoria*. Innsbruck: Institut für Sprachen und Literaturen der Universität Innsbruck (*IBS* 108).

Nickau, Klaus. 1977. *Untersuchungen zur textkritischen Methode des Zenodotos von Ephesos*, Berlin–New York: de Gruyter.

Nieto Izquierdo, Enrique. 2009. *Gramática de las inscripciones de la Argólide*. PhD Madrid. UCM (online publication).

Nieto Izquierdo, Enrique. 2014. La diffusion de la *koiné* en Argolide au IVe siècle: les premières étapes. In Sophie Minon (ed.), *Diffusion de l'attique et expansion des koinai dans le Péloponnèse et en Grèce centrale*. Geneva: Droz. 69–86.

Nieto Izquierdo, Enrique. 2015. El numeral tesalio τρίττος, τρέττος (= τρίτος): ¿arcaísmo o innovación? *Die Sprache* 51/1.83–91.

Nünlist, René. 2009. *The Ancient Critic at Work. Terms and Concepts of Literary Criticism in Greek Scholia*. Cambridge: Cambridge UP.

Nussbaum, Alan. 2017. The Homeric Formulary Template and a Linguistic Innovation in the Epics. In Dieter Gunkel, Olav Hackstein (eds.), *Language and Meter*. Leiden: Brill. 267–318.

Oettinger, Norbert. 2014. Zum anatolischen und indogermanischen Kollektivum. In Sergio Neri, Roland Schuhmann (eds.), *Studies on the Collective and Feminine in Indo-European from a Diachronic and Typological Perspective*. Leiden: Brill. 307–315.

Olsen, Barbara A. 2014. *Women in Mycenaean Greece: The Linear B Tablets from Pylos and Knossos*. London–New York: Routledge.

Olsen, Birgit Anette. 2020. Father Sky and the Wide-Eyed Cow. *Journal of Indo-European Studies* 48/3–4.389–415.

Panagl, Oswald. 1992. Mykenisch und die Sprache Homers: Alte Probleme—neue Resultate. In Jean-Pierre Olivier (ed.), *Mykenaïka, Actes du IX*[e] *Colloque international sur les textes mycéniens et égéens (Athènes, 2–6 octobre 1990). Bulletin de Correspondance Hellénique Supplément* XXV. 499–513.

Parry, Milman. 1928. *L'épithète traditionnelle dans Homère. Essai sur un problème de style homérique*. Paris: Les Belles Lettres (transl. *The traditional epithet in Homer*. In Adam Parry (ed.). *The collected papers of Milman Parry*. Oxford: Clarendon Press. 1971).

Parry, Milman. 1928b. The Homeric Gloss: a Study in Word-sense. *Transactions of the American Philological Association* 59. 233–247 (repr. in Adam Parry (ed.). *The collected papers of Milman Parry*. Oxford: Clarendon Press. 1971).

Peters, Martin. 1980. *Untersuchungen zur Vertretung der indogermanischen Laryngale im Griechischen*, Vienna: Verlag der österreichischen Akademie der Wissenschaften, Phil.-Hist. Klasse Sitzungsberichte 377.

Peters, Martin. 1986. Zur Frage einer 'Achäischen' Phase des griechischen Epos. In Annemarie Etter (ed.), *o-o-pe-ro-si, Festschrift für E. Risch zum 75. Geburtstag*. Berlin–New York: de Gruyter. 303–319.

Petit, Daniel. 1999. **Su̯e- en grec ancien : la famille du pronom réfléchi. Linguistique grecque et comparaison indo-européenne*. Louvain: Peeters.

Petit, Daniel. 2007. L'anastrophe verbale en grec archaïque. Entre syntaxe et poétique. In Alain Blanc and Emmanuel Dupraz (eds.), *Procédés synchroniques de la langue poétique en grec et en latin*. Bruxelles: Safran. 191–214.

Pfeiffer, Rudolf. 1968. *History of classical scholarship. From the beginnings to the end of the Hellenistic age*. Oxford: Clarendon Press.

Pinault, Georges-Jean. 2000. Védique *dámūnas-*, latin *dominus* et l'origine du suffixe de Hoffmann. *Bulletin de la Société de Linguistique de Paris* 95/1.61–117.

Pinault, Georges-Jean. 2017. In the heat of the day. In Ivo Hajnal, Daniel Kölligan and Katharina Zipser (eds.), *Miscellanea indogermanica*, Festschrift für J.-L. García Ramón. Innsbruck: Institut für Sprachen und Literaturen der Universität Innsbruck (*IBS* 154).

Pinault, Georges-Jean. 2019. Résumé des conférences de l'EPHE IVe section, 2017–2018. *Annuaire de l'EPHE*. Paris. 487–494.

Pinault, Georges-Jean. 2020. Le bois, le bâton et la pique. In Claire Le Feuvre and Daniel Petit (eds.), Ὀνομάτων ἵστωρ. *Mélanges offerts à Charles de Lamberterie*. Louvain: Peeters. 353–390.

Pontani, Filippomaria. 2005. *Sguardi su Ulisse. La tradizione esegetica greca all'Odissea*. Rome: Edizioni di storia e letteratura.

Pontani, Filippomaria. 2007. From Budé to Zenodotus: Homeric readings in the European Renaissance. *International Journal of the Classical Tradition* 14.375–430.

Pontani, Filippomaria. 2016. Thoughts on editing Greek Scholia: the case of the Exegesis to the *Odyssey*. In E. Göransson et al. (eds.), *The Arts of Editing Medieval Greek and Latin: A Casebook*, Studies and Texts 203. Pontifical Institute of Mediaeval Studies. 313–337.

Probert, Philomen. 2006. *Ancient Greek Accentuation. Synchronic Patterns, Frequency Effects, and Prehistory*. Oxford: Oxford University Press.

Probert, Philomen. 2015. *Early Greek relative clauses*. Oxford–New York: Oxford University Press.

Pusch, Hermann. 1890. *Quaestiones Zenodoteae. Dissertationes philologicae Halenses vol. XI*. Halle: Niemeyer. 119–216.

Rau, Jeremy. 2018. The Genetic Subgrouping of the Ancient Greek Dialects: Achaean. In Dieter Gunkel et al. (eds.), *Vina Diem Celebrent. Studies in Linguistics and Philology in Honor of Brent Vine*. Ann Arbor: Beech Stave. 380–389.

Renehan, Robert. 1975. *Greek lexicographical notes. A critical supplement to the Greek-English Lexicon of Liddell–Scott–Jones*. Göttingen: Vandenhoeck & Ruprecht.

Rengakos, Antonios. 1992. Homerischer Wörter bei Kallimachos. *Zeitschrift für Papyrologie und Epigraphik* 94.21–47.

Rengakos, Antonios. 1993. *Der Homertext und die hellenistischen Dichter*. Stuttgart: Weiner (*Hermes Einzelschriften* 64).

Rengakos, Antonios. 1994. *Apollonios Rhodios und die antike Homererklärung*. Munich: Beck.

Rengakos, Antonios. 2012. Bemerkungen zum antiken Homertext. In Michael Meier-Brügger (ed.), *Homer, gedeutet durch ein großes Lexikon. Akten des Hamburger Kolloquiums vom 6–8 Oktober 2010 zum Abschluss des Lexikons des frühgriechischen Epos*. Berlin: de Gruyter.

Ringe, Donald. 2006. *A linguistic history of English*. Oxford: Oxford UP.

Risch, Ernst. 1974. *Wortbildung der homerischen Sprache*, 2nd ed. Berlin–New York: de Gruyter.

Rix, Helmut. 1976. *Historische Grammatik des Griechischen. Laut- und Formenlehre*. Darmstadt: Wissenschaftliche Buchgesellschaft.

Rix, Helmut. 1981. Rapporti onomastici fra il panteon etrusco e quello romano. In Giovanni Colonna (ed.), *Gli Etruschi e Roma*. Rome, 104–126 (= *Kleine Schriften* 2001. 272–294).

Ruijgh, Cornelis J. 1966. Observations sur la tablette Ub 1318 de Pylos. *Lingua* 16.130–152.

Ruijgh, Cornelis J. 1967. *Études sur la grammaire et le vocabulaire du grec mycénien*. Amsterdam: Hakkert.

Ruijgh, Cornelis J. 1970. review of Chantraine, DELG. *Lingua* 25.302–320.

Ruijgh, Cornelis J. 1971. review of Chantraine, DELG. *Lingua* 28.162–173.

Ruijgh, Cornelis J. 1985. Le mycénien et Homère. In Anna Morpurgo Davies and Yves Duhoux (eds.), *Linear B, a 1984 Survey: proceedings of the Mycenaean Colloquium of* the VIIIth Congress of the International Federation of the Societies of Classical Studies (Dublin, 27 August–1st September 1984). Louvain: Peeters. 143–190.

Ruijgh, Cornelis J. 2011. Mycenaean and Homeric language. In Anna Morpurgo-Davies and Yves Duhoux (eds.), A Companion to Linear B. Mycenaean Greek Texts and their World, vol. 2. Louvain: Peeters. 253–298.

Ruipérez, Martin. 1972. Le dialecte mycénien. In Martin Ruipérez (ed.), Acta Mycenaea, Actes du cinquième colloque international des études mycéniennes. Salamanca: Universidad de Salamanca. 136–166 (= Minos XI et XII).

Schenkeveld, Dirk M. 1970. Aristarchus and ΟΜΗΡΟΣ ΦΙΛΟΤΕΧΝΟΣ: Some Fundamental Ideas of Aristarchus on Homer as a Poet. Mnemosyne 23.162–178.

Schindler, Jochem. 1967. Das idg. Wort für ‚Erde' und die dentalen Spiranten. Die Sprache 13.191–205.

Schindler, Jochem. 1975. L'apophonie des thèmes indo-européens en -r/n. Bulletin de la Société de Linguistique de Paris 70/1.1–10.

Schironi, Francesca. 2004. I frammenti di Aristarco di Samotracia negli etimologici bizantini. Göttingen: Vandenhoeck & Ruprecht (Hypomnemata 152).

Schironi, Francesca. 2018. The best of the grammarians. Aristarchus of Samothrace on the Iliad. Ann Arbor: University of Michigan Press.

Schmidt, Martin. 1997. Variae lectiones oder Parallelstellen: Was notierten Zenodot und Aristarch zu Homer? Zeitschrift für Papyrologie und Epigraphik 115.1–12.

Schmitt, Rüdiger. 1967. Dichtung und Dichtersprache in indogermanischer Zeit. Wiesbaden: Harrassowitz.

Schulze, Wilhelm. 1888. Zwei verkannte Aoriste. Zeitschrift für vergleichende Sprachforschung 29.230–255.

Schulze, Wilhelm. 1892. Quaestiones epicae. Gütersloh: Bertelsmann (repr. Hildesheim: Olms. 1967).

Sluiter, Ineke. 2011. A champion of Analogy: Herodian's On lexical singularity. In Stephanos Matthaios, Franco Montanari and Antonios Rengakos (eds.), Ancient scholarship and grammar. Archetypes, concepts and contexts. Berlin–New York: de Gruyter. 291–310.

Snodgrass, Anthony M. 2000. The dark age of Greece. An archaeological survey of the eleventh to the eighth centuries BC (2nd ed.). Edinburgh: Edinburgh UP.

Strunk, Klaus. 1976. Griechisch δένδρεον und Zugehöriges. In Wojciech Smoczyński (ed.), Kuryłowicz Memorial volume. Analecta Indoeuropæa Cracoviensia 2.357–363.

Stüber, Karin. 2002. Die primären s-Stämme des Indogermanischen. Wiesbaden: Reichert.

Teodorsson, Sven Tage. 1974. The phonemic system of the Attic dialect 400–340 BC. Göteborg: Acta Universitatis gothoburgensis.

Tichy, Eva. 1995. Die Nomina agentis auf -tar- im Vedischen. Heidelberg: Winter.

Tichy, Eva. 2010. Älter als der Hexameter ? Schiffskatalog, Troerkatalog und vier Einzelszenen der Ilias. Bremen: Hempen.

Tichy, Eva. *Ilias diachronica*. Attempt at a diachronic restitution of the text, several books available online: https://www.indogermanistik.uni-freiburg.de/seminar/pers/tichy/pub.html

Timberlake, Alan. 1977. Reanalysis and actualization in syntactic change. In Charles N. Li (ed.), *Mechanisms of syntactic change*. Austin: University of Texas Press. 141–177.

Vaessen, Rik. 2015. The Ionian migration and ceramic Dynamics in Ionia at the end of the second millenium BC: some preliminary thoughts. In Nicolas Stampolidis et al. (eds.), *Nostoi. Indigenous culture, migration—integration in the Aegean islands—Western Anatolia during the Late Bronze–Early Iron Ages*. Istanbul: Koç UP. 811–834.

Van der Valk, Marchinus. 1963–1964. *Researches on the text and scholia of the* Iliad, 2 vols. Leiden: Brill.

Van der Valk, Marchinus. 1985. A Few Observations on the Homeric Text. *Mnemosyne* 38.376–378.

Van Thiel, Helmut. 1992. Zenodot, Aristarch und andere. *Zeitschrift für Papyrologie und Epigraphik* 90.1–32.

Van Wees, Hans J. 1999. The Homeric Way of War: the *Iliad* and the Hoplite Phalanx. In Irene de Jong (ed.), *Homer Critical assessments, vol. II: the Homeric world*. London: Routledge. 221–238.

Vasilaros, Georgios. 1993. *Der Gebrauch des Genetivus absolutus bei Apollonios Rhodios im Verhältnis zu Homer*. Athens: National and Capodistrian University.

Vine, Brent. 1998. The Etymology of Greek κώμη and Related Problems. In J. Jasanoff, H. C. Melchert and L. Oliver (eds.) *Mír Curad: Studies in Honor of Calvert Watkins*. Innsbruck: Institut für Sprachwissenschaft der Universität Innsbruck (*IBS* 92). 685–702.

Vine, Brent. 1999. A note on the Duenos inscription. *UCLA Bulletin of Indo-European Studies* 1. 293–305.

Vine, Brent. 2006. An alleged case of 'inflectional contamination': on the i-stem inflection of Latin *civis*. *Incontri Linguistici* 29.139–158.

Vine, Brent. 2011. On dissimilatory r-loss in Greek. In T. Krisch, T. Lindner (eds.), *Indogermanistik und Linguistik im Dialog* (Akten der XIII. Fachtagung der Idg. Gesellschaft, Salzbourg 2008). Wiesbaden: Reichert. 1–17.

Visser, Edzard. 1997. *Homers Katalog der Schiffe*. Leipzig: Teubner.

Voigt, Eva Maria: see Hamm.

Wackernagel, Jacob. 1916. *Sprachliche Untersuchungen zu Homer* (1st ed.). Göttingen: Vandenhoeck & Ruprecht.

Wackernagel, Jacob. 1953–1979. *Kleine Schriften*. Göttingen: Vandenhoeck & Ruprecht.

Wathelet, Paul. 1970. *Les traits éoliens dans la langue de l'épopée grecque*. Rome: Ateneo (*SMEA* 37).

West, Martin L. 2001. *Studies in the Text and Transmission of the* Iliad. Munich–Leipzig: Saur.

West, Martin L. 2001a. Some Homeric words. *Glotta* 77.118–135.
West, Martin L. 2002. Zenodotus' text. In Franco Montanari and Paola Ascheri (eds.), *Omero tremilla anni dopo*. Roma: Edizioni di storia e letteratura. 137–142.
West, Martin L. 2011. *The making of the Iliad: disquisition and analytical commentary*. Oxford: Oxford UP.
West, Martin L. 2011b. Recension of Tichy 2010. *Kratylos* 56.156–163.
West, Martin L. 2015: *The making of the Odyssey: disquisition and analytical commentary*. Oxford: Oxford University Press.
White, Heather. 1993. On the languaje (*sic*) and style of Euphorion of Chalcis. *Emerita* 61.181–197.
Wilamowitz-Moellendorf, Ulrich von. 1916. *Die Ilias und Homer*. Berlin: Weidmann.
Willi, Andreas. 2017. *Origins of the Greek verb*. Cambridge: Cambridge University Press.
Willmott, Jo. 2007. *The moods of Homeric Greek*. Cambridge: Cambridge University Press.
Zucker, Arnaud. 1997. Etude épistémologique du mot κῆτος. In Sylvie Mellet (ed.), *Les zoonymes* (proceedings of the Nice conference, January 1997). CNRS, Publications de la faculté des lettres, arts et sciences humaines de Nice vol. 38.425–454.
Zurbach, Julien. 2006. L'Ionie à l'époque mycénienne. Essai de bilan historique. *Revue des Etudes Anciennes* 108/1.271–297.

Index Verborum

NB: the Appendix is not included in the indices.

Alphabetic Greek

ἄαπτος 29
ἄας 107–122, 126, 129–130, 137, 138, 160, 225, 237, 277, 284
ἀγάννιφος 232
Ἀγάπητος 124n42
Ἀγαπωμενός 124n42
ἀγγελίης 25–26
ἀγκών 114, 204
ἄγνυμι: ἔαξα, ἔηξα 35
ἀγχίαλος 34
ἀδανές 131
ἀελλόπος 196
ἀές 115
*ἀές 109–110, 114, 115, 116, 118, 126, 277
ἀεστητόν 108–110, 112, 117, 160
ἀήρ 114
ἀθρόος 143
αἶα 135n8
Αἴας: Αἴαντε 73–74
αἰγανέη 52
αἰέν 114
αἰές 114, 115
αἰθίοψ 210
αἰπεινός 130
αἰπήεις 130
αἶπος αἰπύς 130
αἰχμή 208, 209
αἶψα 151
ἀΐω 151–152, 157
αἰῶ 114
αἰών 114
ἀκαχέω, ἤκαχον 140
Ἀκεσσαμενός 124n42
ἀκίς 208n33
ἄκμων 204
ἀκτή 206
ἀκτηρίς 207–208
ἀκτινωτός 207
Ἄκτιον 206n27
ἀκτίς 202–208, 210, 279
ἀκωκή 208, 209
ἀλαοσκοπίη 21
ἀλγινόεις 240

Ἀλεξαμενός 124n42
Ἀλεξομενός 124n42
ἀλιτήμων 45n61
ἄλφι 98
ἄλφιτον 98
ἀμνίον 20
Ἀμυναμενός 124n42
Ἀμυνομενός 124n42
Ἀμύντας 221
Ἀμφιάραος 32
ἀμφιαχυῖαν see ἰάχω
ἀμφίσταμαι 154
ἀμφίς 154–155
ἀμφιφράζομαι 154–155
ἄμφω 267–269, 277, 284
ἀναπετής 135
ἀναπτάς 132–138, 157, 189, 237, 275, 281, 282, 284, 285, 286, 288
ἀνασεύομαι 266
ἀνδράποδα 10n29
ἀνδραπόδιον 196
ἀνέρχομαι 159n31
ἀνέχω, ἀνασχών 132–133
ἀνήκεστος 66n94
ἄνιπτος 34
ἀνύω, ἄνω 72, 278
ἀξίνη 203
ἀπαρέσκω 156
ἀπό 152, 153, 155
ἀποδίδωμι 156
ἀποέργω 156
ἀποστρέφω 156
ἀπωθέω 155
ἀργαλέος 240
ἀργύρεος, Thess. ἄργυρρος 84–85, 283
ἀρήν: ἀρνέων 41n52
ἀρνεῖος: ἀρνέων 41n52
ἄρουρα 135n8
ἄρρην, ἄρσην 97n43
ἀρχή 61–62, 276
ἀσπίς 209
ἀστήρ 97–98
ἄστρον 97–98
ἄτη 61–62

αὖα, αὖα, αὖας   110–112, 116–118, 120, 126, 127, 160, 277
αὐριβάτης   114
αὐρίζειν   114
αὔριον   106, 107, 112, 114–116, 118, 127
αὐτίκα   151
αὖως (Aeol.), Acc.sg Αὔων   111–113, 115–117, 119n31, 123, 127
ἀφαιρέω   23n7, 155
ἀφικνέομαι, ἀπικνέομαι   29, 159
ἀφοράω   156
ἀχέω1   139, 141
ἀχέω2   see ἰάχω
ἄχνυμαι   137
ἄχομαι   137
ἄψ   152, 153, 155–157, 159, 161–162
Ἀώτῑ   119n31
βάθος   131n61
βαθυδίνης   232
βαθύζωνος   210n37
βαθύκολπος   54
βαθύς   131n61
βακτηρία   208
βάλλω: βεβλήατο, βεβολήατο, βεβολημένος   46–47, 284
βαρύφθογγος   210n37
βένθος   131n61
Βῆσ(σ)αν   38
βλῆτρον   286
βουγάϊε   286
γαῖα   135n8
Γλίσχρων   196
γόνυ   96n37, 99n48
Γοργώ   34
δαίνυμι   137, 221n21
δαίς   9–12, 284
δαίτης   221n21
δαΐφρων   131n61
δαίω   137, 221n21
δάκρυ   98
δακρυόεσσα   103
δάκρυον   98
δαμνίον   20
δειδήμων   44–45, 51, 72, 276, 281
δείδω   44
δείκνυμι   96n38, 133, 137
δένδρεον, δένδρον: δένδρος, δένδρει, δενδρέῳ   82–103, 107, 120, 130, 138, 189, 276, 281–284, 286

δενδρήεις   102–103, 130, 232
δενδρύφιον   90n27
Δεξαμενός   124n42
δέχομαι: δέγμενος, δέχαται, δεικνύμενος   133, 134n6
δήνεα   130–131
διαμπερές   159n31
διαπροέρχομαι   159n31
διδάσκω: ἐδάην, δέδαε, δεδάασθαι   45–46, 72, 131n61
διέρχομαι   159n31
δίκη   96n38
δινήεις   232
Διοκλέης: Διοκλῆος   129
δμήτειρα, μήτειρα   37
δολιχεγχής   144n3
δολιχόσκιος   144n3, 209n34
δονακεύς   234–237, 242, 279, 281, 290
δονακήεις   236–242, 279, 281
δονακόεις   237
δόρυ   95, 96, 98, 99, 209
δρῦς   96, 169
δρυτόμος   96n39
δρύφακτος   36–37, 96n39
δώς   206
δωτίνη   204, 206
ἔγχος   144, 209
ἐέργνυμι   137
ἐέργω   137
ἔζομαι   83
ἑῆος   33
εἰλέω   191
εἴλυμα   172–174, 177, 190, 277
εἰλυσπάομαι   172n6
εἰλυφάζω   171n6
εἰλυφάω   171n6
εἰλύω: εἴλῡμαι, εἰλύσω   170–172, 177, 188n41, 189–191
ἔκαθεν   40
ἑκάς   40
ἑκατηβόλος   103n52
ἐκσεύομαι: ἐξεσύθη   36
Ἐλαιοῦς   237n6
ἐλαφηβόλος   103n52
ἐλεήμων   44–45, 276, 281
ἑλίκωπες   39n45
ἔλπομαι, ἤλπετο   35, 40, 41
(ϝ)ἔλῠμα   168–177, 179, 182, 188–192, 275, 277, 281, 285, 286

INDEX VERBORUM

ἔλῡμα   169, 171, 191–193, 277
ἐλύμνιαι   191–193
ἐλυσθείς   170n3, 172, 176–191, 194, 275, 277, 282, 291
ἔλυτρον   170–172
ἐμπόδιος   196
ἐμωυτόν   33
ἔναρα   258–260
ἐναρίζω   257n23, 258
ἐνοινοχοέω: ἐνῳνοχόει   16–17
ἔντεα   135n8, 258
ἐνύπνιον   66–67
ἐξεναρίζω   257n23
ἐός, ὅς   33, 47–48
ἐπαΐω   152, 153, 157, 165, 278, 285
ἐπέρχομαι   153, 158, 159n31, 160
ἐπηγκενίδες   114
ἐπί, ὀπί   152, 153, 157, 167
Ἐπιλυσαμενός   124n42
ἐπιμάρτυρος   38–39, 54, 83, 102
ἐπιπόδιος   196
ἐπίσταμαι: ἐπιστέαται   32
ἐπιτείνω   162
Ἔραστος   124n42
ἐρίηρος, ἐρίηρες   38, 39n45
ἔρυμα   168–169, 171, 173–176, 277, 281, 283
Ἐρωμένη   124n42
Ἐρῶσα   124n42
ἑσπέρα   106, 116–118, 277
ἕσπερος   106
εὐγενής   89
ἐΰζυγος   43n58, 135n8
εὐθύγραμμος   209
εὐθύκαυλος   209
εὐθυκτέανον   200, 201
εὐθύρριζος   209
εὐθύς   202n14
εὐκλεής: ἐϋκλεῖας   43, 165n37
ἐϋκληΐς   43n58
εὐκτέανον   200, 201
εὐνομίη   53
εὐρυάγυια   164–165
εὐρυεδής   164–165
εὐρυοδείης   164–165
εὐρύοπα   210
εὐρώεις   213n4
εὐτειχής   232
Ἐχευήθεις (Arc.)   123, 126
ἔωθεν   106, 119n31

ἑωθινός   119n31
ἑωυτόν   33, 282
ἕως   106, 113, 119n31
-ϝεντ-   102–103, 128–130, 212, 220, 225–226, 232, 237, 242
ζεύγνυμι   133
ζῳῦφιον   90n27
ἡδυεπής   210n37
ἠήρ   114
ἠϊκανός   115–119
*ἦμι: ἦ   29–30
ἡμιπόδιον   196
Ἡρακλεῖος, Ἡρακληείη   8n23, 43–44, 281, 282
ἠριγένεια   115
ἥρως   213n4
-ήσσιος   227n33
-ησσος   226
ἠχή   140n15
ἠῶθεν   105, 106, 118–120, 122
ἠῶθι   105, 119
ἠώς   104–107, 112, 113
θᾱητός   227
θεάομαι: θαϝέομαι, θηέομαι   227
-θεν   119–120
Θερσίτης   221
θηρίον   196, 197, 211
-θι   119–120
θρασυκάρδιος   210n37
θρασύς   133n4
θρέπτρα   36–37
θυήεις   130, 212n2
θυόεις; θυώεις   212
ἰάχω: ἀχέω, ἀμφιαχυῖαν   139–141, 278–279, 281
ἰδρώεις   213n4
ἰδρώς   213n4
ἱερόσυλος   259
ἴθμα   52
ἰθύθριξ   209
ἰθυκτέανον   200
ἰθυκτίωνα   198–211, 237, 279, 281, 289
ἰθυπτίωνα   194, 210–211, 279, 281, 289, 290
ἰθύς   197, 202, 209
ἰθύφαλλος   209
ἱκνέομαι   52
ἰκτίς   219n16
ἴλλω   191
ἰνίον   196
ἰογάστριος   67–71, 225, 279, 284, 285
-ιον   196–197

ἰός, ἰά (adj.) 68
ἰός, ἰά (subst.) 97n43
ἴχμα 52, 53, 72
ἴχνιον 52
καθέζομαι: ἐκαθέζετο 29, 35, 78n123
καθεύδω: ἐκάθευδε 34–35
Καιάδας 217n11, 229n37
καίατα 217n11
Καιάτας 217n11
Καίβων 221n21
καιέτα 214, 219, 221
καιετάεσσα 214–221, 228, 275
καιέτας 216–219, 229n37
καιετός 216–219
καινός 205
καίνυμαι 221n21
καιτάεις, καιτάεσσα 214–233, 237, 275–276
Καίτας 221
καίω 212
κακκείοντες 144, 164–166
κακοεργίη 43n57
καλλιπάρηος 127
Κάλχας 22
καμμονίη 163n34
κάρα, Gen. κρᾶτός 32
κατά, καταί 153
κατάγνυμι: κατέηγα 35
καταειλύω 171
καταέννυμι 171
κατακαίριος 159n31
κατέρχομαι 159n31
κεῖθι 36
κεῖσε 36
κεῖμαι: κέαται 32
κελάδων 240–241
κῆτος 213, 230
Κητώ 231n42
κητώεις, κητώεσσα 213, 230–233, 276
κηώδης 212–213
κηώεις, κηώεσσα 212, 213, 232, 233
κίς 71n106
κονίη 43n57
κορύφιον 90n27
κράτος, κρατύς, κρατερός 131n61
κρέτος 131n61
κρίνω: ἔκριναν 123
κτηδών 200–202
κτήνεα 131n61
κτιδέη 219n16

κτίς 219n16
κτυπέω, ἔκτυπον 140
κυδάλιμος 240
κύδιμος 240
κύκλος, κύκλα 98
κύκλωψ 210
κυλλοποδίων, κυλλοπόδιον 195–197, 210–211, 279
κυνυλαγμός 10–11, 284
λειριόεσσα 103
μάρτυς, μάρτυρος 22, 33–34, 38–39, 51, 54, 83, 102, 189, 281, 282
μαχήμων 45n61
μέγαθος, μέγεθος 89n22
μεγακήτης 231–232
μεθίημι: ἐμεθίει 35, 68, 70, 281
μελαμπόδιον 196
μέλλω: ἤμελλον 35
μητιάω 21, 37
Μίνως 22
μίτρα 173, 174
μνῆστις 204
ναιχί 70n105
ναός, νηός, νεώς, ναῦος 113, 115, 123, 127
νιφόεις 232
νόμος 53
νῶι 269
ὀγάστριος 67–71, 279, 284
ὀγάστωρ 68
οἶδα: οἶσθας 14, 17
Οἰνοῦσσα 237n6
οἰνοχοέω: ἐῳνοχόει 16–17
οἴχομαι 52
ὀκνείω 144
ὁμογάστριος 67–68, 279, 284
ὀμπέτασον (Aeolic) 135
ὂν (Aeolic) 84
ὀπάτριος 68
ὄπατρος 68
ὀπῑπεύω 210n36
ὄπισθεν, ὄπιθεν 116, 152n22
ὀπίσσω 152n22
ὄπτιλλος 92
ὀπτός 152n21
ὁράω: ὄρημμι, ὀρῆτο, ἰδέσθαι 21, 32
ὀρέγνυμι, ὀρεγνύς 132–133, 137, 138, 189, 275, 281, 284, 288, 289, 290
ὀρέγω 133, 137
ὀρεσίτροφος 286

INDEX VERBORUM 337

ὀρεσκῷος 286
ὄρθρος 106, 120
ὄρχος 98n45
ὅς 'his own' 47
οὐθείς 14, 92n32
οὐκ, οὐκί, οὐχί 35, 68–71, 279
οὐρανίων 195, 211
ὄψ 152, 157, 158, 161–162, 167, 189, 278
Ὀψαγένεις 150
ὀψάγονος 150, 151
ὀψαμάτης 151
ὀψαρότης 151
ὀψέ 150, 152, 157, 158, 162, 278
ὀψείοντες 143, 144–167, 211, 281, 283, 288, 290, 291
ὀψίγονος 150, 152
ὀψιτέλεστος 152
ὄψον 152
πάθος 130n61
παῖς 66n94
παρά, παραί 153–157
παραβάτης, παραιβάτης 154
παρακλίνω 154
παραπόδιος 196
παρατρέπω 154
παράφημι 153, 157
παρειαί, παραύαι 127
παρθενοπῖπα 210n36
πέλεκυς; Acc.pl. πελέκυς, πελέκυας, πελέκεας, πελέκεις 76–77
πενθημιπόδιον 196
πένθος 130n61
περιέρχομαι 159n31
περιρρηδής 240
πετάννυμι/πίτνημι: πετάσσας, πέπταμαι 134–138
πέτομαι: πέταμαι, ἔπτατο, πτάμενος 134, 194
πευκάλιμος 240
πήγνυμι 133
Πιτυοῦς 237n6
πλῆθος 89n22
πληθύς 89n22
πλήθω 89n22
πλήτης 286n8
Πολυδάμας 22
πολυδένδρεος 232
πολυδήνης 131n61
πολύζυγος 43n58, 135n8
πολυκληΐς 43n58

πολύρρην 204
πολύς; Acc.pl. πολέας, πολύς; πολλός 75–78, 84, 102, 275, 282, 286
πολύστονος 232
πολυτελής 128n53
ποτί 31
πότνια 192
προθέλυμνος 192, 193
προμνηστῖνος 204
πρός 31
πρόσθεν 116
πρόσωπον 210
πυκινός 240
πυλεμάχος 286
ῥαδαλός 235–240, 242, 279
ῥαδινός 239–240
ῥοδανός 234, 235
ῥωχμός 229–230
σάκος 209
-σείω 144–147, 165–167, 278, 283
σεύω: ἔσσυτο, ἐσύθη 35
σήμερον 114
σῆτες 114
σπέος 129
σπιδής 238n8
Στράβων 196
στυγέω, ἔστυγον 140
στονόεις 232
συλάω 258–260, 263, 277
συλεύω 258n24
σφός, σφέτερος 47
σφώ, σφῶι, σφῶιν, σφωέ 269
τάλαντα 136
τάνυμαι, τανύω 72
τάχα 151
ταχύπωλος 210n37
Τεισαμενός 124n42
τειχήεις 130, 232
τειχεσιβλῆτα 285–286
τειχεσιπλῆτα 285–286
τειχιόεις 103, 130, 232
τελαμών 136n11
τέλειος 128
τελήεις 103, 128–130
τέμενος 89n22
τεύχεα 135n8
τίκτω 202
τιμή 56–57
τίνυμαι, τίνϝω 72

τλάω: τελάσσαι, ταλάσσαι, ἔτλην   136
τοί, τοι   32, 33
τριημιπόδιον   196
τριπόδιον   196
τρίτος: τρίττος, τρέττος   109n12
Τροίη   30
ὑγιής   121
υἱός: ὑός, υἱέες/υἷες, υἱέας/υἷας, υἱύνς   76, 92n32, 275
ὑλήεις   103
ὑπαί   154
ὑπερέρχομαι   159n31
ὑπέρχομαι   159n31
ὑπό, ὑβ-   154
ὑπογίγνομαι   154
ὑποδεξίη   43n57
ὑποπόδιον   196
ὕπτιος   194
ὕψι   152
φράτρα: φάτρα (Arc.), φρήτρη (Ion.)   37
φημί: ἔφη   30
φθάνω: φθανέει   71–72, 278
Φειδιππίδιον   197
Φιλήμενος   124n42
Φίλητος   124n42
Φιλουμενός   124n42
χάλκεος   49–50, 79, 84–85, 270, 279, 283
χειμών   204
χρύσεος   49–50, 79, 83–85, 283
χυτροπόδιον   196
-ων   195–196

Cyprian
e-ta-we-sa-to   227

Mycenaean Greek
a-ke-ra$_2$-te   123, 124
a-no-we   125
a-pe-e-ke   125n43
a-ro-u-ra   125
a-wo-i-jo   125
a$_3$-ka-sa-ma   208
a$_3$-ku-pi-ti-jo   227
e-re-u-te-ro   125
e-ru-mi-ni-ja   191, 192
e-u-wa-ko-ro, e-wa-ko-ro   125n43
ka-ke-ja-pi   49n72
ka-ki-jo   49n72
ka-za   49
ke-ka-u-me-no   125
ke-ro-si-ja   226n30
ko-ri-si-ja   227
ko-to-na, ko-to-i-na   125
ku-pa-ro$_2$ 123
ku-ru-so   50n72, 84
ku-ru-sa-pi   49, 84n5
me-re-ti-ra$_2$ 123
me-re-ti-ri-ja   123
mi-to-we-sa   226n29
o-ka   98n45
o-u-ki   70n106
o-u-wo-ze   125n43
pa-ra-wa-jo   125
pi-ra-me-no   124n42
pi-ti-ro$_2$-we-sa   226n29
qe-to-ro-we   125
ra-ke-da-mi-ni-jo   227
ta-we-si-jo   226–227, 276
te-o-jo   125
te-re-jo   128
ti-ri-o-we   125
to-qi-de-we-sa   226n29
we-ru-ma-ta   172–175, 277
wi-ri-ne-jo, wi-ri-ni-jo   49n72
wo-ko-de, wo-i-ko-de   125–126
za-ku-si-jo   227
ze-u-ke-si   173

Anatolian
Hittite
  genuas   96n37
  harganāu   133n4
  militt-   206
Palaite
  malitanna-   205
Armenian
  gelum   170, 190, 277

Balto-Slavic
Baltic
  akštìs (Lith.)   205
  ašìs (Lith.)   205
  aušrà (Lith.)   113
  jáunas (Lith.)   206
  svagiù (Lith.)   140n15
Slavic
  drěvo (OCS)   96
  iskoni (OCS)   205

INDEX VERBORUM

junъ (OCS)   206
jutro (Pol.)   115
ostь (R.)   205
osь (R.)   205
ot-voriti (OCS)   191
utro (Ru.)   115

Celtic
aittenn (OIrish)   205
eithinn (MWelsh)   205

Germanic
austr (ON)   113
kniu (Go.)   100n48
triu (Go.)   99
walwjan (Go.)   170, 190

German
Morgen   115

Indo-Iranian
Vedic
  aktú-   202
  ápnas-   131n61
  ávradanta   240
  ā́yu-   96n36, 205
  ā́yuṣ-   114n24
  āvar   191
  íṣu-   97n43
  urú sádas-   165
  urucákṣas-   210n37
  urūcī́   210n36
  uṣás-   113, 115
  usrí   113
  ṛñjate   133, 288
  éjati   52
  énas-   131n61
  kanyā̀   205
  cákra-   98
  jā́nu-   96n37
  tanóti   72
  dáṁsas-   130
  daṇḍá-   97
  dámūnas-   205
  dā́ru-, drós, drúṇas   96
  dāśnóti, dā́ṣṭi   134n6
  dyu-: dyáus, dyávi, dyā́vā   73, 96n38
  dru-ṣád-   96n39
  dhakṣú-   146

dhṛṣṇú-   133n4
dhṛṣṇóti   133n4
dhṛṣṇv́ojas-   210n37
purudáṁsas-   131n61
prátīka-   210
mántra-   206
Mitra-: Mitrá   73
yuñjánti   133
yúvan-   204, 205
rékṇas-   131n61
varutra-   170
varūtár-   171n4
várman-   172n9
vṛṇóti   170, 190, 275, 277
śā́sman-   163n34
sanóti   72
svādurāti-   210n37
hí   70n105
Avestan
  āiiu-   96n36
  dərəzi-   210n37
  mąϑra-   206
  mąϑrān-   206
  vourucašānē   210n37

Italic
L. *abs*   152
L. *abstrahō*   152
L. *aperiō*   191
L. *asportō*   152
L. *aurōra*   111, 113, 117
L. *Castores*   73
L. *diēs*   96n38
L. *diū*   96n38
L. *gens*   205
L. *genu*   96n37
L. *fēnus*   131n61
L. *jungō*   133
L. *Jūpiter*   96n38
L. *juvenis*   206
L. *natiō*, U. *natīne*   204, 205
L. *nudiūs*   96n38
L. *obs-*   152, 157, 165, 278
L. *operiō*   191
L. *opstrudō*   152
L. *oscen*   152
L. *ostendō*   152
L. *pangō*   133
L. *pignus*   131n61

L. *radius* 206
L. *subs-* 152
L. *subscūs* 152
L. *suscipiō* 152
L. *suspendō* 152
L. *sustentō* 152
L. *sustineō* 152
L. *vagīre* 140n15
L. *volūmen* 172, 190, 277

L. *volvō* 170, 190, 277
L. *vulnus* 131n61

Romance languages
French
    matin 106
    matinée 106
    soir 106
    soirée 106

Index Grammaticorum

Apion   120
Apollonius Dyscolus   65n93, 111, 112, 116–117, 229, 277
Apollonius the Sophist   4, 7, 22n4, 26, 120, 145, 171n5, 172, 186, 214n5, 218, 219, 229–231
Aristarchus   2–81, 105, 118, 121, 132, 139, 141, 143, 145, 150–152, 157, 166, 171, 177, 179n24, 196, 197n7, 235, 236, 238, 248n8, 255–260, 263, 264–269, 272n46, 278–291
Aristonicus   3, 6–9, 11, 14n41, 15, 16, 22–68, 75, 83, 86n14, 107, 121, 132, 139, 143, 148, 150, 151, 152, 160, 176, 178, 198, 236, 241, 246, 250, 267, 269, 279, 286–288
Aristophanes of Byzantium   2, 10n29, 12, 15, 24, 37, 40, 42, 52, 66, 70, 74, 168, 169, 175, 190, 200, 235, 236, 238, 241, 287n10

Callistratus   199–200

Didymus   3, 8, 15, 16, 30, 31n23, 52, 55, 56, 66, 148, 256, 265
Dionysius Thrax   16, 235–237

Epimerismi homerici   4, 32, 33, 41n52, 60
Etymologica
   Et. Genuinum   111, 112n16, 183
   Et. Magnum   111, 112, 116, 117, 171n5, 187, 235, 236, 239
Eustathius of Thessalonica   4, 6, 14, 215
   Comm. Il. 1: 454   216–218, 220, 228, 229
   Comm. Il. 1: 691   17
   Comm. Il. 2: 73   36n40
   Comm. Il. 2: 423   241n15
   Comm. Il. 3: 261   231n41

Comm. Il. 3: 500   235–237, 239
Comm. Il. 4: 507   171n5
Comm. Il. 4: 753   187
Comm. Il. 4: 942   183
Comm. Od. 1: 35   284n7
Comm. Od. 1: 140   215
Comm. Od. 1: 354   183
Comm. Od. 2: 34   158n30
Comm. Od. 2: 90   14
Comm. Od. 2: 172   14
Comm. Od. 2: 229   31–32

Herennius Philo   14
Herodian   3, 29, 33, 47, 71, 115, 197n7, 227n33, 245
Pseudo-Herodian   233
Hesychius   37n43, 52, 68, 108–110, 112, 114, 115, 117, 120, 130, 136, 170, 171n5, 191, 192, 194, 200, 214, 217n11, 218, 219, 221, 229, 277, 286n8

Nicanor   3, 245

Orion   112, 170, 171n5

Pollux   147, 169, 207
Ptolemy of Ascalon   238n8
Ptolemy Epithetes   16, 149

Scholia   *see* the reference to the commented line
Suda   9, 130n59, 284n7

Tzetzes   68, 69

Zenodotus   *passim*

Index Locorum

Linear B

KN V(2) 280	70n106
PY An 261	226n30
PY An 616	226n30
PY Ta 707	49
PY Ta 714	84n5
PY Ub(1) 1318	172–173

Inscriptions

IG IV² 1, 121	91–92
IG IV² 1, 123	92
Iscr. di Cos ED 181	94

Homer and Hesiod (reference to the lines and/or the scholia)

Iliad

A 1	41n52
A 4–5	9–12, 17, 284
A 8	269
A 15	83–85, 102
A 24	40–41
A 47	10n29, 176, 177n18, 178–182, 186–190, 275, 277, 279
A 56	8n22
A 59–61	250–255
A 62–64	254
A 66	128
A 68	29, 35, 78n123
A 69	22
A 83	21, 22n4
A 86	22
A 100	60, 61
A 120	159n31
A 129	30–31
A 158–160	56–57
A 170	32n26
A 197	6
A 204	60–61
A 212	60
A 220	6, 155
A 251	24
A 260–261	58, 264
A 271	33
A 299	29, 155
A 351	132–138, 189, 275
A 374	83
A 408–409	261–263
A 412	62n88
A 434	51
A 480	134, 135
A 488–492	287
A 559	77–78
A 577–578	153
A 606	144, 164
A 611	34
B 1	36
B 3–4	75–76, 275
B 12	55
B 13–14	155
B 36	36
B 56–57	66–67
B 111	16
B 123–128	251, 253
B 160–161	27–28
B 187–189	25
B 196	55–56
B 238	69n103
B 268	84n8
B 300	69n103
B 302	22, 38
B 316	140n18
B 349	69n103
B 439–440	143n1
B 484	54
B 490	50, 243
B 528–529	17, 73n112
B 532	38
B 581	13, 213–216, 219, 224–225, 227–230, 233, 275–276, 279
B 597–598	253
B 616	37
B 658	8n23, 43, 281
B 673–675	287
B 681	243, 245–246, 248, 249n9, 250, 264, 276
B 697	34
B 718	19
B 741	53
Γ 56	15, 44–45, 51, 72, 276
Γ 64	49

INDEX LOCORUM

Γ 73–74	60	Z 70–71	255, 256n21, 257, 260, 263, 277
Γ 100	61–62, 276		
Γ 151–152	82, 85–87, 102–103, 122, 276	Z 266	34
		Z 356	61–62, 276
Γ 163	21	H 28	251
Γ 205–206	7, 26	H 127	21
Γ 210–211	267–268	H 133	241
Γ 234–235	254	H 386–388	253
Γ 243–244	47–48, 51	H 475	10n29
Γ 273	41n52	Θ 139	269
Γ 285–286	57	Θ 166	20
Γ 305–306	159	Θ 196	251–252
Γ 324–325	156	Θ 205–207	251, 253
Γ 349	85n10	Θ 335	162
Γ 381	180	Θ 349	34
Γ 453–454	44–45	Θ 470	104–105, 107–108, 112, 118–120, 122, 277
Δ 3	16–17		
Δ 105	259	Θ 493–496	287n9
Δ 116	259–260	Θ 499	161
Δ 137	168–170, 173, 175, 179, 188, 190, 275, 277, 283	Θ 508–509	106n5
		Θ 523–525	104–105, 107, 121–122
Δ 139	56	Θ 526–527	25, 40, 121
Δ 277	51, 63–64	Θ 562	54
Δ 282	63	I 3	7, 46, 284
Δ 523	134	I 9	46, 284
E 23	180–181	I 120	156
E 31	285–286	I 141–142	246, 248, 249n10, 252
E 132	31	I 283–284	246, 248, 249n10, 252
E 146	23	I 335–336	155
E 186	178–179, 181	I 444–445	252
E 194–195	134, 212	I 506	71–72, 278
E 273	251	I 537	41, 284
E 293	35	I 541	192
E 308	155	I 564	6n18
E 321	261, 263	I 587–589	262
E 329	16	K 98	8n22
E 387	50	K 189	152, 157
E 416	23, 65	K 224–226	267, 269n40
E 428	32–33	K 289	161
E 456–457	254	K 337	161
E 466	34	K 343	258
E 502–505	161	K 445	69n103
E 506–507	180n27	K 515	21
E 508–509	262–263	K 547	179n24
E 519–520	262	Λ 27	179n24
E 658	159n31	Λ 76	48
E 778	52	Λ 86	23
E 898	23	Λ 110	258
Z 53–54	24	Λ 140	26

Iliad (cont.)

Λ 142	47–48, 51	Ξ 135	21
Λ 219	24	Ξ 162	33, 282
Λ 233	154	Ξ 169–170	62–63, 248n8
Λ 385	85n10	Ξ 208	23–24
Λ 416–418	154	Ξ 223	17
Λ 437	40	Ξ 259	37
Λ 439	159n31	Ξ 282	180–181
Λ 456–458	264–267, 278	Ξ 322	22
Λ 492	24	Ξ 350	180
Λ 589	27	Ο 39–40	254
Λ 723–724	262–263	Ο 61–62	156
Λ 730	23	Ο 137	69n103
Λ 752	180	Ο 179	21
Λ 831	45, 72	Ο 190–191	270–272, 278
Μ 75	27	Ο 207	55
Μ 105	23	Ο 301–303	74
Μ 115	161	Ο 308	180
Μ 122	135	Ο 356	59, 264
Μ 127–128	24, 74	Ο 416–418	155
Μ 149–150	154	Ο 524	258–259
Μ 231	22	Ο 587–588	67, 282
Μ 248–249	153	Ο 640	25–26
Μ 294–296	28–29	Ο 656–657	143n1
Μ 342–343	73–74	Ο 716	35, 68–71, 281
Μ 390	161	Π 10	31
Μ 419–420	155	Π 58	155, 161
Ν 71–72	52, 72	Π 86	161
Ν 83–84	261, 262–263	Π 141–144	209n34, 287–288
Ν 107	40	Π 155–156	24
Ν 130	23	Π 161	21
Ν 172	8n22, 25	Π 188	7, 42
Ν 288–289	251, 253	Π 202	21, 37
Ν 367	155	Π 301	155
Ν 395–396	156	Π 385	85n10
Ν 425	180	Π 394–395	156
Ν 449	21	Π 507	36
Ν 549	134	Π 762	70n104
Ν 609	35, 41	Π 790	180
Ν 640–641	258	Ρ 149	28
Ν 824	286	Ρ 153	59
Ξ 1–8	163–164	Ρ 173	48
Ξ 27–31	142, 143n2	Ρ 215	35
Ξ 36	66	Ρ 268	22–23
Ξ 37	132, 142, 144–146, 148, 149n16, 160, 163–164, 167, 278–279	Ρ 368	27, 48
		Ρ 371–372	134
		Ρ 406	161
		Ρ 540–544	161
Ξ 40	14	Ρ 551	33
Ξ 90–91	254	Ρ 740–741	153

INDEX LOCORUM

Σ 154–156	28n18	Ψ 393	178, 182, 186–188, 275
Σ 160	138–141, 278	Ψ 592–594	251
Σ 198	15, 45	Ω 34	128
Σ 222	8n22, 49–50	Ω 237–238	156
Σ 247	15–16	Ω 281–282	261
Σ 254–256	154	Ω 287–288	159
Σ 371	195	Ω 472–475	261
Σ 445	155	Ω 510	178, 182, 185–189, 275
Σ 479–480	232	Ω 712	154
Σ 483–606	237	Ω 771	153–154
Σ 576	234–235, 237, 239, 241, 279	*Odyssey*	
		α 3	53
T 79–80	154	α 366	154
T 183	156	α 413	64
T 236–237	143n1	β 434	106n5
T 321–322	252	γ 50	32
T 342	33	δ 1	13, 213–215, 228–229, 275
T 388–391	287–288		
Υ 114	29–30	δ 70	28n18, 36
Υ 150	180	δ 214–215	105, 122
Υ 255	69n103	ε 62	85n10
Υ 270	195–196	ζ 179	172–174, 277
Υ 272	49, 195–196	ζ 256	64
Υ 273	198–199, 209	η 3–4	154
Υ 444	180	η 86	50
Υ 488–489	156	η 288	106n5
Φ 2	53	θ 262–263	154
Φ 89–91	261	θ 562	180
Φ 95	67–68, 70–71, 279	ι 433	178, 183–187, 189, 275, 279
Φ 169–170	194, 198–199, 279		
Φ 262	71–72, 278	λ 15	180
Φ 318–319	177n18	λ 392	135
Φ 331	195, 197, 211, 279	μ 425	83n3
Φ 335	21	μ 438–439	158, 160, 167, 278–279, 291
Φ 531	134		
Φ 575	10–11, 284	ν 278	105
Φ 597	180	ξ 374	159n31
Φ 599	156	ο 20	14
Χ 26–27	105	ο 54–55	261, 263
Χ 37	132	σ 173	99n44
Χ 219–220	253	υ 351–352	181
Χ 276–277	155–156	φ 11–12	203
Χ 348	59	χ 109	203
Χ 348–352	252	*Hymns*	
Χ 368	258	H.Ap. 185	84
Χ 470	49	H.Lun. 6	84
Ψ 135	171	H.Pan 18	141n19
Ψ 306–307	22	H.Ven. 22–23	271
Ψ 345–347	253		

INDEX LOCORUM

Hesiod
Th. 238	231n42
Th. 455–458	271
Op. 129	84
Op. 144	84
Op. 427–429	191
Op. 430	169–171
Op. 436	169
Op. 536	169, 171, 175–176, 277
Op. 577	106n4
Op. 582–583	83
fr. 343	131n61

Other Greek Authors

Aeschylus
Suppl. 476	70
Suppl. 800–801	10–11
fr. 216 *TrGF*	180n25

Alcaeus
fr. 357.4–5 LP	84n6
fr. 367.1 LP	153, 157

Anonymus Londiniensis
88, 94, 218

Anthologia graeca
Anth. Gr. 6.253	130n59
Anth. Gr. 9.418	207
Anth. Appendix, Epigr. sepulcr. 234	87

Apollonius of Rhodes
Arg. 1.829	64n90
Arg. 1.891	64n90
Arg. 1.1034–1035	177n18
Arg. 2.776	64n90
Arg. 2.1251	106
Arg. 3.296–297	184
fr. 8.1	64n90

Archilochus
fr. 191.1	178n22, 183

Aretaeus of Cappadocia
De causis et signis acutorum morborum
1.7.4	135n9

De curatione acutorum morborum 1.2.8;
1.4.5; 1.4.9; 2.10.4   88n21

Aristophanes
Eccl. 796	106
Nub. 175	106
Pax 62	146
Ran. 912	70
Vesp. 165–170	146, 147n11

Callimachus
fr. 303	37n43
fr. 639	215–216

Cratinus
fr. 453	146–147

Dionysius of Halicarnassus
De compositione verborum 5.21
   64n90

Empedocles
fr. 40	203

Euphorion
fr. 51	183–184

Euripides
Hec. 1077	11
HF 1090	203
Phoen. 5	202
Suppl. 641	202

Heliodorus Trag.
fr. 472	135n9

Herodotus
4.155	70
7.49	70
9.96	176, 283

Hippocrates
De mulierum affectibus ii, 15
   188
De natura pueri 26	88, 93–94
De glandulis 9.4	135n9

INDEX LOCORUM

Maxime of Tyre
Diss. 40.6   271n44

Megasthenes
fr. 8   87, 88n17

Mimnermus
fr. 11a 1–2 West   203

Nicaenetus
fr. 1.4   239

Nonnos
Dion. 42.441   266

Oppian
Hal. 2.124   177n18

Plato
Euthyd. 286b7–8   30
Phaedo 117d7   30
Tim. 78d6   203n18

Plutarchus
Marcel. 8.2   200
fr. 158.13–15   200

Ps.-Galenus
Definitiones medicae 19.367
    172n8

Rufus of Ephesus
De partibus corporis humani 25
    135n9

Sappho
fr. 58.19 LP   112
fr. 138 LP   135
fr. 175 LP   110

Septuagint
Deuteronomy 22.6   88

Simonides
fr. 37.24–25   164
fr. 103.23   70n105

Sophocles
Aj. 326   147n11
Aj. 1263   153n23
Trach. 1086   203
fr. 991   146

Stesichorus
fr. 242   286
fr. 255   10

Strabo
Geogr. 8.5.7   216–217, 229
Geogr. 10.4.11   130

Theocritus
Id. 2.44   154
Id. 5.47–48   87

Theophrastus
HP 4.16.6   156

Timon of Phlius
fr. 804.1–3   86

Xenophon
Cyr. 7.1.36   156

Index Notionum

ablaut   72, 76, 95–96, 113–114, 204–206
accent   27, 30, 31n23, 32–33, 37, 69–71, 99, 111–112, 197n7, 238, 265–266, 278
accident (*pathos*)   47, 239
accusative (syntax)
   accusative of direction   26
   double accusative   23, 258, 263
acephalous   169
Achaean   31–33, 50, 68, 79, 84, 85, 103, 107, 118, 126–130, 174, 212–213, 220, 225, 233, 277–278, 283
actualisation   186, 189, 228
adonic   38, 180–181, 184, 249n10, 263
adverb   24, 36, 43, 105, 106, 109, 114–120, 151–163, 167, 209, 262, 277, 278
   adverbial neuter   16, 66
Aeolic   21n3, 31, 32, 33, 39, 49, 71, 82n1, 84, 85, 92, 110–112, 115, 118, 126–128, 130, 184, 203, 222, 266, 283
agreement   24, 34n32, 36, 48, 49, 55, 56, 65, 67, 75n114, 226, 268–269, 272, 277
anacolouthon   244
analogy (linguistics)   32n24, 33, 38–39, 44, 45n61, 47, 49n72, 70n105, 75, 76, 78, 80, 89n22, 90n27, 95, 99, 100, 103, 112, 113, 116, 118, 119n31, 120, 129, 130n61, 133–134, 136, 137, 140n15, 147, 151, 164, 166, 169, 170, 172n9, 190n44, 191, 204, 205n20, 206, 208, 210, 212, 213n4, 232, 233, 240, 275, 277, 288
analogy (composition)   *see* model
analogy (ἀναλογία)   22, 39, 50–51, 54, 78, 81, 83, 102, 134, 164, 177, 269, 270, 282
anaphoric   244, 246, 248, 258, 259, 262–264, 265–266, 278
anastrophe   43n56
animate   67, 76, 113, 114, 121, 159–160, 163n34, 187, 192, 196, 204, 213, 258n24, 265, 266
anthroponym   124n42, 125, 150, 226–227, 276
antisigma   272n46
aorist (morphology)   35, 45–46, 124n42, 134–137, 139–141, 177, 178, 275, 278
Arcadian   37, 123, 124, 126, 221n21
Arcado-Cyprian   39, 115, 126
article   36, 48, 66n94, 105n2, 121, 122, 243–244, 246–248, 281

Asia Minor   127
aspect   21, 124n42, 181
aspiration   *see* psilosis
assibilation   32, 49n72, 203
asyndeton   63, 169, 241
athematicisation   39n45
athetesis   3, 5, 6, 9–10, 15, 17, 18, 22n4, 34n32, 56–57, 73n112, 105, 121, 176, 178, 195, 196, 237, 282, 286–288
Attic, Atticism, Atticisation   14, 19n1, 23, 31, 32, 35, 36, 65, 70, 71, 75, 77, 82, 83, 86n13, 87, 92–95, 114–115, 118, 119n31, 122, 123, 128, 147, 165–167, 268, 278, 283
augment   34–35, 41, 70, 153, 157, 191, 281

barytonesis   32n24, 115–118
Boeotian   108–118, 120, 123, 128n51, 218, 230, 277
brackets (περιγράφειν)   286–288

Caland   130, 210n37, 221n21, 240
cataphoric   244, 260–264
clitic   32–33, 64, 65, 70–71, 153, 225, 265–266
collation   6, 9, 12, 38, 39, 43, 44, 53, 57, 58, 63, 66, 72, 77, 80, 86, 120, 136, 138, 141, 175, 210, 255, 280
collective   96–101, 152n21, 276
commentary (ὑπόμνημα)   2, 8, 9n25, 69, 229, 230, 252
comparative   34, 268
complementary distribution   77, 105, 118, 135n8, 137, 180, 208, 209, 212, 232
compound   11, 34, 68, 89, 96n39, 97, 103n52, 131n61, 150–152, 172n6, 192, 194, 195–196, 202, 204, 207–211, 221, 225, 232, 279, 284, 286
conditional   251–252, 254, 275
conjecture   5, 12, 40n51, 51, 80, 89, 107, 134n7, 150, 175n16, 179, 189, 199, 219n15, 263
consistency   3, 26, 39, 45, 54n78, 56, 77, 78, 80–81, 83, 102, 134, 174, 177, 188–189, 268, 282, 286, 287, 289
contamination (linguistics)   118, 145, 146, 147, 277

INDEX NOTIONUM

contextual permutation 230–231
contraction 22, 34n31, 41n52, 42, 48, 49, 50, 57, 61, 71n107, 72, 84, 104–105, 107, 110–112, 115, 117, 119, 120, 122, 129, 226, 248, 266, 269n40, 278, 284
coordination 22, 53, 63, 137, 169, 222–225, 228, 241, 266
copulative ἀ- 68–69
correction 6, 7, 8, 31n22, 34, 36, 38, 43, 48, 51, 58, 65, 66, 69n102, 77, 89, 91, 137, 149, 166, 169, 234, 235, 237, 265, 269
correlation, correlative 244, 248, 262–263
correptio attica 65n94, 98n44, 286
correptio epica 25, 48, 57, 82, 83–85, 102, 220, 281, 283
crasis 36, 66n94, 281
cretic 43n57, 140
cross-reference 10n29, 46
Cyprian 123n37, 227

dative (syntax) 105, 145, 148, 160, 184, 266, 272
decasuative 113n21, 114n23
decency 58–60, 195, 286
desemanticisation 154
desiderative 144–146, 150, 164–166, 278, 283, 288
diacritic 30–31, 164, 166
diaeresis 31, 41n52
diectasis 42–43, 72
differentiation 46, 96, 99
diffusionist model 31, 126–128, 278
digamma 35, 40, 42, 74, 139, 141, 170, 172, 179, 184, 186, 192, 266
diminutive 90n27, 97, 196–197, 206n27, 211, 279
diphthong 25n9, 37, 66n94, 69n100, 92n32, 103, 115, 118, 123, 125–126, 128, 149n13, 164, 226
diple periestigmene 5, 12, 13, 15, 17, 46
dissimilation 36–37, 97, 128–129
Doric 32n25, 39, 87, 89, 90n28, 91–92, 94–95, 100, 102, 114, 115, 119, 123, 128, 130, 147
dual 24, 73–75, 100n48, 137–138, 262, 268–269, 277, 282n3, 284

economy (formulaic) 181
ekdosis 2, 5–9, 12–14, 16, 20, 29, 57, 66, 77n121, 80, 86, 148, 149, 199, 215, 236, 238, 264, 269, 280, 282, 283, 284n7, 287
elision 19n1, 27n16, 34, 41n52, 45, 48, 70–71, 85, 101, 102, 139, 141, 152, 157, 158
emendation 5, 6, 7, 9, 11, 12, 20, 22, 26, 36, 38, 42, 44, 45, 48, 52, 58, 59, 65, 66, 67, 80, 81, 89, 107, 120, 133, 138, 141n19, 149, 166, 175, 178, 200, 201, 210, 211, 213, 221, 248, 254–255, 264, 268–269, 273, 280–282, 285, 286
emphatic 70–71
enlargement 162n20, 170, 190, 200
ephelcystic *-n* 19, 42
epicene 34, 36n41, 50
ethnonym 123, 227, 233, 276
exegetical scholia 3–4, 32n27

feminisation 34, 226, 228
figura etymologica 28, 169, 174
figure (σχῆμα) 49, 50, 270
first occurrence 31n22, 78n123
future 71, 144–147, 160, 164, 165, 171, 189, 191, 263

geminate 38, 103, 123–127, 130
gender 24, 34, 36n41, 49–50, 67, 75n114, 98, 109, 114–116, 226, 240
genitive (syntax) 23–24, 26, 40, 48, 65, 105–107, 112, 116, 119–120, 122, 145, 151, 155, 165, 266, 268, 278
genitive absolute 265–266, 268, 271–273
Glossai 20, 27, 29, 69, 120
glyconic 82n1

hapax 44, 52, 107, 132, 149, 171, 172, 194, 199, 208, 234, 237, 238, 240, 281
hendiadys 42, 232
heronym 221
hiatus 19n1, 26n9, 27n15, 36, 40, 70, 82, 84, 85, 89n22, 92n32, 125n43, 138, 164, 170
Hoffmann suffix 204–206, 210, 279
homonymy 115, 169, 203
Humbach pattern 42
hyperanalysis 187
hyperarchaism 41n52, 289
hyperbaton 67

INDEX NOTIONUM

hyperdoricism 131
hyperionicism 72
hyphaeresis 43–44, 76, 103

iconic 98
infinitive 31, 140
interpolation 5, 61, 105, 121n32, 197, 224n23
Ionic 14, 18, 23, 24, 27n14, 31–33, 35–37, 39, 41n52, 44, 47n67, 48, 50, 65, 66, 69, 71, 72, 75, 77, 83, 84, 85, 87–95, 100–103, 113–119, 123, 126–130, 154, 162, 184, 210, 220, 268, 277, 278, 283, 285
iotacism 91n30, 194, 251, 252
isochrony 164
iterative 98

koine 3, 41n52, 54, 62, 65, 75, 88, 92n32, 260, 262, 274

Late Helladic 126–127
lectio difficilior 20, 64, 237, 268, 270
lengthening
 compensatory l. 71, 103, 115, 117, 123–124, 126–130, 213n4
 metrical l. 43, 44, 71, 74, 103, 129, 140, 169, 171n4, 196, 205n20, 212–213
 Wackernagel's l. 202, 210
Lesbian 27n14, 31, 32, 71, 84, 103, 111, 112, 115–118, 123, 126–130, 277
lexicalisation 114, 118, 136, 241
lexicographical scholia 3–4
loanword 203, 204
locative 85, 106, 113–116, 119, 120, 277
Luwian 127
Lycian 127

material (adjectives) 49, 84–85
metaplasmos 111, 117
metathesis 41n52, 42, 113, 123, 202, 218, 283
metrics *passim*
 see complementary distribution, contraction, *correptio*, cretic, diectasis, digamma, ephelcystic -*n*, hiatus, hyphaeresis, lengthening, particle, secondary yod, suppletivism, synizesis, tmesis, tribrach, unmetrical, variant
misreading 109
missing lines 17, 57, 196, 254, 287–288
mixed paradigm *see* suppletivism

mode 24, 32, 251–254
model (composition) 10, 26, 43n58, 59, 84, 85, 106n5, 164, 176, 178n22, 179n24, 182, 184, 209, 211, 212, 258, 263, 269, 270, 277, 290
modernisation 23, 24, 36, 38, 41n52, 42, 44, 69, 72, 76, 80, 84, 85n10, 101, 102, 120, 161, 174, 177, 179, 183, 189, 268–269, 275, 278, 280, 283n6, 284, 289
monophthongisation 230
motivation 33, 116, 133, 157, 164–165, 171, 175, 201, 205, 206, 210, 211, 230, 235, 238, 279, 289
Mycenaean 31, 49–50, 70n106, 84, 94n35, 95, 123–130, 172–175, 191, 192, 203n17, 209, 213n4, 225–230, 233, 276, 277, 290

negation 69–71, 125n43, 252, 253, 279
neologism 45, 68n99, 71, 133, 137, 195
nickname 195–197, 211, 227
nominative absolute 267–270, 277
nominativus pendens 268n36, 269
number 22, 24, 27n15, 36, 47–48, 55–56, 74–75, 98–99, 137–138, 203, 268, 282

obelos 3n10, 5, 57, 286–288
optative 31, 92n32, 251–254

palatalisation 49n72, 123, 125n42
papyri 1–3, 6n20, 9, 19n2, 21, 34n30, 35, 39, 58, 78, 85n10, 88, 184n34, 215, 251, 252, 254, 272n46, 273, 281, 288
parataxis 25
parenthetic clause 30
participle
 absolute p. *see* genitive absolute, nominative absolute
 dominant p. 265–267, 278
particle 45, 70n105, 114n23, 137–138, 153, 261–264, 272n25, 273
 modal particle 251–254, 275
partitive 105, 268, 271–272
patronymic 195
peripheral (dialect) 123, 127
phase model 31, 126–128
plus-verse 1, 288
politikai versions 2, 14
polustichos version 1n4

INDEX NOTIONUM

possessive, possession   26, 33, 41n52, 47–48,
    51, 64–65, 122, 128, 206, 208, 212, 232,
    266, 282
pre-Hellenic   226, 233, 276
predicative adjective   24, 66
preverb   29, 35, 43, 83, 92, 137, 152–163, 167,
    191, 192, 210n36, 225
productivity   88–89, 95, 97n42, 99, 100,
    119n31, 128, 134, 136, 170, 196, 220, 263
psilosis   27–29, 32, 48, 69

reanalysis   25–26, 97n42, 101, 139n14, 140,
    163, 165, 171, 186n38, 197, 211, 225–226,
    228–229, 233, 238, 239n10, 240–242,
    260, 263–264
recategorisation   96, 225
recharacterisation   113, 115, 116, 118, 260
redundancy   11, 174, 245, 257–258, 263, 284
reduplication   45, 97–99, 139–140, 180, 191
reflexive   33, 47–48, 51, 57n82, 265–266,
    282
regularisation   33, 38, 39, 80, 94, 100, 113, 177,
    237, 269, 282, 284
reinterpretation   44, 48, 100, 141, 157, 160,
    163, 167, 185–189, 229, 231, 262, 278,
    291
relative clause   24, 244, 248, 250–251, 254,
    262, 264, 275
remodelling (linguistics)   34n31, 39, 46, 47,
    49n72, 71–72, 76, 77, 89n22, 90, 95, 96,
    99, 103, 112, 112–120, 130, 133, 136, 137,
    140n18, 145, 150, 160, 164–167, 171, 172,
    174, 190, 193, 197, 204–206, 209–211,
    219, 225–227, 236, 276–279, 286, 289,
    290
remodelling (line)   30, 35, 74, 85, 266, 268,
    275, 276, 278
resyllabification   205n25
rewriting (μεταγράφειν)   6–7, 26, 80n125, 151,
    246
rhetorics   58–64, 174, 248, 257, 264, 266, 270,
    273–274, 276, 277, 278, 284, 286

sandhi   27, 29
scriptio continua   20, 21, 27, 69, 148, 166
secondary yod   49–50, 84, 85, 279, 283

segmentation   20–21, 27, 34, 39n46, 68–70,
    148–151, 165, 168, 192, 219n16, 224–226,
    233
Sievers' law   72n110, 192n49
simplification (cluster)   37, 152
    see also geminate
singulative   97–99, 101, 152n21, 276
spelling   21, 28, 37–38, 43, 50, 84, 106n5, 110,
    129, 133, 149n13, 197, 213, 226
spurious   286–288
stylistics   3n10, 20n2, 50, 55, 57–59, 63–64,
    174, 197, 249, 250, 251, 254, 264, 266,
    273, 275, 278
sub-Mycenaean   127
suppletivism   38, 83, 91–95, 97, 100–102, 276,
    283
syllepsis   143n2
synchronic etymology   165, 219, 229, 286
syncope   218
synizesis   41, 42, 49, 50, 75–78, 82–85, 102,
    169, 275, 281, 283
system (formulaic)   43n58, 163n34, 180–181,
    230

thematicisation   22, 38, 39n45, 72, 97n43, 99,
    100n48, 171, 192n49
Thessalian   31, 49, 71n106, 84, 85n9, 103,
    109n12, 115, 117, 118, 123, 126, 128, 129, 130
tmesis   37, 43, 152–159, 162, 192, 269n40
toponym   222–228, 233, 237n6, 243–248, 276
tribrach   45, 76, 154

uncials   109
univerbation   225–226, 282
unmetrical   8n22, 14, 15, 36n40, 38, 42–44,
    45, 49, 140, 153, 157, 184n33, 196, 212,
    235–236, 244n2, 281, 282

variant (vocalic/consonantal)   43n58,
    106n5, 135, 258, 260
variant reading   *passim*
voice   21–22, 46, 121, 146, 147, 164
vulgate   *passim*

word order   25, 69–70, 244, 246–248, 253,
    261–263

Printed in the United States
by Baker & Taylor Publisher Services